THE IRWIN GUIDE
TO USING
THE WALL STREET JOURNAL

ABOUT THE AUTHOR

ICHAEL B. LEHMANN is a Professor of Economics at the University of San Francisco. He is a graduate of Grinnell College and received his Ph.D. from Cornell University.

Professor Lehmann lectures extensively on business and investment conditions and has developed a popular seminar based on this book, which he offers to investors, the business community, and corporations as an in-house training program.

THE IRWIN GUIDE
TO USING
THE WALL STREET JOURNAL

SIXTH EDITION

MICHAEL B. LEHMANN

McGraw-Hill

New York San Francisco Washington, D.C. Auckland Bogotá
Caracas Lisbon London Madrid Mexico City Milan
Montreal New Delhi San Juan Singapore
Sydney Tokyo Toronto

Library of Congress Cataloging-in Publication Data

Lehmann, Michael B.
    The Irwin guide to using The Wall Street Journal / Michael B.
    Lehmann. — 6th ed.
       p. cm.
    Rev. ed. of: The Business One Irwin guide to using The Wall Street
    Journal. 4th ed. 1993
      Includes index.
      ISBN 0-07-134649-X
      1. Business cycles—United States. 2. Economic indicators—United
    States. 3. Investments—United States. 4. Wall Street Journal.
    I. Lehmann, Michael B. II. Irwin Professional Publishing. III. Wall
    Street Journal. IV. Title.
HB3743.L44   1999
332.6—dc20   95–45386

McGraw-Hill

A Division of The **McGraw·Hill** Companies

  34567890 AGM/AGM 098765432
ISBN 0-07-134649-X
Printed and bound by Quebecor Printing.

McGraw-Hill books are available at special quantity discounts to use as premiums and sales promotions, or for use in corporate training programs. For more information, please write to the Director of Special Sales, McGraw-Hill, 2 Penn Plaza, New York, NY 10121-2298. Or contact your local bookstore.

 This book is printed on recycled, acid-free paper containing a minimum of 50% recycled de-inked bifer.

PREFACE

When I first proposed this book to Irwin, they asked me if its purpose was to show the reader "how to be your own economist." Not exactly, I said. The objective was to show the reader "how to use *The Wall Street Journal* to be your own economist."

After all, the *Journal* is the authoritative source for business news in America; it is published coast to coast; and it has the largest daily circulation of any newspaper in the country. By focusing on a handful of key statistical reports in the *Journal*, you can acquire a surprisingly quick and firm comprehension of the ups and downs of the American business economy. This book will facilitate that comprehension, clearly and accurately—but, I hope, in a pleasing and nontechnical manner.

The Irwin Guide to Using The Wall Street Journal is designed to help you develop a sound overview of our economy, thus making your grasp of economic events as well as your business and investment decisions more informed and more confident. But it is not a get-rich-quick manual. You should always seek competent professional counsel before placing business or personal capital at risk.

Michael B. Lehmann

ACKNOWLEDGMENTS

I wish to express my gratitude to Angie Pantazis and Wendy Lam for their assistance in preparing the text and organizing *The Wall Street Journal* sources.

Once again, I wouldn't have much to work with had it not been for the editorial assistance on earlier editions of my wife, Millianne Lehmann, and my colleague, Alan Heineman. My indebtedness to them continues through this edition.

Robert H. Meier of DeKalb, Illinois, revised the list of suggested further reading in Appendix D, which he had kindly contributed to the fifth edition. This is an education in itself. Don't miss it.

My thanks also to Stanley Nel, Dean of the University of San Francisco's College of Arts & Sciences, for his past and continuing support of my writing and research efforts.

Finally, my thanks to Kelli Christiansen, my editor at McGraw-Hill, who is a pleasure to work with and for.

M.B.L.

CONTENTS

PART I

THE BIG PICTURE: THE ECONOMIC CLIMATE AND THE INVESTMENT OUTLOOK   1

PART II

YOUR CHOICE OF INVESTMENTS   141

PART III

FINE-TUNING: REFINING YOUR SENSE OF THE ECONOMY AND THE RIGHT INVESTMENT DECISIONS   285

P A R T

THE BIG PICTURE: THE ECONOMIC CLIMATE AND THE INVESTMENT OUTLOOK

1

INTRODUCTION

30,000 ON THE DOW?

ET'S PLUNGE RIGHT IN. Examine Chart 1–1 on page 4 with an investor's eye. The vertical axis provides values for the Dow Jones Industrial Average and the Consumer Price Index, while time is on the horizontal axis.

Although the chart portrays the entire post-World War II era, focus on the years since 1970. Notice that the Dow fluctuated in a range around 1,000 in the 1970s, tripled in the 1980s, flirted with 3,000 by 1990, then tripled again in the 1990s, rising to about 10,000 in 1999.

Since the Dow tripled in the 1980s and 1990s, is it reasonable to assume that it will triple again and go to 30,000 by the year 2010? That seems far-fetched, but who in 1980, let alone 1970, could have anticipated 10,000 on the Dow by the end of the century?

Now you might say, "Wait a minute. Look at the Dow in the 1970s. It fluctuated around 1,000 and went nowhere. Perhaps similar conditions will prevail in the first decade of the new century. The Dow may not triple. Indeed, it might not go anywhere."

These doubts and concerns make sense. What forces held the stock market back in the 1970s? What forces propelled it forward so rapidly in the 1980s and 1990s? Can we shed light on past events and gain a clue to the future?

Could the same force have generated the bust of the 1970s and the boom of the 1980s and 1990s? Yes. It could and did. In a word, *inflation* lay behind both sets of events. *High* inflation held stocks back in the 1970s, and *low* inflation propelled them forward in the 1980s and 1990s.

3

CHART 1–1 Dow vs. CPI: Dow Jones Industrial Average; Change in Consumer Price Index (CPI) at Annual Rate (6-Month Span)

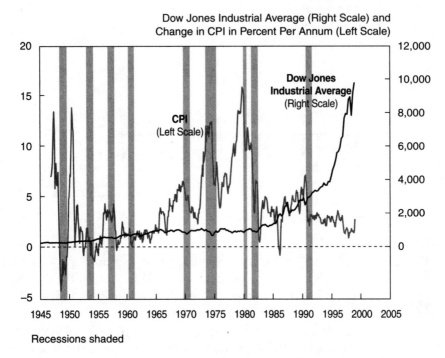

Dow Jones Industrial Average (Right Scale) and
Change in CPI in Percent Per Annum (Left Scale)

Recessions shaded

Source: Dow Jones & Co., Inc.; The Conference Board, *Business Cycle Indicators*, Series P6M320.

Finally, keep an additional point in mind before you move on. The spectacular run-up in stock market values in the 1980s and 1990s coincided with the decline in the rate of inflation after a severe escalation of prices in the 1970s. Suppose prices begin to decline in the first decade of the new century? What effect will *deflation* have on the investment climate in general and upon stocks in particular? Deflation could generate an entirely new dynamic.

ON YOUR OWN

This means you will have to use the investment data on your own, without an interpreter. You will have to decipher the Dow Jones Industrial Average, GDP, capacity utilization, price/earnings ratio, housing starts, advance/decline line, auto sales, and other statistical series and reports. You must use them to gain an understanding of developing business and investment trends so that your judgments and opinions are not merely based on (and therefore biased by) popular analyses and secondary sources.

It's worth some time and effort to learn how to deal with the data on your own, because until you come to grips with the data you can't honestly say that you have formed your own opinion about current economic and business events, let alone about what the future holds. The news media now serve as intermediaries between you and the data. Furthermore, no matter how many experts are quoted, you still aren't dealing with the facts, only with someone else's interpretation of them. And these interpretations are often contradictory—and therefore confusing. At some point you have to wonder: Do the "experts" know what they're talking about? And while you are waiting for them to sort things out, your investment opportunities may have passed.

On the other hand, your desire to master the data may also stem from your own business needs. Will demand for your product be weak or strong two quarters from now or two years from now? Is this the time to lay in additional inventory, hire key personnel, and build more plant? Or, despite the current level of orders, would it be more prudent to cancel those plans? Can you beat the competition to the punch, one way or another? Are interest rates likely to rise or to fall? Is deflation merely a buzzword, or are we truly about to embark upon an era of continuously falling prices? That's just a hint of the issues you can begin to analyze on your own; all it takes is learning to come to grips with a small number of regularly released statistical reports.

You may also wish to conduct your own analysis of current economic events because they form the foundation for so many other social and political developments. Were President Reagan's tax cut and supply-side economics responsible for the early 1980s decline in inflation, or should the Federal Reserve System take the credit? Has the era of federal-budget deficits come to an end, and should we be optimistic about federal budget surpluses for the foreseeable future? And what about our chronic balance of trade deficit? What does it mean and how important is it? Do your answers to these questions reflect your analysis of the data, your political point of view, or the opinions of your favorite commentator? Maybe they should reflect all three, but they can reflect only the last two until you learn to deal with the numbers on your own. Once you do that, your own judgment will be of greater importance to you and others.

Don't misunderstand: Dispensing with expert advice is not the objective. Even the world's leading authority on a subject must consult other experts as a continual check on his or her understanding. This challenges the authority and helps prevent sloppy thinking. The point is: If you become the expert by handling the data on your own, you will know whether or not the other experts make sense. Otherwise, you'll never be certain whether you're receiving sound or flimsy advice.

If you want to be your own economist and investment advisor, if you wish to master the daily data, you need two things: (1) a readily available, reliable, and comprehensive statistical source and (2) a guide to organizing and interpreting the information you receive.

As to the first requirement, *The Wall Street Journal* is your best daily source of investment, business, and economic information; you really don't need anything else. It contains all the reports necessary to conduct your own analysis.

With respect to the second requirement, this book can be your guide. In it, the nature of the statistics will be explained so that what they measure and how they are computed will be clear. GDP, capacity utilization, the price/earnings ratio, and the Dow Jones Industrial Average cannot remain vague and indefinite terms if you are going to be in control of the information.

For example, if the *Journal* reports that the money supply has increased, it is important to know that this fact has virtually nothing to do with the availability of currency. The money supply is composed largely of checking accounts; currency is the petty cash of the economy.

Understanding the nature of the various statistical series is, of course, not enough. You must be able to place them in both historical and contemporary context. For instance, the price/earnings (P/E) ratio for the Dow stocks hit a high of 22 in August 1987, just as the Dow peaked immediately prior to the October crash. But in 1998, the P/E for the Dow climbed to 25, yet there was no crash. Had the rules changed or merely been modified? The savvy investor understood these developments and was prepared to act on them.

These essential skills will develop and gain strength with each chapter. Your historical perspective will deepen, providing the background or benchmark for evaluating contemporary events. When a *Journal* article states that the trade deficit is the largest ever, or that the Dow Jones Industrial Average has hit a new high, the comparison can provide perspective only if you grasp the frame of reference. Knowledge of the past aids evaluation of the present by providing a standard against which recent developments are measured. For instance, motor-vehicle sales and housing starts may be slightly higher or lower than they were a year ago, but your knowledge of their relationship to the historic peaks will provide needed insight.

As you read on, you will become aware that none of the statistical reports stands alone. Understanding the relationships among them provides insight into the economy's operation and the investment scene; each is a piece of the puzzle, and together they compose the picture. For instance, mortgage interest rates and home construction have been featured in the *Journal* lately, and there is a simple, vital link between them: As mortgage interest rates fall, home construction increases.

Consider another example. In 1985 we asked our major trading partners to intervene in the foreign exchange markets in order to depress the value of the dollar. The hope was that cheaper dollars—and hence cheaper prices for American goods in world markets—would boost our exports and reduce our balance-of-trade deficit. Thus, the statistical reports on the value of the dollar and on our ability to export are inextricably linked, as you will see in more detail in Chapter 16.

The great bull market of the 1980s and 1990s seems unprecedented. Or is it? To what extent should the crash of 1929 make us cautious with respect to recent events?

All of the statistics analyzed in this book can be interrelated in this fashion, so they need not be a series of isolated events, released piecemeal on a day-to-day basis. Instead, they will form an unfolding pattern that clearly reveals the direction of economic and business activity.

Finally, you need a framework, a device to give a coherent shape to these historical insights and contemporary interrelationships. The business cycle, the wave-like rise and fall of economic activity, provides that necessary framework. You are already familiar with the cycle in your own investing, business, or personal situation, and the news media have provided increased coverage of the ups and downs of the economy in recent years. Economic expansion and contraction, easy or tight credit conditions, inflation, and unemployment are recurring facts of life. Who escapes them?

The business cycle is the best vehicle for illuminating the *Journal*'s regularly appearing statistical series. Its phases bring life and meaning to the statistical reports and establish the perspective through which the illustrations and examples in the book are interwoven into a unified exposition.

Each chapter will introduce one or more statistical series, and each will be devoted to a theme (such as the money and credit markets) that is used to describe and explain the statistical series introduced in the chapter, beginning with the simplest and most basic elements of the business cycle and proceeding to additional topics that will complete your understanding. This step-by-step progression of topics will not, however, prevent you from breaking into any chapter, out of order, if you wish to examine a particular statistical series or group of series. Indeed, you may already have a firm grasp of some of these topics and need only to fill in the missing elements to round out your comprehension of the essential workings of American business. A complete listing of all the statistical series discussed in this guide can be found in the appendices following Chapter 17.

Each chapter will describe its statistical series in the context of the business cycle and explain the relationship of the new series to the overall picture.

Analysis will be based on charts drawn from official sources so that you can visualize the data and put the current information in perspective. Recent articles in *The Wall Street Journal* containing the statistical series will be reproduced and discussed so that you can interpret the data in light of the visual presentation made by the charts. Finally, you will be alerted to what future developments can be expected.

You will enjoy putting the puzzle together yourself. Anyone can do it, with a little help. The ebb and flow of the business cycle will channel the stream of data that now floods you in seemingly random fashion, and you will experience a genuine sense of accomplishment in creating order out of something that may previously have appeared chaotic.

A word of caution before you begin. This will not be an economics or business cycle course or text, nor will it be a precise forecasting device. There will be no formula or model. The business cycle is used strictly as a vehicle to make the statistical information usable in as easy a manner as possible. The objective is not to make a professional economist out of you, but to enable you to conduct your own analysis of the data just as soon as you are able. You will dive into the data and "get your hands dirty" by taking apart the cycle, analyzing it, and reassembling it. When you have finished this book, you will feel confident that you can deal with the data on your own.

Now, before exploring the business cycle in detail, take time for a leisurely overview.

C H A P T E R

THE BUSINESS CYCLE

A BIT OF HISTORY

THE BUSINESS CYCLE IS NOTHING NEW. It's been a characteristic of every capitalist economy in the modern era. Nations have endured boom followed by bust, prosperity and then depression—periods of growth and confidence trailing off into a decade of despair.

It is all so familiar to us that images of its human effects are scattered among our popular stereotypes. Men in top hats peer at ticker tape emerging from a little glass dome. They wheel and deal, corner wheat markets, play with railroads, and organize steel companies. Fortunes are quickly won and just as quickly lost. Former tycoons are seen selling apples on street corners. Factory gates shut and signs go up saying, "No help wanted." Soup kitchens appear, and desperate families flee the dust bowl in Model A pickup trucks.

These caricatures—based on real history, actual power, blows of ill fortune, human suffering—persist in our collective consciousness, permanently etched by the Great Depression. Although the stock market collapse of 1929 is the most notorious such event in our history, it is by no means unique. Cycles in the American economy can be traced and analyzed going back to the beginning of the 19th century.

The settlement of the West is an example. The frontier assumes such importance in our history and folklore that we tend to think of the westward migration as a smooth, if hazardous, inevitable flow, driven by the doctrine of manifest destiny. It didn't happen that way. The settlement of the West proceeded in a cyclical pattern.

Farmers and ranchers were (and are) businesspeople. The sod house and subsistence farming of the 1800s were temporary inconveniences, converted as quickly as possible to growing cash crops and raising livestock for the market. The settlers wanted to know the bottom line, the difference between revenue and expense. They wanted the best price for their cotton, corn, cattle, wheat, and hogs. They wanted to maximize production and minimize cost by using modern cultivation techniques and the latest equipment. Railroads and banks concerned them, because transportation and interest rates affected the cost of doing business and thus their profit margin. Finally, and most important, farmers wanted their capital to grow. They expected their net worth to increase as their farms appreciated in value and their mortgages were paid.

This experience was not confined to the United States; European settlers in Canada, Australia, and Argentina produced the same commodities under similar conditions. All were part of the growing world economy. Every farmer and rancher counted on industrialization and urbanization at home and in Europe to build demand for his or her commodities.

And worldwide demand for food and fiber did increase rapidly. Farmers responded by boosting production as best they could on existing holdings. Eventually, however, their output reached its limit, even though demand continued to grow. As a result, prices began to creep, and then race, upward. The venturesome dreamed of moving west and doubling or tripling their acreage. Record crop and livestock prices made the costs of moving and financing a new spread seem manageable, and existing farms could always be sold to the less intrepid. Thousands upon thousands of families streamed across the frontier, claiming millions of acres offered by generous government policies or buying from speculators who held raw land.

Nobody planned the westward migration; nobody coordinated it; nobody governed it. Each individual made his or her own calculation of the market. Farmers borrowed in order to purchase land and building materials and to buy livestock, seed, and equipment. Newly opened banks faced an insatiable demand for credit. Towns sprang up at railroad sidings where grain elevators and livestock yards were constructed. Merchants and Main Street followed. High prices brought a land boom, and the land boom brought settlement and opened the West.

It took a while for the newly converted prairie to produce a cash crop. But when it did, thousands of new farms began dumping their output on the market. The supply of agricultural commodities increased dramatically. Shortage changed to surplus, and prices dropped. Time after time during the 19th century, commodity prices fell to record lows after a period of inflation and the subsequent land rush.

Many farmers were wiped out. They could not pay their debts while commodity prices scraped bottom, and banks foreclosed on farm property. If a bank made too many loans that went bad, then it was dragged down too. Merchants saw their customers disappear and had to close up shop. Settlers abandoned their land, and boomtowns became ghost towns.

Prices inevitably remained low for years, and most farmers, living on returns far below expectations, barely made it. In every instance, it took a while before the steady growth in world demand absorbed the excess agricultural commodities.

But as time passed, the cycle would repeat itself. After the inflation that accompanied the Civil War, western settlement continued to occur in waves until the end of the century, despite 30 years of deflation. The process happened at least half a dozen times until the frontier closed in the last years of the 19th century.

By the turn of this century, progress had been spectacular. Many thousands of acres of prairie had been transformed into productive field and pasture. Commodities worth billions of dollars were produced annually for the domestic and world markets. Billions of dollars of wealth had been created in the form of improved farmland. But the discipline of the business cycle governed the advance. For every two steps forward, there had been one step backward, as those who borrowed or lent the least wisely, settled the poorest land, or had the worst luck went broke.

Things haven't changed. Agriculture's fortunes are still guided by the cycle. Remember the boom of the early 70s? Consumption of beef was up; President Nixon negotiated the wheat deal with Russia; the Peruvian anchovy harvest had failed, and soy beans were used to fill the gap (as a protein extender). Agricultural commodity prices doubled, even tripled, causing farm income to shoot up. As a result, farmers spent the rest of the decade investing heavily in land and equipment. Ultimately, supply outstripped demand, and farm prices deteriorated throughout the early 80s.

We've seen the result. It's nothing that hasn't happened before: foreclosures, bankruptcies, falling land values, broken families, and ruined lives. Eventually, of course, prices stabilized—until the next cycle comes along to start the process all over again.

Oil presents a similar picture. Billions were spent on exploration, recovery, and production projects in Texas, Louisiana, Oklahoma, Wyoming, Colorado, and Alaska when prices were high. Houston, Dallas, Denver, and Anchorage were boomtowns in the early 1980s. Then, when prices fell (and they always do), the money dried up. Soon you could get a condominium in Anchorage or Denver for $15,000 because whole city blocks of

new housing developments were abandoned—left by their owners for bank foreclosure.

What was true for farming and oil was equally true for the nation's railroads: They developed in the same cyclical pattern. On the eve of World War I, America's railway system was complete, representing a total capital investment second only to that of agriculture. It was a remarkable feat of creative engineering and equally creative financing.

We marvel at the colorful exploits of the Goulds, Fisks, Drews, Vanderbilts, Stanfords, Hills, and others. History refers to some of them as "robber barons"; they seemed to skim off one dollar for every two invested, and it's a wonder that the railway system was ever completed or operated safely. Yet there it was, the largest in the world, a quarter of a million miles of track moving the nation's freight and passenger traffic with unparalleled efficiency.

Promoters speculatively pushed the railroads westward in anticipation of the freight and passenger traffic that settlement would bring. Federal, state, and local governments, vying for the routes that would generate progress and development, gave the railroad companies 10 percent of the nation's land. Improving rights-of-way; laying track; building trestles, stations, and marshaling yards; and purchasing locomotives and rolling stock required the railway company to raise more capital than had ever been mobilized for any other single business venture. The companies floated billions of dollars in stocks and bonds, and investors eagerly ventured their capital to take advantage of prospective success. Flush with funds, the railroads raced toward the Pacific Coast, hoping that revenue would grow quickly enough to justify their huge investment. Periodically, however, the generous rate of expansion exceeded the growth in traffic. Prospects for profits, which had seemed so bright, grew dim. Investors stopped providing funds, and railroad track construction came to a halt. Since operating revenues could not recover costs, many railroads were forced into receivership and were reorganized. Stock and bond prices plunged, wiping out investors long after the promoters had made off with their killings.

Eventually, traffic grew sufficiently to justify existing lines and raise hopes that construction could profitably resume. Investors were once again lured into advancing their funds, and a new cycle of railway expansion began. It, too, was followed by a bust, and then by another wave of construction, until the nation's railway system was complete.

The tracks spanned a continent, from New York, Philadelphia, and Baltimore to Chicago, and from there to New Orleans, Los Angeles, San Francisco, Portland, and Seattle. Profit had motivated the enterprise, and enormous tangible wealth had been created. Losses had periodically and temporarily

halted the undertaking and impoverished those who had speculated unwisely or who had been duped. Construction had proceeded in waves. It was an unplanned and often disorganized adventure, but, given the institutions of the time, no other method could have built the system as rapidly.

In this century, we have seen the business cycle not only in the heroic proportions of the Roaring Twenties and the Great Depression, but also during every succeeding business expansion or recession. We're in the cycle now, and we will be tomorrow and next year.

Business activity always expands and then contracts. There are periods when production, employment, and profits surge ahead, each followed by a period when profits and output fall and unemployment increases. Then the entire cycle repeats itself once again. During the expansion, demand, production, income, and wealth grow. Homes and factories are constructed, and machinery and equipment are put in place. The value of these assets also grows as home prices and common stock prices increase. But then comes the inevitable contraction, and all the forces that mark the expansion shift into reverse. Demand, production, and income fall. The level of construction and the production of machinery and equipment are drastically curtailed. Assets lose their value as home prices and common stock prices fall.

No doubt you already realize that business cycles occur and repeat themselves in this way. But why? No completely satisfactory theory has yet been created. No one can accurately predict the length and course of each cycle. Economics, unlike physics, cannot be reduced to experiments and repeated over and over again under ideal conditions. There is no economic equivalent to Galileo on the Tower of Pisa, proving that objects of unequal weight fall with equal speed, because the economic "tower" is never quite the same height; the "objects" keep changing in number, size, and even nature; and the "laws of gravity" apply unequally to each object.

Yet one thing is certain: The business cycle is generated by forces within the economic system, not by outside forces. These internal forces create the alternating periods of economic expansion and contraction. And you should recognize that certain crucial feature of the cycle endure.

A THUMBNAIL SKETCH
First, the forces of supply and demand condition every cycle. Our ability to enjoy increasing income depends on our ability to supply or create increased production or output; we must produce more to earn more. But the level of demand, and the expenditures made in purchasing this output, must justify the level of production. That is, we must sell what we produce in order to earn. With sufficient demand, the level of production will be sustained and will

grow, and income will increase; if demand is insufficient, the reverse will occur. During the expansionary phase of the cycle, demand and supply forces are in a relationship that permits the growth of production and income; during the contractionary phase, their relationship compels a decrease in production and income.

Second, neither consumers nor businesses are constrained to rely solely on the income they have generated in the process of production. They have recourse to the credit market; they can borrow money and spend more than they earn. Spending borrowed funds permits demand to take on a life of its own and bid up a constantly and rapidly growing level of production. This gives rise to the expansionary phase of the cycle. Eventually, the growth in production becomes dependent on the continued availability of credit, which sustains the growth in demand. But once buyers can no longer rely on borrowed funds (because of market saturation, the exhaustion of profitable investment opportunities, or tight credit), demand falls and, with it, the bloated level of production and income. The contractionary phase has begun.

Third, every expansion carries with it the inevitability of "overexpansion," the creation of excess productive capacity and subsequent contraction. Overexpansion may be propelled by businesses that invest too heavily in new plant and equipment in order to take advantage of a seemingly profitable opportunity, thereby creating excess productive capacity. Consumers who borrow too heavily in order to buy homes, autos, or other goods can also spur on overexpansion. But when businesses realize the expected level of sales will not support the newly created excess, let alone investments in and purchases of additional plant and equipment, and when consumers realize they will have difficulty paying for that new home or car, then both businesses and consumers curtail their borrowing and expenditures. Since production and income have spurted ahead to meet the growth in demand, they fall when the inevitable contraction in demand takes place.

Fourth, during contractions, production and income recede to a sustainable level; that is, they fall to a level not reliant on a continuous growth in credit. The contraction returns the economy to a more efficient level of operation.

Fifth, every contraction sows the seeds of the subsequent recovery. Income earned in the productive process, rather than bloated levels of borrowing, maintains the level of demand. Consumers and businesses repay their debts. Eventually, lower debt burdens and interest rates encourage consumer and business borrowing and demand. The economy begins expanding once more.

And there is progress over the course of the cycle. Overall growth takes place because some, or even most, of the increase in output remains intact. Nor is all the created wealth subsequently destroyed. The abandoned steel mills of the "rust belt" will be scrapped, but the plant and equipment used to make personal computers will remain on-stream. Residential construction completed in 1986 turned a profit for its developers, while homes completed in 1990, at the peak of the cycle, were liquidated at a loss after standing empty for a year. And so on. The tree grows, but the rings in its trunk mark the cycles of seasons that were often lush but on occasion were beset by drought.

Why did the economy lurch into recession in 1990, but then grow steadily throughout the rest of the decade? Had the business cycle been repealed? Some seem to think so. But others had thought so before them, only to be disappointed by the next recession. Did President Clinton and his policies deserve the credit? Was the Federal Reserve responsible?

The chapters that follow will not only discuss the cycle's dynamic, they will also describe the forces that "stretched out" the cycle in the 1990s and postponed a recession's expected return. Was it reasonable to expect continued prosperity at the end of the 1990s?

But as you may already suspect, the business cycle does not operate in a vacuum. It is conditioned, shortened and stretched, and initiated and forestalled by the institutions of our economy. So, before embarking on an investigation of the cycle, take a quick look at Chapter 3, which discusses the attempts to influence the economy since World War II.

THE TRANSFORMATION OF THE POSTWAR ECONOMY

TO THIS POINT, WE HAVE DISCUSSED THE BUSINESS CYCLE as if it were independent and autonomous. In fact, in modern history, the American business cycle has been influenced by a variety of attempts to guide and direct it. The economic events of the 15 years from 1965 to 1980 provide a vivid example of well-intentioned economic meddling gone awry.

During these years, the federal government and the Federal Reserve System attempted to stimulate demand for goods and services with liberal spending, tax, and credit policies. Their objective was to boost the economy higher and faster, thereby generating increased employment opportunities. They thought that as supply rose to meet demand, increased production would accomplish their objectives. Unfortunately, as demand grew more rapidly than supply, prices spiraled upward. As inflation became more severe, the only solution appeared to be a periodic reversal of those policies of liberal spending, tax, and credit—which invariably helped plunge the economy into recession. These policy reversals exacerbated the cycle so that inflation *escalated* during boom and unemployment rose during bust.

The actions of the Federal Reserve and federal government had their origin in the 1930s, when economists were attempting to cope with the rav-

ages of the Great Depression. At that time, it was obvious that the economy was stagnating due to insufficient demand for the goods and services business could produce. The factories were there; the machines were there; the labor was there; only the customers were missing. The great question of the day was, "How can we generate effective demand for goods and services?"

Traditional economists had no solution to the problem. They viewed the Depression as a trough in a particularly severe cycle that would correct itself with time. Therefore, they prescribed laissez-faire (leave it alone) as the best possible course of action. Why not? It had always worked in the past.

A new generation of economists surveyed the scene and came up with a different diagnosis. They saw the Great Depression as inaugurating an era in which demand was (and might remain) chronically depressed. To deal with the problem, they recommended a two-pronged solution.

First, stimulate demand directly. Clearly, consumers were not going to spend more, for many were unemployed, and those who were working were afraid to spend, because they might lose their jobs. Business was not going to buy new factories and machinery, since existing facilities were underutilized. Only the government was in a position to spend more. Such government spending would involve deficit financing as the level of expenditures exceeded tax revenues, but the New Dealers were prepared to run the risk. If the government had to borrow now, it could pay back later. In this way, the government would be the employer of last resort, hiring people to build dams, bridges, roads, and parks.

Second, the Federal Reserve System (the nation's central bank, known as the Fed) could push interest rates down and thereby depress the cost of borrowing money. This would motivate businesses (to the extent that they could be motivated) to borrow funds in order to buy equipment and machinery and to build additional factories and other establishments. Making credit easy was a way of stimulating economic activity.

These policies, applied in the late 30s, were interrupted by World War II, which generated boom conditions. But when the war came to an end, it was feared that the economy would again slip back into a chronic state of depression. That anxiety was unfounded, but it was so strongly felt that the ideological revolution of the 1930s survived. The new school of economists believed it was the government's duty to stimulate demand until the economy reached its maximum potential of full employment. This attitude meshed with other liberal and progressive views regarding government's responsibility for the social welfare of all.

Conservatives, on the other hand, continued to believe that laissez-faire was the best policy. Thus, throughout the Eisenhower years, the conserva-

tive administration drew fire from progressive economists for not implementing the lessons that had been learned in the 30s. They wanted additional federal spending and easy money in order to spur the economy.

When John F. Kennedy ran for office in 1960, he charged that the Eisenhower administration's conservative policies had reduced the rate of economic growth, and he promised to get the economy moving again. After he took office in 1961, he made good on that pledge by inviting the new school of economists into his administration, urging them to apply the progressive policies that had been developed under Roosevelt.

They did prescribe those policies, but with a new wrinkle. Rather than stimulate demand directly with increased government spending, they proposed putting more purchasing power in the pockets of consumers by cutting taxes. The government would still have to borrow to meet the deficit, but this time it would do so to pay for a shortfall of revenue rather than a growth in expenditure. One way or the other, demand would grow.

Increased consumer spending was just as good as government spending—and, as a rule, politically more advantageous. The extra spending would stimulate economic growth and create jobs as production expanded to meet the surge in consumer demand. At the same time, President Kennedy's economists urged the Federal Reserve to maintain an easy policy so that liberal credit would be available at low rates of interest for consumer and business needs.

These views remained in fashion for two decades. A generation of students was trained to believe that an inadequate level of demand was the paramount problem facing the economy and that they should study economics in order to determine how the federal government and the Federal Reserve could best stimulate the level of economic activity to provide full employment. They all recognized that excessive stimulation of demand could lead to inflation, but they felt that inflation would not be a severe problem until the economy attained full employment.

In each recession the Federal Reserve depressed interest rates, and the government stimulated spending directly with tax cuts for consumers and business. Demand roared ahead in short order, and, when it exceeded supply at current prices, prices surged upward. At this point the federal government and the Federal Reserve reversed course and employed policies designed to dampen inflation. They slammed on the brakes, raising taxes and interest rates, depressing demand temporarily, and causing recession. But as soon as the inflation rate dropped, they reversed course and helped bring on the next round of expanding demand and inflation.

No one—not the economists, not the government, not the Federal Reserve—realized that World War II had profoundly changed the underlying

circumstances and that policies appropriate for the 30s were not suited for the 60s and 70s. The Great Depression, which preceded the war, was a time of inadequate demand. But government borrowing from banks during the war, and the expenditures of those funds, had placed a wealth of liquid assets at the consumer's disposal. When the war ended, consumers were prepared to spend those funds, and they were also increasingly prepared to borrow in order to supplement their expenditures. In the postwar world, demand, buttressed by borrowing, would chronically exceed supply, thus bidding prices upward. Excessive demand, not inadequate demand, would be the problem.

Thus began the first American peacetime period with significant and continuing inflation. In all other eras, inflation had been the product of wartime government spending financed by borrowing, while peacetime had been a period of stable prices or even deflation. Consequently, government spending financed by borrowing, whether in time of war or peace, was viewed by almost everyone as the single source of inflation, and this mindset spilled over into the postwar world. No one comprehended that a new economic dynamic was at work in which inflation would be generated by private (consumer and business) borrowing and spending. Ever greater waves of borrowing by the private sector (not government) would drive the inflationary cycle.

The new generation of economists and their students, whose intellectual mold had been cast during the New Deal, were like generals who conduct a war by fighting the previous campaign. But the real issue facing the postwar world was how to keep demand under control, how to restrain it and prevent it from generating inflation. The Eisenhower years, when demand did seem to stall, confused economists, making them believe that the chronically depressed conditions of the 1930s were a real possibility in the postwar world.

This was a major miscalculation. In fact, the escalating inflation of the 70s showed us that the potential runaway horse of the economy was champing at the bit—and all the while economists and policymakers were wondering how to apply the spurs more vigorously.

By 1980, after two decades of inappropriate policies, the Federal Reserve was determined to come to grips with the problem. New Deal economics had to be discarded. The spurs had to be removed, the reins taken in hand, and the runaway horse restrained. So the Fed tightened up; interest rates reached the stratosphere, borrowing and spending dried up, and the economy came closer to collapsing in 1981–82 than at any time since the war. After the recession of 1981–82 contained demand and eliminated inflation, the Fed slowly began to ease up. But the Fed was determined not to return to the errors of the past; it would not let credit become easy, or demand grow too rapidly, or inflation get out of control again.

Thus, the Fed acted single-handedly to stretch out the business cycle and forestall recession. By squashing the cycle flat in the early 1980s, and then restraining inflation in the mid and late 80s, the Fed interrupted the cycle's regular and periodic oscillations. This created a period of steady expansion during which the economy did not overheat.

But the war with Iraq instigated the recession of 1990–91 and brought an end to the Fed's run of good luck. The Fed responded to the recession by letting interest rates fall sharply and holding them there until recovery was well under way. Then, mindful of its overriding long-run concern with inflation, the Fed sent interest rates upward when the economy expanded rapidly in 1994 and 1995. The Fed hoped its preemptive strike would cool the economy before it overheated, instigate a "soft landing," and prevent a repeat of the cyclical excess of the 1970s. And it worked. The economy took off in the late 1990s, enjoying rapid growth along with continually falling inflation.

So before you consider *The Wall Street Journal*'s reports on business cycle developments, read Chapters 4 and 5 to review the role of the Federal Reserve System and the federal government in today's business and investment scene.

THE FEDERAL RESERVE SYSTEM: MONETARY POLICY AND INTEREST RATES

THE FED AND INFLATION

CHART 1–1 ON PAGE 4 PROVIDES GRAPHIC EVIDENCE that inflation and the business cycle have the greatest imaginable impact on economic conditions and investment values. Because the Federal Reserve System (the Fed) is the only modern American institution that has been able to constructively control and shape these forces, you should begin by learning how to use *The Wall Street Journal* to decipher the Fed's operations.

The Fed is your first order of business because the power of the Fed squashed the business cycle flat in the early 1980s, bringing an end to excessive inflation for the foreseeable future. Before that, during the high-inflation 70s, business cycle fluctuations had grown more severe and inflation's pace had accelerated. *Thus, the Fed's stand against inflation in 1981–82 was the most important turning point in our post World War II economic history.*

The business cycle and inflation had spun out of control in the late 1960s and 70s because consumers and businesses had borrowed ever more heavily to finance ever larger expenditures on homes, cars, and other durable goods,

as well as plant, equipment, and inventory. As oceans of borrowing supported tidal waves of spending (i.e., demand for goods and services), supply could not keep pace, and prices rose.

To understand this phenomenon, consider a hypothetical example in which people had just as much to spend at the end of a given year as at the beginning, but had increased their output of goods and services by 5 percent during that year. Prices would have to fall by 5 percent before the same amount of spending (demand) could absorb an additional 5 percent of goods and services (supply). And if folks continued each year to produce 5 percent more while their spending did not grow, then prices would fall by 5 percent year after year. We would have chronic deflation.

Similarly, if people's ability to spend (demand) grew by 20 percent while output (supply) grew by 5 percent, you can imagine prices being bid up by 15 percent in that year. And if their spending continued to grow by 20 percent a year while their output grew by only 5 percent, you can imagine chronic inflation of 15 percent. Now you understand how changing supply and demand generate deflation and inflation.

You may ask, "How is it possible for spending (demand) to grow more rapidly than the output (supply) of society? You can spend only what you have, after all." No, not if people have access to credit provided by banks. For instance, suppose you earn $50,000 a year and your income is a measure of the value of the goods and services that you produce or supply for the market. Also, suppose that your spending (demand) is limited by your income. Demand and supply ($50,000) are equal, so prices don't change. Now suppose that you have access to bank credit, so that you can borrow $200,000 to have a house built. Your demand (spending) rises to $200,000, even though your income (supply) remains at $50,000. Demand exceeds supply in this case, and if your situation is repeated often enough in others, prices rise. Whenever demand exceeds supply at current prices, a situation made possible by borrowing (credit), inflation (rising prices) occurs.

The $200,000 provided by the banks was *not* produced and saved by someone else, thereby equating earlier supply with new demand. It was created out of thin air by the banking system, and that is why your bank-financed spending is inflationary. It also illustrates the importance of understanding the banking and credit system to comprehend the reasons for the ever-escalating business cycle and inflation of 1965–80 and inflation's subsequent demise.

Private borrowing by consumers and businesses has always been a feature of our economy, but it did not begin to reach heroic proportions and grow at an explosive pace until the late 1960s. From that point on, credit doubled

every five years. There was no way production could keep pace with these surges in demand, so rising inflation filled the gap.

But borrowing and spending did not grow smoothly. They surged forward periodically, generating the wave-like action of the business cycle. The rise of borrowing and spending carried inflation with it; interest rates rose too, as spiraling borrowing drove up the cost of credit. Steep increases in prices and interest rates eventually choked off the boom, discouraging consumers and businesses from continued borrowing and spending. The wave crashed and the cycle completed itself as the economy contracted into recession.

The Fed exacerbated the worst aspects of the cycle in the late 60s and throughout the 70s by attempting to alleviate them. Reining in credit expansion at the peak of the cycle in order to curb inflation merely contributed to the severity of the inevitable downturn and made recession worse. Easing up during recession, in order to encourage borrowing and spending and thus pull the economy out of a slump, contributed to the excesses of the next boom. And with each wave of the cycle, inflation and interest rates ratcheted higher and higher.

The Fed reversed course in 1981–82 and brought an end to 15 years of escalating inflation and cyclical instability by applying a chokehold of high interest rates. The economy was brought to the brink of collapse. But when the Fed relaxed its grip and interest rates declined from exorbitant to merely high, the manic rounds of boom and bust had ceased. The economy set out on a healthy expansion without inflation that lasted through the late 80s until Iraq's invasion of Kuwait eroded consumer sentiment, casting a pall over borrowing and spending that instigated the 1990–91 recession.

That recession prompted the Fed to let interest rates fall to their lowest level in years, as the economy languished in the doldrums of an anemic recovery. But by late 1994, the Fed had ratcheted rates up again in order to rein in a rapidly expanding economy. At the end of the decade the Fed continued to fine-tune the economy, raising interest rates whenever growth seemed excessive and reducing rates when recession threatened.

Borrowing and Inflation

- Bank lending finances spending; spending generates inflation.
- The Fed controls bank lending and can thereby control inflation.
- But a drop in borrowing and spending will reduce inflation and, if sufficiently sharp, will lead to recession.

But what is the Fed? How does it work? What, exactly, did it (and does it) do? Start your investigation with a bit of background.

THE FED'S HISTORY

The United States was the last major industrial nation to establish a central bank. The modern German state commissioned a central bank in 1875; the Bank of France was founded in 1800; and the Bank of England had entered its third century of operation when the Federal Reserve System was created in 1913.

America's tardiness was due to our traditional suspicion of centralized financial power and authority. Historically, we have felt more comfortable with small banks serving a single community. In fact, some states limited branch banking until recently. For instance, the First National Bank of Chicago became one of the nation's biggest, even though Illinois law severely constrained its branch facilities in downstate Illinois. Similarly, the big New York City banks (until after World War II) were hampered by legislation that confined them to the city and its suburbs and kept their branches out of upstate New York. On the other hand, California's liberal branch banking laws once helped Bank of America build its position as the nation's largest bank. To this day, a rational, nationwide scheme for organizing our banking institutions does not exist.

Alexander Hamilton proposed a central bank shortly after the country's founding. The two early attempts to create one failed when confronted with the nation's suspicion of the Eastern financial community. Consequently, our economy grew until the eve of World War I without benefit of coordination or control of its banking activity. Banking, like the sale of alcohol following the repeal of Prohibition, was largely subject to local option.

Under these circumstances, the banks had to fend for themselves, and the business cycle created perils for them as well as opportunities for profit. During recessions, when business income was down (usually following periods of speculative excess), banks found it difficult to collect on loans.

At the same time, nervous businesspersons and investors made large withdrawals, sometimes demanding payment in gold or silver specie. These precious metal coins composed the ultimate reserve for deposits; however, no bank possessed enough of them to secure every depositor, and the banking system functioned on the assumption that only a minority of depositors would demand their funds on any one day. When panic set in and a queue formed out the door and around the block, a bank could be wiped out in a matter of hours. As rumor spread, one bank after another failed, until only the most substantial institutions, with the greatest specie reserve, were left

standing. The chain reaction damaged many people, not the least of whom were innocent depositors who could not reach their funds in time.

Congress took up the issue after the panic of 1907. In that crisis—as the story goes—J.P. Morgan kept New York's most important bankers locked up in his home overnight until they agreed to contribute a pool of specie to be lent to the weakest banks until the run subsided. It worked—but the near-disaster had made it clear that the time had come to establish an American central bank that could lend to all banks in time of panic; the nation's financial system could no longer rely on the private arrangements of J.P. Morgan. Thus, Congress established the Federal Reserve System in 1913. All member banks were required to make deposits to the system, creating a pool of reserves from which financially strapped banks could borrow during a crisis.

The system was originally conceived as a lender of last resort. In times of severe economic stress, it would use the pooled reserves of the banking system to make loans to banks under stress. When conditions improved, the loans were to be repaid. As time went by, however, the Fed discovered two things: first, that the reserve requirement could be used to control banking activity; and second, that control over the banking system provided a means of influencing the business cycle.

The reasoning was straightforward. Bank lending is a key ingredient in the business cycle, driving the cyclic expansion of demand. It cannot, however, grow beyond the limits set by bank reserves; so, when the Fed wants to give the economy a boost by encouraging banks to lend more, it increases reserves. On the other hand, by decreasing reserves and thereby shrinking available credit, the Fed exerts a restraining effect on the economy.

OPEN-MARKET OPERATIONS

The mechanism used by the Fed to manipulate the banking system's reserves is astonishingly simple: It buys or sells securities on the open market. Briefly put, when the Fed buys securities, the sellers deposit the proceeds of the sale in their banks, and the banking system's reserves grow. On the other hand, when the Fed sells securities, buyers withdraw funds from their banks in order to make the purchases, and bank reserves fall.

This illustration may help you understand the process. Imagine that the Fed, a government-securities dealer, and all banks (not an individual bank) are the only players in this example. Keep in mind that there are trillions of dollars of U.S. Treasury securities outstanding and that anyone (domestic and foreign corporations; individuals; state, local, and foreign governments; private banks; and central banks) can buy them. Billions of dollars of securities are traded each day in New York City.

The Fed increases and reduces bank reserves by its actions in this market. It trades in U.S. Treasury securities rather than some other instrument because the government securities market is so broad and Federal Reserve activities have a relatively small impact on the market.

When the Fed purchases a security from one of the dealers, it pays the dealer by instructing the dealer's bank to credit the checking account of the dealer by the amount of the transaction. At the same time, the Fed pays the bank by crediting the bank's reserve account at the Fed.

Returning to the example, Treasury bills are denominated in amounts of $10,000. Thus, when the Fed buys a Treasury bill from a securities dealer, it instructs the dealer's bank to credit the dealer's account by $10,000 to pay for the Treasury bill. At the same time, the Fed credits the dealer's bank's reserve account by $10,000. As a result of the transaction, the dealer has exchanged one asset (Treasury bills ↓ $10,000) for another (checking account ↑ $10,000), the bank's assets (reserves at the Fed ↑ $10,000) and liabilities (dealer's checking account ↑ $10,000) have both increased, and the Fed's assets (Treasury bills ↑ $10,000) and liabilities (bank reserves ↑ $10,000) have both increased.

You may ask, "What gives the Fed the authority to execute these transactions: to pay for a Treasury bill by instructing the dealer's bank to credit the dealer's checking account and then to compensate the bank by crediting its reserve account at the Fed? It's as if the Fed has the right to fund the purchase of an asset by creating its own liability." That's how it works. The Fed has the right under the authority vested in it by the Federal Reserve Act of 1913.

In other words, the Fed can increase the nation's bank reserves by purchasing U.S. Treasury securities from securities dealers, and all it need do to pay for those securities is inform the banks that it has provided them with more reserves. And that's not all; be aware that, unless the Fed continues to buy those securities and pay for them by crediting the banks' reserve accounts, bank reserves won't grow. The Fed can halt the economy's expansion by no longer purchasing Treasury bills. Once the Fed stops buying, bank reserves stop growing, and so must bank lending. If the Fed wishes to keep a growing economy supplied with bank reserves, it must increase its holdings of Treasury securities over the long haul.

But suppose the Fed wishes to slow the economy's growth temporarily by curtailing banks' ability to lend. Easy—it just stops *buying* securities and starts *selling* them. The securities dealer pays for the Treasury bill it acquires (dealer's assets ↑) when the Fed instructs the dealer's bank to debit the dealer's bank account (dealer's assets ↓). The Fed collects from the dealer's bank by debiting the bank's reserve account at the Fed (bank's assets ↓),

and the bank is compensated when it debits the dealer's checking account (bank's liabilities ↓). Consequently, bank lending must cease because the banks are deprived of reserves. Meanwhile, the Fed has merely reduced its assets (Treasury securities ↓) as well as its liabilities (bank reserves ↓).

Consider a few additional points. Don't worry whether or not the securities dealer is willing to buy or sell Treasury securities. There are dozens of dealers competing for the Fed's (and everyone else's) business. There's as much likelihood of the Fed not being able to find a buyer or seller for its Treasury securities as there is of someone not being able to buy or sell a share of stock at the market price. If one stockbroker won't do it, another will.

Also, don't be confused because these open-market operations involve the buying and selling of Treasury securities. Remember, the Fed is not an agency of the U.S. government. The Fed could just as easily deal in common stock or automobiles, but it wouldn't do that because it does not want its actions to upset the stock market or the car market. Nonetheless, keep in mind that the Fed could pay for shares of stock or autos by instructing banks to credit stockbrokers' or auto dealers' accounts (and then credit those banks' reserve accounts) in the same fashion that it instructs banks to credit U.S. Treasury securities dealers' accounts. Then, the Fed would credit the reserve accounts of the banks that held the stockbrokers' and car dealers' accounts. If the Fed sold common stock or used cars, it would drain away bank reserves just as surely as when it sold Treasury bills in the open market.

Finally, keep in mind that the discussion refers to all banks collectively, not to individual banks. This distinction is important. Banks can competitively drain one another of reserves to augment their ability to lend, but this activity does not increase the entire system's reserves, though it does explain the fierce rivalry among banks for deposits. When deposits are moved from one bank to another, the reserves of the first bank fall and those of the second bank increase. The first bank must restrain its lending, while the second bank can lend more. This competitive reshuffling of reserves, however, has not altered the overall level of reserves, and so the lending ability of the banking system remains the same.

To resume the historical account, the Fed has exercised increasing power over the economy since 1913. Periodically, this has led to conflict with the president and Congress. On occasion, politicians took the Fed to task for being too restrictive, for not permitting the economy to grow rapidly enough. At other times, the Fed was criticized for being too lenient and permitting demand to grow so rapidly that inflation threatened.

Why the conflict? Shouldn't the Fed's policy reflect the wishes of Congress and the president? Maybe, but it need not, for—as many do not real-

ize—the Fed is not an agency of the U.S. government, but a corporation owned by banks that have purchased shares of stock. Federally chartered banks are required to purchase this stock and be members of the Federal Reserve System; state-chartered banks may be members if they wish. All banks, however, are subject to the Fed's control.

True, the Fed does have a quasi-public character, because its affairs are managed by a Board of Governors appointed by the president of the United States with the approval of Congress. Nonetheless, once appointed, the Board of Governors is independent of the federal government and is free to pursue policies of its own choosing. New laws could, of course, change its status. That's why the chairman of the board is so frequently called upon to defend the policies of the Fed before Congress, and why Congress often reminds the Fed that it is a creature of Congress, which can enact legislation to reduce, alter, or eliminate the Fed's powers. Indeed, legislators and others do suggest from time to time that the Fed be made an agency of the U.S. government in order to remove its autonomy. So far, however, Congress has kept the Fed independent, and it is likely to remain so, exercising its best judgment in guiding the nation's banking activity.

In some ways, the Fed's control over the banking system's reserves is the most important relationship between any two institutions in the American economy. The Fed can increase or reduce bank reserves at will, making it easier or more difficult for the banks to lend, thus stimulating or restricting business and economic activity.

THE FED AND THE MONEY SUPPLY
But how is it that bank lending increases the supply of money? Where does the money come from? There is an astonishingly simple answer to these questions: The banks create it by crediting the checking account deposits of their borrowers. Thus, bank lending creates money (deposits).

And the only limits to the money supply are:

1. The Fed's willingness to provide the banks with reserves, so that they can lend.
2. The banks' ability to find borrowers.

It may sound strange that banks create money, but, nonetheless, it's true.

The reason so much controversy surrounds the money supply is that many people misunderstand its nature. Checking accounts (or demand deposits, as they are formally called) constitute three-quarters of the money supply, and currency and coins in circulation together make up the remaining quarter. The one-quarter of the money supply that exists as cash comes

from a two-tiered source: The U.S. Treasury mints coins and prints paper money for the Fed, and the Fed distributes them.

These arrangements have an interesting and important history. Before the Civil War, with the exception of the two short-lived attempts at a central bank that were mentioned earlier, all paper money was issued by private banks and was called bank notes. These bank notes resembled modern paper currency and entered circulation when banks lent them to customers.

The banks' incentive to issue bank notes to borrowers, instead of gold and silver coins, came from the limited supply of gold and silver coins (specie). If banks wished to lend more than the specie on hand, they would have to issue bank notes. Each bank kept a specie reserve that was no more than a fraction of its outstanding bank notes. This reserve was used to satisfy those who demanded that a bank redeem its notes with specie; as long as the bank could do so, its notes were accepted at face value and were "good as gold." Bank notes and minted coins circulated together.

After the Civil War, checking accounts replaced bank notes. They were safer and more convenient, because the customer (borrower) had to sign them and could write in their exact amount. In modern times, all customers, whether depositors or borrowers, began to make use of checking accounts. The private bank note passed into history.

The U.S. Treasury first issued paper money during the Civil War, and it continued to do so until some time after World War II. During the 20th century, however, most of our paper money has been issued by the Federal Reserve System, and today the Fed has that exclusive responsibility; if you examine a piece of currency, you will see that it is a "Federal Reserve Note." Thus, ironically, bank notes constitute all of our currency today, just as they did before the Civil War, but the notes are issued by the central bank rather than by a host of private banks.

Since the Treasury prints currency at the Fed's request to meet the public's needs, the common notion that the federal government cranks out more paper money to finance its deficits has no factual basis. The amount of paper money in circulation has nothing to do with the deficits of the federal government. When the federal government runs a deficit (expenditures exceed revenue), the Treasury borrows by issuing bonds that are bought by investors; the government gets the money, and the investors get the bonds. If a bond is sold to a bank (and banks are major purchasers of U.S. Treasury securities), the bank pays for it by crediting the checking account of the U.S. Treasury, thus increasing the total volume of all checking accounts. This is called *monetizing the debt*; it enlarges the money supply but does not affect currency in circulation. (If the bond is purchased by the Fed, the transaction is

also characterized as monetizing the debt, and the effect is similar to an expansionary monetary policy in which the Fed buys U.S. Treasury securities through open-market operations.)

By contrast, the Fed issues paper money in response not to the budget deficits of the *federal government*, but to the *public*'s requirements for cash. It supplies banks with currency, and the banks pay for it with a check written on their reserve account. Checks written to "cash" by bank customers then determine the amount of currency circulating outside banks. This demand for currency has no impact on the money supply because checking accounts decrease by the amount currency increases when the check is "cashed."

How then does the money supply grow? It increases in the same fashion that outstanding bank notes grew in the 19th century. When banks lend, they create demand deposits (checking accounts) or credit an existing demand deposit. The more that banks lend, the more that the money supply (which is mostly demand deposits) increases. Today, as 100 years ago, bank reserves set the only limit on bank lending and, therefore, on the money supply. The difference is that, instead of keeping specie as reserves, the banks must maintain reserves with the Fed.

Remember: Bank loans create deposits (checking accounts), not the other way around. As long as the banking system has sufficient reserves, it can make loans in the form of demand deposits (money). You must abandon the notion that depositors' funds provide the wherewithal for bank lending. That may be true for the traditional mortgage-lending activity of a savings and loan association, but it is not true for commercial banks. After all, where would depositors get the funds if not by withdrawing them from another checking account? But this actually does not increase deposits for the entire system; it only reshuffles deposits among banks. The total is unchanged.

Thus, demand deposits (checking accounts), and with them the money supply, grow when banks lend, and it makes no difference who the borrower is. When a business borrows from its bank in order to stock goods for the Christmas season, the bank creates a deposit (money) on which the business writes checks to pay for merchandise. If you borrow from your bank to buy a car, the loan creates a demand deposit that increases the money supply. Therefore, as you can see, it is not just the federal government that "monetizes debt" when it borrows from the banking system; businesses and consumers "monetize" their debt too.

One last point must be made about the nature of bank reserves. A hundred years ago, these reserves consisted of gold and silver specie; today, they are deposits that banks maintain with the Federal Reserve System. Of what do these reserves consist, if not specie? They are merely checking

accounts that the banks have on deposit with the Fed, very much like the checking account you have at your own bank.

Recall that the banks' checking accounts (reserves) increase when the Fed buys securities from a government securities dealer. In other words, banks' reserves are nothing more than accounts the banks maintain at the Fed, accounts that grow at the Fed's discretion whenever it buys securities in the open market.

If it sounds like a house of cards, or like bookkeeping entries in a computer's memory, that's because it is. Nothing "backs up" the money supply except our faith in it, expressed every time we accept or write a check. Those checking accounts, and hence the money supply, built on borrowing, *must keep growing* if the economy is to grow over the business cycle. The forward surge of the cycle, when demand grows rapidly and pulls the economy's output with it, is founded on spenders' ability and willingness to borrow and to go into debt.

This, then, is the critical significance of the money supply: It measures the increase in demand made possible by bank lending. With that in mind, it is now time to discuss the price borrowers are willing to pay for those funds.

THE FED AND INTEREST RATES

Every commodity has a price; the *interest rate* is the price of money. As with any commodity, that price fluctuates according to the laws of supply and demand.

The demand for money increases and interest rates rise during economic expansion as consumers and businesses finance increased spending. They do so by drawing on three sources of funds: current savings, liquidation of financial assets, and borrowing from banks and other financial intermediaries. It's easy to see that an increase in the demand for funds will drive up interest rates.

During recessions, however, as the economy moves from trough to recovery, cash becomes plentiful again. Savings grow, financial assets accumulate, and debt is repaid. Interest rates fall as the supply of funds exceeds the demand for funds at current rates.

The cyclical rise and fall of interest rates would occur with or without the Federal Reserve System. Yet the Fed's influence on interest rates is so pervasive that it is now time to study the Fed's actions in detail.

Begin with a summary statement of the Fed's objectives and actions that refers to neither the money supply nor interest rates, which will be developed later:

- *Expansionary policy:* If the Fed buys securities, thus increasing member bank reserves, the banks will be able to lend more, stimulating

demand. Such an expansionary policy has traditionally been pursued during a period of recession, when the economy is at the bottom of the business cycle.

- *Contractionary policy:* If the Fed sells securities, and bank reserves are reduced, the banks will not be able to lend as much, which will curtail the share of demand that depends on borrowing and, hence, will reduce the total level of demand. This policy has been followed at the peak of the cycle to restrain the growth of demand and inflationary increases in prices.

These relationships can be easily summarized in the following manner: (Read ↑ as "up," ↓ as "down," and → as "leads to.")

Expansionary policy: Fed buys securities → Bank reserves ↑→ Bank lending ↑→ Demand ↑

Contractionary policy: Fed sells securities → Bank reserves ↓→ Bank lending ↓→ Demand ↓

Now include money in the analysis.

The Fed was traditionally activist, alternately pursuing easy (supplying banks with reserves) or tight (depriving banks of reserves) money policies, depending on the state of the business cycle. During periods of recession and through the recovery stage and the early period of expansion, the Fed's easy money policy contributed to rapid growth in the money supply (demand deposits or checking accounts), as banks lent money (demand deposits or checking accounts) freely in response to plentiful reserves. As the expansionary phase of the cycle reached its peak, the Fed switched to a tight money policy, restricting the growth of bank reserves and, hence, the money supply.

The Fed's actions with respect to the money supply may be added to the earlier set of directed arrows and summarized as shown:

Expansionary policy: Fed buys securities → Bank reserves ↑→ Bank lending ↑→ Money supply ↑→ Demand ↑

Contractionary policy: Fed sells securities → Bank reserves ↓→ Bank lending ↓→ Money supply ↓→ Demand ↓

As you can imagine, the Fed's actions also have an impact on interest rates. The Fed traditionally pursued an "easy money" policy to hold interest rates down and promote relaxed credit conditions in order to boost demand during the recovery phase of the cycle. Eventually, when the expansion was fully under way, the peak of the cycle was not far off, and credit availability

was constricting on its own, the Fed switched to a "tight money" policy, which reduced the supply of credit even further and drove up interest rates.

The Fed's actions with respect to *interest rates* may be included with the directed arrows and summarized as follows:

**Easy money policy: Fed buys securities → Bank reserves ↑→
Interest rates ↓→ Bank lending ↑→ Money supply ↑→ Demand ↑**

**Tight money policy: Fed sells securities → Bank reserves ↓→
Interest rates ↑→ Bank lending ↓→ Money supply ↓→ Demand ↓**

FEDERAL RESERVE POLICY AND THE POSTWAR BUSINESS CYCLE

With these principles in mind, you can examine the Fed's record of expansionary (low interest rates) and contractionary (high interest rates) monetary policies since World War II (see Charts 4–1 and 4–2 below and on page 36). Remember that the Fed's objective had always been to counter-

CHART 4–1 Short-Term Interest Rates: The Prime Rate, the Federal Funds Rate, and the Treasury-Bill Rate

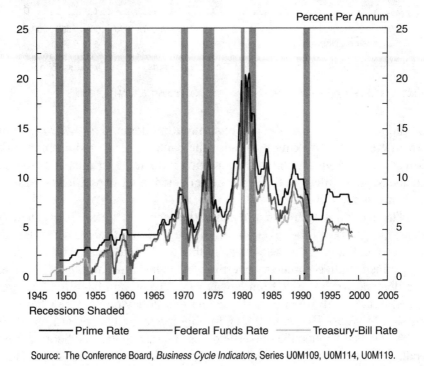

Percent Per Annum

1945 1950 1955 1960 1965 1970 1975 1980 1985 1990 1995 2000 2005
Recessions Shaded

———— Prime Rate   ———— Federal Funds Rate   ———— Treasury-Bill Rate

Source: The Conference Board, *Business Cycle Indicators*, Series U0M109, U0M114, U0M119.

CHART 4–2 Long-Term Interest Rates: Secondary Market Yields on FHA Mortgages, Yield on New Issues of High-Grade Corporate Bonds, and Yield on Long-Term Treasury Bonds

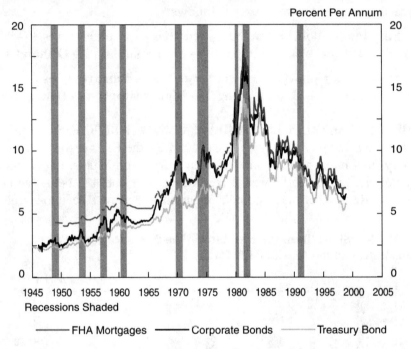

Source: The Conference Board, *Business Cycle Indicators*, Series U0M115, U0M116, U0M118.

act the natural swing of the cycle, stimulating demand at the trough with low interest rates, making it easy for the banks to lend, and curbing inflation at the peak with high interest, making it difficult for the banks to lend. The peaks and valleys of the cycle are reflected in these oscillations. Recessions are shaded in gray.

The economic events that began in the early 70s clearly illustrate these ideas. Do you recall the feverish inflationary boom of 1973, when demand for autos and housing was so insistent that the United Auto Workers Union complained about compulsory overtime and there were shortages of lumber? The demand for borrowed funds was very strong, and bank lending grew apace. Accordingly, the Fed instituted a tight money policy (see Charts 4–1 and 4–2 for years 1973 and 1974), forcing interest rates upward.

As the Fed applied the brakes and raised interest rates, the boom came to a halt. More than 2 million people were thrown out of work when the full force of recession hit in late 1974 and early 1975. So, the Fed switched to an easy

money policy to stimulate the economy from 1975 through 1977, and interest rates fell. By 1977 the economy was expanding once more, and the Fed reversed itself again, adopting a tight money policy. It was 1974 all over again, except that inflation was even more severe. While the Fed pursued its traditional tight money policy, President Carter instituted voluntary wage and price controls.

President Carter reshuffled his cabinet in 1979, appointed Fed Chairman G. William Miller to the position of Secretary of the Treasury, and asked Paul Volcker, president of the Federal Reserve Bank of New York, to replace Mr. Miller. Mr. Volcker accepted the appointment and immediately rallied the members of the Board to maintain the fight against inflation, obtaining a commitment from them to pursue the struggle beyond the cycle's present phase. Interest rates were at a postwar high, the cyclical peak had arrived, and a downturn was inevitable.

The 1980 downturn was so sharp that the Board of Governors set aside its inflation-fighting stance temporarily, providing banks with sufficient reserves and lowering interest rates to prevent undue hardship. Mr. Volcker's battle plan, which will be described more fully in a moment, had been postponed by the exigencies of the moment.

In summary, then, the overall aim of the Fed since World War II had been to curb and, ultimately, reverse the extremes of the cycle: to dampen inflation and to stimulate a depressed economy.

THE MONETARIST CRITIQUE
However, another look at interest rates on pages 35 and 36 reveals that the Fed's policies contributed to the cycle's severity. Like an inexperienced driver with one foot on the gas and the other on the brake, attempting to achieve a steady speed but only able to surge forward after screeching to a halt, the Fed alternately stimulated and restrained the economy. Record interest rates at the cyclical peaks of the late 60s and the middle and late 70s provide evidence of the Fed's desperate attempts to bring inflationary expansion under control. Yet these sudden stops were partly the result of previous attempts, such as those made in 1972 and 1976, to stimulate rapid expansion by providing borrowers with low interest rates. As the economy accelerated and inflation began to go out of control, the Fed hit the brakes.

Meanwhile, the business cycle of the 1970s rose higher and higher, with inflation becoming more severe with each boom and unemployment becoming more severe with each bust. The Fed's policies had failed.

In the 70s, a growing group of economists began to criticize the Fed's policy, accusing the Fed of contributing to the severity of the business cycle instead of reducing cyclical fluctuations. In their view, the Fed's contrac-

tionary policy, applied at the peak of the cycle, only added to the severity of the impending recession, while its expansionary policy, during the early stages of recovery, only set the stage for the subsequent inflations.

These economists, known as the *monetarist* school, believe that the rate of increase in the money supply is the single most important determinant of business cycle conditions. If the money supply grows rapidly, the economy expands; if the money supply does not grow rapidly, or even contracts, economic activity also contracts. The monetarists also believe that because other forces intrinsic to the economy will lead to normal cyclical activity and fluctuation in the rate of growth in the money supply, the Fed's best course of action is to attempt to keep the money supply's growth on an even keel, preferably at a low rate, reflecting the economy's long-range ability to increase output. According to the monetarists' view, anything beyond that rate will lead to inflation, and attempts to reduce the swings of the cycle will instead only exacerbate them.

It's as if the monetarists were saying, "If you want a comfortable temperature, set the thermostat and leave it. Don't fiddle with it by alternately raising and lowering it every time you feel a little chilly or a bit too warm, because this will just cause wide swings in temperature, which only heighten discomfort rather than reduce it."

The Road to Hell Is Paved with Good Intentions

- The effect of the Fed's policies in the 70s was the opposite of its intentions.
- The Fed's policies increased the amplitude of the cycle's swings.
- The rate of inflation and interest rates rose over the course of the cycle.

DEBT AND THE CYCLE

Now, although the Fed was unable to control the cycle or inflation in the 70s, it was not solely responsible for the course of events. You can see tidal waves of consumer and business borrowing (referred to earlier) in Chart 4–3 on page 39, doubling every five years: $100 billion in 1969, $200 billion in 1974, and $400 billion in 1979. This borrowing drove demand forward during the expansionary phase of the cycle, creating the inflationary conditions that provided the Fed's tight money policy and the subsequent crash into recession. The downturn would have occurred in the Fed's absence; the Fed's

CHART 4–3 Total Private Borrowing

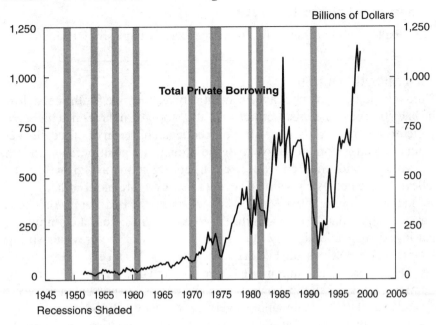

Source: The Conference Board, *Business Cycle Indicators*, Series A0Q110.

policies just made it more severe. Unfortunately, after recession took hold, the quick shift to an easy money policy fostered the next giant wave of borrowing, spending, and inflation, and this inevitably produced (once the wave's internal energy was spent and the Fed tightened up) a major collapse.

Be sure to notice that interest rates rose over time due to the ever-escalating demand for funds and consequent ever-escalating expenditures and inflation. You saw this in Charts 4–1 and 4–2 on pages 35 and 36, when consumer and business borrowing doubled every five years in the 1970s. Since the demand for funds continuously exceeded the supply of funds at current prices, and since prices rose at ever-higher rates, interest rates (the price of borrowed money) climbed in the long run. Certainly lenders would not issue loans at a rate of interest lower than the rate of inflation. Why lend funds at rates too low to offset the decline in the real-dollar value of the amount loaned?

You can see in Charts 4–1 and 4–2 that by the mid 80s interest rates had fallen from their record peaks although private borrowing reached an all-time high. More about this later.

Inflation's Engine: the 1970s

• Explosive borrowing → Explosive spending → Explosive inflation

---

THE FED'S REVOLUTION

Although the Fed may not have been entirely responsible for the debacle of the late 70s, the monetarists' criticism of its "stop-go" policies had hit home. In October 1979, shortly after Mr. Volcker began his term of office, the Fed announced an accommodation with the monetarist position. Henceforth, Mr. Volcker said, the Fed would set targets for monetary growth that it believed were consistent with an acceptable (low) rate of inflation.

In the summer of 1980, Mr. Volcker persuaded the Fed that it would have to renew immediately its commitment to halting inflation, a commitment that it had suspended briefly during the recession of the previous spring. After earlier recessions, the Fed had always reverted to an expansionary policy of a year or two's duration (see Charts 4–1 and 4–2 on pages 35 and 36). Following the 1980 slump, however, the Fed decided to prevent rapid recovery and expansion by maintaining a very tight money policy during the early phases of recovery. Mr. Volcker persuaded the Board of Governors that inflation had become so severe that the economy could not tolerate the usual easy-money-aided recovery. The rate of inflation had risen over each successive cycle and had barely declined during the 1980 recession. Rapid stimulation and recovery of demand would quickly bid prices up once again. This time, tight money was the only appropriate remedy, even if it stunted the recovery.

In consequence, the Fed's 1980, 1981, and 1982 tight money policies drove the prime rate to 21.5 percent and first-mortgage rates to 18 percent, unleashing the worst recession since World War II. For the first time, the Fed had stopped a recovery in its tracks and watched the economy slide off into back-to-back recessions. The Fed had made up its mind that restraining demand in order to control inflation was worth the price of economic contraction.

But the Fed relaxed its grip in the summer of 1982, first, because inflation had been wrung out of the economy and unemployment had reached an intolerable level; and second, because there were strong signs that Congress was losing patience with the Fed's restrictive policies. The Fed had accomplished its objective, so there was no need to further antagonize those who had the power to terminate the Fed's independent status. Yet, despite the eventual relaxation, you should realize that the Fed's 1981 policies

marked a major shift in strategy that had significant and far-reaching consequences for our economy. *If severe inflation has been eliminated for the foreseeable future, it is no exaggeration to say that the Fed beat it back single-handedly.*

The Fed Beats Back Inflation: Early 80s

- Restrictive policy → Bank reserves ↓→ Interest rates ↑→
  Bank lending ↓→ Money supply ↓→ Demand ↓→ Inflation ↓

Events in the 1980s nonetheless required the Fed's constant vigilance. When the Fed permitted easier conditions in late 1982, the economy roared ahead, as you can see from Chart 4–3 on page 39. Business and consumer borrowing grew rapidly in 1983, reaching $500 billion (a record high at the time) by early 1984. Was this to be a repeat of earlier inflationary cycles, where demand, financed by easy credit, would be permitted to leap upward, bidding the rate of inflation to a new record? Would the bitter and wrenching experience of 1981–82, which had brought inflation under control, have been suffered in vain?

Fortunately, because there was so much slack in the economy due to the recession's severity, inflation did not immediately reappear. But swift action was required to avoid just such a painful reoccurrence. So the Fed fine-tuned a mini-slowdown, restricting bank reserves and forcing up interest rates (Charts 4–1 and 4–2 on pages 35 and 36). That solved the problem; the growth in demand was stymied, and the economy cooled off.

The Fed's policies in the early 80s were a radical departure from those of the 60s and 70s. The 1981–82 recession and the mini slowdown of 1984 signaled a new era, a major turning point in postwar economic history. The Fed had abandoned its old game plan: spurring the economy onward during slack conditions only to apply a chokehold when boom and inflation got out of hand, and then dealing with a repeat performance in the next cycle but on a new, higher plateau. General restraint over the course of the cycle was the new master strategy.

Mr. Volcker knew that easy conditions and a pro-growth attitude had contributed to the disaster of the 70s. He also knew that he was on a tightrope, and that the cautious attitude described above could not lapse into complacency. But by the mid-80s, new appointees to the Board of Governors who

favored an easy money policy had begun to undermine Mr. Volcker's go-slow approach. You will notice on pages 35 and 36 that interest rates fell, signaling dramatically easier conditions.

Why did these new appointees to the Board of Governors pursue a policy which appeared to be such a reckless reversal of the Fed's successful approach? And why were they appointed? Because President Reagan and his advisers, who called themselves "supply-side" economists, wanted supply-siders on the Board. Supply-siders favor easy credit and low interest rates. By 1987, at the end of Mr. Volcker's second four-year term as the Board's chair, he was the only veteran of the tight money campaigns of the early 80s. As the supply-siders pushed easier and easier conditions, Mr. Volcker informed President Reagan that he did not wish to be appointed to another term as chair—a term in which the Board's policy of restraint could be undone by a new majority that favored easy money and in which easy money could once again unleash the forces of inflation upon the economy.

President Reagan appointed Alan Greenspan to succeed Mr. Volcker. Many observers were pessimistic and did not believe that Mr. Greenspan would be any more successful in controlling the supply-siders. But these fears were unfounded, because, under Mr. Greenspan, the Board continued to be responsible, refusing to permit a rekindling of the inflation of the 1970s.

You can see in Chart 4–3 on page 39 that private borrowing did not increase in the late 1980s, fluctuating around $600 billion annually. Thus, the Board maintained sufficient restraint to prevent the headlong expansion of private borrowing and, with it, the explosion in demand that precedes a new round of inflation.

(The big jump in borrowing in the last quarter of 1985 was due to state and local government borrowing in anticipation of tax law changes that never came about. State and local borrowing is included with these private borrowing figures, but it is usually quite small.)

The Fed Controls Inflation: Late 80s Throughout 1990s

- Moderate restraint → Moderately high interest rates →
  Moderate borrowing → Moderate spending → Moderate inflation

---

Instead, Mr. Greenspan's board had to confront a new problem at the turn of the 90s. Recession forced them to temporarily suspend the struggle against inflation. As private borrowing plunged to levels not seen since the 1970s (see Chart 4–3 on page 39), the Fed eased and short-term interest rates fell

to 17-year lows, although long-term rates held steady (see Charts 4–1 and 4–2 on pages 35 and 36).

The economy responded as the Fed had hoped. Borrowing and spending recovered and the economy surged forward in 1993 and 1994. Then the Fed switched to a policy of restraint in 1994 and 1995, raising interest rates in order to create a "soft landing" following the mid-decade expansion. Again, the Fed's policy worked and the economy grew rapidly at the end of the decade while inflation remained low.

FINE-TUNING AND DEREGULATION

All of this raises the issue of economic "fine-tuning." How did the Fed manage to bring about an effective mini slowdown in 1984, when it seemed incapable of such sensitive fine-tuning in the 70s? And why should we be optimistic that the Fed can fine-tune in the future? The answer is partly that the Fed had a relatively small and easy task before it in 1984. But that's not all. In the 70s and earlier, interest rate regulations restricted the Fed to operating a switch that was either "off" or "on." But deregulation in the late 70s and early 80s permitted a metamorphosis; the switch became a valve, allowing the flow of credit to be more finely calibrated.

The history of this transition deserves some explanation. Until the end of the 70s, banks and savings-and-loan companies were not permitted to pay more than a statutory maximum of slightly more than 5 percent on consumer savings accounts. During the rapid expansions of 1968–69 and 1973–74, Treasury bill interest rates climbed to well above 5 percent, providing an incentive for large depositors to withdraw their funds from these financial intermediaries and invest them in Treasury bills in order to earn the higher market return.

This process was called *disintermediation* (a coinage only an economist could love), because savers bypassed the financial intermediaries to invest their funds directly in Treasury bills; S&Ls suffered severely due to their dependence on consumer savings accounts.

The upshot was that, as soon as boom conditions developed and the Fed began exercising a tight money policy, driving interest rates up, an ocean of deposits drained out of the banks and especially out of the S&Ls. The savings and loans literally ran out of money. They couldn't make mortgage loans, even if borrowers were willing to pay exorbitant rates of interest.

You can understand, then, why Fed's tight money policies during these earlier periods did not cause credit to constrict gradually as interest rates climbed; instead, the availability of credit suddenly dried up for certain key areas of the economy (e.g., residential construction almost shut down).

Then, when the boom peaked and the economy slipped off into recession, the Fed switched to an easy money policy. As soon as Treasury bill interest rates fell below the statutory maximum that banks and S&Ls were able to pay, depositors sold their Treasury bills and redeposited the funds, propelling a tidal wave of deposits back into the financial intermediaries. As a result, S&Ls practically gave money away to finance home building.

These fund flows out of and then back into the banks and S&Ls exacerbated the business cycle. In 1969 and 1974, analysts didn't talk about tight conditions; they talked about the "credit crunch" and how it had stopped the economy in its tracks. Then, as deposits came flooding back into the system in 1970–72 and 1975–77, demand, fueled by cheap credit, took off like a rocket.

By 1980, deregulation had begun to remove interest rate ceilings from consumer savings accounts. The new, flexible-rate accounts were even called "T-bill accounts" for a while, because they were pegged to the Treasury-bill rate and were designed to prevent savers from defecting to the savings account's chief competitor, the Treasury bill, as interest rates rose.

When the Fed made its desperate stand against inflation in 1981–82, deregulation had been partially accomplished: The T-bill accounts prevented a run on the savings and loan companies' deposits. These accounts required a minimum deposit of $10,000, however, so many savers were attracted by recently-created money-market mutual funds that had much smaller minimum deposit requirements. The money-market funds invested in commercial paper and other short-term instruments, thus providing yields slightly higher than those of Treasury bills. Consequently, banks and S&Ls still faced a partial drain on their deposits.

But deregulation had begun to work. The S&Ls did not run out of money in 1981–82, although they were obliged to raise mortgage rates to prohibitive levels as T-bill account interest rates went up with the yield on Treasury bills. Residential construction was, at last, constrained by the price borrowers had to pay for funds rather than by the availability of those funds.

After the Fed eased up in mid-1982, and as the economy rebounded strongly in 1983, banks and S&Ls received permission to offer "money-market accounts," which competed directly with the money-market funds. Although deregulation was not 100 percent complete, depositors now had little reason to keep their funds elsewhere, and so a large volume of funds returned to the banks and S&Ls from the money-market mutual funds.

Now that the Fed had a finely honed scalpel, it could maintain interest rates at sufficiently low levels to encourage demand, but it could easily nudge them upward whenever inflationary conditions threatened. And it

would not have to fear disintermediation, the destructive flows of funds out of banks and S&Ls.

Early 1984 provided the first test; to confirm the results, review the interest rate record in Charts 4–1 and 4–2 on pages 35 and 36 once again. Interest rates collapsed in late 1982, but the Fed didn't wait long before it began to tighten up again. Demand had roared ahead throughout 1983; and, by the end of the year, there were many alarming signs that inflation was about to be rekindled. Although the Fed had allowed interest rates to drift upward throughout 1983, more decisive, positive action was required by early 1984.

Recall from Charts 4–1 and 4–2 that the Fed's tight money policy in the spring of 1984 had forced interest rates quickly upward, inducing the mini-slowdown of 1984. There was talk of recession, but the Fed had carefully tuned the slowdown and did not let it develop into recession. Once the danger was past, the Fed permitted interest rates to drop sharply, and demand began to grow once again.

Although deregulation became suspect in the late 80s because of the excesses and consequent failures associated with unregulated lending practices by the savings and loan industry, the deregulation of interest rates helped the Fed alter the course of America's economic history.

By the early 1990s, of course, the Fed faced a different problem. Private borrowing tumbled so steeply during the 1990–91 recession (see page 39) that the Fed redirected its efforts to stimulating demand with low interest rates (see pages 35 and 36). By 1994–95, however, the Fed briefly bumped rates upward to prevent demand's rapid growth. Then, failing to see signs of escalating inflation, the Fed eased again and let borrowing grow through the end of the 90s.

THE NEW CREDIT RATIONING
Recall once again the credit craziness of the late 70s, when rampant recourse to borrowed funds pumped up the inflationary balloon. Many observers suggested credit rationing as a solution. That was the only way, they argued, to provide funds for productive business investment in new technology and capital goods, while curtailing unproductive consumer expenditures financed by installment plans, credit cards, and so forth. Otherwise, industry had to compete with consumers in the capital markets for scarce funds. Consumers, the argument continued, were notoriously insensitive to interest rates; all they cared about was the size of the monthly payment, and this could be held down by stretching out the length of payment.

Consequently, as consumers borrowed more and more for second homes, boats, the latest electronic gadget, or whatever, business was forced to pay

ever higher interest rates as it competed for scarce funds. This not only limited industry's ability to modernize and improve our nation's capital stock, it also added *business* debt-financed demand on top of *consumer* debt-financed demand (see Chart 4–3 on page 39). Too many dollars chased too few goods (i.e., supply could not keep pace with demand at current prices), and, therefore, prices inevitably rose too quickly. So, the advocates of credit rationing recommended their solution.

They suggested that legal minimums be set for auto and home-loan down payments and that legal maximums be established for the term of the loan: for instance, 50 percent minimum down payments, with a 10-year maximum loan term for housing and 2 years for autos. Yet, there was no way Congress would enact, or the President sign, such legislation. The auto and construction industries would not permit it.

Then, beginning in the early 80s, the Fed stepped in and throttled inflation with its tight money policy. Inflation collapsed; the Fed was the victor and remained vigilant ever-after.

The Fed had a unique opportunity in the 1990s to keep interest rates at just the right level to maintain an adequate, but not too rapid, growth in demand without inflation. But that meant that interest rates (especially long-term rates) could not return to the low levels of yesteryear, particularly when compared to the rate of inflation. The Fed maintained interest rates well above the rate of inflation, except for an occasional counter-cyclical dip to temporarily deal with weak demand and an occasional counter-cyclical jump to deal with exuberant demand. *High interest rates (which is not to say chronically rising rates) are the new credit rationing, and they will be with us for many years.*

SUMMARY

To summarize this experience, think of the economy as a frisky horse where the rider (the Fed) must continually pull back on the reins (tight money) in order to prevent a runaway, breakneck gallop (inflation). The rider has learned a lesson the hard way, by periodically letting the reins go slack and permitting the horse to break into a gallop, only to be thrown from the horse as it reared when the rider desperately yanked on the reins (pre-1981–82 stop-go policy).

The stop-go policy is over; the Fed has a firm grip on the reins. Its present governors know it must restrain borrowing with high interest rates into the foreseeable future in order to dampen both the business cycle and inflation.

5

C H A P T E R

FEDERAL FISCAL POLICY

THE CONVENTIONAL WISDOM

THE FEDERAL BUDGET NEEDS NO INTRODUCTION. It's been an issue for debate in every presidential election going back further than most folks remember. But by the late 1990s, after decades of deficit, the federal budget flipped into surplus. The focus of debate among our elected officials then switched from what to do about the funds we didn't have to what to do with the funds we did have. This chapter will deal principally with one aspect of that issue: the deficit's impact on the rate of inflation.

Chapter 4 asserted that the Fed had "single-handedly" overcome inflation in the 1980s by the exercise of monetary policy. This runs contrary to the conventional wisdom that it is federal deficits that generate inflation. How do we reconcile the conventional wisdom that deficits generate inflation with the earlier analysis of the Fed's role? Let's look at the evidence.

The Wall Street Journal reports federal budget figures for each month at the end of the subsequent month. See on page 48, for instance, the report for October's budget deficit in the Tuesday, November 24, 1998 issue. Since the federal government's fiscal year concludes on September 30, the *Journal*'s end of October report presents data for the fiscal year just completed. On Thursday, October 29, 1998, the paper reported that the federal government had run a $70 billion budget surplus for fiscal 1998 (see page 49).

Budget Deficit Narrows To $32.46 Billion, a Bit Wider Than Forecast

By a WALL STREET JOURNAL Staff Reporter

WASHINGTON—The federal budget deficit narrowed to $32.46 billion in October from $35.97 billion a year earlier, according to the Treasury Department's monthly report.

The gap is slightly wider than the Congressional Budget Office's estimate of about $31 billion for the month. The CBO said it is anticipating a $63 billion surplus for fiscal year 1999, which began Oct. 1.

The Treasury Department said receipts for October were $119.97 billion, compared with $114.90 billion a year earlier. October outlays were $152.44 billion, compared with $150.87 billion a year earlier.

Treasury Budget Statement

Here is a summary of the Treasury's report, in billions of dollars, through the end of October 1998:

	Fiscal YTD	Comparable Prior Period
Outlays	$152.44	$150.87
Receipts	119.97	114.90
Deficit/Surplus	−32.46	−35.97
Net Interest	20.66	21.77

October Deficit: $32.46 billion (figures rounded).

Since the monthly data are not seasonally adjusted, only the annual data reported at the end of each October is useful for judging the trend of federal budget surplus and deficit.

The facts portrayed in Chart 5–1 on page 50 show that the deficit grew dramatically in 1975 and 1981–82 and shrank to an insignificant number in 1979. If the conventional wisdom made sense, inflation should have jumped in 1975 and 1981–82 with the increase in the federal deficit and subsided in 1979 when the budget balanced.

But that didn't happen. As a matter of fact, the opposite occurred. Inflation narrowed in 1975 and 1981–82 and peaked in 1979. In other words, not only do the facts not support the conventional wisdom, they seem to indicate the opposite. Inflation fell with the increases in the federal deficit (1975 and 1981–82) and rose when the deficit declined (1979). Does this mean that balanced budgets *generate* inflation, while deficits *reduce* inflation? Now that *would* be a scoop.

To resolve the problem, you must put the federal deficit in perspective. Chart 4–3 on page 39, reproduced as Chart 5–2 on page 51, depicts private bor-

U.S. Posts $70 Billion Budget Surplus For Fiscal '98, Dwarfing May Estimate

By JACOB M. SCHLESINGER
Staff Reporter of THE WALL STREET JOURNAL

WASHINGTON—It's official: The U.S. reported a $70 billion budget surplus for fiscal 1998, marking the first time the Treasury has balanced its books since 1969.

The figure, released in the federal government's final report yesterday on the budget for the fiscal year ended Sept. 30, dwarfed the $39.1 billion surplus the Office of Management and Budget projected in late May. "The continued good performance of the economy is contributing to good news on both sides of the ledger," Jacob Lew, the OMB's director, said in an interview.

Tax revenues and other receipts were $17.6 billion higher than anticipated in the spring. Spending, meanwhile, was $13.3 billion less than projected, partly because the strong economy helped reduce social safety net spending. Specifically, payments for welfare, food stamps and unemployment insurance were below the May projections by $1.7 billion, $1.2 billion and $300 million, respectively.

The lower spending indicates that "people are moving to work" and that welfare reform "is working," Mr. Lew said. Still, he added, "it's too early to trumpet it as a major trend. I want to see more information over the next year or two before drawing any major conclusions."

President Clinton used yesterday's announcement to step up his campaign to overhaul Social Security over the next year. "I am very pleased that attempts to spend that surplus, rather than preserve it until we reform the Social Security system to meet the needs of the 21st century, were not successful in the last Congress," he said. "It is important that we maintain this position until we have saved Social Security," he added. "Hopefully, that will occur next year."

The Congressional Budget Office has forecast an $80 billion surplus for the current fiscal year, and $1.5 trillion in total surpluses over the next decade. But some economists have said that, with the economy now apparently weakening, those numbers could erode.

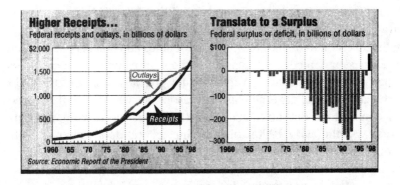

Higher Receipts...
Federal receipts and outlays, in billions of dollars

Translate to a Surplus
Federal surplus or deficit, in billions of dollars

Source: Economic Report of the President

CHART 5–1 Federal Government Expeditures, Revenues, Surplus, or Deficit

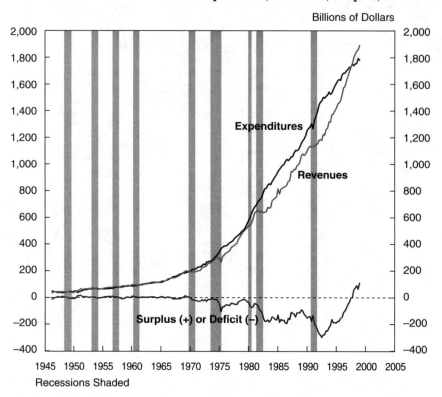

Source: U.S. Department of Commerce, Bureau of Economic Analysis.

rowing. Compare it with the federal deficit in Chart 5–1. Recall that private borrowing includes mortgage borrowing to support residential construction, installment credit to finance the purchase of autos and other consumer durables, and business indebtedness to pay for expenditures on plant, equipment, and inventory. But it also includes (unfortunately, because it is confusing) borrowing by state and local governments, for reasons that need not be developed here.

Keep in mind that both charts portray annual borrowing, not outstanding debt. By the early 1990s, outstanding federal debt was over $4 trillion and outstanding private debt was around $15 trillion. Each year's borrowing added to the outstanding figure, so that an annual federal deficit of $100 billion boosted the outstanding federal figure from $4 trillion to $4.1 trillion, and annual private borrowing of $200 billion lifted the private total to $15.2 trillion. (Don't confuse either of these with the balance of trade deficit, to be examined in Chapter 16.)

CHART 5–2 Total Private Borrowing

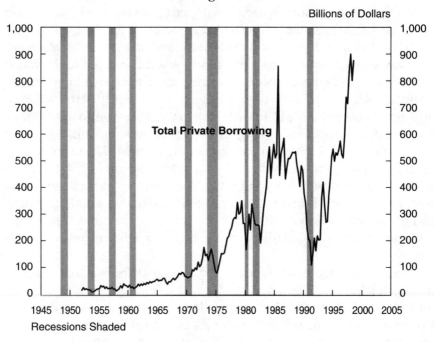

Source: The Conference Board, *Business Cycle Indicators,* Series A0Q110.

Now compare private borrowing with the federal deficit in 1975, and note that both were approximately $100 billion. Then, they move in opposite directions: The federal deficit shrinks to nothing in 1979, and private borrowing balloons to $400 billion. Total borrowing grew from $200 billion in 1975 ($100 billion of private plus $100 billion of federal) to $400 billion in 1979 (all private).

This explains the burst of inflation in the late 70s. Total borrowing doubled, financing the huge increase in demand (greater than the economy's increase in production at current prices) that drove up inflation. Thus, the growth in private borrowing in the late 70s overwhelmed the decline in federal borrowing, generating rapid price increases.

On the other hand, if you continue to look at the record in Charts 5–1 and 5–2, you'll notice that private borrowing slumped in 1981 and 1982, dropping to almost $200 billion annually from its $400 billion peak in 1979. The federal deficit, however, popped back up from next to nothing in 1979 to about $200 billion in 1982. Once again, when you add private and federal borrowing, you see an offset: The total is $400 billion in both years

($400 billion private in 1979 with no federal deficit and $200 billion for each in 1982). When total borrowing stopped growing from 1979 through 1982, the rate of inflation subsided as demand came into line with supply.

This illustrates the fallacy in the conventional wisdom and explains why inflation seemed to behave so perversely when compared to the federal deficit. You can't ignore private borrowing when analyzing inflation. As a matter of fact, the explosion of private borrowing from 1970 to 1973 ($100 billion to $200 billion) and from 1975 to 1979 ($100 billion to $400 billion) explains that decade's two great rounds of inflation. Inflation did not grow in the 1980s, because private borrowing fluctuated in a narrow range (except for 1985) and demonstrated no upward trend after 1984. By the end of the decade, private borrowing was still fluctuating around $600 billion annually, the level it had reached more than five years earlier. When it plunged to $200 billion in the early 90s, inflation withered. Federal borrowing's growth to $400 billion was not large enough to offset private borrowing's decline.

Another development also requires clarification: the burst of private borrowing in late 1985. This burst was due to state and local governments' trying to beat an anticipated change in tax laws that never came to pass. Some Congressmen had suggested that interest paid on state and local bonds no longer be tax-exempt. Enactment of this legislation would have increased state and local interest payments, because their bonds had paid below-market rates for years due to the tax-exempt benefit to investors (i.e., bond holders were willing to receive below market yields, provided they were tax-exempt). State and local governments moved up their borrowing in anticipation of the 1986 change that never came to pass.

But the main point to bear in mind is that the large federal deficits of the 1980s and early 90s did not generate inflation, despite the attention paid them. They were overshadowed by the recessionary drop in private borrowing.

For instance, the drop in private borrowing (see page 51) during the 1990–1991 recession was far larger than the surge in federal borrowing, keeping total borrowing—and hence, inflation—below 1980's levels. By the mid 90s the two remained below 1980's highs.

But by the late 1990s private borrowing had surged to record levels (see page 51), and this time a fluke in state and local government borrowing could not be blamed. Consumers and businesses were truly borrowing and spending record amounts. Why didn't this lead to a surge of inflation? Because, just as in the early 1980s, the economy had sufficient excess capacity to supply all the goods demanded without any strain on productive facilities or any surge of inflation.

Investor's Tip

• Forget about the federal budget deficit or surplus; it won't influence
  our rate of inflation for the foreseeable future, and, therefore, it won't
  influence the value of your investments.

ALONG CAME KEYNES

Nonetheless, you ought to consider the federal government's deficits in
some detail for no other reason than that they have drawn as much attention.
In order to sort out the continuing debate surrounding the federal government's taxing and spending programs and their impact on the economy, you
must go back to the 19th and early 20th centuries. Economics then was governed by an axiom known as *Say's Law*: "Supply creates its own demand."
This meant that economic recession and depression and their accompanying unemployment were temporary and self-correcting phenomena. After
all, capitalists produce goods for market, and workers offer their labor for
hire *so that they, in turn, can demand goods in the marketplace*. If the goods
cannot be sold or the labor is not hired, then a lower price or wage will be
asked, until price and wage cutting permit all of the goods or labor to be
sold. No goods will remain chronically unsold and no labor will remain
chronically unemployed as long as prices and wages remain flexible.

Using this line of reasoning, 19th century economists argued that recession and its concomitant unemployment were transitory phenomena and
should generate neither a great deal of concern nor any corrective policy prescription by the government. Society and government ought to let well enough
alone (i.e., follow the policy of laissez-faire) and let market forces prevail.
The operation of the market would eventually restore full employment.

With Say's Law as their guide, no wonder economists could not understand
the Great Depression, which began in 1929 and hit bottom in 1933. Nor could
they understand why the economy's performance remained anemic for so long
after 1933. After all, they reasoned, the economy should naturally return to conditions of full production and full employment as business cut prices in order to
sell products and workers took wage cuts in order to find employment. If the economy continued in a slump, that was the fault not of the economists and their theories, but of employers and employees who refused to cut prices and wages.

The economists' logic did not help the businesses that were failing or the
workers who were out of jobs. Prices and wages had fallen, yet conditions
remained dismal; something was dreadfully wrong, and somebody had to do
something about it.

In America, President Roosevelt was elected. He responded with massive public-works programs, which, by the way, were funded by federal deficits. The economics community was horrified, and they insisted that the federal government's efforts would merely deny resources to the private sector, and thus provide no net benefit. F.D.R. ignored economic theory. He was a practical man with a practical solution: if people were out of work, then the government would be the employer of last resort and put them to work building roads, parks, bridges, dams, and other public projects.

In 1936, an Englishman named John Maynard Keynes (rhymes with *brains*) gave intellectual credentials to F.D.R.'s practical policies by proposing that the problem was the economists' theories, not the economy. Keynes tackled Say's Law (and the economics establishment) at the knees by declaring that demand could be chronically insufficient and the economy *could* be chronically plagued with substantial excess capacity and unemployment. Keynes scolded his fellow economists for arguing that their theories were right and that the problem lay with the practical world of business and work that was not living up to theoretical expectations. Science—even "the dismal science" of economics—dictates that a theory that does not conform to the facts must be discarded.

Keynes declared that it was ridiculous to expect price and wage cuts to solve the economy's problem. A totally new approach had to be devised. He believed the only answer was to boost demand by the use of some exogenous (outside) force. Workers could not be expected to buy more under conditions of actual and threatened unemployment, nor business to spend more on plant and equipment when excess capacity and weak profits were the rule. But if consumers and business would not spend, how could the economy pull out of its slump? Through government spending, Keynes argued, even if the government had to borrow funds. Once government began to spend on public works, the people who were employed on these projects would spend their earnings on privately produced goods and services. In a multiplier effect, the total level of demand would be lifted and full employment restored. When the pump-priming operation was over and the private economy was back on its feet, the government could gradually withdraw from the economic scene. Pump-priming by government intervention became know as *Keynesian* economics.

Keynesian theory came to dominate economics, rendering Say's Law archaic. The next generation of economists pushed Keynesian theory a bit further, reasoning that a tax cut could be as effective in priming the pump as an increase in government expenditures. Reducing taxes would increase consumers' disposable income and their consumption expenditures. The

new generation believed this would be as effective as an increase in government expenditures for restoring demand to a level sufficient to ensure full employment.

Economists now argued that it didn't matter how the pump was primed, whether through expenditure increases or tax cuts. Putting more into the expenditure stream than was removed from the income stream (in the form of taxes) would always create a net boost in total demand. If government expenditures increased while tax revenues remained the same, the increase in public expenditures would boost demand. If government expenditures remained the same while taxes were cut, the increase in private consumption expenditures would boost demand. In either case, or in both together, the increased government deficit and the borrowing needed to fund that deficit made possible a net addition to total demand.

The increase in the deficit measures the increase in demand, and the government finances that deficit by borrowing from the public through the sale of U.S. Treasury securities. Now, it might seem that borrowing from the public would have the same effect as taxing the public, since it removes funds from the private sector, and would thus neutralize the spending increase. After all, if the public refrains from spending to buy government bonds, isn't the public's expenditure reduced? The answer is yes, if the bonds are purchased by private citizens; however, this is generally not the case. The largest share of bonds is sold to the banking system, which purchases them by creating a demand deposit (checking account) for the government. This is known as "monetizing" the debt, as described in Chapter 4. The fact that the government borrows from the banks permits an increase in government spending without a decrease in private spending.

The federal government's attempts to influence economic activity through its power to tax and spend is known as *fiscal* policy. Although this chapter discusses fiscal policy in the context of the need to stimulate demand in order to deal with recession, it should be clear that fiscal policy could also be employed to deal with inflation. For example, increasing taxes or reducing government expenditures, which would create a surplus, drains spending from the economy, reducing total demand and, consequently, cooling inflation.

As the discussion of fiscal policy continues, remember that it is not the same thing as *monetary policy*, which was discussed in Chapter 4.

Monetary policy refers to the actions of the Federal Reserve System; *fiscal policy* refers to the actions of the federal government. Monetary policy works through its influence on the banking system, the money supply, bank lending, and interest rates, whereas fiscal policy works through its direct impact on aggregate demand.

Also keep in mind that fiscal policy is the province solely of the federal government, not of state or local government. Only the federal government has the flexibility to run the necessary budget deficits or surpluses large enough to influence total demand. Most state and local governments are limited, either de facto or de jure, to operating with a balanced budget.

THE KENNEDY TAX CUT

Keynesian economics, with its emphasis on fiscal policy, had won the hearts and minds of academic economists by the early 1960s. Not everyone, however, was convinced. When President Kennedy assumed office in 1961 and proposed a tax cut to stimulate the level of economic activity, Republicans and conservative Democrats in Congress attacked it as fiscally irresponsible. They demanded a balanced budget and argued that tax cuts would generate unacceptable deficits. President Kennedy's Keynesian reply was that the deficits would disappear as soon as the tax cut stimulated the level of demand, output, and income, providing even greater tax revenues, despite the decline in the tax rate. These arguments did not immediately persuade Congress, and the tax cut did not pass until the spring of 1964, following President Kennedy's assassination.

The nation enjoyed full employment and a balanced budget in 1965, and Keynesian fiscal policy became an accepted method of "fine-tuning" the economy. Indeed, this technique became so legitimate that it was employed by the next two Republican presidents. President Nixon cut taxes to deal with the 1970 recession, and President Ford cut taxes to deal with the 1974–75 recession. In each case, the Federal Reserve also pursued an easy money policy in order to stimulate demand. Conservatives joined liberals and Republicans agreed with Democrats that tax cuts were necessary to get the economy moving.

By the late 1970s, however, severe inflation prompted a new and growing group of economists to conclude that attempts to stimulate demand with easy money and easy fiscal policies had gone awry. Escalating inflation, which reduced real income, had drawn more and more people into the labor force. The new entrants to the labor force, usually the secondary or tertiary wage earners in the family, had fewer skills and thus were more difficult to employ. Unemployment grew as inflation escalated. The economy had the worst of both worlds. Thus, this new group of economists and politicians argued that what was known as "full-employment policy," actually the Keynesian prescription of stimulating demand through easy monetary and fiscal policies, had been a failure.

Moreover, they continued, increased inflation had discouraged savings and investment. Rising prices penalized savers for their thrift, because the

value of real savings fell. This encouraged personal indebtedness rather than saving, and inasmuch as saving is the ultimate source of all funds for investment, the level of investment was bound to shrink over time. These critics charged that the lack of savings and the resulting lack of investment were reflected by the low levels of business investment in new machinery and technology and by the resulting decline in productivity.

Finally, they attacked the progressive income tax, which propelled people into higher tax brackets despite a drop in real income. Higher marginal tax rates, they said, removed the incentive to work more and to work harder. Why should businesses invest in new ideas, new products, and more efficient ways of doing things if higher taxes confiscated the profits? Why should workers put in more hours on the job if higher taxes reduced the additional pay to a meaningless figure?

SUPPLY-SIDE ECONOMICS

The views of these economists and politicians came to be called *supply-side* economics, which they developed in contrast to *demand-side*, or Keynesian, economics. The supply-siders argued that it was more important to support policies that bolstered the economy's ability to supply or produce more goods than to enhance demand. Therefore, the supply-side economists advocated drastic federal income tax reductions over a three-year period, with deficits to be avoided by a parallel reduction in federal spending. Federal expenditure programs, in their view, tended to over-regulate private activity and to waste tax dollars in a variety of boondoggles and unnecessary transfer payments.

Supply-side theory claimed that a massive, across-the-board tax cut would accomplish two major objectives. First, it would provide incentives for increased work, thus boosting output. A greater supply, or output, of goods and services would dampen inflation. Second, increased disposable income would lead to increased savings, providing a pool of funds to finance investment. Once again, the supply of goods and services would be stimulated, and increased output would reduce inflation.

Supply-side economics was a total contradiction of Keynesian fiscal policy, which had prevailed for almost half a century. It was widely and correctly viewed as a device to restrict and contract the federal government, and so it was admired and promoted by conservatives and viewed with suspicion by liberals. The supply-siders began to make their voices heard during President Carter's administration, placing him in a potential quandary. He had pledged to balance the federal budget by the end of his first term in office. Rapid economic expansion and inflation had pushed revenues upward

more rapidly than expenditures; consequently, his goal was in sight by late 1979. The tax cut proposed by the supply-siders would have postponed that goal, unless, of course, it was accompanied by large reductions in federal expenditures, which, as a Democrat, President Carter could not endorse.

The 1980 recession created an even sharper dilemma for him. He might have advocated a tax cut (the traditional Keynesian prescription for recession), but this would have played into the hands of the supply-siders, who would have demanded compensating spending cuts. By now the supply-siders had a presidential candidate, Ronald Reagan, as their principal spokesman. The situation was further complicated for President Carter by the fact that the supply-side tax cut favored upper-income groups, rather than the lower-income groups traditionally targeted for tax cuts by the Democrats. Thus, political circumstances precluded President Carter from trying to deal with the 1980 recession by means of tax reductions.

After his inauguration in 1981, as the economy slid into the 1981–82 recession, President Reagan pushed for and obtained the supply-side tax cuts. What a strange historical reversal: Twenty years after President Kennedy battled Republicans and conservatives for his tax cut, President Reagan now had to battle Democrats and liberals for his. Whereas Democrats had once advocated tax cuts to stimulate the economy and the Republicans had opposed those cuts, it was now the Republicans who were advocating tax cuts over the opposition of the Democrats. The parties had done a complete about-face.

The shift of the mantle of fiscal conservatism from Republicans to Democrats is one of the most important political changes since World War II. President Reagan's supply-side tax cut of 1981–83 accompanied the recession of 1981–82. It generated a chaotic reduction in federal revenue, because a smaller proportion of a declining level of income was collected in taxes. Meanwhile, total expenditures continued to grow, despite reductions in the budget left by President Carter. Democrats criticized the resulting deficit and demanded that the tax cuts be rescinded. Republicans insisted that there be no tax increase, despite the deficits.

The debate occurred in the midst of recession and recovery. The Republicans contended that any tax increase would jeopardize the supply-side expansion. The Democrats countered that continued deficits and the accompanying government borrowing drove up interest rates and jeopardized the expansion. Beneath the economic details of the debate, both sides had ideological positions to defend. The Democrats realized that continued deficits put relentless pressures on domestic expenditures. Only a tax increase could generate the revenue that made these expenditure programs affordable. The Republicans were also aware that the only way to deliver a knockout punch

to the domestic programs, while increasing military expenditures, was to hold taxes down and let the clamor to end the deficits force legislators to curtail domestic spending. So, the real battle was over domestic programs, not taxes, the deficit, or even supply-side economics. Indeed, there are some political analysts who believe that the whole supply-side argument was only a cynical "Trojan horse," the sole purpose of which was to decimate federal social programs and repeal the New Deal.

In the end, no compromise of these issues was attained. The Democrats held on to the social programs, the Republicans held on to the military programs, and President Reagan made it clear that he would veto any tax increase. The deficit remained. Finally, in a desperate attempt to at least seem to be doing something about the problem, Congress passed the Gramm-Rudman Balanced Budget Act in late 1985, mandating gradual elimination of deficits over a five-year period. The political fight was pushed into the future. The Democrats hoped that military expenditures would be cut and taxes raised, the Republicans and the president hoped that domestic expenditures would be cut, and they all hoped that this Procrustean bed would dismember someone else.

In any event, the Gramm-Rudman Act failed in its objective, because Congress and the President ignored it. By the early 90s, it was a dead letter.

CROWDING OUT

Meanwhile, the argument over supply-side economics (never the real issue) was lost in the shuffle, as the political wrangling over the impact of the deficit continued. The Democrats insisted that the increased federal borrowing due to the tax cut would crowd-out private borrowing (and hence capital expenditures). Ironically, Republicans had criticized President Carter's (shrinking) deficits in the late 1970s on precisely the same grounds. Yet, you have seen that private borrowing exploded in those years. The inconsistencies in the political debate provide further evidence that the real issues were not (and are not) economic.

Indeed, any fear about "crowding out" was misplaced, for it was the actions of the Federal Reserve that largely determined whether private borrowing at reasonable rates was possible. Whenever the Fed pursues a tight money policy, private borrowers must compete with the government for funds; whenever the Fed pursues a sufficiently easy policy, there is room for both private and public borrowing. The point is that difficulty or ease of credit conditions is determined largely by the Fed and not by any crowding-out dynamic.

Keep in mind that the Fed's objective throughout the 80s was to restrain the expansion rather than stimulate it, so perhaps a little crowding out, if it

helped prevent credit conditions from becoming too easy, was not so unhealthy. Tight money restricted consumer borrowing more than business borrowing, allocating funds (and resources) away from consumption expenditures and toward investment expenditures in new plant and equipment. And as the economy and tax revenues grew in the late 80s, private borrowing held its own, while federal borrowing shrank (see Chart 5–1 on page 50 and Chart 5–2 on page 51). Then, the recession of 1990–91 and the full impact of the S&L crisis hit, multiplying the deficit, but without crowding-out private borrowing.

Forget about Crowding Out

- The Fed's influence on interest rates is far more important than the federal government's borrowing.

In order to relate this discussion of fiscal policy to the business cycle, you need to know how *not* to relate it. Please realize that the huge federal deficits were responsible for neither the 1981–82 recession or the subsequent recovery and expansion. The Federal Reserve's tight money policy generated the recession; the recession choked off inflation; and the stifling of inflation, along with the release of the Fed's grip, is what produced recovery and expansion in the mid and late 80s.

Thus, President Reagan's administration should be neither blamed for the recession nor lauded for the recovery and expansion or inflation's demise. Those phenomena were created by monetary policy, not fiscal policy.

BALANCING THE BUDGET

You can see from Chart 5–1 on page 50 that the federal deficit grew enormously with each recession—for two chief reasons. First, recession reduced receipts because of lower personal income tax revenues, unemployment (the unemployed paid no income tax), and lower profits-tax revenues. Second, tax cuts accompanied the recessions of 1970, 1974–75, and 1981–82. In addition, note that federal expenditures continued to grow during each recession despite revenue's setback, generating the budget gap. Since the deficit grew with each successive recession, closing this deficit gap became more difficult and took longer every time.

In order to close the deficit gap, receipts must grow more rapidly than expenditures. The gap began to shrink in the late 1980s until the S&L crisis

and the 1990–91 recession hit. The deficit shrank once again in the 1990s as a growing economy generated additional tax revenues and President Clinton's tax increases took hold. By the end of that decade, and sooner than most analysts had forecast, revenues shot past expenditures (see page 50) and the deficit was history. Now analysts were forecasting that a new age of budgetary surplus had begun.

CONCLUSION

Rapidly growing tax revenues generated the federal budget surplus of the late 1990s. Another recession, however, can bring about renewed deficits by reducing tax revenues. To avoid future deficits, a substantial budgetary surplus must be built to provide a cushion for the inevitable decline in revenue that accompanies recession.

6

THE POSTWAR BUSINESS CYCLE: THE ROLE OF CONSUMER DEMAND

CONSUMER DEMAND AND INFLATION

CHAPTER 4 DEVELOPED THREE CONCEPTS:

1. The Fed's policies aided and abetted inflation through the end of the 1970s and exacerbated the business cycle.
2. The Fed's 1981–82 tight money policy was the major turning point in our post-World War II economic history, ending inflation's upward spiral.
3. Fighting inflation continues to be the Fed's primary concern, and, therefore, interest rates will remain relatively high when compared to the rate of inflation.

This chapter will build on these concepts by analyzing the role of the consumer in the post-World War II business cycle, showing how consumer demand led the business cycle by generating ever higher waves of inflation, until that inflation broke on the rocks of the Fed's 1981–82 tight money policy. It will also illustrate how the Fed's fine-tuning smoothed out consumer

demand after the 1981–82 crackdown, thereby reducing inflation in the 1980s and 1990s.

To begin the analysis of inflation, start with a definition and consider that definition in its historical context. *Inflation* is an increase in prices due to excessive spending financed by borrowing from banks. "Too many dollars chasing too few goods" is a standard way of putting it. Economists are more formal: "Inflation occurs when demand exceeds supply at current prices and prices are bid up."

Both explanations conjure up the image of a gigantic auction at which customers bid for both goods and services. The more money the customers have to spend, the higher prices go. Where do they get the money? From banks that create it.

Although we wait and hope for it to subside, we tend to assume that inflation, like death and taxes, is inevitable. In fact, however, chronic inflation is a recent problem. Before the late 1940s, severe inflation was a temporary phenomenon, usually associated with war. When the federal government's wartime expenditures overshot tax revenues and the government covered the difference by selling bonds to the banking system or by printing paper money (which the federal government has not done recently), prices increased swiftly. That's how the conventional wisdom arose that government deficits cause inflation.

From 1789 until after World War II, except for war-related inflations, prices in America fell more often than they rose. As a matter of fact, prices were actually lower in 1914, on the eve of World War I, than they were in 1815, at the end of the Napoleonic Wars and the War of 1812!

Prices dropped during the 19th century because supply grew more rapidly than demand. Railroads and steamships opened new continents and made their agricultural products available throughout the world. Business mobilized the technological advances of the Industrial Revolution to produce standard items of consumption in large quantities at considerably lower cost. Occasionally, prices rose during the upswing of the business cycle, because investment expenditures were financed by bank borrowing or because there were temporary shortages of agricultural commodities. But these increases were more than offset in recession years, when prices tumbled as huge additions to supply were brought to market.

The institutions that, in our day, enabled and encouraged headlong private borrowing and spending had not yet evolved. A hundred years ago it wasn't easy to obtain a home mortgage. Typically, the purchase of a new home required a 50-percent down payment with interest-only mortgage pay-

ments on a seven-year loan, followed by a balloon payment of the entire principal. If you go back far enough, most of the major consumer durables that we now buy on credit were available exclusively to a small portion of the population on a cash-only basis, if they existed at all.

It was not until after World War II that vast amounts of consumer borrowing came into common use, financing residential construction, autos, and other goods. At the same time, new institutions evolved to facilitate business borrowing.

Only the Civil War and World Wars I and II had provided great inflationary experiences; even the period between World War I and World War II was a time of deflation (falling prices). War brought inflation, and peace brought deflation, because government borrowed and spent more massively in wartime than business borrowed and spent in peacetime. The difference was more a matter of degree than a matter of kind; peacetime investment expenditures and borrowing by farmers, railroads, and manufacturers, though substantial, were usually not large enough to boost the growth in demand beyond the increase in supply. Thus, prices fell in most years, because supply exceeded demand at current prices.

To summarize, prices fell unless there was a rapid increase in demand (spending) financed by bank borrowing or the printing press (greenbacks during the Civil War). Only when outside financing provided a boost did demand take on a life of its own and grow more rapidly than supply. It made little difference whether it was government spending for war or business spending for investment, as long as banks printed bank notes or created demand deposits or the government printed paper money. Once demand grew more rapidly than supply, and too many dollars chased too few goods, prices rose.

History does not note or dwell upon the pre-World War II examples of private borrowing and spending that generated inflation, because there were so few of them; they were insignificant when compared to wartime episodes.

But what was responsible for the post-World War II inflationary experience? Why did prices rise so steadily? The answer lies in consumer spending. This period marked the first time that consumers borrowed continually and prodigiously to finance purchases of luxury goods. The level of activity grew decade after decade, and with each cycle, so that in the 1970s tidal waves of credit roared through the system, rapidly swelling demand to record levels.

It started in the 1920s, a kind of brief test run for the full-scale activity that followed World War II. Credit-backed demand included kitchen and laundry appliances; furniture and furnishings; electronic equipment such as television sets, VCRs, stereos, and personal computers; residential construction; and auto-

mobiles. All were financed by credit, and the terms became more liberal over time, even as interest rates rose. The American consumer was encouraged—indeed, came to feel obligated—to mortgage the future so that present expenditures could exceed present income, with borrowing covering the difference.

The economy's health thus developed a dependence on the chronic fix of greater consumer expenditures, financed by borrowing. These circumstances were entirely different from the circumstances of the 19th century; during that era, consumers were largely confined to standard items of consumption purchased with current income (not debt), and economic growth was propelled by increased supply, which pushed prices downward. Now the situation became quite different. Full production and employment became the hostages of ever larger waves of consumer expenditure on discretionary purchases financed by borrowing.

CONSUMER DEMAND AND THE BUSINESS CYCLE

Unfortunately, these surges in consumer demand always led to their own demise, because expansion brought inflation, which depleted real incomes and generated the downturn of the cycle. Only then did inflation abate, real income recover, and expansion begin anew. Thus, every boom inevitably went bust, and each recession was also self-correcting and carried with it the seeds of economic recovery.

But why did the business cycle always rebound from recession, never falling into permanent depression, and why wasn't expansion continuous?

Well, to begin with, every expansion ended inevitably in recession, because every expansion was fueled by credit. Consumers and businesses borrowed to buy new homes, cars, factories, and machinery. The more they borrowed and spent, the faster demand grew, pushing production into high gear in order to keep pace with demand. But, sooner or later, the upward spiral of borrowing and spending came to an end. The strain on productive facilities forced costs higher, pushing prices up, too. Inflation depressed consumer sentiment, and consumers responded by curtailing their expenditures. Consumers also found that their incomes could not support the burden of additional debt repayment. Businesses, having accomplished their targeted growth in plant and equipment, cut back or ceased their expenditures in this area. Once business and consumer borrowing and spending started to decline, the slump began, and production and income fell. Inflation subsided with the drop in demand.

The recessions hit bottom just before consumers recovered their confidence, due to inflation's decline, and began spending again. Components of

demand that were financed by credit stopped shrinking. Remember that these components were a limited, though highly volatile, share of total demand. (The demand for many items that were not financed by credit, such as food and medical care, hardly declined at all during recession.) As consumers and businesses ceased borrowing and turned their attention to liquidating their expansion-generated debts, the price of credit, namely interest rates, fell until, finally, the debt burden and interest rates were low enough that consumers and businesses could borrow and spend again. At this juncture, auto production, home construction, and business investment in new plant and equipment stopped falling, the slide ended, and economic recovery was in sight.

Generally speaking, expansion ceased when consumers were no longer willing to borrow and spend; contraction ended when their confidence returned. In the 1970s, these cyclical changes in consumer confidence were closely tied to the rate of inflation. Rapid economic expansion brought swiftly rising prices with an attendant and sobering drop in real income and consumer confidence. Recession cooled the pace of inflation, encouraging a resurgence of confidence.

In the 1980s, the Fed interrupted the normal course of the cycle by implementing its tight money policy of 1981–82, and then strongly influenced the cycle through its new posture toward inflation. The Fed squashed the cycle flat and squeezed high inflation out of the system, permitting the economy to expand gradually and steadily in the mid and late 80s.

Yet the Fed could not repeal the business cycle. When Iraq invaded Kuwait in the summer of 1990, and it appeared that we would be drawn into the conflict, consumer sentiment plunged and dragged the economy down with it. Consumer demand led the economy out of recession, too, as surging demand for homes and cars brought robust production and employment by the mid 1990s. By then, the Fed had signaled its concern over inflation, raising interest rates frequently in 1994.

In the late 1990s, low inflation inspired consumer confidence, borrowing, and spending. Business responded by borrowing and investing in more plant and equipment. But the economy contained sufficient productive capacity so that supply increased rapidly and inflationary forces remained subdued.

Chapter 4, which examined the Federal Reserve System and the money and credit markets, described the 70s cycle and the new climate of the 80s and 90s in financial terms. Look at the cycle now from a different perspective, weaving in the elements of production, income, and consumer demand.

Consumers borrowed heavily in 1972 and 1973 to make record purchases of new homes and automobiles. Business responded by adding plant

and equipment to meet the demand and by stockpiling inventory to satisfy customers' orders. The sharp growth in consumer and business demand boosted prices rapidly, and the rate of inflation increased from 4 percent in 1972 to 12 percent in 1974. Interest rates moved in parallel fashion. Soon consumers became discouraged, because their incomes failed to keep pace, so their expenditures on homes, autos, and other goods plunged.

This led to a general decline in production, and, by early 1975, unemployment was at a postwar record high. The cycle was complete. The drop in demand reduced both inflation and interest rates, thereby restoring consumer confidence and spending. Recovery and expansion brought boom conditions. Rising inflation and interest rates returned in 1978, eroding consumer confidence once again. Consumer demand fell, and the 1980 recession began; another cycle had come full circle.

Recovery from the 1980 recession had barely begun when the Fed strangled the credit markets in 1981–82. The ensuing recession, designed to curb inflation, had the typical impact on consumer confidence (dramatic improvement due to reduced inflation), and as soon as the Fed relaxed its grip, consumer expenditures surged forward in 1983.

But why didn't the 80s repeat the experience of the 70s? Why didn't burgeoning consumer demand, backed by exploding credit, drive inflation upward once again? Because the Fed fine-tuned demand by maintaining interest rates at relatively high levels. Even though Saddam Hussein had to spoil it all by invading Kuwait on August 2, 1990 and plunging us into recession, the Fed continued to maintain its vigilant stance against inflation, despite the temporary interest rate dip of the early 1990s. The Fed amply illustrated its ability to fine-tune the economy in the mid and late 1990s. At the first signs of strong or weak economic conditions, the Fed adjusted its monetary policy to maintain good growth without inflation. Thus, you should now learn which signposts to observe in order to follow the dynamic of inflation and consumer demand.

So far, the business cycle has been painted with fairly broad strokes. The time has come to take up a finer brush, so that essential details and connections can be clearly drawn. This chapter shows you how to use *The Wall Street Journal* to understand each step in the growth of consumer demand.

The first statistical series to be examined in this chapter is the *consumer price index* (CPI), whose fluctuations chart the course of inflation. Lower inflation leads to improved consumer sentiment and demand, which drives economic expansion forward. You can gauge the latter through data on auto sales, consumer credit, and housing starts, which will serve as the leading indicators of consumer demand.

CONSUMER PRICE INDEX (CPI)

The Bureau of Labor Statistics' CPI release usually appears mid-month in *The Wall Street Journal*. In the Wednesday, November 18, 1998 article on pages 70 and 71, the second paragraph informs you of the CPI's 0.2 percent increase in October. Although multiplying the monthly data by 12 will provide a rough approximation of inflation's annual rate for that month, you can see from the same paragraph that the CPI had increased 1.5 percent in the year ending October 1998. (See pages 70 and 71.)

The CPI compares relative price changes over time. An index must be constructed because consumers purchase such a wide variety of goods and services that no single item could accurately reflect the situation. (See Chart 6–1 on page 72.)

After a base period (1982–84) is selected and assigned an index number of 100.0, prices for other periods are then reported as percentage changes from this base. For instance, if prices rose 5 percent, the index would be 105.0. If prices fell by 10 percent, the index would be 90.0

The Bureau of Labor Statistics (BLS) calculates the CPI by compiling a list of the goods and services purchased by the typical consumer, including such items as food, clothing, shelter, public utilities, and medical care. These make up the "market basket." The base-period price of each item is recorded and assigned a weight according to its relative importance in the basket. Changes in the price of each item are noted, and the percentage change in the total price is reflected in the change of the index number.

The ways consumers spend are continuously shifting, because tastes change, as do incomes and the relative prices of goods. New goods and services are frequently introduced. It would be impossible, however, to generate a consistent index of consumer prices if the components of the market basket were constantly changed; a balance must be struck between the need for consistency and the need for an accurate reflection of consumer buying patterns. Therefore, the BLS revises the contents of the market basket only occasionally, after conducting a survey of consumer expenditure patterns.

Contrary to the popular image, the CPI is not really a "cost-of-living" index. The BLS's market basket is fixed; the individual consumer's is not. Substitutions are made with changes in prices and with changes in income. Your cost of living can vary (or can be made to vary) independently of any change in the CPI.

A final point should be made. In the early 80s, the BLS replaced the cost of home ownership with an imputation (or estimate) of the rental value of owner-occupied homes. The cost of home ownership, which includes mortgage interest rates and home purchase prices, had swiftly escalated in the

Consumer Prices Rose 0.2% in October, But September Inventories Jumped 0.6%

By Michael M. Phillips
Staff Reporter of The Wall Street Journal

WASHINGTON—Despite turmoil elsewhere in the world, the U.S. economy continues to show solid growth and low inflation.

The consumer price index rose a slim 0.2% in October and a mere 1.5% in the past 12 months, according to the latest report by the Labor Department. Separately, the Commerce Department reported that business inventories shot up 0.6% in September, suggesting that the government's initial estimate of third-quarter economic growth might be revised upward.

Last month, the government reported that economic growth, as measured by inflation-adjusted gross domestic product, advanced at an annual rate of 3.3% in the third quarter. But many economists believe that number will now have to be revised upward, thanks to the unexpectedly rapid rise in inventories. Gerald D. Cohen, senior economist at Merrill Lynch & Co. in New York, predicts final figures will show third-quarter GDP growth closer to 4%.

In the inflation report, the Labor Department said the so-called core rate, which excludes the volatile food and energy prices, increased a seasonally adjusted 0.2% in October and 2.3% year over year.

As modest as that figure is, some economists say inflation could move even lower in the months ahead. Since the October inflation data were collected, energy prices have declined, after surging 0.9% in October. "That just means there will be further consumer-price slowdowns in the coming months," predicted Mr. Cohen.

September's rapid accumulation of business inventories came mostly among wholesalers and in the auto industry, which was rebuilding stocks in the wake of the General Motors Corp. strike last summer, the Commerce Department reported.

Commerce had assumed a smaller inventory buildup when last month it issued its preliminary GDP data for the third quarter. Business inventories are one component of the GDP calculation; the faster the inventory buildup, the greater the GDP growth.

The trade deficit data were also missing when Commerce issued its early GDP estimate. The trade figures are due out today and, depending on the size of the deficit, could push the third-quarter GDP data up or down.

While the September inventory buildup may lead to an upward revision of third-quarter economic growth, the large jump in inventories may foretell reduced growth in the fourth quarter, according to Marilyn Schaja, money-market economist for Donaldson, Lufkin & Jenrette in New York. You'd have to expect those inventories to be drawn down," Ms. Schaja said.

Pending today's trade news, Ms. Schaja estimates third-quarter growth at 3.7% with fourth-quarter GDP growth coming in a little under 3%. Merrill Lynch predicts growth in the range of 2% to 2.5% for the fourth quarter.

Separately, the Bureau of Labor Statistics announced that in January it will change the way it calculates the consumer price index, a move that is likely to slightly increase inflation calculations.

The change involves the way the agency assesses the price impact of pollution-control modifications, such as gasoline additives and automobile emissions-control devices. Since 1970, the bureau has considered the cost of those devices to be justified as product-quality improvements, meaning they shouldn't count as inflation-generating price hikes. Now, however, the agency has decided that the cost of pollution-control modifications should be included in the CPI.

Continued

CONSUMER PRICES

Here are the price indexes (1982-1984 = 100) and percentage change for the components of the Labor Department's consumer price index for all urban consumers for October 1998. The percentage changes from the previous month are seasonally adjusted.

	Index	% chg. from Oct. 1998	% chg. from Oct. 1997
All items	164.0	0.2	1.5
Minus food & energy	174.7	0.2	2.3
Food and beverage	162.4	0.5	2.3
Housing	161.4	0.2	2.3
Apparel	135.6	0.1	0.5
Transportation	141.3	0.3	−2.2
Medical care	244.3	0.2	3.6
Entertainment	101.1	−0.3	1.1
Other	241.3	0.3	5.2

October consumer price indexes (1982-1984 equals 100), unadjusted for seasonal variation, together with the percentage increases from October 1997 were:

All urban consumers	164.0	1.5
Urban wage earners & clerical	160.6	1.3
Chicago	165.7	2.0
Los Angeles	163.2	1.3
New York	174.8	1.5
Atlanta	162.0	-
Detroit	161.0	2.0
Houston	148.5	0.8
Miami	161.1	-
Philadelphia	170.3	1.6
San Francisco	167.2	2.9
Seattle	169.3	-

Statistical Summary

CPI—Second Paragraph

The consumer price index rose a slim 0.2% in October and a mere 1.5% in the past 12 months, according to the latest report by the Labor Department. Separately, the Commerce Department reported that business inventories shot up 0.6% in September, suggesting that the government's initial estimate of third-quarter economic growth might be revised upward.

Source: *The Wall Street Journal*, November 18, 1998. Reprinted by permission of *The Wall Street Journal*, ©1998 Dow Jones & Company, Inc. All rights reserved.

**CHART 6–1 Consumer Price Index (CPI) (1982–84 = 100); Change in Index
at Annual Rate (6-Month Span)**

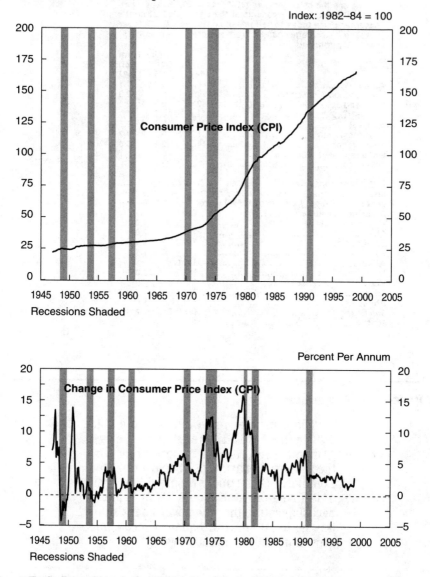

Source: The Conference Board, *Business Cycle Indicators*, Series A0M320 and P6M320.

Jobless Rate Skidded
to 4.4% in November

Report Suggests Economy Remains Vibrant Despite Manufacturing Problems

By ALEJANDRO BODIPO-MEMBA
Staff Reporter of THE WALL STREET JOURNAL

WASHINGTON—Forecasters insisted a few months ago that economic growth was slowing, but statistics tell a different story.

Unemployment Rate

The Labor Department reported that the unemployment rate in November fell to 4.4% from 4.6% in October, dropping it nearly back to April's 28-year low of 4.3%. Not counting agriculture, employers added a surprisingly large 267,000 people to their payrolls last month, suggesting growth is still the trend despite declines in manufacturing employment, headline-making layoff announcements and financial turmoil overseas.

The growth in job creation reflects "the overall dichotomy in the U.S. economy," said Joel L. Naroff, economist at First Union Corp. of Charlotte, N.C. "Manufacturing is in the tank, but consumers are spending like there is no tomorrow," keeping other parts of the economy vibrant.

For the White House, the employment figures were an early Christmas present. Administration insiders said that two Clinton economic advisers, Council of Economic Advisers Chairwoman Janet Yellen and National Economic Council head Gene Sperling, celebrated the news at Friday morning's staff meeting in the staid White House Roosevelt Room with loud whoops and an exuberant, if brief, dance.

"The Grinch hasn't stolen the economy yet," Labor Secretary Alexis Herman declared.

But there was no cheering later Friday when the Commerce Department released its report on factory orders, showing that new orders at the nation's manufacturing plants slowed in October. Orders dropped 1.6% after a 0.8% increase in September, and new orders for durable goods—major appliances, cars and other items intended to last at least three years—fell a revised 2.2% in October.

The slowdown in manufacturing, partly reflecting sluggish growth in foreign economies, is taking a toll on manufacturing employment. Factories lost 47,000 jobs in November, and over the past three months nearly 110,000 jobs have been slashed. "With manufacturing tanking, we are now seeing the primary impact of the world financial problems," said Mr. tion and the services sectors all have yet to fully reflect the impacts."

The decline in manufacturing employment reflects a recent drop in exports as well as a long-term trend. Manufacturing workers now comprise about 25% of the private-sector work force, down from about 45% at the beginning of the 1960s. The portion of Americans working in the service sector has grown and will continue to do so, although that trend may be somewhat overstated because some temporary factory workers are counted in the service sector.

Nonetheless, producing goods remains an important part of the American economy. Goods still account for 50% of the nation's total output. "The goods sector is as important to the U.S. economy as the service sector," measured by the value added by each sector, economists at Chase Securities Inc. in New York observed recently.

Indeed, according to the Federal Reserve's industrial production index, U.S. factories today produce more than 3.5 times as much as they did in 1960. But the manufacturing work force has grown by only 10%. The number of workers on manufacturing payrolls peaked at the end of the 1970s, and has trended down since. For every hour on the job, today's average factory worker churns out more than three times as much as his 1960 counterpart did.

But as factories continue to find ways to produce a greater quantity of goods with fewer workers and as the economy begins to slow, many economists expect factory employment to continue to suffer.

Less certain, however, is exactly how much the economy will slow. Some economists were looking for an economic slowdown months ago, but many indicators continue to point to healthy growth, due in large part to strong consumer spending.

Some economists suggest the economy has enough momentum to continue the current expansion for several more months. With consumption rising and inflation in check, the eventual slowdown might be put off until well into 1999.

"There is nothing that points to a derailment of growth, but clearly there are risks in this economic environment," Dr. Yellen said.

The employment report was a reminder of the American consumer's seemingly insatiable appetite that continues to drive

Continued

the economy's growth. Retailers added 65,000 jobs in November. Hiring at department stores was unusually strong, even by seasonal standards.

The construction industry added 47,000 jobs in November, partly reflecting unusually warm weather. Temporary-help firms, computer and data-processing services, engineering and management services and retail trade all exhibited strength.

"Strong holiday hiring occurred in general merchandise stores, and eating and drinking places added 30,000 workers," said Katharine G. Abraham, commissioner of the Bureau of Labor Statistics.

EMPLOYMENT

Here are excerpts from the Labor Department's employment report. The figures are seasonally adjusted.

	Oct. 1998	Nov. 1998
	(millions of persons)	
Civilian labor force	137.98	138.25
Civilian employment	131.68	132.15
Unemployment	6.30	6.10
Payroll employment	126.51p	126.78p
Unemployment:	(percent of labor force)	
All civilian workers	4.6	4.4
Adult men	3.7	3.5
Adult women	4.0	4.1
Teen-agers	16.0	15.1
White	4.0	3.8
Black	8.6	8.7
Black teen-agers	29.1	28.4
Hispanic	7.2	7.0
Average weekly hours:	(hours of work)	
Total private nonfarm	34.6p	34.6p
Manufacturing	41.7p	41.6p
Factory overtime	4.5p	4.5p

p=preliminary

Statistical Summary

Unemployment Rate—Second Paragraph

The Labor Department reported that the unemployment rate in November fell to 4.4% from 4.6% in October, dropping it nearly back to April's 28-year low of 4.3%. Not counting agriculture, employers added a surprisingly large 267,000 people to their payrolls last month, suggesting growth is still the trend despite declines in manufacturing employment, headline-making layoff announcements and financial turmoil overseas.

Unemployment Rate

UNEMPLOYMENT in July was unchanged at 4.5% of the civilian labor force from the preceding month, the Labor Department reports.

Employment Data—Statistical Summary

EMPLOYMENT

Here are excerpts from the Labor Department's employment report. The figures are seasonally adjusted.

	Oct. 1998	Nov. 1998	
	(millions of persons)		
Civilian labor force.........................	137.98	138.25	
Civilian employment..................	131.68	132.15	
Unemployment...........................	6.30	6.10	
Payroll employment......................	126.51p	126.78p	
Unemployment:	(percent of labor force)		
All civilian workers	4.6	4.4	
Adult men....................................	3.7	3.5	
Adult women	4.0	4.1	
Teen-agers	16.0	15.1	
White	4.0	3.8	
Black	8.6	8.7	
Black teen-agers.........................	29.1	28.4	
Hispanic......................................	7.2	7.0	
Average weekly hours:	(hours of work)		
Total private nonfarm	34.6p	34.6p	Average Workweek
Manufacturing.............................	41.7p	41.6p	
Factory overtime.........................	4.5p	4.5p	Factory Overtime
p=preliminary			

late 1970s, so that this component of the CPI pulled the entire index upward. Many found this an unjustified upward bias. Accordingly, the BLS adjusted the shelter component to estimate the increase in rental value of an owner-occupied home, which more closely approximates its usage value than does actual appreciation in price. Ironically, interest rates and home prices fell soon afterward, so that the old index, had it remained in use, would have displayed a downward bias and risen less rapidly than the new index.

Make a mental note that the *Journal*'s November 18, 1998 report, as well as Chart 6–1 on page 72, confirm inflation's continued abatement since the late 70s peak; the CPI increased by about 5 percent annually in the mid and late 80s, fell to half that level with the 1990–91 recession, and remained at 1 or 2 percent annually at the end of the 1990s. As always, weak demand had done the trick.

EMPLOYMENT DATA

The Wall Street Journal usually publishes the Labor Department's *monthly employment report* on Monday of the second week. November 1998 data

appeared in the Monday, December 7, 1998 *Journal* (see pages 73, 74, and 75). The second paragraph said, "The Labor Department reported that the unemployment rate in November fell to 4.4% from 4.6% in October . . . "

The second paragraph also reported that non-farm employment grew by 267,000 jobs in November. Chart 6–2 below puts this figure in historical perspective.

The illustration on page 74 from the Monday, August 10, 1998 edition is an example of the front-page chart that frequently accompanies such an article, and shows the protracted decline in the unemployment rate throughout 1996, 1997, and 1998.

You should also track the *average workweek* and *factory overtime*, because they, too, portray the economy's strength and are important determinants of consumer sentiment. They appear in the statistical summary at the end of the article, as in the example drawn from the December 7, 1998 story (see page 75). Charts 6–3 and 6–4 on page 77 clearly show that both the workweek and overtime generally improve during expansion, flatten with boom conditions, and plummet in recession. A strong economy provides big paychecks.

CHART 6–2 Job Growth

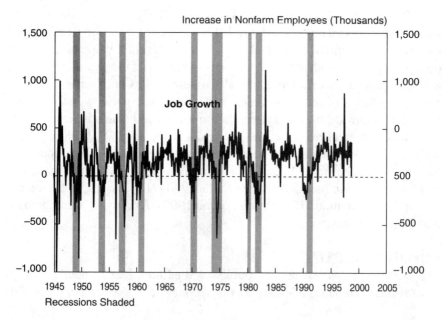

Source: U.S. Department of Labor, Bureau of Labor Statistics.

CHART 6–3 Average Workweek of Manufacturing Production Workers

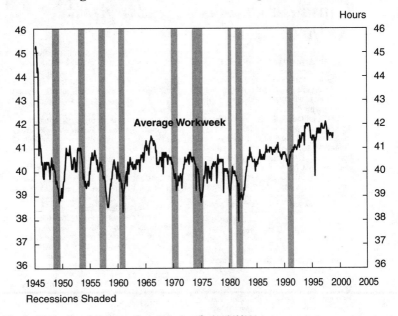

Source: The Conference Board, *Business Cycle Indicators*, Series A0M001.

CHART 6–4 Average Weekly Overtime of Manufacturing Production Workers

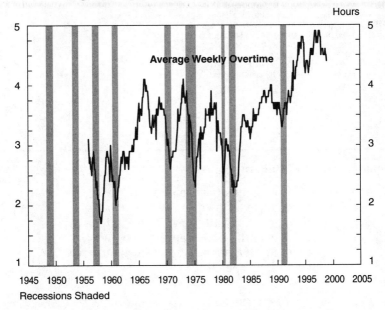

Source: The Conference Board, *Business Cycle Indicators*, Series A0M021.

Consumer Outlays Slowed in April As Income Rose

By ALEJANDRO BODIPO-MEMBA

Staff Reporter of THE WALL STREET JOURNAL

WASHINGTON—Consumer spending eased a bit in April, a hint of a long-awaited slowdown in what has been one of the economy's major drivers.

The Commerce Department said personal-consumption expenditures for April increased 0.4%, following a 0.5% increase in March. Adjusted for inflation, spending was down 0.1%, the first negative monthly reading since November.

"The decline in the personal-consumption numbers was pretty broad based,"

> **Tracking the Economy on Page A14.**

said Steven Ricchiuto, chief economist with ABN-AMRO of New York. "We have probably already seen the strongest consumption numbers we're going to get."

But consumer spirits remain high. The University of Michigan's index of consumer sentiment rose to 106.8 from 104.6 in April. "Consumers' evaluations of current economic conditions in the May 1999 survey have never been more favorable in the 50-year history of the survey," said Richard Curtin, the survey's director. "Consumers were not as exuberant about future economic prospects, however."

Personal Income →
The Commerce Department said personal income, before adjusting for inflation, grew 0.5% after a 0.3% rise in the previous month. That represented the first time in five months that income grew faster than spending.

The report "does not mark the start of a serious weakening in consumption, be-

cause consumers are too happy and too rich to stop spending anytime soon," said Ian Shepherdson, chief U.S. economist for High Frequency Economics in Valhalla, N.Y. "But it is at least a hint that the frantic 6.8% first-quarter surge in spending . . . will not be repeated."

Rising gasoline prices contributed to a 0.5% increase in the Commerce Department's inflation gauge for personal-consumption expenditures. It was the biggest increase since October 1990.

The University of Michigan survey found that consumers expect the inflation rate to edge upward in the coming year. But they see the rise as temporary: Their long-term inflation outlook didn't change in May.

Expenditures for durable goods fell 0.8% before inflation and 1.1% after adjusting for inflation, due to falling motor-vehicle sales.

The Commerce Department's measure of the savings rate—after-tax income minus outlays—was a negative 0.7% in May, matching the record low for the third straight month. The savings measure, which doesn't count capital gains as income, has been negative since November.

Here is the Commerce Department's latest report on personal income. The figures are at seasonally adjusted annual rates in trillions of dollars.

	Mar(r) 1999	Apr(p) 1999
Personal income	7.377	7.413
Wages and salaries	4.328	4.353
Factory payrolls	.760	.763
Transfer payments	1.180	1.182
Disposable personal income	6.240	6.269
Personal outlays	6.285	6.313
Consumption expenditures	6.086	6.113
Other outlays	0.200	0.200
Personal saving	−0.046	−0.044

r-Revised. p—Preliminary.

→ **Statistical Summary**

Personal Income—Fifth Paragraph

The Commerce Department said personal income, before adjusting for inflation, grew 0.5% after a 0.3% rise in the previous month. That represented the first time in five months that income grew faster than spending.

Personal Income—Statistical Summary

Here is the Commerce Department's latest report on personal income. The figures are at seasonally adjusted annual rates in trillions of dollars.

	Mar(r) 1999	Apr(p) 1999
Personal income	7.377	7.413
Wages and salaries	4.328	4.353
Factory payrolls	.760	.763
Transfer payments	1.180	1.182
Disposable personal income	6.240	6.269
Personal outlays	6.285	6.313
Consumption expenditures	6.086	6.113
Other outlays	0.200	0.200
Personal saving	−0.046	−0.044

r-Revised. p—Preliminary.

Source: *The Wall Street Journal*, June 1, 1999. Reprinted by permission of *The Wall Street Journal*, ©1999 Dow Jones & Company, Inc. All rights reserved.

CHART 6–5 Personal Income

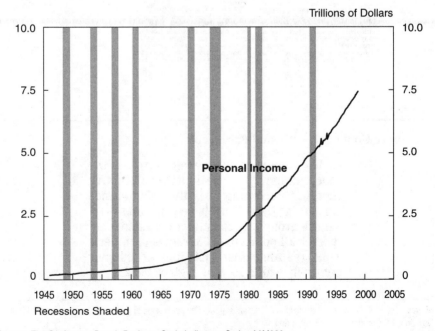

Source: The Conference Board, *Business Cycle Indicators*, Series A0M223.

Consumer Confidence Fell Sharply in October

By JOHN SIMONS

Staff Reporter of THE WALL STREET JOURNAL

WASHINGTON—Battered by global economic crisis, stock market gyrations and signs that the U.S. economy is gearing down, American consumers are losing their financial self-esteem.

Consumer Confidence

Consumer confidence fell sharply in October, dipping for the fourth consecutive month. According to the Conference Board, a New York-based business research group, the consumer confidence index fell 9.1 points to 117.3 from September's 126.4 reading. Just last June, consumer confidence hit a 29-year high of 138.2.

Though confidence is still relatively high, the new numbers dispel any notion that the recent wave of consumer anxiety is temporary. What distinguishes October's slide from those of previous months is that consumers aren't simply pessimistic about the short-term outlook, they are now considerably less optimistic about current economic growth. The board's "present situation index" dropped seven points in October, while the "expectations index" fell more than 10. Confirming that trend, the University of Michigan's survey of consumer sentiment also showed a decline in October.

Spokeswoman Lynn Franco said consumers have the jitters. Their expectations "have deteriorated to a level associated with sluggish economic conditions," she said. "Any further decline in the confidence index could spell a bleak season for retailers."

Sophia Koropeckyj, an economist with Regional Financial Associates in West Chester, Pa., said recently announced layoffs are most to blame for the ongoing anxiety. She expects it may cause some tapering of consumer spending, which accounts for some two-thirds of gross domestic product.

Layoff fears aren't unfounded: According to a Challenger, Gray & Christmas Inc. study, there were announcements of more than 100,000 job cuts in September and early October. And according to the Conference Board, the portion of consumers who believe jobs are plentiful fell to 41.3% in October, from 45.2% in September.

Consumer Confidence
Index (1985 = 100)

Source: Conference Board

Those who perceive jobs as being "hard to get" rose to 16% from 14.3%.

Still, some of the trends that helped to power the economy's seven-year expansion—such as low interest rates and inflation—remain in force. And however low their expectations for future growth, most economists don't foresee a recession. Indeed, ". . .if a recession does start early next year, the circumstances surrounding it will be unique in U.S. business-cycle history," said William Poole, president of the Federal Reserve Bank of St. Louis in a speech earlier this week. As far back as the 1850s, he noted, "there is no case in which the period leading up to a recession was characterized by low-to-declining interest rates in advance of the cycle peak, and high-and-rising money growth," Mr. Poole said.

Even so, consumers apparently don't need a recession to curb their buying plans. L. Douglas Lee, an economist with HSBC Securities Inc. in Washington, believes consumer spending will slow from a 6% rate in the first half to 2% to 2.5% in the next year.

That doesn't bode well for retailers. Most are reluctant to paint a dour picture of the Christmas shopping season, especially since it hasn't officially begun. However, "this is something we are watching very closely," said Carol Sanger, a spokeswoman for **Federated Department** Stores Inc., which owns 400 department stores including the Macy's and Bloomingdale's chains. "It's a question we face every year around this time."

Ms. Sanger insisted that too much fretting about consumer confidence before the holidays "becomes self-fulfilling." Federated predicts a healthy buying season, which translates to 3% to 4% growth over last year's same-store sales, she said.

Ian Richardson, an economist with High Frequency Economics in Valhalla, N.Y., disagrees with those who see further softening of consumer confidence and may have good news for retailers. He doesn't see consumer confidence dipping much more. "The survey doesn't reflect the [second] Fed rate cut since the survey was taken between Oct. 1 and 15," said Mr. Richardson. He added that "stock prices have recovered somewhat as well. A degree of stability has returned."

On Sept 29, the Federal Reserve cut short-term interest rates by a quarter-percentage point, to 5.25%; on Oct. 15, the Fed board trimmed rates another quarter-point.

In a separate report, the Commerce Department said Nevada, Arizona, South Carolina, Utah and Vermont led the nation in personal income growth during the second quarter. Nevada led all states with income growth of 2%; overall, U.S. personal income growth rose 1.1%.

At the bottom were South Dakota, Hawaii, New Jersey and Michigan, all of which posted growth of 0.6% or less.

Consumer Confidence—Second Paragraph

Consumer confidence fell sharply in October, dipping for the fourth consecutive month. According to the Conference Board, a New York-based business research group, the consumer confidence index fell 9.1 points to 117.3 from September's 126.4 reading. Just last June, consumer confidence hit a 29-year high of 138.2.

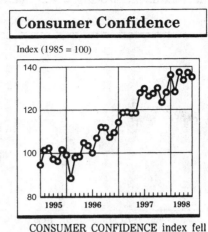

Consumer Confidence

Index (1985 = 100)

CONSUMER CONFIDENCE index fell to 135.2 in May from a revised 137.2 in April, the Conference Board reports. (Article on page A2)

True, manufacturing production workers typically do not control the length of their workweek or whether they will work overtime. Yet the extra income afforded by overtime is welcome and bolsters the consumer sentiment of those earning it. Together with the low rate of inflation, strong overtime helps explain robust consumer sentiment's strong recovery in the mid 1990s. In general, marginal employment adjustments are a reinforcing element of the business cycle through their impact on consumer sentiment.

PERSONAL INCOME

The Commerce Department's monthly personal income report appears in *The Wall Street Journal* during the fourth week or the following week. The statistical summary at the end of the Tuesday, June 1, 1999 *Journal* article on pages 78 and 79 informs you that personal income rose to a seasonally adjusted rate of $7.413 trillion in April of 1999, while the fifth paragraph mentions its percentage growth. These are current, not constant dollars; there is no adjustment for inflation. The statistical summary at the end of the article also breaks out the major components of personal income and its disposition.

Personal income is all the income we earn (wages, salaries, fringe benefits, profit, rent, interest, and so on) plus the transfer payments we receive

CHART 6–6 Consumer Sentiment: Michigan and Conference Board surveys

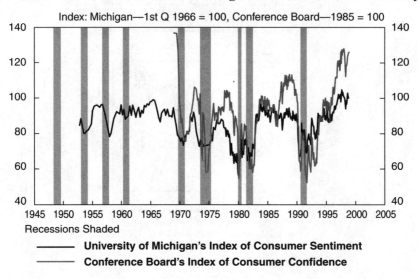

Index: Michigan—1st Q 1966 = 100, Conference Board—1985 = 100

1945 1950 1955 1960 1965 1970 1975 1980 1985 1990 1995 2000 2005
Recessions Shaded

———— **University of Michigan's Index of Consumer Sentiment**

———— **Conference Board's Index of Consumer Confidence**

Source: The Conference Board, *Business Cycle Indicators*, Series U0M058 and U0M122.

(such as veterans' benefits, social security, unemployment compensation, and welfare), minus the social security taxes we pay to the government. Therefore, the federal government's ability to borrow from banks and use these borrowed funds to pay out to us in transfer payments more than it receives from us in taxes provides a cushion that keeps personal income growing even in recession, when earned income is down.

The huge federal deficits generated by the 1990–91 recession helped maintain personal income's growth trend despite rising unemployment in those years. This kept a floor under personal consumption expenditures.

For this reason, as you can see from the historical data (Chart 6–5 on page 79), personal income has grown so steadily that it is difficult to use as a cyclical indicator, even after adjustments for inflation.

CONSUMER SENTIMENT

Let's now consider the impact of inflation on economic recovery in general and on the consumer's leading role in particular.

The Survey Research Center at the University of Michigan compiles the *Index of Consumer Sentiment*. Consumers are asked a variety of questions regarding their personal financial circumstances and their outlook for the

CHART 6–7 Index of Consumer Sentiment and Change in CPI at Annual Rate

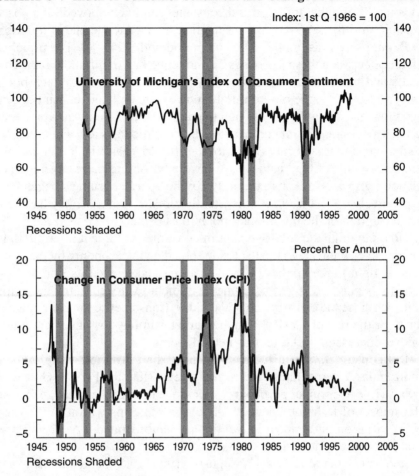

Index: 1st Q 1966 = 100

University of Michigan's Index of Consumer Sentiment

Recessions Shaded

Percent Per Annum

Change in Consumer Price Index (CPI)

Recessions Shaded

Source: The Conference Board, *Business Cycle Indicators*, Series U0M058 and P6M320.

future. Responses are tabulated according to whether conditions are perceived as better or worse than a year earlier, and an index is constructed comparing the outcome to that for a base year (1966).

The Wall Street Journal occasionally reports this index, but more often publishes the Conference Board's *Index of Consumer Confidence*. (See the Wednesday, October 28, 1998 article on page 80, as well as the chart from the May 27, 1998 *Journal* on page 81.) A glance at Chart 6–6 on page 82 shows you that the Michigan and Conference Board indexes have similar records, although the Conference Board index is more volatile.

Compare the CPI with the Michigan index (see Chart 6–7 on page 83), and you will find that inflation and consumer sentiment moved in opposite directions during the 1970s, as consumers responded to the rate of inflation.

Begin by contrasting the 1955–65 period with 1965–80. The principal difference between these periods is the moderate rate of inflation in the first decade and the cyclical increase of inflation after that. With each boom (1969, 1974, 1979), the rate of inflation hit a new high and consumer sentiment reached a new low. Although the mid-70s recession was worse than the 1970 recession, the rate of inflation did not drop to as low a number. No wonder consumer sentiment deteriorated for 15 years: Inflation and the attendant swings of the business cycle were becoming more severe. Once inflation's grip was broken in the early 80s, however, consumers began feeling positively upbeat again for the first time in 20 years. The key had been the interruption of the inflationary boom/bust cycle.

Note the dramatic improvement in consumer sentiment after 1980, as inflation slackened due to the recession forced on the economy by the Fed's 1981–82 tight money policy. Then, when the Fed relaxed its grip and the economy began to recover, consumer sentiment exploded in the most dramatic gain since the construction of the index. Consumer sentiment remained robust for the rest of the 1980s, a dramatic testimony to consumers' relief that ever-increasing inflation was behind them.

But consumers are influenced by more than inflation. Employment opportunities, interest rates, and current events (like the Persian Gulf war) all play a role. Consumer psychology is complicated. Yet you can see the singular impact of inflation before the Fed came to grips with it in the early 1980s; inflation and consumer sentiment demonstrated a clear and predictable inverse relationship.

Iraq's invasion of Kuwait on August 2, 1990 broke that relationship and depressed consumer sentiment for two reasons. First, consumers expected that gasoline prices would rise quickly. Second, and even more important, no one knew whether we would be drawn into the conflict and what the consequences would be. How many lives would be lost? How long would the fighting last? As a result, consumer sentiment plunged dramatically and drastically without a severe and protracted surge of inflation.

Consumer sentiment remained in the doldrums until the fighting stopped, and then snapped back, only to fade as the recession lingered. For the first time in two decades, consumer sentiment seemed to follow the cycle rather than lead it. But by late 1994, consumer confidence had climbed out of the doldrums and was back in its 1980s range. What would restrain it now that the Fed successfully held inflation in check?

U.S. Car, Truck Sales Jumped 9.8% in October

By ANDREA PUCHALSKY
Dow Jones Newswires

New-Vehicle Sales

DETROIT—U.S. consumers bought cars and trucks at a booming 16.7 million annual pace in October, the high-water mark for light-vehicle sales so far this year.

Overall, U.S. car and truck sales rose 9.8% in October, as moderate gains at Ford Motor Co. and General Motors Corp., up 2% and 6%, respectively, were augmented by surging sales at Chrysler Corp. and several European and Asian companies.

GM's market research chief, Michael DiGiovanni, said aggressive incentives have fueled sales in recent months, and based on the rate of sales, "It looks like we are going to exceed our 1998 forecast for 15.4 million in light-vehicle sales." In addition, he said, "The question we are asking ourselves now is whether in 1999 the industry is going to be stronger than we thought."

Ford's 2% sales gain reflected a 10.4% increase in light-truck sales, offsetting an 8% decline in sales of cars. Ford's percentage of the U.S. passenger-vehicle market fell nearly two percentage points in October, to 24.4%.

"Their current product is rather stale, except for a handful of products," said Wes Brown, an analyst at auto consulting firm Nextrend. "Unfortunately for them, on the car side it is going to be difficult . . . to see any improvement in sales for quite a while," he added.

But Ford said the decline in passenger-car sales was the result of its decision to reduce sales of cars to daily rental and other fleet customers.

Jacques Nasser, Ford's president and chief executive officer-elect, played down concerns about the company's slip in car sales. "Car sales aren't in any distress. Our retail performance has been good and we're increasing our quality of market share," he said. Ford has retreated from fleet sales, which mean lower profits, and Mr. Nasser said Taurus and Sable midsize sedan plants are running at full capacity.

GM, fighting to rebuild sales after this summer's 54-day strike, trumpeted a "strong comeback" in October. But its rise in car and light-truck sales wasn't enough to keep its market share above the key 30% level. GM's share dropped to 29.7% in October, in part because it is still ramping up production of its best-selling large pickup models.

GM's rise of 6% in October truck sales benefited from a comparison with a weak year-earlier period. But GM said the improvement in its car sales—also 6%—represented real gains for several recently introduced models. GM also blamed lean inventories caused by the summer strike for slowing its sales growth.

"Our calendar year-to-date truck sales are up 5% over a year ago, even with such a major disruption as the strike and the launch of one of our higher-volume vehicles [the Chevrolet Silverado]," said Don Deveaux, GM's director of North American market analysis. Mr. Deveaux estimated that the new truck launch has shaved about one percentage point off GM's market share in October.

Chrysler, which reported its October sales results Tuesday, posted a 20% increase in sales compared with the year-earlier month. The No. 3 auto maker's 27% surge in October car sales helped it grab a 16.5% share of the U.S. car and truck market, an improvement of 1.5 percentage points over the same month last year.

—*Fara Warner*
contributed to this article.

New Vehicle Sales—First Paragraph

DETROIT—U.S. consumers bought cars and trucks at a booming 16.7 million annual pace in October, the high-water mark for light-vehicle sales so far this year.

By the mid 1990s, both consumer sentiment and consumer demand were robust once more, and the Fed's continued anti-inflation vigilance kept them strong.

Here's the nub of this discussion: *Consumer sentiment drives consumer borrowing and spending*. Strong consumer sentiment propels consumer demand forward, while low consumer sentiment depresses consumer demand. That's why inflation traditionally brought on recession (it depressed consumer sentiment) and why low inflation generated recovery and expansion (it boosted consumer sentiment). Low inflation in the 1980s maintained consumer sentiment and postponed the cycle's peak and the next recession. Credit the Fed's fine-tuning for that. Events in the Persian Gulf depressed consumer sentiment and led to the 1990–91 recession. But low inflation

CHART 6–8 New-Vehicle Sales

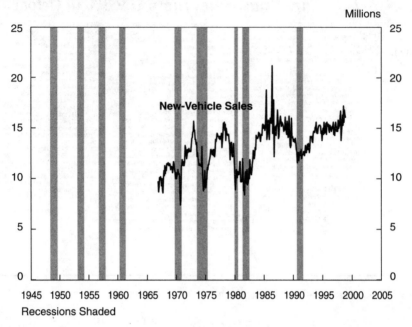

Millions

Source: U.S. Department of Commerce, Bureau of Economic Analysis.

buoyed consumer sentiment throughout the 1990s until it rose to record levels by the end of the decade.

Feelings Are Facts

• When consumer sentiment falters, watch out for recession.

CONSUMER DEMAND

The Wall Street Journal regularly publishes articles on three indicators of consumer demand that merit your close attention: new-vehicle sales, consumer credit, and housing starts. Let's examine each in turn.

New-Vehicle Sales

Around the 5th of the month, *The Journal* reports new-vehicle sales data compiled by the manufacturers. Look at the Thursday, November 5, 1998 report on page 85.

The headline refers to a 9.8 percent jump in car and light truck (pickups, vans, and sport-utility vehicles) sales. But you need the *seasonally*

Consumer Credit Expanded in September

Annual Growth Rate of 7.9% Implies That Confidence Is Better Than Believed

By ALEJANDRO BODIPO-MEMBA
Staff Reporter of THE WALL STREET JOURNAL

**Con-
sumer—
Credit**

WASHINGTON—Consumer credit expanded in September at a seasonally adjusted rate of $8.4 billion, or 7.9% annually, leading a number of analysts to suggest that consumer confidence may be stronger than some first thought.

The latest increase followed a revised rise in August of $4.4 billion, or 4.2% at an annual rate, the Federal Reserve Board said.

Auto credit outstanding expanded an adjusted $1.9 billion in September, after surging $3.8 billion in August. Revolving credit, which includes retail and bank-card borrowing, increased a seasonally adjusted $3.1 billion in September compared with rising $2.2 billion in August. Miscellaneous credit, which includes mobile home loans, cash loans and certain retail financial contracts, expanded $3.4 billion after falling a revised $1.4 billion, surprising some analysts.

Recent stock-market fluctuations not withstanding, Americans appeared eager to continue spending money by borrowing.

Tracking the Economy				Nov. 9, 1998
INDICATOR	**PERIOD COVERED**	**SCHEDULED RELEASE**	**PREVIOUS ACTUAL**	**TECHNICAL DATA CONSENSUS FORECAST**
Nonfarm Productivity	3rd qtr.	Tuesday	+0.1%	+2.0%
Unit Labor Costs	3rd qtr.	Tuesday	+3.9%	+2.0%
Initial Jobless Claims	Week to Nov. 7	Thursday	312,000	310,000
Retail Sales	October	Friday	+0.3%	+0.5%
Producer Prices	October	Friday	+0.3%	+0.1%

Source: Thomson Global Markets

This is occurring even though personal income grew at its slowest pace in 17 months in September and a recent Conference Board report that suggested consumer confidence had fallen.

"Consumer confidence isn't as weak as surveys are showing," said Ian Shepherdson, chief economist for High Frequency Economics, a consulting firm in Valhalla, N.Y. "They are responding with a knee-jerk reaction to the falling stock market."

It is unclear precisely why consumers increased borrowing in September. However, the notoriously volatile consumer-credit figure is often ambiguous about the signals that it sends about the state of the economy.

Many analysts had been expecting an increase in the range of $4.5 billion to $5 billion. But credit watchers said that the relatively sharp monthly increase is consistent with a report last week that September posted the first negative personal-savings rate since the Commerce Department began monthly tracking in 1959.

Some analysts suggest that consumers aren't deterred by the possibility of carrying increasing amounts of debt if conditions begin to deteriorate. In addition, the September increase in consumer borrowing may point to the relative strength of the consumer sector when measured against other areas of the economy.

CONSUMER CREDIT
Here are the seasonally adjusted totals of consumer installment credit outstanding for September 1998, in billions, and percentage changes from August at an annual rate:

Total	$1,285	7.9%
Automobile	437.3	5.2
Revolving	545.7	6.8
Other	302.1	13.8

Consumer Credit—First Paragraph

WASHINGTON—Consumer credit expanded in September at a seasonally adjusted rate of $8.4 billion, or 7.9% annually, leading a number of analysts to suggest that consumer confidence may be stronger than some first thought.

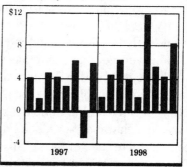

Consumer Credit

Seasonally adjusted, in billions

CONSUMER INSTALLMENT credit outstanding in the U.S. expanded a seasonally adjusted $8.4 billion in September, or at a 7.9% annual rate, the Federal Reserve reports. (Article on page A2)

CHART 6–9 Change in Consumer Installment Credit

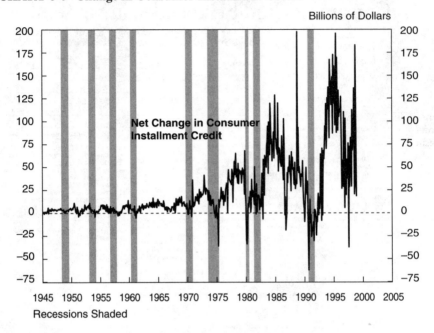

Billions of Dollars

Net Change in Consumer Installment Credit

1945 1950 1955 1960 1965 1970 1975 1980 1985 1990 1995 2000 2005

Recessions Shaded

Source: The Conference Board, *Business Cycle Indicators*, Series A0M113.

adjusted annual rate to make a historical comparison. The first paragraph reports October's new-vehicle sales at a *seasonally adjusted annual rate* of 16.7 million units (see Chart 6-8 on page 86 for a historical comparison).

By the late 1990s new-vehicle sales had reached a sustained level as strong as that of the mid and late 1980s.

The well-equipped auto has symbolized the American consumer economy since the 1920s. The automobile industry pioneered such now familiar techniques as planned obsolescence, mass production, and mass marketing and advertising campaigns in the 1920s and 30s. Henry Ford's Model T was the first mass-produced automobile. His assembly-line production methods were state of the art; his marketing concept, however, was vintage 19th century. He emphasized the cheapest possible serviceable car at the lowest price. Henry Ford reduced the price of a Model T to $300 in the early 1920s and provided customers with any color they wanted, as long as it was black. Ford dominated the market until the late 1920s, when General Motors saw the profit potential in continually inflating the product by offering colors, options, model changes and increased size, weight, and speed. This strategy enabled GM to take the sales lead from Ford; from then on, com-

petition in autos meant more (and different) car for more money, not the same car for a lower price. The option of less car for less money was eliminated until the German and Japanese imports arrived.

Ford had grafted 20th-century technology onto 19th-century marketing techniques, driven the price down as far as it could go, and seen sales go flat in the mid-1920s, as the market became saturated. GM pioneered the 20th-century marketing technique of product inflation on a mass scale and gambled that the consumer would borrow ever more in order to buy next year's model.

Product inflation boosts sales by cajoling the consumer into buying something new at a higher price. The customer isn't swindled, just convinced by marketing and advertising techniques that he or she needs an improved product for more money. Planned obsolescence is a corollary, because style and model changes, as well as product improvement, aid in persuading the consumer that the present (and still serviceable) model should be replaced with a better, more expensive model, not a lower cost repeat of the old model.

That set the pattern for American marketing of consumer goods. You can see it in your kitchen, laundry room, and living room, not just your driveway. TV replaced radio, color TV replaced black-and-white TV, and VCRs are now perceived as near-compulsory accessories. With each innovation, the price goes up and so does debt.

The 1970s and 80s, however, brought a rude shock to the domestic automobile manufacturers. The American public was no longer willing to buy whatever the manufacturers wished to sell. Consumers balked at continued product inflation, especially if it meant buying features, such as increased size and weight, that were no longer attractive. In addition, consumers were willing to accept less car for less money, especially if it meant a better made and more fuel efficient vehicle. As a result, the domestic manufacturers lost market share to the imports, and they have only recently stemmed the tide.

Yet auto sales remained a leading indicator of economic activity. You can see that sales turned down as soon as escalating inflation eroded consumer sentiment (see Chart 6–6 on page 82 and Chart 6–8 on page 86) and recovered quickly when inflation subsided and consumer sentiment improved. Auto sales have led the cycle into both expansion and contraction.

This will help you understand auto sales' role in the economy and why you should regularly track them. It's not just that the auto industry, along with the cluster of industries that depends upon it (e.g., rubber tires, steel, glass, upholstery, fuzzy dice), represents a significant share of total economic activity. It's also that the fortunes of the auto industry lead the cycle, foretelling recession and prosperity. What's good for GM may not necessarily be good for America, but GM's sales are a reliable leading indicator of overall economic activity.

Housing Starts Drop 2.5% as Surge Stumbles

By MICHAEL M. PHILLIPS
Staff Reporter of THE WALL STREET JOURNAL

Housing Starts

WASHINGTON—The residential-construction industry stumbled again last month, but the slip was too slight to indicate a definitive slowdown in one of the economy's strongest sectors.

Housing starts fell 2.5%, to 1.58 million in September from 1.62 million in August, the Commerce Department reported. The August figure already was down from the peak of 1.7 million starts in July. Construction of residences for five or more families registered the sharpest decline, a total of 18.3% in August and September, while single-family housing starts slipped 4.2% over the two months.

"I wasn't disturbed at all by these numbers," said Marilyn Schaja, money-market economist for Donaldson, Lufkin & Jenrette in New York. "The interpretation has to be that it's still a very strong rate of housing starts."

Fueled by extraordinarily low interest rates, the residential-construction industry has been a powerful economic force in the U.S., continuing to prosper even as manufacturers, exporters and farmers have suffered the effects of the global financial crisis.

But even in housing there are signs of weakness. "The one part of the construction market that has been good is residen-

tial," said Stan Shipley, senior economist at Merrill Lynch & Co. in New York. "Now there are parts of that that are starting to pull apart."

In particular, the Commerce Department report showed the fewest multifamily housing starts since May. That could be a sign that builders are having a hard time securing loans to start new projects. "There is some credit disruption in the multifamily market, and we'll probably see it more heavily in the fourth quarter," said Dave Seiders, chief economist at the National Association of Home Builders.

In fact, earlier this month the Federal Deposit Insurance Corp. sent a letter to bank executives advising them to be cautious about lending for real-estate acquisition, development and construction. "The rapid pace of development within various markets may lead to an oversupply of developed property during the next several years," the FDIC letter warned.

Despite credit concerns, however, the overall residential-construction sector is operating at a fast clip. Starts during the first nine months of this year were 9% above the same period of 1997. What weakness there is in the September report was concentrated in the South, where many areas continued to suffer the after-effects of

summer storms and hurricanes. Both the Midwest and the West showed a rise in housing starts, while the Northeast showed a small decline.

Among buyers of single-family homes, low interest rates are helping counter concerns about stock-market volatility and general global turmoil, economists say.

"The quarter overall is still very, very good," Mr. Seiders said.

Home builders still are largely optimistic that a strong housing market will continue into next year. A survey taken at the beginning of October by the home builders' association shows a 12-month high of 68% of builders surveyed consider their sales levels "good," as opposed to "fair" or "poor," while 62% foresee good sales levels through the next six months. Profits have been strong; Pulte Corp. on Tuesday reported a 45% increase in its third-quarter net income.

"Across the board, builders have not seen much in the way of a selling slowdown," said Stuart Miller, president and chief executive of Lennar Corp., a large Miami-based builder active in the South. "Sales are consistently strong. The way order patterns are going, sales will remain consistently strong."

– Carlos Tejada contributed to this article.

Housing Starts—Second Paragraph

Housing starts fell 2.5%, to 1.58 million in September from 1.62 million in August, the Commerce Department reported. The August figure already was down from the peak of 1.7 million starts in July. Construction of residences for five or more families registered the sharpest decline, a total of 18.3% in August and September, while single-family housing starts slipped 4.2% over the two months.

Housing Starts

Annual rate, in millions of dwelling units.

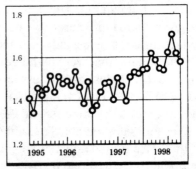

HOUSING STARTS fell to a seasonally adjusted rate of 1,576,000 units from a revised 1,616,000 units in August, the Commerce Department reports. (Article on page A2)

CHART 6–10 Housing Starts

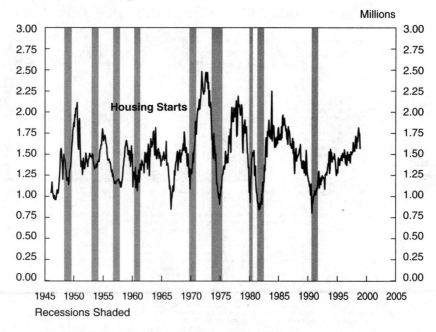

Recessions Shaded

Source: The Conference Board, *Business Cycle Indicators*, Series A0M28.

Consumer Credit

The Wall Street Journal publishes the Commerce Department's release on consumer installment debt in the second week of the month. Changes in consumer credit have been an important barometer of consumer activity, because consumers have borrowed heavily to finance purchases of autos and other expensive and postponable items. The Monday, November 9, 1998 article reproduced on page 87 informs you that consumers borrowed $8.4 billion at a *seasonally adjusted annual rate* in September, for an approximate increase of $100 billion (times 12) at an annual rate. The accompanying chart, which appeared on the front page, shows that September's increase was the second largest of 1998.

Chart 6–9 on page 88 illustrates consumer credit's gradual and cyclical rise until the 1970s. Then, it exploded. You can see the cyclical maximums of $10 billion in the late 60s, $20 billion in the early 70s, $50 billion in the late 70s, $80 billion by the mid 1980s, and $150 billion in the 1990s. But consumer installment borrowing did not spiral ever higher in the late 1990s. By the end of the decade it fluctuated no higher than the levels reached in the early 1990s.

Home Sales Decline an Unexpected 1.1%

Drop of Nearly 5% in South, Partly Due to Hurricane, Hurts September Figure

By Carlos Tejada
Staff Reporter of The Wall Street Journal

Home sales in the South, which has seen the steadiest growth in home building and home sales in recent years, took a hit last month, falling nearly 5%.

Existing-Home Sales

The decline pulled down the national numbers, with sales of existing homes in September dropping an unexpected 1.1% to a seasonally adjusted annual rate of 4.68 million from a rate of 4.73 million in August, according to the National Association of Realtors, which compiles the results. The decline in the South was in contrast to a gain in the West and largely flat activity in the rest of the nation.

Analysts, blamed roughly half of the drop in Southern home sales last month on Hurricane Georges, which caused damage in Mississippi, Louisiana, Alabama and Florida. Even areas that weren't directly hit by the hurricane might have seen ancillary storms, which would have kept potential home buyers indoors instead of out trawling for houses.

But some economists say the region's housing market may simply have peaked. Wesley Basel, senior economist with Regional Financial Associates of West Chester, Pa., said the Southern metropolitan areas of Charlotte, N.C., Birmingham, Ala., and Raleigh, N.C., in particular, show signs of an oversupply in new housing. "It's not a serious crisis, but more a redress of overcapacity," said Mr. Basel, who predicts a 5% drop in the South's existing home sales in the fourth

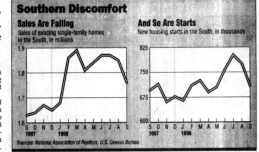

Southern Discomfort

Sales Are Falling
Sales of existing single-family homes in the South, in millions

And So Are Starts
New housing starts in the South, in thousands

Sources: National Association of Realtors, U.S. Census Bureau

quarter and smaller declines in the first half of 1998.

Meanwhile, brisk activity in the summer, combined with a warmer-than-expected winter, spurred additional home-buying activity that may have quelled demand. "It could be they really peaked and ran out of buyers and sellers," said Fred Flick, vice president, economic research, for the realtors' association. "It's been so active over the past three months."

The slowdown in the South could be a prelude to what is in store for the nation as a whole. Although mortgage rates remain unusually low and home prices have been steady, making strong home sales likely, there are other signs suggesting that sales nationwide may slow. Existing home sales have declined twice since July, and in September reached their lowest level since January.

The slower existing home sales follow last week's September housing-starts data, which showed a 12% decline over the past

two months. Given those data, the record level of activity this summer and predictions of an economic slowdown, many economists are predicting sales declines nationwide during the coming months.

To be sure, a slowdown from this summer's lofty numbers still leaves a healthy housing market. Economists generally consider a home-sales number of about four million as indicative of strong home buying, and most forecasts have existing home sales above that number. Meanwhile, home builders have noted a slowing in buyer traffic but remain bullish.

The realtors' association also said the national median price for an existing home fell 1.2% to $131,300 from $132,900. The median sales price in the South fell 3.8% from August. Overall, the inventory of homes for sale remained steady.

Both consumer sentiment and consumer credit fell steeply in the 1990–91 recession, and you can see their historical relationship when you compare Chart 6–9 on page 88 with Chart 6–6 on page 82. In 1991, consumers actually reduced their installment debt appreciably for the first time since World War II. By mid-decade, however, consumer sentiment had recovered, and consumers were once again borrowing at record levels. But by the end of the decade consumer borrowing had tapered off to levels reminiscent of the late 1980s.

Housing Starts

The Commerce Department's monthly release on *housing starts* is usually published in *The Wall Street Journal* between the 17th and the 20th of the month. Always direct your attention to the seasonally adjusted monthly figure, presented at an annual rate. The second paragraph and the front-page chart accompanying the Thursday, October 22, 1998 story on page 90 tells

Existing-Home Sales—Second Paragraph

The decline pulled down the national numbers, with sales of existing homes in September dropping an unexpected 1.1% to a seasonally adjusted annual rate of 4.68 million from a rate of 4.73 million in August, according to the National Association of Realtors, which compiles the results. The decline in the South was in contrast to a gain in the West and largely flat activity in the rest of the nation.

Existing-Home Sales

Annual rate, in millions of dwelling units.

SALES OF EXISTING single-family homes in the U.S. fell in September to a seasonally adjusted annual rate of 4,680,-000 from 4,730,000 in August, the National Association of Realtors reports.

you that there were 1.58 million home and apartment-unit construction starts in September of 1998.

The cyclical sensitivity of housing starts to consumer sentiment and the availability of mortgage credit is striking. (See Chart 6–10 on page 91.) Housing starts turned down well before the onset of recession, as soon as rising inflation reduced consumer confidence and the Fed slammed on the brakes, drying up mortgage credit. But you can see that they often turned back up even before the recession ended, as consumer confidence returned with the decline of inflation and the Fed's switch to an easy money policy.

You have already reviewed the dramatic impact of the Fed's 1981–82 tight money policy on residential construction. The Fed's policy put a new home beyond the reach of most consumers, and mortgage borrowing and housing starts plunged. Although housing starts and mortgage borrowing recovered in the mid 1980s, housing starts did not surpass the record levels of the early 70s (2.5 million at an annual rate in 1972). That fit well with the Fed's plan of restraint.

Residential construction withered during the 1990–91 recession, but had made a modest recovery by mid decade. At the end of the decade (see Chart 6–10 on page 91) housing starts were once again flirting with levels similar to the late 1980s.

New-Home Sales Rose 5.2% in April
To High, Spurred by Healthy Economy

By JOHN SIMONS

Staff Reporter of THE WALL STREET JOURNAL

WASHINGTON—Spurred by a robust job market, high consumer confidence and low mortgage rates, new-home sales climbed to a record in April.

New-Home Sales

Sales of new homes rose 5.2% in April to a seasonally adjusted annual rate of 888,000, up from 844,000 in March. April's record tally is 16.5% above April 1997, the Commerce Department said.

The healthy economic conditions contributing to those robust home sales are expected to continue, according to the Conference Board's index of leading indicators. The index, considered a forecast of business conditions six to nine months in advance, rose slightly in April, to 105.3 from 105.2.

The indicators suggest that the economy is unlikely to be affected by cyclical imbalances and runs almost no risk of recession this year. The pace of economic activity in April was "clearly below" the first quarter's 4.8%, said the Conference Board, a New York business research group.

The Commerce Department said home buying in April was concentrated in the South, where dry, seasonable weather may have played a role. Sales there jumped 18% from March. Sales fell 9% in the Midwest and 3% in the Northeast and were virtually unchanged in the West.

April's overall sales increase dragged the month's supply index down to 3.9 from 4.2 in March. That means at current sales rates, home buyers would deplete the supply of new homes in less than four months.

The department also reported that the median home price fell 2.9% to $147,000 in April. But that drop "doesn't fit the supply/demand character of the residential market, nor the anecdotal evidence of builders," said David Orr, an economist with First Union Corp. in Charlotte, N.C. "Bottom line, new-home prices aren't declining despite what the reported data for April show," he added. Mr. Orr said the April figure is probably skewed by the large portion of sales in the South, where homes are generally cheaper.

New-Home Sales—Second Paragraph

Sales of new homes rose 5.2% in April to a seasonally adjusted annual rate of 888,000, up from 844,000 in March. April's record tally is 16.5% above April 1997, the Commerce Department said.

New-Home Sales

Single-family homes, in thousands.

SALES of new single family homes rose in April to a seasonally adjusted annual rate of 888,000 from a revised 844,000 in March, the Commerce Department reports. (Article on page A2.)

CHART 6–11 Existing-Home Sales

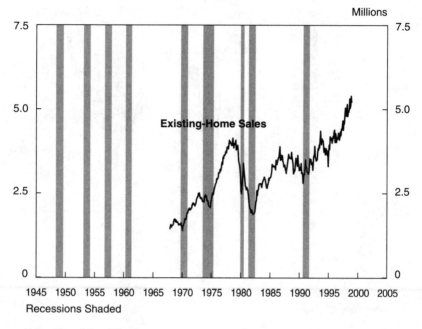

Source: National Association of Realtors.

What was said earlier about industries related to auto sales can be repeated for residential construction. Lumber, cement, glass, roofing materials, heating, plumbing and electrical supplies, kitchen and laundry appliances, and furniture and furnishings are all part of the cluster of industries that fluctuate with housing starts. The Fed's policy of restraint holds all of these activities in check, thereby maintaining moderate levels of inflation in those industries as well.

Home Sales

Two additional reports that exclude apartment-house activity will help you follow the market for single-family homes, and thereby provide an insight into new construction activity.

In the last week of each month, *The Wall Street Journal* publishes the National Association of Realtors' report on existing-home sales for the prior month. The Tuesday, October 27, 1998 report is typical (see pages 92 and 93). According to the headline, second paragraph, and front-page chart, existing-home sales fell in September. Yet the front-page chart shows 1998 activity well ahead of 1997.

CHART 6–12 New-Home Sales

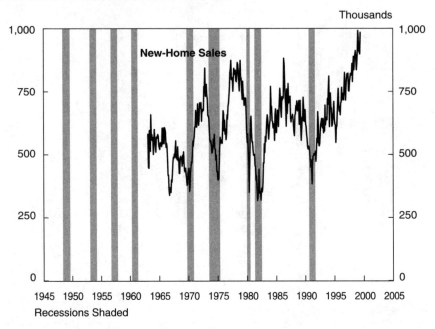

Source: U.S. Department of Commerce, Bureau of the Census.

A week later, usually in the first week of the subsequent month, *The Wall Street Journal* publishes the Commerce Department's release on new-home sales. The example on page 94, drawn from the Wednesday, June 3, 1998 *Journal*, is typical. The headline, second paragraph, and front-page chart, report an increase in April, and the chart reveals the upward trend from 1995 through early 1998.

Charts 6–11 and 6–12 on page 95 and above, when compared with Chart 6–10 on page 91, demonstrate the close correlation between home sales and housing starts.

Retail Sales

The U.S. Department of Commerce's monthly release on *retail sales* appears in *The Wall Street Journal* around the second week of the month. Retail sales are reported in current dollars and include merchandise for personal or house-hold consumption, but do not include services (such as haircuts, dry clean-ing, and restaurant meals). The Thursday, October 15, 1998 report on page 97 states that September retail sales rose 0.3% to a seasonally adjusted $224.9 billion dollars. The front-page chart usually accompanies the report.

Retail Sales Slow Despite Falling Import Prices

By JOHN SIMONS

Staff Reporter of THE WALL STREET JOURNAL

WASHINGTON—The stock market's recent gyrations may have caused consumers to do a bit of belt-tightening, even as falling import prices help keep inflation in check.

Retail | Retail sales rose at a slower-than-expected 0.3% pace in September to a seasonally adjusted $224.9 billion, after practically no increase in August, the Commerce Department said. But even with the general slowdown, retail sales were up 4.3% over September 1997.

Sales | Automotive sales fueled much of last month's increase, rising 0.9% because of a rebound in car-buying after this summer's strike at **General Motors** Corp. Excluding strong auto demand, retail sales rose a scant 0.1% for the second consecutive month.

Meanwhile, the Labor Department said in a separate report that the U.S. import price index declined 0.1% in September, after a 0.3% decrease in August, the Labor Department said. The export price index fell 0.5% during the month of September, following a revised 0.5% decline in August.

The decrease in import prices continued a downward trend, which has amounted to a 6.5% decrease since September 1997. Prices on petroleum imports rose 1.1% in September, after a revised 0.9% rise the previous month. Over the last year, however, petroleum import prices have fallen 32.2%. During the same period, prices of nonpetroleum goods declined 4.2%.

The prices of imports from the newly industrialized Asian countries fell 0.7% in September, down 9.3% from September 1997. Prices on goods coming from Japan fell 0.5% in September, down 5.7% over the last year. The general downward trend in import prices is expected to contribute to declining consumer-goods prices.

While some analysts said the slowdown in retail sales growth portends future penny-pinching among consumers, others cautioned against reading too much into the latest numbers. They note consumers spend a large portion of their income on services, which aren't measured in the retail report.

Sales of clothing and accessories were down 1.3% in September, after a 0.4% decrease in August. Gas-station sales declined 0.8% during the month, after falling 0.4% in August.

September's 0.2% decline in sales of furniture and appliances—the weakest reading in five months—is one of the mysteries contained in the Commerce Department's report. Thanks to low mortgage-interest rates, housing sales remained strong during the period and sales of building materials and supplies rebounded in September, rising 0.4% after a 0.3% decline the previous month. Strong home sales usually are accompanied by a rise in purchases of new furniture and other furnishings. Tim Martin, an economist with NationsBank in Charlotte, N.C., called the furniture spending falloff "puzzling," especially since consumer confidence remains relatively high.

Mr. Martin said that he doesn't believe September's overall slowdown in retail sales portends a wave of consumer cautiousness. "Sales have moderated from the sky-high numbers in the first half of the year, but consumers are still confident about their jobs, and labor markets are going to be fine."

Stan Shipley, an economist with Merrill Lynch in New York, disagrees somewhat, noting that "job growth is slowing and income growth will soon follow." He added that the stock market's so-called wealth effect has added to robust consumer outlays over the past five years and that "the recent stock-market correction should temper consumer spending in the months ahead."

Retail Sales—Second Paragraph

Retail sales rose at a slower-than-expected 0.3% pace in September to a seasonally adjusted $224.9 billion, after practically no increase in August, the Commerce Department said. But even with the general slowdown, retail sales were up 4.3% over September 1997.

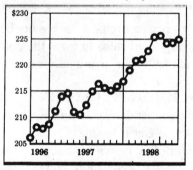

Retail Sales

In billions of dollars, seasonally adjusted.

RETAIL SALES rose in September to a seasonally adjusted $224.94 billion from a revised $224.25 billion in August, according to the Commerce Department.

CHART 6–13 Retail Sales

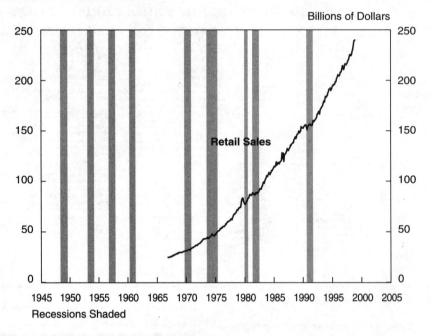

Source: U.S. Department of Commerce, Bureau of the Census.

Because retail sales has not been a volatile series (see Chart 6–13 above), using retail sales to trace the course of the business cycle is not as easy or satisfactory as using auto sales, housing starts, or consumer credit.

SUMMING UP: THE CYCLE AND ITS CONSEQUENCES

Consumer debt and consumer demand provided the leading edge of the post-World War II business cycle. Paradoxically, their strong growth led to cyclical problems with inflation, periodically choking off credit, demand, and economic expansion, and generating recession.

In summary, as the cycle moved from *peak* to *contraction*, rapidly rising inflation depressed consumer real income and consumer sentiment, bringing on a collapse in consumer demand and inevitable recession.

CPI ↑+ Employment data ↓+ Personal income ↓→
Consumer sentiment ↓→ Consumer demand ↓
(Auto sales ↓+ Consumer credit ↓+ Housing data ↓+ Retail sales↓)

Recession let the steam out of the economy, cooling inflation. The temporary reduction in the rate of inflation permitted the business cycle to

resume its course after each recession. Reduced inflation encouraged consumers to indulge in a new wave of borrowing and spending, moving the cycle from *recovery* to *expansion* and launching another round of inflation.

CPI ↓+ Employment data ↑+ Personal income ↑→
Consumer sentiment ↑→ Consumer demand ↑
(Auto sales ↑+ Consumer credit ↑+ Housing data ↑+ Retail sales ↑)

There was no human villain in this drama. Blame the inanimate forces of credit and inflation, which periodically swept over the economy to leave recession's wreckage behind. The Fed finally came to grips with the problem in 1981 when, in its attempt to bring inflation under control, it tightened credit sufficiently to turn recovery into recession.

There are no villains, but there were victims. There is no doubt who bore the burden of recession: the unemployed. Their loss of income is not shared by the rest of us as the economy contracts. Moreover, unemployment hits hardest those industries that depend heavily on big-ticket consumer expenditures financed by borrowing. It is worst in construction, autos, and other durable-goods industries, and in the steel and nonferrous metal industries. Workers in communications, services, finance, and government are largely spared.

Through no fault of their own, therefore, workers (and their families) in a narrow band of industries bore most of the cycle's burden. They are not responsible for the economy's fluctuations, but they are the chief victims in every downturn. Someone must build the homes and cars and mill the lumber and steel. Yet, as if caught in a perverse game of musical chairs, those who do are always left without a seat when the music stops.

WHAT NEXT?

Is the next recession inevitable? Yes, because all economic expansions end in recession. The 1990–91 recession departed from the cyclical pattern described above when the Persian Gulf crisis depressed consumer sentiment even though there was no surge of inflation. That recession created severe slack, and strong growth in the 1990s failed to deplete that slack. Therefore, it does appear that the old cyclical pattern of inflation and recession will reappear. Severe inflation is no longer a concern.

But what have we learned from the past? A strong and rapid expansion, driven by large increases in consumer and business borrowing, and ending in virulent inflation, will produce a sharp and severe recession. A mild and gradual expansion, lacking excessive borrowing and ending with only slight inflation, will produce a mild recession.

Data on auto sales, consumer credit, and housing starts in the late 80s provided evidence that the excesses of the 70s can be avoided if the Fed has the resolve to keep interest rates at restrictive levels. It is better to avoid the rapid growth of demand and the resurrection of inflation, the lethal twins that have killed all previous booms. If demand grows slowly because credit is restrained, expansion will last longer and will not be set back so severely by the next recession.

That explains the Fed's preemptive strike against inflation in the mid 90s, as it forced interest rates upward to cool the interest-sensitive borrowing that finances consumer purchases of new vehicles and new homes. But by the late 1990s consumer demand had reached such strong levels that only continued slack in the economy held inflation at bay. Could it be that the economy might plunge into recession without inflation's resurgence? That was the question of the day.

CHAPTER 7

THE POSTWAR BUSINESS CYCLE: THE ROLE OF COSTS AND INFLATION

THIS CHAPTER WILL DEVELOP THE RELATIONSHIP BETWEEN PRODUCTION, COSTS, AND PRICES, so that you will be able to understand the dynamic whereby rapid growth is transformed into severe inflation. By fathoming this dynamic, you will see why there is little likelihood of inflation's resurgence.

You can find inflation's bellwether in the statistical series that chart output and efficiency. Gross domestic product, industrial production, and capacity utilization measure the economy's output; productivity measures its efficiency. As output increases, efficiency decreases, and inflation (as reported by the producer price index) inevitably becomes a problem.

At the peak of the cycle, when output is at its maximum, production facilities are strained to the point where production costs rise sharply. Overburdened equipment fails, accelerating the expense of maintenance and repair. The quantities of labor added to the production process are relatively greater than the increase in output. Inevitable inefficiencies force up costs

and, consequently, prices, even though the product itself has not changed. As the obvious result, inflation increases rapidly.

With the recession's drop in production, the strain on facilities and labor eases. Costs fall, inflation declines, and the stage is set for a new round of expansion and growth.

The connections between output, efficiency, and inflation form this chapter's central theme. Turn now to an examination of the statistical releases that will be of particular importance in charting the course of production and the interaction of efficiency and inflation as the economy moves from trough to recovery.

GROSS DOMESTIC PRODUCT (GDP)

GDP is a good place to start. As the broadest available measure of economic activity, it provides the official scale with which fluctuations in the economy are measured.

The Wall Street Journal publishes data from the U.S. Department of Commerce's quarterly release on the GDP about one month after the close of the quarter. Then, near the end of the two subsequent months, it reports revisions of the data. The third quarter of 1998 figures appeared in the Monday, November 2, 1998 edition (see pages 103, 104, 105, and 106).

A front-page chart accompanies some articles on the GDP. See for instance, the excerpt from the Monday, August 3, 1998 *Journal* on page 105.

Constant-Dollar (Real) GDP

The headline and second paragraph tell you the economy grew at a 3.3 percent annual rate in the third quarter of 1998. What does this mean?

Constant-dollar (real) GDP measures the final output of goods and services produced in the U.S. in one year, without including the impact of changed prices on the value of those goods. Thus, this year's output (as well as last year's output, next year's, or any year we wish to measure) is calculated in the prices of the base year (1992).

This kind of aggregate measure was once referred to as the Gross National Product (GNP), and there is a slight difference between the two. Put simply, GNP measures the output and earnings of Americans, no matter where they live and work, whereas GDP measures output and earnings in the U.S. regardless of the earner's nationality. For instance, GNP includes the profits of American corporations overseas and excludes the profits of foreign corporations in America, while GDP excludes the former and includes the latter.

GDP includes only final goods and services. This eliminates measuring the same thing more than once at various stages of its production. For

GDP Rise Lifts Hopes for U.S. Economy

Annual Pace of 3.3% Tops
Expectations, Yet Talk
Of a Recession Lingers

By John Simons
And Jacob M. Schlesinger
Staff Reporters of The Wall Street Journal

WASHINGTON—Was all the hand-wringing over an American economic crisis overblown? Or were last week's signs of healthy growth just a brief respite before the collapse?

Developments Friday fueled a new sense of optimism about the U.S. economy. The Commerce Department reported that gross domestic product jumped at an inflation-adjusted annual pace of 3.3% in the third quarter, up from the second quarter's 1.8% pace. The reading was well above analyst estimates, and a far cry from recession. Meanwhile, leaders of the Group of Seven industrialized nations, long accused of foot-dragging amid the recent economic turmoil, unveiled a plan to shore up fragile world markets.

At the same time, investors continued the stock-market rally—launched two weeks ago by surprise Federal Reserve interest-rate cuts—amid fresh signs that Japan is finally fixing its banking mess. The Dow Jones Industrial Average rose 97.07 points to close at 8592.10, the highest

GDP

Turnaround, or Temporary Lull?

GDP Growth Rebounds Sharply...
Percentage change, annual rate

As Markets Stabilize...
DJIA daily closing figure

Still, Consumers Turn More Bearish...
University of Michigan consumer sentiment index

And New Home Sales Ease
Single-family homes, in thousands

Sources: Surveys of consumers at the University of Michigan, Commerce Department

level since Aug. 25.

"Think what's happened in the past month," President Clinton crowed from the White House South Lawn on Friday. "I feel quite good about what my fellow G-7 leaders and others have done," he added. And even "in the face of world-wide economic turmoil," Mr. Clinton said, "our economy remains the strongest in a generation."

But recession talk isn't going away. The

GDP number shows only the state of the economy through Sept. 30, and many analysts say the report contains signs of a slowdown for the rest of the year. Growth was boosted by a sharp jump in inventory investment, often a sign of slower production in the future. Excluding the buildup in stockpiles, growth in the July-to-September period would have been a more modest 2.3%. The mounting trade deficit took
Please Turn to Page A25, Column 1

Continued

instance, bread purchased by the consumer appears in GDP, but both the flour from which the bread is baked and the wheat from which the flour is milled are omitted, because the value of the bread comprises the value of all its ingredients. Thus, the economy's output of *all* goods and services is far greater than its output of *final* (GDP) goods and services. We use very little steel, chemicals, or advertising agency services directly. Their value is subsumed in our purchases of well-promoted Chevrolets and Saran Wrap.

The second paragraph refers to a 3.3 percent increase in final output in the third quarter of 1998. This measurement was made at a *seasonally adjusted annual rate*. Adjusting for seasonal factors merely means correcting the distortion in the data arising from the measurement being taken during this rather than any other quarter. Obviously, no seasonal adjustment is required when a whole year's data is measured, but when the year is divided up and data extracted for a run of months, the risk of distortion attributable to the season is great. For instance, retail trade is particularly heavy around Christmas and particularly light immediately after the first of the year; you could not make a useful comparison of the first quarter's retail sales with the last quarter's without first making a seasonal adjustment.

Latest Rise in GDP Increases Optimism About U.S. Economy

Continued From Page A2

three-quarters of a percentage point off growth, a toll that's expected to increase as economic turmoil abroad continues.

At the same time, business investment, excluding residential construction, dropped in the third quarter, and consumer spending slowed. Many economists think consumption will simply have to slow more, as households apparently are close to being tapped out: The savings rate fell to 0.1% in the quarter, the lowest level in the half century the government has measured the statistic.

Two other economic reports released Friday also pointed toward a slowing: New-home sales fell 1% to a seasonally adjusted annual rate of 822,000 in September from a revised 830,000 in August. It was the third consecutive month of decline. With exception of the Midwest, September home sales declined in all regions. New-home prices rose 1.3% in September and are up 3.9% from a year ago. Lower mortgage rates should help keep housing demand strong, but economists expect to see sales taper somewhat over the next quarter.

Meanwhile, the University of Michigan's consumer-sentiment index was said to have shown a decrease to 97.4 from 98.9 in mid-October, according to people who have seen the report. September's reading was 100.9.

The Michigan survey illustrates that consumers feel good about current economic conditions, but are somewhat uncertain about the future. Indeed, October's "current conditions" index fell to 112.8 from 115.4 in the mid-October. The September level was 111.7. The consumer "expectations" index fell to 87.5 in October from 88.2 in the midmonth report, it was 98.9 in September.

Businesses are beginning to sense a slowdown. Eighty percent of goods-producing businesses say demand was unchanged or fell in the third quarter, the weakest performance since late 1991, according to a survey of corporate economists released last week by the National Association of Business Economists. Profits remained under pressure in the third quarter, the survey said, with 50% of manufacturing respondents reporting lower profit margins in the third quarter compared with 17% with higher margins.

Market Anxiety Remains

Despite the recent stock rally, the market anxiety that has led policy makers to worry about a pending credit crunch remains. Bond markets have calmed a bit over the past couple of weeks. But trading and new issues remain relatively thin, and riskier companies still must pay an unusually high premium to borrow on the markets.

Indeed, many analysts still assume that the Fed will continue to cut the federal funds rate below its current 5% to ease markets and forestall a slowdown. The GDP number "gives me a degree of com-

for that the deceleration is not proceeding too rapidly," said Richmond, Va., Federal Reserve Bank President J. Alfred Broaddus. But he noted, "the problems that have emerged in financial markets that may be having a negative impact on the U.S. economy didn't emerge in force until well into the third quarter. It may well be that all of the impact of the situation has not yet been felt." He added: "We don't want to get cocky."

Still, the GDP report adds to plenty of other signs that the economy is still rather sinewy. Jobless claims have remained low and American workers have received a boost in real disposable personal income, which grew 2.6% in the third quarter, a pace unchanged from the second. Those factors have helped keep consumer spending, which accounts for roughly two-thirds of GDP, at relatively high levels. Indeed, consumption grew a strong 3.9% in the third quarter, down from the lofty 6.1% gains in the first and second periods.

"We continue to have substantial momentum in the economy in spite of all the Asian drag," said Janet Yellen, the chief White House economist. "The economy is in the process of slowing," she said, but to a stable pace of 2% to 2.5%, not to recession. In particular, she noted that "consumption remains extremely strong."

Despite that strong consumption, many analysts agree the economy will slow from here. They are divided, however, over the severity of the ramp-down period. "All along over the past year, we've had respites" in the global economic crisis, said John Makin, an economist with the American Enterprise Institute. "But the problem is essentially still one of overinvestment. We're going to have a fairly significant slowdown."

No 'Turning Upward'

Wesley Basel, an economist with Regional Financial Associates, said he believes the economy is gearing down to a 2.4% rate of growth in the final quarter. "We definitely can't say we've turned the corner and are turning upward," Mr. Basel said. "The inventory bulge will likely slow down, business investment will slow and consumer spending we expect to decelerate."

James O'Sullivan, an economist with J.P. Morgan in New York, said the situation is slightly more dire, pointing out that the real drop in consumer confidence occurred too late in September to be factored into the most recent GDP report. "If employment is weakening, the chances are that consumer spending is going to drop off pretty soon," he said. "And there's no reason to believe that exports are going to pick up anytime soon." The economy is no where near recession now, Mr. O'Sullivan said, "The recession is ahead of us."

He believes the economy will slow to a 1% rate of growth in the fourth quarter; by next year, he sees declining corporate profits, tighter credit conditions and excess capacity combining to cause a falloff in business capital spending. That should tug the economy to a 2% rate of decline by the second quarter of 1999, Mr. O'Sullivan said.

Tracking the Economy
Nov. 2, 1998

INDICATOR	PERIOD COVERED	SCHEDULED RELEASE	PREVIOUS ACTUAL	TECHNICAL DATA CONSENSUS FORECAST
NAPM Mfg. Survey	October	Monday	49.4	49.0
Personal Income	September	Monday	+0.5%	+0.2%
Personal Cons. Expend.	September	Monday	+0.6%	+0.5%
Construction Spending	September	Monday	+0.1%	No change
Leading Indicators	September	Tuesday	No change	No change
NAPM Nonmfg. Survey	October	Wednesday	59.0	58.3
Factory Orders	September	Wednesday	+0.9%	+0.5%
Initial Jobless Claims	Week to Oct. 31	Thursday	301,000	308,000
Nonfarm Payrolls	October	Friday	+69,000	+200,000
Unemployment Rate	October	Friday	4.6%	4.6%
Consumer Credit	September	Friday	+$4.6 billion	+$4.3 billion

Source: Thomson Global Markets

GROSS DOMESTIC PRODUCT
Here are some of the major components of the gross domestic product expressed in seasonally adjusted annual rates in billions of chained (1992) dollars:

	2nd Qtr. 1998	3rd Qtr. 1998
GDP	7,498.6	7,559.5
Inventory chng	38.2	57.2
final sales	7,456.4	7,499.2
Components of Final Sales		
Personal Consumption	5,130.2	5,179.3
Nonresidential Invest.	960.4	958.1
Residential Invest.	309.1	314.3
Net Exports	−245.2	−262.5
Gov't Purchases	1,294.8	1,299.4
implicit Price Deflator	0.9	0.8

Statistical Summary

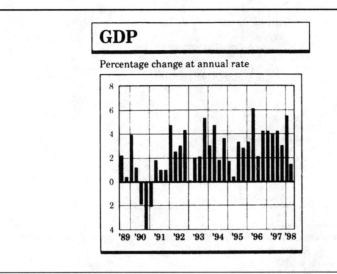

GDP—Second Paragraph

Developments Friday fueled a new sense of optimism about the U.S. economy. The Commerce Department reported that gross domestic product jumped at an inflation-adjusted annual pace of 3.3% in the third quarter, up from the second quarter's 1.8% pace. The reading was well above analyst estimates, and a far cry from recession. Meanwhile, leaders of the Group of Seven industrialized nations, long accused of foot-dragging amid the recent economic turmoil, unveiled a plan to shore up fragile world markets.

Statistical Summary—End of Article

GROSS DOMESTIC PRODUCT

Here are some of the major components of the gross domestic product expressed in seasonally adjusted annual rates in billions of chained (1992) dollars:

	2nd Qtr. 1998	3rd Qtr. 1998
GDP	7,498.6	7,559.5
inventory chng	38.2	57.2
final sales	7,456.4	7,499.2
Components of Final Sales		
Personal Consumption	5,130.2	5,179.3
Nonresidential Invest.	960.4	958.1
Residential Invest.	309.1	314.3
Net Exports	−245.2	−262.5
Gov't Purchases	1,294.8	1,299.4
Implicit Price Deflator	0.9	0.8

The reference to "annual rate" shows that the data for the third quarter, which of course covers only three months' activity, has been multiplied by four to increase it to a level comparable to annual data.

The constant-dollar or real GDP calculation is made in order to compare the level of output in one time period with that in another without inflation's distorting impact. If the inflation factor were not removed, you would not know whether differences in dollar value were due to output changes or price changes. Real GDP gives you a dollar value that measures output changes only.

One last point should be made before moving on. A glance at Chart 7–1 on page 107 shows a steady and robust rise in GDP throughout the 1990s.

A three percent annual increase in GDP is well above the rate of population growth, providing a substantial per capita gain, without getting to an unsustainable rate of more than 5 percent, which, for any length of time, strains our productive capacity.

Statistical Summary

The statistical summary at the end of the article provides a convenient breakdown of the major GDP components.

Now you are ready to put GDP's current performance in historical perspective. Compare it with Chart 7–1 on page 107.

The top graph portrays the actual level of GDP, while the bottom graph depicts quarterly percentage changes at annual rates. When the bottom series is above the zero line, GDP has increased; a drop in GDP is indicated by points below the zero line.

CHART 7–1 Gross Domestic Product (GDP) in Constant (1992) Dollars; Quarterly Change in GDP at Annual Rate

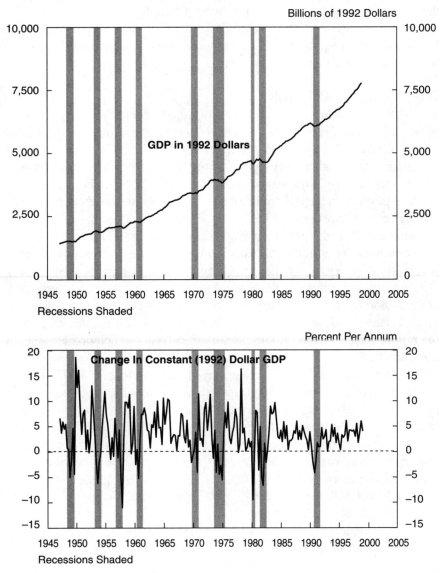

Source: The Conference Board, *Business Cycle Indicators*, Series A0M055 and P1Q055.

As you look at these graphs, pay special attention to the setback to GDP growth during the recession of 1990–91. "Two consecutive quarters of declining GDP" is the traditional definition of recession.

Industrial production and capacity utilization will mirror GDP's performance and also provide important additional detail, so you should now become acquainted with these series.

INDUSTRIAL PRODUCTION

The Wall Street Journal reports data from the Federal Reserve's report on *industrial production* in an article that usually appears mid-month. The Tuesday, November 17, 1998 release (see page 109) is a typical example. The third paragraph, statistical table at the end of the story, and front-page chart summarize matters, while the article provides detail and commentary.

The index of industrial production measures changes in the output of the mining, manufacturing, and gas and electric utilities sectors of our economy. Industrial production is a narrower concept than GDP, because it omits agriculture, construction, wholesale and retail trade, transportation, communications, services, finance, and government. Industrial production is also more volatile than GDP, because GDP, unlike industrial production, includes activities that are largely spared cyclical fluctuation, such as services, finance, and government. The brunt of cyclical fluctuations falls on the mining, manufacturing, and public utilities sectors. Nonetheless, GDP and industrial production move in parallel fashion.

Industrial production is measured by an *index*, a technique that focuses on the relative size and fluctuation of physical output without concern for its dollar value. To construct the index, a base year (1992) was selected to serve as a benchmark and assigned a value of 100.0. (Think of it as 100 percent.) Data for all other months and years is then expressed in relative proportion (numerical ratio) to the data for the base year. For example, according to the statistical summary at the end of the article, industrial production had an index value of 128.3 in October of 1998. This placed October 1998 Industrial production 28.3 percent higher than the average rate of production in 1992.

These developments are reflected in the rate of capacity utilization and in the efficiency with which the economy operates.

CAPACITY UTILIZATION

The Wall Street Journal publishes information from the Federal Reserve's monthly statistical release on *capacity utilization*, or, as it is often called, the *factory operating rate*, along with the industrial production figures. The second to last paragraph of the November 17, 1998 article on page 111 reports

October Manufacturing Rebounded After Plunge

By Jacob M. Schlesinger
Staff Reporter of The Wall Street Journal

Industrial Production

WASHINGTON—Manufacturing rebounded last month after a sharp plunge in September, the Federal Reserve said yesterday.

The latest data are in line with other recent reports on consumer spending and employment showing that the economy, while slowing, seems to remain solid.

Although the Fed's manufacturing index rose 0.3% in October, total American industrial production, which combines factory output with production at utilities and mines, fell by 0.1%, seasonally adjusted. The central bank, in its report, indicated that weak figure was a fluke. The Fed blamed the decline largely on the weather, noting that "utility output, which had been at elevated levels over the summer, fell back as temperatures returned to more normal levels."

Yesterday's industrial production report is one of the last pieces of data that Fed policy makers will see before meeting today to decide whether to continue cutting interest rates. Because of the strong economic data and recent vigor in the stock and bond markets, the decision is increasingly considered a close call.

In a highly unusual move, the U.S. Chamber of Commerce and the AFL-CIO issued a joint statement yesterday urging a further easing of monetary policy. The two recent rate cuts are "not enough," the plea by the two rival organizations said. "Problems continue to grow in the real economy."

The consensus among analysts is that a cut will come. In a Dow Jones/CNBC survey of leading government securities dealers, 26 of 31 firms polled predicted a quarter-point cut today in the target federal funds rate, the rate banks charge each other on loans. Fifteen of 18 economists surveyed by Macroeconomic Advisers

Factories Rebound, Utilities Weaken

U.S. industrial production, manufacturing and utilities indexes, monthly data, seasonally adjusted; 1992=100

Source: Datastream; Federal Reserve

LLC, a St. Louis forecasting firm, also predicted a cut in the rate to 4.75%. The rate currently is 5%.

But the certainty keeps slipping with each new upbeat economic report. Yesterday's manufacturing index was "stronger than expected and is yet one more reason why the Fed today is going to have trouble cutting rates," said Nicholas Perna, chief economist of Fleet Financial Group in Hartford, Conn.

Much of the October manufacturing strength came from a surge in automotive production. But even excluding cars, trucks and auto parts, total manufacturing rose 0.2% over September. "Increases were fairly widespread" in other sectors, the Fed report said, "especially furniture, fabricated metal products, computers and semiconductors."

Despite the improvement, however, manufacturing remains soft. The October rise only partly made up for a 0.6% drop the prior month, and the index remains at its

Capacity Utilization

lowest level since July. Iron and steel production, which has been particularly hard hit by imports, contracted for the second straight month. Other import-vulnerable sectors, like apparel, also cut output.

The decline in the main industrial production index was the fourth in five months. Compared with a year earlier, total industrial production is up by 1.4%. Output at utilities plunged by 3.4% in October from September, while output at mines fell by 1.1%.

The Fed also said the percentage of total industrial production capacity in use fell to 80.6% in October from 81% in September, the lowest level in six years. The biggest drop was in the utilities sector, which saw its capacity-utilization rate fall to 90.9% from 94.2%. But even in manufacturing, the capacity usage rate slipped to 79.4% from 79.5% the prior month—the lowest level since July.

Over the past year, manufacturers have expanded their capacity by 5%, while production has risen by just 1.8%. That implies that, even if production rebounds further, spending on capital equipment is likely to slow.

Statistical Summary

INDUSTRIAL PRODUCTION
Here is a summary of the Federal Reserve Board's report on industrial production in October 1998. The figures are seasonally adjusted.

	% change from	
	Sept. 1998	Oct. 1997
Total	-0.1	1.4
Consumer goods	-0.1	0.6
Business equipment	0.2	5.5
Defense and space	0.9	0.6
Manufacturing only	0.3	1.8
Durable goods	0.6	4.3
Nondurable goods	-0.1	-1.2
Mining	-1.1	-2.1
Utilities	-3.4	-0.2

The industrial production index for October stood at 128.3% of the 1992 average.

capacity utilization's 80.6 percent rate in October. Note that the paragraph also reports manufacturing's 79.4 percent rate.

Capacity utilization is the rate at which mining, manufacturing, and public utilities industries operate, expressed as a percentage of the maximum rate at which they could operate under existing conditions. Putting the matter differently, think of capacity utilization as measuring what these industries are currently producing compared (in percentage terms) to the most they could produce using all of their present resources. Thus, if an industry produces 80 tons of product in a year, while having plant and equipment at its disposal capable of producing 100 tons a year, that industry is operating at 80 percent of capacity; its capacity utilization is 80 percent.

Capacity utilization is a short-run concept determined by a company's current physical limits; at any moment in which capacity utilization is reported, it is assumed that the company's plant and equipment cannot be

**Industrial Production—
Third paragraph**

Although the Fed's manufacturing index rose 0.3% in October, total American industrial production, which combines factory output with production at utilities and mines, fell by 0.1%, seasonally adjusted. The central bank, in its report, indicated that weak figure was a fluke. The Fed blamed the decline largely on the weather, noting that "utility output, which had been at elevated levels over the summer, fell back as temperatures returned to more normal levels."

**Statistical Summary—
End of article**

INDUSTRIAL PRODUCTION

Here is a summary of the Federal Reserve Board's report on industrial production in October 1998. The figures are seasonally adjusted.

	% change from	
	Sept. 1998	Oct. 1997
Total...	-0.1	1.4
Consumer goods............................	-0.1	-0.6
Business equipment	0.2	5.5
Defense and space	0.9	0.6
Manufacturing only	0.3	1.8
Durable goods...............................	0.6	4.3
Nondurable goods	-0.1	-1.2
Mining	-1.1	-2.1
Utilities	-3.4	-0.2

The industrial production index for October stood at 128.3% of the 1992 average.

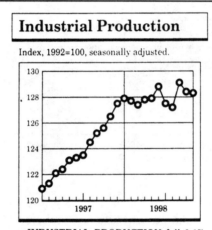

Industrial Production

Index, 1992=100, seasonally adjusted.

INDUSTRIAL PRODUCTION fell 0.1% in October to 128.3 after seasonal adjustments from a revised 128.4 in September, the Federal Reserve reports.

increased, although labor and other inputs can. This defines the short run. Although manufacturing industry continually adds new plant and equipment, it is useful to snap a photograph at a particular moment to enable measurement and comparison.

What bearing does capacity utilization have on the efficiency or productivity of industry? Consider a hypothetical analogy. Your car operates

Capacity Utilization—Second to Last Paragraph

The Fed also said the percentage of total industrial production capacity in use fell to 80.6% in October from 81% in September, the lowest level in six years. The biggest drop was in the utilities sector, which saw its capacity-utilization rate fall to 90.9% from 94.2%. But even in manufacturing, the capacity usage rate slipped to 79.4% from 79.5% the prior month—the lowest level since July.

more efficiently at 50 miles per hour than at 70 miles per hour if its maximum speed is 80, for you will obtain better gas mileage at the lower speed. Efficiency is expressed as a relationship between inputs (gas gallons) and outputs (miles driven). Your car's engine operates more efficiently at lower speeds, or at lower levels of capacity utilization.

You are therefore confronted with the problem of diminishing returns: As your speed increases, you obtain fewer miles for each additional gallon of gas. At 50 miles per hour, you can go 30 miles on an additional gallon of gas; at 52 miles per hour, 29 miles on an additional gallon; at 54 miles per hour, 28 miles; and so on. Your output (miles) per unit of input (gallon) falls as you push toward full capacity utilization (maximum speed).

Likewise, as capacity utilization increases, an industry also passes the point of diminishing returns. This may be at 70 percent, 80 percent, or 90 percent of capacity utilization, depending on the industry, but the point will ultimately be reached where the percentage increases in output will become smaller than the percentage increases in input. For instance, a 15 percent increase in labor input, once we have passed the point of diminishing returns, may provide only a 10 percent increase in output. This phenomenon does not occur because of some mystical mathematical relationship, nor because people are just like automobile engines. There are common-sense reasons for it, and you probably know many of them already.

First, at low levels of capacity utilization, there is ample time to inspect, maintain, and repair equipment; accidental damage can be held to a minimum; and production increases can be achieved easily in a smoothly efficient plant. Above a certain level of capacity utilization, however, manage-

ment finds it more difficult to inspect, maintain, and repair equipment because of the plant's heavier operating schedule. Perhaps a second shift of workers has been added or additional overtime scheduled. There is less time for equipment maintenance, and accidental damage becomes inevitable. The labor force is in place and on the payroll, and production does increase, but not as rapidly as does labor input, because equipment frequently breaks down.

Second, as production increases and more labor is hired, the last people hired are less experienced and usually less efficient than the older workers; furthermore, crowding and fatigue can become a problem if more overtime is scheduled. Poor work quality and accidental damage result. All of this ensures that output will not increase as rapidly as labor input.

Third, low levels of capacity utilization occur at the trough of a recession. Business firms typically suffer a sharp drop in profit, if not actual losses, and, under these circumstances, the employer reduces the work force as much as possible. In fact, he or she usually reduces it more than the drop in output, once the decision to cut back has been made. Why more than the drop in output? Because by the trough of recession, the seriousness of the situation is recognized, and industry has embarked on a thorough restructuring. The alarm has sounded and costs (work force) are slashed. That's why recession often generates the sharpest increases in efficiency.

Even after output has begun to recover, an extended period of labor reduction may continue as part of a general cost-cutting program. As recovery boosts capacity utilization, however, hiring additional workers becomes inevitable. When a factory reaches full capacity utilization near the peak of a boom, the cost-cutting program will be long forgotten as management scrambles for additional labor in order to meet the barrage of orders. At this point, additions to labor are greater than increments in output, even though (to repeat) output will be rising somewhat.

You can summarize business's decisions regarding labor as follows. During rapid expansion and into economic boom, when orders are heavy and capacity utilization is strained, business will sacrifice efficiency and short-run profits to maintain customer loyalty. Management adds labor more rapidly than output increases in order to get the job done. But, when the recession hits in earnest, and it becomes apparent that orders will not recover for some time, management cuts labor costs to the bone with layoffs and a freeze on hiring. This is especially true during a prolonged recession, such as that of 1981–82, which followed on the heels of an earlier recession (in 1980) and an incomplete recovery. Even after recovery and expansion begin, however, business will still attempt to operate with a reduced labor force in order to reap the benefits of cost cutting in the form of higher profits. Oper-

CHART 7–2 Industrial Production Index (1992 = 100)

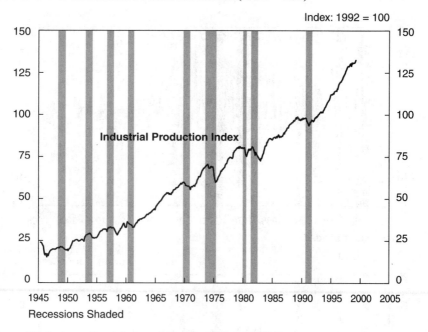

Index: 1992 = 100

Recessions Shaded

Source: The Conference Board, *Business Cycle Indicators*, Series A0M047.

ating efficiency (productivity) improves rapidly, and it will not be threatened until the expansion heats up and boom conditions develop.

Remember the motor in your car? Efficiency is expressed as the relationship between inputs (fuel) and outputs (distance traveled). It is useful to think of the economy as if it were a machine, like the engine in your car. Since your engine is fixed in size (at any moment in time), you can only push a finite amount of fuel through it. Depressing the accelerator rapidly increases your speed and the distance traveled, but the increment in fuel used is greater than the increment in speed and distance. Hence, the efficiency of your engine falls, despite your greater speed and distance. You are getting fewer miles per gallon, and it's taking more fuel to go a mile, because you are driving faster.

Just as a bigger engine would help you accelerate more quickly, more industrial capacity would permit the economy to operate more efficiently. But, for the moment, the economy is limited to the amount of capacity at hand, making it useful to speak about the rate of capacity utilization now. And it is important to realize that, like your car engine, the economy becomes less efficient if it is pushed too hard.

CHART 7–3 GDP and Capacity Utilization

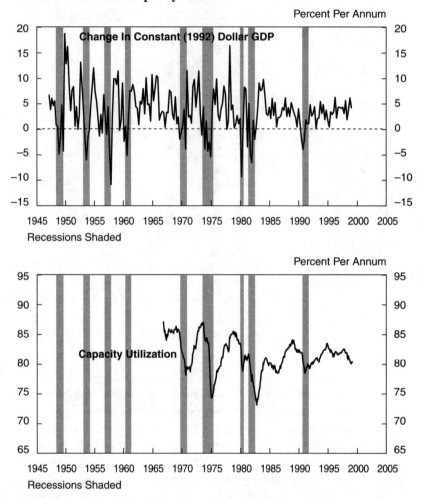

Source: The Conference Board, *Business Cycle Indicators*, Series P1Q055 and A0M124.

Now compare capacity utilization's historical record with that of GDP. (See Chart 7–2 on page 113 and Chart 7–3 above.) Note that the figure did not rise above the 85 percent range throughout the 1990s. This evidence of relaxed growth in GDP kept our economic machinery cool (preventing over-heating), and forestalled inflation's resurgence.

Some economists believe high capacity utilization no longer signals inflation because of the increased availability of imports. But the most prudent reaction is to raise the inflation alarm when it moves beyond 85 percent.

Manufacturing Maintains a Healthy Pace

Orders Index Drops Slightly But Prices for Materials Continue Their Decline

By MICHAEL M. PHILLIPS
Staff Reporter of THE WALL STREET JOURNAL

WASHINGTON — Manufacturing growth eased a bit in April but new orders continued at a healthy clip, indicating that the slowdown was more of a pause than a halt.

Meanwhile, the prices paid by manufacturers for materials to make products fell even faster than in March, the National Association of Purchasing Management reported. And the Commerce Department announced that personal income rose 0.3% in March, down from 0.6% in February. But personal consumption expenditures rose 0.5% during the period, in both current and inflation-adjusted dollars.

Combined, the data show "the economy is still very much on a growth path, with no real signs in our numbers of inflation surfacing," said Norbert J. Ore, chairman of the NAPM business survey committee. "I'm not sure we could go back and find a time in the last 30 or 40 years when we had growth and no increase in inflation."

The purchasing managers' index — the NAPM's principal measure of economic activity — was 52.9 in April, down from 54.8 in March. An overall figure that stays above 43.6 for any length of time generally indicates an expanding economy. Although the new orders index fell very slightly to 56.8 from 57.3, the figure is still considered very strong. "That suggests the dip in the overall number is temporary," said David Orr, an economist at First Union.

The NAPM report, which economists consider a key first look into economic activity in the previous month, did contain a couple of dull spots. New export orders, apparently hurt by the strong dollar and weakened demand in Asia, contracted in April for the fourth consecutive month. The export figure dropped at a somewhat slower pace than in March, however.

"Asia has to be having an impact . . . but it may not be as strong an impact as many thought it could be," said Mr. Ore, who is also director, corporate purchasing, at Chesapeake Corp., a Richmond, Va., tissue and packaging concern.

Factory employment declined in April for the first time in 14 months, although the decrease was very small, the NAPM said. And construction spending was down slightly in March from the strong results posted during the warm weather in January and February, according to the U.S. Bureau of the Census.

The NAPM price data revealed "absolutely no goods price pressures," wrote James McCormick, an economist at J.P. Morgan. The Commerce Department income and spending calculations also showed no uptick of inflation, signs of which might prompt the Federal Reserve Board to raise interest rates.

"The orders are good enough for the Fed to stay on guard, but the prices are going to keep them at bay," predicted Mr. Orr.

Separately, the University of Michigan's consumer sentiment index—a gauge of consumer optimism released only to subscribers—was said to have increased to 108.7 in April from 108 in its midmonth preliminary report, and from 106.5 in March.

Purchasing Managers' Index

Tracking the Economy				May 4, 1998
INDICATOR	PERIOD COVERED	SCHEDULED RELEASE	PREVIOUS ACTUAL	TECHNICAL DATA CONSENSUS FORECAST
Leading Indicators	March	Tuesday	+0.4%	+0.2%
Factory Orders	March	Wednesday	-0.9%	+0.4%
Nonfarm Productivity	1st qtr.	Thursday	+1.6%*	No change
Consumer Borrowing	March	Thursday	+$7.0 billion	+$5.0 billion
Initial Jobless Claims	Week to May 2	Thursday	319,000	315,000
Money Supply: M2	Week to April 27	Thursday	-$23.4 billion	+$0.5 billion
Nonfarm Payrolls	April	Friday	-36,000	+275,000
Unemployment Rate	April	Friday	4.7%	4.7%

* Fourth quarter 1997   *Source: Technical Data*

PERSONAL INCOME
Here is the Commerce Department's latest report on personal income. The figures are at seasonally adjusted annual rates in trillions of dollars.

	Feb. 1998	Mar. 1998
Personal income	7.134	7.158
Wages and salaries	4.074	4.084
Factory payrolls	0.730	0.732
Transfer payments	1.154	1.160
Personal outlays	5.832	5.863
Disposable personal income	6.099	6.122
Consumption expenditures	5.655	5.684
Other outlays	0.178	0.178

Purchasing Manager's Index— Fourth paragraph

The purchasing managers' index — the NAPM's principal measure of economic activity — was 52.9 in April, down from 54.8 in March. An overall figure that stays above 43.6 for any length of time generally indicates an expanding economy. Although the new orders index fell very slightly to 56.8 from 57.3, the figure is still considered very strong. "That suggests the dip in the overall number is temporary," said David Orr, an economist at First Union.

Purchasing Management Index

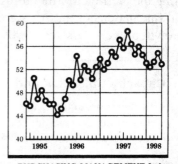

PURCHASING MANAGEMENT Index, which monitors business activity within the manufacturers sector, fell to 52.9 in April from March's level of 54.8.

CHART 7–4 Purchasing Manager's Index

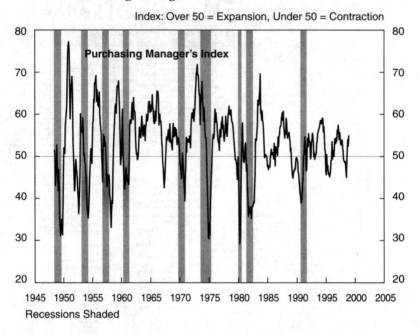

Index: Over 50 = Expansion, Under 50 = Contraction

Recessions Shaded

Source: National Association of Purchasing Management.

When you examine the 1970s, on the other hand, you can see that the rate of capacity utilization periodically rose to the 90 percent level, generating the inefficiency that brings on inflation. That's why the severe cyclical fluctuations of the 70s were bad for the economy and the slow, steady growth of the 1980s and 1990s were good.

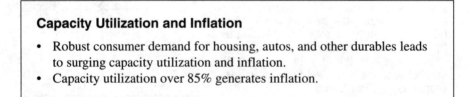

Capacity Utilization and Inflation

- Robust consumer demand for housing, autos, and other durables leads to surging capacity utilization and inflation.
- Capacity utilization over 85% generates inflation.

The next series in this chapter, labor productivity and unit labor costs, will provide the statistical measurements needed to calibrate these fluctuations in efficiency. But first, a brief note on the Purchasing Managers' Index.

Productivity Growth Is Revised Higher

Change to 3% for Quarter Implies Inflation Stays Largely Under Control

By ALEJANDRO BODIPO-MEMBA
Staff Reporter of THE WALL STREET JOURNAL.

WASHINGTON–U.S. productivity in the third quarter rose by more than previously thought, suggesting that inflation is still at bay despite tight labor markets and escalating wages.

Yesterday's Labor Department report, together with the National Association of Purchasing Management's index of nonmanufacturing business activity, points to the generally accepted notion that the economy, while still strong, is slowing a bit.

Productivity — Productivity growth at nonfarm businesses was revised upward to a healthy 3% annual rate for the third quarter, from the previously reported 2.3% increase. That followed a 0.3% growth rate in the second quarter. In addition, growth in unit labor costs for the third quarter was revised downward to 1.1% from 1.7%. All figures are seasonally adjusted.

Growth in manufacturing productivity rose 5.2% in the quarter, reflecting a 0.7% rise in output and a 4.3% drop in hours worked. In addition, unit labor costs fell at a 1.8% rate.

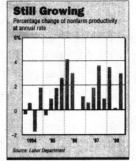

Still Growing
Percentage change of nonfarm productivity at annual rate

Source: Labor Department

"This is unambiguously good news," said Ian Shepherdson, chief U.S. economist for High Frequency Economics in Valhalla, N.Y. "Without productivity growth, there can be no increases in real incomes per head."

Productivity, which measures the ratio of output per hours worked, is important in understanding the economy's relative health. If workers put out more goods and services for each hour they work, businesses can afford to raise wages and benefits without raising prices.

The NAPM's monthly activity index for nonmanufacturing businesses, which make up nearly 80% of the U.S. economy's output, fell slightly to 53 from 53.5 in October. However, some experts expressed concern over declines in the indexes for backlog of orders, below 50 for the second straight month, and for new export orders. If the downward trend in those numbers continues, analysts suggested, business activity may decrease for the next few months.

The business-activity index "is sort of following the manufacturing index downhill a little bit," said Ralph Kauffman, chairman of the NAPM's nonmanufacturing-business survey committee. "But there is no inflationary pressures as indicated by prices paid in this sector."

Separately, first-time jobless claims for the week ended Nov. 28 rose a seasonally adjusted 12,000 to 313,000 from the previous week. Analysts suggested that both the latest week's increase and the previous week's decline were due to seasonal factors, including the Thanksgiving holiday.

The four-week moving average of claims for unemployment benefits, considered a better gauge because it adjusts for weekly fluctuations, rose to 319,250 from 319,000 the previous week.

Productivity—Third Paragraph

Productivity growth at nonfarm businesses was revised upward to a healthy 3% annual rate for the third quarter, from the previously reported 2.3% increase. That followed a 0.3% growth rate in the second quarter. In addition, growth in unit labor costs for the third quarter was revised downward to 1.1% from 1.7%. All figures are seasonally adjusted.

Nonfarm Productivity

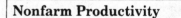

Percentage change at annual rate

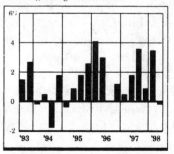

NONFARM business productivity decreased at a 0.2% annual rate in the second quarter from a revised 3.5% increase in the first quarter, the Labor Department reports.

PURCHASING MANAGER'S INDEX

You can buttress your analysis of manufacturing activity by tracking the Purchasing Manager's Index as reported by the National Association of Purchasing Management. A reading over 50 indicates expanding activity; a reading under 50 indicates the opposite.

See the example from the Monday, May 4, 1998 *Journal*, especially the front-page chart and paragraph five, on page 115 and Chart 7–4 on page 116.

LABOR PRODUCTIVITY AND UNIT LABOR COSTS

The Wall Street Journal reports figures from the U.S. Department of Labor's preliminary release on *labor productivity* about a month after the end of the quarter and publishes a revision about a month later. The Friday, December 4, 1998 article presents third-quarter 1998 data (see page 117). Also note the front-page chart that frequently accompanies the report. The example on page 117 is drawn from the August 12, 1998 edition.

Chart 7–5 on page 119 presents the record for all business (including farms).

Labor productivity measures output or production per unit of labor input (e.g., output per hour) and is *the most important gauge* of our nation's efficiency. Its significance cannot be overemphasized, for *per capita real income cannot improve*—and thus the country's standard of living cannot rise—*without an increase in per capita production*.

Unit labor cost measures the cost of labor per unit of output. Thus, unit labor cost is the *inverse* of labor productivity, since unit labor costs fall as labor productivity rises, and vice versa. Unit labor cost tells you how much added labor is required to produce an additional unit of output. Because labor is hired for a wage, requiring more labor time to produce each unit of output will raise labor costs per unit of output, and vice versa.

Consider, for instance, a factory that assembles hand-held calculators. If the production of a calculator has required an hour of labor and a technological innovation permits the production of two calculators per hour, labor productivity has doubled from one to two calculators per hour. The output per hour of work is twice what it was.

If the wage rate is $20 per hour, and before the innovation an hour of work was required to produce a calculator, the labor cost per unit of output was then $20. After the innovation, however, two calculators can be produced in an hour, or one calculator in half an hour, so unit labor cost has fallen to $10. Note that as labor productivity doubled, from one to two calculators per hour, unit labor costs were halved, from $20 to $10 per unit of output. The gain in labor productivity drove down unit labor costs without any change in the wage rate.

CHART 7–5 Productivity: Output per Hour, Business Sector (1992 = 100); Change in Output per Hour (4-Quarter Span)

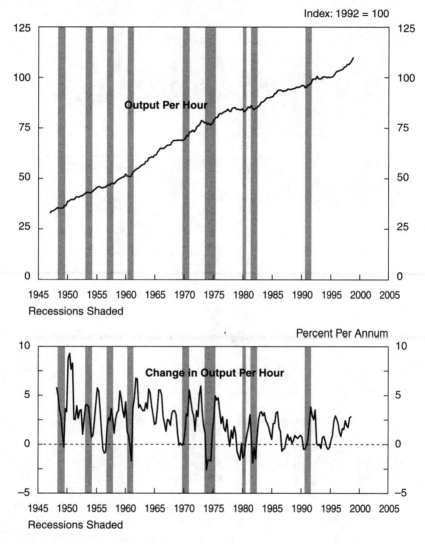

Source: The Conference Board, *Business Cycle Indicators*, Series A0Q370 and P4Q370.

Now compare the record of labor productivity and unit labor costs with the other indicators examined so far (see Chart 7–6 on page 120).

GDP, industrial production, and capacity utilization together define the business cycle in the 1970s. Since 1970, their fluctuations have indicated

CHART 7–6 Manufacturing Unit Labor Cost, Labor Productivity, Capacity Utilization, and GDP

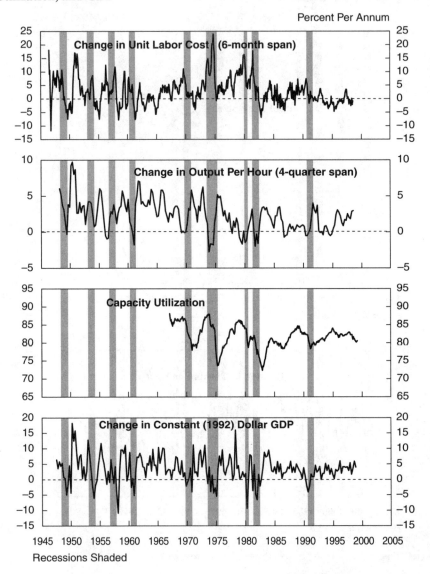

Percent Per Annum

Recessions Shaded

Source: The Conference Board, *Business Cycle Indicators*, Series A6M062, P4Q370, A0M124, and P1Q055.

prosperity and recession. You can also see that labor productivity plunged and unit labor costs soared with the peak of each cycle in the 1970s. Labor productivity improved and unit labor costs declined with each recession and into the next recovery. But as soon as expansion got under way, labor pro-

ductivity's growth began to weaken and unit labor costs began to rise, until productivity slumped and costs peaked at the end of the boom.

And this brings you full circle to the discussion of efficiency included in the earlier investigation of capacity utilization: The economy's efficiency deteriorated in the 70s with each boom and improved in each recession and into recovery. All that this section has done is to provide the labels and devices (labor productivity and unit labor costs) necessary to measure that efficiency. During boom conditions, efficiency (labor productivity) declines and expenses (unit labor costs) mount. During recession the opposite is true.

At first you might ask yourself, "Why would management ever place itself in the position of risking a drop in the efficiency of its operations in order to push output and capacity utilization too far? Why not limit production to an efficient level of operations, at, say, 80 percent capacity utilization, rather than risk declining productivity at 90 percent of capacity utilization?"

The answer is easy, if you put yourself in management's shoes. Suppose you're the boss at Bethlehem Steel, and Ford Motor Co. is your best customer. Suppose also that you're running two production shifts at your mill, 16 hours a day, and a small maintenance crew is employed during the remaining eight-hour shift. The maintenance crew inspects, maintains, and repairs the equipment so that everything is up and running during the daily sixteen hours of production.

Now Ford calls and says their sport-utility vehicles have been a big success and they need more steel in a hurry. Do you tell Ford that you're sorry, that you're running flat out, that you have no idle capacity, and that they should come back during the next recession when you will have plenty of idle capacity and would be happy to take their order? Only if you want to lose your best customer. No, you tell them you will move heaven and earth to fill their order, and you cancel the maintenance shift and put on another production shift.

Putting on another shift of workers increases the size of your production crew (and labor costs) by 50 percent (from 16 to 24 hours a day), yet your output increases by only 30 percent because of periodic breakdowns in equipment that cannot be properly maintained. But if you only require a 30 percent increase in output in order to fill the order, you may very well be willing to put up with a 50 percent increase in labor hours and costs. Sure, output per worker (productivity) falls on this order, and maybe you won't turn a profit either. That's okay as long as you keep your best customer. You're interested in maximizing your profit in the long run, not the short run.

As a result, you've met your deadline by pushing your mill's output to the maximum. Productivity has declined and costs have increased. But that's acceptable, especially if you can pass those higher costs on in the form of higher prices (the subject of the next section of this chapter).

The charts inform you that productivity growth was moderate during the 80s, as output grew more rapidly than labor input. The economy was far better off than in the 70s, when periodic declines in productivity were associated with excessive rates of capacity utilization.

Notice as well that productivity improved nicely coming out of the 1990–91 recession. Labor productivity has continually grown throughout the 1990s, although not at the strong, sustained rate it enjoyed in some previous periods such as the early 1960s.

Productivity and the Cycle

- The economy is like your car's engine—far more efficient at a steady, moderate pace than in stop-and-go traffic.
- If you push the accelerator to the floor and rev the engine (high capacity utilization), efficiency (productivity) drops.

Perhaps by now you are wondering about the long-run influences on productivity. Our economy's efficiency depends on more than cyclical developments. What about industry's efforts to improve efficiency? Where do these fit in?

An economy's productivity improves when enterprise mobilizes improved technology and additional capital goods to raise output per worker and an increasing share of the economy's work shifts to those enterprises that have upgraded their technology and capital goods. These changes occur year-in and year-out, regardless of short-run developments and the cycle's phase. But pushing production to the limit can set these efforts back in the short run.

Turn now to the object of all the effort to contain costs: producer prices.

PRODUCER PRICES

The *producer price index*, until recently referred to as the wholesale price index, is compiled by the U.S. Department of Labor and shows the changes in prices charged by producers of finished goods—changes that are, of course, reflected in the prices consumers must pay. Data from the Labor Department's news release on producer prices is usually published by *The Wall Street Journal* in mid-month.

The Monday, September 14, 1998 article on page 123 is an example, and the headline and first paragraph tell you the producer price index fell 0.4 percent in August of 1998. The illustration on page 123 from the July 13, 1998 edition is an example of the front-page chart that frequently accompanies the article.

Wholesale Prices Slid a Steep 0.4% in August

By Christina Duff
Staff Reporter of The Wall Street Journal

Producer Prices

WASHINGTON—Wholesale prices slid a steep 0.4% in August. Could the deflation goblin finally be at hand?

Certainly, in the goods-producing sector it is. Even after stripping out prices in the volatile food and energy sectors, which dropped a respective 0.4% and 2.3% in August, producer prices still dropped 0.1%, the Labor Department said. For the first

Tracking the Economy on Page A6.

eight months of the year, producer prices have fallen at a 1.4% annual rate, compared with a 1.2% rise for all of 1997.

Such declines, which reflect both a falloff in demand from financially troubled Asian countries and an oversupply for some products, have sparked debate about whether deflation could threaten the U.S. That is a concern because if it should coincide with a period of slackening demand, it could be the nation's closest brush with a repeat of the Great Depression.

"If you ask about the prospect of deflation in the U.S. and you restrict your attention to goods, the answer is yes, and in fact we've had some," said former Fed Vice Chairman Alan Blinder, now teaching at Princeton University.

Indeed, the 0.4% decline in wholesale prices in August is a "significant decline, no question about it," Nobel laureate Milton Friedman said.

But both economists said the prospect of deflation overall, defined as a fall in the general level of consumer prices, is remote. Mr. Blinder noted that prices of services—a huge swath of the economy that includes everything from haircuts to corporate consulting—aren't included in the government's producer price index. While goods generally can be traded world-wide,

and therefore are vulnerable to currency devaluations in other countries, services generally aren't. So a healthy U.S. economy has meant moderate price gains for services.

That should keep the more closely watched consumer price index, then, from falling into deflationary territory as the service sector contributes about 65% of economic output in the U.S.

"People tend to focus too much on goods," Mr. Blinder said. "We cannot emphasize too much that it is a shrinking minority of the economy."

Mr. Friedman added that it would be "very premature" to sound the deflation alarm bells when there are "none of the usual signs." With such a tight labor market and strong economy, he said he worries more about "higher prices than lower prices."

Analyst Ed McKelvey of Goldman, Sachs & Co., New York, noted that even if deflation was imminent, the Federal Reserve has experience in heading it off by lowering interest rates. "We absolutely have the tools to deal with it," he said.

Friday's report, which showed the presence of deflation for many goods, could help give the Fed leeway to reduce short-term interest rates later this year to offset the negative impact of the global crisis. Passenger car prices plunged 1.7% in August. Computer prices continued to drop, sliding a large 4.5%.

There is also an absence of pricing pressure in the pipeline. Prices of intermediate goods, such as flour to make bread, slid 0.3% in August, and prices of crude goods, such as wheat to make that flour, dropped 2.7%.

PRODUCER PRICES
Here are the Labor Department's producer price indexes (1982=100) for August 1998, before seasonal adjustment, and the percentage changes from August 1997.

Finished goods	130.6	-0.8
Minus food & energy	129.2	-1.1
Intermediate goods	123.1	-2.1
Crude goods	94.6	-12.0

Statistical Summary

Producer Prices—First Paragraph

WASHINGTON—Wholesale prices slid a steep 0.4% in August. Could the deflation goblin finally be at hand?

Statistical Summary

PRODUCER PRICES
Here are the Labor Department's producer price indexes (1982=100) for August 1998, before seasonal adjustment, and the percentage changes from August 1997.

Finished goods	130.6	-0.8
Minus food & energy	129.2	-1.1
Intermediate goods	123.1	-2.1
Crude goods	94.6	-12.0

Producer Prices

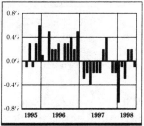

Percentage change from previous month, seasonally adjusted

PRODUCER PRICES of finished goods fell a seasonally adjusted 0.1% in June, according to the Labor Department.

CHART 7–7 Producer Price Index (1982 =100); Change in Index at Annual Rate (6-Month Span)

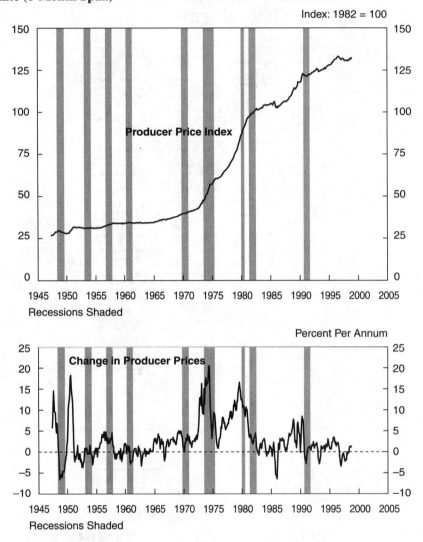

Source: The Conference Board, *Business Cycle Indicators*, Series A0M336 and P6M336.

Chart 7–7 (see above) confirms that in the 1990s, inflation, as measured by the producer price index, continued to fall and remained well below the double-digit levels of the 1970s. The drop since the 1979–80 peak has been dramatic, and many forecasters look forward to deflation (declining prices) in the first decade of the 21st century.

CHART 7–8 Changes in Manufacturing Unit Labor Cost and Producer Prices

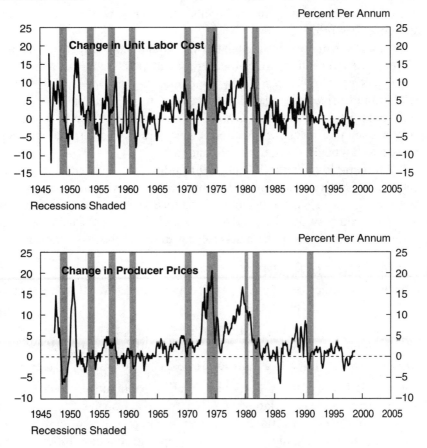

Source: The Conference Board, *Business Cycle Indicators*, Series A6M062 and P6M336.

You can also see from Chart 7–8 above that in the 70s the cyclical trends in producer prices mirrored those of unit labor costs. With each boom in output and capacity utilization, productivity dropped and unit labor costs rose, driving producer prices up. Then, when recession hit and output and capacity utilization fell, improved labor productivity and lower unit labor costs were reflected in reduced inflation. The 1981–82 recession illustrates the principle: Inflation's trend followed unit labor costs downward. As the economy's efficiency improved, stable prices followed on the heels of stable costs. Inflation remained low throughout the 1980s and early 90s because unit labor costs increased at a moderate pace.

"But isn't it true," you may ask, "that moderate wage increases have restrained unit labor costs recently? Perhaps the emphasis on productivity is misplaced and we should instead focus attention on wages as the driving force propelling prices upward."

True, wage increases subsided in the low-inflation 80s and have remained low ever since, contributing to the meager growth in unit labor costs. But generally speaking, *wage rates follow the cycle, they do not lead it*. Wages lagged behind prices during inflation's surge in the late 70s and fell less rapidly than prices in the early 80s. If boom conditions return, and sharp cost increases due to declining productivity are the result, expect wage increases to lag behind inflation once again.

The full employment of the late 1990s didn't generate "wage inflation" because competitive conditions prevented employers from raising prices despite rising wages. As the decade neared its end, employers found themselves squeezed between the need to offer their workers higher wages and the competitive realities of the marketplaces in which they sold their goods.

THE COST/PRICE DYNAMIC

To conclude, summarize the cycle's typical post-World War II progress from *trough* to *recovery* as follows:

GDP ↓→ Industrial production ↓+
Purchasing manager's index ↓→ Capacity utilization ↓→
Labor productivity ↑→ Unit labor costs ↓→ Producer prices ↓

When GDP and industrial production fall, capacity utilization declines. This leads to an increase in labor productivity and a drop in unit labor costs, driving down the rate of inflation as measured by producer prices.

Like the reveler's hangover, recession grips the economy following the bender of boom and inflation. Rest is the only cure, and recovery is marked not by a renewed round of expansion and growth, but by a slack period in which steadiness is restored.

But it would surely be naive to assume that low inflation will be forever with us. What forces can propel it upward once again? Why may we have a renewed round of price increases?

If you ask a businessperson why prices rise, he or she will answer, "Rising costs," probably referring to personal experience. When you ask an economist the same question, the response will be, "Demand exceeds supply at current prices, and therefore prices rise," probably referring to the textbook case. These points of view seem to have nothing in common, yet an analysis of economic expansion shows that they meld into a single explanation. Consider an idealized (and hypothetical) situation.

Suppose all the indicators of economic expansion (demand)—auto sales, consumer credit, housing starts—are strong. This will initiate broad-based growth as incomes increase in the construction, auto, and other durable goods industries, spilling over and boosting demand for other consumer goods. Boom conditions will intensify as business invests in additional factories and machinery to meet the rush in orders.

As the expansion unfolds, capacity utilization increases with the growth in demand and production. Soon factories move from, say, 70 percent to 90 percent of their rated maximum. Productive facilities strain to meet the demand and retain the loyalty of customers.

Next, high levels of capacity utilization drive labor productivity down and unit labor costs up; efficiency is sacrificed for increased output. Machinery that is always in use cannot be adequately maintained, and so it breaks down. Inexperienced workers often do not make the same contribution as old hands. The amount of labor employed increases more rapidly than output, and, as output per worker falls, the labor cost per unit of output rises. This generates a surge in production costs.

Finally, rapidly increasing costs are translated into rapidly increasing prices, and a renewed round of inflation begins.

All the forces that led to a reduction in the rate of inflation are now reversed as the cycle moves from *expansion* to *peak*.

GDP $\uparrow\rightarrow$ Industrial production $\uparrow$+
Purchasing manager's index $\uparrow\rightarrow$ Capacity utilization $\uparrow\rightarrow$
Labor productivity $\downarrow\rightarrow$ Unit labor costs $\uparrow\rightarrow$ Producer prices $\uparrow$

So the practical (businessperson's) and the theoretical (economist's) explanations of inflation are not at odds. During expansion, demand bids production to a level that is inefficient and costly. The businessperson experiences the increased cost and attributes inflation directly to that experience. The economist sees increased demand as the ultimate cause of the production gain that drives costs up. Each explanation covers different aspects of the single phenomenon, economic expansion.

THE 1970s AS AN ILLUSTRATION

The late 1970s illuminate the process graphically. You will need the same statistical series employed earlier to illustrate expansion's impact on inflation: *GDP*, *industrial production*, *capacity utilization*, *labor productivity* and *unit labor costs*, and the *producer price index*. Each of these statistical series has already been introduced, so excerpts from *The Wall Street Journal* will not be presented again.

Although subsequently eclipsed by the 1981–82 recession, the 1974 recession established a postwar record at the time. GNP declined for four quarters, and industrial production tumbled 15 percent. By the spring of 1975, the unemployment rate was more than 9 percent.

Like all recessions, however, this one prepared the way for the subsequent recovery. Capacity utilization fell to a postwar low, and labor productivity began to rise immediately. The resulting decline in unit labor costs cut the rate of inflation.

At the same time, the Federal Reserve System switched from a tight to an easy money policy, reducing interest rates and providing ample credit. A sharp recovery and strong expansion began as the decline in the rate of inflation dramatically improved consumer real income and boosted consumer sentiment. At long last, consumers were pulling ahead of inflation; their pleasure was reflected in demand's rapid increase.

By 1977–78, new housing starts were 2 million annually and domestic automobile sales peaked at approximately 10 million, while consumer installment borrowing hit annual rates of $50 billion.

The evidence of a robust economic expansion was all around as GDP and industrial production surged ahead. Rapid growth in demand, production, and capacity utilization had its inevitable result: The nation's factories and other productive facilities were strained, and increases in the labor force no longer made a proportional contribution to output (see Chart 7–6 on page 120).

In 1979, labor productivity stopped improving and began to fall. As a result, unit labor costs increased steadily, and by early 1980 the rate of inflation, as measured by the producer price index, had reached 15 percent (see Chart 7–8 on page 125).

Declining labor productivity is the focal point of this analysis. Once output is pushed past the point of diminishing returns, unit labor costs become an inevitable problem. Most people believe that rising wages are chiefly responsible for this condition; wages do play a minor role, naturally, but unit labor costs will increase swiftly even if wage gains run well below the rate of inflation (i.e., even if real wages are falling).

Falling real wages, coupled with the forward surge in labor costs, creates one of the cruelest features of inflation. Because labor productivity has declined, there is less per capita output and, therefore, less real income per person. Declining real income pits one segment of American society against another, fighting over a shrinking pie. Labor-management relations become especially bitter in these periods of boom without prosperity. Employers blame workers' wages for rising labor costs and shrinking profits, while

workers blame employers' profits for shrinking real wages; in reality, neither one is responsible for the other's misfortune.

In such times, the public's support for wage and price controls becomes insistent (although, of course, management has a greater interest in controlling wages and labor has a greater interest in controlling prices). Yet you can see from this chapter's analysis that rising costs due to reduced efficiency (falling labor productivity) are responsible for the increase in prices that captures everyone's attention. No one's greed is to blame. Therefore, controls designed to limit greed are bound to be ineffective.

There have been two recent attempts at wage and price controls: the first under President Nixon in 1971–72 and the second under President Carter in 1979–80. President Nixon's controls were certain to "succeed," because they were implemented during the transition from recovery to expansion, while capacity utilization was low and labor productivity was high. As a result, the rate of inflation was still falling from its 1970 cyclical peak. It would have continued to decline in any event and remain low until the expansion gained strength. The controls did slightly dampen inflation, but their impact was marginal.

President Carter's controls were destined to "fail," just as President Nixon's were destined to succeed, because President Carter's were implemented during the virulent expansion of 1977–79. As labor productivity fell and unit costs climbed, business merely passed its increased costs on to the consumer. Rising prices reflected rising costs, not greed, and business did not earn excessive profits.

Keep in mind also that more stringent wage controls could not have restrained business costs. Some of the increase in unit labor costs was due to the increase in wage rates, but most of it was due to declining productivity caused by high capacity utilization. Workers were no more culpable than their employers.

This is an important point. We really can't blame the declines in labor productivity in the 1970s on the American worker, as some are prone to do. Productivity lapses in that decade occurred cyclically, when the economy overheated, and thus they really reflected the limitations of plant equipment under extreme conditions rather than failures of diligence in the labor force.

Harking back to World War II for an example of successful wage and price controls is not the answer, either. Wage and price (and profit) controls worked then because the economy was on a war footing. About half of the economy's output was devoted to the war effort, much of it under a system of planning and direct resource allocation that operated outside ordinary market relationships. You couldn't bid up the price of a car (none were produced because

the auto plants were converted to war production) or buy all the gasoline and steak you wanted (these were rationed). And despite the patriotism aroused by the war effort, black markets arose to subvert the controls. Therefore, it's doubtful whether such a system could work to contain peacetime inflation, for which, unlike war-induced inflation, there is no end in sight.

Imposing wage and price controls during the expansionary phase of the business cycle (as was attempted in the late 70s) is a little like trying to stop the rattle of a boiling kettle by taping down the lid. Demand heats the expansion, and inflation is the natural result. Turning down the heat is the only practical solution.

Finally, there's the question of "supply-side shocks." These are sudden increases in the price of important commodities (imposed by the sellers) or reductions in supply due to forces beyond our control. Some believe that the late 1970s' inflation was due to these sorts of shocks, but this argument should be taken with a grain of salt. First, any explanation that places the blame on others should be suspect; if you wish to find fault, it is always best to look in the mirror. Second, neither OPEC, nor the Russian wheat deal, nor the failure of the Peruvian anchovy harvest can explain the price explosions of the 70s. They may have contributed to the inflation, but they did not cause it. If demand had been weak, prices would have remained stable. After all, prices stopped climbing as soon as recession hit in 1981–82, well before the oil price collapse of early 1986.

And whether you are dealing with free-market farm prices or OPEC, repealing the laws of supply and demand is not easy. Farm prices eased down in the commodity deflation of the 80s, while oil prices collapsed in a matter of months in early 1986. In both cases, high prices and profits in the 70s had attracted investment in new productive facilities and therefore created excess capacity (supply). Once supply exceeded demand at current prices, the price collapse was inevitable.

CONCLUSION
In the 1990s, the forces of supply continued to gain on the forces of demand. By the end of the decade it appeared that inflation would cease, prices would stabilize, and a sustained downward trend might begin by the beginning of the 21st century. Businesses had rapidly added productive capacity, enabling strong growth in supply. At the same time, the Fed had restrained demand so thoroughly that it appeared that the typically inflationary post-World War II dynamic had come to an end. Sustained deflation seemed just around the corner.

C H A P T E R 8

STOCKS

I F YOU RETURN TO THE EXAMINATION OF THE STOCK MARKET'S PER-
FORMANCE (see Chart 8-1 on page 132) first mentioned in Chapter 1,
you will note, to repeat, that stocks did poorly in the high-inflation
70s and well in the low-inflation 80s and 90s. Recall the promise in
Chapter 1 that you would be able to forecast stocks' performance once
you had mastered (1) the forces that shaped inflation and (2) an ability to use
The Wall Street Journal to analyze those forces. Now is the time to put your
knowledge to work.

PROFITS AND STOCKS

Stocks are more complex than commodities, because you must analyze profits first. You can't measure a company's value until you know how much it
can earn. *The Wall Street Journal* survey of corporate profits for over 500
corporations, including industry-wide statistics on earnings and net income
(see page 133), appears about two months after the close of the quarter. The
headline and first paragraph of the Monday, November 2, 1998 article on page
134 reports a three-percent gain over the year-earlier quarter.

Profits measure efficiency by comparing revenues to costs. Recall that
the economy's efficiency improves during the early phases of the cycle and
deteriorates during the latter phases. Thus, profits grow during recovery and
expansion and deteriorate during peak and contraction.

A bit of logic reveals the relationship between general changes in economic efficiency over the cycle and the specific measurement of profit. Efficiency rises early in the cycle, because factories operate with excess capacity
and produce less than maximum output. The general reduction in costs due to

CHART 8–1 Dow vs. CPI: Dow Jones Industrial Average; Change in Consumer Price Index (CPI) at Annual Rate (6-Month Span)

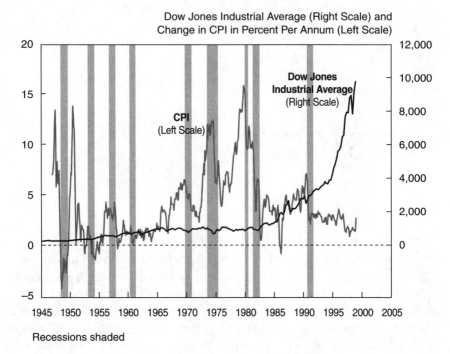

Dow Jones Industrial Average (Right Scale) and
Change in CPI in Percent Per Annum (Left Scale)

Recessions shaded

Source: Dow Jones & Company, Inc.; The Conference Board, *Business Cycle Indicators*, Series P6M320.

enhanced productivity increases the spread between prices and costs, known as the profit margin or profit per unit of output. As sales increase, total profit grows because of both higher output and higher profits per unit of output.

Efficiency deteriorates late in the cycle as factories strain to produce maximum output. Costs rise as productivity falls, and industry is forced into a "profit squeeze," meaning that costs push up against prices. Total profits fall as sales volume stops growing, or actually contracts with the onset of recession, and profit per unit of output (the profit margin) falls.

It may help to think of it in these terms: Costs rise as output increases and industry reaches full capacity utilization. As costs come up from below, they bump prices upward. But competition prevents management from raising prices as rapidly as it would like. If costs rise more rapidly than prices, the margin between price and cost is squeezed. Profit margins decline.

On the other hand, management has the opportunity to rebuild its profit margins in the slack period following recession. Costs are no longer rising as rapidly, because capacity utilization is low. This provides management

Earnings Rise a Lackluster 3% In a Quarter Roiled by Troubles But Prompt Brighter Forecasts

By Tristan Mabry
Staff Reporter of The Wall Street Journal

NET INCOME AT MAJOR U.S. CORPORATIONS rose a modest 3% in the third quarter from a year earlier, as a host of economic crosscurrents, from hurricanes to labor strikes to global financial turmoil, uprooted profits.

While the results were clearly lackluster, they weren't as bad as some had anticipated, and they prompted a number of analysts to forecast stronger profits for the current quarter.

The third period was a "tough quarter, with quite a few negatives," said PaineWebber analyst Thomas Doerflinger. "We were hurt by the strike [at General Motors], by a strong dollar and by financial panic—none of which will be present in the fourth quarter."

Net on continuing operations, a narrower measure of profit that excludes one-time accounting entries, fell 1% during the July-to-September period.

The profit figures are based on The Wall Street Journal's monitoring of 667 publicly traded companies. U.S. corporations posted a 24% gain in net income during the second quarter from a year earlier, but nearly all of that was due to a huge one-time gain by cable-television concern MediaOne Group. Excluding MediaOne's windfall following its separation from U S West, net income at U.S. companies fell 3.6% in the second quarter, and net on continuing operations for the companies in the Wall Street Journal survey fell 2%.

Thomas Galvin, an investment strategist at Donaldson, Lufkin & Jenrette, said companies were able to withstand the multiple challenges they faced in the third quarter because they are nimbler than in previous years and can quickly adapt to changing economic conditions. That flexibility, he said, "helps us avoid the abyss."

The reporting season focuses attention on the growing debate over which profit measure is more telling for investors: net income or operating earnings. Net income includes write-offs and other one-time charges or gains. Operating earnings, however, exclude one-time events and extraordinary items, focusing on day-to-day corporate performance. Wall Street analysts tend to stress operating earnings, although the frequency of write-offs has convinced some that the broader net-income measure is more valuable.

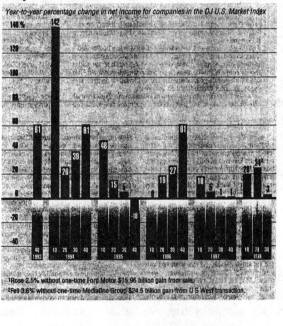

Corporate Profits

Year-to-year percentage change in net income for companies in the DJ U.S. Market Index

[1] Rose 2.5% without one-time Ford Motor $15.96 billion gain from sale.
[2] Fell 3.6% without one-time MediaOne Group $24.5 billion gain from U S West transaction.

with the opportunity to recover profit margins by raising prices more rapidly than costs.

Thus, paradoxically, profit margins shrink when prices rise most rapidly, typically before the peak of the cycle, and grow when inflation abates in the slack period immediately after recession and when recovery begins.

That's why both productivity and profitability recovered nicely as the economy emerged from the 1990-91 recession. There's a strong correlation between productivity and profit margins. As the economy's efficiency improves, so does the spread between price and cost. Business earns more per unit of output. But in the superheated economy at the business cycle's peak, such as during the highly volatile 1970s, efficiency and profitability deteriorated. Profit margins shrank.

Chart 8–2 on page 135 depicts the ratio of price to unit labor cost (i.e., the relative strength of prices and unit labor cost) and is therefore a proxy for profit margins. This informs you of the extent of labor cost's encroachment on prices and of business's ability to hold down labor costs in relation to the prices received. Keep in mind that the ratio of price to unit labor cost is a fraction in which price is the numerator (top half) and cost the denominator (bottom half). In boom conditions, when costs are rising rapidly and pushing prices upward, profit margins are squeezed, because competition prevents management from raising prices as rapidly as costs increase. Thus, the value of the fraction (ratio of price to unit labor cost) falls as the denominator (cost) rises more rapidly than the numerator (price).

In recession and recovery from recession, management can rebuild profit margins, because costs are no longer rising rapidly. Management raises prices somewhat more quickly than costs increase, and profit margins are replenished. As a result the ratio of price to unit labor costs rises as the numerator of the fraction now gains more rapidly than the denominator.

Each of the cycles in the 1970s demonstrates the same sequence of events. Start with a typical recovery and expansion, such as the recovery and expansion of 1970–72 or 1975–77. Unit labor cost was kept down by good gains in labor productivity due to modest levels of capacity utilization. As a result, the ratio of price to unit labor cost (our proxy for the term profit margins) improved and held up well. Since sales volume and output were growing, total real profits grew sharply.

Then, in 1973 and 1978–79, as production and capacity utilization peaked, labor productivity declined and unit labor cost increased. As a result, the ratio of price to unit labor cost fell, pinching profit margins. Since, at the peak of the cycle, sales and output had also stalled, real profits tumbled and continued to fall throughout the ensuing recessions of 1974–75 and 1980.

CHART 8–2 Ratio, Price to Unit Labor Cost, Nonfarm Business

Index: 1992 = 100

Recessions Shaded

Source: The Conference Board, *Business Cycle Indicators*, Series A0Q026.

Chapter 7 discussed wage and price controls, and Chart 8–2 above illustrates the foolishness of this adventure. The rate of inflation declined in 1971–72, during President Nixon's controls, despite rising profit margins (ratio of price to unit labor cost). Since profit margins rose, why didn't inflation climb with them? Because the rate of cost increase subsided due to improved productivity brought about by the recovery phase of the business cycle. In other words, the drop in costs exceeded any increase in margins.

The rate of inflation rose in 1979–80, during President Carter's controls, despite falling profit margins (ratio of price to unit labor cost). Since profit margins fell, why weren't controls effective in limiting inflation? Because the inflation was not due to excessive profit margins; it was due to the increasingly rapid rise in costs brought on by cyclical expansion's negative impact on productivity. Controls could not stem the rising spiral of prices.

In addition, rapidly rising inflation forces interest rates up. Higher yields on interest-earning instruments provide a low-risk alternative to stocks. As investors pull their money out of stocks to take advantage of the lower-risk attractiveness of interest-earning investments, the stock market weakens. That's another reason inflation is so harmful to stocks.

To summarize, profits, when calculated for the entire economy, measure efficiency, not greed. Prices simply can't be controlled by limiting profits.

You can see in Chart 8–2 on page 135 profit margins recovered in the mid 80s, as low rates of capacity utilization boosted labor productivity and held down unit labor costs, providing an increased spread between prices and costs (improved profit margins).

Profit margins stumbled in the late 80s because the economy grew too languidly and slid even further with the start of the 1990–91 recession, an anomaly caused by the Persian Gulf war. Keep in mind, however, that margins did not fall as severely as they had in the 70s during the cyclical course of boom conditions.

The important point (see Chart 8–3 on page 137) is that inflation's cyclical squeeze on profit margins and real earnings in the 1970s regularly depressed the stock market so that it could not advance out of the trading range in which it was trapped. Inflation is murder on profit margins and therefore, is the death of the stock market. On the other hand, once inflation and interest rates subsided, continued strong profit margins and low interest rates provided a boost to the stock market in the 1980s that continued into the 1990s. By the late 1990s, sustained low inflation and interest rates along with strong profit margins propelled the stock market forward at a breakneck pace.

STOCKS AND THE PRICE/EARNINGS RATIO

Let's return to the Dow Jones Industrial Average. You know that the price of a share of stock reflects the ability of the corporation to earn profits. This relationship is expressed as the price/earnings (P/E, or price divided by per share earnings) ratio between the price of the stock and the profits per share of stock earned by the corporation (profits divided by number of shares outstanding). The price/earnings ratio answers this question: "What is the price an investor must pay to capture a dollar of earnings?" For instance, a P/E ratio of 10 might mean that a company earned $10 per share per annum and that a share sold for $100, or it might mean that a company earned $7 per share per annum and that a share sold for $70, and so on.

The investor, of course, seeks the highest yield consistent with safety. The earnings yield is annual profit expressed as a percentage of market price. If you earn $100 a year on an investment of $1,000, the yield is 10 percent. A P/E ratio of 10 (10/1) represents a 10 percent yield, because earnings are 1/10 (10 percent) of the price per share. Similarly, a P/E ratio of 5 (5/1) is the equivalent of a 20 percent yield, because earnings per share are one fifth (20 percent) of invested capital. A P/E ratio of 20 (20/1) represents a 5 percent earnings yield. And so on.

CHART 8–3 Dow Jones Industrial Average (Price), Earnings Per Share, and Price/Earnings Ratio

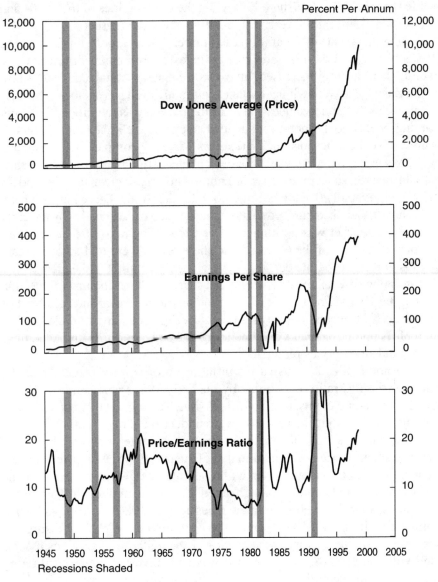

Percent Per Annum

Recessions Shaded

Source: Dow Jones and Company, Inc.

Chart 8–3 on page 137 shows that the Dow's P/E ratio fell from the end of World War II until the beginning of the Korean War, because earnings grew while share prices languished. Following the uncertainties of the 1930s and World War II, investors were still tentative about the market.

Then the great bull market (stock prices fall in a bear market) of the 1950s began, and the P/E ratio rose as investors bid up share prices more rapidly than earnings increased. Investors were at last convinced of a "return to normalcy" and were willing to stake their future in shares of stock. The market was clearly "undervalued" (a P/E ratio of seven was roughly a 15 percent earnings yield), so it is not surprising that stock prices climbed rapidly. Stocks were a good buy, because their price was very low compared to their earnings per share and their potential for even higher earnings. As investors rushed into the market, stock prices soared. Enthusiasm was so great and share prices advanced so rapidly that the P/E ratio rose despite stronger earnings per share.

The P/E ratio had climbed to more than 20 (a 5 percent yield) by the early 60s, so the market was no longer undervalued. The ratio plateaued or fell slightly to the end of the 60s, because share prices were no longer increasing faster than corporate earnings. The great bull market had ended.

Inflation rose and profit margins fell sharply with each burst of inflation during the 1970s. The impact of inflation on interest rates and the effect of severe cyclical fluctuations on profit margins frightened investors. At the first sign of rising interest rates and declining margins, investors unloaded their shares and stock prices plunged.

Yet nominal (not adjusted for inflation) profits rose over the decade, and thus the P/E ratio fell, so that by the early 1980s it was almost as low as it had been at the outset of the Korean War. The market had not kept pace with nominal earnings, and stocks were undervalued once again.

To some, this indicated that we were on the verge of another bull market. The situation seemed similar to that of the late 1940s, with investors hesitant after years of bad news, yet willing to take the plunge when it became clear that the fundamentals had changed. One indication of this sentiment was that stock prices fell little in the recessions of 1980 and 1981–82 when compared with those of 1970 and 1974. (Ignore the early 80s P/E surge. It was clearly the temporary consequence of the collapse in earnings associated with the 1981–82 recession.) It was as if investors were positioning themselves for the bull market that was just around the corner.

There were two very auspicious signs. First, the breaking of the boom-and-bust inflationary spiral with the back-to-back recessions of 1980 and 1981–82 was a key signal that henceforth corporations could enjoy high profit margins. Second, the low P/E ratio meant that stocks were under-valued. Grow-

ing earnings would generate rising share prices, and when sufficient numbers of investors realized that the earnings improvement was permanent, the P/E ratio would rise to higher levels as buying pressure drove stock prices up.

The bull market of the 80s began in the summer of 1982, when it became clear that the Fed had loosened its monetary vise. The decline in interest rates mattered to investors, because interest-earning assets are an alternative to stocks. As interest rates fell, investors moved out of interest-earning instruments and into stocks.

But Chart 8–3 on page 137 demonstrates that investors responded too enthusiastically to the improved profit potential. Speculation bid share prices up must faster than either real or nominal earnings. By August 1987 the Dow had doubled its 1985 level and stood at more than 2700, while earnings per share at $125 were not much greater than they had been four years earlier. The P/E ratio climbed to 22, higher than it had been since the early 60s.

Clearly the market was overvalued, ripe for a correction. It began to fold after its peak of 2722.42 on August 25, 1987, and declined 500 points by October 16. Then on October 19, it crashed another 500 points.

Yet earnings per share continued to grow in a climate of low inflation. They exceeded $200 by early 1989, sending the P/E back down to 12. Now the Dow was undervalued once again, and investors began to recover from their post crash jitters. By early 1990, investors had propelled the Dow passed its 1987 high; in the summer of 1990 it reached 3000.

What was the source of their bullish attitude? Strong margins, low inflation, and a low P/E. What did investors have to fear? Either inflation's return or speculation; the first because of its depressing impact on profit margins, the second because excessive stock market appreciation would create overvaluation (a high P/E) of the kind that existed before the 1987 crash.

Then Iraq invaded Kuwait. As consumer sentiment collapsed and recession unfolded, the Dow fell to 2400. But consumer sentiment rebounded with the success of Operation Desert Storm, and the stock market anticipated economic recovery. The Dow quickly regained the 3000 range and remained there for some time.

Unfortunately, the economic recovery took longer than forecast, and earnings continued to decline. The 1990–91 recession repeated the experience of 1981–82 by sharply depressing earnings. Moreover, as you can see in Chart 8–3 on page 137 the drop in earnings drove the P/E ratio to absurdly high figures. Was that a sign of speculation and a signal for investors to sell?

Clearly not. Abysmal earnings for the Dow stocks, not speculation, had generated the extraordinary P/E ratios. Circumstances at the close of the 1990–91 recession were quite different from those before the crash of 1987.

P/E RATIOS & YIELDS ON INDEXES

	–P/E Ratios–		Dividend Yields	
	1/22/99	Yr. Ago	1/22/99	Yr. Ago
DJ Industrials..........	24.0	20.1	1.67%	1.79%
DJ Tranportations....	16.5	15.1	0.98%	0.88%
DJ Utilities.............	21.7	17.8	3.58%	4.08%
S&P 500	32.17	24.11	1.32%	1.64%

Price earnings ratios for the Dow Jones Averages are based on per share earnings for the most recent four quarters of $379.48 for the 30 Industrials; $185.39 for the 20 transportation issues; $14.18 for the 15 utilities.

Source: *The Wall Street Journal*, January 25, 1999. Reprinted by permission of *The Wall Street Journal*,

Depressed earnings, not speculation, were responsible for the extraordinarily high P/E ratio.

By the mid 1990s, the P/E had fallen back to 15 as earnings passed the $300 per share level. The Dow was poised for and achieved another record ascent. By the end of the 1990s, earnings had reached the $400 per share range and the Dow continued to surge past 10,000, pushing the P/E ratio to 25. But could the bull market continue if earnings stalled with a P/E of 25 to 1?

Follow the earnings and P/E for the Dow stocks each Monday on the third page (C3) of the *Journal*'s third section, called Money and Investing. An example from the Monday, January 25, 1999 *Journal* appears above.

P A R T

YOUR CHOICE OF INVESTMENTS

9

THE STOCK MARKET

A FIRST GLANCE: MARKETS DIARY

The stock market is a good barometer of economic activity, because it reflects the value of owning the businesses responsible for most of our economy's output. *The Dow Jones Industrial Average* is the most popular indicator of stock market performance, and that's why Chapters 1 and 8 employed it to portray the entire market.

The Dow represents share prices of 30 blue-chip industrial corporations, chosen because their operations cover the broad spectrum of industrial America, although you can see from the list presented on page 144 that not all of these firms are literally "industrials" (e.g., American Express, AT&T, Disney, McDonald's, and Wal-Mart are in financial services, communications, entertainment, fast food, and retailing). (Dow Jones publishes separate indexes for public utilities and transportation companies.)

There are broader stock market barometers that include more corporations, but the Dow Industrials remains the most closely watched average because it was first and, more significantly, because its handful of blue-chip companies do reflect stock market activity with surprising precision. Other measures of the stock market's performance will be mentioned shortly.

You probably already know a fair bit of the information in the next several pages, but it will provide a good basis for some more complex ideas presented later in this chapter.

Every day, on the first page of the third section (C1), *The Wall Street Journal* publishes a summary account of the activity of the stock market as measured by several major indexes. It is always the lead item under the heading **Markets Diary** (see the excerpt from the Thursday, December 24, 1998

The 30 Stocks in the Dow Jones Industrial Average (April 1, 1999)

Alcoa	Hewlett-Packard
Allied Signal	IBM
American Express	International Paper
AT&T	Johnson & Johnson
Boeing	McDonald's
Caterpillar	Merck
Chevron	Minnesota Mining
Citigroup	& Manufacturing
Coca-Cola	J. P. Morgan
Disney	Philip Morris
Du Pont	Procter & Gamble
Eastman Kodak	Sears Roebuck
Exxon	Union Carbide
General Electric	United Technologies
General Motors	Wal-Mart
Goodyear	

Journal on page 145). The Dow Jones Industrial Average is featured in the two charts under the **Stocks** caption. The chart on the left pictures the fluctuations in the Dow over the past year-and-a-half, while the one on the right shows the Dow's weekly movement. The table just below the charts features four major domestic stock-market indexes as well as the U.S. component of the Dow Jones Global Index. You should use this chart and table for your first quick assessment of the previous day's stock market activity.

Now take a moment to consider the Dow Industrials in more detail.

CALCULATING THE DOW

Each day, on the third page of the last section (C3), the *Journal* publishes in chart form a detailed summary of the **Dow Jones Averages** over the past six months (see the example from the Thursday, December 24, 1998 *Journal* on pages 146 and 147). It records the progress of the 30 industrials, the 20 stocks in the transportation average, and the 15 stocks in the utility average, as well as trading volume.

After glancing at the top chart of the Dow Jones Averages, your first question—once you know what this index signifies—probably is, "How

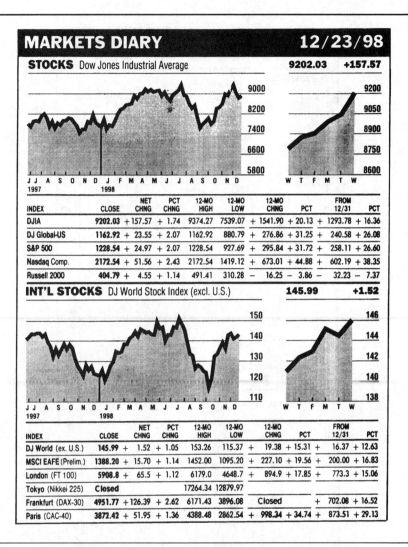

MARKETS DIARY   12/23/98

STOCKS Dow Jones Industrial Average   9202.03   +157.57

INDEX	CLOSE	NET CHNG	PCT CHNG	12-MO HIGH	12-MO LOW	12-MO CHNG	PCT	FROM 12/31	PCT
DJIA	9202.03	+ 157.57	+ 1.74	9374.27	7539.07	+ 1541.90	+ 20.13	+ 1293.78	+ 16.36
DJ Global-US	1162.92	+ 23.55	+ 2.07	1162.92	880.79	+ 276.86	+ 31.25	+ 240.58	+ 26.08
S&P 500	1228.54	+ 24.97	+ 2.07	1228.54	927.69	+ 295.84	+ 31.72	+ 258.11	+ 26.60
Nasdaq Comp.	2172.54	+ 51.56	+ 2.43	2172.54	1419.12	+ 673.01	+ 44.88	+ 602.19	+ 38.35
Russell 2000	404.79	+ 4.55	+ 1.14	491.41	310.28	− 16.25	− 3.86	− 32.23	− 7.37

INT'L STOCKS DJ World Stock Index (excl. U.S.)   145.99   +1.52

INDEX	CLOSE	NET CHNG	PCT CHNG	12-MO HIGH	12-MO LOW	12-MO CHNG	PCT	FROM 12/31	PCT
DJ World (ex. U.S.)	145.99	+ 1.52	+ 1.05	153.26	115.37	+ 19.38	+ 15.31	+ 16.37	+ 12.63
MSCI EAFE (Prelim.)	1388.20	+ 15.70	+ 1.14	1452.00	1095.20	+ 227.10	+ 19.56	+ 200.00	+ 16.83
London (FT 100)	5908.8	+ 65.5	+ 1.12	6179.0	4648.7	+ 894.9	+ 17.85	+ 773.3	+ 15.06
Tokyo (Nikkei 225)	Closed			17264.34	12879.97				
Frankfurt (DAX-30)	4951.77	+ 126.39	+ 2.62	6171.43	3896.08	Closed		+ 702.08	+ 16.52
Paris (CAC-40)	3872.42	+ 51.95	+ 1.36	4388.48	2862.54	+ 998.34	+ 34.74	+ 873.51	+ 29.13

can an average of stock market prices be over $10,000? I don't know of *one* stock that trades that high, much less 30 of them."

The answer involves the manner in which the Dow deals with "stock splits." Companies split their stock (say, two for one) to prevent the stock from becoming too expensive. Shareholders receive two shares for each share they own, and the stock's price is halved; thus, the total value of the shares remains the same.

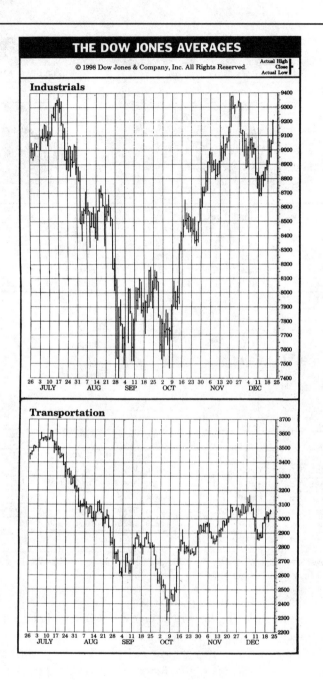

Continued

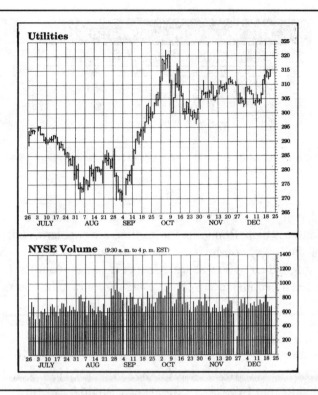

The Dow Divisor on December 23, 1998 →

The Dow Jones Averages Hour by Hour

Following are the Dow Jones averages of INDUSTRIAL, TRANSPORTATION and UTILITY stocks with the total sales of each group for the period included in the chart.

DATE	OPEN	10 AM	11 AM	12 NOON	1 PM	2 PM	3 PM	CLOSE	CHG	%	HIGH*	LOW*	HIGHª	LOWª
30 INDUSTRIALS: (divisor: 0.24275214)											(THEORETICAL)		(ACTUAL)	
Dec 23	9044.72	9086.94	9105.22	9146.16	9156.97	9170.36	9140.24	9202.03	+ 157.57	+ 1.74	9255.84	9022.58	9211.04	9043.17
Dec 22	8989.11	8993.48	8992.97	9007.64	9013.57	9031.07	9035.71	9044.46	+ 55.61	+ 0.62	9122.99	8909.29	9069.44	8948.69
Dec 21	8902.97	8981.13	9051.41	9066.35	9048.84	9071.75	9040.60	8988.85	+ 85.22	+ 0.96	9150.54	8874.28	9079.22	8898.74
Dec 18	8877.63	8892.04	8862.43	8878.91	8891.53	8911.35	8901.31	8903.63	+ 27.81	+ 0.31	9012.28	8789.31	8928.60	8858.57
Dec 17	8787.55	8823.30	8845.96	8869.90	8849.05	8839.52	8845.44	8875.82	+ 85.22	+ 0.97	8959.76	8725.21	8879.94	8785.75
20 TRANSPORTATION COS.: (divisor: 0.24084679)											(THEORETICAL)		(ACTUAL)	
Dec 23	3037.72	3045.50	3051.73	3060.56	3054.59	3044.99	3054.59	+ 18.43	+ 0.61	3102.85	2999.05	3065.75	3035.12	
Dec 22	3025.14	2986.08	2991.27	2996.72	2992.05	3010.02	3018.52	3036.16	+ 0.64	+ 0.35	3084.69	2950.79	3047.06	2977.26
Dec 21	3009.04	3034.22	3042.00	3038.24	3037.98	3044.47	3049.14	3025.52	+ 16.48	+ 0.55	3088.06	2987.90	3053.03	3009.04
Dec 18	2970.64	2989.58	2983.22	2995.94	2996.59	3008.91	3007.49	3009.04	+ 38.40	+ 1.29	3045.76	2934.96	3016.44	2969.34
Dec 17	2870.86	2912.51	2924.32	2940.93	2931.84	2942.48	2956.50	2970.64	+ 100.82	+ 3.51	3003.47	2862.30	2974.01	2866.19
15 UTILITIES: (divisor: 2.0859524)											(THEORETICAL)		(ACTUAL)	
Dec 23	312.72	313.14	313.14	312.99	313.53	312.84	315.05	+ 2.24	+ 0.72	316.28	311.13	315.26	312.69	
Dec 22	314.27	313.53	313.26	313.41	313.08	312.60	312.21	312.81	- 1.55	- 0.49	315.32	310.14	314.33	311.76
Dec 21	313.20	313.38	314.01	314.36	314.04	314.16	313.95	314.36	+ 1.07	+ 0.34	316.73	310.80	314.96	312.42
Dec 18	311.46	310.62	311.13	311.16	311.79	311.79	312.12	313.29	+ 1.65	+ 0.53	314.30	308.70	313.29	310.20
Dec 17	306.57	308.31	307.98	308.64	308.61	308.70	309.33	311.64	+ 5.07	+ 1.65	312.48	305.80	311.64	306.39
65 STOCKS COMPOSITE AVERAGE: (divisor: 1.2674905)											(THEORETICAL)		(ACTUAL)	
Dec 23	2824.23	2834.29	2839.42	2848.84	2850.42	2852.78	2844.10	2861.31	+ 37.37	+ 1.32	2882.81	2809.93	2864.32	2823.54
Dec 22	2813.75	2805.74	2806.28	2810.38	2810.13	2816.01	2818.27	2823.94	+ 10.11	+ 0.36	2852.34	2777.44	2828.13	2795.39
Dec 21	2792.47	2812.42	2828.35	2831.14	2827.09	2833.16	2827.54	2813.83	+ 21.23	+ 0.76	2860.57	2778.87	2837.20	2791.39
Dec 18	2777.26	2782.29	2776.44	2781.83	2785.40	2791.59	2790.04	2792.60	+ 15.34	+ 0.55	2822.06	2749.08	2798.02	2775.42
Dec 17	2732.87	2750.83	2756.68	2765.65	2759.98	2760.23	2764.91	2777.26	+ 43.81	+ 1.60	2800.96	2718.22	2777.26	2731.73

*a-Actual high or low exceeds theoretical value due to computational method. q-Actual. r-Revised.

The Dow Divisor on December 23, 1998 →

The Dow Jones Averages Hour by Hour

Following are the Dow Jones averages of INDUSTRIAL, TRANSPORTATION and UTILITY stocks with the total sales of each group for the period included in the chart.

DATE	OPEN	10 AM	11 AM	12 NOON	1 PM	2 PM	3 PM	CLOSE	CHG	%	HIGH* LOW*		HIGH⁴ LOW⁴	
30 INDUSTRIALS: (divisor: 0.24275214)											(THEORETICAL)		(ACTUAL)	
Dec 23	9044.72	9086.94	9105.22	9146.16	9156.97	9170.36	9140.24	9202.03	+ 157.57	+ 1.74	9255.84	9022.58	9211.04	9043.17
Dec 22	8989.11	8993.48	8992.97	9007.64	9013.57	9031.07	9035.71	9044.46	+ 55.61	+ 0.62	9122.99	8909.29	9069.44	8948.69
Dec 21	8902.97	8981.13	9051.41	9066.35	9048.84	9071.75	9040.60	8988.85	+ 85.22	+ 0.96	9150.54	8874.28	9079.22	8898.74
Dec 18	8877.63	8892.04	8862.43	8878.91	8891.53	8911.35	8901.31	8903.63	+ 27.81	+ 0.31	9012.28	8789.31	8928.60	8858.57
Dec 17	8787.55	8823.30	8845.96	8869.90	8849.05	8839.52	8845.44	8875.82	+ 85.22	+ 0.97	8959.76	8725.21	8879.94	8785.75

This usually occurs when the price of a "round-lot" transaction (100 shares) climbs too high. Round-lot transactions are popular with large investors because of the lower commission per share, and it's much easier to buy a round-lot at $50 than $100 a share. Most companies would rather split their stock than see it become too expensive and discourage investors' purchases.

Here's how this applies to the Dow Jones Industrial Average. Suppose you are calculating the average of a group of 30 stocks (such as the Dow) by adding the share prices of all of them and dividing by 30. If (to make the arithmetic simple and the point clear) each of the 30 were selling at $100, obviously the average would be $100 ($3,000 ÷ 30). However, if each of the 30 happened to split two for one, then each would be worth $50, per share; that is, the average price per share of these 30 stocks would suddenly be $50 not $100. Clearly, it makes no sense to reduce the average because of such splits, since someone who owns the stock has exactly as much equity (ownership value) after a split as before it.

Reducing the divisor from 30 to 15 is one solution: 30 shares at $50 each ($1,500) divided by 15 (not 30) keeps the average at 100. Future stock splits can be handled in a similar fashion with an appropriate adjustment in the divisor.

Another, though less important, reason for changing the divisor is that occasionally Dow Jones replaces one of the 30 industrial stocks with another. Here, too, it wouldn't make sense to change the average; just because one stock is substituted for another doesn't mean the market, itself, has changed. Therefore, the divisor is adjusted at the same time, to keep the average constant.

Now consider a real-life example (see page 149) using the Dow on April 12, 1999. Add the share prices for all 30 companies in the Dow. The total for April 12, 1999 is $2,328.6875, and, when you divide that by a divisor of 0.2252223, you get $10,399.51—the Dow average for April 12, 1999.

Calculating the Dow

Company	NYSE Price: April 12, 1999
Alcoa	45.0625
AlliedSignal	53.25
American Express	135.4375
AT&T	87.9375
Boeing	34.9375
Caterpillar	51.625
Chevron	95.75
Citigroup	74.00
Coca-Cola	61.875
Disney	35.4375
Du Pont	61.0625
Eastman Kodak	63.00
Exxon	75.4375
General Electric	116.375
General Motors	88.125
Goodyear	50.9375
Hewlett-Packard	68.25
IBM	183.4375
International Paper	46.5625
Johnson & Johnson	99.5625
McDonald's	45.875
Merck	85.0625
Minnesota Mining & Manufacturing	71.00
J.P. Morgan	129.625
Philip Morris	35.9375
Procter & Gamble	102.9375
Sears Roebuck	43.625
Union Carbide	49.5625
United Technologies	132.25
Wal-Mart	104.75
Total	**2,328.6875**

$$\frac{\text{Sum of Stocks Prices}}{\text{Divisor}} = \frac{2,328.6875}{0.2252223} = \text{DJIA} = 10,339.51$$

STOCK MARKET DATA BANK — 12/22/98

MAJOR INDEXES

†12-MO HIGH	†12-MO LOW		DAILY HIGH	DAILY LOW	CLOSE	NET CHG	% CHG	†12-MO CHG	% CHG	FROM 12/31	% CHG
DOW JONES AVERAGES											
9374.27	7539.07	30 Industrials	9069.44	8948.69	9044.46	+ 55.61	+ 0.62	+ 1352.69	+ 17.59	+ 1136.21	+ 14.37
3686.02	2345.00	20 Transportation	3047.06	2977.26	3036.16	+ 10.64	+ 0.35	− 88.20	− 2.82	− 220.34	− 6.77
320.51	262.66	15 Utilities	314.33	311.76	312.81	− 1.55	− 0.49	+ 44.38	+ 16.53	+ 39.74	+ 14.55
2960.79	2411.00	65 Composite	2828.13	2795.39	2823.94	+ 10.11	+ 0.36	+ 294.04	+ 11.62	+ 216.57	+ 8.31
1139.37	880.79	DJ Global-US	1145.03	1129.02	1139.37	+ 0.58	+ 0.05	+ 247.25	+ 27.71	+ 217.03	+ 23.53
NEW YORK STOCK EXCHANGE											
600.75	477.20	Composite	580.82	574.13	578.75	+ 1.05	+ 0.18	+ 83.90	+ 16.95	+ 67.56	+ 13.22
736.35	593.49	Industrials	721.00	710.83	718.83	+ 4.63	+ 0.65	+ 110.35	+ 18.14	+ 88.45	+ 14.03
440.61	322.49	Utilities	440.72	435.61	435.90	− 4.71	− 1.07	+ 106.73	+ 32.42	+ 100.71	+ 30.05
537.19	351.13	Transportation	460.69	455.10	459.70	+ 0.49	+ 0.11	+ 11.11	+ 2.48	− 6.55	− 1.40
599.15	399.19	Finance	518.82	513.49	514.79	− 3.92	− 0.76	+ 33.41	+ 6.94	+ 18.83	+ 3.80
STANDARD & POOR'S INDEXES											
1203.57	927.69	500 Index	1209.22	1192.72	1203.57	+ 0.73	+ 0.06	+ 264.44	+ 28.16	+ 233.14	+ 24.02
1442.28	1077.40	Industrials	1448.87	1427.82	1442.28	+ 3.69	+ 0.26	+ 357.92	+ 33.01	+ 320.90	+ 28.62
267.38	225.63	Utilities	261.27	258.25	259.00	− 2.27	− 0.87	+ 27.27	+ 11.77	+ 23.19	+ 9.83
380.67	275.93	400 MidCap	361.23	357.19	359.27	− 1.77	− 0.49	+ 39.15	+ 12.23	+ 25.90	+ 7.77
206.18	128.70	600 SmallCap	168.10	166.72	167.07	− 0.91	− 0.54	− 7.76	− 4.44	− 14.09	− 7.78
252.90	199.07	1500 Index	254.05	250.75	252.89	− 0.01	− 0.00	+ 51.01	+ 25.27	+ 44.09	+ 21.12
NASDAQ STOCK MARKET											
2138.03	1419.12	Composite	2144.61	2105.54	2120.98	− 17.05	− 0.80	+ 611.07	+ 40.47	+ 550.63	+ 35.06
1787.30	938.99	Nasdaq 100	1793.62	1751.68	1767.82	− 19.48	− 1.09	+ 818.25	+ 86.17	+ 777.02	+ 78.42
1408.56	882.40	Industrials	1255.34	1236.45	1242.97	− 9.06	− 0.72	+ 71.47	+ 6.10	+ 21.94	+ 1.80
1945.34	1346.58	Insurance	1743.77	1724.00	1732.07	− 2.93	− 0.17	− 26.93	− 1.53	− 65.88	− 3.66
2297.71	1486.32	Banks	1788.38	1777.83	1777.92	− 10.98	− 0.61	− 246.65	− 12.18	− 305.30	− 14.66
1128.29	584.92	Computer	1133.15	1105.15	1115.48	− 12.81	− 1.14	+ 523.86	+ 88.55	+ 496.82	+ 80.31
475.51	296.22	Telecommunications	477.97	469.31	472.87	− 2.64	− 0.56	+ 175.44	+ 58.99	+ 166.27	+ 54.23
OTHERS											
753.67	563.75	Amex Composite	657.59	652.27	655.35	+ 1.23	+ 0.19	− 5.18	− 0.78	− 29.26	− 4.27
625.38	490.26	Russell 1000	628.36	625.38		+ 0.05	± 0.01	+ 128.36	+ 25.83	+ 111.59	+ 21.72
491.41	310.28	Russell 2000	402.19	399.00	400.24	− 1.59	− 0.40	− 21.79	− 5.16	− 36.78	− 8.42
647.54	509.20	Russell 3000	647.82	639.59	644.97	− 0.14	− 0.02	+ 119.74	+ 22.80	+ 101.92	+ 18.77
508.39	346.66	Value-Line(geom.)	419.64	416.79	417.60	− 2.04	− 0.49	− 22.60	− 5.13	− 36.75	− 8.09
11106.10	8620.80	Wilshire 5000	...	...	10963.13	+ 6.84	+ 0.06	+ 1969.43	+ 21.90	+ 1664.94	+ 17.91

†-Based on comparable trading day in preceding year.

MOST ACTIVE ISSUES

NYSE	VOLUME	CLOSE	CHANGE
AmOnline	22,713,700	138	+ 21
Compaq	10,305,400	14 3/16	+ 1/16
Disney	6,716,800	29 15/16	− 1 1/16
R&B Falcn	6,681,800	7 7/8	− 3/8
Iomega	5,991,900	7 12/16	− 3/8
LucentTch	5,621,600	102 1/4	− 1 5/8
Citigroup	5,440,200	50 7/16	− 11/16
Boeing	5,419,800	31 13/16	.....
Carnival	4,925,600	42 15/16	.....
Hlthsouth	4,830,300	15 1/4	− 1/2
PhilipMor	4,805,800	53 3/8	+ 1 1/16
RJR Nab	4,707,200	30	+ 1 3/4
BostonSci	4,675,200	25 1/8	+ 2 1/4
Mattel	4,483,700	24 1/16	+ 7/8
Gillette	4,367,400	45 15/16	+ 2 15/16
NASDAQ			
CiscoSys	29,385,700	93 13/16	− 7/8
DellCptr	19,445,900	71 7/8	− 1/16
ONSALE	12,348,100	64	− 4
Intel	11,548,300	119 1/16	− 3 3/8
Microsft	10,337,500	138 7/16	− 2
3ComCp	10,321,600	48 5/8	+ 1 1/2
AppleCptr	10,275,000	38	+ 2 15/16
CrtvCmptr	9,783,800	46 59/64	+ 11 35/64
MCI Wrldcm	9,222,800	69 7/8	− 13/16
MicronElec	9,162,600	18 1/16	− 3 5/16
SunMicrsys	8,529,800	83 1/4	− 3 5/8
OracleCp	8,491,700	39 15/16	+ 7/8
Yahoo	8,143,800	245	− 2 1/2
AMEX			
SPDR	5,461,100	120 11/16	+ 17/32
RoyalOak	1,232,600	5/16	.....
FstAusPr	1,229,100	5 3/4	.....
HarkenEngy	1,114,600	1 15/16	.....
Viacom B	1,033,300	70 13/16	+ 1 5/16

DIARIES

NYSE	TUE	MON	WK AGO
Issues traded	3,568	3,574	3,578
Advances	1,289	1,745	1,611
Declines	1,755	1,366	1,488
Unchanged	524	463	479
New highs	81	134	43
New lows	90	64	105
zAdv vol (000)	304,538	447,377	483,252
zDecl vol (000)	339,312	263,451	265,340
zTotal vol (000)	678,355	742,281	774,721
Closing tick¹	−171	+90	+394
Closing Arms² (trin)	.82	.75	.59
zBlock trades	13,756	15,328	16,183
NASDAQ			
Issues traded	5,288	5,288	5,297
Advances	1,751	1,963	2,100
Declines	2,314	2,095	1,916
Unchanged	1,223	1,230	1,281
New highs	93	149	31
New lows	101	78	70
Adv vol (000)	355,908	624,708	532,144
Decl vol (000)	502,266	281,309	192,421
Total vol (000)	906,743	958,387	766,687
Block trades	10,059	11,089	9,321
AMEX			
Issues traded	753	782	752
Advances	219	266	265
Declines	343	352	292
Unchanged	191	164	195
New highs	7	11	5
New lows	32	29	30
zAdv vol (000)	12,772	17,533	19,109
zDecl vol (000)	9,801	9,376	7,431
zTotal vol (000)	27,430	30,194	30,579
Comp vol (000)	38,196	42,441	40,206
zBlock trades	n.a.	564	583

Continued

PRICE PERCENTAGE GAINERS ...

NYSE	VOL	CLOSE	CHANGE	% CHG
ParkElchm	169,300	24 3/8	+ 4 11/16	+ 23.8
NtlDiscBrkr	87,700	11 1/2	+ 2	+ 21.1
AmOnline	22,713,700	138	+ 21	+ 17.9
MusicldStr	1,500,300	11 5/16	+ 1 11/16	+ 17.5
NtlPrpnPtnr	97,900	6 3/4	+ 1	+ 17.4
ZiffDavis	1,392,900	13 1/4	+ 1 9/16	+ 13.4
UtdRentals	322,300	25 5/16	+ 2 15/16	+ 13.2
BAMerchSvc	2,837,100	19 13/16	+ 2 1/4	+ 12.8
AamesFnl	1,509,400	2 1/4	+ 1/4	+ 12.5
LASMO	26,400	5 3/4	+ 5/8	+ 12.2
Hartmarx	169,600	4 5/8	+ 1/2	+ 12.1
MolctrBio	155,500	2 3/4	+ 1/4	+ 10.0
BostonSci	4,675,200	25 1/8	+ 2 1/4	+ 9.8
MSCIndDirA	75,300	25 1/8	+ 2 1/4	+ 9.8
PoloRlphLrn	302,800	17 5/16	+ 1 9/16	+ 9.8
NineWest	292,300	13 5/16	+ 1 1/8	+ 9.2
SmedvigA	3,300	8 7/8	+ 3/4	+ 9.2
PamecoA	71,600	9 11/16	+ 3/4	+ 8.4
BirmghamStl	512,800	4 1/16	+ 5/16	+ 8.3
SunriseMed	110,800	11 7/8	+ 7/8	+ 8.0
NASDAQ NNM				
NovamStl	102,500	8	+ 3 1/2	+ 77.8
AmeriTradeA	6,167,000	34 1/8	+ 13 1/8	+ 62.5
AppldDgtl	550,500	3 1/2	+ 1 5/16	+ 60.0
uBid	6,320,700	134 1/2	+ 50 3/8	+ 59.9
Starmet	8,200	8	+ 2 7/32	+ 38.4
Ariel	297,800	3 1/8	+ 13/16	+ 34.2
CrtvCmptr	9,783,800	46 59/64	+ 11 35/64	+ 32.6
CollabRsch	78,100	4 1/8	+ 1	+ 32.0
FSIInt	625,200	9	+ 2 1/8	+ 30.9
McClainInd	7,000	5 7/8	+ 1 3/8	+ 30.6
Denali	31,100	12	+ 2 5/8	+ 28.0
Zitel	4,364,600	4 5/8	+ 15/16	+ 25.4
Cognos	1,553,900	21 7/8	+ 4 1/4	+ 24.1
OnyxPharm	261,500	6 5/8	+ 1 1/4	+ 23.3
AMEX				
EXXIncA	3,200	2 7/16	+ 5/16	+ 14.7
ecDallasGld	12,000	2 15/16	+ 3/8	+ 14.6
BakerMichl	29,900	9 7/8	+ 1 1/4	+ 14.5
HsptyWldwd	217,300	5 1/16	+ 5/8	+ 14.1
FarmstdTel	59,600	2 5/8	+ 5/16	+ 13.5

AND LOSERS

NYSE	VOL	CLOSE	CHANGE	% CHG
OcwenAsset	449,800	4 5/16	− 1 7/16	− 25.6
IngramMicroA	441,000	37	− 9 1/4	− 20.0
PenncorpFncl.pf	16,300	7 1/2	− 1 5/8	− 17.8
SmartFinal	131,800	8 5/16	− 1 5/16	− 13.6
Chaus	269,500	2 5/8	− 3/8	− 12.5
CyprsSemi	2,707,700	8 45/16	− 1 1/8	− 11.5
Cambrex	108,200	24 13/16	− 3 1/16	− 11.0
CrssTimOil	299,900	5 13/16	− 11/16	− 10.6
CaribnrInt	104,400	8 1/16	− 15/16	− 10.4
SilvrifResrt	69,100	8 1/8	− 15/16	− 10.3
Transmedia	50,600	2 5/16	− 1/4	− 9.8
GraceWR	444,600	14 5/8	− 1 9/16	− 9.7
HuntcoA	35,400	3 5/8	− 3/8	− 9.4
MylanLabs	3,635,000	24 1/4	− 2 1/2	− 9.3
SportsAuth	388,700	4 3/8	− 7/16	− 9.1
Covance	154,600	25 1/2	− 2 1/2	− 8.9
Hercules	2,539,600	26 3/16	− 2 7/16	− 8.5
CabltrnSys	3,103,900	8 3/16	− 3/4	− 8.4
NSGp	161,000	4 1/4	− 3/8	− 8.1
GenCigar	110,200	8 1/2	− 3/4	− 8.1
NASDAQ NNM				
ACSYS	1,340,300	2 31/32	− 2 31/32	− 50.0
MonarchDen	4,255,600	4 13/32	− 4 7/32	− 48.9
AtlDataSvc	1,409,600	7 1/2	− 5 1/2	− 42.3
SilicnVlyBksh	1,156,600	17 3/4	− 6 3/4	− 27.6
CircuitSys	25,200	3 1/16	− 1 5/32	− 27.4
NrthldCrnbr	3,257,900	8 3/32	− 3 3/32	− 27.2
Softech	235,100	2 7/16	− 13/16	− 25.0
DayRunner	661,700	13 3/4	− 4 1/4	− 23.6
InnovsvDvcs	96,300	3	− 3/4	− 20.0
MonroMufflr	756,400	6 1/4	− 1 1/2	− 19.4
LJLBioSys	13,500	2 1/8	− 1/2	− 19.0
ExprtSftwr	44,100	2 1/8	− 7/16	− 17.1
CohesionTch	91,700	3 1/8	− 5/8	− 16.7
Intevac	105,700	5 7/8	− 1 1/8	− 16.1
AMEX				
ExcelMr	25,100	2 1/8	− 13/16	− 28.3
Emultek	42,500	3	− 3/4	− 20.0
JinpanInt	35,500	2 5/8	− 1/2	− 16.0
AppleOrth	105,300	3 7/8	− 11/16	− 15.1
HallwdEngy	23,100	3	− 3/8	− 11.1

VOLUME PERCENTAGE LEADERS

NYSE	VOL	%DIF*	CLOSE	CHANGE
BAMerchSvc	2,837,100	2951.5	19 13/16	+ 2 1/4
NtlDiscBrkr	87,700	1473.9	11 1/2	+ 2
JTIlnkgStr	259,900	1313.5	13 1/4	+ 1/4
TETRA	557,800	1340.5	8 5/16	− 11/16
Sothebys	2,290,100	1323.2	29 3/4	+ 1 3/4
Blkrk1999	322,900	1212.5	9 3/4	.....
ProLogis	1,979,500	1046.4	20 5/8	+ 1/16
Marinemax	119,600	1034.4	8 1/8	+ 5/16
LaidlawOne	76,600	851.4	29 7/16	− 5/8
TelPeruADR	3,229,700	760.9	13	+ 1/4
RogerCommB	409,000	711.0	8 3/8	+ 3/16
Aydin	97,500	693.3	9 15/16	− 1/4
BcoBHIFADR	50,000	666.6	8 5/8	.....
Hercules	2,539,600	645.6	26 3/16	− 2 7/16
BacouUSA	41,500	625.1	21 3/16	+ 3/8
NtlProc	106,700	532.3	5 5/8	.....
DiscntAuto	106,000	525.5	19 1/2	− 1 5/8
SalomonSBF	368,800	474.1	17 13/16	.....
JoAnnStrsA	53,900	473.5	15 7/8	+ 1/8
NewSoAfrFd	69,900	470.8	9 1/8	+ 1/4

NASDAQ NNM	VOL	%DIF*	CLOSE	CHANGE
MonarchDen	4,255,600	6037.3	4 13/32	− 4 7/32
ACSYS	1,340,300	3423.1	2 31/32	− 2 31/32
NrthldCrnbr	3,257,900	2583.0	8 3/32	− 3 3/32
AmeriTradeA	6,167,000	2414.9	34 1/8	+ 13 1/8
AtlDataSvc	1,409,600	2324.6	7 1/2	− 5 1/2
DayRunner	661,700	1596.5	13 3/4	− 4 1/4
YoungInnov	370,700	1569.1	12 7/16	− 1/2
SPSSInc	553,600	1544.7	18 7/8	.....
PkskillFnl	81,000	1301.4	16	+ 1/8
DorchHugtn	74,800	1153.8	10 1/16	− 7/16
ISGIntSftwr	593,400	1141.8	13 1/4	+ 2
Circon	2,256,700	1075.0	14 11/16	.....
BiositeDiag	735,100	1073.2	8	+ 1
ArnoldInd	667,300	976.9	13 3/4	+ 1/8
EncoreWire	1,934,400	935.8	7 5/8	− 7/16
LifeTech	1,406,400	916.8	39 1/4	+ 1/4
AMEX				
MaximPharm	109,500	768.6	14 7/8	+ 1/4
ThermEcotek	59,700	581.5	10 3/4	+ 3/16
AmSciEngrg	43,100	491.5	10 7/16	− 1/8
WEBSCan	68,200	469.4	x11 1/2	− 1/4
Westower	154,500	450.8	32 3/8	+ 2 7/8

*Common stocks of $5 a share or more with average volume over 65 trading days of at least 5,000 shares.
a-has traded fewer than 65 days.   b-10,000% or greater

BREAKDOWN OF TRADING IN NYSE STOCKS (9:30 a.m. to 4 p.m. EST)

BY MARKET	Tues	Mon	WK AGO
New York	678,355,140	742,281,150	774,721,370
Chicago	38,579,400	39,542,870	37,614,600
CBOE	500	24,600	2,400
Pacific	16,817,600	20,627,000	15,451,300
NASD	71,724,015	78,154,928	76,666,339
Phila	6,004,800	6,722,700	5,260,600
Boston	16,475,800	18,406,600	14,091,800
Cincinnati	7,269,900	9,732,300	7,210,200
Composite	835,227,155	915,492,148	931,018,609

1/2-HOURLY	Tues	Mon	WK AGO
9:30-10	79,580,000	85,730,000	97,520,000
10-10:30	73,300,000	84,950,000	70,730,000
10:30-11	57,560,000	62,350,000	68,200,000
11-11:30	50,520,000	53,650,000	61,570,000
11:30-12	43,630,000	46,400,000	45,030,000
12-12:30	37,590,000	42,530,000	44,180,000
12:30-1	36,070,000	35,810,000	38,470,000
1-1:30	33,640,000	36,480,000	39,500,000
1:30-2	39,920,000	39,610,000	42,060,000
2-2:30	48,650,000	41,610,000	43,950,000
2:30-3	45,310,000	44,240,000	56,930,000
3-3:30	52,690,000	54,010,000	62,760,000
3:30-4	79,895,140	114,911,150	103,821,370

NYSE first crossing 1,345,500 shares, value n.a.
Second (basket) 633,689 shares, value $14,780,574
*The net difference of the number of stocks closing higher than their previous trade from those closing lower, NYSE trading only.
*A comparison of the number of advancing and declining issues with the volume of shares rising and falling. Generally, an Arms of less than 1.00 indicates buying demand, above 1.00 indicates selling pressure.
z-NYSE or Amex only.

The figures used on page 149 to compute the Dow are the closing prices for the New York Stock Exchange (NYSE). NYSE *Composite Transactions* prices (to be discussed below) vary slightly from the prices used here. Why the discrepancy? Because the composite includes the closing prices of NYSE stocks listed on other exchanges such as the Pacific Stock Exchange, which continues its operations for half an hour after the New York Exchange closes.

So much for the Dow; you are now ready to move on to a more detailed analysis of the other stock market indicators and stock market performance.

STOCK MARKET DATA BANK

The Stock Market Data Bank appears daily on the second page of the third section (C2). See pages 150, 151, 153, 154, and 155 for an example from the Wednesday, December 23, 1998 *Wall Street Journal*. It presents a comprehensive summary of stock market activity in seven sections: **Major Indexes**, **Most Active Issues**, **Diaries**, **Price Percentage Gainers and Losers**, **Volume Percentage Leaders**, and **Breakdown of Trading in NYSE Stocks**. Look at it after you have examined the **Markets Diary** in order to get a more detailed view of the previous day's trading activity.

Major Indexes on page 153 lists the Dow averages as well as a variety of other domestic indexes in greater detail than provided in the **Markets Diary** on the first page of the third section (C1). These statistics permit you to compare the performance of your own investments with the broadest gauges of stock market activity.

The **U.S. Component of the Dow Jones Global Index** is a very broad-based index (June 30, 1982 = 100) of about 700 stocks (see page 153). A more detailed discussion appears on page 204.

The **New York Stock Exchange Composite** tracks the movements of all stocks listed on that exchange. Notice that this composite, like most others, is broken out into a number of components.

Since this index includes all stocks listed (about 3,000), rather than a sample like the Dow, you may wonder why it isn't preferred to the Dow. Because most investors aren't interested in all the stocks listed, just the most important ones. For that reason, the next measure of the market strikes a compromise.

The Standard and Poor's 500 includes some stocks not listed on the New York Exchange, and it is a composite. Since it weights (measures the importance of) its constituent companies by their market value (share price multiplied by the number of share outstanding), unlike the Dow which weights by price alone, and since it includes far more companies than the Dow, most observers prefer this index to the Dow.

STOCK MARKET DATA BANK   12/22/98

MAJOR INDEXES

— †12-MO — HIGH	LOW		DAILY HIGH	LOW	CLOSE	NET CHG	% CHG	†12-MO CHG	% CHG	FROM 12/31	% CHG
DOW JONES AVERAGES											
9374.27	7539.07	30 Industrials	9069.44	8948.69	9044.46 +	55.61 +	0.62	+ 1352.69 +	17.59	+ 1136.21 +	14.37
3686.02	2345.00	20 Transportation	3047.06	2977.26	3036.16 +	10.64 +	0.35	− 88.20 −	2.82	− 220.34 −	6.77
320.51	262.66	15 Utilities	314.33	311.76	312.81 −	1.55 −	0.49	+ 44.38 +	16.53	+ 39.74 +	14.55
2960.79	2411.00	65 Composite	2828.13	2795.39	2823.94 +	10.11 +	0.36	+ 294.04 +	11.62	+ 216.57 +	8.31
1139.37	880.79	DJ Global-US	1145.03	1129.02	1139.37 +	0.58 +	0.05	+ 247.25 +	27.71	+ 217.03 +	23.53
NEW YORK STOCK EXCHANGE											
600.75	477.20	Composite	580.82	574.13	578.75 +	1.05 +	0.18	+ 83.90 +	16.95	+ 67.56 +	13.22
736.35	593.49	Industrials	721.00	710.83	718.83 +	4.63 +	0.65	+ 110.35 +	18.14	+ 88.45 +	14.03
440.61	322.49	Utilities	440.72	435.61	435.90 −	4.71 −	1.07	+ 106.73 +	32.42	+ 100.71 +	30.05
537.19	351.13	Transportation	460.69	455.10	459.70 +	0.49 +	0.11	+ 11.11 +	2.48	− 6.55 −	1.40
599.15	399.19	Finance	518.82	513.49	514.79 −	3.92 −	0.76	+ 33.41 +	6.94	+ 18.83 +	3.80
STANDARD & POOR'S INDEXES											
1203.57	927.69	500 Index	1209.22	1192.72	1203.57 +	0.73 +	0.06	+ 264.44 +	28.16	+ 233.14 +	24.02
1442.28	1077.40	Industrials	1448.87	1427.82	1442.28 +	3.69 +	0.26	+ 357.92 +	33.01	+ 320.90 +	28.62
267.38	225.63	Utilities	261.27	258.25	259.00 −	2.27 −	0.87	+ 27.27 +	11.77	+ 23.19 +	9.83
380.67	275.93	400 MidCap	361.23	357.19	359.27 −	1.77 −	0.49	+ 39.15 +	12.23	+ 25.90 +	7.77
206.18	128.70	600 SmallCap	168.10	166.72	167.07 −	0.91 −	0.54	− 7.76 −	4.44	− 14.09 −	7.78
252.90	199.07	1500 Index	254.05	250.75	252.89 −	0.01 −	0.00	+ 51.01 +	25.27	+ 44.09 +	21.12
NASDAQ STOCK MARKET											
2138.03	1419.12	Composite	2144.61	2105.54	2120.98 −	17.05 −	0.80	+ 611.07 +	40.47	+ 550.63 +	35.06
1787.30	938.99	Nasdaq 100	1793.62	1751.68	1767.82 −	19.48 −	1.09	+ 818.25 +	86.17	+ 777.02 +	78.42
1408.56	882.40	Industrials	1255.34	1236.45	1242.97 −	9.06 −	0.72	+ 71.47 +	6.10	+ 21.94 +	1.80
1945.34	1346.58	Insurance	1743.77	1724.00	1732.07 −	2.93 −	0.17	− 26.93 −	1.53	− 65.88 −	3.66
2297.71	1486.32	Banks	1788.38	1777.83	1777.92 −	10.98 −	0.61	− 246.65 −	12.18	− 305.30 −	14.66
1128.29	584.92	Computer	1133.15	1105.15	1115.48 −	12.81 −	1.14	+ 523.86 +	88.55	+ 496.82 +	80.31
475.51	296.22	Telecommunications	477.97	469.31	472.87 −	2.64 −	0.56	+ 175.44 +	58.99	+ 166.27 +	54.23
OTHERS											
753.67	563.75	Amex Composite	657.59	652.27	655.35 +	1.23 +	0.19	− 5.18 −	0.78	− 29.26 −	4.27
625.38	490.26	Russell 1000	628.36	619.88	625.38 +	0.05 ‡	0.01	+ 128.36 +	25.83	+ 111.59 +	21.72
491.41	310.28	Russell 2000	402.19	399.00	400.24 −	1.59 −	0.40	− 21.79 −	5.16	− 36.78 −	8.42
647.54	509.20	Russell 3000	647.82	639.59	644.97 −	0.14 −	0.02	+ 119.74 +	22.80	+ 101.92 +	18.77
508.39	346.66	Value-Line(geom.)	419.64	416.79	417.60 −	2.04 −	0.49	− 22.60 −	5.13	− 36.75 −	8.09
11106.10	8620.80	Wilshire 5000	...	...	10963.13 +	6.84 +	0.06	+ 1969.43 +	21.90	+ 1664.94 +	17.91

†-Based on comparable trading day in preceding year.

Source: *The Wall Street Journal*, December 23, 1998. Reprinted by permission of *The Wall Street Journal*, ©1998 Dow Jones & Company, Inc. All rights reserved.

NASDAQ (National Association of Securities Dealers Automated Quotations) stocks are traded over-the-counter (electronically), not on an organized exchange, and typically represent high-tech issues as well as ownership of smaller and less widely-held companies.

The **AMEX** index measures all the stocks (about 1,000) traded on the American Stock Exchange. Most of these companies were traditionally between the New York and over-the-counter companies in size, but this distinction has

MOST ACTIVE ISSUES

NYSE	VOLUME	CLOSE	CHANGE	
AmOnline	22,713,700	138	+	21
Compaq	10,305,400	14 ⁹/₁₆	+	¹/₁₆
Disney	6,716,800	29 ¹⁵/₁₆	–	1 ¹/₁₆
R&B Falcn	6,684,800	7 ¹/₈	–	³/₈
Iomega	5,991,600	7 ¹²/₁₆	–	³/₈
LucentTch	5,621,600	102 ¹/₄	–	1 ⁵/₈
Citigroup	5,440,200	50 ⁷/₁₆	–	¹¹/₁₆
Boeing	5,419,800	31 ¹³/₁₆	.....	
Carnival	4,925,600	42 ¹⁵/₁₆	.....	
Hlthsouth	4,830,300	15 ¹/₄	–	¹/₂
PhilipMor	4,805,800	53 ³/₈	+	1 ¹/₁₆
RJR Nab	4,707,200	30	+	1 ³/₄
BostonSci	4,675,200	25 ¹/₈	+	2 ¹/₄
Mattel	4,483,700	24 ¹/₁₆	+	⁷/₈
Gillette	4,367,400	45 ¹⁵/₁₆	+	2 ¹⁵/₁₆
NASDAQ				
CiscoSys	29,385,700	93 ¹³/₁₆	–	⁷/₈
DellCptr	19,445,900	71 ⁷/₈	–	¹/₁₆
ONSALE	12,348,100	64	–	4
Intel	11,548,300	119 ¹/₁₆	–	3 ⁵/₈
Microsft	10,337,500	138 ⁷/₁₆	–	2
3ComCp	10,321,600	48 ⁵/₈	+	1 ¹/₂
AppleCptr	10,275,000	38	+	2 ¹⁵/₁₆
CrtvCmptr	9,783,800	46 ⁵⁹/₆₄	+	11 ³⁵/₆₄
MCI Wrldcm	9,222,800	69 ⁷/₈	–	¹³/₁₆
MicronElec	9,162,600	18 ¹/₁₆	–	3 ⁵/₁₆
SunMicrsys	8,529,800	83 ¹/₄	–	3 ⁵/₈
OracleCp	8,491,700	39 ¹⁵/₁₆	+	⁷/₈
Yahoo	8,143,800	245	–	2 ¹/₂
AMEX				
SPDR	5,461,100	120 ¹¹/₁₆	+	¹⁷/₃₂
RoyalOak	1,232,600	⁵/₁₆	.....	
FstAusPr	1,229,100	5 ³/₄	.....	
HarkenEngy	1,114,600	1 ¹⁵/₁₆	.....	
Viacom B	1,033,300	70 ¹³/₁₆	+	1 ⁵/₁₆

22.7 million shares of America Online traded on a single day

evaporated with the rapid growth of many of the over-the-counter companies. This exchange was once known as the Curb Exchange, because its business was conducted in the street and it had no premises.

The **Russell 1000, Russell 2000,** and **Russell 3000** track stocks issued by small companies.

The **Value-Line** composite is prepared by the investment service of the same name. It contains about 1,700 stocks traded on the two major exchanges as well as over-the-counter.

DIARIES

NYSE		TUE	MON	WK AGO
Issues traded		3,568	3,574	3,578
Advances		1,289	1,745	1,611
Declines		1,755	1,366	1,488
Unchanged		524	463	479
New highs		81	134	43
New lows		90	64	105
zAdv vol	(000)	304,538	447,377	483,252
zDecl vol	(000)	339,312	263,451	265,340
zTotal vol	(000)	678,355	742,281	774,721
Closing tick[1]		−171	+90	+394
Closing Arms[2] (trin)		.82	.75	.59
zBlock trades		13,756	15,328	16,183
NASDAQ				
Issues traded		5,288	5,288	5,297
Advances		1,751	1,963	2,100
Declines		2,314	2,095	1,916
Unchanged		1,223	1,230	1,281
New highs		93	149	31
New lows		101	78	70
Adv vol	(000)	355,908	624,708	532,144
Decl vol	(000)	502,266	281,309	192,421
Total vol	(000)	906,743	958,377	766,687
Block trades		10,059	11,089	9,321
AMEX				
Issues traded		753	782	752
Advances		219	266	265
Declines		343	352	292
Unchanged		191	164	195
New highs		7	11	5
New lows		32	29	30
zAdv vol	(000)	12,772	17,533	19,109
zDecl vol	(000)	9,801	9,376	7,431
zTotal vol	(000)	27,430	30,194	30,579
Comp vol	(000)	38,196	42,441	40,206
zBlock trades		n.a.	564	583

Labels at left: New Highs→ (New highs); New→Lows (New lows)

Annotations at right:
◄— Declining issues exceeded advancing issues
Decline volume exceeded advance volume
◄— Negative (–) tick indicates more stocks declined than advanced in last trade
◄— Arms index of less than one indicates buying pressure

The **Wilshire 5000** measures all the 5,000 or so stocks that are actively traded on the two major exchanges as well as over-the-counter. This excludes several thousand stocks that are not actively traded.

Now, take a look at **Most Active Issues** on page 154, which lists the day's most heavily traded stocks on the three major markets: the New York Stock Exchange (NYSE), the National Association of Security Dealers Automated Quotation (NASDAQ) system in the over-the-counter (OTC) market, and the

American Stock Exchange (AMEX). For instance, below NYSE you can see that over 22 million shares of America Online changed hands on Tuesday, December 22, 1998 under strong buying pressure for a gain of $21.00 a share.

The Diaries provide other important measures of the day's trading activity: *advances versus declines, new highs versus new lows*, and the *volume of the stocks advancing and declining*. On Tuesday, December 22, 1998, 1,289 issues advanced and 1,755 declined on the New York Exchange (see page 155). Note that although the Dow gained 55 points that day, more NYSE stocks declined than advanced. Moreover, the decliners were more actively traded: 339,312 to 304,538. These figures confirm the overall weakness among NYSE stocks that day despite the Dow's rise.

Closing tick and *Closing Arms (trin)* are even finer measures of stock market strength or weakness.

A *tick* is a measure of movement in closing stock prices; a positive (+) tick means prices were rising at the end of the day, and a negative (–) tick indicates falling prices. The closing tick nets all stocks whose last trade was higher than the previous trade (+) on the NYSE against all stocks whose last trade was lower (–); a "+" closing tick means that more stocks were rising than falling, and a "–" closing tick means that more stocks were falling than rising. On December 22, 1998, 171 more stocks were falling than rising at their last trade, and so the closing tick for the day was –171.

The *Arms index (trin)*, named for Richard W. Arms, Jr., its creator, measures market strength. A trin of less than one indicates money flowing into stocks (bullish sign), as the trin of 0.82 on December 22, 1998 shows. While a trin greater than one indicates money flowing out of stocks (bearish sign). The Arms index is computed by dividing two ratios:

$$\frac{\dfrac{\text{Advances}}{\text{Declines}}}{\dfrac{\text{Advance volume}}{\text{Decline volume}}} = \frac{\dfrac{1,289}{1,755}}{\dfrac{304,538}{339,312}} = \frac{0.73447}{0.89752} = 0.81833 = 0.82 = \text{Arms index}$$

In this example, a trin of less than one indicates that the (denominator) ratio of the volume of advancing stocks to declining stocks ($^{304,538}/_{339,312}$) was greater than the (numerator) ratio of advancing stocks to declining stocks ($^{1,289}/_{1,755}$), *and therefore, a disproportionate share of the trading volume was in advancing stocks (a bullish sign)*. A trin of more than one would indicate the opposite.

This example drawn from the December 23, 1998 *Journal*, is complex because it employs the actual trading data for December 22, 1998. Consider, instead, the following simple hypothetical examples. The first illustrates a bull (rising) market, the second a bear (falling) market.

Use hypothetical numbers of your own to create additional examples. This will establish your understanding of the Arms index.

Bull Market

$$\frac{\dfrac{\text{Advances}}{\text{Declines}}}{\dfrac{\text{Advance volume}}{\text{Decline volume}}} = \frac{\dfrac{1}{1}}{\dfrac{2}{1}} = \frac{1}{2}$$

Although advances and declines were equal, advance volume was twice decline volume, and, therefore, a trin of ½ is a bullish sign.

$$\frac{\dfrac{\text{Advances}}{\text{Declines}}}{\dfrac{\text{Advance volume}}{\text{Decline volume}}} = \frac{\dfrac{1}{2}}{\dfrac{1}{1}} = \frac{1}{2}$$

Although declines exceeded advances, advance volume equaled decline volume, and a trin of ½ remained a bullish sign.

Bear Market

$$\frac{\dfrac{\text{Advances}}{\text{Declines}}}{\dfrac{\text{Advance volume}}{\text{Decline volume}}} = \frac{\dfrac{1}{1}}{\dfrac{1}{2}} = 2$$

Although advances and declines were equal, decline volume was twice advance volume, and, therefore, a trin of 2 is a bearish sign.

$$\frac{\dfrac{\text{Advances}}{\text{Declines}}}{\dfrac{\text{Advance volume}}{\text{Decline volume}}} = \frac{\dfrac{2}{1}}{\dfrac{1}{1}} = 2$$

Although advances exceeded declines, decline volume equaled advance volume, and a trin of 2 remained a bearish sign.

As an investor, you want to know the percentage performance of your stocks. A $1 rise in the price of a stock that you purchased at $100 a share is an event to note, but if you had paid $2 a share for the stock, the same $1 rise is a cause for celebration. In the first case, your investment increased by 1 percent, in the second, by 50 percent.

In **Price Percentage Gainers and Losers** (page 158) you can track this daily. On December 22, 1998 America Online gained 17.9 percent in value.

PRICE PERCENTAGE GAINERS ...

NYSE	VOL	CLOSE	CHANGE		% CHG
ParkElchm	169,300	$24^{3}/_{8}$ +	$4^{11}/_{16}$	+	23.8
NtlDiscBrkr	87,700	$11^{1}/_{2}$ +	2	+	21.1
AmOnline	22,713,700	138 +	21	+	17.9
MusicldStr	1,500,300	$11^{5}/_{16}$ +	$1^{11}/_{16}$	+	17.5
NtlPrpnPtnr	97,900	$6^{3}/_{4}$ +	1	+	17.4
ZiffDavis	1,392,900	$13^{1}/_{4}$ +	$1^{9}/_{16}$	+	13.4
UtdRentals	322,300	$25^{3}/_{16}$ +	$2^{15}/_{16}$	+	13.2
BAMerchSvc	2,837,100	$19^{13}/_{16}$ +	$2^{1}/_{4}$	+	12.8
AamesFnl	1,509,400	$2^{1}/_{4}$ +	$^{1}/_{4}$	+	12.5
LASMO	26,400	$5^{3}/_{4}$ +	$^{5}/_{8}$	+	12.2
Hartmarx	169,600	$4^{5}/_{8}$ +	$^{1}/_{2}$	+	12.1
MolclrBio	155,500	$2^{3}/_{4}$ +	$^{1}/_{4}$	+	10.0
BostonSci	4,675,200	$25^{1}/_{8}$ +	$2^{1}/_{4}$	+	9.8
MSCIndDirA	75,300	$25^{1}/_{8}$ +	$2^{1}/_{4}$	+	9.8
PoloRlphLrn	302,800	$17^{9}/_{16}$ +	$1^{9}/_{16}$	+	9.8
NineWest	292,300	$13^{5}/_{16}$ +	$1^{1}/_{8}$	+	9.2
SmedvigA	3,300	$8^{7}/_{8}$ +	$^{3}/_{4}$	+	9.2
PamecoA	71,600	$9^{11}/_{16}$ +	$^{3}/_{4}$	+	8.4
BirmghamStl	512,800	$4^{1}/_{16}$ +	$^{5}/_{16}$	+	8.3
SunriseMed	110,800	$11^{7}/_{8}$ +	$^{7}/_{8}$	+	8.0
NASDAQ NNM					
NovamStl	102,500	8 +	$3^{1}/_{2}$	+	77.8
AmeriTradeA	6,167,000	$34^{1}/_{8}$ +	$13^{1}/_{8}$	+	62.5
AppldDgtl	550,500	$3^{1}/_{2}$ +	$1^{5}/_{16}$	+	60.0
uBid	6,320,700	$134^{1}/_{2}$ +	$50^{3}/_{8}$	+	59.9
Starmet	8,200	8 +	$2^{7}/_{32}$	+	38.4
Ariel	297,800	$3^{3}/_{16}$ +	$^{13}/_{16}$	+	34.2
CrtvCmptr	9,783,800	$46^{59}/_{64}$ +	$11^{35}/_{64}$	+	32.6
CollabRsch	78,100	$4^{1}/_{8}$ +	1	+	32.0
FSIInt	625,200	9 +	$2^{1}/_{8}$	+	30.9
McClainInd	7,000	$5^{7}/_{8}$ +	$1^{3}/_{8}$	+	30.6
Denali	31,100	12 +	$2^{5}/_{8}$	+	28.0
Zitel	4,364,600	$4^{5}/_{8}$ +	$^{15}/_{16}$	+	25.4
Cognos	1,553,900	$21^{7}/_{8}$ +	$4^{1}/_{4}$	+	24.1
OnyxPharm	261,500	$6^{5}/_{8}$ +	$1^{1}/_{4}$	+	23.3
AMEX					
EXXIncA	3,200	$2^{7}/_{16}$ +	$^{5}/_{16}$	+	14.7
ecDallasGld	12,000	$2^{15}/_{16}$ +	$^{3}/_{8}$	+	14.6
BakerMichl	29,900	$9^{7}/_{8}$ +	$1^{1}/_{4}$	+	14.5
HsptyWldwd	217,300	$5^{1}/_{16}$ +	$^{5}/_{8}$	+	14.1
FarmstdTel	59,600	$2^{5}/_{8}$ +	$^{5}/_{16}$	+	13.5

America Online gained 17.9% in one day

BREAKDOWN OF TRADING IN **NYSE** STOCKS (9:30 a.m. to 4 p.m. EST)								
BY MARKET	Tues	Mon	WK AGO	½-HOURLY	Tues	Mon	WK AGO
New York	678,355,140	742,281,150	774,721,370	9:30-10	79,580,000	85,730,000	97,520,000
Chicago	38,579,400	39,542,870	37,614,600	10-10:30	73,300,000	84,950,000	70,730,000
CBOE	500	24,600	2,400	10:30-11	57,560,000	62,350,000	68,200,000
Pacific	16,817,600	20,627,000	15,451,300	11-11:30	50,520,000	53,650,000	61,570,000
NASD	71,724,015	78,154,928	76,666,339	11:30-12	43,630,000	46,400,000	45,030,000
Phila	6,004,800	6,722,700	5,260,600	12-12:30	37,590,000	42,530,000	44,180,000
Boston	16,475,800	18,406,600	14,091,800	12:30-1	36,070,000	35,810,000	38,470,000
Cincinnati	7,269,900	9,732,300	7,210,200	1-1:30	33,640,000	36,480,000	39,500,000
Composite	835,227,155	915,492,148	931,018,609	1:30-2	39,920,000	39,610,000	42,060,000
				2-2:30	48,650,000	41,610,000	43,950,000
				2:30-3	45,310,000	44,240,000	56,930,000
				3-3:30	52,690,000	54,010,000	62,760,000
				3:30-4	79,895,140	114,911,150	103,821,370

NYSE Volume → (New York)

Composite Volume → (Composite)

NYSE first crossing 1,345,500 shares, value n.a.
Second (basket) 633,689 shares, value $14,780,574
¹The net difference of the number of stocks closing higher than their previous trade from those closing lower; NYSE trading only.
²A comparison of the number of advancing and declining issues with the volume of shares rising and falling. Generally, an Arms of less than 1.00 indicates buying demand, above 1.00 indicates selling pressure.
z-NYSE or Amex only.

Note that America Online's huge dollar gain was not the largest in percentage terms as two other companies traded at lower prices.

Volume Percentage Leaders on page 151 represent the stocks with the largest average gain in trading volume for the previous 65 trading days.

The **Breakdown of Trading in NYSE Stocks** above provides trading volume on all stock exchanges of securities listed on the New York Stock Exchange, as well as trading volume by half-hours. As mentioned earlier in the discussion on how to compile the Dow, shares listed on the NYSE trade on a variety of exchanges as well as electronically, and, therefore, the composite of all trades will be greater than the New York volume. Trading of all NYSE stocks on all exchanges was a composite volume of 835,227,155 shares on Tuesday, December 22, 1998. Note that New York trading of these shares was less than 680 million, and that 150 million shares of NYSE-listed stocks traded on other exchanges that day.

Finally, the **Diaries** component of the **Stock Market Data Bank** on page 155 listed the number of stocks that hit new highs and lows (i.e., the number that closed higher or lower than at any time in the past 52 weeks). You saw that on Tuesday, December 22, 1998, 81 stocks reached new highs and 90 reached new lows. **NYSE Highs/Lows** (in the front-page indexes of the first and last sections) lists these stocks. Consider the example on page 160 from the Wednesday, December 23, 1998 *Journal*.

THE ODD-LOT TRADER

So far this discussion has proceeded without regard to the magnitude of individual investments, except for the observation that companies split their

NYSE HIGHS/LOWS

Tuesday, December 22, 1998

NEW 52-WK. HIGHS — 81

AMP	Firstar	MLySTRYPES6	Sothebys
Abercrombie A	FredMeyer	MrLySP500 MI	SpainFd s
Albertsons	FrmntGnTOPrS	MerLyn pfB	Sprint DECS
AlliantTech	Genentech	MSDWS&PBRn	Swscom ADS n
Alltel	GlaxoWell	MotvePwrInd	SymbolTch s
AmOnline s	Gc1Auto	NtlDataCp	TeleDanmark
AmStores	GlfPwrCpQUIP	NtlWsumin pfA	Teleglobe s
Aquarion	GfPrCpQUIPSB	NewEngBusn	TimeWarn s
BJs WhslClb	HarleyDav	Nokia s	TimesMir PEPS
BellHowell	HiltonHtl wi n	NC Gas s	TotlSysSvc s
BenchmkElec	HomeDepot s	PediatrixMed	Tycolnt
CadburySch	Houstnlnd ACE	PhlSuburbn s	URS Cp
Carnival s	IBP Inc	PSEG pfU	Unisys
ChoicePoint	InfntyBrd A n	PSEG pfT	Unisys pf
ComrcBcpNJ s	IBM	Rayovac	VnKmFL
DillrdCapTr n	JabilCircuit	RubyTues s	Vodafon ADR
EquitResTr n	JacobEngrg	Safeway s	Walgreen
EsteLudr TRAC	Lowes Cos s	SalomonSBF s	WeingtnRly pfn
FDX Cp	MartnMarMat	SchwabC s	WileyJn A
FedlSgnl	Maytag	Solectron	WileyJn B.
FstBrands			

NEW 52-WK. LOWS — 90

AlldPdts	ElderTr n	MarineDrill	R&B Falcn n
Asarco	EntOil	MirageResrt	RLI Cp s
AtlCap pfC n	EqtOfcPropfCn	Morgan JP pfH	RmcoGrshn
AvatexCp pfA	Flowserve	NtlStand	RenaisHldgs
BentonOG	Forcenergy	NYMAGIC	SeagullEngy
BeverlyEnt	Fracmaster n	OcciPete	TCC Ind
BlountInt A	FrptMcCG A	OcciPete pf	TerraNitrgn
BlountInt B	FrptMcCG pfD	OceanEngy n	TETRA
Bunzl ADS n	FrontrOil	Osmonic	TitanInt
BurlgtnCoat	FruitLoom	Paracelsus	TorchEngyTr
CamdnProp p	GaleyLord	ParkPlEnt wi n	Tremont
ChaseMan pfC	GenesisHlth	ParkerDrl	TritonEn A
Conoco A n	GttyPeteMkt	PatinaOil pf	Tuboscope
Copene n	GulfIndoRes	PatAmHspPrd	UALCCpTOPrS
CrescentRE	HRPT Prop	PenncpFnl pf	UnPacRes
CrssTimOil s	HlthCrProp	PnzlQuak wi n	UtdDomnRlty
CrssTimOil pfA	HmstdVlg	PittsMinl	US Restr pfA
CyprusAmax	HowellCp	PlnsAmPipe n	UnocalCp
DECS Tr	KCS Engy	PopeTalbot	Wellman
Dimon	KN Engy wi n	PfdIncoMgt	WstnRes
DominRes Tr	KeyEngy	PrmrFarnl pf	WilshireOil s
Ducommun s	MBNA Cp pfB	QuakerState	WiserOil
EastmanChm	MagellnHlth		

s-Split or stock dividend of 25 percent or more in the past 52 weeks. High-low range is adjusted from old stock. n-New issue in past 52 weeks and does not cover the entire 52 week period.

ODD-LOT TRADING

NEW YORK-The New York Stock Exchange specialists reported the following odd-lot transactions (in shares):

	Customer Purchases	Short Sales	Other Sales	Total Sales
December 21, 1998	3,936,012	145,154	3,611,075	3,756,229

Odd-lot purchases exceeded sales on December 21, 1998. ◄

ODD-LOT TRADING

NEW YORK-The New York Stock Exchange specialists reported the following odd-lot transactions (in shares):

	Customer Purchases	Short Sales	Other Sales	Total Sales
November 12, 1998	2,596,768	104,485	2,667,060	2,771,545

New York Stock Exchange odd-lot trading for all member firms dealing in odd-lots, for the week ended October 30, 1998:

	Shares	Values
Customers' Orders to Buy	13,307,975	$698,258,702
Customers' Orders to Sell	14,122,151	$671,340,476
Customers' Short Sales	758,840	$36,143,486

Round-Lot transactions (in shares) for the week ended October 30, 1998:

	Purchases	Sales (incl. Short Sales)	Short Sales
Total	3,536,297,080	3,536,297,080	393,428,010
For Member Accounts:			
As Specialists-a,b.....	458,595,850	461,683,810	192,512,300
As Floor Traders	854,620	950,200	417,400
Others-a	300,559,194	292,233,680	35,420,680

a-Including offsetting round-lot transactions arising from odd-lot dealer activity by specialists and other members.
b-Includes transactions effected by members acting as Registered Competitive Market Makers.

American Stock Exchange round-lot and odd-lot trading statistics for the week ended October 30, 1998:

	Purchases	Sales (incl. Short Sales)	Short Sales
Total........................	143,711,055	143,711,055	6,120,102
For Member Accounts:			
As Specialists	16,305,154	18,885,670	1,699,870
As Floor Traders	197,500	182,900	56,400
Others....................	7,533,259	8,021,998	969,111
Customer odd-lots...	288,596	276,505	....

Odd-lot sales exceeded odd-lot purchases on November 12, 1998 and odd-lot orders to sell exceeded odd-lot orders to buy for the week ended October 30, 1998.

stock chiefly in order to keep its price within the small investor's reach. Remember that round lots are trades of 100 shares whose commission per share is lower than that on *odd-lot* (less than 100 shares) transactions. Yet many small investors still trade in odd lots because they cannot afford to deal in round lots. For instance, America Online closed at 138 on Tuesday, December 22, 1998, putting the cost of a round-lot purchase at $13,800 ($138.00 multiplied by 100) and out of the reach of many small investors.

Many market analysts used to believe that odd-lot transactions were a contrary (negative) indicator, because they saw the small investor as a market follower who buys more as the market peaks and sells more as it bottoms out (the opposite of the savvy, big time trader who gets in at the bottom and out at the top). Therefore, according to this wisdom, a high ratio of odd-lot buying to selling is a sign of a market peak (time to sell), while the opposite indicates a market trough (time to buy). However, since a great many

NEW YORK STOCK EXCHANGE COMPOSITE TRANSACTIONS

Quotations as of 5 p.m. Eastern Time
Tuesday, December 22, 1998

-A-A-A-

52 Weeks HI Lo	Stock	Sym	Div	Yld %	PE	Vol 100s	HI	Lo	Close	Net Chg
s 32⅝ 17¹⁵⁄₁₆	AAR	AIR	.34	1.4	17	417	24¼	23	24³⁄₁₆	+⁹⁄₁₆
37 25	ABM Indus	ABM	.56f	1.7	26	156	33⁷⁄₁₆	33	33³⁄₁₆	+¼
27¾ 14¼	ABN Am ADR	AAN	.62e	3.0	...	29520³⁄₁₆	20⅝	20⅜	+⅜
n 26⅝ 25	ABN Am pfA		1.88	7.3	...	3104	25¾	25½	25¾	+⅛
s 43 24¾	ACE Ltd	ACL	.36	1.2	9	196	88 28¹¹⁄₁₆	26½	28¹¹⁄₁₆	+1⅝
11½ 7¾	ACM Grt Fd	ACG	.90a	9.8	...	1926	9¹⁵⁄₁₆	9	9¹⁵⁄₁₆	−
8¾ 7¾	ACM OppFd	AOF	.63e	7.9	...	86	8¹⁄₁₆	8	8	−⅛
10¹³⁄₁₆ 7½	ACM SecFd	GSF	.90	10.4	...	2745	8¾	8⁹⁄₁₆	8¹¹⁄₁₆	+⅛
6⅞ 6¼	ACM SpctrmFd	SI	.54	8.6	...	856	6¾	6¼	6⁹⁄₁₆	+¹⁄₁₆
14⁹⁄₁₆ 7¾	ACM MgdDlr	ADF	1.35	15.3	...	1258	8¹⁵⁄₁₆	8⅞	8¹³⁄₁₆	−⅛
10¹⁄₁₆ 7⅞	ACM Mgdinco	AMF	.90a	9.9	...	186	9⅛	9¼	9¼	−⅛
15¾ 13¾	ACM MuniSec	AMU	.87	6.1	...	125	14⅜	14¼	14³⁄₁₆	+⅛
25¹³⁄₁₆ 9¹⁵⁄₁₆	ACX Tch A	ACX	...	...	15	719	10½	10¼	10⁷⁄₁₆	−⁵⁄₁₆
58 23	AES Cp	AES	...	...	28	4083	44	41⅝	42⅞⁄₁₆	−1½
s 42⅜ 22¹¹⁄₁₆	AFLAC	AFL	.26	.6	16	3630	41¹⁵⁄₁₆	41	41⅝	+⅜
30⁹⁄₁₆ 5½	AGCO Cp	AG	.04	.6	3	3488	7	6⅞	6¹⁵⁄₁₆	...
22¾ 17¹¹⁄₁₆	AGL Res	ATG	1.08	4.8	16	870	22⅜	22¼	22⅜	+⅛
18½ 11¼	AgSvcAm	ASV	...	...	12	232	14⅝	14½	14⅝	+⅛
26¼ 24	AICI CapTr pf		2.25	8.9	...	29	25¼	25⅜	25¼	+⅛
13 4⅛	AIM EstEurFd	GTF	...	...	...	238	5³⁄₁₆	5⅞	5¹³⁄₁₆	+⅛
39½ 17¾	AIPC	PLB	...	...	...	288	22¼	21¾	22¼	+⅛
13¾ 4⅛	AJL PepsTr	AJP	1.44	22.8	...	302	6¾	6⅜	6⁹⁄₁₆	+¹⁄₁₆
22¼ 13⅜	AK Steel	AKS	.50	2.3	12	1859	22¼	21¹³⁄₁₆	22¼⁄₁₆	−⁵⁄₁₆
26 20¾	AMB Prop	AMB	1.37	6.5	...	2331	21¾	21	21¹⁄₁₆	−¼
n 25¼ 22¼	AMB Prop pfA		2.13	8.6	...	1024	13⅜ 24¹³⁄₁₆	24⅝	24¹³⁄₁₆	−⁹⁄₁₆
16⅝ 8	AMCOL	ACO	24	2.7	11	290	9⅛	8¹³⁄₁₆	9	−⁵⁄₁₆
31 3⅞	AMF Bowing	PIN	...	...	dd	2144	4¹¹⁄₁₆	4⅜	4⅝	...
24⅜ 18¹⁵⁄₁₆	AMLI Resdntl	AML	1.76	7.9	16	144	22⁷⁄₁₆	22¹⁄₁₆	22⁹⁄₁₆	−⅛
s 50¹³⁄₁₆ 28½	AMP	AMP	1.08	2.2	53	9701	51¾	49¹³⁄₁₆	49¹⁵⁄₁₆	−⅞
n 26 24½	ANZ pf		.50p	...	...	386	25⅜	25⅜	25⅛	−⅛
n 25¹³⁄₁₆ 25½	ANZ II pf		...	...	...	345	25¹³⁄₁₆	25⅜	25¹³⁄₁₆	+⅛
14 2	APT Satelt	ATS	...	...	...	508	4⅛	3⅞	3¹⁵⁄₁₆	−⅛
26¾ 12⁷⁄₁₆	ARM FnlGp A	ARM	.16	.8	15	433	21¼	20¹⁵⁄₁₆	21⅛	+⅜
26⅝ 13¾	ASA	ASA	.80	5.1	...	894	15⅝	15	15³⁄₁₆	−⁵⁄₁₆
n 26⅛ 25	AT&T Cap PINES		...	...	...	439	25⅝	25⁷⁄₁₆	25⁷⁄₁₆	−⅛
76½ 48¾	AT&T	T	1.32	1.8	21	39671	74⅜	72⅝	73⅜	−⅛
23¾ 13¹⁄₁₆	AVX Cp	AVX	.26	1.7	15	919	16	15½	15¼	−¹⁄₁₆
71¼ 36⁹⁄₁₆	AXA UAP	AXA	.74e	1.1	...	446	69½	68¼	68¹³⁄₁₆	+3⅛
15¹¹⁄₁₆ 1	AamesFnl	AAM	.10j	...	...	315094	2¼	1¹³⁄₁₆	2¼	+¼
24¾ 11⅛	AaronRent	RNT	.04	.3	14	225	15⅛	14½	14½	−½
27¹⁄₁₆ 25⅝	AbbeyNtl pfA		2.19	8.2	...	11	26⅝	26⅝	26⅝	+⅛
s 50¹⁹⁄₃₂ 31⅜	AbbotLab	ABT	.60	1.3	33	16071	47⅞	46	47⁹⁄₁₆	+1
Λ63¹¹⁄₃₂ 27¼	Abercrombie A	ANF	...	...	...	7712	65⅞	63⅜	64¹⁵⁄₁₆	+1⅞
16¹³⁄₁₆ 7¾	Abitibi g	ABY	.40	...	...	640	8¹⁵⁄₁₆	8½	8¹¹⁄₁₆	+⅛
9⁹⁄₁₆ 4¾	AcadiaRlty	AKR	...	dd	368	5¾	5½	5½	...
25¾ 16¾	Acceptns	AIF	...	...	9	339	19⅝	18¾	19¹³⁄₁₆	+¹³⁄₁₆
24⅜ 14¾	AckrlyGp	AK	...	...	14	7818	1¹¹⁄₁₆	18¼	18¹¹⁄₁₆	−⁷⁄₁₆
6½ 3¹¹⁄₁₆	AcmeElec	ACE	...	...	9	205	5¼	4¾	5	+⅛
29¾ 19¼	ACNielsen	ART	...	...	31	654	27¹¹⁄₁₆	27¼	27¹¹⁄₁₆	+⅜
20¹¹⁄₁₆ 13⁷⁄₁₆	Acuson	ACN	...	...	21	2658	14⁷⁄₁₆	14¼	14⅜	+⅜
28¼ 21¹³⁄₁₆	AdamsExp	ADX	2.10e	8.1	...	138	26¹⁄₁₆	25¹¹⁄₁₆	25¹³⁄₁₆	−⅛
52¹⁵⁄₁₆ 21¾	Administaff	ASF	...	...	42	283	25⁹⁄₁₆	25¼	25¹³⁄₁₆	−⅝
n 17½ 3	AdvCommGp	ADG	...	...	...	407	4¹³⁄₁₆	4⁷⁄₁₆	4⅜	+⅛
32¾ 12¾	AdvMicro	AMD	...	...	dd	22984	29⁹⁄₁₆	27⅝	29⁷⁄₁₆	+⅛
33¾ 14⅛	Advest	ADV	.16	.8	10	438	19¾	18⅝	19	...
33⅜ 19	Advo	AD	...	...	16	570	25	24⁷⁄₁₆	25	...
10⁹⁄₁₆ 4¾	Advocat	AVC	...	...	31	52	5½	5½	5½	−⅛
s121¾ 43⅛	AEGON	AEG	1.58e	1.3	51	496	120¾	118⅝	118½	−2¼
15¼ 6¼	Aeroflex	ARX	...	...	24	388	13⅜	13	13¹³⁄₁₆	−⅛
72¼ 22	AeroVick	ANV	.88	3.0	9	1181	29⅝	29	29¹³⁄₁₆	−⅛
85¼ 40	AES Tr TECONS		2.69	4.2	...	90	62¹⁵⁄₁₆	64½	64½	−2½
89¾ 60¹⁵⁄₁₆	Aetna	AET	.80	1.0	14	4193	80⅜	78¾	79⅞	+¾
84¼ 62¹⁄₁₆	Aetna pfC		4.76	6.3	...	186	76¼	74⅜	75⅜	+⅝
27¾ 25⁹⁄₁₆	Aetna MIPS A		2.37	9.0	...	67	26⅜	26⅜	26⅜	+⅛
41¾ 22¾	AffilCmptr A	ACS	...	...	33	1371	39½	38¼	39½	+1
39½ 13¾	AffilMangr	AMG	...	...	32	106	29¹¹⁄₁₆	29¼	29⁹⁄₁₆	−⁹⁄₁₆
8 2⅝	AgnicoEgl	.AEM	.02	.5	...	802	4⅛	4	4¹⁄₁₆	−⅛
22¾ 17⅛	AgreeRlty	ATR	1.84	10.2	12	70	18⅛	18⅛	18⅛	−⅜
n 43¾ 21¾	Agribrnt	AGX	...	...	...	1079	29⅝	28⅜	28¹¹⁄₁₆	−⅛
15¾ 7¾	Agrium g	AGU	.11	...	...	975	8⅝	8¾	8⅜	+⅛
n 25½ 23¾	Agrium COPrS		2.00	8.1	...	16524	⁷⁄₁₆ 24¾	24¾	24¾	...
37⅛ 24¹³⁄₁₆	Ahold	AHO	.39e	1.1	38	325	36¹⁵⁄₁₆	36⅞	36⅝	−⅜

52 Weeks HI Lo	Stock	Sym	Div	Yld %	PE	Vol 100s	HI	Lo	Close	Net Chg
29½ 11¹³⁄₁₆	AirNetSys	ANS	...	...	15	604	11¹³⁄₁₆	11¾	11¹³⁄₁₆	−³⁄₁₆
s 45¾ 29	AirProduct	APD	.68	1.8	15	5825	38½	36¾	38⅛	+⅛
s 42½ 14¼	AirbrnFrght	ABF	.16	.5	13	10949	34¹⁄₁₆	30	33¹¹⁄₁₆	+2½
18¹³⁄₁₆ 8	Airgas	ARG	...	...	21	1429	9¼	8¹¹⁄₁₆	8⁴¹⁄₁₆	−¼
14½ 12⅜	Airlease	FLY	1.64	12.5	12	123	13⅜	13	13⅛	+⅛
65⅜ 37⅜	AirTouch	ATI	...	...	62	116649	65⅝	63¼	64⅝	+1⅛
53¾ 33¾	AirTouch pfB		1.74	3.3	...	547	53¼	51½	53¼	+1
92¼ 58	AirTouch pfC		2.13	2.3	...	250	91³⁄₁₆	89½	91¹¹⁄₁₆	+1¹⁄₁₆
25¹¹⁄₁₆ 24	AL Pwr ntsA	ALZ	1.78	7.1	...	421	25⅞	25⅛	25⅞	+⅛
n 25¾ 23¾	AL Pwr ntsB	ACA	1.75	7.0	...	117	25⅛	25⅛	25⅛	...
n 25¾ 24¹¹⁄₁₆	AL Pwr ntsC	ABJ	1.75	6.9	...	113	25¹¹⁄₁₆	25⅝	25⅝	+⅛
26¾ 24⅛	AL PwrCap pfO		1.84	7.2	...	87	25¹¹⁄₁₆	25⅝	25⅝	...
26¹¹⁄₁₆ 24¾	AL PwrCap pfR		1.90	7.3	...	147	26¹¹⁄₁₆	25¹³⁄₁₆	26¹⁄₁₆	+⅛
22¼ 10⅝	AlamoGp	ALG	.44	3.6	14	27	12¼	12⅛	12⅛	...
62⅞ 26	AlaskaAir	ALK	...	...	9	3740	42⁹⁄₁₆	40⅝	41⅜	−¾
29½ 15¹¹⁄₁₆	Albanylnt	ALN	stk	...	12	770	18⁵⁄₁₆	17¾	17⁵⁄₁₆	−½
26¹⁄₁₆ 16	Albemarle	ALB	.40f	1.9	13	1100	21¾	20½	20¹¹⁄₁₆	−¾
26¼ 17¾	AlbEngy g	AGO	.40	...	...	119	22⁹⁄₁₆	21⅝	21⁵⁄₁₆	−⁷⁄₁₆
32⅞ 19¾	AlbertoCl	ACV	.24	1.0	18	622	25	24½	24¾	+¾
28½ 17¹⁵⁄₁₆	AlbertoCl A	ACVA	.24	1.0	17	383	23½	22¾	23¼	+⅛
Λ64¹³⁄₁₆ 44	Albertsons	ABS	.68	1.0	29	5476	65½	63⅞	65¼	+1¾
34½ 18¹¹⁄₁₆	Alcan	AL	.60	2.3	14	4201	27⅜	26⅜	26¹¹⁄₁₆	−1⅛
47¼ 15¹⁵⁄₁₆	Alcatel ADS	ALA	.39e	1.6	...	6621	24¼	23⅜	23¾	−⅜
95¼ 72¼	Alexanders	ALX	...	...	21	18	78¼	77⅝	77⅜	−⅜
34⅝ 25¾	AlexRlEstEq	ARE	1.60	5.1	20	43	31¾	31¹⁄₁₆	31¹⁄₁₆	−⅛
14⅜ 12¼	AllAmTerm	AAT	.96	7.4	...	196	13½	13	13	−⅛
s 248 167¹⁵⁄₁₆	AlleghanyCp	Y	stk	...	12	621	91¹⁄₁₆	183	183	−10
34¹³⁄₁₆ 26¾	AllegEngy	AYE	1.72	5.2	14	2519	33½	33	33⁹⁄₁₆	−¾
29⁹⁄₁₆ 14	AlghnyTidyn	ALT	.64	3.2	15	5628	20⁹⁄₁₆	19½	20¹⁄₁₆	−⅜
s 44¾ 15⅝	Allegiance	AEH	.21	.5	44	6799	43¼	41¹¹⁄₁₆	43¼	+¾
21½ 4¹¹⁄₁₆	AllenTele	ALN	...	...	dd	141	6½	5¹⁵⁄₁₆	6½	+⅛
66½ 31⁹⁄₁₆	Allergan	AGN	.52	.8	dd	3568	61¹⁵⁄₁₆	59¾	61⅜	+1¹⁄₁₆
48 27¾	AllncAll	AMO	3.46e	8.3	...	52	41⁷⁄₁₆	41½	41¹³⁄₁₆	+⅛
s 29 17¾	AllncCapMgt	AC	1.60	6.1	13	831	26⅝	26	26⅜	−¹¹⁄₁₆
n 25¾ 8½	AllncFrstPdt	PFA	...	...	28	9½	9⅝	9⅝	...
s 14⁷⁄₁₆ 7¹¹⁄₁₆	AllncWrld2	AWF	1.32	15.2	...	2625	8¾	8½	8¹¹⁄₁₆	+⅛
s 16⅜ 9¾	AllncWrld	AWG	1.53a	14.4	...	475	10¾	10⅛	10¾	+⅛
Λ 83 53¾	AlliantTech	ATK	...	...	16	596	83¾	82½	82¹³⁄₁₆	+⅛
24 10	AldHldg	AHI	...	...	41	42	13⅜	13¹³⁄₁₆	13¹³⁄₁₆	−⅛
104 55½	AldIrishBk	AIB	1.76e	1.7	...	196	104	102⅝	104	+⅞
† 25⅜ 6¼	AlldPdts	ADP	.16	2.7	12	650	6¹⁄₁₆	5⅞	6	−⁹⁄₁₆
47⅝ 32⅝	AldSgnl	ALD	.60	1.4	19	8693	42¾	42¹⁄₁₆	42⅞	+⅛
75¾ 38⅜	AllmencaFnl	AFC	.20	.4	13	839	57¾	56⅝	56⅛	−⁹⁄₁₆
11¾ 10⅛	AllmrST	ALM	.80	7.0	...	17	11¾	11⅜	11¾	...
s 52¾ 36¹⁄₁₆	Allstate	ALL	.54	1.4	10	18704	38½	37⅜	38¼	+⅛
n 26¼ 24¾	Allstate QUIBS		1.78	7.0	...	75	25¾	25⅛	25¼	−⅜
26¾ 25¼	AllstFng QUIPS		1.99	7.6	...	178	26⅜	26⅛	26⁹⁄₁₆	+⅛
s 57¾ 38¾	Alltel	AT	1.22f	2.1	29	6916	58¾	57¼	57¹³⁄₁₆	+⅛
29¼ 19	Alltrista	ALC	...	...	11	38	24¾	24	24	+⅛
36¹³⁄₁₆ 18⁷⁄₁₆	Alpharma A	ALO	.18	.6	39	1236	33¾	32⁹⁄₁₆	32⁹⁄₁₆	−⅜
17 2½	Alpharma wt		...	...	...	23	13⅜	12⅝	12⅜	+⅛
22¼ 13⅜	AlpineGp	AGI	...	...	15	218	14¼	14	14¹⁄₁₆	+⅛
n 34¹⁄₁₆ 19	Alstom ADS	ALS	...	...	...	318	22	21½	21¾	+⅞
81¼ 58	Alcoa	AA	1.00a	1.4	14	6439	70⅛	69¼	69¼	−⅜
54 29¹⁵⁄₁₆	Alza	AZA	...	...	41	9040	46⅞	45⅜	46½	...
65⁵⁄₁₆ 40⅜	AmbacFnl	ABK	.40	.7	16	3251	58⅜	57	57⅜	+1
n 26½ 24¼	Ambac deb	AKB	1.77	7.1	...	328	25¹¹⁄₁₆	24⅝	25¹¹⁄₁₆	+⅛
24½ 13⅜	Amcastlnd	AIZ	.56	3.0	8	577	19	18½	18¾	+1¼
n 17½ 8¾	Amdocs	DOX	...	...	...	663	17¼	16⅜	17¼	+¼
61¹³⁄₁₆ 46	AmerHess	AHC	.60	1.2	dd	2764	50¾	49⁷⁄₁₆	49¹¹⁄₁₆	−⅜
27¼ 14¾	Amerco pfA		2.13	8.1	...	61	26⅜	26⅝	26⅝	+⅛
n 44¾ 35⁹⁄₁₆	Ameren	AEE	2.54	6.0	14	2153	42⅜	41⅞	42⅝	−⅛
n 9¹³⁄₁₆ 4½	AmFstMtg	MFA	.80e	16.4	...	129	4⅞	4¹¹⁄₁₆	4⅞	−⅛
↓119¾ 26⅜	AmOnline	AOL	...	...	cc	227137	138	114⅜	138	+21
19½ 3	AmWestAir wt		...	...	...	148	6½	6⅜	6¾	...
31⅜ 9¾	AmWstHldg B	AWA	...	...	6	2093	14¹³⁄₁₆	14⅛	14¹³⁄₁₆	+¼
25⅛ 20¹⁵⁄₁₆	AmAnnuity	AAG	.10	.4	9	7	22¾	22⅝	22½	−⅜
27 25	AmAnuty TOPrS		2.32	9.0	...	21	26⅝	25¹³⁄₁₆	25¹¹⁄₁₆	−⁹⁄₁₆
n 18⁷⁄₁₆ 4¾	AmBkNtHolo	ABH	...	...	...	588	16⅝	15⅜	16¾	−¼
66⅜ 30⅛	AmBkrsIns	ABI	.48f	1.0	84	2262	47¾	46¹¹⁄₁₆	46⅞	−⅜
133⅛ 65½	AmBkrsIns pf		3.13	3.2	...	6	96¾	95⅞	96¾	...
5¼ 1¹⁄₁₆	AmBknote	ABN	...	...	29	553	1⅜	1¹⁄₁₆	1¹⁄₁₆	...
n 16 11⅞	AmBusnPdts	ABP	.66	2.8	26	331	23¹¹⁄₁₆	23¾	23¾	−⅛
53¾ 42¼	AEP	AEP	2.40	5.1	15	4709	47¾	46¹¹⁄₁₆	46¹¹⁄₁₆	−½
118¾ 67	AmExpress	AXP	.90	.9	23	70261	02¾	101	101⅜	+⅞
n 26 24½	AmExpress pfA		1.75	6.9	...	613	25⅜	25½	25¹³⁄₁₆	+⅛
27½ 25	AmFnlCap TOPrS		2.28	8.7	...	68	26⅝	26½	26¹³⁄₁₆	−⅛

AMR (American Airlines) →

	39 1/2	17 5/8	AIPC	PLB		...	...	288	22 1/4	21 3/8	22 1/4	+ 1/8
	13 5/8	4 1/8	AJL PepsTr	AJP	1.44	22.8	...	302	6 3/8	6 5/16	6 5/16	+ 1/16
	22 1/4	13 5/8	♣ AK Steel	AKS	.50	2.3	12	1859	22 3/16	21 13/16	22 3/16	– 1/16
	26	20 3/4	AMB Prop	AMB	1.37	6.5	...	2331	21 3/8	21	21 1/16	– 1/4
n	25 7/16	22 1/4	AMB Prop pfA		2.13	8.6	...	10	24 13/16	24 13/16	24 13/16	– 1/16
	16 3/8	8	AMCOL	ACO	.24	2.7	11	290	9 1/8	8 13/16	9	– 5/16
	31	3 7/8	AMF Bowlng	PIN		...	dd	2144	4 11/16	4 3/8	4 5/8	...
	24 3/8	18 7/16	♣ AMLI Resdntl	AML	1.76	7.9	16	144	22 7/16	22 1/16	22 3/16	– 5/16
▲	50 13/16	28 1/8	AMP	AMP	1.08	2.2	53	9701	51 1/4	49 15/16	49 15/16	– 7/8
s	89 15/16	45 5/8	AMR	AMR		...	8	9691	59 1/4	57 7/8	59	– 5/8
n	26	24 1/2	ANZ pf		.50p	...	...	386	25 5/8	25 9/16	25 9/16	– 1/16
n	25 15/16	25 1/2	ANZ II pf			...	...	345	25 15/16	25 5/8	25 15/16	+ 5/16
	14	2	APT Satelt	ATS		...	...	508	4 1/8	3 7/8	3 15/16	– 1/16
	26 3/4	12 7/16	ARM FnlGp A	ARM	.16	.8	15	433	21 1/4	20 15/16	21 1/8	+ 3/16
	26 5/8	13 5/8	ASA	ASA	.80	5.1	...	894	15 9/16	15	15 9/16	– 5/16
n	26 1/8	25	AT&T Cap PINES			...	...	439	25 9/16	25 7/16	25 7/16	– 1/16
	76 1/2	48 3/8	AT&T	T	1.32	1.8	21	39671	74 3/16	72 9/16	73 5/16	– 7/8

AMR (American Airlines)

Source: *The Wall Street Journal*, December 23, 1998. Reprinted by permission of *The Wall Street Journal*,

small investors in recent years have abandoned odd-lots in favor of mutual funds, this omen has become less significant to analysts.

The Journal provides a daily record of **Odd-Lot Trading** for the day preceding the previous trading day. You'll find it beneath **NYSE Highs/Lows**. See the example on page 160 from the Wednesday, December 23, 1998 issue that indicated sales of 3,756,229 shares and purchases of 3,936,012 shares on Monday, December 21, 1998. According to the contrarian wisdom outlined above, this was a *buy* signal for the savvy investor.

A more detailed report appears on Mondays (also beneath **NYSE Highs/Lows**). See for yourself when examining the **Odd-Lot Trading** report from the Monday, November 16, 1998 *Wall Street Journal* on page 161. Odd-lot sales (2,771,545 shares) exceeded odd-lot purchases (2,596,768 shares) on Thursday, November 12, 1998 in NYSE trading by odd-lot specialists, and orders to sell plus short sales (14,122,151 + 758,840 = 14,880,991) exceeded orders to buy (13,207,975) by all NYSE member firms for the week ended Friday, October 30, 1998.

FOLLOW YOUR STOCK

Suppose now that you have studied the various stock market indicators and indexes, decided that the time was right to get into the market, and did so. You will want to follow the progress of your investment. Here's how you do it.

If you own shares of *AMR (American Airlines)*, you can follow their daily performance in *The Wall Street Journal* by turning to **New York Stock**

Exchange Composite Transactions (see page 162). Recall that this composite report includes a small amount of trading activity on regional exchanges. You'll find a reference to all exchanges in the index on the front pages of the first (A1) and third (C1) sections.

In the accompanying excerpts from the Wednesday, December 23, 1998 issue of the *Journal* (pages 162 and 163), the first and second columns tell you the highest and lowest value of one share of the stock in the past 52 weeks expressed in dollars and fractions of a dollar. AMR (American Airlines) stock was as low as $45.62½ cents (45⅝) and as high as $89.93¾ cents (89¹⁵⁄₁₆) in the year preceding December 22, 1998.

Footnotes and symbols, including arrows and underlining, are fully explained in the box on the lower left of the first page of the Composite listings.

The third and fourth columns give the company name and stock ticker symbol (AMR).

The fifth column of data reports the latest annual cash dividend. As you can see, American Airlines paid no dividends in the latest quarter. The dividend is expressed as a percentage of the closing price in the next column.

The seventh column shows the price-earnings (P/E) ratio, which is obtained by dividing the price of the stock by its earnings per share. (This important statistic is discussed in detail in Chapter 8.) On December 22, 1998, American Airline's stock was worth 8 times the profits per share of stock.

The eighth column informs you of the number of shares traded that day, expressed in hundreds of shares: 969,100 shares of American Airlines traded on December 22, 1998. If a *z* appears before the number in this column, the figure represents the actual number (not hundreds) of shares traded.

The ninth, tenth, and eleventh columns reveal the stock's highest, lowest, and closing (last) price for the trading day. On Tuesday, December 22, 1998, American Airlines traded as high as 59¼ and as low as 57⅞, before closing at 59.

The last column provides the change in the closing price of the stock from the price at the close of the previous day. You can see that this stock closed at a price 62.5 cents (⅝ of a dollar) lower than the previous closing price.

You may wonder why share prices are quoted with figures such as ⅛, which must be converted into fractions of a cent. Because trading is usually conducted in round lots of 100 shares, and payment for a round lot eliminates the problem. For instance, 79⅛ × 100 = $7,912.50.

Shares of other companies, usually smaller than those listed on the NYSE, trade on the American Stock Exchange (AMEX). *The Wall Street Journal*'s AMEX report, called **American Stock Exchange Composite Transactions**, is identical in form to **NYSE Composite Transactions**.

Over-the counter (OTC) stocks are not traded on an exchange. Instead, dealers have established a market for them using a computer network referred to as NASDAQ (National Association of Securities Dealers Automated Quotations). You can follow this market in **NASDAQ National Market Issues**, which is similar to the New York and American Exchange listings.

Smaller companies with smaller capitalizations are listed as **NASDAQ Small-Cap Issues** and show trading volume, closing price, and price change only (see page 166).

With this information, you can track the performance of any share of stock traded on the New York or American exchanges or the OTC market.

MUTUAL FUNDS

At this point you may wonder if you can get into the stock market without purchasing a particular stock.

Mutual funds provide a way to invest in the stock market indirectly. Investment companies establish mutual funds to pool the resources of many investors and thus create a large, shared portfolio of investments. Individuals invest in mutual funds by purchasing shares in the fund from the investment company. These mutual funds are open-ended, which means the investment companies are always willing to sell more shares to the public and to redeem outstanding shares. Therefore, the pool of capital, the number of investors, and the number of shares outstanding can expand or contract.

The value of the fund's assets divided by the number of shares outstanding determines the value of each share. Any gain in the fund's portfolio is passed through to the individual investors. Purchases of additional shares by new investors do not reduce the value of existing shares because the purchaser makes a cash contribution equal to the value of the share.

This raises an important point: Mutual fund shares are not traded on the open market. They are purchased from, and sold back to, the investment company.

Mutual funds are popular with individual investors because they permit diversification in a wide variety of securities with a very small capital outlay. In addition, a mutual fund lets you take advantage of the professional management skills of the investment company.

When you purchase a mutual fund share, you own a fraction of the total assets in the portfolio. The price of that share is equal to its net asset value (net value of assets held by the fund divided by the number of mutual fund shares outstanding plus any sales commission). As with any pooled investment in common stock, price appreciation and dividends earned will determine the gain in net asset value.

NASDAQ SMALL-CAP ISSUES

Mutual funds are classified according to whether or not they charge a sales commission called a load. Every day, **Mutual Fund Quotations** lists the major funds available to investors, and it can be found using the indexes on the front pages of the first (A1) and third (C1) sections. Page 168 provides excerpts from the Friday, December 18, 1998 edition of the *Journal*, and reports figures for Thursday, December 17, 1998.

No-Load (NL) Funds don't require a commission to purchase or sell the shares of the fund. There is, however, a "management fee" on these funds', and all other funds', assets that is generally less than 1 percent of the investment. Net asset values are calculated after management takes its fee.

Front-End Loaded Funds charge a one-time admission or sales fee to purchasers of their shares, as well as the management fee levied by all funds. This "sales" or commission fee can be as high as 8 percent, which will effectively reduce your overall rate of return, depending on how long you hold the fund. A *p* after the fund's name indicates there is a distribution charge, or front-load, on the fund.

Back-End Loaded Funds levy a fee of up to 8 percent when the shares are sold back to the investment company. An *r* indicates this *redemption* charge. Some back-loaded funds vary their fees according to the length of time the shares are held. If you sell your shares after one year, the fee may be as high as 8 percent. But if you hold the shares for a long time (say, 30 years), no fee may be charged. (Remember that *all* funds have built-in management fees in addition to any loads.)

When both redemption and distribution fees are charged, the fund is identified by a *t* after the fund's name.

The absence of the letters *p, r,* or *t* after the fund name indicates a no-load fund.

Loaded funds are sold through brokers, which explains the commission fee. The investment company contracts with the broker to act as the fund's marketer.

Since no-load funds are directly marketed and have no outside sales force, there is no commission fee. In order to invest in a no-load fund, you must select the fund (e.g., in response to a newspaper ad or direct-mail solicitation) and contact the investment company directly. A broker customarily will not act for you in the purchase of no-load funds, because he or she will not receive a commission fee of any kind.

Some companies and organizations offer many funds, each with its own special objective. Take the *AARP (American Association of Retired Persons) CaGr (Capital Growth)* fund shown on pages 168 and 169, for example. The first column provides the fund's name. The second column reveals

MUTUAL FUND QUOTATIONS

Capital Appreciation → (Capital Appreciation)

AARP CaGr → (CaGr)

LIPPER INDEXES

Thursday, December 17, 1998

Equity Indexes	Prelim. Close	Percentage chg. since Prev.	Wk ago	Dec. 31
Capital Appreciation ...	2092.73	+ 1.34	+ 0.81	+ 12.06
Growth Fund	7411.83	+ 1.54	+ 1.21	+ 18.27
Small Cap Fund	575.89	+ 1.02	− 0.59	− 8.36
Growth & Income........	6613.20	+ 1.44	+ 0.61	+ 9.61
Equity Income Fd.......	3528.86	+ 1.20	+ 0.52	+ 8.58
Science and Tech Fd ...	676.00	+ 2.46	+ 1.61	+ 34.97
International Fund......	661.14	+ 0.66	− 0.65	+ 9.08
Gold Fund................	71.30	− 1.28	+ 3.36	− 12.46
Balanced Fund...........	4117.65	+ 0.89	+ 0.43	+ 11.65
Emerging Markets......	57.93	− 0.01	− 3.98	− 30.21
Bond Indexes				
Corp A-Rated Debt......	805.27	+ 0.01	− 0.26	+ 7.45
US Government	305.91	+ 0.01	− 0.20	+ 8.07
GNMA	325.50	− 0.01	− 0.11	+ 6.23
High Current Yield......	762.25	− 0.13	− 0.71	− 0.69
Intmdt Inv Grade........	222.21	− 0.03	− 0.16	+ 8.02
Short Inv Grade	198.70	− 0.03	− 0.02	+ 5.67
General Muni Debt......	575.66	− 0.13	− 0.12	+ 5.82
High Yield Municipal ..	278.56	− 0.08	− 0.06	+ 5.54
Short Municipal	121.21	− 0.01	+ 0.08	+ 4.44
Global Income	212.30	+ 0.08	− 0.32	+ 6.28
International Income...	142.32	+ 0.07	− 0.38	+ 13.16

Indexes are based on the largest funds within the same investment objective and do not include multiple share classes of similar funds. The Yardsticks table, appearing with Friday's listings, includes all funds with the same objective.

Source: Lipper Inc. The Lipper Funds Inc. are not affiliated with Lipper Inc.

Ranges for investment companies, with daily price data supplied by the National Association of Securities Dealers and performance and cost calculations by Lipper Inc. The NASD requires a mutual fund to have at least 1,000 shareholders or net assets of $25 million before being listed. NAV-Net Asset Value. Detailed explanatory notes appear elsewhere on this page.

Name	NAV	Net Chg	YTD %ret
AAL Mutual A:			
Balance p	11.35	+0.10	+14.8
Bond p	10.19	...	+6.9
CGrowth p	31.15	+0.47	+21.8
EqInc p	13.35	+0.15	+8.7
HiYBdA	9.09	−0.02	−2.7
Intl p	10.74	+0.03	+7.1
MidCap p	12.72	+0.09	−7.0
MuniBd p	11.58	−0.02	+6.2
SmCap p	10.86	+0.06	−10.1
AAL Mutual B:			
Balance t	11.31	+0.10	+14.0
CGrowth p	30.70	+0.46	+20.6
EqInc p	13.32	+0.15	+7.6
HiYBdB p	9.09	−0.01	−3.5
Intl p	10.57	+0.03	+5.9
MidCap	12.55	+0.09	−8.1
SmCap p	10.74	+0.06	−11.0
AARP Invst:			
BalS&B	21.05	+0.20	+5.1
BdInc	15.33	...	+6.8
CaGr	61.09	+0.75	+17.2
DivGr	18.30	+0.14	+7.1
DivInc	16.45	+0.06	+6.7
GlniM	15.24	...	+6.5
GlblGr	19.69	+0.19	+9.4
GthInc	54.17	+0.85	+3.8
HQSTBd	16.26	−0.01	+5.5
IntlG&I	17.60	+0.04	+6.9
SmCoStk	17.52	+0.12	−12.1
TxFBd	18.76	−0.03	+5.4
USStkI	22.37	+0.34	+23.6
ABN AMRO Funds:			
AsiaTCm	6.61	+0.06	−13.0
Bal Cm	12.17	+0.14	+7.4
FixIncCm	10.58	−0.01	+7.4
Gwth Cm	16.89	+0.25	+21.3
IntFxCm	10.38	−0.01	+8.3
IntlEqCm	18.38	+0.15	+21.2
IntlFICm	11.15	−0.01	+15.7
LatinAm	8.06	+0.07	−37.8
SmCpGrCm	11.19	+0.17	−14.4
TE FICm	10.60	−0.02	+6.1
ValueCm	14.30	+0.33	+3.8
AFBA Equity	10.99x	+0.13	+1.6
AHA Funds:			
Balan	14.50	+0.11	+6.5
DivrEq	20.54	+0.30	+12.6
Full	10.36	...	+8.7
Lim	10.34	...	+6.8
AIM Funds A:			
AdvFlex p	21.49	+0.18	+10.4
AdvIntV p	15.99	+0.09	+7.3
AdvLgCp p	26.48	+0.38	+10.1
AdvMulF p	13.55	+0.10	−3.4
AdvRlEst p	11.64	−0.03	−24.0
Agrsv p	44.24	+0.84	−4.3
AsianGr p	7.64	+0.02	−11.2
Bal p	27.27	+0.26	+7.6
BasicVal p	18.03	+0.28	+4.5
BlChp p	39.33	+0.70	+23.3
CapDev p	13.65	+0.15	−4.9
Chart p	14.55	+0.23	+19.1
Const p	28.59	+0.55	+8.6
DevMkt p	7.42	+0.01	−37.5
EmMkDt p	8.08	−0.06	−30.2
EmMkt p	7.33	+0.01	−39.9
Euro p	15.13	+0.20	+12.5
EuroDev p	13.64	+0.11	+34.5
GlAgGr	16.67	+0.18	−2.2
GlGr p	18.60	+0.25	+15.1
GlGrInc p	9.70	+0.09	+18.3
GlGvInc p	9.19	+0.01	+12.6
GlInc p	10.72	...	+4.9
GlTrend p	10.98	+0.13	+3.3
GlUtil p	21.06	+0.20	+11.9
HiIncMuA p	10.13	−0.01	NS
HYld p	8.78	−0.01	−5.6
Inco p	8.46	...	+5.0
IntGov p	9.61	...	+8.2
IntlEq p	17.84	+0.13	+8.7
IntlGr p	7.48	+0.12	+2.2
JapanGr p	8.74	−0.02	−2.3
LatAmG p	11.33	+0.16	−45.8

Name	NAV	Net Chg	YTD %ret
LimM p	10.18	...	+6.1
MdCpEq p	18.73	+0.22	−10.9
Muni p	8.38	−0.01	+5.5
Pacif p	5.07	+0.04	−21.0
SelGrth p	18.26	+0.36	+16.5
SmCpGr p	15.90	+0.21	+11.4
SmCpOpp p	11.01	+0.30	NS
Strat p	11.11	+0.01	−1.8
Sumit	16.76	+0.35	+23.1
TeCt p	11.10	−0.01	+5.0
TFInt	11.19	−0.01	+5.6
Valu p	40.33	+0.79	+24.4
Weing p	24.25	+0.49	+22.2
Wldw p	14.56	+0.21	+5.7
AIM Funds B:			
Bal t	27.18	+0.26	+6.7
BasicVal t	17.70	+0.27	+3.9
BlChp t	38.84	+0.69	+22.4
CapDev t	13.44	+0.15	−5.6
Chart t	14.45	+0.23	+18.2
Const t	28.28	+0.54	+7.7
EmMkDt t	8.08	−0.05	−30.6
EmMkt t	7.14	+0.02	−40.1
Euro t	14.72	+0.19	+11.7
EuroDev t	13.55	+0.11	+33.5
GlAgGr t	16.29	+0.18	−2.7
GlGr t	18.17	+0.25	+14.5
GlGrInc t	9.69	+0.09	+17.6
GlGvInc t	9.19	+0.02	+12.0
GlInc t	10.72	...	+4.4
GlTrend t	10.91	+0.13	+2.7
GlUtil t	21.04	+0.21	+11.1
HYld t	8.77	−0.02	−6.4
Inco t	8.45	+0.01	+4.3
IntGov t	9.62	...	+7.5
IntlEq t	17.46	+0.13	+7.9
IntlGr t	7.15	+0.11	+1.4
JapanGr t	8.40	−0.02	−3.0
LatAmG	11.23	+0.15	−46.1
MdCpEq t	17.98	+0.21	−11.5
Muni t	8.39	−0.01	+4.6
Pacif t	4.93	+0.05	−21.3
SelGrth t	17.33	+0.34	+15.7
SmCpGr t	15.55	+0.21	+10.6
SmCpOpp t	10.97	+0.29	NS
Strat t	11.12	+0.01	−2.4
Valu t	39.37	+0.78	+23.5
Weing t	23.57	+0.48	+21.4
Wldw t	13.83	+0.20	+5.1
AIM Funds C:			
AdvFlex t	21.46	+0.18	+9.7
AdvIntV t	15.91	+0.09	+6.6
AdvLgCp t	26.29	+0.38	+9.2
AdvMulF t	13.53	+0.09	−4.1
AdvRlEst t	11.62	−0.04	−24.6
Bal p	27.20	+0.25	+6.7
BlChip p	38.83	+0.69	+22.4
CapDev t	13.43	+0.15	−5.6
Chart t	14.48	+0.22	+18.2
Const t	28.27	+0.54	+7.7
GlAgGr t	16.30	+0.18	−2.6
GlGr t	18.17	+0.24	+14.5
Hyld p	8.76	−0.01	−6.3
IntGov t	9.59	...	+7.4
IntlEq t	17.47*	+0.13	+8.0
Valu t	39.38	+0.77	+23.4
Weing t	23.58	+0.47	+21.3
AIM Global Theme:			
ConProdA p	23.94	+0.29	+14.7
ConProdB t	23.41	+0.28	+14.0
FinSerA p	18.50	+0.32	+6.7
FinSerB t	18.13	+0.32	+6.3
HltCrA p	22.17	+0.29	+11.6
HltCrB t	21.30	+0.28	+11.1
InfraA p	14.16	+0.16	+1.1
InfraB t	13.88	+0.15	+0.6
Res A p	10.54	...	−36.9
Res B t	10.34	+0.01	−37.1
TelecomA p	17.55	+0.24	+10.5
TelecomB t	16.96	+0.24	+10.0
AMF Funds:			
AdjMtg	9.92	...	+4.9
IntMtg	9.67	...	+6.9
ShtUSGv	10.62	−0.01	+6.6
USGvMtg	10.72	...	+6.9

Name	NAV	Net Chg	YTD %ret
API Gr fp	13.82	...	+6.1
ARK Funds:			
Balanced	13.45	+0.13	+19.3
BlChpEqA p	17.48	+0.20	+21.3
BlChpEqI	17.51	+0.21	+21.6
CapGr	16.40	+0.29	+32.6
EqIdxI	12.28	+0.18	+24.1
EqInc	11.52	+0.11	+6.2
Income	10.36	...	+6.9
IntlEqSel	10.32	...	+4.0
IntmFixI	10.16	−0.01	+7.8
MidCEq	13.09	+0.20	+9.4
MDTxF A p	10.31	−0.02	+5.6
MDTxFree	10.32	−0.01	+5.9
PATxFBd	10.34	−0.01	+5.5
Small CapI	10.58	+0.17	+11.9
STBond	10.04	−0.01	+6.1
STTreasI	10.13	−0.01	+6.4
USGvtBd	10.02	...	+7.2
ValEq	13.92	+0.17	+14.4
ASM Idx30	19.72	+0.20	+14.0
Accessor Fd:			
Growth	28.98	+0.47	+37.5
IntEq	16.58	+0.13	+11.8
IntFxIn	12.60	...	+8.6
Mortg	12.69	...	+6.2
ShtIntFx	12.52	−0.01	+6.9
SmCap	21.96	+0.27	+3.6
ValInc	22.32	+0.36	+8.9
Achievement Fds:			
BalTr	12.95e	−0.45	+9.4
EqTr	16.10e	+0.06	+12.1
IntTBdTr	10.82	...	+8.6
MuniBd	10.27e	−0.15	+6.0
STBdTr	10.03	−0.01	+5.6
STMuBdTr	10.02e	−0.02	+3.8
IDMuBdTr	10.86e	−0.06	+5.7
Acorn Funds:			
AcornInt	19.80	+0.21	+9.8
Acorn40	10.38	+0.14	NA
AcornF	15.40	+0.15	−3.1
Acorn20	9.72	+0.07	NA
AcornUS	13.62	+0.05	−2.6
AdsnCa p	28.23	+0.35	−3.3
Advance Capital I:			
Balanc p	16.78	+0.14	+10.0
Equity p	18.23	+0.27	+5.7
RetInc p	10.61	...	+6.4
Advantus Fds:			
BondA	10.37	−0.02	+5.5
BondB p	10.40	−0.01	+5.1
CStoneA	15.43	+0.23	−2.5
CStoneB p	15.23	+0.22	−3.2
EnterpA	13.14	+0.16	−9.2
EnterpB p	12.61	+0.15	−9.9
HorznA	24.60	+0.42	+26.4
HorznB p	23.52	+0.40	+25.7
Idx500A p	15.79	+0.24	+21.9
Idx500B p	15.72	+0.24	+20.9
IntBalA	11.04	+0.04	+1.9
MtgSecA	10.67	−0.01	+6.9
SpectmA	17.25	+0.21	+17.6
SpectmB p	17.14	+0.20	+16.9
VentureA	10.72	+0.09	−11.8
Aetna Class A:			
Balanced t	13.49	+0.11	+12.5
Bond t	10.50	−0.01	+7.9
Grow t	18.02	+0.25	+27.1
GrInc t	16.42	+0.24	+9.0
Intl t	12.42	+0.11	+13.9
SmCo t	10.63	+0.10	−4.8
Aetna Class I:			
Ascent	11.57	+0.09	+0.1
Balanced	13.51	+0.11	+12.7
Bond	10.51	...	+8.3
Crossrds	11.45	+0.07	+0.7
Grwth	18.30	+0.25	+27.4
GrwIncm	16.47	+0.24	+9.2
IndPlLgCpI	15.02	+0.24	+26.5
Intl	12.47	+0.11	+14.4
Legacy	10.49	+0.05	+3.9
SmCo	10.93	+0.11	−4.6
Alger Funds A:			
CapApr	28.46	+0.49	+26.9
Growth	12.34	+0.20	+35.0
MidCpGr	19.94	+0.33	+18.6
SmCap	8.55	+0.07	−0.2
Alger Funds B:			
Balncd p	17.00	+0.20	+25.6
CapApr t	27.98	+0.48	+26.0
Growth t	12.12	+0.19	+34.0
MidCpGr t	19.57	+0.32	+17.6
SmCap t	8.40	+0.08	−0.9
Alger Retirement Fds:			
CapAppr	10.49	+0.12	+49.3
Growth	13.88	+0.22	+39.0
MidCpGr	9.64	+0.17	+23.9
SmCap	18.33	+0.18	+11.8
Alliance Advisor Cl:			
GwthAdv	48.72	+0.89	NA
IntlAdv	15.67	+0.09	+7.4
PrGrAdv	28.40	+0.54	+39.4
QusarAdv	22.20	+0.09	−15.5
TechAdv	70.96	+1.86	+48.9
PrGrInst	14.00	+0.28	NS
Alliance Cap A:			
Allian p	5.62	+0.15	−10.1
BalanA p	14.90	+0.12	+11.9
CpBdA p	13.19	−0.02	−0.5
GlbDlGvA p	5.77	...	−24.1
GlbEvA p	5.24	+0.03	−11.6
GlbSA p	9.63	+0.04	−4.0
GlStrInA p	10.35	+0.01	+1.8
GovtA p	7.72	+0.01	+9.0
GrInvA p	14.55	+0.15	+21.0
GrIncA p	3.61	+0.05	+14.2
GwthA p	48.38	+0.89	+21.3
HiYldA p	10.23	−0.02	−1.7
InsMuA p	10.31	−0.01	+5.6
IntlA p	15.70	+0.09	+7.2
LtdMtGA p	9.58	...	+6.9
MrtgA p	8.57	...	+5.7
MMSA p	6.62	+0.01	+6.3
MuCA A p	11.34	...	+6.5
MuFLA p	10.42	−0.01	+6.2
MuICAA p	14.29	−0.01	+6.4
MuMA A p	11.34	−0.01	+6.8
MuNYA p	10.31	−0.01	+5.9
MuPA A p	10.61	−0.03	+6.2
NtlMuA p	11.01	−0.01	+5.8
NEur p	20.35	+0.17	+20.6
NAGvA p	7.62	+0.03	+6.4
PrGrthA p	28.16	+0.53	+39.0
QusrA p	22.08	+0.09	−15.7

Name	NAV	Net Chg	YTD %ret
ReEInvA	10.74	−0.11	−21.0
SelPremA p	10.72	+0.20	NS
StrBalA p	18.85	+0.12	+16.1
TechA p	70.46	+1.85	+48.5
WldPlvA p	10.08	+0.05	+6.2
Alliance Cap B:			
AllAsia t	5.96	−0.02	−15.7
Allian t	5.16	+0.14	−10.7
BalanB t	14.43	+0.12	+11.1
CnstvInv t	12.75	+0.06	+12.2
CpBdB t	13.19	−0.02	−1.1
GlbSB t	8.77	+0.04	−4.7
GlDGvtB t	5.78	...	−24.8
GlStrInB t	10.35	+0.01	+1.2
GovtB t	7.72	...	+8.2
GwthB t	38.37	+0.70	+20.5
GrIncB t	3.57	+0.05	+13.4
GrInvB t	14.65	+0.14	+20.1
HiYldB t	10.23	−0.02	−2.3
InsMuB t	10.30	−0.01	+4.9
IntlB t	14.74	+0.09	+6.4
LtdMtGB t	9.58	...	+6.2
MrtgB t	8.58	...	+5.1
MMSB t	6.64	+0.01	+5.5
MuCA B t	11.33	−0.01	+5.7
MuFLB t	10.42	−0.01	+5.5
MuICAB t	14.29	−0.01	+5.6
MuNJB t	10.52	−0.01	+6.3
MuNYB t	10.31	−0.01	+5.2
MuOHB t	10.42	...	+5.3
MuPAB t	10.61	−0.02	+5.6
NtlMuB t	11.00	−0.01	+5.1
NEurB t	19.30	+0.17	+19.9
NAGvB t	7.64	+0.03	+5.6
PrGrthB t	26.93	+0.51	+38.1
QusarB t	19.87	+0.08	−16.4
ReEInvB t	10.71	−0.11	−21.5
SelPremB p	10.67	+0.20	NA
StrBalB t	15.33	+0.10	+15.3
TechB t	67.29	+1.76	+47.5
UtilInc t	15.00	+0.12	+18.7
WldPrivB t	9.83	+0.04	+5.5
Alliance Cap C:			
Allian t	5.15	+0.14	−11.0
CpBdC t	13.19	−0.02	−1.1
GlbDlGvC p	5.78	...	−24.8
GovtC t	7.72	...	+8.2
GrIncC t	3.58	+0.05	+13.7
GwthC t	38.39	+0.70	+20.5
HiYldC p	10.23	−0.02	−2.3
InsMuC t	10.30	−0.01	+4.9
IntlC t	14.74	+0.08	+6.4
LtdMtGC t	9.58	...	+6.2
MMSC t	6.64	+0.01	+5.5
MrtgC t	8.58	...	+5.1
MuCA C t	11.33	−0.01	+5.7
MuFLC t	10.42	−0.01	+5.5
MuNJC t	10.52	−0.01	+6.3
MuNYC t	10.31	−0.01	+5.2
MuOHC t	10.42	...	+5.3
N EurC t	19.31	+0.16	+19.8
NtlMuC t	11.00	−0.01	+5.1
NAGvC t	7.64	+0.03	+5.6
PrGrthC t	26.97	+0.51	+38.1
QuasarC t	19.88	+0.07	−16.4
ReEInvC t	10.72	−0.10	−21.4
TechC t	67.27	+1.76	+47.4
WldprivC t	9.83	+0.04	+5.4
AlpineIntlRe	13.30	...	−0.7
AlpineUSRe	12.45	−0.06	−25.6
Am Skandia Adv Fds:			
ACStBaX t	11.57	+0.10	+14.0
FHiYdBB t	9.79	−0.01	+4.0
FHiYdBX p	9.78	−0.02	+3.9
FSmCapX t	9.79	+0.11	−3.9
INV EqX	12.24	+0.09	+12.5
InvEqIA	12.24	+0.09	+12.9
InvEqIB	12.25	+0.10	+12.5
InvEqIC t	12.25	+0.10	+12.4
JanCapA	16.49	+0.30	+47.2
JanCapB	14.72	+0.27	+46.6
JanCapC	14.69	+0.27	+46.5
JanCapX	14.73	+0.28	+46.6
JanOvrA p	11.23	+0.12	+12.3
JanOvrB p	11.18	+0.12	+11.8
JanOvrC p	11.19	+0.12	+11.9
JanOvrX	11.17	+0.12	+11.7
LabGlA p	11.03	+0.17	+10.6
LabGlB p	11.03	+0.16	+10.3
LabGlC p	11.01	+0.16	+10.1
LabGlX p	11.02	+0.17	+10.2
MarCpGrB p	11.06	+0.19	NA
MarCpGrC p	11.05	+0.19	NA
MarCpGrX p	11.08	+0.20	NA
RSVaGrX p	11.69	+0.26	+16.9
TotRtBdB p	10.70	...	+5.8
TotRtBdX p	10.70	−0.01	+5.7
TRInEqX t	10.02	+0.10	+9.9
TRSmCVA	8.85	+0.01	−15.7
TRSmCVB p	8.80	+0.02	−16.1
TRSmCVC p	8.80	+0.01	−16.2
TRSmCVX	8.79	+0.01	−16.2
AmanaGrowth	8.00	+0.09	+7.5
AmanaIncome	19.59	+0.04	+10.6
AmUtlFd	31.91	+0.42	+13.2
Amer AAdvant Inst:			
BalInst	14.82	+0.10	+7.1
GrInInst	21.39	+0.22	+3.8
IntBdInst	10.56	...	+8.9
IntlInst	17.27	+0.07	+7.9
S&PInst	16.14	+0.25	+23.6
StBndInst	9.58	...	+5.5
Amer AAdvant Plan:			
BalPlan	14.60	+0.10	+6.8
GrInPlan	21.12	+0.22	+3.5
IntlPlan	17.09	+0.07	+7.7
Amer Century:			
Balanced	20.13	+0.19	+12.7
EqGro	21.94	+0.35	+18.9
EqInc	6.19	+0.05	+10.8
GlGold f	5.68	...	NE

Name	NAV	Net Chg	YTD %ret
IncGro	29.11	+0.43	+22.1
NatRes	10.53	−0.02	−7.3
Real	12.61	−0.08	−19.1
StrAgg	6.59	+0.07	+9.3
StrConv	5.61	+0.02	+8.5
StrMod	6.26	+0.05	+9.5
Util	16.91	+0.24	+22.9
Value	5.91	+0.05	+2.6
Amer Century Benham:			
AZIntMu	10.81	−0.01	+6.0
Bond	9.80	...	+7.0
CaHYMu	9.85	−0.02	+6.8
CaInsTF	10.60	−0.03	+6.5
CaIntTF	11.33	−0.02	+5.9
CaLgTF	11.69	−0.03	+6.7
CaLtdTF	10.47	−0.01	+4.9
FlIntMu	10.67	−0.01	+6.6
GNMA	10.69	...	+6.1
HighYld	9.07	−0.03	−1.3
HiYldMu	10.23	−0.01	NS
Int TF	10.61	−0.01	+5.9
IntlBnd	12.40	...	+17.5
IntTrBd	10.19	...	+7.7
ITreas	10.76	...	+9.3
Lg TF	10.82	−0.02	+6.4
LtdBnd	9.99	...	+6.3
Ltd TF	10.23	...	+5.1
LTreas	10.77	−0.01	+13.2
PrmBnd	10.32	...	+8.0
SGov	9.56	...	+6.0
STreas	9.93	...	+6.4
Tg2000	94.25	−0.01	+8.9
Tg2005	76.50	+0.05	+15.1
Tg2010	61.28	+0.04	+16.1
Tg2015	49.11	+0.04	+15.5
Tg2020	36.08	+0.05	+16.7
Tg2025	31.36	+0.06	+22.8
Amer Century 20th:			
EmgMkt	3.26	+0.01	−22.0
Gift	18.40	+0.23	−21.0
Gl Grwth	5.15	+0.07	NA
Grwth	30.88	+0.42	+28.6
Heritage	10.61	+0.18	−7.7
IntDisc	9.14	+0.09	+12.1
Intl Gr	9.37	+0.14	+14.4
New Opp	5.36	+0.05	+2.1
Select	54.73	+0.96	+28.5
Ultra	34.06	+0.52	+24.8
Vista	9.82	+0.15	−20.9
Amer Express IDS A:			
BluCpA	11.00	+0.17	+17.3
BondA	5.16	−0.01	+5.6
CalA	5.41	−0.01	+6.0
DEIA	9.99	+0.15	+8.4
DiscvA	10.79	+0.14	−8.0
EmgMkA	3.54	+0.01	−33.1
EqSelA	14.75	+0.19	+8.0
EqValA	12.19	+0.18	+6.1
ExtlA	3.93	−0.01	−5.0
FdInA	5.11	...	+6.7
GlBal	6.13	+0.02	+16.0
GlBdA	6.29	−0.01	+7.7
GloGrA	8.41	+0.05	+21.2
GwthA	36.54	+0.50	+15.4
HiYdA	4.69	...	+5.7
InsrA	5.68	−0.01	+5.6
IntlA	11.38	+0.04	+11.7
MassA	5.61	...	+6.0
MgdAllA	11.27	+0.09	+5.5
MichA	5.61	−0.01	+5.8
MinnA	5.44	...	+5.9
MutlA	14.37	+0.14	+7.3
NYA	5.35	...	+5.8
NwDA	28.62	+0.45	+20.0
OhioA	5.55	...	+5.8
PreMtA	5.64	−0.09	−9.5
ProgA	8.59	+0.10	−8.5
RschOpA	7.32	+0.13	+16.6
SelectA	9.37	...	+8.3
SmColA	5.94	+0.07	−10.1
StockA	27.24	+0.29	+12.6
StrAgA	20.73	+0.38	+7.4
TE BdA	4.18	−0.01	+5.6
UtilInA	9.68	+0.13	+17.7
Amer Express IDS B:			
BluCpB t	10.91	+0.17	+16.5
BondB t	5.16	−0.01	+4.8
DiscvB t	10.48	+0.13	−8.7
DivrEqB t	9.99	+0.14	+7.6
EmgMkB p	3.49	+0.01	−33.5
EqSelB t	14.49	+0.18	+7.2
EqValB t	12.17	+0.18	+5.3
ExtlB t	3.93	−0.01	−5.7
FdInB t	5.11	...	+5.9
GlBal	6.10	+0.01	+15.1
GlBdB t	6.29	−0.01	+7.0
GloGrB t	8.27	+0.05	+20.4
GwthB t	35.47	+0.48	+14.6
HiYdB t	4.69	...	+4.9
InsrB t	5.68	−0.01	+4.9
IntlB t	11.28	+0.03	+10.8
MgdAllB t	11.19	+0.09	+4.8
MNTaxB p	5.44	...	+5.2
MutlB t	14.26	+0.13	+6.4
NwDB t	28.12	+0.44	+19.2
PreMtB t	5.54	−0.08	−10.1
ProgB t	8.43	+0.09	−9.2
RschOpB	7.19	+0.13	+15.8
SelectB t	9.37	...	+7.5
SmColB t	5.85	+0.08	−10.6
StockB t	27.06	+0.30	+11.8
StrAgB t	20.02	+0.36	+6.6
TE BdB t	4.18	−0.01	+4.8
UtilInB t	9.67	+0.12	+16.7
Amer Express IDS Y:			
BluCpY	11.01	+0.18	+17.4
BondY	5.16	−0.01	+5.7
DiscvY	10.81	+0.14	−7.9
DEIY	9.99	+0.14	+8.4
FdInY	5.11	...	+6.8
GloGrY	8.42	+0.05	+21.4
GrwthY	36.71	+0.50	+15.5
HiYdY	4.69	...	+5.8
IntlY	11.38	+0.03	+11.7
MgdAllY	11.27	+0.09	+5.6
MutlY	14.37	+0.14	+7.3
NwDY	28.65	+0.44	+20.1
ProgY	8.60	+0.10	−8.4
SelectY	9.37	...	+8.3
StockY	27.25	+0.30	+12.7
AmerExpStrGT p	31.72	+0.50	+20.0
AmerExpStrGr p	38.54	+0.52	+15.3
American Funds:			
AMutl p	28.86	+0.34	+11.7

Name	NAV	Net Chg	YTD %ret
A Bal p	16.58	+0.10	+9.1
Amcp p	16.77	+0.27	+23.1
Bond p	13.69	...	+5.1
CapIB p	46.92	+0.40	+10.4
CapW p	16.20	+0.02	+10.2
CapWGr p	24.77	+0.20	+13.2
Eupac p	27.58	+0.23	+12.2
FdInv p	30.32	+0.50	+12.2
Govt p	13.44	...	+8.0
Gwth p	23.15	+0.42	+23.3
HiInMuni	16.07	−0.01	+5.0
HI Tr p	14.12	...	+0.8
Inco p	18.57	+0.09	+8.0
IntBd p	13.58	...	+6.9
ICA p	29.93v	−2.31	+18.4
LtdTEBd p	15.04	...	+5.6
NEco p	24.25	+0.41	+21.6
N Per p	22.14	+0.27	+24.0
SmCp p	24.46	+0.27	−5.9
TxEx p	12.63	−0.01	+6.2
TECA p	16.68	−0.02	+6.3
TEMd p	16.24	...	+5.9
TEVA p	16.61	−0.01	+5.8
Wsh p	34.82	+0.61	+16.2
A GthD	9.44	+0.13	+0.1
A Heritg	0.32	−0.01	−67.3
A HeritgGr	0.12	...	−14.3
Amer Natl Funds:			
Grth	5.51	+0.09	+13.3
Inco	27.78	+0.28	+10.1
Triflex	19.28	+0.17	+11.2
Am Perform:			
AggGro	11.76	+0.05	−19.2
Balan p	13.27	+0.14	+18.8
Bond	9.74	...	+8.4
Equity	17.11	+0.26	+19.4
GroEq p	13.59	+0.21	+39.2
IntBd	10.47	...	+6.8
IntmTxF	11.00	−0.01	+5.9
ShTrInc	10.12	...	+7.2
Amerindo Tch	12.27	+0.30	+66.7
Amsouth Fds Classic:			
Balance	14.39	+0.10	+11.0
Bond	11.26	...	+9.6
EqInc	11.89	+0.14	+8.6
Equity	22.73	+0.27	+13.1
FlaTxF	10.55	...	+5.5
LtdMat	10.58	...	+7.4
MuniBd	10.20	−0.01	+5.5
RegEq	23.63	+0.35	−11.8
Amsouth Fds Premier:			
Balance	14.38	+0.10	+11.2
Bond	11.26	...	+9.8
Equity	22.70	+0.27	+13.4
FlaTxF	10.55	−0.01	+5.5
LtdMat	10.58	...	+7.5
MuniBd	10.21	...	+5.6
RegEq	23.65	+0.35	−11.6
AmeriStar Funds:			
CapGro p	NA	...	NA
CoreInc p	NA	...	NA
DivGr p	NA	...	NA
LimDurInc p	NA	...	NA
LimDurTn p	NA	...	NA
LimDurUS p	NA	...	NA
TnTEBd p	NA	...	NA
AmeriStar Trust Shs:			
CapGro	NA	...	NA
CoreInc	NA	...	NA
DivGro	NA	...	NA
LimDurInc	NA	...	NA
TnTe	NA	...	NA
AmeristockMF	34.28	+0.59	+27.9
AmwayTr p	8.43	+0.10	+9.1
Anchor Funds:			
CapAccum	20.41	+0.12	+14.4
IntlBd	8.21	−0.01	+10.1
ResrcComm	8.37	−0.01	−14.9
StratAsst	3.91	−0.06	NA
Aon Funds:			
AstAllo	16.23	+0.11	+0.7
GovSec	11.13	...	+10.9
IntlEq	11.96	+0.11	+10.8
REIT	11.33	−0.06	−17.5
S&P500	17.71	+0.27	+23.5
ApexMCapGr	6.07	−0.01	−11.1
Aquila Funds:			
AZ TF A	10.97	−0.01	+5.8
CO TF A	10.67	−0.01	+5.1
HI TF A	11.79	−0.01	+5.6
KY TF A	10.85	−0.01	+5.3
Nrgnt TF A	10.59	−0.01	+6.0
OR TF A	10.84	−0.02	+5.5
UT TF A	10.33	−0.02	+5.9
Aquinas:			
Balance	11.91	+0.10	+4.7
EqGrth	16.81	+0.31	+11.2
EqInc	15.09	+0.19	+2.6
FxInc	10.42	...	+7.5
ARCH Fds Inst Shares:			
Balance	11.75	+0.10	+8.3
GrInc	17.67	+0.19	+7.8
SmCap	11.65	+0.17	−15.7
ARCH Funds Inv A:			
GroEq	18.37	+0.33	+22.6
GroInc	17.67	+0.19	+7.8
IntmCorBd	10.33	−0.01	+9.0
MOTF	12.08	−0.01	+5.3
ShIntmMu	10.28	−0.01	+4.7
SmCap	11.69	+0.17	−15.7
ARCH Funds Trust:			
Balance	11.79	+0.09	+8.6
BdIdx	10.41	...	+9.1
EqIdx	14.57	+0.23	+23.0
EqInc	7.96	+0.09	+7.2
GrInc	17.75	+0.19	+8.1
GroEq	18.43	+0.33	+23.1
GvtCorpBd	10.57	...	+9.2
Intl	12.58	+0.10	+13.1
IntmCorBd	10.33	...	+9.3
MOTF	12.08	−0.02	+5.5

Source: *The Wall Street Journal*, December 18, 1998. Reprinted by permission of *The Wall Street Journal*,

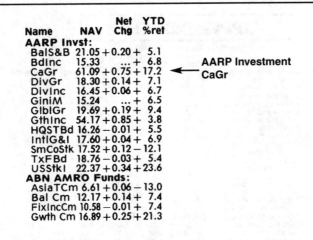

Name	NAV	Net Chg	YTD %ret
AARP Invst:			
BalS&B	21.05	+0.20	+ 5.1
BdInc	15.33	...	+ 6.8
CaGr	61.09	+0.75	+17.2
DivGr	18.30	+0.14	+ 7.1
DivInc	16.45	+0.06	+ 6.7
GiniM	15.24	...	+ 6.5
GlblGr	19.69	+0.19	+ 9.4
GthInc	54.17	+0.85	+ 3.8
HQSTBd	16.26	−0.01	+ 5.5
IntlG&I	17.60	+0.04	+ 6.9
SmCoStk	17.52	+0.12	−12.1
TxFBd	18.76	−0.03	+ 5.4
USStkl	22.37	+0.34	+23.6
ABN AMRO Funds:			
AsiaTCm	6.61	+0.06	−13.0
Bal Cm	12.17	+0.14	+ 7.4
FixIncCm	10.58	−0.01	+ 7.4
Gwth Cm	16.89	+0.25	+21.3

AARP Investment
CaGr

the fund's net asset value of $61.09. As you recall, this is calculated by totaling the market value of all securities owned by the fund and then dividing by the number of fund shares outstanding. In short, net asset value (NAV) equals a dollar value of the pool per mutual fund share. The third column reveals the increase or decrease in net asset value. In this case, AARP's capital growth fund increased by 75 cents a share. The last column reveals that the fund's shares had gained 17.2 percent for the year.

Each day's **Mutual Fund Quotations** begin with the **Lipper Indexes**, which show large funds' performances grouped by investment objective (see pages 168 and 170). For instance, you will note that the largest capital-appreciation funds had a year-to-date gain of 12.06 percent.

On Fridays *The Wall Street Journal* publishes **Performance Yardsticks** (see page 171). This table provides more detail than the daily **Lipper Indexes**, and summarizes the performance of all funds within categories, not just large funds. Note for instance that on page 171 the year-to-date gain of *all* capital appreciation funds was 11.71 percent, slightly less than the 12.06 percent gain of the largest funds. Friday's **Performance Yardsticks** also provide half-a-dozen key indexes with which investors can compare their fund's performance. You can also use this table to check the performance over the previous four weeks of the best- and worst-performing funds, as well as the year-to-date performance of the largest stock and bond funds.

LIPPER INDEXES

Thursday, December 17, 1998

| | Prelim. | Percentage chg. since | | |
Equity Indexes	Close	Prev.	Wk ago	Dec. 31
Capital Appreciation ...	2092.73	+ 1.34	+ 0.81	+ 12.06
Growth Fund	7411.83	+ 1.54	+ 1.21	+ 18.27
Small Cap Fund	575.89	+ 1.02	− 0.59	− 8.36
Growth & Income.......	6613.20	+ 1.44	+ 0.61	+ 9.61
Equity Income Fd	3528.86	+ 1.20	+ 0.52	+ 8.58
Science and Tech Fd ...	676.00	+ 2.46	+ 1.61	+ 34.97
International Fund	661.14	+ 0.66	− 0.65	+ 9.08
Gold Fund..................	71.30	− 1.28	+ 3.36	− 12.46
Balanced Fund...........	4117.65	+ 0.89	+ 0.43	+ 11.65
Emerging Markets......	57.93	− 0.01	− 3.98	− 30.21
Bond Indexes				
Corp A-Rated Debt......	805.27	+ 0.01	− 0.26	+ 7.45
US Government	305.91	+ 0.01	− 0.20	+ 8.07
GNMA	325.50	− 0.01	− 0.11	+ 6.23
High Current Yield......	762.25	− 0.13	− 0.71	− 0.69
Intmdt Inv Grade........	222.21	− 0.03	− 0.16	+ 8.02
Short Inv Grade	198.70	− 0.03	− 0.02	+ 5.67
General Muni Debt......	575.66	− 0.13	− 0.12	+ 5.82
High Yield Municipal ..	278.56	− 0.08	− 0.06	+ 5.54
Short Municipal	121.21	− 0.01	+ 0.08	+ 4.44
Global Income	212.30	+ 0.08	− 0.32	+ 6.28
International Income...	142.32	+ 0.07	− 0.38	+ 13.16

← Capital Appreciation

Indexes are based on the largest funds within the same investment objective and do not include multiple share classes of similar funds. The Yardsticks table, appearing with Friday's listings, includes all funds with the same objective.
Source: Lipper Inc. The Lipper Funds Inc. are not affiliated with Lipper Inc.

Ranges for investment companies, with daily price data supplied/by the National Association of Securities Dealers and performance and cost calculations by Lipper Inc. The NASD requires a mutual fund to have at least 1,000 shareholders or net assets of $25 million before being listed. NAV–Net Asset Value. Detailed explanatory notes appear elsewhere on this page.

The *Journal* publishes a report daily on the third-to-last page of the third (C) section called **Mutual Fund Scorecard**. (See the example from the Friday, December 18, 1998 *Wall Street Journal* on page 172.) It lists the top and bottom performers of a wide variety of mutual funds.

Each day, on the next-to-last page of the third section, the *Journal* publishes a chart and table titled **Fund Performance Derby**. It covers the same fund category as the **Mutual Fund Scorecard** which appears on the previous page of that day's edition. The chart compares the performance over the past year of the highlighted fund with the performance of similar funds, while the table provides data on the performance of the largest funds in the highlighted category. (See the example from the Friday, December 18, 1998 *Journal* on page 173.)

Performance Yardsticks

How Fund Categories Stack Up

INVESTMENT OBJECTIVE	YEAR-TO-DATE	FOUR WEEKS	ON A TOTAL RETURN BASIS ONE YEAR	3 YRS (annualized)	5 YRS (annualized)
Capital Appreciation	+ 11.71%	+ 3.37%	+ 13.74%	+ 14.53%	+ 13.67%
Growth	+ 16.28	+ 3.34	+ 17.57	+ 20.61	+ 18.14
Small-Cap Stock	— 8.24	+ 0.91	— 5.83	+ 10.43	+ 11.64
Mid-Cap Stock	+ 2.84	+ 1.84	+ 5.81	+ 13.98	+ 13.40
Growth & Income	+ 12.42	+ 1.74	+ 13.31	+ 20.63	+ 18.23
Equity Income	+ 7.79	+ 0.91	+ 8.82	+ 18.01	+ 16.32
Global (inc U.S.)	+ 7.98	+ 2.21	+ 9.03	+ 12.74	+ 10.76
International (non U.S.)	+ 8.81	+ 2.32	+ 8.32	+ 9.01	+ 7.23
European Region	+ 16.80	+ 2.87	+ 16.97	+ 20.15	+ 15.43
Latin America	— 41.72	— 11.98	— 39.37	+ 0.41	— 5.94
Pacific Region	— 9.19	+ 0.74	— 10.16	— 12.05	— 8.06
Emerging Markets	— 31.20	— 4.95	— 29.90	— 9.02	— 9.99
Science & Technology	+ 37.26	+ 9.16	+ 41.68	+ 21.21	+ 20.88
Health & Biotech	+ 17.09	+ 2.64	+ 18.91	+ 17.92	+ 20.24
Natural Resources	— 26.65	— 8.07	— 25.96	+ 0.04	+ 3.00
Gold	— 11.48	— 7.46	— 8.83	— 19.12	— 13.03
Utility	+ 13.74	+ 2.52	+ 17.23	+ 17.13	+ 13.23
Balanced	+ 10.41	+ 1.87	+ 11.34	+ 15.09	+ 13.38
Intermediate Corp. Debt	+ 7.81	+ 1.40	+ 8.25	+ 6.92	+ 6.51
Intermediate Gov't	+ 8.23	+ 1.21	+ 8.65	+ 6.76	+ 6.07
Long-Term Govt.	+ 8.94	+ 1.31	+ 9.57	+ 6.97	+ 6.62
High-Yield Taxable	— 1.33	+ 0.63	— 1.20	+ 8.21	+ 7.50
Mortgage Bond	+ 5.79	+ 0.70	+ 6.13	+ 6.32	+ 5.94
Short-Term US	+ 6.57	+ 0.81	+ 6.84	+ 5.91	+ 5.40
Long Term	+ 7.03	+ 1.76	+ 7.53	+ 7.03	+ 6.85
General US Taxable	+ 2.05	+ 1.05	+ 2.41	+ 7.27	+ 6.30
World Income	+ 2.90	+ 0.97	+ 3.14	+ 6.79	+ 5.44
Short-Term Muni	+ 4.66	+ 0.52	+ 4.94	+ 4.67	+ 4.34
Intermed.-Term Muni	+ 5.65	+ 0.86	+ 6.14	+ 5.81	+ 5.25
General L-T Muni	+ 5.69	+ 0.85	+ 6.34	+ 6.53	+ 5.67
High-Yield Muni	+ 5.31	+ 0.63	+ 6.00	+ 6.89	+ 6.07
Insured Muni	+ 5.86	+ 0.85	+ 6.49	+ 6.25	+ 5.61

← Capital Appreciation

Capital Appreciation	+ 11.71%	+ 3.37%	+ 13.74%	+ 14.53%	+ 13.67%
Growth	+ 16.28	+ 3.34	+ 17.57	+ 20.61	+ 18.14
Small-Cap Stock	— 8.24	+ 0.91	— 5.83	+ 10.43	+ 11.64
Mid-Cap Stock	+ 2.84	+ 1.84	+ 5.81	+ 13.98	+ 13.40
Growth & Income	+ 12.42	+ 1.74	+ 13.31	+ 20.63	+ 18.23
Equity Income	+ 7.79	+ 0.91	+ 8.82	+ 18.01	+ 16.32
Global (inc U.S.)	+ 7.98	+ 2.21	+ 9.03	+ 12.74	+ 10.76
International (non U.S.)	+ 8.81	+ 2.32	+ 8.32	+ 9.01	+ 7.23
European Region	+ 16.80	+ 2.87	+ 16.97	+ 20.15	+ 15.43
Latin America	— 41.72	— 11.98	— 39.37	+ 0.41	— 5.94
Pacific Region	— 9.19	+ 0.74	— 10.16	— 12.05	— 8.06
Emerging Markets	— 31.20	— 4.95	— 29.90	— 9.02	— 9.99

← Capital Appreciation: year to date (first column) of 11.71%

Mutual Fund Scorecard/Money Market

INVESTMENT OBJECTIVE: Holds financial instruments with average maturity of 90 days or less: intends to keep constant net asset value

(Ranked by 12-month return)	NET ASSET VALUE[1] NOV. 30	TOTAL RETURN[2] IN PERIOD ENDING NOV. 30				ASSETS SEPT. 30 (In millions)
		1 MONTH	SINCE 12/31	12 MONTHS	5 YEARS*	
TOP 15 PERFORMERS						
Zurich Yieldwise Money	$1.00	0.40%	5.11%	5.64%	**%	$1104.0
Olde Premium Plus MM[3]	1.00	0.42	5.09	5.57	5.48	2337.5
Wt:Money Market;K[3,5]	1.00	0.42	5.04	5.54	**	334.2
Aon:Money Market;Y[3,5]	1.00	0.42	5.02	5.50	5.25	774.7
Strong Heritage:Money[3]	1.00	0.42	4.99	5.49	**	1478.8
Scudder MM;Prem[3,5]	1.00	0.42	5.01	5.48	**	735.9
Transam Prem:Csh R;Inv[3,5]	1.00	0.42	5.00	5.48	**	72.3
Marshall:MM;A[3,5]	1.00	0.41	4.98	5.47	5.16	1620.8
TIAA/CREF:Money Market	1.00	0.41	4.96	5.45	**	178.0
Elfun Money Market[3,6]	1.00	0.41	4.95	5.44	5.20	182.8
Fremont:Money Market[3]	1.00	0.42	4.94	5.43	5.14	681.9
Vngrd MM Rsv:Pmm;Inv[3,5]	1.00	0.41	4.94	5.42	5.17	32328.3
Preferred:Money Market[3]	1.00	0.40	4.96	5.41	5.02	130.7
Citifunds Prem:Liq Rsvs[3]	1.00	0.41	4.93	5.41	5.19	724.6
JPM:Prime MM[3]	1.00	0.40	4.91	5.40	5.11	2600.4
AVG. FOR CATEGORY		0.37%	4.46%	4.89%	4.74%	
NUMBER OF FUNDS		330	312	310	200	
BOTTOM 10 PERFORMERS						
ASAF:JPM MONY Mkt;B[5]	$1.00	0.24%	3.08%	3.38%	**%	$13.3
Eaton Vance Money Mkt[3]	1.00	0.29	3.45	3.80	**	39.5
Franklin/Temp Money II[3]	1.00	0.34	4.01	4.40	**	88.9
Unified:Taxable MM[3]	1.00	0.34	4.02	4.41	**	65.4
Vintage Mut:Liqd Ast;S[3,5]	1.00	0.32	4.07	4.48	4.44	80.0
Equitrust MM Fund[3]	1.00	0.34	4.09	4.49	3.83	27.2
Oppenheimer Cash Rsv;A[3,5]	1.00	0.35	4.19	4.59	4.27	232.1
AIM:Money Market;A[5]	1.00	0.34	4.19	4.61	4.39	603.2
Five Arrows Shtm:USD;Shs[5]	1.00	N.A.	4.16	4.64	**	0.1
AIM Dollar;A[3,5]	1.00	0.34	4.26	4.65	4.38	299.1

[1] Some funds don't qualify for newspaper share price quotation
[2] Change in net asset value with reinvested dividends and capital gains
[3] No initial load
[4] Low initial load of 4.5% or less
[5] Fund has other share classes
[6] Fund may not be open to all investors

** Fund didn't exist in period
N.A.=Not available
* Annualized

Source: Lipper

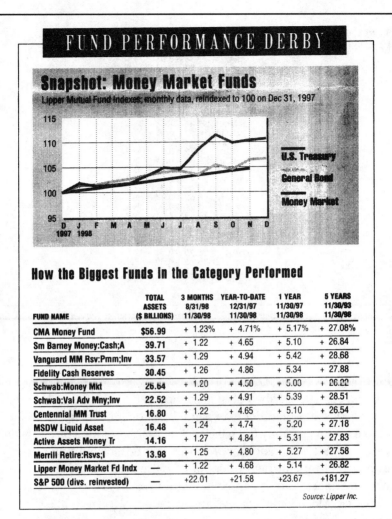

FUND PERFORMANCE DERBY

Snapshot: Money Market Funds

Lipper Mutual Fund Indexes; monthly data, reindexed to 100 on Dec 31, 1997

U.S. Treasury

General Bond

Money Market

How the Biggest Funds in the Category Performed

FUND NAME	TOTAL ASSETS ($ BILLIONS)	3 MONTHS 8/31/98 11/30/98	YEAR-TO-DATE 12/31/97 11/30/98	1 YEAR 11/30/97 11/30/98	5 YEARS 11/30/93 11/30/98
CMA Money Fund	$56.99	+ 1.23%	+ 4.71%	+ 5.17%	+ 27.08%
Sm Barney Money:Cash;A	39.71	+ 1.22	+ 4.65	+ 5.10	+ 26.84
Vanguard MM Rsv:Pmm;Inv	33.57	+ 1.29	+ 4.94	+ 5.42	+ 28.68
Fidelity Cash Reserves	30.45	+ 1.26	+ 4.86	+ 5.34	+ 27.88
Schwab:Money Mkt	26.64	+ 1.20	+ 4.50	+ 5.00	+ 26.22
Schwab:Val Adv Mny;Inv	22.52	+ 1.29	+ 4.91	+ 5.39	+ 28.51
Centennial MM Trust	16.80	+ 1.22	+ 4.65	+ 5.10	+ 26.54
MSDW Liquid Asset	16.48	+ 1.24	+ 4.74	+ 5.20	+ 27.18
Active Assets Money Tr	14.16	+ 1.27	+ 4.84	+ 5.31	+ 27.83
Merrill Retire:Rsvs;I	13.98	+ 1.25	+ 4.80	+ 5.27	+ 27.58
Lipper Money Market Fd Indx	—	+ 1.22	+ 4.68	+ 5.14	+ 26.82
S&P 500 (divs. reinvested)	—	+22.01	+21.58	+23.67	+181.27

Source: Lipper Inc.

But you can still invest in the overall stock market by selecting an *index fund* that places your capital in one of the better-known stock market barometers. For instance, *Vanguard Group* has an index fund, called the *500* (see page 174), that places all of its resources in the S & P 500. On Thursday, December 17, 1998, Vanguard's Index 500 had a net asset value of $110.10.

Vanguard 500
Net Asset Value $110.10 ➞

Vanguard Index Fds:

500	110.10	+1.70	+23.4
Balanced	18.26	+0.16	+14.3
EmerMkt r	7.88	+0.05	−21.1
Europe	24.88	+0.27	+23.9
Exten	30.21	+0.33	− 0.7
ExtenIst	30.25	+0.33	− 0.6
Growth	30.26	+0.43	+35.1
GrwthIst	30.27	+0.42	NS
InstIdx	109.42	+1.68	+23.5
InstPlus	109.43	+1.68	+23.6
ITBond	10.62	−0.01	+10.5
LTBond	11.44	+0.01	+12.5
MidCp	9.79	+0.15	NS
MidCpIst	9.80	+0.15	NS
Pacific	7.75	+0.02	+ 0.4
SmCap	21.41	+0.21	− 9.3
SmCapIst	21.44	+0.22	− 9.1
SmGth	8.68	+0.14	NS
SmVal	8.21	+0.07	NS
STBond	10.18	−0.01	+ 7.7
TotBd	10.34	...+	8.7
TotBdIst	10.34	...+	8.7
TotIntl	11.02	+0.09	+11.7
TotSt	26.25	+0.38	+17.0
TotStIst	26.26	+0.38	+17.1
Value	22.62	+0.39	+11.4
ValueIst	22.63	+0.39	NA

CLOSED-END FUNDS

The mutual funds described above are open-ended because they continually issue new shares in order to expand their pool of capital. They sell their shares to investors and buy them back. But after their initial offering, *closed-end funds* do not issue additional shares and do not buy them back. The shares of the close-end fund trade on an organized exchange or over-the-counter, and appreciate or depreciate with investor demand like any other share of stock. Meanwhile, the investment company has its initial (fixed) pool of capital with which to make investments.

The success of the fund's investments determines the net asset value of the fund's shares (a fluctuating numerator to be divided by a fixed denominator), which can differ from their market value (stock price) as determined by supply and demand. The stock price may be above net asset value, trading at a premium, or below, trading at a discount. Either way, the fund's management takes its fee for administering the fund.

Why would fund managers choose to be confined by a close-end fund rather than grow with a conventional open-end mutual fund? Because their pool of capital is not subject to the volatile swings generated by purchases and redemptions.

CLOSED END FUNDS

Thursday, December 24, 1998

Closed-end funds sell a limited number of shares and invest the proceeds in securities. Unlike open-end funds, closed-ends generally do not buy their shares back from investors who wish to cash in their holdings. Instead, fund shares trade on a stock exchange. The following list, provided by Lipper, shows the ticker symbol and exchange where each fund trades (A: American; C: Chicago; N: NYSE; O: Nasdaq; T: Toronto; z: does not trade on an exchange). The data also include the fund's most recent net asset value, share price and the percentage difference between the market price and the NAV (often called the premium or discount). For equity funds, the final column provides 52-week returns based on market prices plus dividends. For bond funds, the final column shows the past 12 months' income distributions as a percentage of the current market price. Footnotes appear after a fund's name. a: the NAV and market price are ex dividend. b: the NAV is fully diluted. c: NAV is as of Thursday's close. d: NAV is as of Wednesday's close. e: NAV assumes rights offering is fully subscribed. v: NAV is converted at the commercial Rand rate. w: Convertible Note-NAV (not market) conversion value. y: NAV and market price are in Canadian dollars. All other footnotes refer to unusual circumstances; explanations for those that appear can be found at the bottom of this list. N/A signifies that the information is not available or not applicable.

Thursday, December 24, 1998

Fund Name (Symbol)	Stock Exch	NAV	Market Price	Prem /Disc	52 week Market Return
General Equity Funds					
Adams Express (ADX)	♣N	32.13	26 1/2	– 17.5	23.3
Alliance All-Mkt (AMO)	N	42.96	42 3/8	– 1.4	52.1
Avalon Capital (MIST)	O	17.88	10 7/16	– 41.6	–13.0
Baker Fentress (BKF)	♣N	19.37	15 5/16	– 21.0	6.7
Bergstrom Cap (BEM)-s	A	199.00	172	– 13.6	33.5
Blue Chip Value (BLU)	♣N	10.31	10 1/8	– 1.7	5.1
Central Secs (CET)	A	28.68	24 7/8	– 13.2	–7.7
Corp Renaissance (CREN)-c	O	9.08	6 3/8	– 29.8	8.5
Engex (EGX)	A	9.44	6 13/16	– 27.9	–28.3
Equus II (EQS)	♣N	N/A	16 1/4	N/A	–25.5
Gabelli Equity (GAB)	N	11.20	11 7/8	+ 6.1	14.1
General American (GAM)	♣N	34.19	30 5/16	– 11.3	34.8
Librty AllStr Eq (USA)	♣N	13.98	12 13/16	– 8.4	13.3
Librty AllStr Gr (ASG)	♣N	12.66	11 1/8	– 12.1	7.1
MFS Special Val (MFV)	N	14.61	16 7/8	+ 15.5	–2.8
Morgan FunShares (MFUN)-c	O	N/A	8	N/A	49.5
Morgan Gr Sm Cap (MGC)	♣N	10.98	9 7/16	– 14.0	–11.3
NAIC Growth (GRF)-c	C	12.68	10	– 21.1	–39.9
Royce Micro-Cap (OTCM)	♣O	9.73	8 7/16	– 13.3	–15.4
Royce Value (RVT)	♣N	15.13	13 1/2	– 10.8	0.7
Salomon SBF (SBF)	N	18.54	18 7/16	– 0.5	25.1
Source Capital (SOR)	N	45.20	48 1/2	+ 7.3	5.3
Tri-Continental (TY)	♣N	33.92	28 1/4	– 16.7	27.4
Zweig (ZF)	♣N	11.84	10 15/16	– 7.6	–7.1
Specialized Equity Funds					
C&S Realty (RIF)	♣A	8.96	9 13/16	+ 9.5	–6.8
C&S Total Rtn (RFI)	♣N	14.00	14	0.0	–9.1
Chartwell D & I (CWF)	N	13.90	13 5/8	– 1.9	N/A
Delaware Gr Div (DDF)	N	15.33	18 3/8	+ 19.9	11.9
Delaware Grp Gl (DGF)	N	15.41	15 3/4	+ 2.2	–4.5
Duff&Ph Util Inc (DNP)	N	10.36	11 5/16	+ 9.2	20.9
Emer Mkts Infra (EMG)	♣N	9.58	7 5/16	– 23.7	–31.7
Emer Mkts Tel (ETF)	♣N	13.06	10 3/4	– 17.7	–11.0
First Financial (FF)	N	8.92	9 1/8	+ 2.4	–32.6
Gabelli Gl Media (GGT)	N	11.83	[illegible]	– 10.0	[illegible]
H&Q Health Inv (HQH)	♣N	18.66	14 5/16	– 23.3	–6.2
H&Q Life Sci Inv (HQL)	♣N	15.40	11 15/16	– 22.5	–6.4
Jardine Fl China (JFC)	♣N	7.58	5 5/8	– 25.7	–40.0
Jardine Fl India (JFI)-c	♣N	6.83	5 1/16	– 25.9	–25.7
Korea (KF)	N	9.42	8 11/16	– 7.7	28.7
Korea Equity (KEF)	N	3.78	3 1/2	– 7.4	9.8
Korean Inv (KIF)	N	4.66	3 7/8	– 16.7	–4.5
Latin Am Sm Cos (LLF)-a	N	5.99	5 15/16	– 0.8	–37.8
Latin Amer Disc (LDF)	N	8.50	6 13/16	– 19.9	–21.3
Latin Amer Eq (LAQ)	♣N	10.38	7 1/2	– 27.7	–36.6
Latin Amer Inv (LAM)	♣N	12.13	8 3/4	– 27.9	–29.6
Malaysia (MF)	N	2.88	4	+ 38.9	–40.2
Mexico (MXF)-c	♣N	N/A	11 9/16	N/A	–38.4
Mexico Eqty&Inc (MXE)-ac	N	7.07	5 5/16	– 24.9	–38.0
Morgan St Africa (AFF)	N	12.24	9 3/16	– 24.9	–14.1
Morgan St Asia (APF)	N	8.55	6 13/16	– 20.4	–4.0
Morgan St Em (MSF)	N	10.28	8 3/8	– 18.5	–13.8
Morgan St India (IIF)	N	8.99	6 5/8	– 26.3	–13.8
Morgan St Russia (RNE)	N	12.67	9 5/8	– 24.0	–44.9
New South Africa (NSA)	♣N	N/A	9 1/16	N/A	–18.1
Pakistan Inv (PKF)	N	2.53	1 15/16	– 23.3	–59.2
Portugal (PGF)	♣N	22.90	21 5/8	– 5.5	36.2
ROC Taiwan (ROC)	N	7.74	6 3/8	– 17.6	–17.9
Royce Global Trust (FUND)	♣O	5.33	4 3/4	– 10.9	–2.6
Scud Spain & Por (IBF)	N	15.13	14 11/16	– 2.9	33.3
Scudder New Asia (SAF)	N	11.56	9 1/4	– 20.0	0.0
Scudder New Eur (NEF)	N	23.71	20 1/8	– 15.1	34.8
Singapore (SGF)-c	♣N	7.75	6 9/16	– 15.4	–4.8
Southern Africa (SOA)	N	11.23	9	– 19.9	–21.3
Spain (SNF)	N	23.08	20 1/4	– 12.3	54.4
Swiss Helvetia (SWZ)	♣N	19.00	15 3/4	– 17.1	26.5
Taiwan (TWN)-ac	N	16.24	12 13/16	– 21.1	–13.7
Taiwan Equity (TYW)-ac	♣N	11.66	9 3/8	– 19.6	–6.6
Templeton China (TCH)-c	N	6.19	6 3/16	0.0	–18.6
Templeton Dragon (TDF)	N	10.15	7 5/8	– 24.8	–19.1
Templeton Em App (TEA)-c	N	9.69	9 11/16	0.0	–7.1
Templeton Em Mkt (EMF)	N	9.06	10 1/4	+ 13.1	–8.1
Templeton Russia (TRF)-c	N	9.19	9	– 2.1	–64.1
Templeton Vietnm (TVF)	N	9.04	6 7/8	– 23.9	–8.3
Thai (TTF)	N	3.75	6 1/4	+ 66.7	20.7
Thai Capital (TC)	♣N	N/A	4	N/A	10.4
Third Canadian (THD)-cy	T	20.28	16 35/64	– 18.4	–11.1
Turkish Inv (TKF)	N	5.48	4 7/16	– 19.0	–35.2
United Corps Ltd (UNC)-cy	T	64.82	46 1/2	– 28.3	9.4
United Kingdom (UKM)-a	♣N	15.36	14 1/4	– 7.2	16.7
Z-Seven (ZSEV)	O	N/A	7 9/16	N/A	–1.7

Fund Name (Symbol)	Stock Exch	NAV	Market Price	Prem /Disc	12 Mo Yield 11/30/98
U.S. Gov't. Bond Funds					
ACM Govt Inc (ACG)	N	8.60	9 5/16	+ 8.3	9.5
ACM Govt Oppty (AOF)	N	8.33	7 15/16	– 4.7	7.8
ACM Govt Secs (GSF)	N	8.56	8 9/16	0.0	10.3
ACM Govt Spec (SI)	N	6.99	6 5/16	– 9.7	8.7
Excelsior Income (EIS)-c	♣N	18.69	16 1/2	– 11.7	6.7
Kemper Int Govt (KGT)	♣N	7.78	7 9/16	– 2.8	7.7
MFS Govt Mkts (MGF)	N	7.43	6 1/2	– 12.5	7.2
MSDW Govt Inc (GVT)	♣N	9.52	8 7/8	– 6.7	6.6
RCM Strat Glbl (RCS)-a	N	11.30	9 11/16	– 14.2	9.8
U.S. Mortgage Bond Funds					
2002 Target Term (TTR)-c	N	15.06	14 3/16	– 5.8	6.1
Amer Sel Port (SLA)-c	N	13.11	11 7/8	– 9.4	9.1
Amer Str Inc II (BSP)-c	N	13.15	11 7/8	– 9.7	8.4
Amer Str Inc III (CSP)-c	N	12.56	11 5/8	– 7.4	8.9
Amer Str Income (ASP)-c	N	13.03	11 7/8	– 8.8	8.0
Franklin Univ (FT)	N	9.57	9 3/4	+ 1.9	8.4
High Inc Opp (HIO)	♣N	11.18	10 9/16	– 5.5	10.0
High Yld Income (HYI)	N	6.94	7	+ 0.9	10.0
High Yld Plus (HYP)-g	N	7.58	7 7/8	+ 4.0	10.0
Kemper High Inc (KHI)	♣N	8.71	9 15/16	+ 14.1	9.1
MSDW Hi Inc (YLD)	♣N	4.13	5 5/16	+ 28.6	11.7
MSDW Hi Inc II (YLT)	♣N	4.63	5 3/16	+ 12.1	13.4
MSDW Hi Inc III (YLH)	♣N	5.05	6 1/16	+ 20.0	11.7
Managed High Inc (MHY)	♣N	10.78	10 1/4	– 4.9	9.7
Managed High Pls (HYF)	N	12.56	12 5/16	– 2.0	N/A
Managed High Yld (PHT)	N	12.10	11 13/16	– 2.4	10.2
Morgan St Hi Yld (MSY)	N	14.52	15 15/16	+ 9.8	8.8
New Amer Hi Inc (HYB)	N	4.21	4 7/16	+ 5.5	11.8
Pacholder (PHF)-ac	♣A	15.19	16 1/4	+ 7.0	10.3
Prospect St High (PHY)-a	♣N	8.20	9 7/8	+ 20.5	12.2
Putnam Mgd HiYld (PTM)	N	12.38	14 1/2	+ 17.1	9.3
S B Hi Inc II (HIX)	N	13.17	12 1/4	– 7.0	N/A
Salomon HIF (HIF)	N	12.68	15 1/16	+ 18.8	9.3
Senior Hi Inc (ARK)	N	8.38	8 5/16	– 0.8	10.5
VK High Inc (VIT)	N	5.86	6 5/16	+ 7.7	10.2
VK High Inc II (VLT)	N	7.58	8 5/8	+ 13.9	10.5
Zenix Income (ZIF)	N	5.98	6 3/16	+ 3.5	11.0
Other Domestic Taxable Bond Funds					
ACM Mgd $ (ADF)	N	8.67	9 1/8	+ 5.3	14.0
ACM Mgd Income (AMF)	N	8.42	9 1/4	+ 9.9	10.0
Allmerica Secs (ALM)	N	11.82	11 1/4	– 4.8	7.6
BEA Income (FBF)	♣N	7.74	7 1/2	– 3.1	9.1
BEA Strategic Gl (FBI)	♣N	9.28	8 9/16	– 7.8	10.8
Bull&Bear US Gvt Sec (BBG)	♣A	14.30	13 1/2	– 5.6	8.7
CNA Income (CNN)-c	N	9.79	10 9/16	+ 7.9	8.9
Colonial Intrmkt (CMK)	♣N	10.96	10 9/16	– 3.6	8.7
Duff&Ph Util Cor (DUC)	N	14.41	15 1/8	+ 5.0	7.7
Franklin MultiInc (FMI)	N	10.97	9 7/8	– 9.9	7.6
J Han Income (JHS)	♣N	16.48	15 13/16	– 4.1	7.4
J Han Investors (JHI)	♣N	21.57	21 9/16	0.0	7.0
Kemper Multi Mkt (KMM)	♣N	10.24	9 1/2	– 7.2	8.8
Kemper Strat Inc (KST)	♣N	13.16	15 7/16	+ 17.3	10.6
Lincoln Income (LND)-c	♣N	N/A	14 5/16	N/A	8.1
MFS Charter (MCR)	N	10.30	9 7/8	– 4.1	8.2
MFS Intmdt (MIN)	N	7.66	6 15/16	– 9.4	7.3
MFS Multimkt (MMT)	N	7.28	6 9/16	– 9.9	8.7
MassMutual Corp (MCI)	N	N/A	23 9/16	N/A	4.7
MassMutual Part (MPV)	N	N/A	12 1/8	N/A	5.6
Op Fd Multi-Sec (OMS)	N	9.95	8 7/8	– 10.8	8.9
Putnam Mas Inc (PMT)	N	8.33	8 1/16	– 3.2	9.0
Putnam Mas Int (PIM)	N	8.00	8 1/16	+ 0.8	8.7
Putnam Prem Inc (PPT)	N	8.00	8 1/4	+ 3.1	8.8
USLife Income (UIF)	N	10.44	10 1/16	– 3.6	7.8
VK Income Tr (VIN)	N	7.80	7 7/8	+ 1.0	9.1
Zweig Total Rtn (ZTR)	♣N	8.32	8 7/8	+ 6.7	9.4
World Income Funds					
Alliance Wld $ (AWG)	N	10.20	11 1/16	+ 8.4	13.5
Alliance Wld $ 2 (AWF)	N	8.67	8 11/16	+ 0.2	13.4
BlckRk North Am (BNA)-c	N	11.83	10 1/16	– 15.0	8.4
Dreyfus Str Govt (DSI)	♣N	10.13	9 1/8	– 9.9	12.9
Emer Mkts Float (EFL)	N	10.56	10 15/16	+ 3.6	13.5
Emer Mkts Inc (EMD)	N	9.80	11 3/8	+ 16.1	16.0
Emer Mkts Inc II (EDF)	N	8.65	9 13/16	+ 13.4	13.9
First Aust Prime (FAX)	A	6.58	5 11/16	– 13.5	11.2
First Commonwlth (FCO)	N	13.18	10 11/16	– 18.9	8.7
Global Hi Inc $ (GHI)-a	N	13.12	10 11/16	– 18.5	11.3
Global Income Fund (GIF)	A	6.17	5 5/8	– 8.8	12.6
Global Partners (GDF)	N	10.18	[illegible]	[illegible]	[illegible]
Kleinwort Aust (KBA)-a	♣N	7.99	6 3/4	– 15.5	7.9

Source: *The Wall Street Journal*, December 28, 1998. Reprinted by permission of *The Wall Street Journal*,

The Wall Street Journal publishes a report on closed-end funds each Monday under the heading **Closed-End Funds**. You can find it in the index on page C1. Shown above is an example from the Monday, December 28, 1998 issue. Notice the broad array of investments and investment objectives. Notice also that you may be able to purchase shares in a fund at a substantial discount from its net asset value. This may signal an unusual and temporary investment opportunity.

RISKY BUSINESS

Margin and Option Trading

If you are confident a stock will rise, you may purchase it and realize your gain if your prediction proves true. But there are a number of ways you can

leverage your purchase in order to increase your gain (i.e., you can capture the increase on a larger number of shares of stock than you can currently afford to purchase). Your *leverage* is the ratio between the value of the shares you control (and from which you will reap a profit) and the amount of capital (money) you have invested. The smaller your investment and the larger the value of the shares you control, the greater your leverage.

For instance, under current regulations set by the Fed, you may borrow from your broker up to half the initial value of the shares of stock you purchase, which provides leverage of two to one. It's called *buying on margin*. If you buy $200 worth of stock from your broker, with a margin (your capital) of $100 (50 percent margin) and a $100 loan from the broker, and the stock doubles in value (from $200 to $400), you have made $200 on a $100 investment (less interest and brokerage costs) instead of $100 on a $100 investment that was not margined. That's leverage.

Options provide another opportunity to leverage your investment. They give you the right (option) to buy or sell stock at a stated price for future delivery at a premium (cost to buy the option). People do this for the same reason they buy or sell any stock: They think it's going up or down in value. Only in this case, they believe the market price of the stock will be higher or lower than the price at which they agreed to buy or sell it. Investors stand to gain if they can buy a stock below its market price (and can then sell it at the market price), or can sell it above market price (after having purchased it below market price).

For instance, suppose you had the option to buy a share of stock for $25 in a few months' time that currently trades at 23½, and you were convinced the stock would be trading at 28 by then. Wouldn't you pay a premium for the right to buy a $28 stock for $25? That's a good deal, as long as the premium is smaller than the spread between $25 and the $28 price at which you think the stock will trade. Conversely, if you were convinced that a stock, currently trading at 23½, would fall to 18, wouldn't you pay a fee (premium) for the right to sell it at $20, knowing you could obtain it at $18?

The excerpt from the Thursday, October 22, 1998 *Journal* shown on page 177 presents a summary of options trading on Wednesday, October 21, 1998. This report, called **Listed Options Quotations**, appears daily, and you can find it listed in the front-page indexes of the first (A1) and last (C1) sections. The excerpt on page 178 takes America Online (AOL) as an example.

The first column informs you that America Online closed at 106½ on Wednesday, October 21, 1998.

LISTED OPTIONS QUOTATIONS

Wednesday, October 21, 1998

Composite volume and close for actively traded equity and LEAPS, or long-term options, with results for the corresponding put or call contract. Volume figures are unofficial. Open interest is total outstanding for all exchanges and reflects previous trading day. Close when possible is shown for the underlying stock on primary market. CB-Chicago Board Options Exchange. AM-American Stock Exchange. PB-Philadelphia Stock Exchange. PC-Pacific Stock Exchange. NY-New York Stock Exchange. XC-Composite. p-Put.

MOST ACTIVE CONTRACTS

Option/Strike		Vol	Exch	Last	Net Chg	a-Close	Open Int
I B M	Nov 140	p 8,147	CB	4¼	− 3¼	142⅜	3,789
Infrmx	Nov 5	7,429	XC	⅞	+ ⅜	5½	33,124
Aliste	Nov 45	6,212	XC	1¼	− 2⅞	42½	4,284
Micsft	Nov 100	p 6,153	PC	1⅞	− 2¾	106⅞₁₆	6,910
ProvFn	Nov 70	5,910	PC	8⅜	+ ⅛	76¹¹⁄₁₆	9,494
DellCptr	Nov 55	5,839	AM	5⅜	+ 1¼	56¹⁵⁄₁₆	18,455
Aliste	Nov 40	5,609	XC	3⅞	− 3⅜	42½	864
I B M	Nov 140	5,575	CB	7	+ 1½	142⅜	7,793
Intel	Nov 90	5,480	AM	2	+ ⅝	87¹⁄₁₆	27,635
Ph Mor	Mar 47½	p 5,450	AM	2¹³⁄₁₆	− 1⁵⁄₁₆	49¹⁵⁄₁₆	2,002
Micsft	Jan 90	5,366	PC	19	+ 4	106⁷⁄₁₆	26,767
Micsft	Nov 105	5,173	PC	5⅛	+ 1¾	106⁷⁄₁₆	8,442
Intel	Jan 70	5,025	AM	17¾	− ⅛	87¹⁄₁₆	22,153
Intel	Jan 95	4,749	AM	3	+ ½	87¹⁄₁₆	22,536
DellCptr	Nov 60	4,537	AM	3	+ ¾	56¹⁵⁄₁₆	28,745
Disney	Jan 23⅜	4,305	XC	5	+ 2⅝	27⁹⁄₁₆	34,294
A M P	Nov 40	4,199	CB	1¾	− 1¼	40¹⁄₁₆	11,389
I B M	Nov 145	4,195	XC	4	+ ⅝	142⅜	5,518
Stratus	Nov 35	4,000	PC	2	− ¾		4,453
Microsft	Jan 00 80	3,920	PC	4	− 1½	106⁷⁄₁₆	37,805

Option/Strike		Vol	Exch	Last	Net Chg	a-Close	Open Int
Lucent	Nov 75	p 3,678	XC	2¾	− 2	79	8,370
Micsft	Nov 110	3,597	PC	2½	+ ⅝	106⁷⁄₁₆	11,058
I B M	Nov 135	3,589	CB	2¾	− 2¼	142⅜	3,238
Citigrp	Mar 40	3,571	XC	8½	− ¼	43¹⅜₁₆	13,412
AmBankrs	Nov 35	3,530	XC	⅝	− ⅜	42⁷⁄₁₆	5,907
Boeing	Jan 00 40	3,510	XC	7⅜	− ¾	36⅝	4,611
Citigrp	Mar 40	3,507	XC	3¼	+ ⅛	43¹⅜₁₆	11,034
I B M	Nov 130	3,483	CB	11¹⁄₁₆	− 1⁹⁄₁₆	142⅜	4,283
Boeing	May 35	3,170	XC	3½	...	36⅝	125
I B M	Nov 150	3,139	XC	1⅞	+ ⅛	142⅜	4,605
Microsft	Jan 00 85	3,120	PC	5⅝	− 1	106⁷⁄₁₆	18,420
Housh	Jan 35	3,119	XC	8⅞	− ¾	36⁷⁄₁₆	6,138
Microsft	Jan 01 85	3,104	PC	8	− 1⅞	106⁷⁄₁₆	56,551
Micsft	Nov 100	3,060	PC	8⅜	+ 3¼	106⁷⁄₁₆	9,372
Boeing	Nov 30	3,053	XC	5¼	− ¾	36⅝	2,580
Wm Lm	Nov 30	3,012	AM	5½	+ 1¼	72¹¹⁄₁₆	1,809
DellCptr	Nov 65	2,874	AM	1⅜	+ ⅜	56¹⁵⁄₁₆	25,715
AmBankrs	Nov 40	2,770	XC	2⅜	− ⁵⁄₁₆	42⁷⁄₁₆	1,871
Lucent	Nov 80	2,727	XC	3¼	+ 1¹¹⁄₁₆	79	29,793
AmBankrs	Jan 55	2,700	XC	...	− ¼	42⁷⁄₁₆	3,905

(Detailed call/put options listings table — Option/Strike, Exp., Call Vol./Last, Put Vol./Last — reproduced as printed.)

←Boeing

America Online →

Amazon	70	Nov	5	36¾	236	1¾
110	80	Nov	...	...	235	2⅝
110	95	Nov	23	20	216	5¼
110	100	Nov	249	16⅛	262	7⅛
110	105	Nov	527	13¼	231	8¾
110	110	Nov	188	10¾	199	11⅝
110	115	Nov	262	8	5	15½
110	120	Nov	321	6¼	3	18½
110	125	Nov	348	4⅜	135	23
110	130	Nov	633	3⅝	25	25
AmOnline	50	Jan	...	...	600	1⅛
106½	70	Nov	210	34⅞	38	⅝
106½	95	Nov	85	16¾	280	3⅞
106½	100	Nov	166	13	389	4¾
106½	105	Nov	1733	9½	651	7
106½	105	Jan	209	15⅜	60	12
106½	110	Nov	1898	6⅝	515	9⅛
106½	110	Jan	245	13	30	14½
106½	115	Nov	493	5⅛	13	12¼
106½	120	Nov	815	3⅜	17	15⅛
106½	125	Nov	228	2⅛	...	...
106½	130	Nov	974	1¼	...	...
106½	130	Jan	312	6¼	...	...
106½	140	Nov	261	7/16	...	...
AmBankrs	35	Nov	15	7	3530	⅝
42 7/16	35	Jan	...	...	1525	2½
42 7/16	40	Nov	518	3¾	2770	2⅜
42 7/16	40	Jan	766	6½	110	4½
42 7/16	45	Jan	229	3⅞	...	...
42 7/16	45	Apr	230	5⅞	...	...
42 7/16	50	Jan	1230	1⅞	...	...
42 7/16	55	Jan	2700	1	...	...
AmExpr	90	Nov	616	3¾	70	5⅞
87 1/16	95	Nov	1124	2 1/16	86	9¾

America Online call option at 6¼ on October 21, 1998

　　The second column lists the **strike prices**—from $50.00 to $140.00—at which you have the option of buying or selling the stock in the future. Note that some prices are higher and some prices are lower than the current price (106½). Think of the strike price as the price at which you strike a deal. The third column lists the month—on the third Friday—that your option expires.

　　The last four columns list the volume of options traded and the premium you must pay per share to purchase the option to buy *(call)* or sell *(put)* America Online stock at the applicable strike price of the months listed. Take January as an example. You could purchase an option at a strike price of 130. On October 21, 1998 you had to pay a premium of $6.25 (6¼) for the right (option) to buy a share of America Online stock at $130.00 (130) by the close of trading on January 15, 1999 (third Friday of January). Once the deal was struck, the seller (writer) of the option would be bound to deliver the stock to you at that price at any time before the close of business on January 15, 1999, *at your option*. That is, the decision to purchase is up to you. You can take it or leave it once you have paid the premium.

AmOnline	75	Jan	798	72	...	...
145 9/16	75	Jul	18	83 3/8	383	4 3/4
145 9/16	100	Jan	1316	45	35	1/16
145 9/16	100	Feb	...	...	552	2 7/16
145 9/16	115	Jan	60	30 7/8	390	3/16
145 9/16	120	Feb	130	33 1/2	788	6 3/8
145 9/16	120	Jul	729	46 1/2	7	18 3/4
145 9/16	130	Jan	445	16	1098	13/16
145 9/16	130	Feb	185	25 1/8	889	9 1/2
145 9/16	130	Apr	687	33 1/4	32	16 1/2
145 9/16	130	Jul	2211	43 3/4	112	23 5/8
145 9/16	135	Jan	773	11	678	1
145 9/16	135	Feb	122	24 1/4	408	11 3/4
145 9/16	135	Jul	440	43	10	25 3/8
145 9/16	140	Jan	1764	7 5/8	2329	2 3/8
145 9/16	140	Feb	830	20 3/8	564	14
145 9/16	140	Jul	743	36 3/4	6	26 5/8
145 9/16	145	Jan	2400	4 7/8	2320	3 5/8
145 9/16	145	Feb	634	20	423	16 1/2
145 9/16	150	Jan	3770	2 5/8	1393	7
145 9/16	150	Feb	3040	15 1/4	175	20
145 9/16	150	Apr	553	25 1/8	106	26
145 9/16	155	Jan	2697	1 1/4	2174	10 7/8
145 9/16	155	Feb	805	13	86	22 1/2
145 9/16	160	Jan	3439	15/16	489	16
145 9/16	160	Feb	1753	11 3/4	184	24 7/8
145 9/16	160	Apr	440	19 7/8	...	...
145 9/16	165	Jan	1393	7/16	21	16 3/8
145 9/16	165	Feb	814	10	39	25 1/8
145 9/16	170	Jan	756	3/16	43	26
145 9/16	170	Feb	1093	8 1/2	41	32
145 9/16	175	Jan	1324	3/16	44	30
145 9/16	175	Feb	706	7 3/4	167	36 1/4

America Online call option at 16 on January 13, 1999.

Source: *The Wall Street Journal*, January 14, 1999. Reprinted by permission of *The Wall Street Journal*,

Why would you buy such a contract? Because you were convinced that America Online would trade at more than \$136.25 (strike price of \$130 plus premium of \$6.25) plus commissions at any time before the third Friday in January of 1999. Then you would have the option to buy it at \$130.00 (the strike price) from the option writer and sell it at the higher market price. When the call price rises above the strike price, an option is said to be *in the money*.

Trading is done in round lots of 100 shares. Thus, on Wednesday, October 21, 1998, when America Online was \$106.50, you could have purchased an option for \$625 (100 × \$6.25) to buy 100 shares at \$130.00 by the close of business on Friday, January 15, 1999. How would you have done?

Not bad. As you can see above in the excerpt from the Thursday, January 14, 1999 *Journal*, America Online traded at 145 9/16 (\$145.5625) on Wednesday, January 13, 1999, just two days before the option expired. Back in November 1998 you paid a \$625.00 premium (100 × \$6.25) for the option to call (buy) 100 shares at \$130.00. By January 13, 1999 those shares were worth \$14,556.25 (100 × \$145.5625) on the market. Thus, by exercising

your option you could have purchased (called) $14,556.25 worth of securities for $13,000 (100 × $130.00), less your premium of $625.00, for a gain of $931.25 ($14,556.25 – $13,000.00 – $625.00 = $931.25) on your $625.00 investment in only a few months time. That's leverage!

Notice that purchasing the option provided you with a much higher return than buying America Online (AOL) stock at $106.50 on October 21, 1998. By January 13, 1999 AOL stock had appreciated by 36.7 percent ($145.5625 – $106.50 = $39.0625 return of 36.7 percent on $106.50 investment), considerably less than the 149 percent ($931.25 return on $625.00 investment) gain on the option. But also notice that the option carried considerably greater risk. When a stock does not appreciate, you at least preserve your capital (you still have the stock). When an option expires, your money's gone (you have nothing).

You should know, however, that you need not purchase a stock underlying an option in order to realize your gain. You can sell the option instead. For instance, using the American Online example in the previous paragraphs, you will notice on page 179 that the option was in the money a few days before its expiration and traded at $16.00, a little more than the difference ($15.5625) between the market price ($145.5625) and the call price ($130.00). In other words, you could have sold the option for $16.00 on January 13, 1999 to another investor and reaped your gain of $975.00 ($16.00 × 100 – $6.25 × 100 = $975.00) on an initial investment of $625.00 ($6.25 × 100) for a return of 156 percent ($975.00 / $625.00) without purchasing the underlying stock. As a matter of fact, most investors never intend to buy the underlying stock. Instead, they hope to sell their option at a profit.

Thus, if you buy a call, you're speculating that the stock's price will rise sufficiently to earn you a return (spread) over and above the premium you must pay to buy the option. But suppose it doesn't? Suppose the stock rises only a little, or even falls in value, so that you have the option to buy a stock at a price greater than market value? What then? Would you have to buy the stock from the option writer at the strike price? No, because you have only purchased an option to buy. There's no requirement to do so. You can let the option expire without exercising it, and you have only lost your premium.

A rising market motivates investors to buy calls. They hope the price of their stock will shoot up and they will be able to exercise their option and recover their premium, and then some. This does not necessarily mean that option writers (people who sell the option) are counting on the market to stay flat or even fall. The call writer may have decided to sell a stock if it reaches a certain target level (i.e., take his or her gain after the stock rises a certain number of points). If it does rise, the call writer will receive the increment and the

premium; even if it doesn't, he or she will still receive the premium. Thus, income is the primary motive for writing the option. Instead of waiting for the stock to move up to the target level, the seller writes a call. If it doesn't move up to that price, he or she will still have earned the premium. If it does, he or she will get premium plus capital gain.

Now let's consider the other kind of option and turn to the Wednesday, November 11, 1998 issue of the *Journal* (see below), using *Boeing* as our example. Suppose you had believed on Tuesday, November 10, 1998 that Boeing stock would fall substantially below its current market value of $41.1875 (41³⁄₁₆) and had purchased a put contract. The option writer would have been obliged to buy Boeing from you at the strike price regardless of current market value. Your option to sell at the strike price would give you an opportunity to buy at the lower market value (assuming your forecast was correct) and sell at the strike price to profit on the difference.

The last column in the example provides the put-contract premiums. Notice the $1.25 (1¼) premium for the May 1999 contract at a strike price of 35. If Boeing fell below $33.75 (strike price less premium, or $35.00 – $1.25) before the May 1999 expiration date, you could buy Boeing at the (lower) market price and sell (put) it to the option writer at the (higher) contract price of $35.00. The difference, less the premium and any brokerage fees, would be your profit.

Let's turn to page 182 to see what happened. You did not have to wait until May 1999. Boeing fell to $31.8750 (31⅞) by December 3, 1998, and your put was *definitely* in the money. You could have purchased Boeing at the market price of $31.8750 and sold it to the option writer for $35.00, for a gain of $3.125 per share less the $1.25 premium and any brokerage fees.

To be precise, your premium would have been $125.00 (100 × $1.25). When Boeing fell to $31.875, you could have purchased 100 shares at $3,187.50 (100 × $31.8750) in the market and exercised your option to sell for $3,500 (100 × $35.00), for a gain of $187.50 ($312.50 of gain on the stock less $125.00 of premium) on an initial investment of $125.00. Again you have to subtract the broker's fee from your profit.

Boeing	35	May	5	8¾	205	1¼	← Boeing put option at 1¼ on
41³⁄₁₆	40	Dec	58	2⅞	240	1¼	November 10, 1998
41³⁄₁₆	40	Feb	105	4	3114	2¼	
41³⁄₁₆	45	Nov	622	³⁄₁₆	222	4⅛	
41³⁄₁₆	45	Feb	266	1¾	...	...	

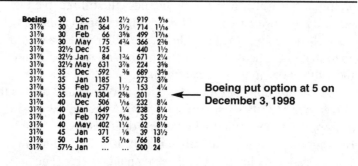

Boeing	30	Dec	261	2 1/2	919	9/16
31 7/8	30	Jan	364	3 1/2	714	1 1/16
31 7/8	30	Feb	66	3 5/8	499	1 7/16
31 7/8	30	May	75	4 3/4	366	2 3/8
31 7/8	32 1/2	Dec	125	1	440	1 1/2
31 7/8	32 1/2	Jan	84	1 3/4	671	2 1/4
31 7/8	32 1/2	May	631	3 7/8	224	3 5/8
31 7/8	35	Dec	592	3/8	689	3 5/8
31 7/8	35	Jan	1185	1	273	3 7/8
31 7/8	35	Feb	257	1 1/2	153	4 1/4
31 7/8	35	May	1304	2 5/8	201	5
31 7/8	40	Dec	506	1/16	232	8 1/4
31 7/8	40	Jan	649	1/4	238	8 1/4
31 7/8	40	Feb	1297	9/16	35	8 1/2
31 7/8	40	May	402	1 1/4	62	8 1/8
31 7/8	45	Jan	371	1/8	39	13 1/2
31 7/8	50	Jan	55	1/16	766	18
31 7/8	57 1/2	Jan	...	...	500	24

← **Boeing put option at 5 on December 3, 1998**

Source: *The Wall Street Journal*, December 4, 1998. Reprinted by permission of *The Wall Street Journal*,

Once again, be aware that most options buyers do not exercise their options. They sell them if they show a profit or let them expire if they do not. In this case, the premium had risen to \$5.00 for a net gain of \$3.75 (\$5.00 – \$1.25 = \$3.75, i.e. premium at sale less premium at purchase equals your gain). For 100 shares, that works out to \$375.00 (\$3.75 × 100 = \$375.00). What a bonanza on an initial investment of \$125.00!

If you guessed wrong and Boeing rose, so that the market price exceeded the strike price, you wouldn't want to exercise your option to sell at a price below market. Instead, you would permit your option to expire without exercising it. Your loss would be only the premium you paid.

Why would someone write a put? Because he or she is prepared to buy a stock if it should drop to a particular price. The writer earns the premium whether or not the option is exercised. If he or she believes the stock will rise in price, then the writer has little concern that an option holder will put it to him or her at less than the market price. And the writer has collected the premium. But if the market does fall, and falls sufficiently that the contract comes in the money, the writer will have to buy the stock at the contract price, which will be above market. That's not necessarily bad, since the writer had already planned to buy the stock if it fell to the strike price, and he or she has collected a premium, too.

In addition to simply playing the options market for profit, an investor can use options to hedge against price fluctuations of his or her investment in the underlying security. For instance, you can write (sell) call options against a stock you own. If the stock falls in value, you at least get to keep the premium. If it rises above the strike price, you keep the premium and realize a gain on the stock.

On the other hand, if you like a stock but think it will fall in value, write (sell) a put instead of buying the stock. If it doesn't fall, you collect the premium anyway. If it does fall, you still collect the premium and purchase the stock at a lower price.

These strategies involve *covered* options, i.e. stock you own or intend to buy. You can write *naked* options on stock you don't own and do not intend to buy. It seems like an easy way to collect a premium. But suppose you've written a call option thinking the stock couldn't possibly rise that far, and it does. You'll have to buy that stock at the market price if the option is exercised and then sell it at the lower strike price. That could hurt.

Conversely, you can write naked put options and collect your premium if you believe a stock could never fall *that* far. But if there's another crash like the one in 1987 and the market collapses, you may find yourself in the embarrassing position of having to buy stock at prices substantially above market in order to meet your obligation to sell the stock at the much lower market price. Where will you obtain the funds to cover the difference between the high price at which you purchased the stock and the low price at which you must sell it?

That's one of the reasons options are risky business.

One more comment above leverage. You can minimize risk if you buy options whose strike price is close to the market price, but you also reduce your relative gain. Leverage increases as the strike price increasingly deviates from the market price. That is, not surprisingly, risk and reward move together.

You can spread the risk of options investing by purchasing *index options* (see pages 184 and 185) in the entire market rather than an option on an individual stock. Instead of buying all the stocks in one of the stock market averages (or buying an index mutual fund), you can buy a put or call on an index option (such as the S & P 100), just as you can invest in options on individual stocks.

Take a look at the Wednesday, November 11, 1998 *Journal* excerpt from **Index Options Trading** on pages 184 and 185. You can see that options on the *Dow Jones Industrial Average*, the *NASDAQ*, and the *S & P 500* permit you to speculate on changes in the broad market without purchasing a large number of stocks.

But the index options on the *S & P 100* are the most widely traded (see page 185). Among the S & P 500 companies, options trading regularly occurs in the stocks of these 100 companies.

Finally, the investor can purchase longer-term options on some stocks. *The Journal* publishes a daily listing of **Leaps-Long Term Options**, as the example on page 186 illustrates.

INDEX OPTIONS TRADING

Tuesday, November 10, 1998

Volume, last, net change and open interest for all contracts. Volume figures are unofficial. Open interest reflects previous trading day. p–Put c–Call

CHICAGO

Strike	Vol.	Last	Net Chg.	Open Int.
CB TECHNOLOGY(TXX)				
Nov 295p	10	7/16 – 315/16		10
Call Vol.	10	Open Int.		571
Put Vol.	10	Open Int.		1,964

			Net	Open
DJ INDUS AVG(DJX)				
Dec 64p	170	1/8	...	8,591
Dec 65p	25	1/8	...	12
Dec 69p	16	1/4 – 11/16		25
Dec 70p	16	5/16	...	611
Dec 72p	105	9/16	...	30,653
Nov 76p	300	1/16	...	10,102
Dec 77p	10	1/2 + 1/16		6,730
Dec 78p	5	9/16 – 1/16		516
Nov 80c	12	93/8 + 1/4		4,425
Nov 80p	90	1/16 – 1/16		11,518
Dec 80c	2	95/8 – 1/4		8,566
Dec 80p	60	7/8	...	22,143
Mar 80c	18	123/8 – 1/8		262
Mar 80p	21	215/16 – 3/16		7,776
Jun 80p	35	35/8	...	1,171
Nov 82p	50	3/16 + 1/16		3,705
Nov 83c	5	57/8 – 1/8		880
Dec 83p	3	11/8 – 1/8		1,932
Nov 84c	25	53/8 – 5/8		907
Nov 84p	10	1/4 – 1/16		3,431
Dec 84c	103	61/2 + 1/4		1,796
Dec 84p	85	11/4 – 1/16		11,073
Mar 84c	1	91/8 – 1/8		393
Mar 84p	19	33/4 + 1/8		5,389
Jun 84p	2	45/8 + 1/2		420
Nov 85c	16	4 – 1/8		1,463
Nov 85p	74	3/8 – 1/8		3,906
Dec 85c	17	53/4 – 1/8		1,839
Nov 86c	41	3 – 3/4		1,258
Nov 86p	54	3/8 – 3/16		4,926
Dec 86c	1	5	...	1,293
Dec 86p	66	15/8 – 1/8		2,713
Nov 87p	32	1/2 – 5/16		1,820
Dec 87p	19	21/4 + 1/8		811
Nov 88c	56	23/16 + 1/8		1,303
Nov 88p	688	11/8 + 1/8		2,532
Dec 88c	168	31/4 – 3/8		6,907
Dec 88p	126	21/4	...	7,879
Mar 88c	2	63/8 – 1/4		376
Mar 88p	71	45/8 + 1/8		6,545
Jun 88p	8	53/4 + 3/8		2,112
Nov 89c	140	1 – 3/8		938
Nov 89p	383	19/16 + 1/16		2,297
Dec 89c	12	211/16 – 3/16		173
Dec 89p	117	213/16	...	532
Nov 90c	151	5/8 – 3/16		1,897
Nov 90p	318	21/8 + 5/16		880
Dec 90c	636	23/16 – 1/16		4,492
Dec 90p	30	3 – 1/8		4,076
Mar 90c	2	5 – 1/8		1,030
Mar 90p	42	53/8 + 1/8		226
Nov 91c	45	3/8 – 1/16		140
Nov 91p	3	23/8 – 3/8		170
Dec 91c	3	111/16 – 1/4		10
Nov 92c	43	1/4	...	481
Nov 92p	34	31/2 + 1/4		429
Dec 92c	3	13/16 + 1/16		1,854
Dec 92p	27	41/8 – 1/4		971
Mar 92c	3	37/8 – 3/8		1,155
Nov 93c	86	1/16 – 1/16		55
Nov 93p	5	41/4	...	
Dec 93c	5	1	...	
Nov 94c	5	1/16	...	2,952
Dec 94p	12	55/8 – 15/16		382
Nov 96p	40	71/8 – 47/16		12
Dec 96c	61	1/4 – 1/16		1,404
Mar 96c	450	27/8 – 1/8		8,103
Mar 100p	5	111/8 + 1/16		5,373
Call Vol.	2,350	Open Int.		97,336
Put Vol.	3,641	Open Int.		284,189

DJ TRANP AVG(DTX)				
Dec 280p	20	5 + 1		50
Nov 285p	2	31/8 + 11/2		8
Dec 300c	30	31/2 – 21/4		170
Dec 300p	50	41/2 + 25/8		40
Dec 310c	2	11/2 – 5/8		40
Call Vol.	32	Open Int.		1,296
Put Vol.	72	Open Int.		1,328

RANGES FOR UNDERLYING INDEXES

Tuesday, November 10, 1998

	High	Low	Close	Net Chg.	From Dec. 31	% Chg.
DJ Indus (DJX)	89.28	88.55	88.64	– 0.34	+ 9.56	+ 12.1
DJ Trans (DTX)	291.00	286.00	286.48	– 4.49	– 39.17	– 12.0
DJ Util (DUX)	311.10	306.84	310.08	+ 2.70	+ 37.01	+ 13.6
S&P 100 (OEX)	557.27	550.86	553.40	– 0.22	+ 93.46	+ 20.3
S&P 500 -A.M.(SPX)	1135.37	1122.80	1128.26	– 1.94	+ 157.83	+ 16.3
CB-Tech (TXX)	335.62	325.91	330.96	+ 3.63	+ 115.17	+ 53.4
CB-Mexico (MEX)	88.28	86.71	87.17	– 1.11	– 39.81	– 31.4
CB-Lps Mex (VEX)	8.83	8.67	8.72	– 0.11	– 3.98	– 31.3
MS Multintl (NFT)	652.07	642.48	647.40	+ 1.46	+ 115.85	+ 21.8
GSTI Comp (GTC)	200.65	195.68	198.69	+ 1.14	+ 55.23	+ 38.5
Nasdaq 100 (NDX)	1488.01	1457.67	1477.48	+ 9.85	+ 486.68	+ 49.1
NYSE (NYA)	560.17	555.47	557.42	– 1.72	+ 46.23	+ 9.0
Russell 2000 (RUT)	398.53	395.59	396.86	– 1.57	– 40.16	– 9.2
Lps S&P 100 (OEX)	111.45	110.17	110.68	– 0.04	+ 18.69	+ 20.3
Lps S&P 500 (SPX)	113.54	112.28	112.83	– 0.19	+ 15.79	+ 16.3
S&P Midcap (MID)	349.05	346.02	347.05	– 2.00	+ 13.68	+ 4.1
Major Mkt (XMI)	968.52	958.18	961.59	+ 0.31	+ 124.74	+ 14.9
HK Fltg (HKO)	192.60	192.57	192.60	– 2.42	– 21.96	– 10.2
IW Internet (IIX)	445.72	434.43	439.23	+ 4.60	+ 178.98	+ 68.8
AM-Mexico (MXY)	93.39	91.73	92.62	– 0.77	– 48.91	– 34.6
Institut'l -A.M.(XII)	654.49	645.06	649.31	+ 0.40	+ 124.23	+ 23.7
Japan (JPN)		145.88		– 0.83	– 11.76	– 7.5
MS Cyclical (CYC)	474.44	466.25	466.67	– 7.77	– 8.34	– 1.8
MS Consumr (CMR)	535.89	527.95	533.37	+ 3.47	+ 87.73	+ 19.7
MS Hi Tech (MSH)	691.76	671.80	681.58	+ 4.67	+ 234.06	+ 52.3
Pharma (DRG)	722.49	708.25	717.55	+ 5.43	+ 183.81	+ 34.4
Biotech (BTK)	169.83	166.15	166.38	– 3.45	+ 3.96	+ 2.4
Comp Tech (XCI)	665.92	647.41	658.70	+ 6.47	+ 219.71	+ 50.1
Gold/Silver (XAU)	80.54	77.75	78.10	– 0.93	+ 3.91	+ 5.3
OTC (XOC)	267.29	262.16	264.95	+ 1.09	– 473.00	– 64.1
Utility (UTY)	348.47	341.56	347.54	+ 6.46	+ 37.51	+ 12.1
Value Line (VLE)	890.46	883.67	885.77	– 4.69	+ 8.93	+ 1.0
Bank (BKX)	763.76	753.99	754.54	– 12.44	– 0.81	– 0.1
Semicond (SOX)	278.07	270.76	275.98	+ 0.20	+ 12.35	+ 4.7
Top 100 (TPX)	1119.75	1104.44	1111.53	+ 0.57	+ 201.91	+ 22.2
Oil Service (OSX)	68.49	64.59	64.66	– 4.51	– 49.71	– 43.5
PSE Tech (PSE)	379.26	372.24	376.21	+ 1.20	+ 85.65	+ 29.5

Strike	Vol.	Last	Net Chg.	Open Int.
GS TECH COMPOSITE(GTC)				
Dec 180c	1	24	...	
Call Vol.	0	Open Int.		0
Put Vol.	0	Open Int.		0

NASDAQ-100(NDX)				
Nov 1100p	2	7/16 – 1/2		342
Nov 1200p	20	3/8 – 3/8		543
Dec 1200p	5	7 – 23/8		733
Nov 1220p	20	3/4 – 5/8		618
Dec 1240p	1	10 – 22		162
Nov 1260p	34	1 – 11/4		385
Dec 1300c	1	170 + 41/4		1,185
Dec 1300p	288	11/2 – 3/4		1,114
Dec 1300p	1	14 – 7		661
Nov 1320p	111	21/4 – 11/2		251
Nov 1340p	52	2 – 11/2		136
Dec 1360p	63	31/2 – 31/2		170
Nov 1380c	10	102 + 7		624
Nov 1380p	67	61/2 – 2 1/4		541
Dec 1380c	53	129 + 17		150
Dec 1380p	3	251/8 – 51/8		164
Nov 1400c	10	771/4 + 31/4		336
Nov 1400c	511	7 – 71/4		309
Dec 1400p	1	118 – 29		540
Dec 1400p	107	30 – 15/8		236
Jan 1400p	2	49 – 14		30
Nov 1420c	45	787/8 + 281/8		332
Nov 1420p	22	11 – 21/2		383
Nov 1440c	2,004	611/8 + 245/8		2,643
Dec 1440p	402	133/4 – 111/4		309
Dec 1440c	2	85 + 61/2		198
Nov 1440p	2,276	44 – 121/4		264
Nov 1460c	46	433/4 + 77/8		666

Strike	Vol.	Last	Net Chg.	Open Int.
Nov 1460c	28	173/4 – 95/8		159
Nov 1480c	649	25 + 21/8		2,023
Nov 1480c	14	263/8 – 87/8		133
Dec 1480c	1	587/8 + 5		46
Dec 1480p	122	55 – 353/8		17
Nov 1500c	531	16 + 4		622
Nov 1500p	87	421/2 – 1/2		10
Dec 1500c	4	501/2 + 11/4		123
Dec 1520c	39	107/8 + 45/8		827
Dec 1520c	2,250	40 + 14		68
Nov 1540c	92	51/8 + 33/16		832
Nov 1540c	1	33 + 8		53
Nov 1560c	32	21/4 + 11/4		111
Nov 1580c	3	3/4 + 3/8		271
Dec 1580c	23	171/2 + 45/8		536
Dec 1580p	1	112 – 587/8		4
Call Vol.	5,802	Open Int.		18,221
Put Vol.	4,602	Open Int.		20,852

RUSSELL 2000(RUT)				
Dec 285p	10	115/16 – 213/16		6
Nov 300p	3	1/8 – 13/16		103
Nov 345p	10	1/2 – 9/16		235
Dec 345c	6	543/4 – 13/4		56
Dec 345p	6	23/4 + 1/4		67
Dec 360c	3	353/8 – 6		1
Dec 360c	4	31/2 ...		4,114
Jan 360p	2	40 + 11		100
Nov 370c	1	251/2 – 35/8		1,736
Nov 370p	100	13/8 – 1/8		1,431
Dec 370c	4	131/8 + 121/16		251
Nov 375c	4	213/4 – 41/8		2,017
Nov 380c	15	181/4 – 23/8		380
Dec 380c	4	233/8 – 1/4		360

Continued

Strike		Vol.	Last	Net Chg.	Open Int.
Dec	380p	4	7	− 2 1/8	404
Nov	385c	1	16 1/8	− 1/4	360
Jan	385c	2	26	+ 5 3/8	45
Jan	385p	2	12 3/8	− 2 5/8	45
Nov	390c	103	11	− 1/4	743
Nov	390p	38	3 1/4	− 1 3/8	66
Dec	390c	5	16 1/4	− 2 3/4	173
Nov	395c	16	6	− 5	964
Nov	395p	10	4 5/8	− 1 1/8	750
Jan	395c	5	20 5/8	− 3/8	14
Nov	400c	173	4	− 2	2,438
Nov	400p	500	7 5/8	− 1 1/8	72
Dec	400c	32	10 1/8	− 2 3/4	1,079
Jan	400c	3	17 1/8	− 2 1/4	3,688
Nov	405c	5	1 7/8	− 1 3/8	67
Jan	405c	1	14	...	2
Nov	410c	6	1 3/16	− 1/4	67
Dec	410c	25	6 1/4	− 2 3/8	126
Dec	410p	4	17 1/2	+ 1 3/8	41
Dec	420c	157	3 1/8	− 1	96
Dec	430c	22	1 3/4	− 1/8	525
Call Vol.		**648**	**Open Int.**		**41,427**
Put Vol.		**696**	**Open Int.**		**40,227**

S & P 100 INDEX(OEX)

Strike		Vol.	Last	Net Chg.	Open Int.
Nov	410p	256	1/16	...	15,192
Dec	410p	465	13/16	− 1/16	3,792
Nov	420p	73	1/16	...	11,317
Dec	420p	111	13/16	− 3/16	1,148
Nov	430p	481	1/16	− 1/16	8,915
Dec	430p	12	1 1/4	...	3,793
Jan	430p	1	3 3/8	+ 1/4	1,468
Nov	440p	229	1/8	− 1/16	8,952
Jan	440p	5	3 1/4	+ 1/8	210
Nov	450c	5	105 1/2	+ 9 1/2	124
Nov	450p	121	1/8	− 1/8	10,938
Dec	450p	444	1 5/8	− 7/16	3,119
Jan	450p	60	4	...	507
Nov	455p	360	3/16	− 1/16	3,293
Nov	460p	439	1/8	− 3/16	11,032
Dec	460p	148	2	− 1/2	2,002
Nov	465p	475	1/4	− 1/8	4,026
Nov	470c	72	82 5/8	− 2 3/8	383
Nov	470p	359	1/4	− 1/8	9,454
Dec	470c	10	87	+ 6 1/2	51
Dec	470p	38	2 1/2	− 1/4	1,261
Jan	470p	6	5 1/2	− 1	982
Feb	470c	10	96	...	...
Feb	470p	2	9 1/8	+ 1 1/8	9
Nov	475c	104	77 3/4	+ 4 3/4	653
Nov	475p	169	3/8	− 1/16	4,748
Nov	480c	283	72 3/4	− 1/4	3,050
Nov	480p	1,213	5/16	− 3/16	9,670
Dec	480p	19	3 3/8	− 3/8	3,692
Jan	480c	1	82	+ 2	481
Feb	480p	65	10 1/4	− 1/4	523
Nov	485c	110	73 3/8	+ 3 1/4	1,511
Nov	485p	451	7/16	− 1/8	5,689
Dec	485p	52	3 1/8	− 1/2	402
Nov	490c	5	64	...	2,842
Nov	490p	1,259	9/16	− 1/16	12,963
Dec	490p	49	4	− 1/4	3,727
Nov	495c	84	61 5/8	+ 2 5/8	1,068
Nov	495p	340	9/16	− 1/8	4,661
Dec	495p	46	4 3/8	− 3/8	479
Nov	500c	207	54	+ 7/8	2,384
Nov	500p	936	11/16	− 3/16	13,481
Dec	500c	5	60 5/8	− 1/8	2,276
Dec	500p	162	4 7/8	− 1/4	6,846
Jan	500c	3	67	+ 6 1/4	152
Jan	500p	165	9 1/4	+ 1/8	3,460
Feb	500p	20	13 1/2	+ 1 1/4	112
Nov	505c	331	48 5/8	− 2 3/8	1,789
Nov	505p	1,451	13/16	− 3/16	4,844
Nov	510c	208	47 1/2	+ 2 1/2	2,524
Nov	510p	2,026	1	− 1/8	9,348
Dec	510p	23	6	− 1/8	2,488
Nov	515c	455	42 7/8	+ 1 7/8	3,537
Nov	515p	1,208	1 1/4	− 1/16	7,007
Dec	515p	2	6	− 1/2	1,535
Nov	520c	438	34 1/2	− 1/4	6,184
Nov	520p	1,721	1 1/2	− 1/8	14,025
Dec	520c	1,924	43 1/2	+ 1/2	3,573
Dec	520p	193	7 1/2	+ 1/8	2,953
Jan	520c	6	51 1/4	− 1/8	1,581
Jan	520p	1	12 1/2	+ 1	611
Nov	525c	260	33 7/8	+ 2	4,962
Nov	525p	1,100	2	...	9,786
Dec	525p	30	8	− 1 1/2	2,098
Jan	525p	3	13 1/2	− 1 1/2	2
Nov	530c	732	25 7/8	− 1 3/8	7,717
Nov	530p	3,059	2 5/8	+ 1/8	13,035
Dec	530c	155	36 1/8	+ 2 1/8	2,013
Dec	530p	294	9	− 1 7/8	2,809
Jan	530p	4	14	− 1 1/4	746
Nov	535c	655	23 1/2	− 1/8	6,110
Nov	535p	2,392	3 3/8	+ 1/4	6,334
Dec	535c	6	33	+ 1/2	2,348
Dec	535p	154	12	+ 1 1/4	1,105
Jan	535c	3	36 3/8	− 1/8	53
Nov	540c	2,048	17	− 2 1/4	8,429
Nov	540p	4,122	4 1/4	+ 1/4	9,642
Dec	540c	1	27	− 1/2	4,082
Dec	540p	886	13	+ 1/4	3,534
Jan	540c	2	35 3/4	+ 1 3/4	531
Nov	545c	523	13	− 1 1/2	6,959
Nov	545p	2,858	5 1/2	+ 3/8	6,198
Dec	545c	4	25 1/2	+ 2 1/2	1,201
Dec	545p	13	13 1/8	− 1 1/4	274
Jan	545p	2	17 7/8	− 3 3/4	443
Nov	550c	3,212	9 3/4	− 1 3/4	8,402
Nov	550p	7,711	7 1/4	+ 7/8	8,807
Dec	550c	2,005	22	+ 7/8	3,290
Dec	550p	261	16 1/2	+ 3/4	1,759
Jan	550c	363	28 1/2	+ 1/2	4,738
Jan	550p	88	20 1/4	− 1 3/4	1,335
Feb	550p	172	25 3/4	+ 7/8	14
Nov	555c	5,455	6 3/4	− 1 1/2	9,628
Nov	555p	2,544	9 1/4	+ 1	4,007
Dec	555c	119	17	+ 1/2	2,885
Dec	555p	213	17 1/8	− 7/8	577
Jan	555c	32	26 1/8	+ 2 1/8	578
Jan	555p	30	23 1/2	+ 1/2	119
Nov	560c	5,149	4 3/8	− 1 1/8	14,520
Nov	560p	721	11 1/2	+ 3/4	3,290
Dec	560c	148	15 7/8	+ 1 3/8	3,157
Dec	560p	69	17 3/4	− 2 3/4	1,900
Jan	560c	50	20 1/4	− 1 1/8	300
Jan	560p	5	24 3/4	...	85
Feb	560p	5	31 1/4	+ 2 3/4	22
Nov	565c	3,642	2 5/8	− 7/8	6,721
Nov	565p	346	14 1/8	− 1 1/8	105
Dec	565c	27	12 7/8	+ 2 1/4	2,388
Jan	565p	2	26 3/4	+ 2 1/4	10
Nov	570c	3,574	1 5/8	− 1/2	7,811
Nov	570p	62	19 5/8	+ 3/8	206
Dec	570c	115	9	+ 1/4	4,595
Dec	570p	8	23 1/2	+ 1 1/2	99
Jan	570c	50	15 5/8	+ 1 1/8	1,018
Feb	570c	100	21 1/2	− 1/4	243
Nov	575c	1,392	13/16	− 5/16	5,890
Dec	575c	12	7 3/8	− 1/8	806
Nov	580c	1,822	7/16	− 1/8	9,398
Dec	580c	111	5 5/8	+ 3/8	5,782
Dec	580p	4	31 1/4	− 1 1/4	35
Jan	580c	1	10 7/8	− 1/4	1,051
Jan	580p	1	33 3/4	+ 1 3/4	105
Feb	580c	100	16 1/2	...	...
Nov	585c	324	3/16	− 1/16	6,668
Dec	585c	136	4 3/8	...	8
Nov	590c	230	1/8	− 1/16	4,219
Nov	590p	2	39	+ 1 7/8	4
Dec	590c	18	2 7/8	...	1,721
Nov	595c	50	1/16	− 1/8	996
Nov	600p	2	49 1/2	+ 10 1/4	2
Dec	600c	19	1 1/2	− 1/8	46
Jan	600c	112	4 1/2	− 1/4	198
Dec	610c	6	3/4	...	1,293
Dec	620c	209	3/8	− 1/16	1,235
Nov	630c	80	1/8	+ 1/16	467
Dec	630c	80	1/4	− 1/16	889
Call Vol.		**37,493**	**Open Int.**		**215,772**
Put Vol.		**42,844**	**Open Int.**		**316,497**

S & P 500 INDEX-AM(SPX)

Strike		Vol.	Last	Net Chg.	Open Int.
Dec	550p	27	1/8	...	8,436
Dec	700p	510	5/16	− 3/16	10,035
Nov	750p	50	1/16	− 1/16	2,290
Dec	750p	5,600	5/8	...	46,125
Nov	800p	151	1/16	...	9,006
Dec	800p	5,668	7/8	− 1/4	40,723
Nov	825p	30	1/8	− 1/8	3,075
Nov	850p	20	1/8	− 1/16	9,829
Dec	850p	1,177	1 3/4	− 1/4	20,570
Jan	850p	1,003	4 3/8	+ 3/8	2,867
Dec	875p	1	2 3/4	+ 1/2	15,707
Nov	900p	136	1/4	...	17,277
Dec	900p	2,223	2 1/2	− 1	62,576
Jan	900p	1,005	6 5/8	− 1/8	5,248
Dec	920p	11	3 1/4	− 7/8	2,065
Nov	925p	8	5/16	+ 1/16	9,229
Dec	925p	6	4 1/2	...	29,878
Jan	925p	5	8 3/4	+ 1	1,430
Nov	950p	183	3/8	− 3/8	20,997
Dec	950c	4	189 1/2	+ 3 1/2	6,384
Dec	950p	5,067	5 1/4	+ 1/4	43,861
Jan	950p	361	10	− 1	1,161
Dec	960p	5	5 1/8	− 1/8	1,730
Nov	975c	1	152	+ 2	7,485
Nov	975p	16	1/2	− 1/8	11,424
Dec	975p	45	6 5/8	+ 1/8	24,640
Dec	980p	100	7 3/8	− 2	6,545
Nov	995p	15	3/4	− 1/2	10,275
Dec	995c	20	142 3/4	+ 20 3/4	13,920
Dec	995p	131	7 1/2	− 1 7/8	23,043
Jan	995p	2	15	+ 1/2	186
Nov	1005p	373	1 3/16	− 5/16	17,165
Dec	1005c	21	136 1/2	− 1/2	39,751
Dec	1005p	8	8	− 1	22,443
Jan	1005p	10	14 1/4	− 2 3/4	1,908
Dec	1010p	30	9	+ 3/8	4,410
Nov	1020p	6	1 1/4	+ 1/16	1,218
Nov	1025c	1	108 1/2	+ 2 1/2	8,486
Nov	1025p	33	1 1/8	− 3/8	16,603
Dec	1025c	130	120	− 1	20,484
Dec	1025p	372	11	+ 1/2	32,306
Jan	1025p	40	17 1/2	− 2	4,877
Nov	1030c	2	106 1/2	+ 9	2,151
Nov	1030p	10	1 1/4	− 3/8	4,961
Dec	1040p	23	13	+ 1/8	6,241
Nov	1050c	300	76 1/2	− 1 1/2	13,538
Nov	1050p	1,277	2 1/2	− 1/4	12,168
Dec	1050c	26		...	18,230
Dec	1050p	806	13 1/2	+ 1/4	38,704
Jan	1050p	12	23	− 1	3,385
Nov	1055p	2	2 1/2	...	123
Nov	1060c	129	79 1/2	+ 7 3/4	3,250
Nov	1060p	57	3	− 1/2	3,628
Dec	1060c	20	90	+ 2 1/2	6,223
Dec	1060p	5	14 1/2	− 1/2	6,309
Nov	1070p	121	3 1/8	− 1 7/8	4,120
Nov	1075c	23	63 1/2	+ 3 1/2	12,569
Nov	1075p	323	3 1/8	− 1 1/8	13,450
Dec	1075c	2	77	− 2 1/2	41,809
Dec	1075p	1,329	16	− 1	25,712
Jan	1075p	31	28	+ 1/2	1,636
Nov	1080p	320	3 7/8	− 1 3/4	1,803
Dec	1080p	105	17 1/4	+ 1 1/4	1,265
Nov	1085p	1	4 7/8	− 2 3/8	224
Nov	1090c	12	50	+ 8	1,535
Nov	1090p	33	6 1/4	− 1/2	1,279
Dec	1090p	2	21	− 1	4,423
Nov	1095p	47	7 1/2	+ 1/4	1,359
Nov	1100c	210	35	− 5	13,079
Nov	1100p	671	7 3/8	+ 1/4	8,436
Dec	1100c	129	52	− 6 1/2	40,798
Dec	1100p	3,470	25	+ 2	38,734
Jan	1100c	15	69	− 9	1,478
Jan	1100p	64	32 1/2	− 3	3,303
Nov	1105p	2	8 7/8	− 1 3/8	55
Nov	1110c	30	31	+ 1 1/8	754
Nov	1110p	64	10 1/2	+ 1 1/4	1,029
Dec	1110c	15	50	− 2	642
Nov	1115p	13	10	+ 1	720
Nov	1120c	18	20 1/8	− 3 7/8	256
Nov	1120p	1,232	13 1/2	+ 1 1/2	752
Dec	1120c	1	44	− 1/2	4,941
Dec	1120p	93	27	− 3 3/8	3,528
Nov	1125c	501	22	+ 1	10,390
Nov	1125p	1,726	15 1/2	+ 2 1/2	7,064
Dec	1125c	2,591	40 1/2	− 3/4	23,488
Dec	1125p	3,071	32 1/2	+ 1	22,936
Jan	1125c	377	54 1/2	+ 7/8	6,432
Jan	1125p	217	41	− 1/2	3,563
Nov	1130c	129	14	− 5	1,741
Nov	1130p	170	17 1/4	[illegible] 1 1/4	[illegible]
Nov	1140c	29	13 1/8	+ 7/8	929
Nov	1140p	18	18	− 2 1/2	2,636
Nov	1145p	4	24 1/4	+ 6 1/4	29
Dec	1145c	260	28	− 1	2,072
Dec	1145p	195	38	...	2,164
Nov	1150c	3,240	5 1/2	− 2 3/4	21,737
Nov	1150p	43	29 3/4	+ 1 5/8	5,298
Dec	1150c	6,512	24	+ 1 1/2	63,284
Dec	1150p	2,631	38 1/2	− 1/2	11,210
Jan	1150c	53	40	+ 1	4,368
Nov	1160c	8	3 1/4	− 1	294
Dec	1160c	123	21 1/2	− 2 1/2	8
Nov	1170c	152	2 1/2	− 3/8	807
Dec	1170p	200	52	...	80
Nov	1175c	222	2	− 3/4	5,905
Nov	1175p	43	47	+ 1/2	303
Dec	1175c	240	12 3/4	− 1 1/4	18,080
Dec	1175p	7	51 1/2	− 4	4,050
Jan	1175c	13	26 3/4	+ 3/4	648
Jan	1175p	1	64	+ 4	95
Nov	1180c	50	1 1/8	− 7/8	37
Nov	1185c	104	7/8	...	...
Nov	1200c	39	3/8	− 1/8	7,804
Dec	1200c	3,054	5 1/8	− 1 1/2	21,658
Dec	1200p	1	72	+ 5 1/2	4,135
Dec	1225c	66	2 7/8	− 1/8	8,928
Dec	1240c	1	1 1/2	− 1/2	2,631
Dec	1250c	33	1 1/4	...	12,692
Dec	1275c	51	1/2	− 1/8	1,157
Jan	1275c	5	1 3/4	− 1 1/4	113
Nov	1300p	250	171	+ 7	595
Dec	1300p	350	169	+ 13	1,650
Dec	1350c	250	1/8	+ 1/16	11,100
Call Vol.		**30,940**	**Open Int.**		**923,412**
Put Vol.		**53,170**	**Open Int.**		**1,239,952**

AMERICAN

COMP TECH(XCI)

Strike		Vol.	Last	Net Chg.	Open Int.
Dec	565p	9	4 1/2	− 4 1/2	247
Dec	570c	10	93 3/4	+ 68 1/2	10
Dec	580p	10	7 7/8	...	...
Nov	595p	5	7/8	...	...

Source: *The Wall Street Journal*, November 11, 1998. Reprinted by permission of *The Wall Street Journal*,

LEAPS — LONG TERM OPTIONS

Option/Strike		Exp.	Call Vol.	Call Last	Put Vol.	Put Last
AT&T	45	Jan 01	1003	24	200	3
63 1/4	75	Jan 01	1002	8 5/8	...	...
AMD	15	Jan 01	...	...	500	1 15/16
25 3/4	20	Jan 00	174	10 1/4	10	2 3/4
AmerOn	155	Jan 00	137	38 1/4	100	36 1/4
AppleC	30	Jan 00	135	11 1/4	7	4 1/2
35 1/8	45	Jan 00	144	5 1/4	...	...
BellSth	55	Jan 01	3	30 1/4	450	2 3/4
Boeing	50	Jan 00	194	4	...	...
CBS	25	Jan 00	35	8	175	2 1/2
Cendant01	10	Jan 01	161	7 1/2	...	...
CUC Int	30	Jan 00	200	1 5/16	...	...
ChaseManh	60	Jan 01	207	12 1/2	...	...
Travelers	25	Jan 00	6	21 1/8	315	1 1/8
43 1/2	30	Jan 00	20	17	159	2 1/4
43 1/2	40	Jan 00	79	11 1/8	155	5 5/8
43 1/2	50	Jan 00	235	6 7/8	180	10 5/8
43 1/2	60	Jan 00	333	3 7/8	...	...
CocaCola	80	Jan 00	1501	7 3/4	30	12 1/8
ColHCA	25	Jan 00	150	3 7/8	...	...
22 1/2	40	Jan 00	250	1	...	...
Compaq	25	Jan 01	5	14	626	4
32 7/16	30	Jan 01	195	11 7/8	105	6 1/8
32 7/16	30	Jan 00	142	9 1/4	50	4 3/4
32 7/16	35	Jan 00	186	7	8	7 1/2
32 7/16	40	Jan 00	190	5 1/8	2	10
DellCptr	35	Jan 01	178	45 3/4	16	6 1/4
70 5/16	45	Jan 00	36	34 1/4	4030	6 1/2
70 5/16	50	Jan 00	238	31 3/4	41	7 3/4
70 5/16	60	Jan 00	298	25 3/4	654	11 1/2
70 5/16	65	Jan 01	1518	29 3/4	10	17 3/4
70 5/16	65	Jan 00	300	23 1/8	77	13 7/8
70 5/16	70	Jan 00	2261	20 1/4	1	16 1/2
70 5/16	70	Jan 01	197	28 1/4	90	20
70 5/16	75	Jan 00	370	19 1/8	16	18 3/4
70 5/16	80	Jan 01	147	23 3/8	10	26 1/2
70 5/16	90	Jan 01	386	20 1/4	6	32
DiamOffs	55	Jan 01	140	3 1/8	...	...
Disney	33 3/8	Jan 00	2003	3 3/4	2	6 1/4
EMC Cp	22 1/2	Jan 00	...	...	400	7/16
GenElec	90	Jan 00	135	14	...	...
GnMotr o	70	Jan 99	16	4 1/8	277	3 1/8
HewlettPk	75	Jan 00	214	7 1/4	...	...
Intel	90	Jan 00	181	22 3/8	69	9 1/4
97 9/16	90	Jan 01	295	30	3	13 5/8
97 9/16	100	Jan 00	361	17	15	13 1/4
97 9/16	110	Jan 00	511	13	4	19 3/4
97 9/16	120	Jan 00	2293	9 1/2	...	...
IBM	40	Jan 00	296	33 1/2	4	11
155 5/16	100	Jan 00	1	62 1/4	208	2 11/16
155 5/16	110	Jan 00	5	50 7/8	176	4 5/8
155 5/16	150	Jan 00	440	27 1/2	46	15 1/8
155 5/16	160	Jan 00	159	22 3/8	20	19 7/8
155 5/16	170	Jan 00	35	17	250	27 3/4
Lucent	90	Jan 01	377	23 1/2	6	17 1/8
MerrLyn	75	Jan 01	6	13 3/8	200	21
MicronTc	40	Jan 01	305	17 1/2	300	9 1/2
MicrnT	40	Jan 00	652	13 1/2	31	7 1/2
Microsft	75	Jan 00	3	43 3/8	1800	2 3/8
112 1/16	110	Jan 00	186	21 3/8	113	12
112 1/16	120	Jan 00	372	16 1/2	...	...
112 1/16	140	Jan 00	131	9 1/4	...	...
NorTel	55	Jan 00	...	...	250	14 1/4
Novell	15	Jan 00	153	3 1/4	...	...
Oracle	30	Jan 00	143	7 3/8	3	4 1/8
Pfizer	110	Jan 00	256	19 5/8	...	...
PhilMor	50	Jan 00	137	10	...	...
54 1/8	50	Jan 01	231	11	10	6 1/2
54 1/8	60	Jan 01	296	7 7/8	14	11 7/8
PlacerD	17 1/2	Jan 00	500	4	...	...
TelBrasl	50	Jan 00	215	3 1/8	...	...
TexInst	45	Jan 00	...	...	333	3 1/4
TWA	5	Jan 01	155	2	100	1 13/16
WalMart01	75	Jan 01	175	15 3/8	10	14 5/8
Yahoo	75	Jan 01	...	...	155	7 3/4

VOLUME & OPEN INTEREST SUMMARIES

CHICAGO BOARD			
Call Vol:	27,148	**Open Int:**	2,273,799
Put Vol:	21,369	**Open Int:**	2,018,321
AMERICAN			
Call Vol:	19,110	**Open Int:**	1,457,091
Put Vol:	7,888	**Open Int:**	750,310
PACIFIC			
Call Vol:	5,638	**Open Int:**	816,474
Put Vol:	4,215	**Open Int:**	536,104
PHILADELPHIA			
Call Vol:	2,159	**Open Int:**	570,513
Put Vol:	738	**Open Int:**	241,253
TOTAL			
Call Vol:	54,055	**Open Int:**	5,117,877
Put Vol:	34,210	**Open Int:**	3,545,988

Source: *The Wall Street Journal*, November 11, 1998. Reprinted by permission of *The Wall Street Journal*, ©1998 Dow Jones & Company, Inc. All rights reserved.

Many of these possibilities sound intriguing, easy, and potentially profitable. Keep in mind, however, that there are substantial commission costs. Furthermore, as in any leveraged situation, the potential for considerable loss exists. Options are not for novices, and even buying on margin exposes you to up to twice the risk of simply buying a stock with your own money. With leverage you can move a big rock with a small stick—but the stick can also break off in your hands, and the rock can roll back over your feet.

In fact, the whole options game is tricky and multifaceted. Consequently, before you can invest in options, your broker will evaluate your past investment experience and your current financial position. It will not be easy to qualify.

Short Interest

Instead of speculating on a price increase, some investors borrow stock from their broker in the hope of a price *decrease*. They sell the stock and leave the proceeds of the sale with their broker. If the stock falls, the borrower buys it back at the lower price and returns it to the broker, at which time the broker returns the funds from the original sale to the borrower. The advantage to the borrower is obvious: He or she pockets the difference between the high price when he or she borrowed and sold the stock and the low price when he or she bought and returned the stock.

Short Interest On Big Board Drops by 1.3%

Figure for Month Decreased
To 4.15 Billion Shares;
Amex Declined by 4.1%

By GREG IP
Staff Reporter of THE WALL STREET JOURNAL

NEW YORK—Short interest on the New York Stock Exchange fell this month from its record in September. Activity on the American Stock Exchange also fell.

Short interest on the Big Board fell 1.3% to 4,151,71,024 shares on Oct. 15 from 4,206,357,899 shares in mid-September.

On the Amex, the figure fell 4.1% to 195,354,322 shares from a revised 203,631,751 shares in mid-September.

The level of negative sentiment measured by the Big Board's short-interest ratio—sometimes considered a contrarian indicator, as short-interest shares eventually must be purchased—fell to 5.16 from 5.45 in the previous trading period. The short-interest ratio is the number of trading days at the exchange's average daily trading volume required to convert the total short-interest position.

Investors who sell securities "short" borrow stock and sell it, betting the stock's price will decline and that they will be able to buy the shares back later at a lower price for repayment to the lender. Short interest is the number of shares that haven't been purchased for return to lenders, and as such, is often viewed as an indicator of the degree of negative sentiment among investors in the stocks.

Investors may rely on short selling for other purposes, including as a hedging strategy related to corporate mergers and acquisitions, to hedge convertible securities and options, or for tax-related purposes.

Average daily Big Board volume was 805,126,000, up from 771,201,550 shares in the previous month. Short positions were calculated for the month including the 22 trading days through Oct. 15.

The next Big Board short-interest report will be published Nov. 20.

SHORT INTEREST HIGHLIGHTS

Largest Short Positions

Rank		Oct. 15	Sep. 15	Change
	NYSE			
1	Walt Disney Hl	72,549,631	75,350,099	−2,800,458
2	AT&T	48,887,859	41,616,230	7,271,629
3	Royal Dtch Ptri-1.25	41,067,683	6,486,371	34,581,312
4	Micron Technology	35,763,042	35,620,879	142,163
5	Wal-Mart Stores	35,435,033	37,758,929	−2,323,896
6	SBC Comm	33,904,389	33,246,460	657,849
7	Columbia/HCA	33,596,235	33,403,803	192,432
8	Home Depot	31,939,082	33,736,094	−1,796,402
9	Norwest	29,726,469	21,944,465	7,782,004
10	Compaq Comp	28,973,364	27,300,501	1,672,863
11	AmerHomeProd	28,893,453	27,976,265	1,017,188
12	Kmart	27,750,913	31,402,473	−3,711,560
13	Albertson's	25,263,917	18,072,600	7,191,317
14	Citigroup n	25,196,549	0	25,196,549
15	American Intl Group	24,873,294	17,547,925	7,325,369
16	Waste Management	24,324,065	23,991,604	332,461
17	Medianne Group	24,031,134	24,935,440	−904,306
18	Iomega	23,644,493	27,831,452	−4,186,959
19	Coca Cola	23,569,299	23,171,781	397,518
20	Conseco	22,547,525	22,625,304	−77,779
	AMEX			
1	Standard&Poors	28,619,498	27,684,288	935,210
2	Cablevision Sys	10,046,550	9,758,144	288,406
3	Trans World Cm	9,760,676	10,290,575	−529,899
4	Nabors Ind	7,664,480	9,576,856	−1,912,376
5	Viacom Clb	7,581,569	8,003,689	−422,120

Largest Changes

Rank		Oct. 15	Sep. 15	Change
	NYSE			
1	Royal Dtch Ptri-1.25	41,067,683	6,486,371	34,581,312
2	Citigroup n	25,196,549	0	25,196,549
3	Bankamer(New)	19,018,271	4,596,355	14,421,916
4	Furr's/Bishop's	8,983,289	3,287	8,980,192
5	Norwest	29,726,469	21,944,465	7,782,004
6	American Intl Group	24,873,294	17,547,925	7,325,369
7	AT&T	48,887,859	41,616,230	7,271,629
8	Albertson's	25,263,917	18,072,600	7,191,317
1	Tyco Intl Ltd	8,406,757	26,745,408	−18,338,652
2	Halliburton Co-Hldg	9,825,367	17,541,450	−4,816,083
3	Hilton Hotels	5,755,577	13,661,193	−7,905,616
4	Philip Morris	11,147,170	18,216,159	−7,068,989
5	Ctl & South West	2,118,666	8,181,649	−6,062,983
6	Bethlehem Steel	10,786,467	15,977,054	−5,190,587
7	Ikon Office Solution	4,829,726	9,976,295	−5,146,569
8	Bell Atlantic	16,771,142	21,725,506	−4,954,364
	AMEX			
1	Standard&Poors	28,619,498	27,684,288	935,210
2	Diamonds	2,434,392	1,507,679	926,713
3	Harken Energy	3,079,888	2,381,482	698,406
4	Softnet Systems	1,046,627	368,509	678,118
1	Nabors Ind	7,664,480	9,576,856	−1,912,376
2	Royal Oak Mines	2,683,172	4,496,129	−1,812,957
3	Standard&Poors	1,514,301	2,962,963	−1,448,362
4	Oncor	1,720,160	2,547,277	−797,117

NYSE Short Interest (In millions of shares)

Short Interest Ratio (NYSE)

Largest Short Interest Ratios

The short interest ratio is the number of days it would take to cover the short interest if trading continued at the average daily volume for the month.

		Oct. 15 Short Int	Avg Dly Vol-a	Days to Cover
	NYSE			
1	M.D.C Hld	3,946,516	39,814	99
2	Grupo TribasaADR	10,168,916	169,714	60
3	Penn Traffic	2,014,937	34,504	58
4	Homebase	4,995,177	85,580	58
5	Planet Hollywood	5,400,020	93,242	58
6	Amer Retirement	1,318,278	23,019	57
7	WHX Hldg	4,705,370	84,700	56
8	Applied Magnetics	11,228,804	213,176	53
9	Total System Svcs	3,208,861	61,819	52
10	MGM Grand	3,583,488	70,861	51
11	Fila Holding (Ads)	2,198,381	43,847	50
12	Oakley	7,620,670	154,309	49
13	Teleglobe	4,795,198	99,871	48
14	Titan	3,822,649	80,433	48
15	Fini Sec Assur Hld	3,419,080	73,747	46
16	Biovail Intl	5,123,985	122,266	42
17	Arcadia Financial	7,159,757	172,233	42
	AMEX			
1	Canadian Occ	3,439,015	51,319	67
2	Milestone Scientific	1,224,227	22,271	55
3	Thermolase	1,099,177	20,152	54
4	NVR	1,131,264	23,222	49
5	US Cellular	2,710,714	61,352	44

a-Includes securities with average daily volume of 20,000 shares or more. n-New. r-Revised. Issues that split in the latest month are excluded. The largest percentage increase and decrease sections are limited to issues with previously established short provisions in both months.

Largest % Increases

Rank		Oct. 15	Sep. 15	%
	NYSE			
1	Furr's/Bishop's	8,003,399	3,207	249,460.3
2	Scudder Sp+Fort	326,059	3,271	9,869.2
3	Kmart Financing I	956,070	10,809	8,745.1
4	Fletcher Ch-Ads Prst	466,642	8,300	5,522.2
5	Mediaone Group	568,106	12,200	4,556.6
6	Republic Services	272,150	5,970	4,458.6
7	Conseco Feline	287,030	8,672	3,209.8
8	TVX Gold	928,012	28,000	1,757.2
9	Astra AB (Cl A Adss)	1,134,708	90,411	1,155.1
10	Cable+Wireless(Ads)	537,450	64,958	727.4
11	Royal Dtch Ptri-1.25	41,067,683	6,486,371	533.1
12	Carramerica Realty	561,971	100,774	457.7
13	APT Inv&Mgt-Cl A	3,239,325	592,929	446.3
14	Wallace Computer	909,700	210,900	331.4
15	Bankamer	19,018,271	4,596,355	313.8
16	Banco Bilbao (ADR)	542,006	136,175	298.0
17	Converys	423,874	113,608	273.2
18	Gabelli Equity Trst	352,270	96,292	265.8
19	Rhone-Poulenc (Ads)	1,466,498	424,453	245.5
20	Crestar Financial	741,286	218,546	239.2
	AMEX			
1	Softnet Systems	1,046,627	368,509	184.0
2	Diamonds	2,434,392	1,507,679	61.5
3	Merrill Lynch Mlf	552,714	350,159	57.8
4	Tubos D Acero	943,722	645,134	46.3
5	Telephone&DataS	1,612,173	1,154,772	39.6

Largest % Decreases

Rank		Oct. 15	Sep. 15	%
	NYSE			
1	Usec	7,350	273,443	−97.3
2	Cascade Natural Gas	25,477	623,150	−95.9
3	Enron 6 1/4% '98	27,500	599,054	−95.4
4	Ctl Vermont Pub Svc	29,301	852,903	−95.4
5	DLJ High Yield Bond	74,846	1,296,735	−94.2
6	Allegheny Energy	243,441	2,645,826	−90.8
7	Wash. Water Pwr	66,296	705,519	−90.6
8	Cooker Rest	50,090	494,488	−89.9
9	Toronto-Domin	34,333	309,250	−88.9
10	CMP Group	90,601	778,430	−88.2
11	NB Capitl-D/S A	153,252	1,033,669	−85.2
12	Westcoast Energy	66,080	368,609	−81.5
13	Eastern Util Assoc	126,163	708,098	−80.8
14	Midamer Energy	126,757	608,383	−79.2
15	Energy East Hld	152,950	718,537	−78.7
16	Pilgrim Am Prime	113,152	512,092	−77.9
17	Banco Frances De	487,676	2,102,199	−76.8
18	Betafearborn	177,416	752,761	−76.4
19	Ashland	179,637	755,921	−76.4
20	Cliffs Drilling	129,000	519,630	−75.4
	AMEX			
1	Canadian 88 Energy	175,600	603,800	−70.9
2	Aqua Alliance	150,390	479,500	−68.0
3	Keane	283,914	864,328	−67.2
4	Standard&Poors Mid	1,514,301	2,962,963	−48.9
5	Royal Oak Mines	2,683,172	4,496,129	−40.3

	10/15/98 Volume	9/15/98 Volume	% Chg
Boston Properties	838,773	415,016	99.2
Boston Scientific	7,531,631	9,741,328	−22.7
Bowater Inc	356,225	1,029,624	−65.4
BP Prudhoe Bay Rlty	576,064	566,710	1.8
Briggs & Stratton	718,343	653,730	9.9
Brinker Intl	646,299	759,040	−14.9

	10/15/98 Volume	9/15/98 Volume	% Chg
Dover Corp	6,302,387	4,585,451	37.4
Dow Chemical Co	4,558,958	2,658,429	71.5
Dow Jones & Co Inc	3,033,636	3,749,779	−19.1
DPL Inc	686,662	1,005,719	−31.7
DST Systems Inc	1,669,675	1,268,970	31.6
DTE Energy Co-Hldg	8,016,289	8,306,016	−3.4

	10/15/98 Volume	9/15/98 Volume	% Chg
Helmerich & Payne	1,259,138	1,408,052	−10.6
Hercules Inc	1,354,325	1,327,589	10.3
Hershey Foods Corp	2,647,354	2,443,726	34.7
Hewlett-Pack (Dw)	10,254,456	7,417,238	38.3
Hibernia Corp (Cl A)	652,632	1,164,087	−43.9
Hilton Hotels Corp	5,755,577	13,661,193	−57.9

For example, if you borrow a $2 stock from your broker and sell it, you have $2. If it falls to $1, you can buy it on the market and return the stock to the broker and you keep the other dollar. This is called *selling short*. But what advantage does the broker gain? Brokers lend stocks because you have to leave the cash from your sale of the stock with them as collateral for the borrowed stock, and they can then lend (or invest) the cash at interest.

If you borrow a $2 stock from your broker in the hope that if falls to $1, you can easily return the stock to your broker if the market heads south. But what happens if you guess wrong and the stock rises to $3? You have only $2 and, therefore, cannot repurchase the stock for $3 in order to return it to your broker. How can the broker protect him or herself?

Your broker will insist that you maintain a substantial deposit (margin) at the brokerage firm in order to cover that risk, and, if the stock does appreciate, you will be required to deposit additional margin. This risk can be

appreciably reduced if you have a buy-stop order with your broker that instructs the broker to repurchase the stock for your account as soon as it rises to a level slightly higher than the price at which you borrowed it. Your loss will be held to a minimum.

Around the twentieth of each month, *The Wall Street Journal* reports **Short Interest Highlights** for stocks traded on the New York and American stock exchanges. It publishes a report for NASDAQ issues one week later (check the front-page index of the first section). The Thursday, October 22, 1998 and Wednesday, November 25, 1998 *Journal* excerpts (see page 187 and below) serve as examples. You can also use these reports to trace the short-interest position in individual stocks.

Short interest is the number of borrowed shares that have not been returned to the lender. A great deal of short interest in a stock indicates widespread speculation that a stock will fall. Remember, however, that these shares must be repaid, and that those who owe stock must buy it in order to repay it. Their stock purchases could bid the stock up.

SHORT INTEREST HIGHLIGHTS

NASDAQ ISSUES

Largest Short Positions

Rank		Nov. 13	Oct. 15	Change
1	Dell Computer	35,783,222	54,658,375	-18,875,152
2	MCI Worldcom	34,627,098	32,181,261	2,445,837
3	Cisco Sys	23,901,116	22,046,489	1,854,627
4	Boston Chicken	22,194,113	22,834,094	-639,981
5	Intel	20,770,992	17,675,820	3,095,172
6	Apple Computer	20,756,520	16,756,878	3,999,642
7	Tele Comm A TCI	20,744,345	19,008,820	1,735,525
8	Microsoft	17,081,255	21,053,859	-3,972,604
9	Ascend Comm	16,904,844	24,315,046	-7,410,202
10	Tel-Save Hldgs	16,564,823	18,966,500	-2,401,677
11	Staples Inc	16,522,667	18,068,251	-1,545,584
12	Baan	16,078,263	20,971,778	-4,893,515
13	Syquest Tech	14,577,852	14,502,855	74,997
14	Networks Assoc	14,510,222	18,488,073	-3,977,851
15	HBO Co	13,686,751	18,808,689	-5,121,938

Largest Changes

Rank		Nov. 13	Oct. 15	Change
1	Apple Computer	20,756,520	16,756,878	3,999,642
2	BMC Software	11,058,658	7,225,473	3,833,185
3	Synetic	4,236,794	1,137,578	3,099,216
4	Intel	20,770,992	17,675,820	3,095,172
5	Sun Microsys	10,474,003	7,466,751	3,007,252
6	MCI Worldcom	34,627,098	32,181,261	2,445,837
7	Tele Comm A Lby	11,556,120	9,350,917	2,205,203
1	Dell Computer	35,783,222	54,658,375	-18,875,152
2	Ascend Commun	16,904,844	24,315,046	-7,410,202
3	Allied Waste Inds	2,995,600	9,698,125	-6,702,525
4	HBO Co	13,686,751	18,808,689	-5,121,938
5	Baan	16,078,263	20,971,778	-4,893,515
6	Nextel Com A	12,304,086	16,754,124	-4,450,038
7	Washington Mutual	10,299,123	14,668,095	-4,368,972

Largest Short Interest Ratios

The short interest ratio is the number of days it would take to cover the short interest if trading continued at the average daily volume for the month.

Rank		Nov. 13 Short Int	Avg Dly Vol-a	Days to Cover
1	Synetic	4,236,794	66,586	64
2	Hmmngbrd Comm	2,719,219	56,177	48
3	Hibbett Sporting	1,365,614	31,600	43
4	TRO Learning	714,524	21,098	34
5	WFS Financial	1,196,249	37,508	32
6	Parkervision	970,164	32,242	30
7	Scandinavin Brdcas	1,530,670	54,021	28
8	Wyman Gordon	5,192,531	184,224	28
9	Nexstar Pharm	2,722,451	96,793	28
10	Ohio Casualty	2,811,225	101,180	28
11	Newport	1,172,985	42,894	27
12	Littelfuse	2,516,250	97,897	26
13	Northfield Labs	639,734	25,042	26
14	Zoltek	3,618,157	146,092	25
15	Optical Cable	818,744	33,510	24
16	Vltech America	1,208,426	49,765	24
17	Ugly Duckling	1,315,000	54,840	24
18	Credit Acceptance	2,849,796	119,044	24
19	Data Transmission	2,535,133	106,839	24
20	Actrade Intl	1,610,216	70,769	23
21	Qiagen	660,844	29,837	22
22	Res-Care	3,486,380	159,151	22
23	Avatar Hldgs	663,824	30,914	21
24	Gardenburger	2,015,559	96,211	21
25	World Acceptance	421,726	20,321	21
26	Emcor Group	1,080,671	54,996	20
27	Ultratech Stepper	2,669,159	137,115	19

a-Includes securities with average daily volume of 20,000 shares or more. n-New. r-Revised.
Issues that split in the latest month are excluded.
The largest percentage increase and decrease sections are limited to issues with previously established short positions in both months.

Largest % Increases

Rank		Nov. 13	Oct. 15	%
1	Photoelectron	159,869	2,050	7,698.5
2	Jetform	492,759	10,643	4,529.9
3	Rank Group Adr	121,386	3,534	3,334.8
4	Genesis Direct	164,844	6,532	2,423.6
5	Il Fornaio (Amer)	248,469	10,800	2,200.6
6	Natural Health	279,443	14,718	1,798.6
7	WPP Group Adr	219,899	14,415	1,425.5
8	Terayon Comm Sys	306,661	20,606	1,388.2
9	Genesis Microchip	186,538	12,604	1,380.0
10	Ozemail Adr	170,297	12,295	1,285.1
11	Starbase	112,663	11,054	919.2
12	Sonic Solutions	220,336	22,359	885.4
13	PC Connection	193,967	23,426	728.0
14	Telegroup	539,837	80,058	574.3
15	Infonautics A	434,823	74,702	482.1

Largest % Decreases

Rank		Nov. 13	Oct. 15	%
1	TCI Comm Pfd A	27	204,351	-100.0
2	Home Health	1,514	214,077	-99.3
3	Iridex	1,136	140,970	-99.2
4	Il Superconductor	3,011	153,033	-98.0
5	Consilium	5,096	115,399	-95.6
6	Cortex Pharm	12,643	255,770	-95.1
7	Michael Foods	10,340	144,947	-92.9
8	Globo Cabo Adr	59,912	722,620	-91.7
9	Esenjay Explor	21,745	237,616	-90.8
10	Kelley Oil & Gas	90,471	891,329	-89.8
11	Oravax	63,312	565,925	-88.8
12	Methanex	34,804	305,143	-88.6
13	Mercer Intl SB	33,046	279,724	-88.2
14	Thermo Tech Techni	78,575	542,753	-85.5
15	Republic Sec Fin C	495,185	2,978,305	-83.4

WORLD STOCK MARKETS

Markets End Day Mostly Lower as Investors Keep Their Focus on Latin America and Floating Real

By Sara Webb
Staff Reporter of The Wall Street Journal.

World stock markets mostly ended lower as investors continued to focus on Latin American markets in the wake of Brazil's decision last week to devalue its currency and allow the real to float freely.

Brazil's key stock market index, the Bovespa, ended up 3.8%, while elsewhere in the region Argentina was up 1.9%, Mexico down 0.9%, Venezuela down 3.4% and Chile down 0.6%.

The Dow Jones World Stock Index rose 0.41 point, or 0.20%, to 205.37.

European stocks, which were buoyed by merger news and relief at Brazil's apparently calm devaluation in the past couple of trading sessions, had a mixed day. Among the bigger markets, Germany lost 0.8%, France fell 0.9%, Switzerland lost 0.6%, Italy dropped 1.8% and London fell 1.6%.

Meanwhile, in Asia, volume was light following Monday's holiday in the U.S. and with stock markets in Singapore, Malaysia and Indonesia closed for holidays. Hong Kong fell 1.1%, South Korea shed 0.7% and Tokyo slipped 0.3%.

In trading in Asia Wednesday, Tokyo closed the morning session down 0.2%, while South Korea was up 0.7% in late-morning dealings. Hong Kong had gained 0.4% in early trading.

In SAO PAULO Tuesday, the Bovespa Index closed up 267 points, or 3.8%, at 7380. Stock-market bellwether Telebras preferred receipts gained 3.6%, to end at 109.30 reais.

Late Monday, Brazil raised interest rates to support the currency. Yesterday, the Brazilian real ended firmer against the dollar, closing at 1.56 reais per dollar compared with Monday's closing of 1.59 reals per dollar.

Investors are still waiting for important developments this week regarding measures aimed at cutting the fiscal deficit, and many observers fear that if no progress is made with these measures, the real will fall sharply against the dollar.

Gerard Lyons, chief economist at DKB International in London, said in a note to clients "the Brazilian government did the worst of all worlds and hiked a key rate from 29% to 41%. . . . The outcome will not be positive for the Real (which will still fall) or for the economy (which will still suffer from high interest rates as well as from a tough fiscal stance)."

Meanwhile, David Malpass, chief international economist at Bear Stearns in New York, described the latest developments in exchange-rate policy as "a huge step backwards for Brazil," in a note to clients yesterday.

"Unless Brazil comes up with a whole new approach to the constitution, currency stability, structural reforms and growth, it is difficult to see how the situation will avoid getting worse," he said. Mr. Malpass sees gross domestic product shrinking 7% in 1999, with inflation hitting at least 10%, putting pressure on interest rates.

"Brazil's fiscal situation is much worse than those encountered in Asia," Mr. Malpass added, going on to say that "constitutional constraints will make dramatic policy improvements difficult for Brazil. In addition, as Brazil's economic situation worsens, it will be difficult to dispel market concerns over the fiscal deficit, inflation, debt, the possibility of additional currency depreciation, capital controls, internal

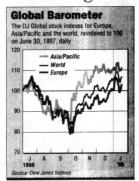

Global Barometer
The DJ Global stock indexes for Europe, Asia/Pacific and the world, reindexed to 100 on June 30, 1997, daily

Source: Dow Jones Indexes

debt restructuring and the uncertainty over the actual levels of debt."

In SEOUL, the Kospi index ended 4.4 points, or 0.7%, lower at 618.12, despite good news on the credit-rating front. Expectations of an upgrade in the country's credit rating by Fitch IBCA—which were actually announced after the market had closed—gave stocks a boost, but the rally ran out of steam.

The rating agency said it has restored South Korea's sovereign rating to investment grade, citing an "unprecedented recovery in external liquidity." Fitch IBCA said it upgraded South Korea's long-term foreign currency rating to triple B minus from double B plus.

South Korean stocks have soared in the last three months on hopes that improving economic fundamentals would result in a better credit rating for the country and

Continued

This ambivalence illustrates the difficulty in using short-interest data as an analytical tool. For instance, the charts included with **Short Interest Highlights** for New York Stock Exchange issues (see page 187) indicate approximately 4 billion shares had not yet been returned to brokers (NYSE Short Interest) and that this was nearly 5 times recent trading volume (Short Interest Ratio). Despite the fact that this indicates considerable sentiment that stocks will fall, a short-interest ratio of over two has been a rule of thumb that stocks will rise, because these borrowed stocks must be repurchased to be repaid. Now you can see why it is difficult to find meaning in the ratio.

Nonetheless, this does not mean that you should remain unconcerned if there is a substantial short interest increase in an individual stock in your portfolio. The forces that move the entire market may not be the same as those

Down in Dollars
The DJ Global stock indexes in U.S. dollar terms for Mexico, Brazil and Venezuela, reindexed to 100 on June 30, 1997, daily

Source: Dow Jones Indexes

companies.

Among the big-cap stocks followed by foreign investors, **Samsung Electronics** ended 0.4% lower at 90,400 won, while **Pohang Iron & Steel**, known as Posco, rose 0.8% to 63,000 won and **Korea Electric Power**, or Kepco, rose 2.5% to 32,500 won.

In **HONG KONG**, the Hang Seng Index finished down 1.1%, or 112.43 points, at 10290.11.

But mainland-China-backed stocks, known as red-chips, fell more heavily on concerns about bad loans and a spate of profit warnings. The red-chip index dropped 2.2%, or 16.71 points, to 754.84.

Yizheng Chemical Fibre, a mainland-Chinese enterprise listed in Hong Kong, Monday warned shareholders of financial losses for 1998, which led its stock price to fall 6.8% on Monday and a further 3.6%—to HK53 cents—yesterday.

Jilin Chemical Industrial tumbled 10% to close at HK30.5 cents, while **China Eastern Airlines** fell 7.5% to HK43 cents after the carrier warned it will likely report a loss for 1998.

Among the blue-chip stocks, shares in banking giant **HSBC Holdings** rose 0.5% to HK$203, while property giant **Cheung Kong (Holdings)** inched up 0.4% to HK$59.25 and its conglomerate affiliate **Hutchison Whampoa** ended unchanged at HK$58.50.

Hotel stock **Hong Kong & Shanghai Hotels** tumbled 5% to HK$5.65, while **Shangri-la Asia** lost 4.5% to HK$6.40.

Meanwhile, Hong Kong's economy shows no sign of improving with the latest unemployment figures—released on Monday after the market had closed—showing the jobless rate for the three months ended December surged to a record high of 5.8%.

In **TOKYO**, the Nikkei 225 ended down 34.62 points, or 0.3%, at 13770.44.

Advancing issues outnumbered decliners by 602 to 487, while 186 issues were unchanged.

A slightly firmer dollar during Tokyo trading helped support some of Japan's export-oriented stocks.

Cosmetics group **Shiseido** gained 4.3% to 1299 yen after Shiseido and U.S-based **Johnson & Johnson** said they would form a strategic alliance.

Communications- and Internet-related stocks made good gains, following recent euphoria in the sector in Europe and the U.S.

Nippon Telegraph and Telephone rose 0.3% to 870,000 yen, while **NTT Mobile Communications Network** gained 2% to 4.68 million yen.

Shares in **Yahoo Japan** rose 13% to a all-time high of 17 million yen. Its parent, **Softbank**, rose 7.8% to 8,990 yen.

In Europe, "markets were rather undecided," said James Cornish, European equity strategist at BT Alex.Brown in London. "There was much less going on, with only the odd bit of merger news, such as the British Aerospace-Marconi deal," he added.

In **LONDON**, the FTSE 100 share index closed down 96.3 points, or 1.6%, at 6027.60, despite news that British Aerospace is acquiring Marconi, the defense electronics arm of Britain's **General Electric Co.**, or GEC.

But shares in British Aerospace plummeted 14% to 425.5 pence, while GEC shares fell 5.4% to 546.5 pence.

Telecom stocks, which rocketed higher on Monday following news of **Vodafone's** purchase of AirTouch Communications of the U.S., lost some of those gains yesterday. Vodafone fell 8.4% to 1,123 pence and **Orange** fell 6.6% to 1000.5 pence.

In **MADRID**, the IBEX-35 index closed down 99.80 points, or 1%, at 9971.70, after gaining 5% on Monday.

Spanish banks, which have rallied recently on merger news and speculation, had a mixed day. **Banco Santander**—which is merging with **Banco Central Hispanoamericano**, or BCH—gained 2.7% to 17.28 euros, while BCH closed down 2.4% at 10.22 euros. **Banco Bilbao Vizcaya** ended 2.9% lower, at 13.60 euros.

In **LISBON**, where the Bolsa de Valores de Lisboa index finished down 0.3 points, or 0.2%, at 5022.59, shares in **Banco Portugues do Investimento** rose 4.1% to 32.97 euros on speculation it could be a merger target.

Retailer **Jeronimo Martins e Filhos** climbed 2.1% to 46.01 euros, bouncing back from recent losses that were driven by concern over its exposure to the Brazilian market.

In **MILAN**, the Mibtel index fell 1.8%, or 432 points, to 23846.

Bank shares lost ground after days of merger speculation.

BCI and **Banca Di Roma** ended lower after BCI failed to discuss a merger with Banca Di Roma in a BCI board meeting on Monday. BCI fell 1.8% to 5.760 euros, while Banca Di Roma fell 5% to 1.37 euros.

In **FRANKFURT**, the Xetra DAX closed down 38.4 points, or 0.8%, at 5038.45, but telecom stocks there continued to rally.

Deutsche Telekom closed up 6.9% at 37.30 euros while **Mobilcom** ended 9.4% higher at 426.10 euros.

Earlier in the session, Deutsche Telekom reported a 27% jump in net profit.

DaimlerChrysler shares ended 1.4% lower at 90 euros in response to news that British Aerospace would acquire the Marconi defense and aerospace operations, as this is seen as reducing the likelihood of a merger between British Aerospace and DaimlerChrysler Aerospace AG.

In **PARIS**, where the CAC-40 index fell 35.69 points, or 0.9%, to 4115.99 points, defense stocks also responded to the British Aerospace news.

Shares in **Thomson-CSF** fell 5% to 33.00 euros on fears that its own merger options have now diminished.

Shares of resort-group **Club Mediterranee** rose 5.9% to 77.95 euros, after it reported net profit of 171 million francs in the fiscal year ending Oct. 31, 1998, compared with a loss the previous year.

---

that move an individual stock. What does the smart money know about your stock that you don't? It's an important question, and one that you should ask. So follow this report each month in the *Journal*.

Foreign Markets

Finally, you can buy shares on stock exchanges throughout the world. *The Journal* provides daily listings of these issues, and you can find a reference to them on the front-page indexes of the first and last sections under **World**

Stock Market Indexes

EXCHANGE	INDEX	1/19/99 CLOSE	NET CHG		PCT CHG		YTD NET CHG		YTD PCT CHG	
Argentina	Merval Index	380.55	+	6.92	+	1.85	−	49.51	−	11.51
Australia	All Ordinaries	2855.80	+	25.40	+	0.90	+	42.40	+	1.51
Belgium	Bel-20 Index	3478.72	−	7.63	−	0.22	−	35.79	−	1.02
Brazil	Sao Paulo Bovespa	7380.00	+	267.00	+	3.75	+	596.00	+	8.79
Britain	London FT 100-share	6027.60	−	96.30	−	1.57	+	145.00	+	2.46
Britain	London FT 250-share	4874.60	−	29.20	−	0.60	+	19.90	+	0.41
Canada	Toronto 300 Comp.	6758.90	−	63.92	−	0.94	+	272.96	+	4.21
Chile	Santiago IPSA	89.94	−	0.54	−	0.60	−	10.06	−	10.06
China	Dow Jones China 88	124.94	+	0.27	+	0.22	+	3.74	+	3.09
China	Dow Jones Shanghai	153.17	+	0.72	+	0.47	+	3.83	+	2.56
China	Dow Jones Shenzhen	147.35	+	0.95	+	0.65	+	2.02	+	1.39
Europe	DJ Stoxx (Euro)	287.34	−	1.76	−	0.61	+	8.14	+	2.92
Europe	DJ Stoxx 50 (Euro)	3456.53	−	6.33	−	0.18	+	136.28	+	4.10
Euro Zone	DJ Euro Stoxx (Euro)	306.64	−	1.50	−	0.49	+	8.27	+	2.77
Euro Zone	DJ Euro Stoxx 50 (Euro)	3515.69	+	0.26	+	0.01	+	173.37	+	5.19
France	Paris CAC 40	4115.99	−	35.69	−	0.86	+	173.33	+	4.40
Germany	Frankfurt DAX	5073.15	+	22.75	+	0.45	+	70.76	+	1.41
Germany	Frankfurt Xetra DAX	5038.45	−	38.40	−	0.76	+	31.88	+	0.64
Hong Kong	Hang Seng	10290.11	−	112.43	−	1.08	+	241.53	+	2.40
India	Bombay Sensex	3218.91	−	59.67	−	1.82	+	163.50	+	5.35
Italy	Milan MIBtel	23846.00	−	432.00	−	1.78	+	151.00	+	0.64
Japan	Tokyo Nikkei 225	13770.44	−	34.62	−	0.25	−	71.73	−	0.52
Japan	Tokyo Nikkei 300	213.10	−	0.78	−	0.36	−	2.99	−	1.38
Japan	Tokyo Topix Index	1074.80	−	0.99	−	0.09	−	12.19	−	1.12
Malaysia	DJ Malaysia	Closed								
Mexico	I.P.C. All-Share	3603.43	−	34.34	−	0.94	−	357.35	−	9.02
Netherlands	Amsterdam AEX	540.00	+	4.67	+	0.86	+	10.52	+	1.95
Singapore	Straits Times	Closed								
South Africa	Johannesburg Gold	983.60	+	5.10	+	0.52	+	112.10	+	12.86
South Korea	Composite	618.12	−	4.40	−	0.71	+	55.66	+	9.90
Spain	IBEX 35	9971.70	−	99.80	−	0.99	+	135.10	+	1.37
Sweden	Stockholm General	3312.39	+	6.34	+	0.19	+	77.93	+	2.41
Switzerland	Zurich Swiss Market	7207.70	−	40.40	−	0.56	+	47.00	+	0.66
Taiwan	Weighted Index	6343.36	−	33.89	−	0.53	−	75.07	−	1.17

Markets. A Representative sample is included on pages 189 and 190 from the Wednesday, January 20, 1999 issue.

But foreign investing can be risky for Americans, as the events of 1997 and 1998 made abundantly clear. Remember, when you invest in foreign markets you must be concerned with the fluctuation of foreign currency values as well as the value of the shares you purchase. A rise in the dollar's value against the currency in which your shares are denominated can wipe out your gain, while a fall in the dollar's value could accentuate that gain. In

FOREIGN MARKETS

Americas

MONTREAL in Canadian dollars

	CLOSE	NET CHG.
Bio Pha	42.25	– 0.90
BombrdrB	22.90	– 0.15
Cambior	8.00	– 0.05
Cascades	7.85	– 0.15
Donohue A	30.75	– 0.05
NatBk Cda	24.45	– 0.70
Power Corp	35.00	– 0.10
Provigo	17.10	+ 0.05
Quebecr B	33.25	– 0.75
Quebecr P	35.20	+ 0.20
SNC-Lavalin	12.80	– 0.05
Teleglobe	61.00	+ 5.00
Videotron	26.10	

TORONTO in Canadian dollars

	CLOSE	NET CHG.
Abitibi C	14.40	– .40
AirCanada	6.85	– .20
Alcan	42.30	– .45
AltEnergy	36.05	– 1.20
Anderson	13.90	– .50
Atco I f	37.75	– .50
Aur Res	2.60	...
BC Gas	29.75	...
BCE Inc	61.75	– 1.10
BCE Mobl	46.75	+ .25
BCTelcom	41.35	– .35
BGR A	9.50	...
Bank Mtl	65.90	– 1.10
Bank N S	32.70	– .75
Barick gld	30.15	– .40
C Util B	48.70	– .20
CAE	8.85	+ .05
CCL B f	16.15	– .15
CIBkCom	39.40	– .55
CP Ltd	31.70	– .30
CTire A f	39.90	+ .15
Cambior	8.00	...
Cambridg	12.30	– .50
Cameco	37.25	+ 1.45
Canfor	5.55	+ .10
Cdn Airline	2.35	– .04
Cdn Tire	52.00	...
CdnNatRes	25.20	+ .05
Co Steel	12.65	– .10
Cominco L	18.30	– .75
Crestar	13.50	– .35
Dia a o f	16.00	...
Dofasco	20.20	+ .10
Domtar	9.40	+ .10
DundeeAf	14.10	+ .05
Dupont A	45.00	+ .25
Dylex Ltd	4.15	– .05
Enbridge	69.75	– .50
Euro Nev	24.60	...
FSesnHlf	47.05	– .20
Fairfax f	567.00	– 18.00
Falcnbrg	17.40	– .10
Finning	10.05	– .35
FletCCanA	15.60	– .40
Franco	28.75	– .25
GeacComp	42.00	...
Gendis A	5.10	...
GoldcorpAf	8.40	– .20
Gulf Can	4.41	– .20
H Bay Co	17.30	– .30
I Comfort	11.20	+ .40
IForestAf	3.60	– .15
Imasco L	32.10	– .65
ImperialOil	24.10	– .40
Inco	18.40	– .35
Ipsco	25.95	– .05
Ivaco A f	3.35	...
Jannock	14.25	...
Loblaw Co	38.50	+ .20
MDS B	33.65	– .20
Mackenzie	20.45	– .25
Macmilan	15.50	– .20
Maritime f	35.50	+ .25
MolsonAf	22.05	– .45
Moore	18.00	+ .05
NatBkCan	24.40	– .70
Noma A f	9.00	+ .30
Noranda I	16.75	– .20
Onex C f	45.35	– .65
PanCan P	17.00	– .25
PetroCCV	17.70	– .45
PlacerDm	18.05	– .55
Poco Pete	11.85	+ .10
Ptash Cor	103.10	+ 1.60
Ranger	7.05	– .10
Renisanc	17.65	– .95
RogersBf	19.80	+ .05
Royal Bnk	78.80	– .70
Sears Can	20.15	+ .05
Shell Can	23.50	+ .55
Southam	25.00	...
Spar Aero	9.30	...
Stelco A	8.25	+ .20
TIPS	36.80	– .65
Talisman	27.85	– .55
Teck B f	11.00	– .30
Telus Corp	31.85	– .15
ThomCor	37.70	– .90
TorDmBk	58.85	+ .10
TorstarBf	17.60	– .30
TrAlt corp	23.00	– .20
TrCan PL	21.45	– .10
Trilon A	11.75	– .05
Trimac	7.20	– .05
TrizecHaf	31.90	+ .05
Wcoast E	30.20	– .15
Weston	61.50	+ 1.65

MEXICO CITY in pesos

	CLOSE	NET CHG.
Alfa A	24.10	– 0.90
Apasco A	30.75	– 0.25
Banacci B	9.14	– 0.44
Bimbo A	17.20	– 0.10
Cemex B	21.80	– 0.20
Cifra C	10.46	+ 0.22
Cifra V	10.52	+ 0.22
Femsa B	20.90	– 0.30
Gcarso A1	26.80	– 1.00
GModeloC	20.95	– 0.45
Kimber A	23.80	– 0.90
Maseca B	8.10	– 0.12
Tamsa	68.50	– 2.00
Telecom A1	29.50	– 0.50
Televisa	116.50	– 4.70
Telmex L	24.55	– 0.15
Vitro	14.30	– 0.30

BRAZIL in real

	CLOSE	NET CHG.
BcoBrdscoPfd	6.30	+ 0.10
BrahmaPfd	590.00	+ 60.00
CemigPfd	22.00	+ 1.50
ItaubancoPfd	550.00	+ 20.00
LightServ	79.01	– 3.98
PetrobrasPfd	112.00	+ 2.00
Sabesp	57.50	+ 0.50
TelebrasPfd	109.30	+ 5.50
TelespPfd	166.00	+ 4.00
VaiRioDocPfd	23.29	+ 1.79

CHILE in pesos

	CLOSE	NET CHG.
Cervezas	1410.00	....
Chilectra	2275.00	– 25.00
Copec	910.00	+ 10.00
CTC-A	2190.00	+ 40.00
D&S	310.00	– 5.00
Endesa	146.00	– 5.00
Enersis	218.50	– 4.50
Falabella	215.00	– 5.00
Gener	93.00	+ 1.00
Santander	25.99	– 0.01

VENEZUELA in bolivars

	CLOSE	NET CHG.
BcoPrvincial	565.00	– 5.00
CANTV	1250.00	– 0.25
ElecCaracas	205.00	– 12.00
Sivensa	27.00	– 3.00
Vancemos	270.00	– 20.00

Europe

AMSTERDAM in euros

	CLOSE	NET CHG.
ABN Amro	17.75	– 0.10
Aegon	98.05	– 1.05
Ahold	35.05	+ 1.50
Akzo Nobel	34.60	+ 1.60
AMEV	36.95	+ 0.55
Bols Wessanen	10.20	....
DSM	77.75	– 0.45
Elsevier	12.40	....
Hagemeyer	33.15	+ 0.55
Heineken	50.30	– 1.00
Hoogovens	24.65	– 0.70
Hunter Douglas	22.30	+ 0.30
ING Groep N.V.	53.35	+ 0.85
KLM	24.00	– 0.30
KNP BT	11.50	+ 0.10
Nedlloyd	9.95	– 0.10
Oce-van Grntn	26.15	– 0.45
Pakhoed Hldg	22.20	– 0.20
Philips Elec	64.50	+ 1.25
Randstad	46.10	+ 0.10
Robeco	105.50	+ 0.90
Rodamco	21.75	– 0,20
Rolinco	91.40	+ 0.40
Rorento	60.55	+ 0.25
Royal Dutch	39.00	– 0.40
Royal PTT	50.40	– 1.30
Unilever	72.55	+ 2.00
Van Ommeren	26.50	+ 0.20
VNUVerBez	37.40	+ 1.40
Wolters Kluwer	179.05	– 0.95

BRUSSELS in euros

	CLOSE	NET CHG.
Arbed	62.50	....
BarcoNV	221.00	+ 2.50
Bekaert	368.00	– 5.00
CBR	82.00	– 2.15
Delhaize	75.95	+ 2.30
Electrabel	412.00	– 0.10
Fortis	35.80	+ 0.35
Gevaert	63.95	+ 0.95
GIB	37.07	– 0.99
Kredietbank	71.80	– 0.05
Petrofina	406.50	– 0.90
Solvay	60.80	+ 0.90
Tractebel	165.10	– 6.40

FRANKFURT in euros

	CLOSE	NET CHG.
Adidas Salmn	83.35	+ 0.35
Allianz	326.80	– 3.70
BASF	32.85	– 0.90
Bayer	33.00	– 1.04
Beiersdorf	58.40	+ 0.09
BMW	611.00	– 7.10
Byr Vereinsbk	60.11	– 2.89
Commerzbank	27.63	– 0.05
Continental	22.15	– 0,35
Daimler Chrysler	90.00	– 1.25
Degussa	41.51	– 2.03
Deutsche Bank	50.00	+ 0.21
Deutsche Tel	37.30	+ 2.40
Dresdner Bank	37.60	– 1.05
Gehe	56.00	+ 0.90
Heidlbg Zemnt	65.10	– 2.90
Henkel	66.50	+ 1.30
Hochtief	29.90	– 0.60
Hoechst	35.90	– 0.11
Karstadt	355.50	– 27.50
Linde	466.00	+ 4.00
Lufthansa	19.40	+ 0.26
MAN	235.00	– 0.10
Mannesmnn	119.20	+ 2.60
Metallges	12.75	+ 0.10
Metro AG	69.80	+ 1.73
Munchen Rk	439.85	+ 0.85
Porsche	2000.00	....
Preussag	440.00	– 28.00
RWE	39.00	– 0.30
SAP	276.90	– 8.60
SAP Pfd	313.00	– 15.00
Schering	110.80	– 2.20
SchwarzPhar	48.60	– 0.30
Siemens	54.60	– 0.85
Thyssen	151.00	+ 7.50
Veba	45.50	– 2.10
Viag	448.00	– 10.00
Volkswagen	68.65	– 0.35

LONDON in pound/pence

	CLOSE	NET CHG.
3-I Group Plc	6.150	– 0.140
Abbey National	12.940	....
Allied-Domecq	4.860	+ 0.120
AlliedZurich	9.155	– 0.145
Arjo Wiggins	1.075	– 0.005
Assoc Brit Fds	5.545	– 0.055
BAA Plc	7.215	– 0.080
Barclays	14.140	+ 0.090
Bass	7.595	– 0.395
BG	3.990	– 0.065
Blue Circle	2.710	– 0.100
BOC Group	8.330	– 0.235
Body Shop	0.850	– 0.025
Boots	8.870	– 0.430
BPB Indus	1.943	+ 0.018
Brit Sky Brd	4.273	– 0.068
BritAmTob	6.570	– 0.180
British Aero	4.255	– 0.680
British Airwys	3.890	– 0.088
British Land	4.550	– 0.100
British Pete	8.995	– 0.240
British Steel	1.045	– 0.015
British Telcom	9.815	– 0.055
BTR	1.095	+ 0.005
Burmah Castrol	7.035	– 0.215
Cable&Wireless	9.460	+ 0.175
Cadbury Schwp	9.545	– 0.205
Caradon	1.220	– 0.010
CGU	8.815	– 0.300
Charter Plc	3.650	– 0.010
Coats Viyella	0.290	– 0.010
Compass	7.970	+ 0.130
Cookson Group	1.240	– 0.029
Diageo	6.700	– 0.120
EMI	3.630	– 0.120
Eng Ch Clay	2.400	+ 0.005
Enterprise Oil	2.550	– 0.045
Euro Tunnel	0.750	– 0.020
Gen Electric	5.465	– 0.310
GKN	7.660	– 0.085
Glaxo Wellcome	21.960	– 0.040
Granada	10.595	– 0.405
Great Universl	6.790	+ 0.095
Guardian Royal	3.488	+ 0.005
Hanson Plc	4.218	– 0.270
Hillsdown	0.690	– 0.010
Imp Chem Ind	4.595	– 0.250
Imperl Tobac	6.860	– 0.010
Inchcape Plc	1.310	– 0.040
Jefferson Smurf	1.141	+ 0.011
Johnson Mathy	3.640	+ 0.010
Kingfisher	6.340	– 0.075
Ladbroke Grp	2.205	– 0.090
Land Securs	7.615	– 0.030
LASMO	1.030	– 0.035
Legal & Genl	8.130	– 0.105
Lloyds TSB Grp	8.320	– 0.010
Lucas Varity	2.260	+ 0.010
Marks & Spencr	3.473	– 0.108
MEPC	3.985	– 0.065
Nat Power Plc	5.310	+ 0.010
Nat Wstmn Bk	11.300	....
Next Plc	5.633	– 0.025
NFC	1.120	+ 0.040
P & O	6.290	+ 0.140
Pearson	13.020	+ 0.010
Pilkgtn Bros	0.560	– 0.005
PowerGen Plc	8.920	– 0.130
Prudential	8.955	+ 0.135
Rank Gp	1.893	– 0.078
Reckit&Colman	7.300	– 0.265
Reed Intl	4.988	– 0.070
Rentokil	4.680	– 0.010
Reuters	7.800	– 0.155
Rexam Plc	1.770	+ 0.020
Rio Tinto	6.990	– 0.090
RMC	5.870	– 0.220
Rolls Royce	2.368	– 0.033
Royal and Sun	4.818	+ 0.053
Royl Bk Scot	11.020	– 0.085
Safeway	2.793	– 0.063
Sainsbury J	4.355	– 0.133
Scottish Pwr	6.565	– 0.015
Sears	3.470	– 0.012
Severn Trent	9.580	– 0.120
Shell	3.353	– 0.100
Siebe Plc	2.050	....
Smith & Nephew	1.745	– 0.005
SmithKline B	8.920	– 0.150
Smiths Ind	8.250	– 0.260
Std Chartrd	8.110	– 0.140
SunLife & Prov	5.810	– 0.115
Tarmac	1.043	– 0.043
Tate & Lyle	3.920	+ 0.130
Tesco	1.815	– 0.058
Thames Wtr	10.700	– 0.320
TI Group	3.118	....
Tomkins	2.038	– 0.043
Unilever	6.480	– 0.055
United Util	7.955	– 0.065
Utd Biscuits	1:870	+ 0.015
Utd News	4.800	– 0.130
Vodafone	11.230	– 1.025
Williams	3.125	– 0.003
Wolseley	3.623	– 0.178
WPP Group	4.035	– 0.053
Zeneca Grp	27.680	+ 0.030

MADRID in euros

	CLOSE	NET CHG.
ACESA	13.65	– 0.51
Argentaria	23.60	– 0.80
Bco Bil Viz	13.60	– 0.41
Bco Cntrl Hisp	10.22	– 0.25
Bco de Sntdr	17.28	+ 0.45
Bco Inter Esp	30.60	– 0.77
Bco Populr Esp	66.00	– 1.70
Centr Com Pry	20.48	– 0.05
Crp Mapfre	20.42	– 0.50
ENDESA	24.95	+ 0.05
Fomnto Constr	56.85	– 2.55
Gas Natrl SDG	88.10	– 0.90
Iberdrola I	15.80	+ 0.12
Petroleos	32.20	– 0.05
Repsol	46.33	+ 0.50
Sevillana Elec	13.13	– 0.06
Tabacalera A	20.80	– 0.75
Telefonica	41.03	– 0.47
Valen Cem Port	12.00	– 0.20

MILAN in euros

	CLOSE	NET CHG.
Alleanza	11.65	– 0.40
Banca Com	5.76	– 0.08
Benetton	1.59	+ 0.03
CIGA	0.63	– 0.02
CIR	0.91	+ 0.01
ENI	5.32	– 0.17
FIAT Com	2.86	– 0.18
FIAT Pref	1.60	– 0.07
Generali	37.65	– 0.15
Instituto Naz	2.24	– 0.02
Mediobanca	10.85	– 0.45
Montedison	1.03	– 0.02
Olivetti Com	3.07	– 0.10
Olivetti NC	2.86	– 0.14
Pirelli Co	1.55	– 0.05
Pirelli SpA	2.42	– 0.08

Continued

	CLOSE	NET CHG.
RAS	11.05 −	0.45
Rinascente	9.20	....
Rolo Banca	22.00 −	1.00
Saipem	3.20 −	0.03
Snia	1.46 +	0.01
Telecm Ital	5.96 −	0.20
Telecm Itl Ord	8.10 −	0.10
UniCredito Ital	5.06 +	0.03

PARIS in euros

	CLOSE	NET CHG.
Accor	183.00 −	9.20
Air Liquide	144.00 −	5.00
Alcatel Alstm	96.35 −	8.95
AXA Group	128.40 +	1.40
Bic	45.01 −	0.44
BNP	77.15 +	0.55
Carrefour	621.00 −	11.00
Club Med	77.95 +	4.35
Danone	225.10 −	9.60
Dassault Avitn	170.00 −	5.00
Elf Aquitaine	97.00 −	2.75
Euro Disneyld	1.14	....
FrTelecom	76.00 +	0.20
Imetal	98.35 −	0.65
L'Oreal	615.00 −	12.00
Lafarge	78.55 +	0.85
Lagardere Grp	36.75 +	2.24
LVMH	213.00	....
Michelin	31.90 −	0.09
Paribas	83.50 +	0.80
Pernod Ricard	53.00 −	1.60
Peugeot	134.50 −	4.00
Pinault Prnt	156.00 −	1.00
Renault	44.00 +	0.21
Rhone Poulnc	45.25 −	1.10
Saint Gobain	108.00 −	5.70
Sanofi	174.90 −	5.70
Schneider	49.55 −	2.20
Soc Generale	155.00 +	6.00
Sodexho	165.80 +	1.60
STMicroelect	79.00 −	3.00
Suez Lyonnaise	187.50 +	4.40
Thomson CSF	33.00 −	1.72
Total Francais	91.30 −	0.10
Usinor	10.30 +	0.03
Vivendi	257.50 +	4.30

STOCKHOLM in krona

	CLOSE	NET CHG.
ABB'B'	75.50 −	1.00
AGA	105.50	....
Astra	170.00 +	0.50
Atlas Copco	168.00 −	4.50
Electrolux	128.50 +	1.00
Ericsson	197.50 −	0.30
FoerSparbk	216.50 +	1.00
Hennes&Mau B	703.00 −	9.00
Investor B	377.00 −	2.00
Nordbanken	59.50 +	2.50
Sandvik A	146.50 −	2.00
SE Bank	83.50 +	2.00
Skanska	228.50 −	0.50
SKF	99.50	....
Svenska Hndbk	331.00 +	4.00
Volvo	223.50 +	8.50

SWITZERLAND in Swiss francs

	CLOSE	NET CHG.
ABB AG	1516 −	13
ABB AG reg	307 −	3
Adecco	643 +	18
Alusuisse	1515 −	10
Ciba Sp Chem	111 −	2
CredSuisseGp	219 −	3
Hof LaRoch br	25200	....
Holderbank	1515 −	40
Nestle reg	2630 −	39
Novartis br	2850 +	11
Novartis reg	2845 +	9
Richemont	2400	....
Roche div rt	17980 −	20
Sulzer reg	751 −	15
Swiss Reins reg	3560 −	25
Swissair	307 −	5
Swisscom	617 −	4
UBS reg	430 +	1
ZurAlliedAG	1040 −	29

Africa

JOHANNESBURG in rand

	CLOSE	NET CHG.
Amalgmt Bk	30.80 +	1.30
Anglo Am Ind	96.00 −	3.00
Anglo Am Inv	82.00 −	1.50

	CLOSE	NET CHG.
Anglo Am Plat	84.50 −	0.50
Anglo Am SA	178.60 −	1.40
Barlow Ltd	25.25 −	0.55
De Beers	86.30 −	0.30
Firstrand	7.10 +	0.25
Gencor Ltd	10.50 −	0.10
Goldfileds	37.00 +	0.70
Imperial Hldg	39.00	....
Investec Bk	206.00	....
Johnnies Ind	29.90 −	0.35
Lib Life Assoc	86.00 +	1.00
Lib Life Strat	13.70	....
Liberty Hldgs	217.00 −	0.60
Nedcor	113.60 +	3.00
Rem Cntig Inv	24.15 +	0.15
Rem Grp	43.50 +	0.80
SA Brew	97.20 +	0.20
Sasol	23.55 −	0.05
Smith CG	13.50 −	0.20
Stand Bk Inv	17.25 +	0.05
Tiger Oats	60.00 +	0.40

S. AFRICAN MINES in U.S. $

	CLOSE	NET CHG.
Anglo Amer Plat	14.00 −	0.25
Impala Pltm	14.68 −	0.15

Asia

HONG KONG in H.K. dollars

	CLOSE	NET CHG.
Bank E Asia	12.25 −	0.20
Cathay Pacific	8.25 −	0.55
Cheung Kong	59.25 +	0.25
China L & P	37.00 −	0.50
CITIC Pacific	16.65 −	0.65
Hang Seng Bk	74.25 −	2.00
Hendrson Land	39.30	....
HK & Chn Gas	9.85 −	0.05
HK Electric	23.80	....
HK Telecom	13.25 −	0.30
HSBC Hldgs	203.00 +	1.00
Hutchan Whmp	58.50	....
Hysan Develop	10.90 −	0.25
New World Dev	17.55 −	0.60
Sun Hung Kai	56.25 −	0.75
Swire Pacific	37.50 −	0.60
Tsingtao Brew	0.74	....
Wharf Holdings	11.05 −	0.15
Wheelock	6.00 −	0.20

SHANGHAI in renminbi
Asian investors only

	CLOSE	NET CHG.
Anshan Trust	6.65 +	0.03
Beijing Wanfuj	6.75 +	0.08
Cai Hong Dis	7.31 −	0.03
GD Meiyan Ent	7.71 −	0.06
Harbin Pharm	6.90 +	0.02
Hubei Xinghua	14.31 +	0.25
Jinan Qinqi	6.28 −	0.02
Maannshan I&S	2.31 +	0.01
No China Pharm	4.12	....
Orient	6.32 −	0.06
QD Haier	17.93 +	0.15
SC ChangHong	17.76 +	0.29
SH AJ	13.05 +	0.03
SH Feilo	7.16 +	0.06
SH Lujiazui	14.81 −	0.14
SH Petrochem	2.83 +	0.02
SH Raw Water	6.66	....
SH Shenua	12.28 +	0.20
SHENERGY	8.11 +	0.01
SY Jinbei Auto	4.39 +	0.17

SHENZHEN in renminbi
Asian investors only

	CLOSE	NET CHG.
China Baoan	3.93 +	0.03
GD DongGuan	5.28 −	0.05
GD Elect Pwr	9.30 −	0.08
GD Marco	5.44 +	0.16
GD Meiya Stk	7.90 −	0.10
HN New Contl	7.06	....
LZ Old Cellar	11.58 +	0.19
MD Hldg	7.80 +	0.07
SZ Dev Bk	14.85 −	0.03
SZ Energy Inv	6.15 +	0.25
SZ Fountain	5.31 −	0.03
SZ Jintian Ind	4.29 −	0.04
SZ Kaifa Tech	24.86 −	0.15
SZ Konka Elec	17.70 +	0.45
SZ Liaotong	5.58 +	0.15
SZ Vanke	8.04 +	0.06
SZ Zhenye	10.13 +	0.09
Wuhan Phnx	4.33 +	0.10
ZH Gr Elec Apl	17.70 −	0.14

TAIWAN in new Taiwan dollars

	CLOSE	NET CHG.
Acer	38.40 −	0.10
ASE	61.50 +	0.50
Asustek Cptr	286.00 −	4.00
Cathay Life	104.00 +	2.00
China Dev	56.50	....
China Stl	17.80 −	0.10
Chng Hwa Bk	43.40 +	0.10
First Com Bk	43.80	....
Formosa Plas	46.60	....
Hou Hai Prec	176.00 −	2.00
Hua Nan Bk	46.30 −	0.40
ICBC	29.90	....
Inventec	119.00 −	1.50
Mosel Vitelic	35.40 +	0.20
Nan Ya Plas	41.90 −	0.60
Shin Kg Life	49.80 −	0.20
Tai Semi Mfg	85.50 −	2.50
Tatung	30.40 +	0.10
Utd Micro Elec	45.60 −	0.50
Winbond Elec	39.50 −	0.70

INDONESIA closed

KOREA in won

	CLOSE	NET CHG.
Dacom	63600 +	2600
Daewoo Hv Ind	5810 −	20
Hyun Eng & Con	10300	....
Hyundai Elec	25250 +	50
Hyundai Motor	21900	....
Kepco	32500 +	800
Kia Motors	1450 −	150
Kookmin Bk	9390 +	190
LG Chemical	15200	....
LG Electrnc	16200 +	150
LG Info & Comm	44500 −	1000
LG Semicon	13900 −	200
Posco	63000 +	500
Shinhan Bk	7900 −	100
SK Telecom	608000	....
Smsg Elec Dev	56500 −	400
Smsg Electrnc	90400 −	400
Ssngyng Oil Rf	19050 +	50
Yukong	18900 −	100

KUALA LUMPUR closed

SINGAPORE closed

TOKYO in yen

	CLOSE	NET CHG.
Aiwa	2860 +	100
Ajinomoto	1240 +	3
Alps Elec	1969 +	1
Amada Co	337 +	...
ANA	365 +	1
Ando Elec	710 +	4
Anritsu	878 −	2
Asahi Chem	508 −	11
Asahi Glass	692 −	9
Banyu Pharm	1925 +	17
Bk of Yokohama	255	....
Bridgestone	2460 −	90
Brother Ind	327 +	12
Canon Inc	2450 −	95
Canon Sales	1567 −	3
Casio Computer	800	....
Chubu Pwr	2235 −	10
Chugai Pharm	1210 −	2
Citizen Watch	671 −	2
CSK	2450 +	20
Dai Nippon Print	1531 −	24
Dai-ichi Kangyo	634 +	6
Daiei	320 −	13
Daiichi Seiyaku	1760 −	190
Dainippon Ink	288 −	2
Dainippon Pharm	500 +	4
Daiwa House	1138 −	4
Daiwa Securities	369 −	4
Denso	2125 +	15
Eisai	2145 +	15
Ezaki Glico	675 +	19
Fanuc	3770 +	10
Fuji Bank	448 −	8
Fuji Hi	550 −	2
Fuji Photo Film	4040 −	50
Fujisawa Pharm	1545 +	33
Fujitsu	1473 +	3
Furukawa Elec	430 −	20
Hirose Elec	7870 +	90
Hitachi Cable	644 −	5
Hitachi Credit	2150 −	5
Hitachi Ltd	772 −	14
Hitachi Maxell	1762 +	27
Hitachi Metals	334 −	2
Honda Motor	3890 −	170

	CLOSE	NET CHG.
Hosiden Elec	2165	....
Hoya	5010 −	160
IHI	185 −	5
Ind Bank Japan	559 +	7
Intec	1195 +	25
Isetan	1149	....
Isuzu	226	....
Itto-yokado	6980 +	220
Itochu Corp	216 +	6
Iwatsu Elec	147 +	8
JAL	299 +	3
Japan Aviat El	315 +	5
Japan Energy	116 +	4
Japan Radio	497	....
JEOL	531 +	1
JUSCO	2160 −	15
Kajima	275 −	5
Kandenko	722 +	4
Kansai Elec	2395 +	30
Kao Corp	2420 +	75
Kawasaki Hi	232 −	6
Kawasaki Steel	155 −	1
KDD	3760	....
Kirin	1448 −	16
Kobe Steel	80 −	1
Kokuyo	1655 +	15
Komatsu Ltd	605	....
Konica	518 +	13
Kubota	319 −	11
Kumagai Gumi	79 +	1
Kuraray	1210 +	22
Kureha Chem	312 −	2
Kyocera	5870 −	30
Kyowa Hakko	614	....
Kyushu Matsushit	1138 +	20
Lion	483 −	5
Makino Milling	640	....
Makita Elec	1125 −	5
Marui	2040 +	5
Mats' Elec Ind	1940 −	35
Mats' Elec Wrks	1160 −	11
Matsushita Com	5120 −	120
Mazda	446 +	4
Meiji Seika	454 +	3
Minolta	599 +	42
Mitsubishi Chem	228	....
Mitsubishi Corp	601 −	18
Mitsubishi Elec	385 −	5
Mitsubishi Hi	402 −	10
Mitsubishi Matl	176	....
Mitsubishi Real	902 −	38
Mitsubishi Trust	749 +	18
Mitsubishi Whse	1345 +	22
Mitsui & Co	588 −	2
Mitsui Fudosan	832 +	2
Mitsui Mar&Fire	598 −	1
Mitsui Trust&Bank	104 −	2
Mitsukoshi	289 +	3
Mochida Pharm	491 +	32
NCR Japan	690 −	7
NEC	1174 −	9
NGK Spark	1171 +	10
NIFCO	880 +	5
Nihon Unisys Ltd	1463 −	34
Nikko Securities	310 −	1
Nikon Corp	1426 +	55
Nintendo	9760 −	40
Nippon Chemi-con	417 +	39
Nippon Columbia	235 +	1
Nippon El Glass	1459 −	10
Nippon Express	581 −	9
Nippon Hodo	570 +	6
Nippon Meat	1757 +	12
Nippon Oil	361 −	8
Nippon Paper	457 +	12
Nippon Sanso	360 +	13
Nippon Steel	197 −	4
Nissan Motor	408 −	8
Nissin Food	2685	....
Nitsuko	515 +	5
NKK	69 −	1
Nomura Securitie	991 −	3
NSK	425 −	8
NTN	366 −	1
NTT	870000 +	3000
Obayashi Corp	520 +	3
Odakyu Railway	401 −	3
Oji Paper	562 −	14
Oki Elec Ind	333 +	6
OKK	188 +	6
Okuma Corp	547 +	12
Olympus Optical	1280 +	49
Omron	1367 +	49
Ono Pharm	4100 −	20
Onward	1300 +	18
Pioneer Electron	1955 −	36
Ricoh Co	1050 −	14

Continued

	CLOSE	NET CHG.
Royal Co	1401	− 1
Sakura Bank	264	+ 1
Sankyo Co	2495	+ 30
Sanrio	1408	+ 23
Sanwa Bank	986	− 15
Sanyo Elec	325	....
Sapporo Brewery	511	+ 8
Secom	9410	+ 80
Sekisui House	1143	+ 11
Seven-eleven	8550	+ 70
Sharp	1064	− 21
Shimizu Corp	400	+ 10
Shin-etsu Chem	2865	+ 75
Shionogi	867	....
Shiseido	1299	+ 54
Showa Denko	87	− 1
Skylark	1697	+ 7
SMK	390	+ 20
Sony	7900	+ 20
Sony Music Ent	4860	+ 60
Sumitomo Bank	1271	+ 20
Sumitomo Chem	407	− 12
Sumitomo Corp	555	+ 13
Sumitomo Elec	1205	− 7
Sumitomo Marine	700	− 1
Sumitomo Metal	121	+ 5
Sumitomo Realty	333	− 5
Sumitomo Trust	260	− 5
Suzuki Motor	1356	....
Taiheiyo Cmnt	270	− 5
Taisei	207	− 4
Taisho Pharm	3110	− 40
Taiyo Yudln	1455	+ 44
Takeda Chem	4110	+ 90
TDK	9910	+ 80
Teijin	404	+ 8

	CLOSE	NET CHG.
Toho Co	15600	+ 40
Tok Mtsubsh Bk	1240	− 10
Tokio Mar&Fire	1366	+ 5
Tokyo Denki Kom	395	....
Tokyo Elec Pwr	2635	− 10
Tokyo Electron	5320	+ 80
Tokyo Gas	285	− 1
Tokyo Style	1080	− 11
Tokyu Corp	284	− 1
Tonen Corp	615	− 6
Toppan Print	1282	− 8
Toray	505	− 12
Toshiba	721	− 2
Toto	907	+ 3
Toyo Seikan	2075	+ 10
Toyobo	151	+ 2
Toyoda Mach	1056	+ 10
Toyota Motor	2805	− 45
Tsugami	122	....
Uny	2035	− 15
Ushio	1156	+ 8
Wacoal	1366	− 34
Yamaha	1226	+ 5
Yamanouchi Phm	3460	− 20
Yamatake Corp.	1022	+ 7
Yamato Tran	1610	− 25
Yamazaki Baking	1540	− 15
Yasuda Fire	553	+ 3
Yokogawa Elec	574	− 13

Pacific

	CLOSE	NET CHG.
NEW ZEALAND in N.Z. $		
Cart Holt Har	1.75	....
FletchChBui	3.16	+ 0.14
FletchChEne	3.92	+ 0.02
FletchChPap	1.41	+ 0.01
Telecom NZ	9.25	+ 0.22
SYDNEY in Australian dollars		
Amcor	7.12	+ 0.08
ANZ Group	10.53	+ 0.06
Boral	2.35	− 0.02
Bougainville	0.20	....
Brambles Inds	42.80	+ 0.62
Brokn Hil Prp	12.13	+ 0.03
Centrl Norsemn	0.47	....
CocColaAm:at	6.91	+ 0.16
Coles Myer	8.62	+ 0.18
Comalco	5.93	− 0.07
Commwlth Bk	23.10	+ 0.25
CSR	3.78	+ 0.11
Foster's	4.75	+ 0.11
Goodman	1.63	− 0.02
Leighton	6.37	− 0.01
Lend Lease	21.31	− 0.29

	CLOSE	NET CHG.
Mayne Nickless	6.28	+ 0.14
MIM Holdings	0.73	....
Nat Aust Bnk	26.00	+ 0.58
News Corp	10.06	+ 0.06
Normdy Mining	1.40	+ 0.04
North Ltd	2.56	....
Pacific Dunlop	2.75	....
Pioneer Intl	3.35	....
Publsh & Brd	7.60	....
Qantas Airways	3.38	+ 0.09
QCT Res	0.98	+ 0.00
Rio Tinto	19.41	− 0.15
S Pac Pete	1.59	− 0.01
Santos	4.64	+ 0.02
StarCityHlds	1.58	− 0.01
Telstra	8.10	+ 0.20
Westpac	11.17	+ 0.15
WMC Ltd	5.06	− 0.02
Woodside	7.52	− 0.07
Woolworths	5.62	+ 0.07

a-U.S. dollars x-Ex-dividend

Source: *The Wall Street Journal*, January 20, 1999. Reprinted by permission of *The Wall Street Journal*, ©1999 Dow Jones & Company, Inc. All rights reserved.

addition, information on foreign stocks is often not as complete and accurate as on U.S. stocks. Let the buyer beware.

Each day, the *Journal*'s **World Stock Markets** feature (see the front-page indexes under **World Markets**) carries a number of reports on foreign stock markets that provide detail on recent developments as well as historical trends (see pages 189 and 190). Note that one or two charts are typically included as well as a report on **Stock Market Indexes** that summarizes the key stock-market indexes in exchanges around the world (see page 191). The **Foreign Markets** portion lists the most important firms on the most important exchanges around the world (see pages 192, 193, and above).

Also note that the front-page indexes refer you to the Dow Jones global indexes and global industry groups. You can find these reports listed as **Dow Jones Global Indexes, DJ Global Groups Biggest Movers,** and **Dow Jones Global Industry Groups**. These indexes provide additional important data by country and by industry. Be sure to note, however, that the U.S. and foreign indexes have different base years. (See the examples on pages 195 through 199.)

If these disparities alarm you, there is a way you can invest in foreign firms while keeping your money in dollars and in the U.S. American Depository

DOW JONES GLOBAL INDEXES

5:30 p.m., Tuesday, January 19, 1999

REGION/ COUNTRY	DJ GLOBAL INDEXES, LOCAL CURRENCY	PCT. CHG.	IN U.S. DOLLARS								
			5:30 P.M. INDEX	CHG.	PCT. CHG.	12-MO HIGH	12-MO LOW	12-MO CHG.	PCT. CHG.	FROM 12/31	PCT. CHG.
Americas			288.44	+ 1.82	+ 0.63	294.31	219.47	+ 58.08	+ 25.21	+ 4.66	+ 1.64
Brazil†	740 + 4.39		181.35	+ 7.62	+ 4.39	489.24	155.25	−223.91	− 55.25	−57.24	−23.99
Canada	203.49 − 1.07		153.72	− 2.01	− 1.29	181.01	117.73	+ 4.55	+ 3.05	+ 7.48	+ 5.11
Chile	148.81 − 0.50		116.36	− 1.11	− 0.94	184.66	96.32	− 42.07	− 26.55	−14.58	−11.13
Mexico	262.16 − 0.95		79.07	− 0.37	− 0.47	136.26	60.60	− 47.84	− 37.70	− 9.95	−11.18
U.S.	1190.53+ 0.70		1190.53	+ 8.26	+ 0.70	1212.76	900.71	+262.70	+ 28.31	+21.19	+ 1.81
Venezuela	313.06 − 2.79		33.91	− 1.01	− 2.89	79.45	23.01	− 40.24	− 54.27	− 6.02	−15.08
Latin America			106.69	+ 1.32	+ 1.25	221.07	90.39	− 87.73	− 45.13	−21.64	−16.86
Europe/Africa			239.62	− 1.46	− 0.61	251.61	185.07	+ 50.12	+ 26.45	+ 4.62	+ 1.97
Austria	109.06 − 0.95		98.19	− 0.99	− 1.00	141.18	93.22	− 10.31	− 9.50	− 7.13	− 6.77
Belgium	323.51 − 0.34		291.54	− 1.13	− 0.39	307.75	179.80	+111.74	+ 62.15	+ 2.13	+ 0.74
Denmark	204.97 − 0.29		189.34	− 0.38	− 0.20	210.95	161.03	+ 1.76	+ 0.94	− 0.79	− 0.42
Finland	839.78 + 2.38		678.53	+15.47	+ 2.33	678.53	320.54	+357.99	+111.69	+74.01	+12.24
France	249.00 − 1.04		228.04	− 2.48	− 1.08	238.23	154.89	+ 73.15	+ 47.23	+ 7.02	+ 3.18
Germany	280.84 − 0.21		252.27	− 0.65	− 0.26	280.68	190.55	+ 61.64	+ 32.33	+ 4.26	+ 1.72
Greece	489.53 − 1.03		308.89	− 2.62	− 0.84	315.88	137.69	+165.14	+114.89	+26.90	+ 9.54
Ireland	402.74 + 0.50		354.27	+ 1.60	+ 0.45	369.89	247.45	+104.60	+ 41.90	+18.63	+ 5.55
Italy	313.78 − 2.05		231.81	− 4.96	− 2.09	252.46	165.27	+ 66.54	+ 40.26	− 2.61	− 1.11
Netherlands	381.65 + 0.69		342.85	+ 2.20	+ 0.65	366.66	258.60	+ 76.37	+ 28.66	− 3.18	− 0.92
Norway	155.74 + 0.48		125.57	+ 0.86	+ 0.69	190.12	96.85	− 34.50	− 21.55	+ 9.44	+ 8.13
Portugal	400.74 − 0.30		313.26	− 1.09	− 0.35	361.91	221.49	+ 69.36	+ 28.44	+15.37	+ 5.16
South Africa	162.78 + 0.63		73.88	− 0.24	− 0.32	136.11	57.78	− 23.85	− 24.41	+ 3.17	+ 4.49
Spain	399.47 − 0.92		271.60	− 2.64	− 0.96	293.48	192.05	+ 79.55	+ 41.42	+ 0.97	+ 0.36
Sweden	383.40 + 0.37		274.44	+ 4.21	+ 1.56	317.82	190.08	+ 39.69	+ 16.91	+20.98	+ 8.28
Switzerland	405.96 − 0.52		399.63	− 1.65	− 0.41	421.91	295.28	+ 74.35	+ 22.86	+ 3.70	+ 0.94
United Kingdom	227.93 − 1.50		202.29	− 2.32	− 1.13	209.30	162.40	+ 24.97	+ 14.08	+ 3.72	+ 1.87
Europe/Africa (ex. South Africa)			249.09	− 1.53	− 0.61	260.76	191.94	+ 54.38	+ 27.93	+ 4.70	+ 1.93
Europe/Africa (ex. U.K. & S. Africa)			278.13	− 1.08	− 0.39	292.44	206.68	+ 71.44	+ 34.57	+ 5.24	+ 1.92
Asia/Pacific			81.36	+ 0.28	+ 0.35	89.49	62.38	+ 0.18	+ 0.22	+ 0.33	+ 0.40
Australia	178.75 + 1.18		150.05	+ 2.72	+ 1.85	150.63	112.56	+ 12.13	+ 8.79	+ 9.04	+ 6.41
Hong Kong	205.96 − 1.20		206.75	− 2.49	− 1.19	241.43	134.48	+ 9.06	+ 4.58	+ 2.69	+ 1.32
Indonesia	160.78 0.00		38.45	0.00	0.00	55.52	15.47	+ 1.30	+ 3.50	− 2.00	− 4.95
Japan	66.67 − 0.39		73.34	+ 0.28	+ 0.38	81.42	57.38	− 1.53	− 2.04	− 0.85	− 1.15
New Zealand	143.18 + 1.87		141.91	+ 2.66	+ 1.91	170.63	99.94	− 23.84	− 14.39	+12.51	+ 9.67
Philippines	203.64 − 0.91		137.89	− 1.04	− 0.75	153.00	60.68	+ 34.44	+ 33.29	+10.60	+ 8.33
Singapore	119.49 0.00		115.23	+ 0.18	+ 0.16	125.42	59.89	+ 16.60	+ 16.83	+ 5.83	+ 5.33
South Korea	102.40 − 0.65		66.07	− 0.10	− 0.15	72.10	25.38	+ 24.22	+ 57.87	+ 4.84	+ 7.91
Taiwan	152.92 − 0.54		122.24	− 0.77	− 0.63	176.76	106.17	− 21.29	− 14.83	− 1.05	− 0.85
Thailand	67.29 − 0.74		43.19	− 0.56	− 1.28	52.94	20.88	+ 11.47	+ 36.13	+ 3.43	+ 8.64
Asia/Pacific (ex. Japan)			136.23	+ 0.32	+ 0.24	150.29	91.45	+ 9.81	+ 7.76	+ 5.54	+ 4.24
World (ex. U.S.)			148.95	− 0.52	− 0.35	153.61	115.37	+ 18.69	+ 14.34	+ 1.93	+ 1.31
DJ WORLD STOCK INDEX			205.37	+ 0.41	+ 0.20	209.97	160.36	+ 35.76	+ 21.08	+ 2.58	+ 1.27

Indexes based on 6/30/82=100 for U.S., 12/31/91=100 for World.
†Local currency index shown in 000s.

Source: *The Wall Street Journal*, January 20, 1999. Reprinted by permission of *The Wall Street Journal*, ©1999 Dow Jones & Company, Inc. All rights reserved.

DJ GLOBAL GROUPS BIGGEST MOVERS

Tuesday, January 19, 1999, as of 5:30 p.m.

Groups Leading

Strongest Stocks	5:30 P.M.	CHG.	PCT. CHG.
Oil Drilling	**199.63**	**+ 6.42**	**+ 3.32**
NoblDrll (US)	15.50	+ 1.13	+ 7.83
GloblMar (US)	9.81	+ 0.69	+ 7.53
Transocean (US)	28.63	+ 0.94	+ 3.39
DmndOffshr (US)	25.81	+ 0.81	+ 3.25
ParkerDrl (US)	4.13	+ 0.13	+ 3.13
Cable/Brdcast	**357.60**	**+ 10.93**	**+ 3.15**
TeleComm (US)	67.94	+ 5.56	+ 8.92
ComcastCp (US)	67.81	+ 4.69	+ 7.43
Canal+ (FR)	221.00	+ 11.10	+ 5.29
MediaOne (US)	54.88	+ 2.63	+ 5.02
ClearChanl (US)	63.13	+ 2.69	+ 4.45
Entertainment	**386.53**	**+ 11.10**	**+ 2.96**
TimeWarner (US)	65.00	+ 3.19	+ 5.16
GrammyEnt (TH)	189.00	+ 7.00	+ 3.85
Pathe (FR)	259.00	+ 7.50	+ 2.98
SonyMusicEnt (JP)	4860.00	+ 60.00	+ 1.25
KingWorld (US)	28.88	+ 0.25	+ 0.87
Software	**677.52**	**+ 19.12**	**+ 2.90**
OracleCp (US)	51.69	+ 4.56	+ 9.68
Autodesk (US)	48.50	+ 3.44	+ 7.63
HmmngbrdCmm (CA)	37.00	+ 2.25	+ 6.48
Peoplesoft (US)	24.50	+ 0.94	+ 3.98
Microsoft (US)	155.63	+ 5.88	+ 3.92
Comp-w IBM	**483.31**	**+ 12.38**	**+ 2.63**
SunMicrsys (US)	105.31	+ 4.88	+ 4.85
Gateway 2000 (US)	58.19	+ 2.50	+ 4.49
SeagateTch (US)	44.00	+ 1.75	+ 4.14
Compaq (US)	48.88	+ 1.94	+ 4.13
DellCptr (US)	82.13	+ 3.13	+ 3.96
Telephone Sys	**322.49**	**+ 8.03**	**+ 2.55**
AirTouch (US)	92.88	+ 9.50	+ 11.39

Groups Lagging

Weakest Stocks	5:30 P.M.	CHG.	PCT. CHG.
Biotechnology	**180.91**	**− 5.83**	**− 3.12**
Monsanto (US)	37.44	− 4.56	− 10.9
Biogen (US)	90.06	− 5.94	− 6.19
GenzymeCp (US)	51.88	− 1.63	− 3.04
BrBiotech (UK)	0.26	− 0.01	− 2.78
BiochemPharma (CA)	42.00	− 1.15	− 2.67
Aero & Defens	**260.98**	**− 6.79**	**− 2.54**
BrAerosp (UK)	4.26	− 0.68	− 13.8
ThomsnCSF (FR)	33.00	− 1.72	− 4.95
SamsungAero (SK)	8600.00	− 400.00	− 4.44
SmithsInd (US)	8.25	− 0.26	− 3.06
LockhdMartin (US)	39.13	− 1.00	− 2.49
Tobacco	**177.26**	**− 4.28**	**− 2.36**
Seita (FR)	50.65	− 2.85	− 5.33
USTInc (US)	32.00	− 1.38	− 4.12
Tabclera serA (SP)	20.80	− 0.75	− 3.48
UnivCp (US)	31.31	− 1.06	− 3.28
JpnTobacco (JP)	1080000	− 30000.	− 2.70
Medical Suppls	**226.25**	**− 5.06**	**− 2.19**
BectonDksn (US)	38.38	− 1.38	− 3.46
Omnicare (US)	33.38	− 1.13	− 3.26
Hillenbrnd (US)	50.25	− 1.63	− 3.13
HoyaCp (JP)	5010.00	− 160.00	− 3.10
BostonSci (US)	23.75	− 0.75	− 3.06
Hvy Machnry	**105.48**	**− 2.33**	**− 2.16**
Caterpillar (US)	45.94	− 1.63	− 3.42
Kubota (JP)	319.00	− 11.00	− 3.33
Deere (US)	33.94	− 1.13	− 3.21
Partek (FI)	7.68	− 0.17	− 2.17
Furukawa (JP)	160.00	− 3.00	− 1.84
Health Care	**164.45**	**− 3.42**	**− 2.04**
HlthMgt A (US)	15.00	− 1.63	− 9.77

AU - Australia	FI - Finland	IR - Ireland	PH - Philippines	SW - Sweden
AS - Austria	FR - France	IT - Italy	PT - Portugal	SZ - Switzerland
BE - Belgium	GR - Germany	JP - Japan	SI - Singapore	TW - Taiwan
BZ - Brazil	GC - Greece	MX - Mexico	SA - South Africa	TH - Thailand
CA - Canada	HK - Hong Kong	NV - Netherlands	SK - South Korea	UK - United Kingdom
CH - Chile	IN - Indonesia	NZ - New Zealand	SP - Spain	US - United States
DK - Denmark		NW - Norway		VZ - Venezuela

NOTE: Stock prices are in local currencies.   ©1999 Dow Jones & Co. Inc., All Rights Reserved

Source: *The Wall Street Journal*, January 20, 1999. Reprinted by permission of *The Wall Street Journal*, ©1999 Dow Jones & Company, Inc. All rights reserved.

DOW JONES GLOBAL INDUSTRY GROUPS

Industry Group Performance

	WORLD 5:30 P.M. 01/19/99	%CHG. YTD		U.S. 5:30 P.M. 01/19/99	%CHG. YTD	AMERICAS 5:30 P.M. 01/19/99	%CHG. YTD	EUROPE 5:30 P.M. 01/19/99	%CHG. YTD	ASIA/PACIFIC 5:30 P.M. 01/19/99	%CHG. YTD
112.33 +	0.26	**Basic Materials**	649.86 +	3.08	148.77 +	2.72	165.40 −	2.81	57.61 −	1.38
149.71 +	8.22	Aluminum	626.96 +	12.72	192.06 +	9.96	180.95 +	5.21	45.62 −	0.71
65.74 +	1.65	Other non-ferrous	202.82 +	0.86	67.35 +	4.55	75.56 +	0.76	57.68 −	1.75
158.82 −	1.11	Chemicals	932.29 +	2.44	195.14 +	2.25	197.06 −	4.53	73.54 −	0.71
181.38 −	0.38	Chem-commodity	1009.18 +	3.84	225.97 +	3.88	230.95 −	3.93	82.90 −	1.02
120.27 −	2.38	Chem-specialty	816.80 +	0.29	148.05 −	0.16	136.42 −	5.60	55.68 +	0.08
128.52 +	5.87	Forest products	466.47 +	5.09	151.42 +	4.72	262.73 +	12.94	44.33 +	12.08
101.72 +	3.16	Mining, diversified	508.98 +	0.25	101.65 +	5.52	130.18 +	0.36	92.18 +	4.43
98.11 −	1.84	Paper products	625.52 −	1.80	124.25 −	1.40	110.56 −	0.78	53.04 −	4.98
69.78 +	3.58	Precious metals	147.98 +	6.59	95.47 +	3.17	192.32 −	11.84	55.12 +	0.63
56.31 −	1.31	Steel	144.18 +	6.29	92.30 −	0.79	113.73 +	3.93	40.22 −	4.71
196.24 +	0.38	**Independent**	2444.58 −	0.75	439.50 −	0.93	124.31 +	0.86	89.47 +	3.84
252.71 +	0.66	Conglomerates	2444.58 −	0.75	439.50 −	0.93	128.32 +	0.96	154.66 +	7.30
47.44 −	3.06	Overseas Trading	0.00	0.00	0.00	0.00	36.43 −	0.55	47.35 −	3.64
135.94 −	2.19	Plantations	0.00	0.00	0.00	0.00	0.00	0.00	135.94 −	2.19
204.55 +	2.04	**Consumer, Cyclical**	1386.79 +	3.43	299.37 +	3.45	205.52 +	0.78	109.31 −	2.76
486.25 −	1.38	Advertising	2677.85 −	3.52	469.03 −	3.52	513.10 +	9.73	0.00	0.00
142.56 +	5.80	Airlines	757.10 +	11.41	210.84 +	11.42	172.19 −	3.05	56.71 +	5.53
84.11 −	4.76	Apparel	982.17 −	1.13	115.88 −	1.23	137.95 −	7.45	55.77 −	6.51
75.78 −	4.65	Clothing/Fabrics	710.70 −	0.68	101.90 −	0.84	144.77 −	5.54	57.03 −	6.39
124.07 −	5.08	Footwear	1406.01 −	1.71	134.07 −	1.71	90.17 −	12.17	25.81 −	11.96
259.87 +	4.50	Auto manufacturers	1128.68 +	14.52	532.20 +	14.52	235.06 +	4.95	168.51	3.34
159.83 −	0.61	Auto parts & equip	570.94 +	0.52	205.13 +	0.09	243.69 −	1.08	120.17 −	0.84
116.04 +	1.60	Casinos	984.00 +	5.70	167.54 +	5.70	146.07 −	8.95	72.34 +	8.03
124.34 −	1.87	Home construction	1107.08 +	1.41	254.35 +	1.41	85.41 −	2.89	112.34 −	3.64
129.80 −	1.67	Home furnishings	547.15 −	0.07	218.95 −	0.07	142.92 −	6.76	119.40 −	1.62
126.50 −	1.62	Consumer electronics	0.00	0.00	0.00	0.00	177.35 +	10.35	127.80 −	1.72
140.32 −	1.76	Other furnishings	547.15 −	0.07	219.48 −	0.07	157.85 −	8.07	66.29 +	0.02
125.27 +	0.91	Lodging	914.26 +	11.11	321.77 +	11.11	161.16 −	1.51	53.55 −	1.58
288.06 +	7.58	Media	1789.76 +	9.97	337.37 +	9.73	245.62 +	4.70	229.36 +	1.37
357.60 +	11.19	Cable/Broadcasting	2624.78 +	14.86	456.95 +	14.80	233.55 +	0.10	340.24 +	5.47
239.01 +	4.03	Publishing	1119.68 +	1.49	235.14 +	2.15	246.98 +	7.08	220.94 −	0.47
204.15 +	4.03	Recreation products	943.49 +	6.03	339.82 +	6.36	80.40 −	5.06	93.15 −	4.34
386.53 +	4.93	Entertainment	1038.24 +	5.26	425.59 +	6.11	138.46 −	4.74	130.21 −	3.47
187.58 +	5.47	Other Rec Products	847.28 +	8.00	300.99 +	8.00	52.32 −	5.46	105.42 −	2.15
92.71 −	7.57	Toys	725.62 −	5.66	188.91 −	5.66	0.00	0.00	67.23 −	9.29
244.37 +	1.30	Restaurants	1683.16 +	1.78	291.24 +	1.79	129.07 +	0.31	76.61 +	0.16
243.11 +	5.06	Retailers,apparel	3194.57 +	4.41	288.16 +	4.41	606.72 +	10.06	40.73 −	2.33
188.72 −	3.50	Retailers,broadline	1780.72 −	1.36	238.53 −	1.77	220.77 −	6.13	91.36 −	5.79
435.46 −	5.36	Retailers,drug-based	3496.49 −	4.71	657.31 −	4.71	177.62 −	12.40	0.00	0.00
233.13 −	0.11	Retailers,specialty	1777.95 −	1.28	296.32 −	1.32	178.75 +	8.02	55.40 −	0.55
236.24 −	2.75	**Consumer, Non-Cycl**	2079.62 −	5.14	260.18 −	5.18	266.93 +	1.79	114.91 −	1.81
133.57 −	2.68	Beverages, distillers	1297.23 −	0.10	180.64 −	1.66	133.22 −	5.49	111.33 +	2.15
284.60 −	4.49	Beverages, soft drinks	3237.51 −	5.09	298.52 −	5.25	608.38 +	11.94	107.13 +	14.09
328.22 −	0.62	Consumer services	1652.66 −	3.33	324.58 −	3.56	155.20 +	15.48	132.70 −	1.24
311.42 +	0.24	Cosmetics	2019.26 +	2.80	291.03 +	2.80	530.06 −	0.77	167.11 −	6.18
159.02 −	5.20	Food	1608.70 −	4.50	165.62 −	4.64	212.59 −	6.69	64.82 +	0.53
23.76 −	3.44	Fishing	0.00	0.00	0.00	0.00	0.00	0.00	23.76 −	3.44
161.13 −	5.20	Other food	1608.70 −	4.50 •	165.62 −	4.64	212.59 −	6.69	68.37 +	0.69
231.75 −	2.82	Food retailers	1848.20 −	6.09	265.53 −	5.39	253.63 +	0.50	152.61 −	4.44
164.45 −	5.28	Health care	635.87 −	5.53	186.54 −	5.55	1032.61 +	27.68	46.04 +	6.82
268.15 −	6.57	**Household products**	2394.05 −	6.52	300.61 −	6.73	99.17 −	7.43	56.14 +	6.77
104.80 −	2.78	Durable	1233.76 −	4.15	128.37 −	4.15	0.00	0.00	45.14 +	10.74
307.41 −	6.86	Non-durable	2481.65 −	6.69	332.83 −	6.91	99.17 −	7.43	83.99 +	2.97
226.25 −	5.28	Medical supplies	1451.28 −	5.38	239.31 −	5.38	190.12 +	2.12	165.20 −	9.73
310.49 −	1.37	Pharmaceuticals	2466.33 −	5.82	325.26 −	5.81	363.00 +	6.11	144.51 −	1.76
177.26 −	1.77	Tobacco	1866.69 −	5.22	181.10 −	4.98	222.73 +	13.34	129.62 −	5.06

Household Procucts →

Continued

Bio-technology ➡

168.63 − 7.34	**Energy**	515.13 − 1.47	187.99 − 1.75	201.88 − 3.58	46.31 + 2.92
66.69 − 2.87	Coal	193.23 − 9.69	81.88 − 9.69	0.00 0.00	30.89 + 5.62
199.63 + 7.87	Oil drilling	183.71 + 7.97	273.72 + 7.74	49.97 + 13.26	0.00 0.00
194.93 − 10.14	Oil cos, major	702.65 − 3.12	208.53 − 3.09	209.47 − 4.27	0.00 0.00
97.79 − 2.11	Oil cos, secondary	182.90 − 2.68	109.20 − 4.31	145.06 − 1.25	47.45 + 2.85
157.99 + 7.27	Oilfield equip/svcs	224.58 + 7.43	160.39 + 7.42	173.33 + 5.93	22.38 + 2.46
293.96 + 1.92	Pipelines	583.13 + 1.52	273.28 + 0.67	156.99 + 4.91	0.00 0.00
188.24 + 0.83	**Financial**	1308.23 + 0.35	358.09 + 0.17	280.56 + 0.78	59.22 + 2.68
158.25 + 1.03	Banks, all	1198.07 − 0.60	367.85 − 0.85	273.73 + 0.94	53.67 + 5.19
132.91 + 3.75	Major int'l	836.89 + 6.23	332.85 + 5.86	255.50 + 1.36	56.53 + 5.96
190.63 − 1.96	Regional banks	1441.20 − 3.89	381.54 − 4.68	314.73 + 0.25	49.25 + 3.57
0.00 0.00	U.S. east	1400.61 − 3.67	0.00 0.00	0.00 0.00	0.00 0.00
0.00 0.00	U.S. central	1859.86 − 4.66	0.00 0.00	0.00 0.00	0.00 0.00
0.00 0.00	U.S. south	1162.46 − 3.13	0.00 0.00	0.00 0.00	0.00 0.00
0.00 0.00	U.S. west	1871.23 − 3.14	0.00 0.00	0.00 0.00	0.00 0.00
320.33 + 0.69	Diversified financial	1705.69 + 1.21	432.68 + 0.98	290.33 + 1.86	100.36 − 7.47
282.86 + 0.32	Insurance, all	1225.16 − 0.09	322.85 − 0.03	323.88 + 0.30	78.46 + 1.93
329.64 − 0.48	Full line	672.41 − 1.17	305.79 − 1.17	333.90 − 0.43	161.61 + 2.55
266.30 − 8.30	Life	1892.93 − 2.07	337.56 − 2.07	318.06 + 0.93	170.96 + 3.93
230.77 + 2.91	Property/Casualty	1569.37 + 1.02	319.75 + 1.10	279.99 + 6.49	70.71 + 1.36
93.65 + 0.27	Real estate	433.61 + 1.53	64.34 + 1.44	105.04 − 1.09	90.29 − 1.13
0.00 0.00	Savings & loan	1221.47 + 1.84	0.00 0.00	0.00 0.00	0.00 0.00
149.47 + 4.48	Securities brokers	2306.54 + 6.89	477.94 + 6.89	271.69 + 0.08	51.22 + 0.17
127.24 − 1.19	**Industrial**	725.94 − 1.58	195.01 − 1.68	187.42 − 0.12	68.70 − 1.47
299.35 − 8.61	Air freight	652.56 − 8.61	333.72 − 8.61	0.00 0.00	0.00 0.00
106.28 − 4.47	Building materials	994.59 − 1.94	171.64 − 3.25	132.51 − 6.90	64.44 + 0.10
93.46 + 2.52	Containers & pkging	914.66 + 1.24	132.03 + 1.24	92.34 + 4.80	61.97 + 6.36
158.65 − 2.44	Elec comps & equip	788.18 − 2.63	217.96 − 2.67	232.83 − 6.40	116.42 − 0.41
76.74 − 3.11	Factory equipment	377.59 + 5.33	119.90 + 5.33	116.23 − 5.77	68.06 − 1.73
49.21 − 3.26	Heavy construction	270.80 − 0.48	83.81 − 0.94	132.78 − 3.99	24.10 − 2.85
105.48 − 0.20	Heavy machinery	373.80 + 0.91	257.61 + 0.91	50.35 − 9.21	50.52 − 1.30
206.21 − 0.61	Industrial, diversified	887.21 − 3.31	263.25 − 3.43	263.67 + 4.03	59.58 − 6.13
85.35 − 5.25	Marine transport	427.45 − 1.19	84.69 − 1.18	147.90 − 5.98	48.09 − 4.97
107.28 + 6.96	Pollution control	877.20 + 7.62	97.10 + 7.61	268.43 − 1.68	65.06 + 1.66
204.03 − 0.39	Other industrial svcs	670.60 − 1.73	211.33 − 1.67	318.24 + 4.30	119.39 − 4.05
118.26 − 0.95	Railroads	846.18 − 2.98	183.99 − 2.46	33.47 − 2.44	88.95 + 0.25
85.42 + 11.50	Transportation equip	498.08 + 4.69	207.05 + 4.69	165.22 + 52.83	30.05 − 3.63
87.01 − 1.41	Trucking	309.39 + 0.21	114.14 + 0.30	0.00 0.00	80.76 − 2.15
397.97 + 7.47	**Technology**	1581.09 + 9.28	508.75 + 9.33	339.67 + 2.30	135.22 + 5.22
260.98 − 3.55	Aerospace/Defense	1062.36 − 1.41	273.56 − 0.89	268.55 − 10.90	54.21 + 7.94
430.45 + 10.89	Communications tech	1906.44 + 10.80	458.19 + 10.85	492.10 + 11.69	120.58 − 0.21
483.31 + 9.70	Computers w/IBM	1023.13 + 10.17	578.46 + 10.31	12.59 + 9.58	149.50 + 3.21
0.00 0.00	Computers wo/IBM	1836.52 + 13.29	0.00 0.00	0.00 0.00	0.00 0.00
185.57 + 2.97	Diversified technology	665.06 + 1.58	234.78 + 1.58	247.20 + 3.53	97.37 + 7.31
141.42 + 2.20	Industrial technology	391.14 + 2.04	127.46 + 2.04	218.82 − 9.04	139.38 + 3.77
228.93 − 4.43	Medical/Bio tech	2551.94 − 4.57	249.57 − 4.47	127.57 − 5.39	102.42 + 0.63
290.50 − 4.57	Advcd Med Devices	3012.64 − 4.54	320.13 − 4.31	119.22 − 7.07	162.81 − 0.99
180.91 − 4.31	Biotechnology	2163.87 − 4.59	200.56 − 4.59	17.18 − 1.07	76.13 + 5.71
265.61 − 0.91	Office equipment	1317.39 − 1.41	456.67 − 1.41	167.21 − 15.51	154.43 + 1.56
918.50 + 16.12	Semiconductors	4541.87 + 17.13	1534.05 + 17.13	132.44 + 16.92	248.51 + 9.98
677.52 + 7.85	Software	18715.23 + 11.52	773.79 + 11.50	277.31 − 14.84	92.35 − 1.86
225.50 + 5.93	**Utilities**	665.18 + 5.35	228.62 + 4.13	348.90 + 9.60	94.31 + 1.70
132.66 − 2.75	Electric	310.24 − 3.95	127.38 − 5.30	289.01 + 1.47	83.37 − 3.35
134.52 − 3.27	Gas	239.26 − 5.32	154.06 − 5.19	268.17 − 2.98	74.73 − 1.87
322.49 + 9.79	Telephone	1220.14 + 9.01	318.47 + 7.97	409.71 + 13.34	184.77 + 6.11
280.95 + 5.21	Water	955.85 − 6.92	165.87 − 20.88	288.17 + 7.23	0.00 0.00
205.37 + 1.27	**DJ Global Indexes**	1190.53 + 1.81	288.44 + 1.64	249.09 + 1.92	81.36 + 0.40

Indexes based on 6/30/82=100 for U.S., 12/31/91=100 for World

311.42 + 0.24	Cosmetics	2019.26 + 2.80	291.03 + 2.80	530.06 − 0.77	167.11 − 6.18
159.02 − 5.20	Food	1608.70 − 4.50	165.62 − 4.64	212.59 − 6.69	64.82 + 0.53
23.76 − 3.44	Fishing	0.00 0.00	0.00 0.00	0.00 0.00	23.76 − 3.44
161.13 − 5.20	Other food	1608.70 − 4.50 •	165.62 − 4.64	212.59 − 6.69	68.37 + 0.69
231.75 − 2.82	Food retailers	1848.20 − 6.09	265.53 − 5.39	253.63 + 0.50	152.61 − 4.44
164.45 − 5.28	Health care	635.87 − 5.53	186.54 − 5.55	1032.61 + 27.68	46.04 + 6.82
268.15 − 6.57	Household products	2394.05 − 6.52	300.61 − 6.73	99.17 − 7.43	56.14 + 6.77
104.80 − 2.78	Durable	1233.76 − 4.15	128.37 − 4.15	0.00 0.00	45.14 + 10.74
307.41 − 6.86	Non-durable	2481.65 − 6.69	332.83 − 6.91	99.17 − 7.43	83.99 + 2.97
226.25 − 5.28	Medical supplies	1451.28 − 5.38	239.31 − 5.38	190.12 + 2.12	165.20 − 9.73
430.45 + 10.89	Communications tech	1906.44 + 10.80	458.19 + 10.85	492.10 + 11.69	120.58 − 0.21
483.31 + 9.70	Computers w/IBM	1023.13 + 10.17	578.46 + 10.31	12.59 + 9.58	149.50 + 3.21
0.00 0.00	Computers wo/IBM	1836.52 + 13.29	0.00 0.00	0.00 0.00	0.00 0.00
185.57 + 2.97	Diversified technology	665.06 + 1.58	234.78 + 1.58	247.20 + 3.53	97.37 + 7.31
141.42 + 2.20	Industrial technology	391.14 + 2.04	127.46 + 2.04	218.82 − 9.04	139.38 + 3.77
228.93 − 4.43	Medical/Bio tech	2551.94 − 4.57	249.57 − 4.47	127.57 − 5.39	102.42 + 0.63
290.50 − 4.57	Advcd Med Devices	3012.64 − 4.54	320.13 − 4.31	119.22 − 7.07	162.81 − 0.99
180.91 − 4.31	Biotechnology	2163.87 − 4.59	200.56 − 4.59	17.18 − 1.07	76.13 + 5.71
265.61 − 0.91	Office equipment	1317.39 − 1.41	456.67 − 1.41	167.21 − 15.51	154.43 + 1.56
918.50 + 16.12	Semiconductors	4541.87 + 17.13	1534.05 + 17.13	132.44 + 16.92	248.51 + 9.98

Household Procucts → Household products

Bio-technology → Biotechnology

Receipts (ADRs) are negotiable instruments representing foreign securities that trade like stocks in the U.S. They are listed each day in the *Journal* at the end of **NASDAQ Small-Cap Issues**. For instance, see the page 200 **ADRS** listing from the Thursday, January 14, 1999 edition.

EARNINGS AND DIVIDENDS

Many investors focus so heavily upon the potential capital gain (increase in price) of their stock that they ignore the dividends it pays. These dividends can be an important part of a stock's total return, so take a moment to consider corporate earnings and dividends.

Corporations issue stock to raise capital; investors buy shares of it to participate in the growth of the business, to earn dividends, and to enjoy possible capital gains. The ability of a corporation to pay dividends and the potential for increase in the value of a share of stock depend directly on the profits earned by the corporation: The greater the flow of profit (and anticipated profit), the higher the price investors will pay for that share of stock.

ADRS

Wednesday, Jan 13, 1999

ABB AB s .27e	510	$10\frac{1}{4}$	+	$\frac{1}{8}$
AngSA 1.37e	487	$28\frac{3}{4}$	+	$\frac{1}{4}$
AngAG .23e	74	$3\frac{15}{16}$	+	$\frac{1}{8}$
BurmhC .44e	1	$27\frac{1}{2}$	−	$\frac{1}{2}$
CSK .11e	3	$22\frac{13}{16}$	+	$1\frac{1}{16}$
CnPacMin	3	$4\frac{7}{16}$	−	$\frac{1}{32}$
DBeer 1.02e	5834	$14\frac{3}{16}$	+	$\frac{1}{16}$
DriefC .15e	96	$4\frac{3}{8}$	−	$\frac{1}{16}$
FujiPh .16e	323	$33\frac{1}{8}$	−	$\frac{3}{8}$
Ftrmdia	866	$\frac{15}{16}$	+	$\frac{1}{16}$
GoldFd	209	$1\frac{7}{8}$	−	$\frac{1}{8}$
GrtCtrl .11e	20	$2\frac{9}{16}$	+	$\frac{1}{32}$
Highvld .12e	6	$2\frac{5}{16}$	−	$\frac{1}{16}$
KirinBr .93e	4	$124\frac{5}{8}$	−	$4\frac{7}{8}$
LundnOil n .03e	39	$2\frac{1}{4}$	−	$\frac{1}{4}$
Minorc .30e	963	$15\frac{1}{2}$		...
Nissan .10j	5467	$7\frac{1}{4}$	−	$\frac{1}{8}$
RankGrp .71e	37	$7\frac{1}{16}$	+	$\frac{1}{16}$
StHIGd .62e	48	$2\frac{11}{16}$	+	$\frac{1}{16}$
Santos .64e	5	$11\frac{3}{4}$		...
Sanyo .18e	24	$14\frac{1}{4}$	−	$1\frac{1}{4}$
Sasol .27e	622	4	−	$\frac{1}{4}$
Senetek	1809	$1\frac{19}{32}$	+	$\frac{3}{32}$
SoPacPet	70	2	+	$\frac{1}{16}$
TelefMex .07e	1301	2	−	$\frac{1}{8}$
Telepart	350	3	−	$\frac{1}{4}$
Telpart wt	100	$\frac{29}{32}$	+	$\frac{1}{32}$
Toyota .33e	538	$47\frac{5}{16}$	−	$2\frac{1}{4}$
TrnBio	1220	$1\frac{5}{8}$	+	$\frac{1}{16}$

Source: *The Wall Street Journal*, January 14, 1999. Reprinted by permission of *The Wall Street Journal*, ©1999 Dow Jones & Company, Inc. All rights reserved.

The ownership value of assets depends on the income they generate, just as the value of farmland reflects profits that can be reaped by raising crops on it and the value of an apartment building reflects rent that can be collected. Similarly, the value of a share in the ownership of a corporation ultimately depends on the ability of that corporation to create profits. Note that the value of an asset depends not only on the income it currently earns, but also on its potential for greater earnings and on investors' willingness to pay for these actual and potential earnings.

A corporation's profit is one of the most important measures of its success. Profit indicates the effectiveness and efficiency with which its assets are managed and employed. Profits calibrate the ability of a firm to make and sell its product or service for more than the cost of production. Profit means that the firm has efficiently combined the labor, material, and capital necessary to produce and market its product at a price that people will pay and that will provide the owners with the financial incentive to expand the

DIGEST OF EARNINGS REPORTS

Figures in parentheses are losses.

ARV ASSISTED LIVNG (A)

Quar Sept 30:	1998	1997
Revenues	$34,886,000	$25,735,000
Inco cnt op	(5,608,000)	(3,729,000)
Inco dis op	....	(354,000)
Net income	(5,608,000)	(4,083,000)
Avg shares	15,881,000	11,109,000
Shr earns:		
Inco cnt op	(.35)	(.34)
Net income	(.35)	(.37)
9 months:		
Revenues	93,318,000	73,627,000
Inco cnt op	(13,068,000)	(5,333,000)
Inco dis op	....	(2,194,000)
Net income	(13,068,000)	(7,527,000)
Avg shares	15,881,000	10,152,000
Shr earns:		
Inco cnt op	(.82)	(.52)
Net income	(.82)	(.74)

ASA INT'L LTD. (Nq)

Quar Sept 30:	1998	1997
Revenues	$9,464,000	$6,239,000
Net income	73,000	140,000
Avg dil shs	3,661,000	3,469,000
Shr earns (diluted):		
Net income	.02	.04
9 months:		
Revenues	24,630,000	17,921,000
Net income	242,000	393,000
Avg dil shs	3,663,000	3,475,000
Shr earns (basic):		
Net income	.07	.12
Shr earns (diluted):		
Net income	.07	.11

AVI BIOPHARM INC. (Nq)

Quar Sept 30:	1998	1997
Revenues	$4,970	$5,345
Net inco	a(21,257,957)	(944,635)
Avg shares	11,539,885	11,012,743
Shr earns:		
Net inco	(1.84)	(.09)
9 months:		
Revenues	16,780	9,100
Net inco	a(14,242,779)	(2,802,725)
Avg shares	11,286,190	9,735,018
Shr earns:		
Net inco	(2.16)	(.29)
a-Includes a nonrecurring charge of $19,476,091.		

Abercrombie & Fitch ➤ **ABERCROMBIE FITCH (N)**

13 wk Oct 31:	1998	1997
Sales	$229,869,000	$148,516,000
Net income	24,943,000	10,403,000
Shr earns (basic):		
Net income	.48	.20
Shr earns (diluted):		
Net income	.47	.20
39 weeks:		
Sales	511,226,000	309,472,000
Net income	41,849,000	13,021,000
Shr earns (basic):		
Net income	.81	.26
Shr earns (diluted):		
Net income	.79	.25

AVTEL COMMUNICTNS (Nq)

Quar Sept 30:	1998	1997
Revenues	$10,589,000	a$12,403,000
Net income	(1,209,000)	(166,000)
Avg shares	9,526,410	9,366,667
Shr earns:		
Net income	(.13)	(.02)
9 months:		
Revenues	34,329,000	39,244,000
Net income	(4,944,000)	7,000
Avg shares	9,518,132	9,366,522
Shr earns:		
Net income	(.53)	(.01)
a-Corrected by company.		

AYDIN CORP. (N)

Quar Sept 26:	1998	r1997
Sales	$20,803,000	$21,006,000
Inco cnt op	1,470,000	a2,708,000
Inco dis op	(3,990,000)	(814,000)
Net income	(2,520,000)	1,894,000
Avg shares	5,220,936	5,210,984
Shr earns (diluted):		
Inco cnt op	.28	.52
Net income	(.48)	.36
9 months:		
Sales	65,211,000	69,640,000
aInco cnt op	(19,791,000)	375,000
Inco dis op	(6,659,000)	(2,490,000)
Net income	(26,450,000)	(2,115,000)
Avg shares	5,213,463	5,149,461
Shr earns (diluted):		
Inco cnt op	(3.80)	.07
Net income	(5.07)	(.41)
a-Includes nonrecurring charge of $1,548,000 in the nine months of 1998, compared with gain of $1,800,000 in the quarter and charge of $812,000 in the nine months of 1997.		

BANCO FRANCES DEL (N)

Quar Sept 30:	1998	1997
Net income	$38,801,000	$23,597,000
ADS earns:		
Net income	.62	.48

BANYAN STRAT RLTY (Nq)

Quar Sept 30:	1998	1997
Net income	$1,257,000	$1,730,000
Shr earns (diluted):		
Net income	.10	.16
9 months:		
Income	4,132,000	2,578,000
Extrd item	(141,000)	....
Net income	3,991,000	2,578,000
Shr earns (diluted):		
Income	.30	.24
Net income	.29	.24

BASF GROUP (F)

Quar Sept 30:	1998	1997
Sales	12,635,000,000	13,658,000,000
Net income	959,000,000	847,000,000
9 months:		
Sales	41,373,000,000	41,455,000,000
Net income	2,576,000,000	2,264,000,000
Amounts in German marks.		

COLORADO MEDTECH (Nq)

Quar Sept 30:	1998	1997
Sales	$13,408,421	$7,260,230
Net income	1,318,905	663,709
Avg shares	12,336,377	11,821,519
Shr earns (basic):		
Net income	.12	.07
Shr earns (diluted):		
Net income	.11	.06

COMMERCL NET LEASE (N)

Quar Sept 30:	1998	1997
Net income	$9,951,000	$7,622,000
Avg shares	29,463,000	23,826,000
Shr earns:		
Net income	.34	.32
9 months:		
Net income	23,854,000	21,575,000
Avg shares	29,202,000	23,034,000
Shr earns:		
Net income	.82	.94

COMPUSA INC. (N)

13 wk Sept 26:	1998	1997
Sales	$1,392,140,000	$1,191,812,000
Net income	8,140,000	23,459,000
Avg shares	93,041,000	95,514,000
Shr earns (basic):		
Net income	.09	.26
Shr earns (diluted):		
Net income	.09	.25

CORPORATE OFFICE PRP (N)

Quar Sept 30:	1998	1997
Net income	$1,339,000	$86,000
Shr earns (diluted):		
Net income	.12	.06
9 months:		
Net income	1,769,000	264,000
Shr earns (diluted):		
Net income	.26	.19

CRYSTAL OIL CO. (A)

Quar Sept 30:	1998	1997
Revenues	$6,556,000	$4,660,000
Net income	510,000	163,000
Avg dil shs	2,741,239	2,728,255
Shr earns (diluted):		
Net income	.19	.06
9 months:		
Revenues	20,103,000	13,317,000
Net income	881,000	1,472,000
Avg dil shs	2,741,239	2,728,016
Shr earns (basic):		
Net income	.33	.55
Shr earns (diluted):		
Net income	.32	.54

DICK CLARK PROD (Nq)

Quar Sept 30:	1998	1997
Revenues	$13,138,000	$14,055,000
Net income	46,000	115,000
Avg shares	8,808,000	8,801,000
Shr earns:		
Net income	.01	.01

operation. When costs exceed revenues and the firm takes a loss, the amount that the public is willing pay for the firm's product no longer justifies the cost of producing it.

If you are a stock owner, then, in addition to following the market indexes, you will need to monitor the earnings of particular stocks. You can do so by using *The Wall Street Journal*'s **Digest of Earnings Report**, above,

ABERCROMBIE FITCH (N)

13 wk Oct 31:	1998	1997
Sales..............	$229,869,000	$148,516,000
Net income.....	24,943,000	10,403,000
Shr earns (basic):		
Net income..	.48	.20
Shr earns (diluted):		
Net income..	.47	.20
39 weeks:		
Sales..............	511,226,000	309,472,000
Net income.....	41,849,000	13,021,000
Shr earns (basic):		
Net income..	.81	.26
Shr earns (diluted):		
Net income..	.79	.25

listed as **Earnings Digest** in the front-page index of the first and last sections. The **Digest of Earnings Report** occasionally appears in the second section of the *Journal*.

Find *Abercrombie and Fitch* in the Wednesday, November 11, 1998 reprint above. The statement reports earnings for the quarter ending October 31, 1998 and compares them with the figures for the same period one year earlier. Note also the figures for the first three-fourths of each year at the bottom half of the report. Look for revenues, net income, and net income per share (i.e., total earnings divided by total shares of stock outstanding). As you can see, Abercrombie and Fitch's performance improved very strongly in 1998.

Improved earnings are important, because (among other things) they permit corporations to pay dividends, an important source of income for many stockholders. The stock pages list current annual dividends, and you can also use the *Journal*'s daily **Corporate Dividend News** (see the Thursday, January 14, 1999 excerpt on page 203), listed in the front-page indexes of the first and last sections, to be informed of future dividend payments.

The January 14, 1999 report provides dividend news for January 13. The companies listed under the heading **Regular** will pay regular cash dividends on the payable date to all those who were stockholders on the record date.

For instance, the January 14, 1999 excerpt on page 204 reports that Procter & Gamble announced a quarterly dividend of 28.5 cents per share payable on February 16, 1999 to all stockholders of record on January 22, 1999.

Some companies prefer to pay dividends in extra stock rather than cash. Returning to the report, you can see that Walgreen Co. announced a 2-for-1

CORPORATE DIVIDEND NEWS

Dividends Reported January 13

Company	Period Amt.	Payable date	Record date
REGULAR			
AAR Corp	Q .08¹⁄₂	3– 3–99	2– 1
AmerGenlCap pfB	M .1693	2– 1–99	1–29
Applied Pwr clA	Q .01¹⁄₂	2–26–99	2– 9
ArizonaPubSvc un	M .2083	2– 1–99	1–29
Burlington Resourc	Q .13³⁄₄	4– 1–99	3–12
Conn Water Service	Q .2933	3–15–99	3– 1
G&L Rlty 10.25%pfA	M .2135	2–15–99	2– 1
G&L Rlty 9.8%pfB	M .2042	2–15–99	2– 1
General Amer Inv pfd	Q .45	3–23–99	3– 8
Household Intl $4.30 pfd	S 2.15	3–31–99	2–26
ICN Pharmaceutical new	Q .06	2– 1–99	1–22
Laidlaw Inc	Q b.07	2–15–99	1–22
Linear Technology	Q .07	2–10–99	1–22
Procter & Gamble	Q .28¹⁄₂	2–16–99	1–22
PugetSoundEnrgy7.45%pfIII	Q .465⁵⁄₈	4– 1–99	3–15
PugetSoundEnrgy8.50%pfIII	Q .53¹⁄₈	4– 1–99	3–15
PugetSoundEnrgy adipfB	Q .223¹⁄₄	2– 2–99	12–28
Richardson Elec	Q .04	3– 2–99	2–11
Skaneateles Bancorp	Q .07	2–17–99	2– 3
Unum Corp 8.8%mids	M .1833	2– 1–99	1–29
Westcorp Inc	Q .05	2– 8–99	1–22

FUNDS · REITS · INVESTMENT COS · LPS

Company	Period Amt.	Payable date	Record date
AetnaCap LLC mipsA	M .1979	2– 1–99	1–29
AmerGenlCap pfAmip	M .1760	2– 1–99	1–29
AmerGenlDel pfAmip	M .25	2– 1–99	1–29
CL&P Captl LP pfA	M .19³⁄₈	2– 1–99	1–29
CapitalReLLC pfAmip	M .159³⁄₈	2– 1–99	1–29
CommonwithGenlLLC pfrmip	M .1849	2– 1–99	1–29
ComsatCapl LP mips	M .1693	2– 1–99	1–29
CorningDel LP mips	M .25	2– 1–99	1–29
DLJ Cap Trl 8.42%pf	M .1754	1–29–99	1–28
Duquesne Capital pfA	M .1745	2– 1–99	1–29
GTE Delaware LP pfA	M .1927	2– 1–99	1–29
GTE Delaware mipsB	M .1823	2– 1–99	1–29
General Amer Inv	k1.36	3–10–99	1–25
GA Power CapLP pfA	M .18³⁄₄	2– 1–99	1–29
IIIPwrCapLP pfAmip	M .196⁷⁄₈	2– 1–99	1–29
JCP&L CapLP pfAmip	M .1783	2– 1–99	1–29
Liberty Term Tr'99	M .03	2– 1–99	1–22
LoewenGpCap pfAmip	M .196⁷⁄₈	2– 1–99	1–29
MCN MI LP pfA	M .1953	2– 1–99	1–29
MEI-EdCapLPpfv².mip	M .18¹⁄₄	2– 1–99	1–29
MissionCap 8.5% mipsB	M .1771	2– 1–99	1–29
MissionCap 9 7/8%mips	M .2057	2– 1–99	1–29
PLC CapLLC pfAmips	M .18³⁄₄	2– 1–99	1–29
PWG Capl 8.3%pfTrSec	M .1729	2– 1–99	1–29
PWG Capll 8.08%pf	M .1683	2– 1–99	1–29
PECOEngvCap pfAmip	M .18³⁄₄	2– 1–99	1–29
PenelecCap mipsA	M .1823	2– 1–99	1–29
PSE&G CapLP mipsB	M .1667	2– 1–99	1–29
PSE&G CapLP mipsA	M .1953¹⁄₈	2– 1–99	1–29
St PaulCapLLC 6%mps	M .25	2– 1–99	1–29
Texaco Cap mipsA	M .1432	2– 1–99	1–29
Texaco Cap pfB	M .09³⁄₈	2– 1–99	1–29
TorchmkCap LLC pfA	M .19¹⁄₈	2– 1–99	1–29
Transam Del LP mip	M .1901	2– 1–99	1–29
USX Captl pfAmips	M .1823	2– 1–99	1–29
Utd Cap Fd LP pfA	M .2005	2– 1–99	1–29
UtilicpCapL PpfAmip	M .1849	2– 1–99	1–29

STOCK

Company	Period Amt.	Payable date	Record date
Linear Technology	s	2–19–99	1–29
s-2-for-1 stock split.			
Northrim Bank	5%	2–16–99	2– 2
Walgreen Co	s	2–12–99	1–27
s-2-for-1 stock split.			

INCREASED

Company	Period	Amounts New	Old	Payable date	Record date
FCNB Corp	Q	.15¹⁄₂	n.15	2– 5–99	1–22
Harbor FL Bncshs	Q	.07¹⁄₂	.06¹⁄₂	2–19–99	1–29
Home Loan Financl	Q	.06	.05	2–12–99	1–29
Nordic Amer Tanker	Q	.32	.30	2–12–99	1–27

Company	Period	Amount	Payable date	Record date
NthCarolNatGas	Q	.26¹⁄₂	3–15–99	3– 1
Pall Corp	Q	.16	.15¹⁄₂ 2– 8–99	1–25
Raychem Corp	Q	.09	.08 3–10–99	2–10
Rite Aid Corp	Q	.11¹⁄₂	.10³⁄₄ 1–25–99	1–20

FOREIGN

Company	Period	Amount	Payable date	Record date
BCH Intl PR Inc pfA'94	M	.2057	2– 1–99	1–28
Embotellad AndinaADS A	–	t0.0610	– –	1–20
Embotellad AndinaADS B	–	t0.0671	– –	1–20

INITIAL

Company	Period	Amount	Payable date	Record date
Associates1stCapCorpA new	Q	.05¹⁄₂	3– 1–99	2– 1
Walgreen Co new	Q	n.03¹⁄₄	3–12–99	2–19

n-Increased amount payable on post split shrs.
A-Annual; b-Payable in Canadian funds; c-Corrected; h-From Income; k-From capital gains; M-Monthly; Q-Quarterly; r-Revised; S-Semi-annual; t-Approximate U.S. dollar amount per American Depositary Receipt/Share before adjustment for foreign taxes.

* * *

Stocks Ex-Dividend January 15

Company	Amount	Company	Amount
Capstead Mtge pfB	.10¹⁄₂	PutnamMngMuniInco	.063¹⁄₂
Caterpillar Inc	.30	PutnamMuniOppsTr	.075¹⁄₂
Embotlld AndnaA	t.0609911	PutnamNYInvGrdMuni	.06³⁄₄
EmbotlldaADS B	t.0670902	PutnamPremInco	.063
		PutnamTaxFrHlth	.07¹⁄₂
HeritageUS GovInco	.06	Rite Aid Corp	.11¹⁄₂
PutnamCAInvGrdMuni	.07¹⁄₄	Southwest Energy	.06
PutnamConvOpp&Inc	.155	SuperiorTeleCom	.078¹⁄₈
PutnamDivdndInco	.056	Union El $3.50pf	.87¹⁄₂
PutnamHiIncoCnv&Bd	.071	Union El $4.00pf	1.00
PutnamHiYldMuni	.05³⁄₄	Union El $4.50pf	1.12¹⁄₂
PutnamInvGrdMuni	.08	Union El $4.56pf	1.14
PutnamInvGrdMuniII	.08	West Co	.16
PutnamInvGrdMuniIII	.0667	t-Approximate U.S. dollar amount per American Depositary Receipt/Share before adjustment for foreign taxes.	
PutnamMngHiYld	.116		
PutnamMasterInco	.063		
PutnamMasterInter	.06		

Procter & Gamble →

Walgreen →

		REGULAR		
AAR Corp .... Q	.08½	3– 3–99	2– 1
AmerGenlCap pfB .... M	.1693	2– 1–99	1–29
Applied Pwr clA .. .. Q	.01½	2–26–99	2– 9
ArizonaPubSvc un .... M	.2083	2– 1–99	1–29
Burlington Resourc .... Q	.13¾	4– 1–99	3–12
Conn Water Service .... Q	.2933	3–15–99	3– 1
G&L Rlty 10.25%pfA .... M	.2135	2–15–99	2– 1
G&L Rlty 9.8%pfB .... M	.2042	2–15–99	2– 1
General Amer Inv pfd .... Q	.45	3–23–99	3– 8
Household Intl $4.30 pfd ...... S	2.15	3–31–99	2–26
ICN Pharmaceutical new ..... Q	.06	2– 1–99	1–22
Laidlaw Inc .... Q	b.07	2–15–99	1–29
Linear Technology .... Q	.07	2–10–99	1–22
Procter & Gamble .... Q	.28½	2–16–99	1–22
PugetSoundEnrgy7.45%pfI I .. Q	.465⅝	4– 1–99	3–15
PugetSoundEnrgy8.50%pfI I I Q	.53⅛	4– 1–99	3–15
PugetSoundEnrgy adipfB ..... Q	.223¼	2– 2–99	12–28
Richardson Elec .... Q	.04	3– 2–99	2–11
Skaneateles Bancorp .... Q	.07	2–17–99	2– 3
Unum Corp 8.8%mids .... M	.1833	2– 1–99	1–29

Procter & Gamble → (points to Procter & Gamble line)

stock split effective February 12, 1999 for all holders of record on January 27, 1999. That is, each shareholder received an additional amount of stock equal to the number of shares in his or her current holdings, thereby reducing each share's value by half. Companies split their stock in this fashion in order to reduce its price and make round-lot purchases of 100 shares more accessible to more investors.

INDUSTRY GROUPS

This chapter began with a look at the **Markets Diary**, which appears on the first page of the *Journal*'s third section (C1) (see example on page 145). That discussion mentioned the **Dow Jones Global Index** (June 30, 1982 = 100).

Each day the *Journal* breaks out the performance of these stocks in **Dow Jones Global Industry Groups** (see page 197) and **Dow Jones U.S. Industry Groups** (see page 205) (you can find the index on pages A1 or C1). The latter report presents the five industries that enjoyed the greatest relative gain in value the previous trading day and the five that suffered the biggest loss, together with the three most important contributing firms in each case. You can use this information to compare the performance of your stock with the average for the entire industry or to compare the performance of a variety of industries.

For instance, under **Technology** in the Thursday, January 14, 1999 report on pages 197 through 199 note that *Household Products* and *Biotechnology* had increased equally since June 30, 1982. That is, the index for each had risen by approximately the same amount since 1982.

Test yourself, but be honest. Do you think you could have forecast these industry performances back in 1982?

DOW JONES U.S. INDUSTRY GROUPS

January 19, 1999, 4:30 p.m. Eastern Time

GROUPS LEADING (and strongest stocks in group) **GROUPS LAGGING** (and weakest stocks in group)

GROUP	CLOSE	CHG	%CHG	GROUP	CLOSE	CHG	%CHG
Telephone	1220.14	+ 63.51	+ 5.49	**Biotechnology**	2163.87	− 74.16	− 3.31
AirTouch	92⁵/₈	+ 9¹/₄	+ 11.09	Biogen	90¹/₁₆	− 5¹⁵/₁₆	− 6.18
BellAtl	57⁷/ₓ	+ 4³/₄	+ 8.94	Monsanto	37⁷/₁₆	− 1⁹/₁₆	− 4.01
GTE	67⁷/₈	+ 5⁵/ₓ	+ 8.60	Genzyme	51⁷/₈	− 1⁵/₈	− 3.04
Broadcasting	2624.78	+ 115.13	+ 4.59	**Paper products**	625.52	− 21.06	− 3.26
TeleComm A	67¹⁵/₁₆	+ 5⁹/₁₆	+ 8.92	ChampInt	38¹/₄	− 2¹/₄	− 5.56
Comcast spA	67¹³/₁₆	+ 4¹¹/₁₆	+ 7.43	ConsldPaper	25³/₁₆	− ¹⁵/₁₆	− 3.59
MediaOne	54³/₄	+ 2¹/₂	+ 4.78	IntPaper	43³/₈	− 1¹/₂	− 3.34
Auto manufacturers	1128.68	+ 45.27	+ 4.18	**Heavy machinery**	373.80	− 11.31	− 2.94
GenMotor	88	+ 4¹¹/₁₆	+ 5.63	Caterpillar	45¹⁵/₁₆	− 1⁵/₈	− 3.42
FordMotor	63¹⁵/₁₆	+ 1¹⁵/₁₆	+ 3.13	Deere	33¹⁵/₁₆	− 1¹/₈	− 3.21
				Harnisch	10	− ³/₁₆	− 1.85
Entertainment	1038.24	+ 40.29	+ 4.04	**Banks-South**	1162.46	− 34.39	− 2.87
TimeWarn	65¹/₄	+ 3⁷/₁₆	+ 5.56	BB&T Cp	38⁷/₁₆	− 2	− 4.95
KingWorld	28⁷/₈	+ ¹/₄	+ 0.87	SunTrustBk	72⁵/₈	− 2⁹/₁₆	− 3.41
Viacom B	79¹/₁₆	+ ¹/₂	+ 0.63	Wachovia	87	− 3	− 3.33
Software	18715.23	+ 658.40	+ 3.65	**Tobacco**	1866.69	− 51.97	− 2.71
OracleCp	51¹¹/₁₆	+ 4⁹/₁₆	+ 9.68	UST Inc	32	− 1³/₈	− 4.12
Autodesk	48¹/₂	+ 3⁷/₁₆	+ 7.63	UnvlCp	31⁵/₁₆	− 1¹/₁₆	− 3.28
Peoplesoft	24¹/₂	+ ¹⁵/₁₆	+ 3.98	PhilipMor	50¹³/₁₆	− 1⁷/₁₆	− 2.75

Source: *The Wall Street Journal*, January 20, 1999. Reprinted by permission of *The Wall Street Journal*, ©1999 Dow Jones & Company, Inc. All rights reserved.

INSIDER TRADING

Finally, if you want to see what the officers and directors of the company in which you own stock are doing, you can follow the **Insider Trading Spotlight** in Wednesday's *Wall Street Journal*. An example from the Wednesday, January 20, 1999 issue is provided on page 206.

If you have an interest in a particular company, it may be worth your while to know whether its key executives and members of its board of directors have purchased its stock recently. Sales are not as important, because they can occur for a variety of reasons. Sellers may wish to diversify their portfolios or need cash. Yet you should be alert for massive selloffs by a number of insiders.

Insider purchases of a company's stock are a better indicator of long-term company prospects (why else buy the stock?) because, according to law, insiders must keep their purchases for six months. Nor may insiders sell stock short. This protects the public from insiders profiting from their knowledge at the public's expense.

Whereas insider trading may be a good clue to the fortunes of a particular company, that does not mean that insider trading can be used to successfully forecast stock market trends and turning points. They may know more than

INSIDER TRADING SPOTLIGHT

Biggest Individual Trades

(Based on reports filed with regulators last week)

COMPANY NAME	EXCH.	INSIDER'S NAME	TITLE	$ VALUE (000)	NO. OF SHRS. IN TRANS. (000)	% OF HLDNG. EXCLD. OPTNS.	TRANSACTION DATES
BUYERS							
Quorum Health Group	O	R. Carson x	D	6,810	590.0	34.00	12/22-30/98
Vista Info Solutions	O	R. J. Freeman x	D	5,000	837.5	n	12/31/98
US Timberlands Com U	O	J. M. Rudey x,s	CB	2,023	148.4	65.00	12/3-31/98
NBI Pfd A	N	J. H. Lustig	O	1,743	185.0	n	12/31/98
Unova	N	A. J. Brann	CB	1,651	100.1	99.00	12/4-10/98
Enterprise Prdts Com U	N	O. S. Andras	P	1,529	100.0	n	12/23-28/98
Infinity Brdcstng Com A	N	M. Karmazin	CB	1,025	50.0	n	12/10/98
Providian Finl	N	J. D. Grissom	D	930	10.0	10.00	12/9/98
Ford Motor (Del)	N	W. C. Ford x	D	675	12.0	1.00	12/1-2/98
Emeritus Corp	A	D. R. Baty x	CB	751	73.7	2.00	12/4-30/98
SELLERS							
Wal-Mart Stores	N	S. R. Walton	CB	56,928	750.0	1.00	12/9-16/98
EMC (Ma)	N	M. E. Egan	D	38,122	500.0	9.00	12/1-2/98
Bindview Development	O	P. L. Bloom x	D	37,567	1,883.0	39.00	12/8-9/98
Schering-Plough	N	R. P. Luciano	D	33,391	631.9	63.00	12/3-8/98 r
Autozone	N	J. R. Hyde III x	D	28,707	900.7	24.00	12/15-23/98
Oracle Corp	O	R. J. Lane	P	26,301	634.3	99.00	12/22-29/98 r
Skymall	O	R. M. Worsley	CB	23,195	650.0	12.00	12/28/98 r
SFX Entrtnmnt Com A	O	D. B. Falk	D	16,519	325.5	53.00	12/3-10/98
Edwards (JD)	O	J. L. Thompson	D	15,200	600.0	6.00	12/17-31/98
Dell Computer	O	D. K. Maxwell	O	14,308	200.7	41.00	12/21-22/98 r

Companies With Biggest Net Changes

(Based on actual transaction dates in reports received through Friday)

COMPANY NAME	EXCH./SYMBOL	NET % CHG. IN HOLDINGS OF ACTIVE INSIDERS' LATEST 12 WEEKS	NET % CHG. IN HOLDINGS OF ACTIVE INSIDERS' LATEST 24 WEEKS	LATEST 12 WKS. NO. OF BUYERS-SELLERS	LATEST 12 WKS. MULTIPLE OF HIST. NORM²	LATEST 24 WKS NO. OF BUYERS-SELLERS	LATEST 24 WKS MULTIPLE OF HIST. NORM²
BUYING							
Massachusetts Fincorp	O/MAFN	2952	2952	13-0	1.0	13-0	1.0
US Office Products	O/OFISD	1727	-	3-0	1.0	4-0	1.0
Cohoes Bancorp	O/COHB	822	822	12-0	1.0	12-0	1.0
First Place Financial	O/FPFC	801	801	11-0	1.0	11-0	1.0
Willow Grove Bancorp	O/WGBC	727	727	11-0	1.0	11-0	1.0
Security of Penn. Finl	A/SPN	635	635	10-0	1.0	10-0	1.0
Employee Solutions	O/ESOL	261	261	7-0	1.0	7-0	1.0
Baldwin Piano & Organ	O/BPAO	233	233	3-0	5.1	3-0	2.6
Unova	N/UNA	178	206	3-0	1.0 *	4-0	1.0
Bank Plus	O/BPLS	170	172	4-0	18.7 *	4-0	9.3
SELLING							
Medimmune	O/MEDI	− 78	− 78	0-3	1.0	0-3	1.0
Verity Inc	O/VRTY	− 77	− 77	0-4	1.0 *	0-4	1.0
North American Vaccine	A/NVX	− 46	− 46	0-3	4.5	0-3	2.3
Firstplus Finl Group	N/FP	− 43	− 72	1-3	1.4 *	2-3	0.7
Cable Design Tech	N/CDT	− 42	− 42	0-4	5.3	0-4	2.7
Digital Courier Tech	O/DCTI	− 34	− 34	0-3	1.0 *	0-3	1.0
Spyglass Inc	O/SPYG	− 33	− 38	0-4	3.4	0-5	2.1
Inso	O/INSO	− 29	− 34	0-5	1.0	0-6	1.0
Unitil	A/UTL	− 29	− 24	1-3	7.2	4-3	3.6
Thrustmaster	O/TMSR	− 26	− 19	0-4	1.0	1-4	1.0

NOTE: Shows purchases and sales by most officers and directors, which must be reported to the SEC and other regulators by the 10th of the month following the month of the trade. Includes both open-market and private transactions involving direct and indirect holdings. Excludes stocks valued at less than $2 a share, acquisitions through options and companies being acquired.

n-No prior holdings. r-sale within two weeks of option exercise equal to 90% or more of shares sold.s-Holds other class of stock. x-Reflects shares held indirectly. †-Late filing.*-Base period is less than 3 years.

CB-chairman. P-president. D-director. VP-vice president. O-officer. Z-other.

¹Ranked by the net change in shares held by those insiders who bought or sold during the last 12 weeks, expressed as a percentage change of only their holdings at the start of the period. Reflects companies for which filings made last week showed some insider activity during the latest 12 weeks. Excluded: companies with total trades valued under $75,000; option-related sales, unexercised options, companies with fewer than three buyers or sellers, or fewer buyers or sellers than the historical average for the period.

²Based on the previous three years.

Source: CDA/Investnet, Rockville, MD.

you do about their company, but that doesn't necessarily mean they know more than you do about the entire market. You're better off using the guidelines in this book.

GREED VERSUS FEAR

Perhaps this chapter has made clear to you how complex the stock market can be, and how many ways there are to invest in stocks. No wonder that even major investors feel they need an expert's advice before they venture their capital.

There is a saying, "Greed and fear drive the stock market." For example, greedy investors fueled the blaze of speculative gains before the crash of 1987, while fear held the market back after the crash.

So far, there has been no discussion of investors' psychological dynamics, the herd instinct created by greed and fear. Instead, these chapters treated the fundamentals of investing and then applied that analysis to a variety of stock market indicators. Here is a brief summary of these approaches.

Fundamental analysis tries to determine the intrinsic value of stocks by discovering their future earnings potential within the context of the business environment, and then concludes whether or not their present market value accurately reflects that intrinsic value.

This book's version of fundamental analysis began with a review of business cycle conditions and inflation's outlook and the impact of monetary and fiscal policy on them. From there, the analysis proceeded to a discussion of profits under a variety of cyclical and inflationary settings, and delved into the importance of these settings. At the same time, it dealt with the importance of the price-earnings ratio and the importance of current stock market valuation as a determinant of potential appreciation.

This chapter provided some additional assistance in the fundamental analysis of a particular stock. You learned how to compare that stock's performance to its industry's performance and then compare the industry to the overall market. A company's earnings and its price-earnings ratio are also ingredients in fundamental analysis. Final steps include an appraisal of a company's management and a forecast of future prospects founded upon its marketing and technological outlook and the ability to control costs.

If that makes sense, you must nonetheless keep in mind that *technical analysis*, a school with a number of passionate advocates, takes a different approach. It studies the historical price trend of the stock market, a group of stocks, or a single stock to forecast future trends. Technical analysis makes extensive use of charts to comprehend historical developments and thereby predict price movements. This reduces an understanding of the psychology

of the market and the forces of greed and fear to an analysis of charts of past price movements. For instance, if stock prices (or the price of a stock) rise and then fall back, only to rise again above the previous high, one school of technical analysis views this as a sign of market strength. On the other hand, failure of the stock to surpass its earlier peak is viewed as a sign of weakness.

Investor's Tip

- To avoid greed and fear, take the long-run view developed in these chapters.

CONCLUSION

You can make money in the stock market if you have the time and expertise required to study it closely. But as you know from Chapters 1 and 8, timing is crucial. You have to know when to get in and when to get out, because it's very difficult to find a stock that will buck the market's trend for long. Just remember that, by investing in an index fund, you can invest in that trend without investing in an individual stock.

10

COMMODITIES AND PRECIOUS METALS

INTRODUCTION

CHAPTER 9 REVIEWED INVESTMENT OPPORTUNITIES IN THE STOCK MARKET. It's now time to turn to commodities and precious metals as investment opportunities. But before you do, let's take a historical step backward to gain a little perspective on commodity and commodity futures markets, where gold (among other things) is traded for delivery and payment at a later date.

Drastic price fluctuations plagued the farmers and producers of commodities throughout our nineteenth-century westward expansion. After a period of rapid western settlement, new farms and ranches flooded the market with their output. Prices plummeted, devastating farmers and ranchers who had hoped for higher prices to cover their debts. Only after the market absorbed the excess capacity did prices firm and rise again, instigating a new round of price increases and cyclical expansion.

Wildly fluctuating prices for cotton, grain, and meat hurt the farmer and rancher as well as the textile manufacturer, flour miller, and meat packer. In order to protect themselves from unpredictable swings in market prices, these "producers" and "consumers" began contracting to buy and sell output (*commodities*) at predetermined prices for future delivery (*forward contracts*). That way both parties could more accurately forecast revenues and costs and remove some of the uncertainty and risk from their operations.

The contracting parties custom tailored the quantity, quality, delivery date, and other conditions of the forward contracts. Soon, buyers and sellers felt the need for greater flexibility. Suppose either party wanted to get out of the deal, for whatever reason. Who would take the cotton, hogs, or cattle? As a result, commodity producers and users established exchanges to trade these commodities, just as stock exchanges had been established to trade ownership in corporations. And just as a share of stock became a standardized unit of corporate ownership to be exchanged on the open market, commodity contracts were standardized with respect to quantity, quality (grade), delivery date, and price so that they could be traded, too. That established the modern *futures* contract, which can be bought and sold anonymously without any special reference to initial producer or ultimate user.

The futures contract is settled at the price initially agreed to when the contract is entered into, regardless of the commodity's market price (cash or spot price) at the time of future delivery and payment, and regardless of any subsequent change in the value of the contract due to changes in the market price. In this way, producers, such as farmers and ranchers, who contract to sell their output for future delivery, protect themselves from potentially lower spot (cash) prices, while foregoing the possibility that the actual cash prices might be higher at the time of delivery. Conversely, manufacturers, millers, meat packers, and other commodity processors who contract to buy goods for future delivery forego potentially low spot prices at time of delivery to avoid the possible risk of higher prices later. Futures contracts limit both the potential risk and the potential reward of the cash market for producers and consumers; the price risk is hedged.

For instance, if you are a wheat farmer and wheat's spot and future price is $4 a bushel, you can contract to sell it for the $4 futures price. If the spot price falls to $3, you have protected yourself by hedging (hemming in) your risk. You will have sold your wheat for $1 more than the spot price. Should the price rise to $5, you will not be able to take advantage of that opportunity, although you will have protected yourself (hedged) against the downside risk. In other words, hedging permits you to guarantee a good price while foregoing the risk and reward of extreme prices.

The miller may have the same motivation to lock in $4 with a futures contract and forego either high or low prices.

The futures market protects buyers and sellers of commodities, but it also provides a market for speculative trading. Speculators do not produce or consume the commodities they trade; they hope to profit from fluctuations in commodity prices. The possibility for speculative profits arises as futures prices fluctuate with spot prices.

If wheat sells for $4 a bushel in spot and futures markets, farmers and millers will contract for future delivery of the crop at that price. But if you are smart enough to correctly forecast that wheat will rise to $6 a bushel by the time of future delivery, you may wish to also contract to buy wheat for future delivery at $4 a bushel. Why? Because if you are right, the wheat you bought for delivery at $4 can be resold for $6 on the spot market at a gain of $2 when the day of future delivery arrives.

Moreover, you won't have to take delivery of the wheat, because as the spot price starts to rise, the price of futures contracts will also rise. After all, other speculators will begin to buy futures contracts when they see the spot price rise, bidding its price up. Therefore, when the price of the futures contract for which you paid $4 reaches $5, you can offset it by contracting for a futures sale at $5. You earn $1 by selling a bushel of wheat for $5 for which you paid only $4.

Conversely, if wheat is $6 a bushel and you correctly forecast that it will fall to $4, you can enter into a contract to sell wheat for future delivery at $6 and then fulfill your obligation on that date by purchasing wheat in the spot market for $4 and reselling it for $6 at a gain of $2. As the futures price falls to $5 with the spot price, you can make $1 with a $5 purchase of a contract for future delivery by using it to discharge your obligation to sell a contract for $6.

Speculation is important to the futures market because it provides liquidity by increasing sales and purchases of futures contracts. Speculative buying and selling broadens and deepens the market for producers and processors. As a result, fewer than 5 percent of futures contracts are held for actual delivery. The business of the exchange is conducted by traders who make a market for others and buy and sell on their own account.

LONG POSITION

Miller and manufacturer enter into futures contracts to buy commodities for future delivery at a set price. This is called a *long* position.

Investors also take long positions (i.e., purchase futures contracts that enable them to buy commodities at a stipulated price for future delivery) when they expect market prices at the time of delivery to be higher than the present futures price. If the investors' forecast of future cash prices is accurate, they will profit by selling at a high spot price the commodity they purchased for a low futures price. For instance, if you expect gold prices to be higher in October than the current October gold futures contract, you will buy that contract. If you are correct, and in October the spot prices *are* higher than the October futures contract price, your gain will be the difference

between the low futures price at which you purchased the gold and the high spot price at which you sell it.

In practice, however, fewer than 5 percent of all futures contracts are actually held to delivery; investors rarely trade the actual commodity. An investor who has taken a long position (i.e., bought a contract for future delivery) can sell the contract before the delivery date. Again, as above, if you are correct, and gold prices are rising, the October contract will have risen as well, because market forces push future prices toward spot prices as the date of delivery approaches. You will be able to sell your contract to buy gold to someone else at a higher price than you paid for it.

SHORT POSITION

Farmers, ranchers, and miners enter into futures contracts to sell commodities for future delivery at an agreed upon price. This is known as a *short* position.

Investors take short positions when they anticipate that spot prices will be lower than present futures prices. If, for example, you anticipate falling gold prices and feel that spot prices will be lower than present futures contract prices, you can take a short position in gold and thereby contract to sell gold at favorable futures prices. If you wait until the time of delivery, you can buy gold in the cash market at the low spot price and then complete or perform the contract to sell the gold at the higher contracts' futures price.

But as you learned earlier, futures contracts are rarely performed; they are generally offset with an opposing trade. As gold prices fall, and therefore futures prices with them, you can buy a contract at the new low price and discharge your obligation to sell a contract at the old high price. Your gain is the difference between the two prices.

MARGIN

Finally, be aware that whether you buy (long position) or sell (short position) a futures contract, your broker will ask you for only a small portion (say, 10 percent) of the contract's value. This margin deposit will protect the broker in the event that prices fall, should you have gone long, or rise, if you have sold short. The broker can liquidate your position quickly, as soon as prices move the wrong way, and cover the loss from your deposit. Obviously, your margin can disappear in a hurry.

If wheat's spot price is $4, and you go long because you think it will rise, but instead it falls to $3, will you be able to buy it at $4 in order to sell it at $3? Where will you get the money? That's why your broker will demand more margin.

But if wheat prices move the right way, your potential profits will accrue in your account.

INVESTING SHORT

The Wall Street Journal reports commodity prices on a daily basis (see the first or last section's index). **Future Prices** provides quotes for future delivery of specified amounts of each commodity (see pages 214–218 for excerpts from the Wednesday, October 7, 1998 *Wall Street Journal*). The line in boldface across the top tells you the name of the commodity, the exchange where it is traded, the size of a contract, and the unit in which the price is quoted. Take **Crude Oil** (see page 215) as an example. This commodity trades on the New York Mercantile Exchange (NYM) in contracts of 1,000 barrels as prices quoted in dollars per barrel. The quotations are for delivery in November and December of 1998 and January, February, March and subsequent months of 1999, continuing through December of 2004.

Using March 1999 for an example from page 215 and the top excerpt on page 220, note how the *Journal* provides the following information by column (note the column headings on the top of page 215):

Open—opening price: $15.80 per barrel for March 1999 delivery

High—highest price for trading day: $16.02

Low—lowest price for trading day: $15.77

Settle—settlement price or closing price for the trading day: $16.00

Change—difference between the latest settlement price and that of the previous trading day: an increase of ten cents (plus 0.10) for March 1999 delivery

Lifetime High—highest price ever for the March 1999 contract: $20.20

Lifetime Low—lowest price ever for the March 1999 contract: $14.40

Open Interest—number of contracts outstanding for March 1999 delivery (for the previous trading day): 19,027 contracts have not been offset by an opposing trade or fulfilled by delivery

The bottom line provides the estimated volume (number of contracts) for the day (75,722) as well as the actual volume for the prior trading day (97,792). Finally, the total open interest is given for all crude oil contracts (483,090) along with the change in the open interest from the previous trading day (–1,169).

Recall that you sell (short) futures contracts when you expect commodity prices to fall, because you anticipate a lower spot price than the futures contract price for which you are obligated. If you held the contract to maturity, you could buy at the (lower) spot price and sell at the (higher) contract price. But you also

FUTURES PRICES

Tuesday, October 6, 1998

Open Interest Reflects Previous Trading Day

GRAINS AND OILSEEDS

CORN (CBT) 5,000 bu.; cents per bu.

	Open	High	Low	Settle	Change	Lifetime High	Lifetime Low	Open Interest
Dec	209	211	208¾	210¼	+ ½	299½	196	172,500
Mr99	220½	222½	220½	222	+ ½	305	209½	70,098
May	229	230½	228¼	229½	+ ¼	299	217	27,941
July	235	236	235	235½	....	312	223½	36,652
Sept	242	242¼	241¼	241½	....	280	232	6,704
Dec	249¾	250	249	249½	– ½	291½	238	18,290
Dc00	266	267	264¼	265½	– 1	279½	254	392

Est vol 35,000; vol Mon 66,896; open int 332,713, +2,338.

OATS (CBT) 5,000 bu.; cents per bu.

	Open	High	Low	Settle	Change	Lifetime High	Lifetime Low	Open Interest
Dec	111½	113	111½	112½	....	177½	106¼	10,152
Mr99	....	....	....	121¼	+ ¼	166½	114½	3,530
May	126	126	125¼	125¾	– ¼	161	119½	485
July	130½	130¾	130½	130¾	....	150	124½	538

Est vol 800; vol Mon 849; open int 15,615, +51.

SOYBEANS (CBT) 5,000 bu.; cents per bu.

	Open	High	Low	Settle	Change	Lifetime High	Lifetime Low	Open Interest
Nov	519½	520¾	519	522¾	+ 1¾	717	508½	91,922
Ja99	530	531	529½	532¾	+ 1½	701½	518	30,799
Mar	541	544	540	542½	+ 1½	694	527	22,635
May	551	553½	550¾	551¾	+ 1	671	539½	9,541
July	558½	560	558½	....	– ½	728	549	13,370
Aug	560	....	....	560½	– ½	608	553	599
Nov	570	572	568	570½	– 1½	680	564½	5,047

Est vol 36,000; vol Mon 52,237; open int 174,011, –241.

SOYBEAN MEAL (CBT) 100 tons; $ per ton.

	Open	High	Low	Settle	Change	Lifetime High	Lifetime Low	Open Interest
Oct	125.10	126.80	125.10	126.70	+ 1.60	226.00	123.80	8,664
Dec	128.90	130.60	128.70	130.20	+ 1.30	231.00	127.40	77,379
Ja99	131.50	133.00	131.30	132.50	+ 1.10	215.50	129.80	18,169
Mar	136.00	137.40	135.80	136.70	+ .80	195.00	134.60	16,269
May	140.30	141.50	140.20	140.60	+ .60	192.50	138.60	9,622
July	144.80	146.20	144.80	145.40	+ .60	188.00	143.50	9,175
Aug	147.30	147.50	146.50	147.10	....	178.90	145.60	2,019
Sept	148.50	149.50	148.50	149.10	....	183.50	147.50	1,906
Oct		....	....	150.30	– .20	180.50	143.50	618
Dec	155.00	155.20	154.00	154.10	....	181.50	152.50	2,061

Est vol 25,000; vol Mon 37,985; open int 145,882, –1,164.

SOYBEAN OIL (CBT) 60,000 lbs.; cents per lb.

	Open	High	Low	Settle	Change	Lifetime High	Lifetime Low	Open Interest
Oct	24.55	24.57	24.31	24.35	– .23	29.55	23.05	5,920
Dec	24.33	24.42	24.17	24.24	– .10	29.30	23.15	56,300
Ja99	24.32	24.44	24.20	24.30	– .02	29.05	23.35	14,692
Mar	24.35	24.46	24.23	24.34	– .01	28.80	23.50	17,835
July	24.33	24.40	24.18	24.35	....	27.50	23.68	10,989
Sept	24.27	24.30	24.20	24.20	– .07	25.43	23.75	626
Oct		....	....	24.15	– .12	25.20	23.75	381
Dec	24.26	24.30	24.26	24.28	+ .03	25.60	23.71	2,812

Est vol 17,000; vol Mon 20,948; open int 118,555, –1,210.

WHEAT (CBT) 5,000 bu.; cents per bu.

	Open	High	Low	Settle	Change	Lifetime High	Lifetime Low	Open Interest
Dec	286½	287	282¼	283¾	– 2¾	417	251	79,519
Mr99	301	302	297	298¾	-2½	384½	266	29,416
May	310	310½	306¼	307¾	-2¼	355	278	5,325
July	319	320	315¾	317½	-1½	389	287½	12,288
Sept	327½	327½	324	325½	– 1	327½	297	396

Est vol 21,000; vol Mon 38,816; open int 127,512, +1,524.

WHEAT (KC) 5,000 bu., cents per bu.

	Open	High	Low	Settle	Change	Lifetime High	Lifetime Low	Open Interest
Dec	316½	318½	313½	314¼	– 4½	418½	277	32,247
Mr99	328½	331¼	325½	327¾	– 3¾	410½	292	14,393
May	336½	337	333	333	– 4	370	300	3,826
July	342	343½	339	340¼	– 4¼	370	308	7,715

Est vol 8,614; vol Mon 10,505; open int 59,274, +2,128.

WHEAT (MPLS) 5,000 bu.; cents per bu.

	Open	High	Low	Settle	Change	Lifetime High	Lifetime Low	Open Interest
Dec	357	360¼	352½	354¼	– 6¼	422	311½	14,390
Mr99	365½	367½	361	362½	– 4	398	319	5,922
May	370½	372	365½	366	– 4½	401	326	2,236
July	376	377	371	371¼	– 4¾	377	337	734

Est vol 5,129; vol Mon 5,780; open int 23,344, +503.

CANOLA (WPG) 20 metric tons; Can. $ per ton

	Open	High	Low	Settle	Change	Lifetime High	Lifetime Low	Open Interest
Nov	362.00	366.50	362.00	366.10	+ 3.80	397.50	349.60	35,485
Ja99	365.50	369.90	365.50	369.60	+ 3.40	401.00	354.10	17,685
Mar	371.00	372.50	369.30	372.20	+ 3.50	403.50	359.00	6,841
May		....	....	375.50	+ 4.50	409.00	364.00	581
July	377.50	380.00	376.50	379.70	+ 3.80	386.00	359.50	341
Nov	356.00	356.00	352.00	352.00	– 3.60	369.00	352.00	1,413

Est vol 7,255; vol Mn 7,119; open int 62,346, +735

WHEAT (WPG) 20 metric tons; Can. $ per ton

	Open	High	Low	Settle	Change	Lifetime High	Lifetime Low	Open Interest
Oct	142.00	142.00	141.50	141.50	– 0.80	180.50	133.40	460
Dec	143.50	143.80	142.50	142.50	– 2.00	170.00	136.60	6,002
Mr99	146.60	146.80	146.00	146.00	– 1.00	164.00	140.40	1,369
May		....	....	147.50	– 2.00	167.00	142.10	2,573
July		....	....	149.00	– 1.50	155.00	149.50	379

Est vol 110; vol Mn 395; open int 10,783, +10

BARLEY-WESTERN (WPG) 20 metric tons; Can. $ per ton*

	Open	High	Low	Settle	Change	Lifetime High	Lifetime Low	Open Interest
Oct	120.00	121.00	120.00	120.80	+ 0.20	158.00	111.50	2,104
Dec	123.50	124.40	123.50	124.00	– 0.10	151.50	114.90	7,342
Mr99	127.70	127.70	127.40	127.40	– 0.40	142.50	118.00	2,797
May	128.50	128.50	128.50	128.50	– 2.00	142.70	128.50	191

Est vol 1,000; vol Mn 909; open int 12,434, –134

LIVESTOCK AND MEAT

CATTLE-FEEDER (CME) 50,000 lbs.; cents per lb. ←Cattle

	Open	High	Low	Settle	Change	Lifetime High	Lifetime Low	Open Interest
Oct	68.45	69.15	68.40	68.80	+ .32	83.00	65.50	4,534
Nov	69.25	70.52	69.25	70.25	+ .75	83.60	66.85	5,819
Ja99	70.80	71.85	70.80	71.55	+ .50	81.75	68.05	2,811
Mar	70.90	71.70	70.85	71.50	+ .60	79.55	68.10	951
Apr	71.07	71.85	71.07	71.75	+ .65	78.62	68.30	521

Est vol 1,864; vol Mon 1,835; open int 15,191, +127.

CATTLE-LIVE (CME) 40,000 lbs.; cents per lb.

	Open	High	Low	Settle	Change	Lifetime High	Lifetime Low	Open Interest
Oct	59.30	60.47	59.27	60.30	+ .92	74.05	57.42	15,784
Dec	62.00	63.17	62.00	62.97	+ .87	74.20	59.75	42,397
Fb99	63.05	63.85	63.05	63.60	+ .50	73.50	61.00	21,688
Apr	64.75	65.35	64.75	65.30	+ .52	73.25	62.57	11,155
June	62.30	62.87	62.30	62.80	+ .40	70.20	60.97	8,067
Aug	62.40	62.85	62.40	62.55	+ .20	65.40	61.00	3,033
Oct	64.35	64.45	64.35	64.35	+ .30	64.45	61.90	149

Est vol 25,323; vol Mon 17,144; open int 102,273, +1,702.

HOGS-LEAN (CME) 40,000 lbs.; cents per lb.

	Open	High	Low	Settle	Change	Lifetime High	Lifetime Low	Open Interest
Oct	41.10	41.25	40.70	40.85	– .70	66.00	35.40	6,569
Dec	38.20	39.25	38.05	38.60	+ .12	58.50	35.52	14,995
Fb99	41.80	42.85	41.70	42.40	+ .45	59.50	40.60	8,175
Apr	42.75	44.15	42.65	43.67	+ .75	58.20	42.65	2,291
June	51.70	53.00	51.70	52.20	+ .35	65.50	51.50	2,180
July	51.90	53.05	51.75	52.35	+ .40	64.50	51.62	1,064
Aug	51.90	52.80	51.80	51.92	+ .37	63.30	51.25	1,203

Est vol 11,108; vol Mon 6,074; open int 36,810, +288.

PORK BELLIES (CME) 40,000 lbs.; cents per lb.

	Open	High	Low	Settle	Change	Lifetime High	Lifetime Low	Open Interest
Feb	44.20	46.00	43.65	44.85	+ .65	61.90	42.45	3,057
Mar	43.90	45.80	43.50	45.00	+ 1.10	61.80	42.20	227

Est vol 1,933; vol Mon 574; open int 3,391, +89.

FOOD AND FIBER

COCOA (CSCE)-10 metric tons; $ per ton.

	Open	High	Low	Settle	Change	Lifetime High	Lifetime Low	Open Interest
Dec	1,525	1,546	1,525	1,541	+ 16	1,863	1,500	32,550
Mr99	1,566	1,582	1,566	1,579	+ 17	1,901	1,538	21,825
May	1,593	1,600	1,593	1,605	+ 16	1,911	1,568	6,952
July	1,632	1,632	1,632	1,632	+ 16	1,850	1,598	2,023
Sept		....	....	1,658	+ 16	1,858	1,628	1,721
Dec		....	....	1,684	+ 16	1,885	1,653	4,974
Mr00		....	....	1,717	+ 16	1,910	1,695	3,814

Est vol 6,357; vol Mn 2,894; open int 73,859, +836.

COFFEE (CSCE)-37,500 lbs.; cents per lb.

	Open	High	Low	Settle	Change	Lifetime High	Lifetime Low	Open Interest
Dec	104.50	105.90	103.80	105.50	+ 1.70	157.50	98.75	18,350
Mr99	102.75	103.70	102.00	103.50	+ 1.60	154.00	98.50	9,052
May	103.90	104.50	103.50	104.50	+ 1.65	155.50	100.00	3,499
July	104.75	105.50	105.50	105.50	+ 1.60	131.00	101.50	1,702
Sept	105.75	106.50	106.00	106.50	+ 1.60	123.00	103.00	1,486
Dec		....	....	108.50	+ 1.60	123.00	105.30	549

Est vol 4,816; vol Mn 4,490; open int 34,638, –213.

SUGAR-WORLD (CSCE)-112,000 lbs.; cents per lb.

	Open	High	Low	Settle	Change	Lifetime High	Lifetime Low	Open Interest
Mr99	7.36	7.46	7.26	7.27	– .09	11.87	7.20	96,479
May	7.51	7.59	7.39	7.40	– .11	11.68	7.35	16,499
July	7.61	7.65	7.50	7.50	– .11	11.68	7.48	9,968
Oct	7.89	7.93	7.88	7.81	– .11	11.58	7.79	9,341
Mr00	8.15	8.16	8.05	8.05	– .11	10.00	8.05	7,859
May	8.18	8.23	8.18	8.07	– .11	9.05	8.18	471

Est vol 10,906; vol Mn 9,698; open int 140,686, –384.

SUGAR-DOMESTIC (CSCE)-112,000 lbs.; cents per lb.

	Open	High	Low	Settle	Change	Lifetime High	Lifetime Low	Open Interest
Nov	21.68	21.69	21.57	21.59	– .10	22.51	21.57	1,819
Ja99	21.70	21.73	21.70	21.73	....	22.44	21.68	3,601
Mar	21.82	21.86	21.82	21.84	+ .02	22.42	21.81	4,037
May	22.12	22.12	22.12	22.13	+ .01	22.37	22.10	2,379
July	22.33	22.33	22.30	22.32	– .05	22.46	22.10	1,814
Sept	22.41	22.41	22.41	22.38	– .08	22.47	22.28	1,156
Nov	22.03	22.05	22.03	22.03	+ .03	22.45	21.99	280
Jan	22.00	22.00	21.80	21.80	– .20	22.20	21.75	244

Est vol 785; vol Mn 733; open int 15,330, +11.

COTTON (CTN)-50,000 lbs.; cents per lb.

	Open	High	Low	Settle	Change	Lifetime High	Lifetime Low	Open Interest
Oct		....	....	74.25	+ 1.70	81.20	65.60	20
Dec	74.55	75.45	74.25	75.17	+ 1.17	78.10	66.90	35,266
Mr99	73.70	74.15	73.45	73.67	+ .48	77.25	68.50	21,805
May	73.80	74.25	73.75	73.85	+ .55	76.80	69.50	10,462
July	73.90	74.35	73.85	74.11	+ .61	77.31	69.80	6,539
Oct	71.70	71.70	71.70	71.75	....	77.05	70.80	896
Dec	70.70	70.85	70.70	70.80	– .03	74.10	69.40	8,268
Mr00	71.75	71.75	71.75	71.78	– .12	71.80	70.90	164

Est vol 14,000; vol Mn 5,809; open int 83,486, –883.

ORANGE JUICE (CTN)-15,000 lbs.; cents per lb.

	Open	High	Low	Settle	Change	Lifetime High	Lifetime Low	Open Interest
Nov	101.25	102.50	99.90	102.20	+ .90	120.90	80.95	17,319
Ja99	103.80	105.00	103.00	104.75	+ .80	122.00	83.40	7,699
Mar	106.30	107.50	105.90	107.50	+ 1.35	123.75	86.05	4,711
May		....	....	109.75	+ 1.25	126.00	90.80	922
July	110.50	111.00	110.50	111.00	+ .05	128.30	106.10	252

Est vol 3,400; vol Mn 3,929; open int 30,955, +210.

Continued

Column Headings →

METALS AND PETROLEUM

COPPER-HIGH (Cmx.Div.NYM)-25,000 lbs.; cents per lb.

	Open	High	Low	Settle	Change	Lifetime High	Lifetime Low	Open Interest
Oct	71.50	71.70	71.50	71.65	+ .65	99.40	70.75	1,966
Nov	71.85	72.10	71.70	71.90	+ .55	98.80	70.90	2,155
Dec	72.30	72.50	71.25	72.15	+ .65	102.00	70.80	32,846
Ja99	72.25	72.25	72.25	72.40	+ .60	96.80	71.30	2,038
Feb		....	....	72.65	+ .60	94.60	71.80	1,254
Mar	73.30	73.40	72.60	72.95	+ .60	98.20	71.90	5,662
Apr	73.45	73.45	73.45	73.20	+ .55	96.00	72.40	1,118
May	73.70	73.70	73.60	73.40	+ .55	98.50	72.50	2,957
June		....	....	73.60	+ .55	91.00	72.80	949
July	74.15	74.20	73.90	73.85	+ .55	95.75	72.75	2,967
Aug		....	....	74.00	+ .55	90.50	73.50	748
Sept	74.80	74.80	74.40	74.25	+ .55	94.60	73.75	2,139
Oct	74.80	74.80	74.80	74.45	+ .55	90.00	74.00	516
Nov	74.80	74.80	74.80	74.65	+ .55	86.90	74.00	480
Dec	74.90	75.10	74.80	75.05	+ .55	86.00	73.75	3,231

Est vol 7,000; vol Mn 14,084; open int 61,294, +2,711.

GOLD (Cmx.Div.NYM)-100 troy oz.; $ per troy oz.

	Open	High	Low	Settle	Change	Lifetime High	Lifetime Low	Open Interest
Oct	294.90	296.50	294.90	296.10	– .80	367.80	271.60	407
Dec	299.30	299.30	296.10	298.30	– .70	505.00	273.80	99,569
Fb99	300.80	300.80	297.80	299.90	– .70	349.50	277.50	18,086
Apr	299.60	301.50	299.50	301.40	– .70	351.20	280.00	13,629
June	301.00	303.30	300.70	302.80	– .70	520.00	282.00	14,563
Aug	302.20	304.20	302.20	304.10	– .70	327.00	289.80	5,047
Oct	303.50	305.50	303.50	305.30	– .70	308.40	287.00	1,470
Dec	305.60	307.00	305.00	306.60	– .70	506.00	286.50	10,506
Fb00		....	....	307.70	– .70	312.00	303.00	1,067
Apr		....	....	308.90	– .70	307.00	304.00	890
June		....	....	310.00	– .70	473.50	290.50	10,155
Dec		....	....	313.60	– .70	474.50	299.00	5,644
Ju01		....	....	317.40	– .70	447.00	347.00	2,290
Dec		....	....	321.30	– .70	429.50	317.00	4,691
Ju02		....	....	325.60	– .70	385.00	325.00	1,614
Dec		....	....	330.00	– .70	....	....	943
Ju03		....	....	334.20	– .70	....	....	180

Est vol 30,000; vol Mn 44,130; open int 190,751, +1,400.

PLATINUM (NYM)-50 troy oz.; $ per troy oz.

	Open	High	Low	Settle	Change	Lifetime High	Lifetime Low	Open Interest
Oct	341.00	341.00	338.50	342.20	+ 4.80	425.00	337.00	327
Ja99	339.50	345.00	338.40	344.20	+ 4.80	418.00	337.50	12,311
Apr	341.50	341.50	341.50	344.70	+ 4.80	410.00	341.50	256
Oct		....	....	347.20	+ 4.80	350.00	350.00	431

Est vol 3,163; vol Mn 3,980; open int 13,396, +257.

SILVER (Cmx.Div.NYM)-5,000 troy oz.; cnts per troy oz.

	Open	High	Low	Settle	Change	Lifetime High	Lifetime Low	Open Interest
Oct	507.5	507.5	507.5	505.0	+ 2.5	521.0	471.0	[illegible]
Dec	512.0	512.0	505.0	509.0	+ 2.5	734.0	448.5	47,392
Mr99	515.5	515.5	510.5	512.5	+ 2.5	690.0	471.0	11,685
May	515.0	518.5	512.0	514.3	+ 2.5	656.0	473.5	2,360
July	517.5	517.5	515.5	515.4	+ 2.6	680.0	472.0	2,952
Sept		....	....	516.7	+ 2.7	698.0	485.0	884
Dec	520.0	521.0	518.0	517.7	+ 2.8	720.0	482.0	3,256
Mr00				519.3	+ 2.8	555.0	515.0	118
July		....	....	523.2	+ 2.8	590.0	510.0	1,043
Dec	534.0	534.0	534.0	526.3	+ 2.8	685.0	500.0	1,357
Dc01		....	....	533.8	+ 2.8	680.0	510.0	221
Dc02	545.0	545.0	545.0	539.3	+ 2.8	613.0	520.0	253

Est vol 8,000; vol Mn 16,992; open int 71,581, –787.

Crude Oil →

CRUDE OIL, Light Sweet (NYM) 1,000 bbls.; $ per bbl.

	Open	High	Low	Settle	Change	Lifetime High	Lifetime Low	Open Interest
Nov	15.38	15.56	15.17	15.50	+ 0.11	20.63	13.28	108,239
Dec	15.50	15.67	15.32	15.61	+ 0.11	20.74	13.60	85,826
Ja99	15.64	15.77	15.45	15.74	+ 0.11	20.30	13.90	51,841
Feb	15.68	15.88	15.64	15.87	+ 0.10	20.32	14.18	20,741
Mar	15.80	16.02	15.77	16.00	+ 0.10	20.20	14.40	19,027
Apr	15.90	15.95	15.90	16.12	+ 0.09	20.27	14.65	12,249
May	16.05	16.18	16.05	16.24	+ 0.08	20.29	14.83	10,843
June	16.24	16.40	16.19	16.36	+ 0.07	20.47	15.00	23,166
July	16.32	16.53	16.32	16.47	+ 0.06	20.14	15.17	13,451
Aug	....	....	....	16.58	+ 0.06	19.47	15.33	12,699
Sept	....	....	....	16.68	+ 0.05	20.10	15.47	9,580
Oct	....	....	....	16.76	+ 0.05	20.14	15.73	5,748
Nov	16.73	16.80	16.73	16.83	+ 0.05	19.90	15.86	4,043
Dec	16.80	16.96	16.80	16.90	+ 0.05	20.75	15.90	28,056
Dc00	....	....	....	17.65	+ 0.05	20.75	17.00	16,962
Jan	16.88	16.88	16.88	16.98	+ 0.05	19.15	16.08	5,590
Feb	....	....	....	17.06	+ 0.05	20.16	16.54	2,007
Mar	....	....	....	17.14	+ 0.05	20.10	16.38	8,507
Apr	....	....	....	17.20	+ 0.05	19.16	17.27	882
May	....	....	....	17.26	+ 0.05	19.16	17.32	1,094
June	....	....	....	17.32	+ 0.05	20.10	16.55	6,222
July	....	....	....	17.37	+ 0.05	17.88	17.33	890
Aug	....	....	....	17.43	+ 0.05	17.47	17.43	2,995
Sept	....	....	....	17.49	+ 0.05	17.70	16.80	1,878
Oct	....	....	....	17.55	+ 0.05	17.55	17.28	1,461
Nov	....	....	....	17.60	+ 0.05	17.68	17.35	4,391
Dec	....	....	....	17.65	+ 0.05	20.75	17.00	16,962
Ju01	....	....	....	17.81	+ 0.04	18.13	17.85	2,412
Dec	....	....	....	18.00	+ 0.01	20.98	17.00	6,872
Dc02	....	....	....	18.33	+ 0.01	21.38	17.15	5,633
Dc03	....	....	....	18.66	+ 0.01	22.00	16.95	3,877
Dc04	....	....	....	18.88	+ 0.01	19.27	17.20	5,683

Est vol 75,722; vol Mon 97,792; open int 483,090, –1,669.

HEATING OIL NO. 2 (NYM) 42,000 gal.; $ per gal.

	Open	High	Low	Settle	Change	Lifetime High	Lifetime Low	Open Interest
Nov	.4194	.4250	.4145	.4237	+ .0048	.5905	.3635	49,284
Dec	.4300	.4370	.4270	.4361	+ .0047	.5900	.3790	28,522
Ja99	.4410	.4465	.4390	.4461	+ .0042	.5950	.3925	26,087
Feb	.4515	.4525	.4455	.4521	+ .0037	.5850	.4040	20,175
Mar	.4480	.4540	.4480	.4536	+ .0032	.5830	.4090	16,954
Apr	.4515	.4515	.4500	.4526	+ .0027	.5900	.4130	7,057
May	.4480	.4505	.4480	.4521	+ .0027	.5330	.4150	6,549
June	.4490	.4530	.4490	.4536	+ .0027	.5300	.4190	9,420
July	.4550	.4550	.4550	.4561	+ .0027	.5290	.4220	5,440
Aug	.4615	.4615	.4615	.4621	+ .0027	.5120	.4300	5,348
Sept	.4650	.4650	.4650	.4701	+ .0027	.5200	.4400	1,444
Oct	....	....	....	.4781	+ .0027	.5200	.4500	1,139
Nov	....	....	....	.4861	+ .0027	.5235	.4575	620
Dec	....	....	....	.4941	+ .0027	.5275	.4675	2,423
Ja00	....	....	....	.4996	+ .0027	.5170	.4715	2,434

Est vol 23,205; vol Mon 19,354; open int 183,318, +790.

GASOLINE-NY Unleaded (NYM)) 42,000 gal.; $ per gal.

	Open	High	Low	Settle	Change	Lifetime High	Lifetime Low	Open Interest
Nov	.4710	.4740	.4550	.4737	+ .0048	.5585	.4005	36,569
Dec	.4605	.4695	.4590	.4683	+ .0036	.5450	.4090	12,279
Ja99	.4635	.4680	.4625	.4695	+ .0038	.5350	.4180	6,306
Feb	.4705	.4730	.4695	.4746	+ .0039	.5275	.4280	4,685
Mar	.4800	.4800	.4800	.4831	+ .0039	.5230	.4433	3,442
Apr	.5070	.5085	.5070	.5111	+ .0034	.5500	.4710	5,802
May	.5135	.5135	.5135	.5156	+ .0034	.5500	.4730	4,082
June	.5145	.5160	.5145	.5161	+ .0034	.5250	.4800	1,974
July	.5115	.5145	.5115	.5146	+ .0034	.5260	.4820	3,610
Aug	....	....	....	.5126	+ .0034	.5215	.4800	155

Est vol 26,959; vol Mon 24,774; open int 79,229, –2,802.

NATURAL GAS, (NYM) 10,000 MMBtu.; $ per MMBtu's

	Open	High	Low	Settle	Change	Lifetime High	Lifetime Low	Open Interest
Nov	2.395	2.395	2.295	2.346	– .047	2.830	1.860	46,367
Dec	2.595	2.595	2.505	2.550	– .043	2.940	1.950	36,087
Ja99	2.660	2.660	2.590	2.624	– .029	2.950	2.085	31,958
Feb	2.525	2.525	2.465	2.494	– .021	2.770	2.025	19,827
Mar	2.370	2.370	2.330	2.350	– .017	2.600	1.945	17,650
Apr	2.210	2.215	2.200	2.205	– .012	2.440	1.910	10,749
May	2.150	2.160	2.145	2.150	– .010	2.380	1.960	8,458
June	2.155	2.155	2.140	2.145	– .010	2.384	1.860	9,567
July	2.150	2.150	2.135	2.142	– .010	2.390	1.960	7,408
Aug	2.150	2.155	2.135	2.142	– .010	2.390	1.975	6,479
Sept	2.150	2.150	2.140	2.142	– .010	2.380	1.970	5,687
Oct	2.170	2.185	2.170	2.182	– .010	2.415	2.042	4,026
Nov	2.333	2.333	2.315	2.323	– .010	2.535	2.140	3,688
Dec	2.455	2.455	2.440	2.447	– .010	2.680	2.213	5,603
Ja00	2.490	2.500	2.485	2.493	– .010	2.680	2.295	6,933
Feb	2.385	2.400	2.385	2.388	– .010	2.565	2.242	3,267
Mar	2.266	2.280	2.266	2.271	– .010	2.475	2.119	2,713
Apr	2.166	2.180	2.166	2.171	– .010	2.360	2.015	3,296
May	2.155	2.155	2.155	2.144	– .010	2.339	1.960	2,958
June	2.155	2.155	2.135	2.145	– .010	2.320	2.061	2,925
July	2.140	2.155	2.140	2.149	– .010	2.325	2.005	1,679
Aug	2.165	2.165	2.165	2.152	– .010	2.320	2.005	1,237
Sept	2.161	2.161	2.145	2.164	– .010	2.270	2.145	1,068
Oct	2.195	2.195	2.195	2.185	– .010	2.346	2.100	1,232
Nov	....	....	....	2.316	– .010	2.469	2.240	844
Dec	....	....	....	2.457	– .010	2.620	2.380	2,099
Ja01	....	....	....	2.478	– .010	2.675	2.477	2,050
Feb	....	....	....	2.359	– .010	2.522	2.358	1,160
Mar	....	....	....	2.270	– .010	2.420	2.269	805
Apr	....	....	....	2.169	– .010	2.315	2.174	1,213
May	....	....	....	2.156	– .010	2.305	2.161	1,029
June	2.145	2.145	2.145	2.156	– .010	2.301	2.145	293
July	2.160	2.160	2.160	2.157	– .010	2.310	2.150	855

Est vol 40,519; vol Mon 23,656; open int 251,966, +208.

BRENT CRUDE (IPE) 1,000 net bbls.; $ per bbl.

	Open	High	Low	Settle	Change	Lifetime High	Lifetime Low	Open Interest
Nov	14.00	14.14	13.81	14.12	+ .05	19.15	12.24	58,660
Dec	14.20	14.42	14.07	14.39	+ .13	18.53	12.59	52,765
Ja99	14.35	14.56	14.25	14.54	+ .15	17.95	12.82	43,810
Feb	14.46	14.69	14.41	14.68	+ .17	17.35	13.01	19,144
Mar	14.59	14.78	14.54	14.79	+ .16	17.80	13.13	13,835
Apr	14.73	14.85	14.69	14.90	+ .15	16.15	13.49	9,660
May	14.81	14.90	14.81	15.01	+ .14	16.17	13.69	8,048
June	14.97	15.02	14.90	15.12	+ .13	17.30	13.75	8,676
July		....	....	15.22	+ .12	15.48	13.96	4,805
Aug		....	....	15.32	+ .11	15.55	14.10	3,921
Sept		....	....	15.42	+ .11	16.79	14.38	2,183
Dec	15.58	15.64	15.58	15.72	+ .11	17.80	14.62	17,256
Ju00		....	....	16.12	+ .11	16.58	15.30	1,014
Dec	16.33	16.39	16.33	16.52	+ .11	17.63	15.85	3,283
Ju01	16.57	16.57	16.52	16.70	+ .11	16.57	16.28	200

Est vol 56,000; vol Mn 45,413; open int 247,310, –1,571.

GAS OIL (IPE) 100 metric tons; $ per ton

	Open	High	Low	Settle	Change	Lifetime High	Lifetime Low	Open Interest
Oct	122.75	123.75	122.00	123.50	+ 1.25	182.00	106.50	21,679
Nov	126.00	126.75	125.25	126.75	+ 1.25	184.00	110.50	32,379
Dec	129.00	129.75	128.50	129.50	+ 1.25	179.75	113.75	36,846
Ja99	131.25	132.25	131.00	132.00	+ 1.25	175.00	117.25	18,986
Feb	134.00	134.25	133.25	134.25	+ 1.50	162.00	119.75	13,994
Mar	134.75	135.25	134.50	135.75	+ 1.75	160.50	122.00	9,209
Apr		....	....	137.00	+ 1.75	186.00	12400	5,928
May	138.25	138.25	138.25	138.25	+ 1.75	150.50	129.00	2,930
June	138.75	139.50	138.75	139.50	+ 1.75	153.00	129.75	5,302
July		....	....	141.00	+ 1.75	145.50	133.25	1,082
Aug		....	....	142.50	+ 1.75	143.75	140.50	1,716
Sept	143.25	143.75	143.25	144.25	+ 2.00	175.00	138.25	1,834
Dec		....	....	149.00	+ 2.25	157.25	140.75	14,703

Est vol 16,500; vol Mn 17,573; open int 166,588, +2,819

Continued

INTEREST RATE

TREASURY BONDS (CBT)-$100,000; pts. 32nds of 100%

	Open	High	Low	Settle	Change	Lifetime High	Lifetime Low	Open Interest
Dec	133-30	134-08	133-14	134-04	– 17	135-08	103-13	739,675
Mr99	133-18	133-28	133-03	133-24	– 17	134-26	103-04	73,511
Sept	....	....	....	132-21	– 17	131-06	115-11	4,171

Est vol 575,000; vol Mon 608,339; open int 818,095, +11,149.

TREASURY BONDS (MCE)-$50,000; pts. 32nds of 100%

	Open	High	Low	Settle	Change	Lifetime High	Lifetime Low	Open Interest
Dec	133-31	134-12	133-14	134-10	– 8	135-08	118-30	16,698

Est vol 7,000; vol Mon 10,089; open int 16,716, +969.

TREASURY NOTES (CBT)-$100,000; pts. 32nds of 100%

	Open	High	Low	Settle	Change	Lifetime High	Lifetime Low	Open Interest
Dec	122-19	122-23	122-04	122-19	– 16	123-19	111-11	463,013
Mr99	123-00	123-01	122-16	122-31	– 15	123-22	112-04	15,320

Est vol 155,000; vol Mon 123,705; open int 478,582, +4,657.

5 YR TREAS NOTES (CBT)-$100,000; pts. 32nds of 100%

	Open	High	Low	Settle	Change	Lifetime High	Lifetime Low	Open Interest
Dec	115-19	115-24	115-09	15-195	– 11.5	116-07	108-30	386,101

Est vol 77,000; vol Mon 44,406; open int 387,301, –3,962.

2 YR TREAS NOTES (CBT)-$200,000, pts. 32nds of 100%

	Open	High	Low	Settle	Change	Lifetime High	Lifetime Low	Open Interest
Dec	106-20	06-235	06-162	106-21	– 5.0	106-29	04-047	35,643

Est vol 2,500; vol Mon 4,176; open int 35,643, –2,305.

30-DAY FEDERAL FUNDS (CBT)-$5 million; pts. of 100%

	Open	High	Low	Settle	Change	Lifetime High	Lifetime Low	Open Interest
Oct	94.760	94.760	94.745	94.755	– .025	94.890	94.320	13,320
Nov	94.95	94.95	94.90	94.91	– .05	94.96	94.27	7,751
Dec	95.07	95.11	95.06	95.08	– .05	95.13	94.25	7,113
Ja99	95.18	95.23	95.18	95.20	– .06	95.26	94.25	2,308
Feb	95.43	95.43	95.41	95.41	– .06	95.52	94.31	1,684
Mar	95.48	95.48	95.47	95.47	– .06	95.53	94.38	643

Est vol 5,555; vol Mon 4,571; open int 32,886, +772.

MUNI BOND INDEX (CBT)-$1,000; times Bond Buyer MBI

	Open	High	Low	Settle	Change	Lifetime High	Lifetime Low	Open Interest
Dec	129-11	129-22	129-09	129-12	– 17	130-07	123-07	22,628

Est vol 3,300; vol Mon 3,809; open int 22,647, –864.
The index: Close 129-05; Yield 4.96.

TREASURY BILLS (CME)-$1 mil.; pts. of 100%

	Open	High	Low	Settle	Chg	Discount Settle	Discount Chg	Open Interest
Dec	95.99	96.04	95.99	96.00	– .04	4.00	+ .04	1,480
Mr99	96.36	96.40	96.33	96.32	– .06	3.68	+ .06	165

Est vol 134; vol Mon 123; open int 1,668, +38.

LIBOR-1 MO. (CME)-$3,000,000; points of 100%

	Open	High	Low	Settle	Chg	Discount Settle	Discount Chg	Open Interest
Oct	94.71	94.71	94.64	94.66	– .06	5.34	+ .06	19,666
Nov	94.86	94.87	94.85	94.86	– .06	5.14	+ .06	12,202
Dec	94.84	94.85	94.82	94.84	– .04	5.16	+ .04	6,690
Ja99	95.17	95.19	95.16	95.18	– .06	4.82	+ .06	1,786
Feb	95.29	95.32	95.28	95.30	– .06	4.70	+ .06	1,201
Mar	95.36	95.40	95.36	95.39	– .07	4.61	+ .07	130

Est vol 4,212; vol Mon 7,366; open int 41,783, +711.

EURODOLLAR (CME)-$1 million; pts of 100%

	Open	High	Low	Settle	Chg	Yield Settle	Yield Chg	Open Interest
Oct	94.77	94.77	94.72	94.74	– .05	5.26	+ .05	38,191
Nov	94.93	94.95	94.91	94.92	– .05	5.08	+ .05	12,005
Dec	95.10	95.10	95.03	95.05	– .05	4.95	+ .05	497,526
Ja99	....	....	....	95.24	– .06	4.76	+ .06	2,962
Feb	95.34	95.38	95.34	95.36	– .06	4.64	+ .06	941
Mar	95.49	95.51	95.39	95.44	– .07	4.56	+ .07	492,600
June	95.66	95.66	95.52	95.58	– .08	4.42	+ .08	415,928
Sept	95.71	95.72	95.58	95.64	– .08	4.36	+ .08	323,642
Dec	95.59	95.59	95.46	95.53	– .07	4.47	+ .07	278,912
Mr00	95.56	95.60	95.52	95.57	– .08	4.43	+ .08	225,388
June	95.47	95.50	95.42	95.48	– .07	4.52	+ .07	151,046
Sept	95.37	95.40	95.33	95.38	– .08	4.62	+ .08	119,462
Dec	95.19	95.22	95.16	95.20	– .08	4.80	+ .08	111,031
Mr01	95.17	95.20	95.14	95.19	– .07	4.81	+ .07	88,916
June	95.09	95.12	95.07	95.11	– .07	4.89	+ .07	70,935
Sept	95.04	95.05	95.00	95.03	– .07	4.97	+ .07	65,792
Dec	94.88	94.91	94.86	94.89	– .07	5.11	+ .07	51,433
Mr02	94.88	94.91	94.86	94.90	– .06	5.10	+ .06	48,531
June	94.82	94.85	94.81	94.84	– .06	5.16	+ .06	51,474
Sept	94.78	94.81	94.76	94.79	– .06	5.21	+ .06	30,903
Dec	94.69	94.72	94.68	94.69	– .06	5.31	+ .06	32,818
Mr03	94.70	94.73	94.69	94.71	– .06	5.29	+ .06	29,580
June	94.66	94.69	94.65	94.67	– .05	5.33	+ .05	20,830
Sept	94.63	94.66	94.62	94.64	– .05	5.36	+ .05	16,576
Dec	94.58	94.58	94.56	94.55	– .05	5.45	+ .05	13,806
Mr04	94.60	94.60	94.58	94.58	– .04	5.42	+ .04	11,903
June	94.57	94.57	94.55	94.55	– .04	5.45	+ .04	11,648
Sept	94.55	94.58	94.53	94.53	– .04	5.47	+ .04	10,216
Dec	94.47	94.47	94.44	94.44	– .04	5.56	+ .04	10,342
Mr05	94.49	94.49	94.46	94.47	– .03	5.53	+ .03	8,912
June	94.48	94.48	94.43	94.44	– .03	5.56	+ .03	7,485
Sept	94.46	94.46	94.41	94.42	– .03	5.58	+ .03	7,712
Dec	94.38	94.38	94.34	94.33	– .03	5.67	+ .03	4,175
Mr06	94.41	94.41	94.37	94.36	– .03	5.64	+ .03	5,816
June	94.38	94.38	94.34	94.34	– .02	5.66	+ .02	6,192
Sept	94.36	94.36	94.32	94.32	– .02	5.68	+ .02	6,180
Dec	94.25	94.26	94.23	94.23	– .02	5.77	+ .02	7,721
Mr07	94.28	94.29	94.26	94.26	– .02	5.74	+ .02	5,751
June	94.25	94.26	94.23	94.24	– .01	5.76	+ .01	6,176
Sept	94.23	94.24	94.21	94.22	– .01	5.78	+ .01	5,442
Dec	94.14	94.16	94.12	94.13	– .01	5.87	+ .01	5,491
Mr08	94.16	94.18	94.14	94.16	....	5.84	....	3,998
June	94.13	94.15	94.11	94.13	....	5.87	....	3,342
Sept	94.11	94.13	94.09	94.11	....	5.89	....	1,764

Est vol 668,450; vol Mon 533,586; open int 3,321,494, –35,549.

EUROYEN (CME) -Yen 100,000,000; pts. of 100%

	Open	High	Low	Settle	Change	Lifetime High	Lifetime Low	Open Interest
Dec	99.37	99.39	99.37	99.38	+ .04	99.52	96.39	16,637
Mr99	99.41	99.42	99.41	99.42	+ .02	99.56	96.67	12,195
June	99.46	99.47	99.45	99.46	+ .01	99.56	97.45	11,960
Sept	99.41	99.41	99.41	99.41	+ .01	99.53	97.28	5,534
Dec	99.26	99.26	99.26	99.26	+ .01	99.39	97.09	6,810
Mr00	99.19	99.20	99.19	99.19	....	99.36	96.92	6,988
June	....	....	....	99.12	....	99.27	98.09	2,092
Sept	....	....	....	99.06	+ .01	99.17	98.00	461
Dec	....	....	....	98.97	....	99.10	97.92	593
Mr01	....	....	....	98.92	....	98.96	98.07	573

Est vol 3,910; vol Mon 3,348; open int 63,855, –2,657.

SHORT STERLING (LIFFE)-£500,000; pts of 100%

	Open	High	Low	Settle	Change	Lifetime High	Lifetime Low	Open Interest
Dec	93.14	93.15	93.02	93.08	– .07	93.25	91.27	191,268
Mr99	93.60	93.61	93.45	93.51	– .10	93.65	91.45	159,962
June	93.94	93.95	93.81	93.86	– .09	93.99	91.53	149,849
Sept	94.12	94.12	94.00	94.05	– .08	94.16	91.92	124,677
Dec	94.17	94.17	94.04	94.10	– .08	94.20	91.94	138,079
Mr00	94.29	94.30	94.19	94.24	– .06	94.32	91.96	116,126
June	94.31	94.33	94.21	94.27	– .06	94.35	92.47	91,321
Sept	94.29	94.31	94.20	94.25	– .05	94.31	93.01	58,206
Dec	94.24	94.24	94.19	94.72	– .04	94.28	93.22	32,930
Mr01	94.24	94.24	94.17	94.20	– .05	94.26	93.29	28,291
June	94.20	94.20	94.14	94.18	– .04	94.24	93.37	15,210
Sept	94.15	94.18	94.15	94.17	– .04	94.23	93.50	9,237
Dec	....	....	....	94.15	– .03	94.00	93.53	100
Mr02	....	....	....	94.15	– .03	93.80	93.58	401

Est vol 216,779; vol Mon 121,674; open int 1,115,734, –9,586.

LONG GILT (LIFFE) (Decimal)-£50,000; pts of 100%

	Open	High	Low	Settle	Change	Lifetime High	Lifetime Low	Open Interest
Dec	118.48	118.53	117.45	117.66	– .86	118.95	107.90	142,234

Est vol 65,237; vol Mon 45,605; open int 142,234, +656.

5 YR. GILT (LIFFE)-£50,000; pts of 100%

	Open	High	Low	Settle	Change	Lifetime High	Lifetime Low	Open Interest
Dec	....	....	....	108.99	– .43	107.40	104.81	1,674

Est vol ; vol Mon0; open int 1,674, .

3-MONTH EUROMARK (LIFFE)
DM 1,000,000; pts of 100%

	Open	High	Low	Settle	Change	Lifetime High	Lifetime Low	Open Interest
Oct	96.47	96.47	96.47	96.46	– .01	96.52	96.28	13,669
Dec	96.51	96.53	96.50	96.51	+ 0	96.54	93.40	513,403
Mr99	96.72	96.74	96.67	96.68	– .03	96.74	93.24	532,371
June	96.78	96.80	96.69	96.72	– .04	96.80	93.29	320,823
Sept	96.80	96.81	96.69	96.72	– .06	96.81	93.80	243,550
Dec	96.67	96.70	96.58	96.61	– .05	96.70	94.19	203,812
Mr00	96.73	96.75	96.65	96.66	– .06	96.76	94.24	186,651
June	96.66	96.69	96.58	96.58	– .06	96.69	93.97	129,898
Sept	96.57	96.58	96.49	96.49	– .07	96.60	93.84	84,275
Dec	96.41	96.41	96.33	96.33	– .08	96.44	93.68	26,917
Mr01	96.36	96.36	96.28	96.28	– .08	96.40	93.50	38,110
June	96.26	96.26	96.21	96.20	– .08	96.33	93.85	19,355
Sept	96.18	96 18	96.10	96.10	– .08	96.25	94.01	15,270
Dec	....	....	....	95.97	– .08	96.14	94.50	4,494
Mr02	....	....	....	95.91	– .08	96.04	94.75	2,225
June	....	....	....	95.83	– .08	95.94	94.93	828
Sept	....	....	....	95.75	– .08	95.89	95.56	274

Est vol 332,654; vol Mon 268,829; open int 2,335,925, –3,723.

3-MONTH EUROSWISS (LIFFE)
SFr 1,000,000; pts of 100%

	Open	High	Low	Settle	Change	Lifetime High	Lifetime Low	Open Interest
Dec	98.56	98.57	98.46	98.48	– .06	98.60	96.99	92,939
Mr99	98.60	98.61	98.49	98.50	– .08	98.62	96.90	57,213
June	98.58	98.58	98.46	98.46	– .09	98.58	97.34	28,190
Sept	98.48	98.50	98.38	98.39	– .09	98.50	97.34	16,988
Dec	98.28	98.28	98.18	98.19	– .09	98.28	97.19	9,022
Mr00	....	....	....	98.15	– .08	98.21	97.10	4,515
June	....	....	....	98.00	– .08	98.07	96.99	1,744
Sept	....	....	....	97.84	– .08	97.90	97.45	491

Est vol 49,263; vol Mon 45,287; open int 211,102, +9,757.

EXCHANGE ABBREVIATIONS
(for commodity futures and futures options)

CBT-Chicago Board of Trade; CME-Chicago Mercantile Exchange; CSCE-Coffee, Sugar & Cocoa Exchange, New York; CMX-COMEX (Div. of New York Mercantile Exchange); CTN-New York Cotton Exchange; EUREX-European Exchange; FINEX-Financial Exchange (Div. of New York Cotton Exchange; IPE-International Petroleum Exchange; KC-Kansas City Board of Trade; LIFFE-London International Financial Futures Exchange; MATIF-Marche a Terme International de France; ME-Montreal Exchange; MCE-MidAmerica Commodity Exchange; MPLS-Minneapolis Grain Exchange; NYFE-New York Futures Exchange (Sub. of New York Cotton Exchange); NYM-New York Mercantile Exchange; SIMEX-Singapore International Monetary Exchange Ltd.; SFE-Sydney Futures Exchange; TFE-Toronto Futures Exchange; WPG-Winnipeg CommodityExchange. CBT, CME, NYMX/CMX, CTN, FINEX, NYFE reflect overnight trading.

Continued

	Open	High	Low	Settle	Change	Lifetime High	Low	Open Interest
3-MONTH EURO LIRA (LIFFE)								
ITL 1,000,000,000; pts of 100%								
Dec	96.31	96.38	96.30	96.33	+ 0	96.39	92.84	186,293
Mr99	96.69	96.72	96.64	96.65	− .03	96.72	92.78	275,041
June	96.76	96.76	96.67	96.69	− .03	96.76	94.03	69,422
Sept	96.77	96.77	96.67	96.69	− .04	96.77	94.41	42,309
Dec	96.65	96.65	96.56	96.56	− .04	96.65	94.91	45,069
Mr00	96.69	96.69	96.60	96.60	− .05	96.70	95.23	45,524
June	96.61	96.61	96.52	96.53	− .05	96.62	95.40	33,271
Sept	96.48	96.48	96.45	96.45	− .04	96.49	96.12	1,614
Est vol 42,865; vol Mon 42,550; open int 698,545, − 1,026.								
GERMAN GOVT. BOND (LIFFE)								
250,000 marks; pts of 100%								
Dec	115.20	115.20	115.20	114.93	− .19	115.22	107.21	4,911
Est vol 5; vol Mon 166; open int 4,911, − 207.								
ITALIAN GOVT. BOND (LIFFE)								
ITL 200,000,000, pts of 100%								
Dec	111.64	111.84	111.40	111.56	+ .02	112.43	106.35	78,655
Est vol 25,412; vol Mon 30,196; open int 78,665, − 3,957.								

CANADIAN BANKERS ACCEPTANCE (ME)-C$1,000,000								
Oct	94.69	94.73	94.68	94.71	− .05	94.80	93.90	2,995
Nov				94.81	− .02	94.80	94.50	315
Dec	94.95	95.00	94.90	94.96	− .01	95.04	93.37	107,638
Mr99	95.37	95.45	95.35	95.40	− .02	95.46	93.55	66,726
June	95.50	95.58	95.48	95.54	− .01	95.58	93.70	38,281
Sept	95.51	95.57	95.50	95.54	− .02	95.57	93.80	22,629
Dec	95.33	95.39	95.33	95.37	− .02	95.40	93.77	12,736
Mr00	95.35	95.35	95.34	95.36	− .01	95.37	93.85	11,332
June				95.25	− .01	95.23	93.87	3,631
Sept	95.17	95.17	95.17	95.19	− .01	95.21	94.36	1,018
Est vol 30,002; vol Mn 26,759; open int 267,363, − 145.								
10 YR. CANADIAN GOVT. BONDS (ME)-C$100,000								
Dec	129.65	129.90	129.40	129.77	− .23	130.35	120.65	56,621
Est vol 5,942; vol Mn 6,610; open int 56,621, + 1,159.								
5 YR. FRENCH GOVT. BONDS (MATIF)								
FFr 500,000; 100ths of 100%								
Dec	103.73	103.82	103.55	103.59	− .12	111.64	99.00	21,861
Est vol 4,905; vol Mn 3,843; open int 21,861, − 47.								
10 YR. FRENCH GOVT. BONDS (MATIF)								
FFr 500,000; 100ths of 100%								
Dec	111.55	111.72	111.18	111.28	− .27	111.72	102.35	94,320
Est vol 73,341; vol Mn 71,827; open int 94,320, + 607.								
PIBOR-3 MONTH (MATIF) FF5,000,000								
Dec	96.55	96.55	96.52	96.52		96.57	93.77	80,490
Mr99	96.69	96.72	96.66	96.68	− .02	96.72	93.52	50,279
June	96.79	96.79	96.70	96.70	− .04	96.79	93.37	20,752
Sept	96.78	96.78	96.70	96.71	− .04	96.78	94.23	16,119
Dec	96.62	96.63	96.59	96.61	− .03	96.67	94.45	12,004
Mr00	96.74	96.74	96.64	96.65	− .04	96.74	94.42	6,900
June	96.69	96.69	96.69	96.59	− .04	96.69	74.48	3,483
Sept				96.48	− .04	96.53	94.36	2,252
Dec				96.34	− .04	96.23	95.00	1,238
Mr01				96.49	− .05	95.82	95.28	420
June				96.21	− .04	95.62	95.62	160
Sept				96.11	− .05			160
Est vol 8,809; vol Mn 14,989; open int 194,257, − 3,047.								
3 YR. COMMONWEALTH T-BONDS (SFE)-A$100,000								
Dec	95.57	95.58	95.48	95.50	− .05	95.58	94.03	191,730
Est vol 33,370; vol Mn 2,722; open int 191,730, + 8,502.								
EUROYEN (SIMEX)-Yen 100,000,000 pts. of 100%								
Dec	99.34	99.38	99.34	99.38	+ .30	99.49	96.37	129,258
Mr99	99.39	99.42	99.39	99.42	+ .15	99.55	96.24	117,515
June	99.46	99.47	99.45	99.46	− .05	99.56	96.65	81,751
Sept	99.41	99.42	99.41	99.41		99.53	96.99	37,910
Dec	99.24	99.24	99.24	99.25		99.59	97.23	53,828
Mr00	99.20	99.20	99.19	99.20		99.40	97.10	41,995
June				99.14		99.28	97.39	14,293
Sept	99.06	99.06	99.06	99.06	+ .01	99.15	97.94	2,965
Dec				98.97	+ .01	99.03	97.90	2,632
Mr01				98.92	+ .01	98.93	98.08	2,030
June				98.85	+ .01	99.40	98.26	845
Sept				98.80	+ .01			110
Est vol 23,583; vol Mn 24,675; open int 485,132, − 3,467.								
BOBL-5 YR. GERMAN GOVT. BOND (EUREX)								
DM 250,000; DM per $								
Dec	108.92	109.03	108.64	108.76	− .17	109.03	105.69	357,864
Mr99	108.31	108.31	108.31	108.31	− .27	108.50	108.31	3,453
Est vol 173,344; vol Mn 149,623; open int 361,317, − 740.								
BUND-10 YR. GERMAN GOVT. BOND (EUREX)								
DM 250,000; pts of 100%								
Dec	115.23	115.33	114.78	115.00	− .30	115.38	107.93	973,645
Mr99	115.77	115.83	115.38	115.52	− .37	115.87	111.49	16,719
Est vol 470,977; vol Mn 404,895; open int 990,364, + 14,924.								

SCHATZ-2 YR. GERMAN GOVT. BOND (EUREX)								
DM 250,000; DM per $								
Dec	104.75	104.80	104.66	104.69	− .06	104.88	104.10	159,232
Est vol 38,888; vol Mn 35,161; open int 159,232, + 1,989.								

INDEX

DJ INDUSTRIAL AVERAGE (CBOT)-$10 times average

	Open	High	Low	Settle	Chg	High	Low	Open Interest
Dec	7765	7920	7710	7775	+ 10	9515	7415	15,391
Mr99	7945	7970	7780	7828	+ 'c	9586	7550	1,332
June	7854	7925	7854	7881	+ 11	9150	7670	323
Est vol 16,500; vol Mon 148,173; open int 17,195, − 340.								
Idx prl: High 7880.98; Low 7683.51; Close 7742.98 + 16.74								

S&P 500 INDEX (CME)-$250 times index

Dec				104,264;				
Dec		101900	982.10	994.30	− .20	121210	890.85	395,246
Mr99	102050	102800	991.50	100280	....	122500	902.85	6,910
June				101080	....	123810	914.85	2,183
Dec				102450	+ .20	126390	980.70	630
Est vol 104,264; vol Mon 148,173; open int 405,102, +5,277.								
Idx prl: High 1008.77; Low 974.81; Close 984.59 − 3.97								

MINI S&P 500 (CME)-$50 times index

Dec	994.50	101900	982.00	994.75	− .25	121175	943.00	14,805
Vol Mon 28,356; open int 14,835, +2,584.								

S&P MIDCAP 400 (CME)-$500 times index

Dec	297.00	298.90	288.00	292.50	+ 1.50	392.00	283.00	15,789
Est vol 866; vol Mon 1,178; open int 15,790, +318.								

NIKKEI 225 STOCK AVERAGE (CME)-$5 times index

Dec	13030.	13160	13030.	13150.	+ 270	17330.	12715.	17,951
Est vol 1,384; vol Mon 2,502; open int 18,070, +271.								
Idx prl: High 13216.28; Low 12927.78; Close 13021.64 +73.52								

NASDAQ 100 (CME)-$100 times index

Dec	121700	126600	118500	119500	− 22.00	151300	113800	7,457
Est vol 5,208; vol Mon 6,261; open int 7,507, +309.								
Idx prl: High 1250.40; Low 1174.40; Close 1184.76 −22.92								

GSCI (CME)-$250 times nearby index

Oct	150.40	152.20	150.30	151.80	+ .10	175.10	139.70	21,514
Nov	152.90	154.10	152.50	153.70	+ .10	169.90	142.70	4,526
Dec				156.30	+ .20	170.30	146.30	279
Est vol 2,005; vol Mon 511; open int 26,319, − 1,067.								
Idx prl: High 152.27; Low 150.31; Close 152.24 +.67								

RUSSELL 2000 (CME)-$500 times index

Dec	345.00	345.00	331.25	333.30	− 3.00	508.85	331.25	11,661
Est vol 530; vol Mon 1,259; open int 11,662, +333.								
Idx prl: High 340.85; Low 330.94; Close 332.55 −4.25								

U.S. DOLLAR INDEX (FINEX)-$1,000 times USDX

Dec	94.87	95.21	94.26	94.50	− .40	102.60	94.26	5,715
Mr99	94.50	94.50	94.50	94.32	− .40	102.03	94.50	2,022
Est vol 2,500; vol Mon 294; open int 7,745, + 37.								
Idx prl: High 95.24; Low 94.40; Close 94.53 −.45								

ALL ORDINARIES SHARE PRICE INDEX (SFE)

A$25 times index								Open
	Open	High	Low	Settle	Chg	High	Low	Interest
Dec	2506.0	2528.0	2498.0	2508.0	− 19.0	2920.0	2426.0	133,941
Mr99				2524.0	− 19.0	2940.0	2590.0	1,251
June				2535.0	− 19.0	2850.0	2570.0	1,766
Sept				2540.0	− 19.0			137
Est vol 10,739; vol Mn 3,603; open int 137,181, +6,101.								
The index: High 2515.7; Low 2490.7; Close 2491.2 −24.5								

CAC-40 STOCK INDEX (MATIF)-FFr 50 per index pt.

Oct	2971.0	3154.0	2970.0	3145.0	+ 162.0	4045.0	2888.5	249,616
Nov	3041.5	3160.0	3041.5	3153.0	+ 161.0	3371.0	2953.0	5,319
Dec	3000.0	3167.5	3000.0	3160.0	+ 162.5	4448.5	2807.5	84,952
Mr99				3185.0	+ 164.0	4499.0	2890.0	29,465
Sept				3163.0	+ 168.0	4519.5	3407.5	31,785
Mr00				3217.0	+ 170.0	4569.4	4204.0	6,180
Est vol 87,851; vol Mn 109,931; open int 407,317, + 16,057.								

DAX-30 GERMAN STOCK INDEX (EUREX)

DM 100 times index								
Dec	3998.0	4204.0	3989.0	4196.0	+ 215.0	6285.0	3861.0	87,986
Mr99	4035.0	4235.0	4035.0	4235.0	+ 222.0	5206.5	3930.0	1,324
June	4242.0	4242.0	4242.0	4242.0	+ 202.5	4242.0	4027.0	837
Est vol 31,928; vol Mn 35,266; open int 90,147, + 210.								
The index: High 4190.80; Low 3963.38; Close 4185.39 na								

FT-SE 100 INDEX (LIFFE)-£10 per index point

Dec	4778.0	4925.0	4755.0	4920.0	+ 221.0	6285.0	4648.0	222,022
Mr99	4910.0	4910.0	4910.0	4956.0	+ 221.0	6234.0	4773.0	1,942
Est vol 32,602; vol Mn 28,483 ; open int 223,944, + 949.								

Continued

recall that contracts are usually not held to maturity. If your forecast of falling prices proves accurate, you can offset your short position to sell (*at the contract price that has remained unchanged*) with an offsetting purchase of a lower-priced long position. The price difference is your profit per barrel. Follow the step-by-step example below in order to sharpen your understanding.

1. Turn to page 220 (top excerpt) and note from the excerpt of the Wednesday, October 7, 1998 *Wall Street Journal* the $16.00 price on Tuesday, October 6, 1998 for the March 1999 crude-oil contract. Suppose at that time you sold short a March 1999 crude-oil futures contract because you believed crude oil prices would fall. Your broker would adjust your account by $16,000 ($16.00 × 1,000 barrels) to reflect the sale and ask for a good-faith deposit (margin) of, say, 10 percent ($1,600) in the event prices rose.

2.   By Wednesday, November 11, 1998 (see the Thursday, November 12, 1998 *Journal* excerpt on page 220), your forecast proved accurate, as the March 1999 crude-oil contract price dropped to $14.22 a barrel.

3.   On Friday, January 29, 1999 (see the Monday, February 1, 1999 excerpt on page 220) the March 1999 crude-oil contract traded for $12.75. You then instructed your broker to purchase a long position to buy crude oil for March 1999 delivery at the March price of $12.75 in order to offset your obligation to sell at $16.00. In other words, you *bought* a contract in order to meet your need to *sell* a contract.

4.   In that way, you realize the difference ($3.25) between the initial high futures price at which you sold ($16.00) and the present low price ($12.75) at which you bought. Your net gain on Friday, January 29, 1999, after about 4 months, is $3,250 ($3.25 per barrel × 1,000 barrels) reflecting the difference between the contract's original value of $16,000 (see number 1 above) and its current value of $12,750 ($12.75 × 1,000 barrels).

Keep in mind that you need never take possession of the commodity or actually buy or sell it. Your broker handles all transactions and maintains a running record of your gain or loss.

Return for a moment to your margin deposit of $1,600. This is a performance bond or good faith money, not a down payment. It says you are prepared to meet your contractual obligation to sell crude oil at the contract price. But remember that you must first buy the crude oil in order to sell it. Since you agreed to deliver crude oil at $16.00 a barrel, a higher spot price would have placed you in the embarrassing position of buying high in order to sell low. Had crude oil increased rather than fallen in value, your broker would have asked you to deposit additional margin to cover the difference in price.

For instance, if the spot and futures price rises to $18.00 a barrel, how does your broker know that you will be able to meet the $2,000 difference ($2.00 × 1,000 barrels) between the $18.00 you will pay for crude oil and the $16.00 at which you must deliver it? Your margin deposit of $1,600 does not cover the loss, and your broker does not wish to be responsible for it. Your broker will demand a bigger margin (deposit) from you as crude oil prices increase.

Should the price surge suddenly and unexpectedly before you can respond to your broker's call for more margin, your broker will liquidate your position to cover the difference and protect his or her own position. After all, your broker is liable for the orders he or she exercises on your behalf. You will lose your margin before your broker takes a loss on your behalf.

Commodities trading is risky.

CRUDE OIL, Light Sweet (NYM) 1,000 bbls.; $ per bbl.

March 1999 Crude-Oil Contract, $16.00 barrel →

Nov	15.38	15.56	15.17	15.50	+ 0.11	20.63	13.28	108,239
Dec	15.50	15.67	15.32	15.61	+ 0.11	20.74	13.60	85,826
Ja99	15.64	15.77	15.45	15.74	+ 0.11	20.30	13.90	51,841
Feb	15.68	15.88	15.64	15.87	+ 0.10	20.32	14.18	20,741
Mar	15.80	16.02	15.77	16.00	+ 0.10	20.20	14.40	19,027
Apr	15.90	15.95	15.90	16.12	+ 0.09	20.27	14.65	12,249
May	16.05	16.18	16.05	16.24	+ 0.08	20.29	14.83	10,843
June	16.24	16.40	16.19	16.36	+ 0.07	20.47	15.00	23,166
July	16.32	16.53	16.32	16.47	+ 0.06	20.14	15.17	13,451
Aug	....	....	....	16.58	+ 0.06	19.47	15.33	12,699
Sept	....	....	....	16.68	+ 0.05	20.10	15.47	9,580
Oct	....	....	....	16.76	+ 0.05	20.14	15.73	5,748
Nov	16.73	16.80	16.73	16.83	+ 0.05	19.90	15.86	4,043
Dec	16.80	16.96	16.80	16.90	+ 0.05	20.75	15.90	28,056
Dc00	....	....	....	17.65	+ 0.05	20.75	17.00	16,962
Jan	16.88	16.88	16.88	16.98	+ 0.05	19.15	16.08	5,590
Feb	....	....	....	17.06	+ 0.05	20.16	16.54	2,007
Mar	....	....	....	17.14	+ 0.05	20.10	16.38	8,507
Apr	....	....	....	17.20	+ 0.05	19.16	17.27	882
May	....	....	....	17.26	+ 0.05	19.16	17.32	1,094
June	....	....	....	17.32	+ 0.05	20.10	16.55	6,222
July	....	....	....	17.37	+ 0.05	17.88	17.33	890
Aug	....	....	....	17.43	+ 0.05	17.47	17.43	2,995
Sept	....	....	....	17.49	+ 0.05	17.70	16.80	1,878
Oct	....	....	....	17.55	+ 0.05	17.55	17.28	1,461
Nov	....	....	....	17.60	+ 0.05	17.68	17.35	4,391
Dec	....	....	....	17.65	+ 0.05	20.75	17.00	16,962
Ju01	....	....	....	17.81	+ 0.04	18.13	17.85	2,412
Dec	....	....	....	18.00	+ 0.01	20.98	17.00	6,872
Dc02	....	....	....	18.33	+ 0.01	21.38	17.15	5,633
Dc03	....	....	....	18.66	+ 0.01	22.00	16.95	3,877
Dc04	....	....	....	18.88	+ 0.01	19.27	17.20	5,683

Est vol 75,722; vol Mon 97,792; open int 483,090, −1,669.

Crude Oil Futures Prices on October 6, 1998

Source: *The Wall Street Journal*, October 7, 1998. Reprinted by permission of *The Wall Street Journal*, ©1998 Dow Jones & Company, Inc. All rights reserved.

CRUDE OIL, Light Sweet (NYM) 1,000 bbls.; $ per bbl.

March 1999 Crude-Oil Contract, $14.22 barrel →

Dec	13.49	13.90	13.48	13.55	+ 0.03	20.74	13.23	99,281
Ja99	13.73	14.14	13.73	13.81	+ 0.04	20.30	13.50	85,216
Feb	14.01	14.30	13.95	14.02	+ 0.03	20.32	13.77	41,625
Mar	14.30	14.50	14.25	14.22	+ 0.03	20.20	13.95	23,712
Apr	14.55	14.55	14.53	14.40	+ 0.02	20.27	14.15	14,837
May	14.68	14.85	14.57	14.57	+ 0.02	20.29	14.49	14,348
June	14.88	14.97	14.88	14.74	+ 0.02	20.47	14.62	23,285
July	15.05	15.10	15.02	14.90	+ 0.02	20.14	14.82	17,480
Aug	15.20	15.20	15.20	15.06	+ 0.02	19.47	15.10	11,714
Sept	15.36	15.36	15.25	15.22	+ 0.02	20.10	15.25	12,299
Oct	15.50	15.50	15.50	15.36	+ 0.02	20.14	15.39	8,169
Nov	15.60	15.60	15.60	15.49	+ 0.01	19.90	15.52	6,093
Dec	15.78	15.87	15.75	15.63	+ 0.01	20.75	15.60	40,611
Dc00	....	....	....	16.90	....	20.75	17.00	18,554
Jan	....	....	....	15.75	+ 0.01	19.15	15.80	8,429
Feb	....	....	....	15.87	+ 0.01	20.16	16.19	4,274
Mar	....	....	....	15.97	+ 0.01	20.10	16.38	8,693
Apr	....	....	....	16.07	+ 0.01	19.16	16.12	976
May	....	....	....	16.17	+ 0.01	19.16	16.59	1,046
June	....	....	....	16.27	+ 0.01	20.10	16.45	7,190

Crude Oil Futures Prices on November 11, 1998

Source: *The Wall Street Journal*, November 12, 1998. Reprinted by permission of *The Wall Street Journal*, ©1998 Dow Jones & Company, Inc. All rights reserved.

March 1999 Crude-Oil Contract, $12.75 barrel →

CRUDE OIL, Light Sweet (NYM) 1,000 bbls.; $ per bbl.

Mar	12.45	12.80	12.35	12.75	+ 0.30	20.20	11.10	112,385
Apr	12.47	12.82	12.44	12.79	+ 0.30	20.27	11.35	54,369
May	12.54	12.94	12.54	12.86	+ 0.28	20.29	11.63	42,700
June	12.70	13.00	12.68	12.96	+ 0.26	20.47	11.48	31,542
July	12.83	13.07	12.80	13.07	+ 0.24	20.14	12.20	24,137
Aug	13.01	13.25	12.99	13.19	+ 0.23	19.47	12.51	16,275
Sept	13.09	13.33	13.08	13.31	+ 0.22	20.10	12.72	12,795
Oct	13.22	13.48	13.22	13.43	+ 0.21	20.14	12.92	11,245
Nov	....	....	....	13.56	+ 0.20	19.90	13.07	15,232
Dec	13.52	13.75	13.47	13.69	+ 0.19	20.75	13.14	52,559

Crude Oil Futures Prices on January 29, 1999

Source: *The Wall Street Journal*, February 1, 1999. Reprinted by permission of *The Wall Street Journal*, ©1999 Dow Jones & Company, Inc. All rights reserved.

On the other hand, as noted on page 220, your broker will add your potential profits to your margin account if gold prices fall.

Finally, note the higher contract prices in the examples on page 220 as settlement dates extend further into the future. Does that mean that traders always anticipated a price increase despite continuously falling prices? No. The increases reflect the time value of money. A dollar tomorrow is worth less than a dollar today at any positive rate of interest.

INVESTING LONG

Therefore, the price of a barrel of oil for delivery a year from now must be greater than the price of a barrel of oil today in order to compensate the owner for the interest foregone by holding oil instead of an interest-earning asset.

Commodity prices do not always march in lock step. Cattle prices rose at the same time that crude-oil prices fell in the examples above. Use the excerpts from the *Journal* below to track cattle futures on the first and last dates.

Test your understanding of these concepts by asking yourself (and answering) these questions:

March 1999 Contract →

LIVESTOCK AND MEAT

CATTLE-FEEDER (CME) 50,000 lbs.; cents per lb.

Oct	68.45	69.15	68.40	68.80	+	.32	83.00	65.50	4,534
Nov	69.25	70.52	69.25	70.25	+	.75	83.60	66.85	5,819
Ja99	70.80	71.85	70.80	71.55	+	.50	81.75	68.05	2,811
Mar	70.90	71.70	70.85	71.50	+	.60	79.55	68.10	951
Apr	71.07	71.85	71.07	71.75	+	.65	78.62	68.30	521

Est vol 1,864; vol Mon 1,835; open int 15,191, +127.

Cattle Futures Prices on October 6, 1998

March 1999 Contract →

LIVESTOCK AND MEAT

CATTLE-FEEDER (CME) 50,000 lbs.; cents per lb.

Mar	72.80	73.10	72.30	72.60	−	.32	79.55	65.80	5,122
Apr	73.10	73.50	72.80	73.00	−	.12	78.62	66.85	2,709
May	73.40	73.60	72.95	73.35	−	.05	76.25	67.70	3,701
Aug	74.60	75.00	74.40	74.75		....	76.00	69.00	1,772
Sept	74.50	74.95	74.25	74.57	+	.17	75.45	69.00	406
Oct	74.75	75.25	74.40	74.90	+	.17	75.55	69.30	453

Est vol 1,662; vol Thu 2,060; open int 15,623, +294.

Cattle Futures Prices on January 29, 1999

FUTURES OPTIONS PRICES

Friday, January 29, 1999.

AGRICULTURAL

CORN (CBT)
5,000 bu.; cents per bu.

Strike	Calls-Settle			Puts-Settle		
Price	Mar	May	Jly	Mar	May	Jly
190	24½	....	....	⅛	⅝	1⅜
200	15	21¼	....	½	1¾	2⅞
210	6⅝	14	20¾	2⅛	4	5½
220	2⅛	8½	15	7⅝	8¼	9½
230	⅝	5	10⅝	16	14¾	15¼
240	¼	3	7¾	25⅝	22½	22⅛

Est vol 8,200 Th 5,958 calls 4,772 puts
Op int Thur 141,892 calls 112,747 puts

SOYBEANS (CBT)
5,000 bu.; cents per bu.

Strike	Calls-Settle			Puts-Settle		
Price	Mar	May	Jly	Mar	May	Jly
450	56¾	62½	....	⅛	1¾	2¾
475	.....	42	....	1⅛	5½	8
500	13⅝	25	32	6⅞	13	15¾
525	4⅛	13¼	21	22⅜	26½	29⅞
500	1⅛	6⅝	13½	44¼	44¾	47⅛
575	⅜	3⅝	8½	68½	66¾	66

Est vol 15,000 Th 7,608 calls 9,745 puts
Op int Thur 133,532 calls 79,984 puts

SOYBEAN MEAL (CBT)
100 tons; $ per ton

Strike	Calls-Settle			Puts-Settle		
Price	Mar	May	Jly	Mar	May	Jly
120	....	....	....	.50	....	2.35
125	6.40	8.00	....	1.25	3.25	3.90
130	3.00	5.25	7.25	2.75	5.25	6.25
135	1.50	3.50	5.50	5.90	8.60	9.25
140	.50	2.25	4.25	10.00	12.40	12.45
145	.15	1.50	3.00	14.75	16.60	16.75

Est vol 2,500 Th 1,163 calls 2,140 puts
Op int Thur 48,742 calls 32,398 puts

SOYBEAN OIL (CBT)
60,000 lbs.; cents per lb.

Strike	Calls-Settle			Puts-Settle		
Price	Mar	May	Jly	Mar	May	Jly
2100	....	....	....	....	.300	....
2150	....	....	....	.350	.490	.600
2200	.300	.650	.900	.600	.770	.810
2250	.180	.470	.700	.970	1.090	1.100
2300	.100	.370	.550	1.400	1.395	1.450
2350	.050	.250	.430	1.840	1.860	1.830

Est vol 3,500 Th 4,482 calls 1,098 puts
Op int Thur 37,505 calls 18,999 puts

WHEAT (CBT)
5,000 bu.; cents per bu.

Strike	Calls-Settle			Puts-Settle		
Price	Mar	May	Jly	Mar	May	Jly
260	17¼	29	40¼	2¼	4	5⅝
270	10½	22¼	33¼	5½	7	8¾
280	6¼	16¾	27¼	10½	11½	12½
290	3¾	12¼	22	18¼	16½	17
300	2	8⅝	17½	26	23	22¼
310	1	7	13¾	35¼	30¾	27¾

Est vol 4,000 Th 6,408 calls 949 puts
Op int Thur 84,811 calls 64,896 puts

COTTON (CTN)
50,000 lbs.; cents per lb.

Strike	Calls-Settle			Puts-Settle		
Price	Mar	May	Jly	Mar	May	Jly
59	1.96	4.15	5.04	.28	1.54	....
60	1.27	3.54	4.46	.59	1.92	2.44
61	.76	3.00	3.93	1.08	2.37	2.89
62	.40	2.52	3.45	1.72	2.87	3.38
63	.21	2.10	3.00	2.53	3.44	3.91
64	.11	1.73	2.60	3.43	4.06	4.49

Est vol 3,000 Th 2,749 calls 1,662 puts
Op int Thur 79,622 calls 30,184 puts

ORANGE JUICE (CTN)
15,000 lbs.; cents per lb.

Strike	Calls-Settle			Puts-Settle		
Price	Mar	May	Jly	Mar	May	Jly
95	9.50	10.25	11.00	.70	2.30	2.70
100	5.30	6.75	8.20	1.50	3.75	4.70
105	2.40	4.25	5.90	3.75	6.00	7.00
110	1.20	2.60	3.80	7.00	9.00	10.00
115	.70	1.50	2.50	11.50	12.50	13.50
120	.35	.90	1.50	16.15	....	....

Est vol 3,000 Th 927 calls 937 puts
Op int Thur 38,564 calls 19,047 puts

COFFEE (CSCE)
37,500 lbs.; cents per lb.

Strike	Calls-Settle			Puts-Settle		
Price	Mar	Apr	May	Mar	Apr	May
97.5	6.97	9.62	10.80	.58	1.80	3.00
100	5.09	7.93	9.11	1.20	2.60	3.80
105	1.98	5.19	6.90	2.90	4.85	6.55
110	.60	3.30	5.00	6.69	7.93	9.62
115	.15	2.20	3.70	11.24	11.81	13.29
120	.10	1.40	2.70	16.19	16.00	17.26

Est vol 2,838 Th 1,690 calls 1,969 puts
Op int Thur 25,426 calls 19,512 puts

SUGAR-WORLD (CSCE)
112,000 lbs.; cents per lb.

Strike	Calls-Settle			Puts-Settle		
Price	Mar	Apr	May	Mar	Apr	May
600	1.13	.96	1.01	.03	.10	.15
650	.67	.59	.66	.07	.23	.29
700	.30	.30	.39	.20	.42	.52
750	.11	.11	.22	.50	.73	.85
800	.04	.04	.11	.93	1.16	1.24
850	.01	.02	.04	1.40	1.64	1.69

Est vol 12,186 Th 9,181 calls 3,070 puts
Op int Thur 131,212 calls 81,316 puts

COCOA (CSCE)
10 metric tons; $ per ton

Strike	Calls-Settle			Puts-Settle		
Price	Mar	Apr	May	Mar	Apr	May
1250	81	117	124	1	5	12
1300	37	76	88	7	14	26
1350	10	45	57	29	33	45
1400	2	21	34	70	57	70
1450	1	10	20	119	96	104
1500	1	5	11	169	141	147

Est vol 585 Th 460 calls 302 puts
Op int Thur 24,844 calls 15,144 puts

OIL

CRUDE OIL (NYM)
1,000 bbls.; $ per bbl.

Strike	Calls-Settle			Puts-Settle		
Price	Mar	Apr	May	Mar	Apr	May
1200	.94	1.21	1.43	.19	.42	.58
1250	.60	.89	1.15	.35	.63	.79
1300	.37	.66	.89	.62	.87	1.03
1350	.21	.48	.69	.96	1.19	1.33
1400	.11	.34	.53	1.36	1.54	1.66
1450	.05	.15	.31	2.30	2.35	2.43

Est vol 27,049 Th 9,419 calls 8,842 puts
Op int Thu 232,518 calls 176,423 puts

HEATING OIL No.2 (NYM)
42,000 gal.; $ per gal.

Strike	Calls-Settle			Puts-Settle		
Price	Mar	Apr	May	Mar	Apr	May
31	....	....	....	.0045	.0080	.0110
32	.0210	.0294	.0385	.0068	.0113	.0150
33	.0158	.0185	.0321	.0116	.0203	.0185
34	.0100	.0150	.0267	.0158	.0267	.0230
35	.0070	.0115	.0200	.0228	.0332	.0263
36	.0040	.0093	.0165	.0297	.0409	.0327

Est vol 821 Th 1,343 calls 770 puts
Op int Th 38,857 calls 16,827 puts

GASOLINE-Unlead (NYM)
42,000 gal.; $ per gal.

Strike	Calls-Settle			Puts-Settle		
Price	Mar	Apr	May	Mar	Apr	May
35	.0362	....	....	.0028	....	....
36	.0285	....	....	.0051	.0055	.0060
37	.0215	....	....	.0080	....	.0085
38	.0160	....	....	.0125	.0100	.0100
39	.0110	.0342	....	.0175	.0130	.0125
40	.0085	.0280	.0376	.0250	.0168	.0175

Est vol 1,735 Th 538 calls 36 puts
Op int Th 18,310 calls 12,631 puts

NATURAL GAS (NYM)
10,000 MMBtu.; $ per MMBtu.

Strike	Calls-Settle			Puts-Settle		
Price	Mar	Apr	May	Mar	Apr	May
170	.149	....	....	.072	.090	.090
175	.123	....	....	.096	.112	.110
180	.103	.145	.172	.123	.138	.134
185	.083	.124	.150	.156	.171	.160
190	.066	.104	.129	.189	.200	.191
195	.052	.088	.111	.224	.234	.222

Est vol 8,932 Th 7,727 calls 5,698 puts
Op int Th 143,278 calls 118,178 puts

BRENT CRUDE (IPE)
1,000 net bbls.; $ per bbl.

Strike	Calls-Settle			Puts-Settle		
Price	Mar	Apr	May	Mar	Apr	May
1050	.92	1.25	1.49	.07	.33	.44
1100	.53	.92	1.19	.18	.50	.64
1150	.27	.66	.94	.42	.74	.89
1200	.11	.46	.73	.76	1.04	1.18
1250	.04	.31	.56	1.19	1.39	1.51
1300	.02	.20	.42	1.67	1.78	1.87

Est vol 2,105 Th 35 calls 2,220 puts
Op int Thur 19,178 calls 15,930 puts

GAS OIL (IPE)
100 metric tons; $ per ton

Strike	Calls-Settle			Puts-Settle		
Price	Feb	Mar	Apr	Feb	Mar	Apr
9000	5.55	12.00	13.50	.10	2.00	1.70
9500	2.25	8.25	10.05	.55	3.55	3.10
10000	.90	5.40	7.25	2.25	5.75	5.25
10500	.50	3.35	5.10	5.90	8.60	7.85
11000	.15	1.95	3.55	10.50	12.05	11.05
11500	.05	1.05	2.45	15.15	15.95	14.70

Est vol 0 Th 10 calls 0 puts
Op int Thur 5,857 calls 1,934 puts

LIVESTOCK

CATTLE-FEEDER (CME)
50,000 lbs.; cents per lb.

Strike	Calls-Settle			Puts-Settle		
Price	Mar	Apr	May	Mar	Apr	May
7200	1.75	2.77	3.12	1.15	1.80	1.80
7250	....	....	....	....	....	....
7300	1.10	....	....	1.50	....	....
7350	....	....	....	....	....	....
7400	.87	1.50	2.00	2.27	2.47	2.65
7450	....	....	....	....	....	....

Est vol 456 Th 256 calls 236 puts
Op int Thur 3,423 calls 7,222 puts

CATTLE-LIVE (CME)
40,000 lbs.; cents per lb.

Strike	Calls-Settle			Puts-Settle		
Price	Feb	Apr	Jun	Feb	Apr	Jun
60	2.07	5.47	....	.12	.45	.82
61	1.25	4.65	....	.30	.60	....
62	.60	3.85	3.47	.65	.80	1.30
63	.25	3.12	....	1.30	1.07	....
64	.07	2.52	2.35	2.12	1.45	2.15
65	.02	1.92	....	3.07	1.85	....

Est vol 2,817 Th 539 calls 1,306 puts
Op int Thur 32,473 calls 40,429 puts

HOGS-LEAN (CME)
40,000 lbs.; cents per lb.

Strike	Calls-Settle			Puts-Settle		
Price	Feb	Apr	Jun	Feb	Apr	Jun
38	3.47	6.27	16.57	.45	1.30	.17
39	2.72	....	....	.70	1.60	....
40	2.02	5.05	14.67	1.00	2.05	.30
41	1.42	....	....	1.40	2.30	....
42	1.00	3.82	12.77	1.97	2.80	.40
43	.60	3.27	....	2.57	3.25	....

Est vol 652 Th 1,040 calls 571 puts
Op int Thur 17,116 calls 14,712 puts

METALS

COPPER (CMX)
25,000 lbs.; cents per lb.

Strike	Calls-Settle			Puts-Settle		
Price	Mar	Apr	May	Mar	Apr	May
60	4.75	5.55	6.45	.25	.65	1.15
62	3.15	4.10	5.00	.70	1.20	1.70
64	1.90	2.90	3.80	1.40	1.95	2.50
66	1.05	1.95	2.85	2.50	3.00	3.50
68	.50	1.25	2.05	4.00	4.30	4.65
70	.20	.75	1.45	5.70	5.80	6.05

Est vol 300 Th 215 calls 48 puts
Op int Thu 20,563 calls 4,920 puts

GOLD (CMX)
100 troy ounces; $ per troy ounce

Strike	Calls-Settle			Puts-Settle		
Price	Mar	Apr	Jun	Mar	Apr	Jun
275	13.60	13.90	17.10	.60	1.50	2.60
280	8.80	10.00	13.00	.80	2.00	3.20
285	4.70	6.20	9.80	1.50	3.00	5.00
290	1.90	3.80	7.30	3.80	5.60	7.30
295	.70	2.00	4.80	7.60	9.20	10.10
300	.30	.90	3.50	12.10	13.10	13.50

Est vol 6,200 Th 5,008 calls 2,361 puts
Op int Thu 306,401 calls 121,192 puts

Source: *The Wall Street Journal*, February 1, 1999. Reprinted by permission of *The Wall Street Journal*,

1.   What were the prices for the March 1999 (October 7, 1998 and February 1, 1999 excerpts) contracts on page 221, and how much did they change?

2.   How could an investor have profited from these price movements by purchasing long contracts? By how much would the investor have profited in each case? Note that prices are quoted in cents per pound and that a contract is 50,000 pounds.

OTHER FUTURES AND OPTIONS ON FUTURES CONTRACTS

Turn once again to the excerpt from the Monday, February 1, 1999 *Journal* on pages 214–218 and notice that you can purchase futures contracts on investments other than commodities. For instance, futures contracts are available on **Treasury Bonds**, **Eurodollars**, the **S & P 500**, the **NYSE Composite Index**, and the **Dow Jones Industrial Average**. Whereas futures began with commodities like wheat, trading activity is now far heavier for instruments like Treasury bonds. *Futures options* let you buy options on futures contracts (see page 222).

TRACKING COMMODITIES

Every day, on the first page of the third section (C1), *The Wall Street Journal* summarizes recent **Commodities** activity under the **Markets Diary** heading. A sample from the Monday, February 1, 1999 edition appears on

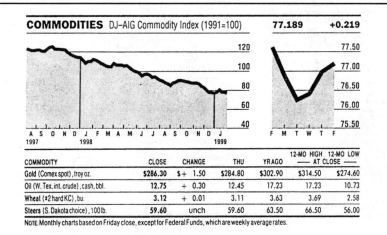

COMMODITY	CLOSE	CHANGE	THU	YR AGO	12-MO HIGH — AT CLOSE —	12-MO LOW
Gold (Comex spot), troy oz.	**$286.30**	$+ 1.50	$284.80	$302.90	$314.50	$274.60
Oil (W. Tex. int. crude), cash, bbl.	**12.75**	+ 0.30	12.45	17.23	17.23	10.73
Wheat (#2 hard KC), bu.	**3.12**	+ 0.01	3.11	3.63	3.69	2.58
Steers (S. Dakota choice), 100 lb.	**59.60**	unch	59.60	63.50	66.50	56.00

NOTE: Monthly charts based on Friday close, except for Federal Funds, which are weekly average rates.

the previous page. The chart presents the **DJ-AIG Commodity Index** and spot prices for **Gold**, **Oil**, **Wheat**, and **Steers**.

The Wall Street Journal carries a commodities article daily in the third section; on Mondays it includes the Dow Jones **Commodity Indexes**. See the example from the Monday, February 1, 1999 issue below.

You can use the daily or weekly indexes to follow commodity price movements. These indexes will be your most sensitive barometers of inflation.

Gold Rallies as Duisenberg Parries Gore's Plan

COMMODITIES

By Betsy Dowling Stephens
Dow Jones Newswires

NEW YORK—Gold futures rallied Friday, helped by comments by European Central Bank President Wim Duisenberg indicating that European central banks will hang onto their gold reserves.

Mr. Duisenberg's remarks held sway over those of U.S. Vice President Al Gore, who proposed selling "a small proportion" of gold held by the International Monetary Fund for a debt-relief fund. Mr. Gore and Mr. Duisenberg were attending the World Economic Forum, in Davos, Switzerland.

In trading Friday at the Comex division of the New York Mercantile Exchange, the most-active April gold contract rose $1.60 to $288.20 a troy ounce, while the February contract rose $1.50 to $286.30 an ounce.

Mr. Duisenberg said gold reserves held by central banks are "reserves to hold and not reserves to spend." That helped placate some of the continuing concerns about sales by European central banks, which last year drove prices to a 19-year low.

"The market had a near obsession with central-bank sales last year and the year before. That seems to have diminished with the successful launch of the Euro," said Jim Steel, commodities analyst at Refco Inc. in New York. Mr. Duisenberg's remark "brings transparency. It's good for gold," he added.

One concern in the market was that the central banks of the 11 nations involved in European economic and monetary union would sell gold to meet the fiscal criteria for EMU's launch on Jan 1, that concern is redundant.

Robin Alssid, precious metals manager at Mitsubishi International Corp. in New York, said Mr. Gore and Mr. Duisenberg almost canceled out each other's comments but that Mr. Duisenberg had more impact.

"The idea of using gold from the IMF to fund developing nations is something that I think we've heard so many times before and will be overhanging the market, but

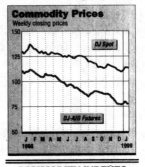

Commodity Prices
Weekly closing prices

DJ Spot

DJ-AIG Futures

J F M A M J J A S O N D J
1998   1999

COMMODITY INDEXES

Friday, January 29, 1999

	Close	Net Chg.	Yr. Ago
Dow Jones-AIG Futures	77.189	+ .219	111.926
Dow Jones Spot	112.69	+ .21	137.02
Reuter United Kingdom	1438.2	− 5.7	1756.8
C R B BRIDGE Futures	189.74	+ .42	234.39

Dow Jones REIT Indexes

Friday, January 29, 1999

	Close	Net Chg	% Chg	YTD % Chg	Yld
Equity REIT	127.94	− 0.68	− 0.53	− 2.64	7.42
Equity REIT-tot ret	245.31	− 1.28	− 0.52	− 2.40	....
Composite REIT	116.03	− 0.43	− 0.37	− 2.56	7.58
Composite REIT-tot ret	230.59	− 0.84	− 0.36	− 2.26	....

Indexes of publicly traded Real Estate Investment Trusts. Jan 1990 = 100. Yield based on indicated annualized dividend.

until it happens, I'm not sure it's going to have any effect," Ms. Alssid said, referring to Mr. Gore's proposal.

Refco's Mr. Steel also pointed out that gold prices had continued to rise Thursday and Friday despite strength in both U.S. stocks and the dollar, factors that usually spell weakness for the precious metal.

Ms. Alssid said gold seemed to find strength after falling on Wednesday below $285 an ounce, recognized by traders as a key level on price charts. She said buying came in at $282, giving the metal good support that brought it up to Friday's high of $287.70 an ounce. However, she said it could be tough for gold to push above its next key resistance area of $290 to $292 an

ounce.

COPPER: Futures prices rose slightly on the Comex division of the New York Mercantile Exchange, after earlier falling to a 12-year low Friday. The March contract added 0.15 cent to 64.50 cents a pound after hitting an intraday low of 63.60 cents. Jim Steel, analyst at Refco Inc. in New York, said short covering—the buying of futures to balance previous sales—started as participants became nervous about prices dropping below 64 cents.

SOYBEANS: Futures fell to an 11-year low for the fourth straight session at the Chicago Board of Trade. The March contract dropped 3.50 cents to $5.0675 a bushel. "The big story continues to be the pretty much ideal weather in South America," said Don Roose, analyst with U.S. Commodities in West Des Moines, Iowa.

—Daniel Rosenberg
contributed to this article.

CASH PRICES

Friday, January 29, 1999
(Closing Market Quotations)
GRAINS AND FEEDS

	Fri	Thur	Year Ago
Barley, top-quality Mpls., bu	u2.25	2.25	z
Bran, wheat middlings, KC ton	u59-63	58-62	81.50
Corn, No. 2 yel. Cent. Ill. bu	bpu2.05½	2.07½	2.61½
Corn Gluten Feed, Midwest, ton	60-70	65-80	77.50
Cottonseed Meal, Clksdle, Miss. ton	97.50	97.50	135.00
Hominy Feed, Cent. Ill. ton	58.00	58.00	81.00
Meat-Bonemeal, 50% pro. Ill. ton	145.00	c145.00	160.00
Oats, No. 2 milling, Mpls., bu	u1.21¼	1.21½	z
Sorghum, (Milo) No. 2 Gulf cwt	u409-14	407-16	5.08
Soybean Meal, Cent. Ill., rail, ton 44%	u123½-6½	124-7	191.00
Soybean Meal, Cent. Ill., rail, ton 48%	u132½-4½	133-5	201.50
Soybeans, No. 1 yel Cent.-Ill. bu	bpu4.96½	4.99	6.67
Wheat, Spring 14%-pro Mpls. bu	u389-404	390¾-405¾	4.13½
Wheat, No. 2 sft red, St.Lou. bu	bpu2.50	2.47	3.39
Wheat, hard KC, bu	3.11½	3.10½	3.62½
Wheat, No. 1 sft whf, del Port Ore	u3.20	3.19	3.68

FOODS

Beef, Carcass, Equiv.Index Value, choice 1-3,550-700lbs.	u91.88	92.54	94.24
Beef, Carcass, Equiv.Index Value, select 1-3,550-700lbs.	u88.36	87.28	93.00
Broilers, Dressed "A" lb.	ux.5877	.5968	.5281
Broilers, 12-Cty Comp Wtd Av	u.5889	.5889	.5455
Butter, AA, Chgo., lb.	u1.35½	1.42¾	1.36
Cheddar Cheese, barrels, Chgo lb.	n122.50	122.00	143.00
Cheddar Cheese, blocks, Chgo lb.	n126.00	126.00	136.00
Cocoa, Ivory Coast, $metric ton	1,539	1,534	1,731
Coffee, Brazilian, NY lb.	n1.01½	1.01½	1.86½
Coffee, Colombian, N Y lb.	n1.11½	1.11½	1.96½
Eggs, Lge white, Chgo doz.	u.68-73	.73-8	.77½
Flour, hard winter KC cwt	9.15	9.15	9.70
Hams, 17-20 lbs, Mid-US lb fob	u.47½	.46	z
Hogs, Iowa-S.Minn. avg. cwt	u27.00	27.00	37.25
Hogs, S. Dakota avg. cwt	u26.50	28.25	37.00
Pork Bellies, 12-14 lbs Mid-US lb	u.53-4	.53-4	.52½
Pork Loins, 13-19 lbs. Mid-US lb	u.85½	.89½-101	1.14
Steers, Tex.-Okla. ch avg cwt	u60.50	z	63.00
Steers, Feeder, Okl Cty, av cwt	u81.00	81.00	88.00
Sugar, cane, raw, world, lb. 100	7.59	7.15	11.43

FATS AND OILS

Coconut Oil, crd, N. Orleans lb.	xxn.35	.35	.26½
Corn Oil, crd wet/dry mill, Chgo.	u28-29	28½-9¼	.27
Grease, choice white, Chgo lb.	n.12½	.12½	.13½
Lard, Chgo lb.	.15	.15	.16
Palm Oil, ref. bl. deod. N.Orl. lb.	n.31	.31	.29¼
Soybean Oil, crd, Centrai Ill. lb.	u2151-71	2171-191	.2517
Tallow, bleachable, Chgo lb.	.13½	.13½-14	.16¼
Tallow, edible, Chgo lb.	.16	.16	.18½

FIBERS AND TEXTILES

Burlap, 10 oz 40-in NY yd	n.3300	.3300	.3000
Cotton 1 1/16 str lw-md Mphs lb	.5918	.5955	.6362
Wool, 64s, Staple, Terr. del. lb.	u1.05	1.05	2.60

METALS

Aluminum ingot lb. del. Midwest	p.58½-9½	c58¾-9¾	.73½
Copper high gr lb., Cmx sp price	.64	.64	.79
Copper Scrap, No 2 wire NY lb	h.49½	.49½	.64
Lead, lb.	pna	c.43689	.45042
Mercury 76 lb. flask NY	q165-85	165-85	187.5
Steel Scrap 1 hvy mlt EC ton	83-5	83-5	145.5
Tin composite lb.	q3.5136	3.5189	3.5637
Zinc Special High grade lb	q.48200	.48100	.52750

MISCELLANEOUS

Rubber, smoked sheets, NY lb.	n.38½	38¾	.43½
Hides, hvy native steers lb., fob	u68-71	68-71	70.5

PRECIOUS METALS

Gold, troy oz			
Engelhard indust bullion	286.54	284.68	306.02
Engelhard fabric prods	300.86	298.92	321.32
Handy & Harman base price	285.40	283.55	304.85
Handy & Harman fabric price	299.67	297.73	320.09
London fixing AM 285.65 PM	285.40	283.55	304.85
Krugerrand, whol	a295.00	293.00	309.00
Maple Leaf, troy oz.	a296.50	294.50	313.50
American Eagle, troy oz.	a296.50	294.50	313.50
Platinum, (Free Mkt.)	344.50	342.00	386.50
Platinum, indust (Engelhard)	346.00	344.00	390.00
Platinum, fabric prd (Engelhard)	446.00	444.00	490.00
Palladium, indust (Engelhard)	341.00	335.00	238.00
Palladium, fabrc prd (Englhard)	356.00	350.00	253.00
Silver, troy ounce			
Engelhard indust bullion	5.270	5.190	6.280
Engelhard fabric prods	5.902	5.813	7.034
Handy & Harman base price	5.275	5.155	6.255
Handy & Harman fabric price	5.908	5.774	7.006
London Fixing (in pounds)			
Spot (U.S. equiv.$5.2375)	3.1791	3.0852	3.6895
Coins, whol $1,000 face val	a5,323	5,330	4,251

a-Asked. b-Bid. bp-Country elevator bids to producers. c-Corrected. h-Reuters. n-Nominal. na-Not available. p-Producer price via Platt's Metals Week. q-Platt's Metals Week. r-Rail bids. u-U.S. Dept. of Agriculture. x-Less than truckloads. z-Not quoted. xx-f.o.b. tankcars.

The Wall Street Journal reports **Cash Prices** for immediate delivery on a wide variety of commodities on a daily basis. On Monday, February 1, 1999, the *Journal* published cash prices for Friday, January 29, 1999 (see above).

All of these series can be located using the indexes on the front pages of the first and last sections.

CONCLUSION

Commodities investing is far riskier than stock market investing, because positions are highly leveraged. You can lose your entire investment if prices move the wrong way. Moreover, individual commodities can be drastically affected by random events–droughts, floods, wars, and political upheavals. Yet these markets also present tremendous opportunities for those who can accurately forecast inflation's trend.

11

LONG-TERM INTEREST RATES

INTRODUCTION

Chapter 9 investigated the stock market; this chapter will examine long-term debt instruments. You will discover why they, like stocks, appreciate when prices are stable, but become poor investments when inflation turns severe. Begin your investigation with a general discussion of the origin of these investments.

Governments and businesses turn to the credit markets and issue long-term debt instruments to raise large sums whenever their internally generated funds, such as tax revenues or profits, fall short of their current or capital expenditures. The federal government, for instance, began the 1990s by annually borrowing hundreds of billions of dollars in the capital markets, because recession suppressed revenue growth while expenditures continued to climb.

Corporations, on the other hand, issue debt (i.e., sell bonds that are redeemed after a long period throughout which they pay interest) in order to finance the purchase of new plants and equipment. Take public utilities for example. Profits cannot cover the cost of new generating and switching stations, satellites, and transmission lines, so the difference has to be made up by borrowing. Since the projects of public utility companies are long-term and generate income for these companies over several decades of useful life, it's appropriate that the financing be long-term too. The stretch-out in earnings on these assets will provide for the regular payment of interest and principal.

You already know that corporations can raise funds by selling shares via the stock market (see Chapter 9). In that process, the ownership of a corporation is subdivided by the issue of new stock. The situation is very different when corporations borrow funds in the credit markets. Ownership does not change hands, although, of course, the debt burden increases.

New credit market debt, whether sold by government or business, is subdivided into discrete units called notes or bonds and is issued for a specified length of time. At the conclusion of that period, the issuer redeems the note or bond and repays the initial purchase price. Notes are medium-term debt instruments that are redeemed in one to 10 years, whereas bonds are issued with maturities of more than 10 years. (Chapter 12 discusses debt instruments with maturities of less than a year.)

Notes and bonds are sold or auctioned in the *primary* (initial issue) market and then traded on the *secondary* market until they mature (redeemed by the issuer). They have a specific face or *par value* (such as $1,000) and pay a specified annual, semiannual, or quarterly amount, known as *coupon interest*. When you purchase a bond, expect to receive an interest return (called the *current* or *true* yield) determined by the relationship between the fluctuating market price of the bond (more, less, or equal to its fixed $1,000 par value) and the fixed periodic payment of coupon interest. If you hold the bond to maturity (i.e., until it is redeemed by the issuer), you will also receive back its par value.

But you need not hold the note or bond to maturity, because there is a secondary market for notes and bonds that is separate from the initial-issue market. The existence of this secondary or resale market makes it much easier for government and business to sell bonds in the initial primary market. If note and bond buyers could not sell and resell these instruments over and over again, it would be very difficult for government and businesses to issue them in the first place. Now you know why these instruments are issued in discrete units (such as $1,000) for convenient trading.

Trading on the secondary market determines all notes' and bonds' market prices and thereby determines their current yields. The secondary market dog wags the primary market tail. Not only are primary market auction or issue prices determined by secondary market trading, but primary-market coupon rates will quickly reflect true yields established in the secondary market.

There are three principal issuers of bonds: the United States government and its agencies; corporations; and state and local governments. Examine each of their issues in turn.

TREASURY AND AGENCY ISSUES

Both the U.S. Treasury and a variety of federal agencies issue long-term debt instruments. Treasury debt is classified as bonds, notes, and bills. The Treasury bill will be discussed in Chapter 12. Treasury notes (maturities of 1 to 10 years) and bonds (over 10 years) are issued in $1,000 denominations and pay a stated coupon interest payment semiannually.

Treasury bills, bonds, and notes are referred to collectively as **Treasury Securities**. These securities are the safest of all debt instruments, because they are backed by the full taxing power of the U.S. government.

The government sells Treasury securities when it needs funds. These primary market sales are made at auction to securities dealers. Dealers then resell them on the secondary market to investors, where they are traded freely until maturity. The value of daily trading in the secondary market (an over-the-counter market in New York) far exceeds the value of the daily trades on the New York Stock Exchange. *The Wall Street Journal* reports activity in the primary and secondary markets for long-term Treasury securities in its daily **Credit Markets** article in the third (C) section (see front-page index).

The Treasury announces its auction of 2-year notes once a month. The auction takes place during the last full week of the month, and the notes are issued on the last day. Five-year, two-month (62-month) notes are auctioned and issued with the two-year notes.

The Treasury generally auctions 3-year notes and 10-year notes quarterly, during the first week of February, May, August, and November and issues them shortly afterward, on the 15th of the same month. Thirty-year bonds are issued twice a year in February and August.

Bonds and notes are almost always issued in denominations of $1,000, which is referred to as the par value of the bond. Each bond has a coupon rate indicating the dollar amount the security will pay annually until maturity. Interestingly, bonds are seldom auctioned at precisely their par value, because market conditions will influence buyers' bids at the auction.

The Treasury entertains bids at the primary auction and arrays them from highest to lowest. The Treasury accepts bids starting at the highest price and works down until it has accepted a sufficient number of bids to realize its target funding. The par value and coupon interest rate is established before the auction begins, but the true yield is determined by the price established at the auction. It can be higher or lower than the $1,000 par value. If higher, the true yield will be less than the coupon rate. If lower, the true yield will be more than the coupon rate.

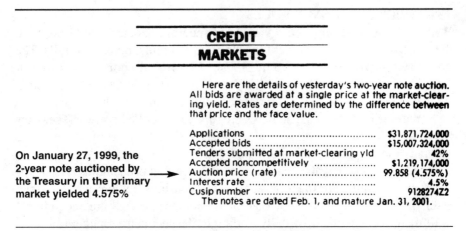

CREDIT MARKETS

Here are the details of yesterday's two-year note auction. All bids are awarded at a single price at the market-clearing yield. Rates are determined by the difference between that price and the face value.

On January 27, 1999, the 2-year note auctioned by the Treasury in the primary market yielded 4.575%

Applications	$31,871,724,000
Accepted bids	$15,007,324,000
Tenders submitted at market-clearing yld	42%
Accepted noncompetitively	$1,219,174,000
Auction price (rate)	99.858 (4.575%)
Interest rate	4.5%
Cusip number	9128274Z2

The notes are dated Feb. 1, and mature Jan. 31, 2001.

Look at the Thursday, January 28, 1999 *Journal* excerpt above from the **Credit Markets** article (see the front-page index) that reports on the previous day's 4.575% two-year note issue. Noncompetitive bids totaled $1.2 billion. These small bidders took the market (average) price established at the auction. Notice that (on the average) successful bidders paid 99.858% of par ($1,000), so that a $1,000 2-year note cost $998.58 (on the average), which is $1.42 less than par. The coupon rate (interest rate) was 4.5% or $45.00 annually per $1,000 note. But since successful bidders paid only $998.50 on the average, the true yield was a slightly higher 4.575%. Therefore, the 4.575% true yield on these 2-year notes was slightly higher than the coupon rate of 4.5%.

Major financial institutions, not individuals, bid in the primary market for Treasury securities, but your bank or broker can act as your agent if you wish to purchase a Treasury note or bond in the secondary (resale) market. This market is very liquid, which means that you should have no trouble buying or selling securities on any business day. The third section of *The Wall Street Journal* reports trading on the secondary market for Treasury notes and bonds on a daily basis under **Treasury Bonds, Notes & Bills**. (See the report on pages 231 and 232 for Friday, January 29, 1999 in the Monday, February 1, 1999 *Wall Street Journal*. You can locate it using the front-page index of the first or last section.)

The first column of **Treasury Bonds, Notes & Bills** begins with figures headed **Govt. Bonds & Notes**. Turn to the *bellwether* (named after the lead

sheep in the flock that wears a bell) 30-year Treasury bond on page 232 and in the next-to-last blowup on page 234. It is listed last among **Govt. Bonds and Notes** because it has the most recent date of issue and, therefore, has the longest span of time until maturity. The first two columns describe the bond or note in question. Begin with the coupon rate in the first column (*Rate*). Since it is 5¼, a $1,000 note or bond will pay $52.50 annually (5.25% of $1,000). The

TREASURY BONDS, NOTES & BILLS

Friday, January 29, 1999

Representative and Indicative Over-the-Counter quotations based on $1 million or more.

Treasury bond, note and bill quotes are as of mid-afternoon. Colons in bond and note bid-and-asked quotes represent 32nds; 101:01 means 101 1/32. Net changes in 32nds. Treasury bill quotes in hundredths, quoted in terms of a rate discount. Days to maturity calculated from settlement date. All yields are to maturity and based on the asked quote. Most recently auctioned treasury bonds and notes, and current 13-week and 26-week bills are boldfaced. For bonds callable prior to maturity, yields are computed to the earliest call date for issues quoted above par and to the maturity date for issues quoted below par. n-Treasury note. i-Inflation-indexed. wi-When issued. iw-Inflation-indexed when issued; daily change is expressed in basis points.

Source: Dow Jones/Cantor Fitzgerald.

U.S. Treasury strips as of 3 p.m. Eastern time, also based on transactions of $1 million or more. Colons in bid-and-asked quotes represent 32nds; 99:01 means 99 1/32. Net changes in 32nds. Yields calculated on the asked quotation. ci-stripped coupon interest. bp-Treasury bond, stripped principal. np-Treasury note, stripped principal. For bonds callable prior to maturity, yields are computed to the earliest call date for issues quoted above par and to the maturity date for issues below par.

Source: Bear, Stearns & Co. via Street Software Technology Inc.

GOVT. BONDS & NOTES

Rate	Maturity Mo/Yr	Bid	Asked	Chg.	Ask Yld.
5	Feb 99n	99:31	100:01	....	4.08
8 7/8	Feb 99n	100:04	100:06	....	3.78
5 1/2	Feb 99n	100:00	100:02	....	4.55
5 7/8	Feb 99n	100:01	100:03	....	4.50
5 7/8	Mar 99n	100:05	100:07	....	4.40
6 1/4	Mar 99n	100:07	100:09	..	4.38
7	Apr 99n	100:14	100:16	....	4.39
[illegible]	Apr 99n	100:12	100:14	....	4.40
6 1/[illegible]	Apr 99n	100:13	100:15	....	4.46
6 3/8	May 99n	100:14	100:16	....	4.53
9 1/8	May 99n	101:07	101:09	....	4.48
6 1/4	May 99n	100:15	100:17	....	4.55
6 3/4	May 99n	100:20	100:22	-1	4.56
6	Jun 99n	100:17	100:19	-1	4.51
6 3/4	Jun 99n	100:27	100:29	-1	4.48
6 3/8	Jul 99n	100:25	100:27	....	4.46
5 7/8	Jul 99n	100:18	100:20	....	4.59
6 7/8	Jul 99n	101:02	101:04	....	4.56
6	Aug 99n	100:22	100:24	....	4.57
8	Aug 99n	101:24	101:26	-1	4.55
5 7/8	Aug 99n	100:21	100:23	....	4.59
6 7/8	Aug 99n	101:07	101:09	....	4.58
5 3/4	Sep 99n	100:22	100:24	....	4.57
7 1/8	Sep 99n	101:18	101:20	....	4.58
6	Oct 99n	100:28	100:30	-1	4.61
5 5/8	Oct 99n	100:21	100:23	....	4.62
7 1/2	Oct 99n	102:00	102:02	-1	4.63
5 7/8	Nov 99n	100:28	100:30	-1	4.63
7 7/8	Nov 99n	102:14	102:16	....	4.58
5 5/8	Nov 99n	100:24	100:26	....	4.60
7 3/4	Nov 99n	102:15	102:17	....	4.58
5 5/8	Dec 99n	100:26	100:28	-1	4.63
7 3/4	Dec 99n	102:22	102:24	-1	4.63
6 3/8	Jan 00n	101:16	101:18	-1	4.68
5 3/8	Jan 00n	100:21	100:23	-1	4.63
7 3/4	Jan 00n	102:30	103:00	-1	4.64
5 7/8	Feb 00n	101:05	101:07	-1	4.66
8 1/2	Feb 00n	103:26	103:28	-1	4.63
5 1/2	Feb 00n	100:26	100:28	-1	4.65
7 1/8	Feb 00n	102:16	102:18	-1	4.65
5 1/2	Mar 00n	100:28	100:30	-1	4.65
6 7/8	Mar 00n	102:13	102:15	-1	4.66
5 1/2	Apr 00n	100:29	100:31	-2	4.65
5 5/8	Apr 00n	101:03	101:05	-1	4.65
6 3/4	Apr 00n	102:13	102:15	-2	4.67
6 3/8	May 00n	102:02	102:04	-1	4.64
8 7/8	May 00n	105:05	105:07	-1	4.63
5 1/2	May 00n	101:00	101:02	-2	4.66
6 1/4	May 00n	101:31	102:01	-1	4.65
5 3/8	Jun 00n	100:29	100:31	-2	4.65
5 7/8	Jun 00n	101:19	101:21	-1	4.65
5 3/8	Jul 00n	100:31	101:01	-2	4.65
6 1/8	Jul 00n	102:01	102:03	-2	4.66

Rate	Maturity Mo/Yr	Bid	Asked	Chg.	Ask Yld.
6	Aug 00n	101:29	101:31	-2	4.66
8 3/4	Aug 00n	105:31	106:01	-1	4.65
5 1/8	Aug 00n	100:20	100:22	-2	4.66
6 1/4	Aug 00n	102:10	102:12	-3	4.67
4 1/2	Sep 00n	99:22	99:24	-2	4.65
6 1/8	Sep 00n	102:08	102:10	-2	4.66
4	Oct 00n	98:27	98:29	-3	4.66
[illegible]/4	Oct 00n	101:24	101:26	-2	4.65
5 3/4	Nov 00n	101:25	101:27	-3	4.66
8 1/2	Nov 00n	106:15	106:17	-3	4.64
4 5/8	Nov 00n	99:29	99:31	-3	4.64
5 5/8	Nov 00n	101:20	101:22	-3	4.65
4 5/8	Dec 00n	99:26	99:27	-6	4.71
5 1/2	Dec 00n	101:16	101:18	-1	4.63
4 1/2	**Jan 01n**	**99:26**	**99:27**	**-1**	**4.58**
5 1/4	Jan 01n	101:02	101:04	-4	4.65
5 3/8	Feb 01n	101:12	101:14	-2	4.63
7 3/4	Feb 01n	105:30	106:00	-2	4.63
11 3/4	Feb 01	113:19	113:23	-2	4.63
5 5/8	Feb 01n	101:28	101:30	-2	4.63
6 3/8	Mar 01n	103:13	103:15	-3	4.66
6 1/4	Apr 01n	103:09	103:11	-2	4.66
5 5/8	May 01n	102:04	102:05	-2	4.62
8	May 01n	107:04	107:06	-3	4.64
13 1/8	May 01	118:04	118:08	-3	4.61
6 1/2	May 01n	103:29	103:31	-2	4.68
6 5/8	Jun 01n	104:10	104.12	-2	4.68
6 5/8	Jul 01n	104:15	104:17	-3	4.68
7 7/8	Aug 01n	107:15	107:17	-3	4.69
13 3/8	Aug 01	120:16	120:22	-1	4.65
6 1/2	Aug 01n	104:10	104:12	-2	4.67
6 3/8	Sep 01n	104:04	104:06	-2	4.68
6 1/4	Oct 01n	103:29	103:31	-2	4.69
7 1/2	Nov 01n	107:07	107:09	-1	4.68
15 3/4	Nov 01	128:15	128:21	-2	4.65
5 7/8	**Nov 01n**	**103:04**	**103:06**	**-1**	**4.66**
6 1/8	Dec 01n	103:28	103:30	....	4.66
6 1/4	Jan 02n	104:08	104:10	-1	4.69
14 1/4	Feb 02	126:22	126:28	-1	4.67
6 1/4	Feb 02n	104:12	104:14	....	4.68
6 5/8	Mar 02n	105:18	105:20	....	4.69
6 5/8	Apr 02n	105:22	105:24	-1	4.69
7 1/2	May 02n	108:12	108:14	-1	4.69
6 1/2	May 02n	105:15	105:17	....	4.68
6 1/4	Jun 02n	104:26	104:28	....	4.69
3 5/8	Jul 02i	99:28	99:29	+ 1	3.65
6	Jul 02n	104:05	104:07	+ 1	4.68
6 3/8	Aug 02n	105:12	105:14	+ 1	4.69
6 1/4	Aug 02n	105:00	105:02	....	4.69
5 7/8	Sep 02n	103:29	103:31	+ 1	4.68
5 3/4	Oct 02n	103:17	103:19	....	4.69
11 5/8	Nov 02	123:18	123:24	....	4.70

Rate	Maturity Mo/Yr	Bid	Asked	Chg.	Ask Yld.	
5 3/4	Nov 02n	103:19	103:21	....	4.69	
5 5/8	Dec 02n	103:09	103:11	+ 1	4.68	
5 1/2	Jan 03n	102:30	103:00	+ 1	4.67	
6 1/4	Feb 03n	105:23	105:25	+ 1	4.66	
10 3/4	Feb 03	121:27	122:01	....	4.70	
5 1/2	Feb 03n	103:00	103:02	+ 1	4.66	
5 1/2	Mar 03n	103:02	103:04	+ 1	4.66	
5 3/4	Apr 03n	104:02	104:04	+ 1	4.67	
10 3/4	May 03	123:01	123:07	+ 2	4.70	
5 1/2	May 03n	103:07	103:09	+ 1	4.65	
5 3/8	Jun 03n	102:28	102:30	+ 1	4.63	
5 1/4	Aug 03n	102:19	102:20	+ 2	4.60	
5 3/4	Aug 03n	104:14	104:16	+ 2	4.64	
11 1/8	Aug 03	125:28	126:02	+ 3	4.69	
4 1/4	**Nov 03n**	**98:23**	**98:24**	**+ 2**	**4.54**	← November 2003 Note
11 7/8	Nov 03	129:31	130:05	-2	4.75	
5 7/8	Feb 04n	105:19	105:21	+ 3	4.60	
7 1/4	May 04n	112:00	112:04	+ 3	4.63	
12 3/8	May 04	135:08	135:14	+ 2	4.72	
7 1/4	Aug 04n	112:14	112:18	+ 3	4.65	
13 3/4	Aug 04	143:12	143:18	+ 3	4.72	
7 7/8	Nov 04n	115:30	116:02	+ 4	4.67	
11 5/8	Nov 04	134:14	134:20	+ 4	4.71	
7 1/2	Feb 05n	114:19	114:23	+ 4	4.68	
6 1/2	May 05n	109:23	109:25	+ 4	4.68	
8 1/4	May 00-05	104:11	104:13	+ 1	4.67	
12	May 05	138:29	139:03	+ 4	4.73	
6 1/2	Aug 05n	109:30	110:00	+ 4	4.71	
10 3/4	Aug 05	133:07	133:13	+ 4	4.75	
5 7/8	Nov 05n	106:22	106:24	+ 4	4.70	
5 5/8	Feb 06n	105:14	105:16	+ 5	4.70	
9 3/8	Feb 06	127:10	127:16	+ 5	4.74	
6 7/8	May 06n	112:31	113:03	+ 4	4.73	
7	Jul 06n	113:26	113:30	+ 5	4.76	
6 1/2	Oct 06n	110:30	111:02	+ 5	4.77	
3 3/8	Jan 07i	97:07	97:08	-2	3.78	
6 1/4	Feb 07n	109:24	109:26	+ 5	4.77	
7 5/8	Feb 02-07	108:00	108:02	+ 3	4.75	
6 5/8	May 07n	112:14	112:18	+ 5	4.77	
6 1/8	Aug 07n	109:10	109:12	+ 5	4.78	
7 7/8	Nov 02-07	110:21	110:25	+ 2	4.73	
3 5/8	Jan 08i	98:27	98:28	....	3.77	
5 1/2	Feb 08n	105:27	105:29	+ 6	4.69	
5 5/8	May 08n	106:17	106:18	+ 3	4.74	
8 3/8	Aug 03-08	114:15	114:19	+ 4	4.76	
4 3/4	**Nov 08n**	**100:24**	**100:25**	**+ 4**	**4.65**	
8 3/4	Nov 03-08	116:11	116:15	+ 3	4.85	
3 7/8	Jan 09i	100:28	100:29	-2	3.76	
9 1/8	May 04-09	119:16	119:20	+ 4	4.87	
10 3/8	Nov 04-09	127:10	127:16	+ 4	4.86	
11 3/4	Feb 05-10	135:15	135:21	+ 4	4.87	
10	May 05-10	127:09	127:15	+ 4	4.87	← May 2005–2010 T-Bond
12 3/4	Nov 05-10	144:27	145:01	+ 3	4.87	← November 2005–2010 T-Bond
13 7/8	May 06-11	154:10	154:16	+ 7	4.89	
14	Nov 06-11	157:31	158:05	+ 4	4.92	
10 3/8	Nov 07-12	137:27	138:01	+ 4	4.98	
12	Aug 08-13	152:13	152:19	+ 5	5.00	
13 1/4	May 09-14	165:09	165:15	+ 4	5.02	← May 2009–2014 T-Bond
12 1/2	Aug 09-14	160:11	160:17	+ 5	5.03	
11 3/4	Nov 09-14	155:08	155:14	+ 4	5.03	← November 2009–2014 T-Bond
11 1/4	Feb 15	165:11	165:17	+ 20	5.18	
10 5/8	Aug 15	158:31	159:05	+ 20	5.24	
9 7/8	Nov 15	150:25	150:31	+ 19	5.26	
9 1/4	Feb 16	144:01	144:07	+ 18	5.28	
7 1/4	May 16	121:23	121:29	+ 14	5.30	
7 1/2	Nov 16	124:25	124:31	+ 15	5.31	
8 3/4	May 17	139:21	139:27	+ 16	5.32	
8 7/8	Aug 17	141:13	141:19	+ 16	5.32	
9 1/8	May 18	145:09	145:15	+ 15	5.32	
9	Nov 18	144:10	144:16	+ 16	5.33	
8 7/8	Feb 19	143:00	143:06	+ 16	5.34	
8 1/8	Aug 19	134:05	134:11	+ 16	5.35	
8 1/2	Feb 20	139:09	139:15	+ 16	5.35	
8 3/4	May 20	142:23	142:29	+ 16	5.35	
8 3/4	Aug 20	142:31	143:05	+ 17	5.35	
7 7/8	Feb 21	132:06	132:12	+ 15	5.36	

Continued

Treasury Bonds

Rate	Maturity Mo./Yr	Bid	Asked	Chg.	Ask Yld.
8⅛	May 21	135:19	135:25	+15	5.36
8⅛	Aug 21	135:25	135:31	+15	5.36
8	Nov 21	134:12	134:18	+15	5.36
7¼	Aug 22	125:01	125:07	+16	5.35
7⅝	Nov 22	130:07	130:13	+17	5.35
7⅛	Feb 23	123:24	123:30	+15	5.35
6¼	Aug 23	112:09	112:13	+14	5.34
7½	Nov 24	130:07	130:13	+17	5.32
7⅝	Feb 25	132:03	132:09	+14	5.32
6⅞	Aug 25	121:24	121:30	+14	5.32
6	Feb 26	109:23	109:25	+12	5.31
6¾	Aug 26	120:12	120:18	+14	5.32
6½	Nov 26	116:29	117:01	+12	5.32
6⅝	Feb 27	118:29	119:01	+12	5.31
6⅜	Aug 27	115:17	115:21	+11	5.30
6⅛	Nov 27	112:11	112:15	+10	5.28
3⅝	Apr 28i	98:25	98:26	-5	3.69
5½	Aug 28	104:25	104:26	+13	5.18
5¼	**Nov 28**	102:12	102:13	+9	5.09

← Bellwether T-Bond (5¼ Nov 28)

U.S. TREASURY STRIPS

Mat.	Type	Bid	Asked	Chg.	Ask Yld.
Feb 99	ci	99:27	99:27	....	4.79
Feb 99	np	99:26	99:26	....	5.10
May 99	ci	98:23	98:23	....	4.59
May 99	np	98:23	98:23	....	4.59
Aug 99	ci	97:19	97:19	....	4.60
Aug 99	np	97:19	97:19	....	4.60
Nov 99	ci	96:15	96:16	....	4.62
Nov 99	np	96:15	96:15	....	4.65
Feb 00	ci	95:11	95:11	....	4.65
Feb 00	np	95:12	95:12	....	4.62
May 00	ci	94:09	94:10	....	4.62
May 00	np	94:07	94:08	....	4.68
Aug 00	ci	93:05	93:06	....	4.68
Aug 00	np	93:04	93:05	....	4.68
Nov 00	ci	92:04	92:05	....	4.64
Nov 00	np	92:02	92:03	....	4.68
Feb 01	ci	91:02	91:03	....	4.64
Feb 01	np	91:02	91:03	....	4.64
May 01	ci	90:00	90:02	....	4.65
May 01	np	90:00	90:02	....	4.65
Aug 01	ci	88:30	89:00	....	4.66
Aug 01	np	88:30	88:31	....	4.66
Nov 01	ci	87:29	87:31	....	4.67
Nov 01	np	87:28	87:30	....	4.68
Feb 02	ci	87:01	87:03	+1	4.61
May 02	ci	86:02	86:03	+1	4.61
May 02	np	85:31	86:01	+1	4.64
Aug 02	ci	85:01	85:03	+1	4.62
Aug 02	np	84:30	85:00	+1	4.65
Nov 02	ci	84:18	84:21	+1	4.45
Feb 03	ci	83:01	83:04	+1	4.63
Feb 03	np	83:01	83:04	+1	4.63
May 03	ci	82:02	82:05	+1	4.64
Aug 03	ci	81:08	81:11	+1	4.60
Aug 03	np	81:06	81:10	+1	4.62
Nov 03	ci	80:12	80:15	+1	4.59
Feb 04	ci	79:10	79:14	+4	4.63
Feb 04	np	79:17	79:21	+4	4.57
May 04	ci	78:13	78:16	+4	4.63
May 04	np	78:14	78:18	+4	4.62
Aug 04	ci	77:26	77:30	+4	4.55
Aug 04	np	77:14	77:18	+4	4.64
Nov 04	ci	76:13	76:17	+4	4.68
Nov 04	bp	76:08	76:12	+9	4.72
Nov 04	np	76:14	76:18	+4	4.67
Feb 05	ci	75:09	75:13	+3	4.73
Feb 05	np	75:16	75:20	+3	4.68
May 05	ci	74:11	74:15	+3	4.75
May 05	np	74:06	74:11	+3	4.78
Aug 05	ci	73:13	73:18	+3	4.75
Aug 05	bp	73:09	73:13	+3	4.78
Aug 05	np	73:19	73:24	+3	4.71
Nov 05	ci	72:21	72:26	+3	4.79
Nov 05	np	72:27	73:00	+3	4.70
Feb 06	ci	71:18	71:23	+3	4.78
Feb 06	np	71:25	71:29	+3	4.74
Feb 06	np	71:31	72:04	+3	4.70
May 06	ci	70:23	70:28	+3	4.78
Aug 06	ci	69:30	70:03	+3	4.77
Nov 06	ci	69:09	69:14	+3	4.79
Feb 07	ci	67:30	68:03	+6	4.84
May 07	ci	67:02	67:07	+2	4.86

Mat.	Type	Bid	Asked	Chg.	Ask Yld.
Aug 07	ci	66:06	66:12	+2	4.86
Nov 07	ci	65:23	65:29	+2	4.81
Feb 08	ci	64:10	64:16	+3	4.91
May 08	ci	63:14	63:20	+3	4.93
Aug 08	ci	62:21	62:26	+3	4.93
Nov 08	ci	61:21	61:27	+3	4.97
Feb 09	ci	60:21	60:27	+4	5.01
May 09	ci	59:25	59:30	+4	5.04
Aug 09	ci	58:25	58:31	+2	5.08
Nov 09	ci	58:00	58:05	+5	5.09
Nov 09	bp	57:12	57:18	+4	5.19
Feb 10	ci	57:01	57:07	+7	5.12
May 10	ci	56:05	56:11	+7	5.15
Aug 10	ci	55:10	55:16	+7	5.17
Nov 10	ci	54:16	54:22	+7	5.19
Feb 11	ci	53:21	53:27	+4	5.21
May 11	ci	52:27	53:02	+4	5.23
Aug 11	ci	52:01	52:07	+4	5.25
Nov 11	ci	51:08	51:14	+4	5.27
Feb 12	ci	50:15	50:21	+3	5.29
May 12	ci	49:23	49:29	+3	5.30
Aug 12	ci	48:31	49:05	+3	5.32
Nov 12	ci	48:07	48:14	+3	5.33
Feb 13	ci	47:16	47:22	+2	5.35
May 13	ci	46:25	46:31	+2	5.36
Aug 13	ci	46:02	46:08	+2	5.38
Nov 13	ci	45:11	45:17	+2	5.39
May 14	ci	44:20	44:26	+2	5.41
Aug 14	ci	43:31	44:05	+2	5.42
Aug 14	ci	43:09	43:16	+3	5.43
Nov 14	ci	42:30	42:26	+2	5.45
Feb 15	ci	41:31	42:06	+3	5.46
Feb 15	bp	42:24	42:30	+3	5.34
May 15	ci	41:11	41:17	+3	5.47
Aug 15	ci	40:23	40:29	+3	5.48
Aug 15	bp	41:00	41:07	+3	5.43
Nov 15	ci	40:02	40:09	+4	5.49
Nov 15	bp	40:06	40:12	+3	5.48
Feb 16	ci	39:14	39:20	+2	5.51
Feb 16	bp	39:20	39:26	+4	5.48
May 16	ci	38:28	39:02	+3	5.51
May 16	bp	39:05	39:11	+4	5.47
Aug 16	ci	38:09	38:15	+3	5.52
Nov 16	ci	37:23	37:29	+4	5.53
Nov 16	bp	37:31	38:06	+4	5.49
Feb 17	ci	37:04	37:11	+3	5.54
May 17	ci	36:20	36:26	+3	5.54
May 17	bp	36:24	36:30	+3	5.52
Aug 17	ci	36:02	36:09	+2	5.55
Aug 17	bp	36:08	36:14	+3	5.52
Nov 17	ci	35:20	35:26	+3	5.54
Feb 18	ci	35:03	35:09	+3	5.55
May 18	ci	34:19	34:25	+2	5.55
May 18	bp	34:22	34:28	+3	5.54
Aug 18	ci	34:06	34:13	+2	5.54
Nov 18	ci	33:22	33:28	+3	5.55
Nov 18	bp	33:23	33:29	+3	5.54
Feb 19	ci	33:04	33:10	+4	5.56
Feb 19	bp	33:08	33:14	+3	5.56
May 19	ci	32:22	32:28	+3	5.56
Aug 19	ci	32:07	32:13	+3	5.56
May 19	bp	32:12	32:18	+2	5.54
Nov 19	ci	31:25	31:31	+3	5.56
Feb 20	ci	31:11	31:17	+3	5.56
Feb 20	bp	31:15	31:21	+4	5.56
May 20	ci	30:29	31:03	+3	5.54
May 20	bp	31:02	31:08	+3	5.54
Aug 20	ci	30:16	30:22	+3	5.54
Aug 20	bp	30:20	30:27	+3	5.54
Nov 20	ci	30:03	30:09	+3	5.56
Feb 21	ci	29:24	29:30	+3	5.55
Feb 21	bp	29:30	30:05	+3	5.55
May 21	ci	29:10	29:17	+3	5.55
May 21	bp	29:15	29:21	+3	5.55
Aug 21	ci	28:30	29:05	+3	5.55
Aug 21	bp	29:03	29:10	+3	5.52
Nov 21	bp	28:20	28:26	+3	5.54
Nov 21	bp	28:24	28:30	+3	5.52
Feb 22	ci	28:07	28:13	+3	5.54
May 22	ci	27:28	28:02	+3	5.53
Aug 22	ci	27:17	27:23	+3	5.53
Aug 22	bp	27:26	28:00	+3	5.48
Nov 22	ci	27:06	27:12	+3	5.52
Nov 22	bp	27:14	27:20	+3	5.48

Mat.	Type	Bid	Asked	Chg.	Ask Yld.
Feb 23	ci	27:00	27:06	+2	5.49
Feb 23	bp	27:08	27:14	+2	5.45
May 23	ci	26:22	26:28	+2	5.48
Aug 23	ci	26:12	26:19	+2	5.47
Aug 23	bp	26:26	27:00	+2	5.41
Nov 23	ci	26:03	26:09	+2	5.47
Feb 24	ci	25:28	26:02	+3	5.44
May 24	ci	25:18	25:24	+3	5.44
Aug 24	ci	25:08	25:14	+3	5.43
Nov 24	ci	25:01	25:07	+3	5.42
Feb 25	ci	25:08	25:14	+4	5.38
Feb 25	bp	24:26	25:00	+2	5.4C
Feb 25	bp	24:31	25:06	+3	5.37
May 25	ci	24:16	24:22	+3	5.39
Aug 25	ci	24:06	24:12	+3	5.39
Aug 25	bp	24:11	24:17	+3	5.36
Nov 25	ci	23:31	24:05	+3	5.40
Feb 26	ci	23:16	23:22	+3	5.40
Feb 26	bp	23:30	24:04	+3	5.33
May 26	ci	23:08	23:13	+3	5.39
Aug 26	ci	22:30	23:04	+3	5.39
Aug 26	bp	23:06	23:12	+3	5.35
Nov 26	bp	22:29	23:03	+3	5.35
Feb 27	ci	22:21	22:27	+3	5.34
Feb 27	bp	22:25	22:31	+3	5.32
May 27	ci	22:04	22:10	+3	5.37
Aug 27	ci	22:05	22:11	+3	5.32
Aug 27	bp	22:10	22:16	+1	5.29
Nov 27	ci	22:13	22:19	+3	5.23
Nov 27	bp	22:14	22:20	+3	5.23

Bellwether Strip → (Nov 27 bp 22:14 22:20)

TREASURY BILLS

Maturity	Days to Mat.	Bid	Asked	Chg.	Ask Yld.
Feb 04 '99	3	4.62	4.54	-0.09	4.60
Feb 11 '99	10	4.58	4.50	+0.09	4.57
Feb 18 '99	17	4.50	4.42	+0.04	4.49
Feb 25 '99	24	4.49	4.41	+0.03	4.48
Mar 04 '99	31	4.51	4.47	+0.02	4.55
Mar 11 '99	38	4.52	4.48	+0.05	4.56
Mar 18 '99	45	4.52	4.48	+0.05	4.57
Mar 25 '99	52	4.49	4.45	+0.03	4.54
Apr 01 '99	59	4.51	4.47	+0.03	4.57
Apr 08 '99	66	4.48	4.46	+0.05	4.57
Apr 15 '99	73	4.48	4.46	+0.04	4.56
Apr 22 '99	80	4.48	4.46	+0.05	4.57
Apr 29 '99	87	4.37	4.36	-0.01	4.47
May 06 '99	94	4.45	4.43	....	4.54
May 06 '99	94	4.34	4.33	-0.02	4.44
May 13 '99	101	4.43	4.41	+0.05	4.53
May 20 '99	108	4.42	4.40	+0.05	4.52
May 27 '99	115	4.41	4.39	+0.03	4.51
Jun 03 '99	122	4.39	4.37	+0.02	4.50
Jun 10 '99	129	4.39	4.37	+0.03	4.50
Jun 17 '99	136	4.38	4.36	+0.02	4.49
Jun 24 '99	143	4.35	4.33	+0.03	4.47
Jul 01 '99	150	4.35	4.33	+0.02	4.47
Jul 08 '99	157	4.35	4.33	+0.02	4.47
Jul 15 '99	164	4.34	4.32	+0.02	4.47
Jul 22 '99	171	4.35	4.33	+0.02	4.48
Jul 29 '99	178	4.29	4.28	....	4.43
Aug 05 '99	185	4.30	4.29	+0.02	4.45
Aug 19 '99	199	4.35	4.33	+0.03	4.49
Sep 16 '99	227	4.35	4.33	+0.03	4.49
Oct 14 '99	255	4.34	4.32	+0.01	4.49
Nov 12 '99	284	4.36	4.34	+0.03	4.52
Dec 09 '99	311	4.36	4.34	+0.03	4.53
Jan 06 '00	339	4.33	4.32	+0.03	4.52
Feb 03 '00	367	4.30	4.29	....	4.50

INFLATION-INDEXED TREASURY SECURITIES

Rate	Mat.	Bid/Asked	Chg.	*Yld.	Accr. Prin.
3.625	07/02	99-28/29	+01	3.634	1024
3.375	01/07	97-07/08	-02	3.773	1035
3.625	01/08	98-27/28	....	3.766	1015
3.875	01/09	100-28/29	-02	3.757	1000
3.625	04/28	98-25/26	-05	3.690	1014

*-Yld. to maturity on accrued principal.

Source: *The Wall Street Journal*, February 1, 1999. Reprinted by permission of *The Wall Street Journal*, ©1999 Dow Jones & Company, Inc. All rights reserved.

second column, titled *Maturity-Mo/Yr* (maturation date), provides the year and month of maturity: November 2028. If the security has two maturity dates, such as 09–14, the bond matures in 2014 but can be called (redeemed) by the Treasury as early as 2009. Thus, if market interest rates drop below the 2009–14 bond's rate, the Treasury may redeem the security in 2009 and reissue the debt at the lower interest rate. For instance, the 11¾ November 2009–14 pays $117.50 per $1000 bond. If in 2009 the current interest rate is less than 11¾%, the Treasury can redeem the 11¾% 2009–14 bonds and reissue new securities with lower coupon payments, thus reducing the Treasury's annual coupon obligation.

The letter *n* following the date indicates that the security is a note. All other issues are bonds. You will notice in the example on page 231 that there are no *n*'s after November 2008, because there are no notes with maturities greater than 10 years. The bond issues that mature in less than 10 years (those with no letter following the month) are seasoned issues, sold sometime in the past.

The third (*Bid*) and fourth (*Asked*) columns on pages 231, 232, and 234 represent the prices buyers bid or offered and sellers asked. The price quoted is a percentage of par ($1,000) value, with a number after the colon representing 32nds. Thus, a price of 102:12 for the November 2028 (bellwether) bond means that on January 29, 1999 buyers were willing to pay 102¹²⁄₃₂ percent of the par ($1000) value, or $1,023.75 (102 + 0.375% of par, or $1,000 × 1.02375). Whenever the price exceeds par value, the security trades at a *premium*; securities below par trade at a *discount*. Thus the bellwether bond traded at a premium on January 29, 1999.

The second-to-last column (*Chg.*) is the change in bid price, expressed in 32nds, from the previous trading day. The bellwether bond on pages 232 and 234 rose $2.8125 on January 29, 1999 (⁹⁄₃₂ of 1% of $1,000 equals $2.8125).

The last column (*Ask Yld.*) is the yield to maturity of 5.09%, which is slightly less than the coupon rate of 5.25% because the bond traded at $1,023.75, somewhat above its $1,000 par.

Here's a rough and ready way to approximate the yield:

$$\text{Approximate yield} = \frac{\text{Coupon rate}}{\text{Market price}}$$

$$= \frac{\$52.50}{\$1,023.75}$$

$$= 5.128\%$$

$9\frac{1}{8}$	May 04-09	119:16 119:20	+ 4	4.87	
$10\frac{3}{8}$	Nov 04-09	127:10 127:16	+ 4	4.86	
$11\frac{3}{4}$	Feb 05-10	135:15 135:21	+ 4	4.87	
10	May 05-10	127:09 127:15	+ 4	4.87	←
$12\frac{3}{8}$	Nov 05-10	144:27 145:01	+ 3	4.87	←
$13\frac{7}{8}$	May 06-11	154:10 154:16	+ 7	4.89	
14	Nov 06-11	157:31 158:05	+ 4	4.92	
$10\frac{3}{8}$	Nov 07-12	137:27 138:01	+ 4	4.98	
12	Aug 08-13	152:13 152:19	+ 5	5.00	
$13\frac{1}{4}$	May 09-14	165:09 165:15	+ 4	5.02	←
$12\frac{1}{2}$	Aug 09-14	160:11 160:17	+ 5	5.03	←
$11\frac{3}{4}$	Nov 09-14	155:08 155:14	+ 4	5.03	←

May 2005–2010 T-Bond
$100 annual coupon payment,
$1,272.8125 price, 4.87% yield

November 2005–2010 T-Bond
$127.50 annual coupon payment,
$1,448.4375 price, 4.87% yield

May 2009–2014 T-Bond
$132.50 annual coupon payment,
$1,652.8125 price, 5.02% yield

November 2009–2014 T-Bond
$117.50 annual coupon payment,
$1,552.50 price, 5.03% yield

$5\frac{3}{8}$	Jun 03n	102:28 102:30	+ 1	4.63
$5\frac{1}{4}$	Aug 03n	102:19 102:20	+ 2	4.60
$5\frac{3}{4}$	Aug 03n	104:14 104:16	+ 2	4.64
$11\frac{1}{8}$	Aug 03	125:28 126:02	+ 3	4.69
$4\frac{1}{4}$	**Nov 03n**	**98:23 98:24**	+ 2	4.54
$11\frac{7}{8}$	Nov 03	129:31 130:05	-2	4.75
$5\frac{7}{8}$	Feb 04n	105:19 105:21	+ 3	4.60
$7\frac{1}{4}$	May 04n	112:00 112:04	+ 3	4.63
$12\frac{3}{8}$	May 04	135:08 135:14	+ 2	4.72
$7\frac{1}{4}$	Aug 04n	112:14 112:18	+ 3	4.65
$13\frac{3}{4}$	Aug 04	143:12 143:18	+ 3	4.72

November 2003 Note,
$987.1875 price

$6\frac{1}{8}$	Nov 27	112:11 112:15	+10	5.28
$3\frac{5}{8}$	Apr 28i	98:25 98:26	-5	3.69
$5\frac{1}{2}$	Aug 28	104:25 104:26	+13	5.18
$5\frac{1}{4}$	**Nov 28**	**102:12 102:13**	+ 9	5.09

Bellwether T-Bond
$1,023.75 price

U.S. TREASURY STRIPS

Mat.	Type	Bid	Asked	Chg.	Ask Yld.
Feb 99	ci	99:27	99:27	....	4.79
Feb 99	np	99:26	99:26	....	5.10

Aug 27	bp	22:10	22:16	+ 1	5.29
Nov 27	ci	22:13	22:19	+ 3	5.23
Nov 27	bp	22:14	22:20	....	5.23

Bellwether Strip
$224.375 price

TREASURY BILLS

Maturity	Days to Mat.	Bid	Asked	Chg.	Ask Yld.
Feb 04 '99	3	4.62	4.54	−0.09	4.60
Feb 11 '99	10	4.58	4.50	+0.09	4.57

In this particular example, the approximate yield to maturity (5.128%) does not equal the actual yield to maturity (5.09%), but it nonetheless offers a good approximation.

Why do securities sell at premiums (prices above the $1,000 par value) and discounts (prices below par)? Once again, market forces provide the answer. If the economy is awash in cash and, therefore, demand for Treasury securities (the next best thing to cash) is strong on the part of those who desire an interest return, securities buyers will bid their price up. Since the coupon rate is fixed, a higher market price will reduce the yield (see the approximate yield example on page 233). Conversely, a cash shortage will prompt sales of securities on the part of those who need cash, reducing their price and increasing yields.

To illustrate this, note on pages 231 and 234, that two Treasury bonds with similar maturities can have markedly different coupon rates although they have similar yields. For example, the 10% ($100.00 annually) May 2005–2010 bond yields 4.87%, whereas the 12¾% (127.50 annually) November 2005–2010 bond also yields 4.87%. Why is there no difference in the yield when there is a large ($127.50 – $100 = $27.50) difference in the coupon payment? Because these securities have different prices. The May bond's bid price is 127⁹⁄₃₂, or $1,272.8125, while the November bond's price is 144²⁷⁄₃₂ or $1,448.4375. In other words, the $27.50 coupon difference is off-set by a $175.625 difference in market price. Thus, differing prices will ensure that Treasury bonds and notes with similar maturity dates and features will have similar yields, whether the coupon is markedly different or not.

Treasury bonds are almost risk-free when held to maturity, yet their value will fall when interest rates rise, and you will suffer a loss if you must sell your bonds before they mature. For instance, the 4¼ November 2003 note traded at $987.1875 on January 29, 1999 (see pages 231 and 234), or $12.8125 below par, because interest rates had increased somewhat since its issue in 1993. If you had purchased it then, and had been obliged to sell it six years later, you would have suffered a loss.

On the other hand, looking at the 13¼ May 2009–2014 bond on pages 231 and 234, you see that its price had risen to $1,652.8125 since its 1979 issue at high interest rates. Substantial capital gains can be earned in low-risk Treasuries, while enjoying a comfortable yield (13¼% at issue or $132.50 annually in this case).

Bond prices converge on par and fluctuate very little as the maturity date approaches. Thus, bonds with the longest time to maturity offer the greatest opportunities for speculation, the greatest risk of loss, and (usually) the highest yields.

Finally, examine the data on pages 232 and 234 under **U.S. Treasury Strips**. You can purchase Treasuries in the secondary market that pay no annual interest but are offered at a deep discount so that you receive the equivalent of interest as the price appreciates. For instance, turning to the February 1, 1999 publication of the January 29 data, you can see that the most recently issued (bellwether) bond traded at $224.375 (22$^{14}\!/_{32}$). If you had purchased it that day, you could count on it appreciating almost five-fold by maturity. Many investors purchase these securities in order to accumulate a nest egg for a special purpose, such as a child's college education.

Investor's Tip

- Bonds are a good investment in low inflation times, because falling interest rates send bond prices upward.
- Unload your bonds when inflation threatens, because rising interest rates will depress bond prices.

Since fluctuations in market interest rates are crucial in determining the value of your investment, make a habit of tracking **Key Interest Rates** in Tuesday's *Wall Street Journal* (check the last section's index). See Tuesday, January 26, 1999's report on page 237 for the week ending Friday, January 22, 1999.

The Treasury is not the only government agency that issues long-term debt. The *Journal* publishes a **Government Agency & Similar Issues** report daily, which you can find using the front-page index of the first or last sections (under Treasury/Agency Issues). The Monday, February 1, 1999 edition (see page 238) covered Friday, January 29, 1999 trading activity for these agencies: **FNMA (Federal National Mortgage Association), Federal Home Loan Bank, Federal Farm Credit Bank, Student Loan Marketing, World Bank Bonds, Financing Corporation, Inter-American Development Bank, GNMA (Government National Mortgage Association), Tennessee Valley Authority, Farm Credit Financial Assistance Corporation**, and the **Resolution Funding Corporation**. The columns read **Rate, Mat. Bid, Asked**, and **Yld**, and provide the same information as Treasury securities. The discussion below deals with some of these issues.

FNMA (called "Fannie Mae") stands for the Federal National Mortgage Association, a publicly owned corporation sponsored by the federal government and established to provide a liquid market for mortgage investors. Fannie Mae buys mortgages from mortgage bankers and other mortgage writers, earns the interest payments made by homeowners, and pays for

these mortgages with the sale of bonds (debentures) to investors in $10,000 and $5,000 denominations. Pension funds, insurance companies, mutual funds, and other large institutional investors are the principal purchasers of these bonds, which are called Fannie Maes.

The **Federal Home Loan Bank** (FHLB) is a federally chartered, privately owned company charged with regulating the S&L industry. The FHLB borrows by issuing bonds in $10,000 denominations to provide funds to weaker S&Ls with temporary liquidity problems.

The **Federal Farm Credit Bank** assists farmers by helping financial institutions, such as small commercial banks and S&Ls, provide credit to farmers for the purchase and sale of commodities and the financing of buildings and new equipment. It is an independent agency of the U.S. government primarily funded by short-term debt, although it also issues longer-term notes that trade in the secondary market and are listed in the report.

Student Loan Marketing ("Sallie Mae") is a privately owned, government-sponsored corporation that provides a secondary market for government-guaranteed student loans. Sallie Mae sells bonds to investors to raise funds for the purchase of these student loans from financial institutions. The yields on these issues tend to be higher than other government agency issues because of the higher risk of default on student loans.

Key Interest Rates

Annualized interest rates on certain investments as reported by the Federal Reserve Board on a weekly-average basis:

	Week Ended:	
	Jan. 22, 1999	Jan. 15, 1999
Treasury bills (90 day)-a	4.26	4.35
Commrcl paper (Non-Finl., 90 day)-a	4.76	4.79
Commrcl paper (Finl., 90 day)-a	4.79	4.84
Certfs of Deposit (Resale, 3 month)	4.87	4.91
Certfs of Deposit (Resale, 6 month)	4.88	4.92
Federal funds (Overnight)-b	4.64	4.75
Eurodollars (90 day)-b	4.84	4.90
Treasury bills (one year)-c	4.49	4.51
Treasury notes (two year)-c	4.63	4.61
Treasury notes (three year)-c	4.62	4.61
Treasury notes (five year)-c	4.60	4.61
Treasury notes (ten year)-c	4.70	4.75
Treasury bonds (30 year)-c	5.14	5.17

a-Discounted rates. b-Week ended Wednesday, Jan. 20, 1999 and Wednesday, Jan. 13, 1999. c-Yields, adjusted for constant maturity.

GOVERNMENT AGENCY & SIMILAR ISSUES

Friday, January 29, 1999

Over-the-Counter mid-afternoon quotations based on large transactions, usually $1 million or more. Colons in bid-and-asked quotes represent 32nds; 101:01 means 101 1/32.

All yields are calculated to maturity, and based on the asked quote. * -- Callable issue, maturity date shown. For issues callable prior to maturity, yields are computed to the earliest call date for issues quoted above par, or 100, and to the maturity date for issues below par.

Source: Bear, Stearns & Co. via Street Software Technology Inc.

FNMA Issues

Rate	Mat.	Bid	Asked	Yld.
9.55	3-99	100:15	100:18	4.05
5.55	3-99	100:04	100:07	3.64
6.00	3-99	100:08	100:11	3.62
5.65	5-99	100:07	100:10	4.60
6.60	6-99	100:19	100:22	4.79
8.45	7-99	101:18	101:21	4.63
5.86	7-99	100:12	100:15	4.89
6.35	8-99	100:25	100:28	4.63
5.47	8-99	100:06	100:09	4.93
8.55	8-99	102:03	102:06	4.65
5.81	10-99	100:13	100:16	5.02
5.73	10-99	100:14	100:17	4.91
6.07	10-99	100:27	100:30	4.70
8.35	11-99	102:19	102:22	4.74
5.78	11-99	100:16	100:19	5.01
5.83	12-99	100:18	100:21	5.01
5.34	1-00	100:08	100:11	4.99
6.10	2-00	100:28	100:31	5.11
9.05	4-00	104:10	104:13	5.15
5.58	4-00	100:20	100:23	4.97
5.65	4-00	100:23	100:26	4.96
6.41	5-00	102:04	102:07	4.64
5.79	6-00*	100:08	100:11	4.69
5.80	6-00*	100:07	100:10	4.84
5.75	6-00*	100:06	100:09	4.89
8.90	6-00	104:25	104:28	5.14
6.20	6-00	101:30	102:01	4.69
5.90	7-00	101:16	101:19	4.72
5.56	7-00	100:24	100:27	4.97
5.97	7-00	101:20	101:23	4.76
5.69	8-00*	100:11	100:14	4.83
5.49	8-00	100:14	100:17	5.13
9.20	9-00	106:15	106:18	4.90
5.20	9-00	100:04	100:07	5.06
5.97	10-00	101:27	101:30	4.74
5.83	10-00	101:04	101:07	5.07
6.03	10-00	102:01	102:04	4.73
4.90	11-00*	99:10	99:13	5.26
5.86	11-00	101:22	101:25	4.78
5.05	11-00*	99:18	99:21	5.26
8.25	12-00	105:20	105:23	5.01
5.72	1-01	101:20	101:23	4.77
5.55	1-01	101:00	101:04	4.95
5.44	1-01	101:06	101:10	4.73
5.78	1-01*	100:12	100:16	4.77
5.50	2-01	101:03	101:07	4.85
5.37	2-01	99:01	99:05	5.82
5.65	2-01*	99:14	99:18	5.88
5.41	2-01	98:08	98:12	6.27
5.36	2-01	99:00	99:04	5.82
5.63	3-01	101:14	101:18	4.84
6.16	4-01	102:02	102:06	5.07
6.63	4-01	103:02	103:06	5.07
6.45	4-01	103:15	103:19	4.72
6.00	4-01*	100:08	100:12	4.45
6.74	5-01*	100:26	100:30	3.11
7.00	5-01*	100:25	100:29	3.58
6.59	5-01	103:04	103:08	5.08
5.95	7-01*	100:10	100:14	3.57
6.67	8-01	104:01	104:05	4.88
6.69	8-01	104:03	104:07	4.89
6.70	8-01*	100:20	100:24	5.22
6.38	8-01	102:29	103:01	5.08
5.43	9-01*	99:20	99:24	5.54
6.58	10-01	104:02	104:06	4.88
4.63	10-01	99:07	99:11	4.89
5.00	11-01*	99:30	100:02	4.97
5.00	11-01*	99:05	99:09	5.28
5.26	11-01*	100:02	100:06	5.02
6.44	11-01*	100:22	100:26	5.36
6.38	1-02	103:26	103:30	4.93
6.41	2-02	104:04	104:08	4.87
7.50	2-02	106:10	106:14	5.17
6.23	3-02	103:20	103:24	4.90
6.49	3-02	104:21	104:25	4.82
7.12	4-02*	100:12	100:16	4.66
7.55	4-02	107:23	107:27	4.89
6.82	4-02	105:22	105:26	4.86
6.70	5-02	105:10	105:14	4.88
6.61	5-02	104:29	105:01	4.92
6.59	5-02	104:30	105:02	4.91
6.22	7-02	103:30	104:02	4.93
6.23	7-02	103:31	104:03	4.93
6.26	7-02	103:16	103:20	5.11
6.54	9-02*	102:22	102:26	4.72
6.09	9-02	103:24	103:28	4.91
6.48	10-02*	100:28	101:00	4.95
6.06	10-02	103:02	103:06	5.10
5.90	10-02	103:02	103:06	4.95
6.40	10-02*	101:27	101:31	5.19
6.21	10-02	104:00	104:04	4.98
5.89	11-02	103:07	103:11	4.90
7.05	11-02	107:00	107:06	4.94
6.00	11-02	103:23	103:29	4.85
6.32	12-02*	100:22	100:28	5.29
6.80	1-03	105:24	105:30	5.12
6.06	1-03*	100:22	100:28	5.10
6.01	1-03*	100:20	100:26	5.12
5.25	1-03	100:27	101:01	4.96
6.15	1-03*	100:10	100:16	3.88
5.99	2-03*	100:12	100:18	5.42
5.78	2-03*	101:06	101:12	5.05
6.14	3-03*	100:02	100:08	3.15
5.75	4-03	102:26	103:00	4.95
5.96	4-03*	103:06	103:12	4.34
6.00	4-03*	101:26	102:00	5.03
6.19	4-03*	101:07	101:13	4.99
6.10	4-03*	101:05	101:11	4.96
6.16	5-03*	101:02	101:08	5.12
6.06	5-03*	101:30	102:04	5.07
6.71	5-03	107:03	107:09	4.81
6.20	5-03*	101:04	101:10	5.14
6.03	6-03*	101:28	102:02	5.09
6.16	6-03*	101:06	101:12	5.10
6.20	6-03*	100:10	100:16	4.92
5.89	7-03*	101:24	101:30	5.05
5.94	8-03*	101:27	102:01	5.07
6.09	8-03*	100:10	100:16	5.14
5.86	8-03*	101:18	101:24	5.12
5.91	8-03*	100:30	101:04	5.16
5.50	9-03*	99:22	99:28	5.53
5.26	10-03*	99:04	99:10	5.43
5.45	10-03	102:00	102:06	4.92
5.43	11-03*	100:02	100:08	5.10
5.46	11-03*	100:04	100:10	5.00
4.75	11-03	98:27	99:01	4.98
5.53	12-03*	100:04	100:10	5.34
5.80	12-03	102:24	102:30	5.11
6.85	4-04	107:22	107:28	5.09
6.79	6-04	109:04	109:10	4.79
7.55	6-04*	100:22	100:28	4.99
7.40	7-04	109:26	110:00	5.26
7.70	8-04*	101:18	101:24	4.26
7.85	9-04*	101:16	101:22	4.96
8.25	10-04*	101:22	101:28	5.46
8.40	10-04*	102:03	102:09	5.15
8.63	11-04*	103:19	103:25	3.59
6.00	1-05*	101:23	101:29	5.29
8.50	2-05*	103:11	103:17	4.83
7.88	2-05	115:08	115:14	4.90
6.25	2-05*	100:23	100:29	5.36
7.65	3-05	113:00	113:06	5.11
6.35	5-05*	102:28	103:02	4.93
6.35	6-05	105:25	105:31	5.23
5.75	6-05	103:20	103:26	5.04
6.55	9-05	108:13	108:19	5.01
6.85	9-05*	101:30	102:04	5.45
6.40	9-05	107:21	107:27	5.00
6.70	11-05*	101:30	102:04	5.41
5.94	12-05	105:10	105:16	4.98
5.88	2-06	103:18	103:24	5.23
6.41	3-06	107:20	107:26	5.08
6.22	3-06	106:20	106:26	5.07
6.89	4-06	110:12	110:18	5.12
7.90	6-06*	100:26	101:00	5.30
7.07	7-06	110:24	110:30	5.28
7.93	9-06*	101:16	101:24	5.09
7.59	10-06*	101:22	101:28	4.71
7.50	11-06*	101:10	101:16	5.52
6.88	11-06*	103:02	103:08	5.61
6.96	4-07	110:15	110:21	5.33
6.64	7-07	108:11	108:17	5.37
6.99	7-07*	103:06	103:12	5.88
6.52	7-07	109:26	110:00	5.05
6.54	9-07	109:29	110:03	5.08
7.13	9-07*	101:26	102:00	5.80
6.59	9-07	107:30	108:04	5.40
6.39	9-07	108:14	108:20	5.14
6.87	10-07	102:04	102:10	6.51
6.83	10-07*	102:00	102:06	5.44
6.34	10-07	108:10	108:16	5.12
6.94	10-07*	101:26	102:00	5.70
6.97	10-07*	101:26	102:00	5.73
6.65	11-07*	101:16	101:22	5.63
6.15	12-07	107:10	107:16	5.09
6.56	12-07*	103:04	103:10	5.59
6.16	12-07	107:08	107:16	5.10
6.48	12-07*	103:08	103:16	5.47
6.40	12-07*	102:26	103:02	5.51
6.17	1-08*	102:06	102:14	5.47
6.41	1-08*	100:15	100:23	6.01
6.29	1-08*	101:07	101:15	5.49
6.24	1-08*	102:20	102:28	5.43
6.27	2-08*	102:05	102:13	5.59
6.43	2-08*	101:05	101:13	5.68
6.42	2-08*	101:16	101:24	5.50
5.75	2-08	103:28	104:04	5.18
6.38	2-08*	101:13	101:21	5.51
6.58	5-08*	101:12	101:20	5.81
6.00	5-08	105:17	105:25	5.21
6.22	8-08*	102:26	103:02	5.45
6.20	8-08*	102:18	102:26	5.49
6.14	9-08*	100:28	101:04	5.67
6.00	9-08*	100:00	100:08	5.96
6.00	11-08*	100:02	100:10	5.56
6.01	11-08*	99:22	99:30	6.01
0.00	7-14	42:28	43:04	5.53
10.35	12-15	148:04	148:12	5.81
8.20	3-16	127:27	128:03	5.62
8.95	2-18	136:00	136:08	5.78
8.10	8-19	128:23	128:31	5.69
0.00	10-19	30:24	31:00	5.74
7.13	4-26	121:16	121:22	5.57
6.09	9-27	102:02	102:10	5.92
6.03	10-27	106:30	107:06	5.53
6.75	2-28*	102:09	102:17	6.03
5.63	4-28	100:30	101:06	5.54

Federal Home Loan Bank

Rate	Mat.	Bid	Asked	Yld.
6.44	4-99	100:12	100:15	4.14
8.60	6-99	101:14	101:17	4.59
6.11	6-99	100:14	100:17	4.77
8.45	7-99	101:23	101:26	4.61
6.26	8-99	100:21	100:24	4.77
8.60	8-99	102:00	102:03	4.77
5.87	10-99	100:17	100:20	4.96
8.38	10-99	102:14	102:17	4.80
5.00	10-99*	100:01	100:04	4.82
5.80	11-99	100:15	100:18	5.02
8.60	1-00	103:12	103:15	4.91
5.53	2-00	100:14	100:17	5.00
5.78	5-00*	100:06	100:09	4.76
4.49	11-00	99:00	99:03	5.03
5.62	1-01	101:15	101:18	4.77
5.20	9-01	100:04	100:08	5.08
4.86	10-01	99:14	99:18	5.03
4.63	10-01	98:30	99:02	5.00
4.66	10-01	98:31	99:03	5.02
4.64	10-02	98:09	98:13	5.12
4.68	10-02	100:10	100:14	4.55
6.18	10-02	103:27	103:31	5.00
5.66	1-03	102:18	102:24	4.88
5.37	1-03	100:30	101:04	5.05
6.25	1-03*	99:26	100:00	6.25
5.42	1-03	101:30	102:04	4.82
6.07	1-03*	100:10	100:16	3.98
6.05	2-03*	100:00	100:06	5.43
6.03	5-03*	101:30	102:04	5.01
5.76	6-03	103:08	103:14	4.88
5.57	9-03	101:29	102:03	5.06
5.63	9-03	101:30	102:04	5.11
5.13	9-03	100:10	100:16	5.00
4.78	10-03	98:14	98:20	5.11
5.06	10-03*	99:27	100:01	5.05
6.02	10-03*	99:12	99:18	6.13
9.50	2-04	121:00	121:06	4.75
6.00	5-04*	99:12	99:18	6.09
7.00	7-07*	101:24	101:30	5.61
7.00	8-07*	102:00	102:06	5.49
5.80	9-08	103:20	103:28	5.28

Federal Farm Credit Bank

Rate	Mat.	Bid	Asked	Yld.
5.60	5-99	100:09	100:12	4.05
5.55	7-99	100:06	100:09	4.83
8.65	10-99	102:12	102:15	4.81
6.28	6-01	103:02	103:06	4.84
6.10	9-01	102:30	103:02	4.84
5.70	6-03	102:22	102:28	4.96
6.75	6-07	111:18	111:24	5.02

Student Loan Marketing

Rate	Mat.	Bid	Asked	Yld.
5.52	6-99	100:06	100:09	4.63
5.66	2-00*	100:00	100:03	5.56
5.56	3-00*	100:01	100:04	4.01
7.50	3-00	102:16	102:19	5.04
6.05	9-00	101:26	101:29	4.81
7.00	12-02	106:25	106:31	4.98
7.30	8-12	119:18	119:26	5.24
0.00	10-22	24:27	25:03	5.93

World Bank Bonds

Rate	Mat.	Bid	Asked	Yld.
8.38	10-99	102:12	102:15	4.56
8.13	3-01	107:00	107:04	4.49
6.38	5-01	103:20	103:24	4.63
6.75	1-02	104:21	104:25	4.99
12.38	10-02	123:04	123:10	5.35
5.25	9-03	102:02	102:08	4.70
6.38	7-05	107:30	108:04	4.90
6.63	8-06	110:12	110:20	4.92
8.25	9-16	127:30	128:06	5.69
6.63	10-16	132:02	132:10	5.70
9.25	7-17	140:02	140:10	5.69
7.63	1-23	127:00	127:08	5.55
8.88	3-26	141:29	142:05	5.78

Financing Corporation

Rate	Mat.	Bid	Asked	Yld.
10.70	10-17	152:21	152:29	5.96
9.80	11-17	147:29	148:05	5.62
9.40	2-18	138:23	138:31	5.95
9.80	4-18	148:07	148:15	5.63
10.00	5-18	150:01	150:09	5.68
10.35	8-18	154:00	154:08	5.70
9.65	11-18	147:02	147:10	5.64
9.90	12-18	149:16	149:24	5.68
9.60	12-18	146:02	146:10	5.68
9.65	3-19	147:02	147:10	5.67
9.70	4-19	147:13	147:21	5.70
9.00	6-19	138:12	138:20	5.75
8.60	9-19	134:05	134:13	5.74

Inter-Amer. Devel. Bank

Rate	Mat.	Bid	Asked	Yld.
7.13	9-99	101:12	101:15	4.79
8.50	5-01	106:28	107:00	5.16
6.13	3-06	106:26	107:00	4.94
6.63	3-07	110:14	110:20	5.01
12.25	12-08	151:17	151:25	5.41
8.88	6-09	127:06	127:14	5.38
8.40	9-09	124:14	124:22	5.32
8.50	3-11	126:10	126:18	5.47
7.13	3-23*	105:08	105:16	6.26
7.00	6-25	116:12	116:20	5.76
6.80	10-25	113:30	114:06	5.75

GNMA Mtge. Issues Feb99

Rate	Mat.	Bid	Asked	Yld.
5.50	30Yr	96:26	96:28	5.95
6.00	30Yr	99:08	99:10	6.16
6.50	30Yr	101:06	101:08	6.33
7.00	30Yr	102:15	102:17	6.48
7.50	30Yr	103:12	103:14	6.44
8.00	30Yr	104:07	104:09	6.18
8.50	30Yr	106:01	106:03	5.74
9.00	30Yr	106:22	106:24	6,09
9.50	30Yr	107:10	107:12	6.88

Tennessee Valley Authority

Rate	Mat.	Bid	Asked	Yld.
8.38	10-99	101:22	101:25	5.56
6.00	11-00	101:10	101:13	5.15
6.50	8-01	103:08	103:12	5:07
6.38	6-05	106:04	106:10	5.19
3.38	1-07	96:10	96:16	3,89
8.05	7-24*	102:27	103:03	4.37
6.75	11-25	112:22	112:30	5:79
8.63	11-29*	104:07	104:15	8,22
8.25	9-34*	103:26	104:02	3,47
8.25	4-42*	114:19	114:27	6.81
7.25	7-43*	105:18	105:26	6:78
6.88	12-43*	105:30	106:06	6,19

Farm Credit Fin. Asst. Corp.

Rate	Mat.	Bid	Asked	Yld.
9.38	7-03	116:29	117:03	5.05
8.80	6-05	121:06	121:12	4,85
9.20	9-05*	107:22	107:28	4.22

Resolution Funding Corp

Rate	Mat.	Bid	Asked	Yld.
8.13	10-19	132:22	132:30	5.45
8.88	7-20	143:03	143:TT	5,43
9.38	10-20	143:31	144:07	5:78
8.63	1-21	140:09	140:17	5,44
8.63	1-30	138:00	138:08	5,92
8.88	4-30	150:22	150:30	5.46

Source: *The Wall Street Journal*, February 1, 1999. Reprinted by permission of *The Wall Street Journal*,

BANK CREDIT CARD INTEREST RATES

February 1999

Banks or savings institutions with low interest rates offering bank credit cards nationally. Rates shown are for regular, not premium cards. Though not listed, some cards may be through affiliate or agent banks. Temporary or promotional interest rates are excluded. Grace period (interest free period for cardholders paying purchase balance in full each month) is calculated from the date of billing unless footnoted.

Bank / Location	Int. Rate	Annual Fee	Grace Days
Wachovia Bnk, Atlanta	v7.75%	$88.00	20
Ark. Natl Bnk, Bentonville, Ark.	x7.92	r50.00	25
Huntington Natl Bnk, Cleveland	v8.75	39.00	25
Simmons FrstNatlBnk, Pine Blf,Ark.	v9.50	35.00	25
Capital One, Richmond, Va.	f9.90	0.00	25
First USA Bnk, Wilmington, Del.	f9.99	0.00	20
AFBA Industrial Bnk, Colo.Sp.,Colo.	v10.25	35.00	25
Amalgamated Bnk Chicago, Chicago	v10.50	45.00	25
Central Carolina Bank, Columb., Ga.	v11.25	20.00	25
Commerce Bnk, Omaha, Neb.	v11.35	29.00	25
AFBA Industrial Bnk, Colo.Sp.,Colo.	v11.40	0.00	25
USAA FSB, San Antonio, Texas	v11.65	0.00	25
Pullman Bnk & Trust, Chicago	v11.75	0.00	25
Partner's First, Annapolis. Md.	v12.25	18.00	25
Wachovia Bnk, Atlanta	v12.40	18.00	20
AFBA Industrial Bnk, Colo.Sp., Colo.	v12.65	0.00	25
Amalgamated Bnk Chicago, Chicago	v13.25	0.00	25
Commerce Bnk, Omaha, Neb.	v13.35	0.00	25
First Union, Charlotte, N.C.	v13.65	20.00	25
AmSouth Bnk, Hoover, Ala.	v13.75	0.00	25
Liberty Savings Bank, Denver	f13.90	0.00	25
People's Bnk, Bridgeport, Conn.	f13.99	0.00	25
Chase Manhattan, New York	v14.48	0.00	25
Wachovia Bnk, Atlanta	v14.65	0.00	20
Washington Trust Bnk, Riversd,R.I.	v14.75	0.00	25

Banks offering credit cards nationally with no annual fee.

Bank / Location	Interest Rate Structure	Grace Days
Capital One, Richmond, Va.	9.90%-Fixed	25
First USA Bnk, Wilmington, Del.	9.99%-Fixed	20
AFBA Industrial Bnk, Colo.Sp.,Colo.	Prime +2.90%	25
USAA Fed Savings Bnk, San Antonio	26 wk TB +7%	25
Pullman Bnk & Trust, Chicago	Prime +4.00%	25
AFBA Industrial Bnk, Colo.Sp., Colo.	Prime +4.90%	25
Amalgamated Bnk Chicago, Chicago	Prime +5.50%	25
Commerce Bnk, Omaha, Neb.	Prime +5.60%	25
AmSouth Bnk, Hoover, Ala.	Prime +6.00%	25
Liberty Savings Bnk, Denver	13.90%-Fixed	25

Interest rates offered by the 10 largest U.S. issuers.

Bank	Int. Rate	Annual Fee Regular	Annual Fee Premium	Grace Days
Bank One	9.99-22.99%	$ 0.00	$ 0.00	22.5
Citibank	13.40-20.90	0.00	0.00	22.5
MBNA America	12.99-18.40	0.00	0.00	25
Dean Witter Dscvr	12.99-22.99	0.00	0.00	25
Chase Manhattan	13.49-21.99	0.00	0.00	25
Bank of America	16.49-20.99	0.00	0.00	25
Fleet	9.90-23.99	0.00	0.00	20
Household Bank	16.40-20.90	0.00	39.00	25
Capital One	9.90-24.99	0.00	0.00	25
Providian	16.99-23.99	59.00	0.00	0

c-Higher rate charged for cash advances. d-Security deposit required. e-Estimated amount, actual fees not disclosed. f-Fixed rate. k-Interest rate based on credit risk of cardholder. n-No annual fee available on some cards.p-interest rate guaranteed for at least one year. r-Relationship required. s-Special lower rate available on some cards. t-Tiered (or lower) rates based on account balance. u-Monthly user fee applies. v-Variable rate. w-Fee waived under special conditions. x-Interest charged from date of purchase. z-Interest charged from date of posting.

CP-High grade commercial paper rate. Prime-Prime rate. QA-Quarterly average. TB-Treasury Bill rate. TTIA-Top 10 Issuers Average.

Source:Cardweb Inc. (www.cardweb.com) Gettysburg, Pa.

World Bank Bonds are debt instruments issued by the International Bank for Reconstruction and Development (World Bank) to finance its lending activities to less-developed countries.

GNMA ("Ginnie Mae"), the Government National Mortgage Association, is a government-owned corporation that purchases, packages, and resells mortgages and mortgage purchase commitments in the form of mortgage-backed securities called Ginnie Maes. Each Ginnie Mae bond is backed by a package of residential mortgages, and the holder of a GNMA bond thereby owns a portion of these underlying mortgages. New GNMA bonds cost $25,000, but older, partially repaid GNMAs can cost as little as $5,000.

Mortgage payments of interest and principal are "passed through" to the Ginnie Mae holders. Thus, unlike holders of Treasuries, who receive their principal at maturity, investors in Ginnie Maes are paid interest and principal each month.

Ginnie Maes don't have stated maturity dates, because the bond's flow of income depends on the repayment of the underlying mortgages. If all

homeowners pay their mortgages regularly for the mortgage's life, with no prepayments, the Ginnie Mae holder receives regular monthly checks for 30 years. However, a homeowner may choose to pay off his or her mortgage prior to maturity, or may pay additional principal in some months. The pre-payment or excess principal payments are passed through to the Ginnie Mae holder, who receives a larger monthly check. This prepayment reduces the subsequent monthly payments and the Ginnie Mae's par value.

Ginnie Maes offer higher rates than Treasury bonds because of the unpre-dictable nature of interest and principal payments. The U.S. Treasury backs these government bonds to remove the risk of homeowner default.

Finally, you can see the mortgage interest rates associated with the var-ious Ginnie Mae pools, as well as the range of prices that determine these bonds' yields.

Federal Land Banks are privately owned organizations, backed by the fed-eral government, that are organized to finance agricultural activities. They pri-marily provide first mortgage loans on farm properties with original maturities of around 20 years and fund these mortgages by issuing Consolidated Federal Farm Loan Bonds. The Federal Farm Credit Agency examines the activities of the Federal Land Bank.

There are almost as many U.S.-agency bond issuers as bank credit-card issuers in the excerpt from the February 8, 1999 *Journal* on page 239.

CORPORATE BONDS

Corporations are the second principal issuer of long-term debt, and they, like the government and government agencies, issue credit instruments in order to finance long-term needs.

Most bonds are exchanged over-the-counter, like Treasury securities, by large investment banking firms on behalf of institutional investors. A lim-ited amount of small-lot trading is conducted on the New York Stock Exchange by brokerage firms for individual investors. If you wish to track a corporate bond that is listed on the New York Stock Exchange, you will find it in *The Wall Street Journal* under **New York Exchange Bonds**. Consult the front page of the first or last section for the daily listing. An example from the Monday, February 1, 1999 issue appears on pages 241 and 242. (American stock exchange bonds appear under **Amex Bonds** on pages 241 and 243.)

The top portion of the New York Exchange Bonds quotations provides important information about the previous trading day. **Volume** is the par value of bonds traded on Friday, January 29, 1999: $11,325,000. **Issues traded** lists the number of different bonds sold on that day. **Advances** is the number of bonds that traded at a price higher than the previous day; **Declines** is the num-

NEW YORK EXCHANGE BONDS

Quotations as of 4 p.m. Eastern Time
Friday, January 29, 1999

Volume $11,325,000

SALES SINCE JANUARY 1
(000 omitted)

1999	1998	1997
$267,622	$367,124	$565,794

	Domestic Fri	Domestic Thu	All Issues Fri	All Issues Thu
Issues Traded	203	192	212	202
Advances	82	81	87	85
Declines	77	70	80	75
Unchanged	44	41	45	42
New highs	11	6	11	7
New lows	4	5	4	5

Dow Jones Bond Averages

–1998– High	–1998– Low	–1999– High	–1999– Low		–1999– Close	–1999– Chg.	–1999– %Yld	–1998– Close	–1998– Chg.
107.17	104.42	106.88	106.35	20 Bonds	106.45	– 0.23	6.64	105.18	+ 0.19
104.71	101.88	104.72	104.20	10 Utilities	104.41	– 0.31	6.67	102.48	– 0.17
109.81	106.48	109.44	108.13	10 Industrials	108.49	– 0.15	6.62	107.89	+ 0.55

CORPORATION BONDS
Volume, $10,948,000

Bonds	Cur Yld	Vol	Close	Net Chg.
AES05	...	25	92½	...
ATT 5⅛01	5.1	25	100⅛	+ ⅛
ATT 7⅛02	6.8	75	105⅛	+ ¼
ATT 6¾04	6.3	15	106⅝	– ⅛
ATT 8.2s05	7.9	35	104	...
ATT 8⅛22	7.6	40	107⅝	+ ¼
ATT 8⅝31	7.6	23	113⅜	– ⅛
Aames 10½02	11.2	21	93½	+ 1⅝
Aetna 6⅜03	6.4	25	99⅜	+ ⅞
AlldC zr2000	...	18	90⅝	...
AlldC zr01	...	5	86	...
AlldC zr09	...	50	50¾	+ ¾
Alza 5s06	cv	68	138	+ 7½
Alza zr14	...	80	66	+ 8¾
ARetire 5¾02	cv	30	87	+ ⅞
Amresco 10s03	11.8	20	84½	– ⅞
Amresco 10s04	12.4	50	80⅞	+ ⅛
AnnTaylr 8¾00	8.6	53	101⅞	+ ½
Argosy 13¼04	11.9	20	111⅝	+ ½
ARch 9⅛11	7.4	6	122⅞	...
BellPa 7⅛12	7.0	20	101⅞	– ⅜
BellsoT 6¼03	6.0	3	104¾	+ ¼
BellsoT 6½05	6.1	4	106½	– ⅛
BellsoT 7⅞32	7.3	15	107¼	– ¼
BellsoT 6¾33	6.5	2	103¾	+ ¼
BethSt 8.45s05	8.4	198	100¾	...
Bevrly 9s06	8.6	6	104½	– ¼
BlockF 6¾04	6.8	20	99½	...
Bluegrn 8¼12	cv	62	93⅞	– 1⅝
Bordn 8⅜16	8.5	63	99⅛	...
BosCelts 6s38	9.8	7	61	– ⅛
BurN 6.55s20K	6.5	10	100⅞	...
CalEgy 9⅞03	8.9	177	111	+ 2⅞
CaterpInc 6s07	6.0	50	100	+ ¾
ChaseM 7⅞04	7.8	30	101¼	– ⅞
ChaseM 6½05	6.2	5	104⅛	+ ⅛
CPoM 7¼12	7.1	16	101⅞	...
ChckFul 7s12	cv	15	93½	...
ChryF 13¼99	12.6	10	105 1/32	– 3/32
Clardge 11¾02f	...	127	72⅞	– 3⅛
ClrkOil 9½04	9.5	110	100½	– ¼
CoeurDA 7¼05	11.5	72	63	+ ½
Coeur 6⅜04	cv	51	63	– ½
CmclFd 7.95s06	7.8	5	101½	+ ½
CompUSA 9½00	9.4	54	100⅝	+ ⅜
CompMgt 8s03	cv	20	17	– 1
ConPort 10½04	14.6	10	72	+ 1¾
ConPort 10s06	15.1	7	66⅛	– 1⅞
Convrse 7s04	cv	305	33	+ 1⅛
DVI 9⅞04	9.9	61	99½	...

Bonds	Cur Yld	Vol	Close	Net Chg.
DataGen 6s04	cv	148	99½	– ⅛
DiaSTel 7s08	6.9	10	101¼	+ ⅞
DukeEn 7s00	6.8	25	103⅜	+ 1
DukeEn 6¼04	6.1	65	102½	+ ¼
DukeEn 6⅞23	6.7	3	102½	+ ½
DukeEn 7s33	6.8	13	103⅝	– ⅜
Eckerd 9¼04	8.8	80	104 31/32	+ 5/16
FUnRE 8⅞03	9.1	65	97⅜	– 1⅞
Florsh 12¾02	12.2	15	104½	– ½
FordCr 6⅜08	6.1	5	104¾	+ ⅝
GMA 7⅛99	7.1	10	100 5/32	...
GMA 9⅝00	9.2	10	105⅛	– ⅛
GMA 7s00	6.9	74	101⅝	+ ¼
GMA 5½01	5.5	10	100	...
GMA 6¾02	6.5	9	104	+ ⅝
GMA 7s02	6.7	50	104	– ¼
GMA 6⅝02	6.4	49	103¼	+ ½
GMA 5⅞03	5.8	36	101	– ⅜
GMA [illegible]05	7.0	10	112¾	2¼
GMA dc6s11	6.1	111	99⅛	– ⅞
GMA zr12	...	22	400	...
GMA zr15	...	12	327⅛	– ⅞
GenesisH 9¾05	10.1	24	97	– 1
GrnTrFn 10¼02	9.7	100	105½	+ ⅛
HRPT 7½03	cv	10	99¼	– 1¼
Hexcel 7s03	cv	17	90	– 1½
Hills 12½03f	...	60	96	– 2
Hilton 5s06	cv	142	96¼	...
HomeDpt 3¼01	cv	2	257⅜	– 1⅝
IBM 6⅜00	6.3	45	101⅝	– ⅛
IBM 7½13	6.5	50	116	...
IBM 7s25	6.4	7	109⅜	– ⅝
IBM 6½28	6.1	12	106	...
IntShip 9s03	8.8	10	102⅛	...
JCPL 6⅜03	6.2	5	102⅛	– 2¾
JCP 6¾25	6.7	5	100⅜	+ 2⅛
KCS En 8⅞08	15.9	135	56	+ ⅝
KaufB 9⅜03	9.1	94	102¾	+ ⅛
KaufB 7¾04	7.8	125	99⅝	+ ¼
KentE 4½04	cv	22	77⅜	– ⅝
LeasSol 6⅞03	cv	100	25¼	– ¼
Leucadia 8¼05	7.9	160	104	...
Leucadia 7⅞06	7.9	210	100⅜	+ ⅜
Leucadia 7¾13	7.8	163	100	...
Lilly 7⅛25	6.7	1	106½	+ 1
Loews 3⅛07	cv	54	80½	+ ½
MacNS 7⅞04	cv	5	93	...
MarO 7s02	6.9	118	101⅛	...
Mascotch 03	cv	121	79½	– ¼
McDnl 6⅜03	6.7	10	101¼	– ⅛
Medtrst 7½01	cv	80	96	...
MPac 4¾20f	...	25	73¼	– 1¾
Motrla zr09	...	6	130⅛	+ 1⅛
Motrla zr13	...	1	83⅝	+ ⅝
Nabis 8.3s99	8.3	25	100 1/16	...
NatData 5s03	cv	26	113	– ⅛
NETelTel 6¼03	6.0	5	103½	+ 1⅛
NETelTel 7⅜07	7.3	10	101¼	– ½
NETelTel 6⅜08	6.3	15	100⅞	...
NETelTel 7⅞29	6.7	10	118	+ 5

Bonds	Cur Yld	Vol	Close	Net Chg.
NJBTl 7¼11	7.1	20	102⅛	– ⅜
NJBTl 7⅜12	7.3	36	101⅝	– ⅛
NYEG 7⅝01	7.5	10	101⅝	– 1¼
NYTel 4¼00	4.3	13	99⅛	+ 23/32
NYTel 4⅝02	4.7	64	98¾	+ ¾
NYTel 5⅝03	5.5	50	102⅜	+ 1
NYTel 7⅜11	7.2	35	102½	+ ⅜
NYTel 7⅝23	7.1	65	107	...
NYTel 7s25	6.8	9	103⅜	– ⅜
NYTel 7s33	6.6	5	105½	+ ⅝
Noram 6s12	cv	102	97⅞	+ ⅛
Novacr 5½2000	cv	232	79¼	– ¼
OcciP 10⅛01	9.3	49	109⅜	+ ⅜
OffDep zr08	...	25	83½	+ ½
OreStl 11s03	10.5	38	105⅛	...
Oryx 7½14	cv	14	99	...
OwensM 10⅞06	9.9	5	109½	+ ¾
PacBell 7½33	7.0	2	106⅞	+ ¾
PacBell 6⅝34	6.4	7	102⅞	...
ParkerD 5½04	cv	256	62¼	– 1⅛
PennTr 9⅝05f	...	27	7½	– ¼
PennzE 4.95s08	cv	5	96	– ½
PhilEl 7¼24	7.0	33	103⅝	...
PotEl 5s02	cv	70	97	+ ¼
PotEl 7s18	cv	3	101⅛	+ ⅛
Pride 6¼06	cv	10	80	– 2
PSEG 6s00	6.0	35	100½	...
Quanx 6.88s07	cv	22	92¾	+ 1
RJR Nb 8s00	7.9	121	101¼	+ 5/32
RJR Nb 8s01	7.8	12	102½	+ ⅛
RJR Nb 8⅝02	8.3	35	104⅛	– ⅛
RJR Nb 7⅝03	7.5	80	101¼	– ¼
RJR Nb 8¾05	8.4	181	104½	– ¼
RJR Nb 8¾07	8.3	131	105⅛	– ⅛
RJR Nb 9¼13	8.6	25	108	– ⅛
RJR Nb 8.3s99	8.3	5	100 5/32	+ 1/32
RJR Nb 8¾04	8.4	55	104⅜	– ⅜
Rallys 9⅞00	11.1	124	89	+ 8½
RalsP 7⅞25	7.1	13	111	+ 2⅝
RelGrp 9s00	8.7	225	104	– ¼
RelGrp 9¾03	9.4	10	104	+ ⅛
Revl 9½99	9.5	30	100 1/32	– 1/16
RobMyr 63	cv	20	96½	+ ½
Safwy 10s01	9.1	81	110¼	– ⅛
Safwy 9.65s04	8.4	20	114⅞	– ⅞
Safwy 9⅞07	8.1	40	121¼	+ ⅜
SallM zr14	...	125	31	...
Seagrm zr06	...	3	86	+ ½
Sears 9½99	9.4	5	100 17/32	+ 1/32
Sequa 9⅜03	9.1	50	103	...
SvcMer 8⅜01f	...	2	54	– 1
SvcMer 9s04f	...	651	21	+ ½
SilicnGr 5¼04	cv	40	92	+ ½
SoCG 5¾03	5.6	1	102	– ⅜
SwBell 6⅛00	6.1	25	100⅝	– ½
SwBell 6⅝05	6.3	5	106	
StdPac 10½00	10.3	20	102	...
StdPac 8½07	8.3	25	101⅞	– ⅛
StoneC 11½99	11.4	82	101 5/16	+ 3/16

AMEX BONDS

Volume $791,000

SALES SINCE JANUARY 1

1999	1998	1997
$11,627,000	$29,371,000	$37,393,000

	Fri.	Thu.	Wed.	Tue.
Issues Traded	6	18	12	13
Advances	1	5	2	2
Declines	3	7	9	9
Unchanged	2	6	1	2
New highs	0	0	0	0
New lows	2	3	4	1

	Bonds	Cur Yld	Vol	Close	Net Chg
	AssisLiv cv02	7.4	5	80¾	– 3¼
	BentPh 12s06	cv	63	105	...
	ThmoInst 4s05	cv	3	84	+ 1⅝
	Thrmtrx 3/07	cv	3	73½	+ 1½
	TWA 11½04	15.9	25	72½	– 1½
TWA →	TWA 11¾06	19.6	1	58	– 1
	Trump 11¾03f	...	145	87	+ ⅝
	US Cell zr15	...	15	44½	...
	Viacom 10¼01	9.3	2	110	+ 2
Viacom →	Viacom 8s06	7.8	15	103	...

Continued

Bonds	Cur Yld	Vol	Close	Net Chg
StoneC 9 7/8 01	9.7	124	101 7/8	– 1/8
StoneC 11 1/4 02A	11.2	126	100 5/8	+ 1/2
StoneC 10 3/4 02O	10.3	26	104 1/8	– 1/4
StoneC 11 1/2 04	10.9	35	105 1/8	...
StoneCn 6 3/4 07	cv	61	87	– 1
TVA 8 3/8 99	8.2	35	101 7/8	+ 9/16
TVA 6 1/8 03	6.1	156	101 1/4	+ 1/8
TVA 8.05s24	8.0	108	100 3/4	– 1/8
TVA 8 5/8 29	8.0	12	108 1/8	+ 1/8
TVA 8 1/4 34	8.2	20	101 1/8	...
TVA 6 7/8 43	6.6	38	103 3/4	– 1/2
Tenet 05	cv	10	85	– 1/2
TerR 4s19	4.7	10	85 1/8	...

EXPLANATORY NOTES
(For New York and American Bonds)
Yield is Current yield.

cv-Convertible bond. cf-Certificates. cld-Called. dc-Deep discount. ec-European currency units. f-Dealt in flat. il-Italian lire. kd-Danish kroner. m-Matured bonds, negotiability impaired by maturity. na-No accrual. r-Registered. rp-Reduced principal. st, sd-Stamped. t-Floating rate. wd-When distributed. ww-With warrants. x-Ex interest. xw-Without warrants. zr-Zero coupon.

vj-In bankruptcy or receivership or being reorganized under the Bankruptcy Act, or securities assumed by such companies.

Bonds	Cur Yld	Vol	Close	Net Chg
Texco 9s99D	8.8	25	102 1/8	– 1/8
TmeWar 7.95s00	7.8	55	102 1/4	+ 1/8
TmeWar 8.11s06	7.2	14	112 3/4	+ 3/8
TmeWar 8.18s07	7.2	14	113 1/4	+ 1/8
TmeWar 7.48s08	6.9	10	109	– 3
TmeWar 9 1/8 13	7.3	3	125 1/8	– 3/8
TolEd 8s03	7.9	10	101 1/8	– 1 7/8
TollCp 9 1/2 03	9.3	10	102	...
TollCp 8 3/4 06	8.4	5	104 3/4	– 1/8
URS 8 5/8 04	8.6	25	100	– 1 1/2
US Timb 9 5/8 07	9.5	10	101 1/2	+ 1/4
US Filt 4 1/2 01	cv	183	95 3/4	+ 3/4
Utilicp 6 5/8 11	cv	2	140	– 1/2
Webb 9 3/4 03	9.6	10	102	...
Webb 9s06	8.8	86	102 5/8	+ 1/8
WebbDel 9 3/8 09	9.6	289	97 1/2	
Weirton 10 7/8 99	10.9	20	100 1/8	+ 1/8
Weirton 11 3/8 04	12.2	10	93 1/4	+ 1/4
Weirton 10 3/4 05	12.1	71	88 1/2	+ 3/8
WhlPit 9 3/8 03	8.7	25	108 3/8	...
WldColor 07	cv	5	96	...

FOREIGN BONDS
Volume, $342,000

Bonds	Cur Yld	Vol	Close	Net Chg
Inco 7 3/4 16	8.5	25	91 1/8	– 1/2
SeaCnt 12 1/2 04A	11.4	10	109 1/4	+ 1/4
TrnMarMx 03	...	90	82	...
SeaCnt 9 1/2 03	9.2	20	103	+ 1/8
EmplCA 5s04	...	40	61 1/4	– 1 1/4
CGDina 8s04	...	143	46	+ 1/4
TelArg 11 7/8 04	11.3	33	105	– 1/8
MBL Int 3s02	...	10	102 1/2	+ 1/2
APP Fn zr12	...	18	16 1/2	+ 2 1/2

NASDAQ

Convertible Debentures

Friday, January 29, 1999

Issue	Vol.	Close	Net Chg.
Baker 7s02	70	75 3/4	+ 1/4
CalMicr 5 1/4 03	90	66	– 1
DrgEmp 7 3/4 14	25	88	+ 2
DuraPh 3 1/2 02	100	75 3/4	...
Exectne 7 1/2 11	10	68	+ 5
Hechng 5 1/2 12	200	25	– 3 1/2
Jacobsn 6 3/4 11	300	82	...
Metamor 2.94s04	5	85 1/4	– 1 7/8
OHM 8s06	25	96	+ 1/2
PhyCor 4 1/2 03	88	67 3/4	+ 1/4
RemOG 8 1/4 02	100	99 3/4	+ 1 1/4
SBS Bdc 7 1/4 05	20	102 1/4	– 3/4
Schuler 6 1/2 03	18	84	+ 2 1/2
Synetic 5s07	50	100 51/64	+ 1 51/64
SysSftwr 7s02	25	68 1/2	+ 1 1/2
Telxon 7 1/2 12	100	73	+ 4 1/2
VLSI 8 1/4 05	200	97 3/4	– 1/4

Source: *The Wall Street Journal*, February 1, 1999. Reprinted by permission of *The Wall Street Journal*,

ber that traded at a price below the previous trading day's, and **Unchanged** is the number of bonds whose price did not change. **New highs** lists the number trading at all-time highs. **Dow Jones Bond Averages** is a straight arithmetic summary and average of 20 selected utility and industrial bonds.

If you wish to follow the performance of a particular bond, consider the following illustration from the Monday, February 1, 1999 edition under **Amex Bonds**.

Bonds	**Cur. Yld.**	**Vol.**	**Close**	**Net Chg.**
TWA 11⅜ 06	19.6	1	58	–1
Viacom 8s 06	7.8	15	103	...

You will find a key to all footnotes under **Explanatory Notes** at the bottom of the listing.

In the case of the *Viacom* bond shown above and on pages 241, 243, and 244, the coupon rate at issue per $1000 bond (8 percent) and the year of maturity (2006, the year the bond is due for redemption), follows the company's name. (You'll find an "s" after the interest rate when a fraction is absent.)

Corporate bonds are issued in denominations of $1,000, and this particular Viacom bond originally paid an annual fixed-dollar interest return of $80.00

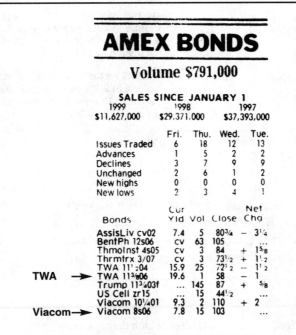

AMEX BONDS

Volume $791,000

SALES SINCE JANUARY 1

1999	1998	1997
$11,627,000	$29,371,000	$37,393,000

	Fri.	Thu.	Wed.	Tue.
Issues Traded	6	18	12	13
Advances	1	5	2	2
Declines	3	7	9	9
Unchanged	2	6	1	2
New highs	0	0	0	0
New lows	2	3	4	1

Bonds	Cur Yld	Vol	Close	Net Chg
AssisLiv cv02	7.4	5	80¾	− 3¼
BentPh 12s06	cv	63	105	...
Thmolnst 4s05	cv	3	84	+ 1⅝
Thrmtrx 3/07	cv	3	73½	+ 1½
TWA 11⅞04	15.9	25	72½	− 1½
TWA 11¾06	19.6	1	58	− 1
Trump 11¾03f	...	145	87	+ ⅝
US Cell zr15	...	15	44½	...
Viacom 10¼01	9.3	2	110	+ 2
Viacom 8s06	7.8	15	103	...

TWA → (arrow pointing to TWA 11¾06)

Viacom → (arrow pointing to Viacom 8s06)

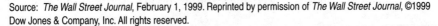

(8 percent of $1,000 = $80.00). Thus, Viacom promised to pay the bearer $80.00 a year until it redeemed the bond at maturity for its face value of $1,000.

You can see from the next column that the current yield is 7.8 percent. Volume is reported in thousands of dollars: 15 bonds with a face (par) value of $1000 were traded on January 29, 1999. The closing price for the day follows. Since bonds are issued in denominations of $1,000, the reported prices are a percentage of the face value of $1,000. Thus, 103 means this bond traded at a price of $1,030 (103 percent of $1,000 = $1,030) at the day's close. The last column informs you that the January 29 closing price was unchanged from the previous close.

Now, if you bought this bond on January 29, 1999, your yield would be 7.8 percent, slightly *less* than the coupon rate of 8 percent, because on January 29 the bond had a value of $1,030, *more* than its par value of $1,000. An annual payment of $80.00 on an investment of $1,030 provides a lower yield than a payment of $80.00 on an investment of $1,000.

If the current yield on securities of similar risk and maturity as the Viacom bond falls below the coupon rate of 8 percent (as they have here), an

AssisLiv cv02	7.4	5	80¾	−	3¼	
BentPh 12s06	cv	63	105		...	
Thmolnst 4s05	cv	3	84	+	1⅝	
Thrmtrx 3/07	cv	3	73½	+	1½	
TWA 11¼04	15.9	25	72½	−	1½	
TWA 11⅜06	19.6	1	58	−	1	
Trump 11¾03f	...	145	87	+	⅝	
US Cell zr15	...	15	44½		...	
Viacom 10¼01	9.3	2	110	+	2	
Viacom 8s06	7.8	15	103		...	

On 1/29/99 the TWA Bond that will mature in 2006 was worth $580 and paid a $113.75 annual coupon interest rate for a yield of 19.6%

On 1/29/99 the Viacom Bond that will mature in 2006 was worth $1,030 and paid an $80 annual coupon interest rate for a yield of 7.8%

investor will pay more than the par value for the bond. When commentators speak of the bond market rising and falling, they mean the *price* of the bond, not the *interest rate*. Bondholders want interest rates to fall so that the value of their bonds will rise. You can see that the Viacom bond went from $1,000 to $1,030 as its yield fell from 8 percent to 7.8 percent.

Investor's Tip

- Rising inflation, or fear of inflation, which drives interest rates up, hurts corporate bonds as well as Treasuries. Bond prices fall as interest rates rise.

You may have noticed that some of these bonds carry a "cv" notation in the *current yield* column. These bonds can be converted to a designated amount of common stock at the discretion of the bond holder, who will ordinarily make the conversion when the stock rises above a certain level. Because of this added feature, convertible bonds trade at a higher price and lower yield than bonds of comparable maturity and credit-worthiness. They are attractive to investors who are drawn to a company's stock but wish to earn interest while waiting to see whether the stock will appreciate.

Not only interest rates, but also the relative strength of the issuing company will affect the price of its bonds. Viacom is an investment of high quality because of its healthy financial condition and secure earnings potential. On the other hand, the TWA 11⅜ 2006 bond (see pages 241, 242, 243, and above) carries a higher coupon payment *and* yield than the Viacom bond, because TWA, a much weaker company in severe financial difficulty, had to pay a higher yield to attract investors' funds.

"Junk" bonds (like TWA) offer higher rates of interest because of their inherently risky nature. They are issued by companies that have high debt-

to-equity ratios and high debt-to-cash flow ratios and must therefore pay high interest rates to attract investors' money. Any fluctuation in the business of the issuing corporation could affect the timely payment of interest and the repayment of principal on the bonds.

Junk, or high-yield bonds, have been around for a long time and should be distinguished from their well-heeled cousins, the investment-grade bonds issued by financially secure corporations. Interest in junk bonds, especially on the part of institutions such as insurance companies and S&Ls, grew in the early 1980s, when falling interest rates boosted the prices of all bonds. Investors used the proceeds form the sale of junk bonds to purchase the stock of corporations, particularly conglomerates, that had fallen on hard times. These new owners often hoped to service their junk-bond debt by selling off divisions of the company they had purchased. Sometimes the company was worth more dead than alive and was dismembered. Sometimes top management bought a company from stockholders (called "going private") and then shrank it down to a profitable base. Often, however, the highly-leveraged surviving company was burdened with a huge, high-yield debt. Many companies failed and defaulted on their bonds, so that by the end of the 1980s, and especially during the 1990–91 recession, junk bonds fell out of favor and their prices sank and their yields soared. But the 1992 recovery and falling interest rates resuscitated many of these bonds, so that some investors realized strong capital gains as their prices climbed.

Junk bonds can bring substantial speculative rewards if a troubled company works its way out of difficulty and survives. Consider the TWA example on page 244. If an investor bought this bond on January 29, 1999, he or she would have earned $113.75 in annual coupon payments. Moreover, the investor would have paid $580.00 (58 percent of $1,000) for a bond that would mature seven years later and have a redemption value of $1,000. That would be a gain of $420.00 on a $580.00 investment in a seven-year stretch, on top of $113.75 in annual coupon payments. But if TWA filed for bankruptcy before this bond matured in 2006, the investor could be badly hurt.

Every day the *Journal* publishes **High-Yield Bonds** (see the Monday, January 25, 1999 example from the Tuesday, January 26, 1999 *Journal* on page 246) that summarizes activity in key junk bonds. You should note from the index that in early 1999, junk bonds had doubled in value over the past 8½ years to 253.04 (July 1, 1990 = 100).

You will notice that High-Yield Bonds lists a number of companies that have issued junk bonds. The column immediately after the company name provides a rating for these firms. The table on page 246 summarizes the format used by the two major rating-services.

HIGH-YIELD BONDS

Monday January 25, 1999

Junk-bond index up 153.04% since July 1, 1990 →

	Total Daily Return	Index Value	Average Price Change	Vol.
Flash Index	+ 0.21%	253.04	+ 0.17	M
Cash Pay	+ 0.16	276.11	+ 0.13	M
Deferred Int	+ 0.68	274.14	+ 0.49	M
Distressed	− 0.08	23.43	− 0.07	M
Bankrupt	+ 0.02	171.13	unch	M

Volume Key: H = Heavy, M = Moderate, L = Light
The Flash Index comprises more than 650 issues.

Key Gainers

	Type/ Coup.	Mat.	3:00P.M. Bid Price	Price Change	Principal Return	Yld.-y
NTL Incorp	c/ 0.000	4/08	68 1/2 +	4	+ 6.20	9.46
Trump AC	d/11.250	5/06	92 1/2 +	1	+ 1.06	12.86
Level 3 Com	a/ 9.125	5/08	98 +	1	+ 1.01	9.45

Key Losers

	Type/ Coup.	Mat.				
Winstar	b/10.000	3/08	78 −	2	− 2.39	14.399
Park Place	b/ 7.875	12/05	98 1/2 −	1	− 1.00	8.16

Name	Type/Rating	Coup.	Mat.	3 PM Bid	Net Chg.	Yld.-y
AK Steel	a/BB-	9.125	12/06	106 1/2 +	1/4	7.72
Advantica	a/B	11.250	1/08	101	unch	11.04

Name	Type/Rating	Coup.	Mat.	3 PM Bid	Net Chg.	Yld.-y
American Std	a/BB-	7.375	2/08	100 1/2	unch	7.30
Chancellor	b/B	8.125	12/07	103 3/4 −	1/4	7.41
Fed. Mogul	a/BB+	8.800	4/07	107	unch	7.63
Global Xing	a/B	9.625	5/08	104 1/2	unch	8.77
HMH Prop	a/BB	7.875	8/08	96	unch	8.50
Integrated	b/B-	9.250	1/08	95 1/2	unch	10.02
Intermedia	a/B	8.600	6/08	95 1/4	unch	9.37
Level 3 Com	a/B	9.125	5/08	98	+ 1	9.45
Nextel Comm	c/CCC+	0.000	9/07	68	+ 2 1/2	10.77
Ocean Enrgy	b/BB-	8.875	7/07	97 1/2	unch	9.31
Paging Ntwk	b/B	10.000	10/08	96	unch	10.67
Qwest Comm	c/BB+	0.000	10/07	78	unch	7.92
Revlon	a/B	8.125	2/06	93 1/2	unch	9.41
Stone	a/B	9.875	2/01	101 1/2	unch	8.29
Trump AC	d/B	11.250	5/06	92 1/2	+ 1	12.86
US Air	a/B	9.625	2/01	103 1/4	unch	7.84
Vintage Pet	b/B+	8.625	2/09	94 1/2 +	1/4	9.48

Volume indicators are based solely on the traders' subjective judgment given the relative level of inquiry and trading activity on any given day.

Bid Prices are indicative only and may not represent actual bids by a dealer.

Price quotes follow accrued interest conventions.

a-Senior. b-Senior Sub. c-Senior, Zero To Full. d-Secured. y-yield is the lower of yield to maturity and yield to call. z-omitted for reset or bankrupt bonds, negative yields, or yields above 35%.

Source: Salomon Smith Barney

Bond Ratings

Moody's	Standard & Poor's	Rating
Aaa	AAA	
Aa	AA	Investment Grade
A	A	
Baa	BBB	
Ba	BB	
B	B	
Caa	CCC	Junk
Ca	CC	
C	C	

You can also follow **New Securities Issues** daily in the *Journal* (check the index in the first or last section). It lists all new corporate, municipal, government agency, and foreign bonds issued on the previous day and provides pertinent information regarding these securities, including their ratings. (See the excerpt from the Monday, January 25, 1999 *Journal* on page 247.)

NEW SECURITIES ISSUES

The following were among Friday's offerings and pricings in U.S. and non-U.S. capital markets, with terms and syndicate manager, based on information provided by Dow Jones Newswires. (A basis point is one-hundredth of a percentage point; 100 basis points equals a percentage point.)

CORPORATE

Aristar Inc. – $200 million of notes were priced via lead manager Merrill Lynch & Co., according to MCM CorporateWatch. Terms: maturity: Jan. 27, 2004; coupon: 5.85%; issue price: 99.85; yield: 5.885%; spread: 125 basis points above Treasurys; call: noncallable; debt ratings: A3 (Moody's), single-A-minus (S&P).

Dime Bancorp – $200 million of notes were priced via lead managers Merrill Lynch and Credit Suisse First Boston Corp., according to MCM CorporateWatch. Terms: maturity: Jan. 30, 2001; coupon: 6.375%; issue price: 99.803; yield: 6.481%; spread: 187.5 basis points above Treasurys; call: noncallable; debt ratings: Ba1 (Moody's), triple-B-minus (S&P).

Fannie Mae – $100 million of notes were priced via lead manager Merrill Lynch, according to MCM CorporateWatch. Terms :maturity: Feb. 2, 2004; issue price: par; yield: 5.68%; call: noncallable for one year.

Fannie Mae – $100 million of notes were priced via lead manager J.P. Morgan Securities Inc., according to MCM CorporateWatch. Terms: maturity: Feb. 4, 2009; issue price: par; yield: 6%; call: noncallable for three years.

Fannie Mae – $200 million of medium-term notes were priced via lead manager Bear, Stearns & Co., according to BondData-Corporate Service. Terms: maturity: Feb. 1, 2001; issue price: par; yield: 5.07%; call: noncallable for one year.

Fannie Mae – $200 million of notes were priced via lead managers First Tennessee Bank, Goldman, Sachs & Co., and HSBC Securities Inc., the managers announced. Terms: maturity: Feb. 1, 2002; issue price: par; yield: 5.3%; spread: 78 basis points; call: noncallable for one year.

Federal Farm Credit Banks – $101 million of notes were priced via lead manager Fuji Securities Inc., according to MCM CorporateWatch. Terms: maturity: Feb. 4, 2002; issue price: par; yield: 5.38%; call: noncallable for six months.

Federal Home Loan Bank System – $50 million of bonds were priced via lead managers Prudential Securities Inc. and First Chicago Capital Markets, according to MCM CorporateWatch. Terms: maturity: Aug. 7, 2001; issue price: par; yield: 5.055%; call: noncallable for three months.

Federal Home Loan Bank System – $50 million of bonds were priced via lead manager Norwest Investment Services Inc., according to MCM CorporateWatch. Terms: maturity: Feb. 5, 2004; issue price: par; yield: 5.5%; call: noncallable for two years.

Federal Home Loan Bank System – $50 million of notes were priced via lead managers Morgan Keegan & Co. and Chase Securities Inc., according to MCM CorporateWatch. Terms: maturity: Feb. 9, 2004; issue price: par; yield: 5.625%; call: noncallable for nine months.

Federal Home Loan Bank System – $80 million of notes were priced via lead manager Salomon Smith Barney Inc., according to MCM CorporateWatch. Terms: maturity: Feb. 4, 2002; issue price: par; yield: 5.33%; call: noncallable for one year.

Federal Home Loan Bank System – $3 billion of global bonds were priced via lead manager Salomon Smith Barney, according to MCM CorporateWatch. Terms: maturity: Jan. 26, 2001; coupon: 4.875%; issue price: 99.991; yield: 4.88%; spread: 35 basis points above Treasurys; call: noncallable.

Freddie Mac – $25 million of notes were priced via lead manager First Tennessee, First Tennessee announced. Terms: maturity: July 27, 2001; issue price: par; yield: 5.31%; spread: 79 basis points; call: noncallable for three months.

Freddie Mac – $25 million of notes were priced via lead manager First Tennessee, First Tennessee said. Terms: maturity: Jan. 29, 2003; issue price: par; yield: 5.61%; spread: 108 basis points; call: noncallable for three months.

Freddie Mac – $50 million of notes were priced via lead manager First Tennessee, First Tennessee said. Terms: maturity: Jan. 28, 2014; issue price: par; yield: 6.43%; spread: 178 basis points; call: noncallable for one year.

Freddie Mac – $300 million of notes were priced via lead manager Salomon Smith Barney, according to MCM CorporateWatch. Terms: maturity: Feb. 3, 2009; coupon: 6.25%; issue price: 99.80; yield: 7.064% (to call); yield: 6.277% (to maturity); call: noncallable for three months.

Toll Corp. – $170 million of senior subordinated notes were priced via lead manager Salomon Smith Barney, according to MCM CorporateWatch. Terms: maturity: Feb. 1, 2009; issue price: par; yield: 8.125%; spread: 343 basis points; call: noncallable for five years, then at 104.063; debt ratings: Ba3 (Moody's), double-B-plus (S&P).

EQUITY

First Community Financial Corp. – Initial public offering is filed for 2.38 million shares at a price of $15 apiece.

ASSET-BACKED

Bombardier Capital Inc. – $167.43 million of manufactured housing asset-backed securities were priced in eight parts via lead manager Prudential Securities, according to MCM CorporateWatch. Terms follow, citing amount (in millions of dollars), class, rating, coupon, yield and spread. Part I: 35; A-1; AAA (Moody's, S&P); 5.825%; 5.65%; N/A. Part II: 31; A-2; AAA (Moody's, S&P); 5.795%; 5.781%; 113 basis points above 6.25% Treasury of February 2002. Part III: 22; A-3; AAA (Moody's, S&P); 5.98%; 6%; 137 basis points above 5.875% Treasury of February 2004. Part IV: 34; A-4; AAA (Moody's, S&P); 6.475%; 6.527%; 178 basis points above 5.625% Treasury of May 2008. Part V: 14.375; A-5; AAA (Moody's, S&P); 6.7%; 6.769%; 168 basis points above 5.25% Treasury of November 2028. Part VI: 13.503; M-1; Aa3 (Moody's), double-A-minus (S&P); 6.785%; 6.846%; 210 basis points above 5.625% Treasury of May 2008. Part VII: 9.002; M-2; A2 (Moody's), single-A (S&P); 7.665%; 7.746%; 300 basis points above 5.625% Treasury of May 2008. Part VIII: 8.552; B-1; Baa3 (Moody's), triple-B-minus (S&P); to be announced; TBA; TBA.

First Consumers – $250 million of credit-card asset-backed securities were priced in two parts via lead manager J.P. Morgan Securities Inc., according to MCM CorporateWatch. Terms follow, citing amount (in millions of dollars), coupon, yield and spread. Part I: 214; 5.8%; 5.888%; 135 basis points above 4.25% Treasury of November 2003. Part II: 36; 6.28%; 6.388%; 175 basis points above 5.825% Treasury of February 2007.

EUROBOND

Associates Capital Corp. (U.K.) – Increased its offering of floating-rate Eurobonds due Jan. 2004 at 99.782 by HSBC Markets by £50 million, bringing total to £200 million

Banca Popolare di Brescia (Italy) – $200 million of floating-rate note Eurobonds due Feb. 5, 2001, priced at 99.924 by ABN Amro. Coupon pays 12.5 basis points above three-month London interbank offered rate. Fees 0.125%.

Council of Europe – Increased its inverse floating-rate note due Feb. 1, 2019, at 100.50 by Lehman Brothers International by 20 million euros, bringing total to 145 million euros.

BGB Finance PLC (German parent) – Increased its offering of structured Eurobonds due Jan. 28, 2019, at 99.75 by Morgan Stanley Dean Witter by 40 million euros, bringing total to 100 million euros.

Credit Local de France – $100 million of callable step-down Eurobonds due Feb. 22, 2011, reoffered at 99.85 by Sanwa International. Callable from Feb. 22, 2000. Coupon pays 7⅛% for first year; 6% thereafter. Fees 2%.

Cregem Finance NV (Netherlands) – 75 million euros of zero-coupon Eurobonds due Feb. 11, 2005, indexed to the BEL 20 stock index, priced at par by Dexia Capital Markets. Fees 1.875%.

European Bank for Reconstruction and Development – 100 million euros of step-down Eurobonds due Feb. 22, 2029, reoffered at 99.80 by TD Securities. Coupon pays 10% in year one, 5% in years two and three, 4% in year three and four, zero in years five to 16, 4% in years 17 and 18, 5% in year 19 and 10% in year 20. Fees 2%.

European Investment Bank – 30 billion Greek drachmas of 6% Eurobonds due Feb. 4, 2002, reoffered at 99.5875 by RBC DS Global Markets. Fees 1.375%.

GE Capital Corp. (U.S.) – 275 million euros of 2.875% Eurobonds due Feb. 8, 2000, reofferd at 99.927 by Paribas to yield seven basis points above the French government BTAN bond due Jan. 2000. Fees 1%.

GE Capital Corp (U.S.) – 350 million euros of 3% Eurobonds due Feb. 8, 2001, reoffered at par by Paribas to yield 10 basis points above the French government BTAN bond due Oct. 2000. Fees 1.125%.

GMAC Australia Finance Ltd. (U.S. parent) – 100 million Australian dollars of 5.5% Eurobonds due Feb. 25, 2004, priced at 100.56 by RBC DS Global Markets. Fees 2%.

Japan General Finance Co. – $324 million equivalent asset-backed Eurobonds via Deutsche Bank through special purpose vehicle Hexagon Funding Ltd. Tranche 1 comprised of $80 million of 1.032-year notes to yield 46 basis points above one-month Libor. Tranche 2 comprises 210 million euros of 1.032-year notes to yield 38 basis points above one-month European interbank offered rate.

John Hancock Global Funding Ltd. (U.S.) – 300 million euros of 3⅞% Eurobonds due Feb. 8, 2006, priced at 99.429 by ABN Amro Bank and Lehman Brothers to yield 53 basis points above the 7¼% OAT due April 2006 or 45 basis points above the bund due Jan. 2006. Fees 0.325%.

Kiwi Co-operative Dairies Ltd. (New Zealand) – $125 million of 6% Eurobonds due Feb. 12, 2009 priced at 99.063 by Salomon Brothers International to yield 140 basis points above the 4¾% Nov. 2008 Treasury. Fees 0.425%.

Ricoh Leasing Co. (Japan) – $320 million collateralized Euro/144a floating-rate notes due Feb. 2, 2004, priced at 99.96 by Morgan Stanley Dean Witter offered through special purpose vehicle R Funding Corp. Coupon pays 55 basis points above one-month Libor. Fees 0.3%.

Source: *The Wall Street Journal*, January 25, 1999. Reprinted by permission of *The Wall Street Journal*,

Finally, Monday's **Securities Offering Calendar** (see the excerpt from the Monday, January 25, 1999 edition on page 249) provides information on the week's new issues (check the third section's index under *New Offerings*).

MUNICIPAL BONDS

You may wish to purchase municipal (state and local government) or tax-exempt bonds, as they are sometimes called, because earnings from these bonds are not subject to federal income tax and may not be subject to income tax in your state. These bonds were granted tax exemption in order to reduce the borrowing cost of the states, cities, and local districts that issue them. Investors purchase them knowing their return is not taxable, and they will therefore be satisfied with a yield below that of comparable federal or corporate bonds. State and local governments save billions in interest costs as a result of this indirect subsidy.

Each Friday, the *Journal* publishes a **Municipal Bond Index** prepared by Merrill Lynch (see the last section's index). The excerpt from the Friday, February 12, 1999 *Journal* on page 250 serves as an example. In addition to an overall index, this report presents the latest yield on a variety of municipal bond categories.

Before deciding on the purchase of a tax-exempt municipal bond, an investor must weigh four considerations: the yield available on the municipal bond, the yield on a taxable bond with the same maturity, the investor's tax bracket, and whether the bond is callable.

If, for example, you are in a 28 percent tax bracket, use the "equivalent tax-exempt yield formula" to calculate your after-tax yield on a security whose income is taxable. This will be the minimum yield a municipal bond must pay you to be of equivalent value to the taxable bond.

Here's an example using a 10 percent yield on the security whose interest is taxable.

$$\text{Equivalent tax - exempt yield} = (1 - \text{Tax bracket}) \times \text{Taxable yield}$$
$$= (1 - .28) \times .10$$
$$= .072$$
$$= 7.2 \text{ percent}$$

Thus, in your 28 percent tax bracket, a 7.2 percent tax-exempt yield is the equivalent of a 10 percent taxable yield.

Therefore, if you had the opportunity, you would purchase an 8 percent tax-exempt bond rather than a 10 percent taxable bond with similar maturity and credit-worthiness.

SECURITIES OFFERING CALENDAR

The following U.S. Treasury, corporate and municipal offerings are tentatively scheduled for sale this week, according to Dow Jones Newswires:

TREASURYS
Monday
$15 billion in three- and six-month bills.

Wednesday
$15 billion in two-year notes.

CORPORATE
Investment-Grade Debt
One Day in the Week
Federal Farm Credit Bank System – $1.584 billion two-part consolidated system-wide bond offering via selling group. $1.195 billion 3-month tranche and $389 million 6-month tranche. (Aaa/AAA).
BRE Properties (BRE) – $50 million offering of perpetual preferred securities via Morgan Stanley Dean Witter. Two million shares at $25 per share. (Baa3/BBB–). Offer range: 8.375% to 8.50% area.
Liberty Property Trust – $100 million six-year offering via Donaldson, Lufkin & Jenrette Securities. Rule 144a market. (Baa3/BBB-). Offer range: 300 basis points over Treasurys.
Kinder Morgan Energy LP (ENP) – $200 million 10-year senior notes offering via Goldman Sachs & Co. (Baa1/BBB+).
MTR Corp – $500 million of 10-year global, via Merrill Lynch and Goldman, Sachs & Co. (A3/A).

High-Yield Debt
One Day in the Week
Bresnan Communications Group LLC – $295 million of Rule 144a, two-part offering via Salomon Smith Barney. $170 million of senior notes, due 2009, noncallable five years. $125 million (proceeds) of senior discount notes, due 2009, noncallable five years, with five-year zero coupon. (B2/B+). Offer range: Senior notes at 8% to 8.125%, senior discount notes at the yield on the cash pay notes plus 125 basis points.
Carmike Cinemas Inc. (CKE) – $200 million of Rule 144a senior subordinated notes, due 2009, noncallable five years, via Goldman, Sachs & Co. (B2/–).
Cinergy Corp. (Cin) – $117 million of senior secured notes, due 2016, with 13.6-year average life, via Salomon Smith Barney. Will be sold under special purpose vehicle, Cincap V LLC.
Completel Europe N.V. – $200 million of Rule 144a senior notes, due 2009, noncallable five years, cash pay with 2.5-year interest escrow account, via Salomon Smith Barney. (Caa2/–).
Consumers Packaging Inc. (T.CGC) – $75 million of Rule 144 senior notes, due 2005, callable 2001, via BT Alex.Brown Inc. (B1/–).
Dynacare Inc. – $65 million of Rule 144a senior notes add-on to 10.75s of 2006, callable on 2001, via Credit Suisse First Boston. (B2/–). Original issue priced at $125 million.
Integrated Electrical Services Inc. (IEE) – $150 million of Rule 144a senior subordinated notes, due 2009, noncallable five years, via Merrill Lynch & Co. (B2/B+). Offer range: 9.5% to 9.75%.
Luigino's Inc. – $100 million of Rule 144a senior subordinated notes, due 2006, noncallable four years, via First Chicago Capital Markets.
Oglebay Norton Co. (OGLE) – $100 million of Rule 144a senior subordinated notes, due 2009, noncallable five years, via CIBC Oppenheimer. (B3/B-). Offer range: 10% area.
Pac-West Telecom Inc. – $150 million of Rule 144a senior notes, due 2009, noncallable five years, with one-year interest reserve, via Nationsbanc Montgomery Securities. (B3/–).
Panolam Industries – $145 million of Rule 144a senior subordinated notes, due 2009, noncallable five years, via Donaldson, Lufkin & Jenrettes Securities. (–/B-).
Phoenix Color Corp. – $100 million of Rule 144a senior subordinated notes, due 2009, noncallable five years, via First Union Capital Markets. (B3/B-).
Tokheim Corp. (TOK) – US$210 million of Rule 144a senior subordinated notes due 2008, in two-parts, both noncallable five years, via BT Alex.Brown Inc. (B3/B). Split between $135 million tranche and Euro65 million tranche. Offer range: US$ tranche at 10.75% to 11%, Euro tranche at 11% area.
Waste Systems International Inc. (WSII) – $100 million of Rule 144a senior subordinated notes, due 2006, noncallable four years, via First Albany Companies. (–/B).

Willis Corroon Corp. – US$550 million of Rule 144a senior subordinated notes, due 2009, noncallable five years, via Chase Securities. (Ba3/B+). Guaranteed by Willis Corroon Group Limited.

Initial Public Offerings
One Day in the Week
American Axle & Manufacturing Holdings Inc. – Seven million shares via Merrill Lynch & Co. Offer range: $16 to $18.
CNB Inc. – 1.25 million shares via Ryan. Offer range: $10 to $12.
Entercom Communications Corp. – 10.85 million class A shares via Credit Suisse First Boston. Offer range: $18 to $21.
Packaged Ice Inc. – Nine million shares via NationsBanc Montgomery Securities Inc. and Jefferies & Co. Offer range: $11 to $13.
Smith-Gardner & Associates Inc. – 4.41 million shares via BT Alex.Brown Inc. Offer range: $8 to $10.
Tower Financial Corp. – Two million shares via Roney & Co. Offer range: $10.
Tut Systems Inc. – 2.5 million shares via Lehman Brothers Inc. Offer range: $14 to $16.

Other Corporate Offerings
One Day in the Week
AHL Services Inc. (AHLS) – Four million shares via Salomon Smith Barney Inc.
Franchise Finance Corporations of America (FFA) – Six million shares via Merrill Lynch & Co. and Bear Stearns & Co.
ITT Educational Services Inc. (ESI) – Seven million shares via Credit Suisse First Boston.
Mettler-Toledo International Inc. (MTD) – 5.587 million shares via Merrill Lynch & Co.
Provant Inc. (POVT) – 3.485 million shares via Merrill Lynch & Co.
Quanta Services Inc. (PWR) – 3.5 million shares via BT Alex.Brown Inc.
Stewart Enterprises Inc. (STEI) – 12.5 million class A shares via Bear Stearns & Co.
Tiffany & Co. (TIF) – 3.88 million shares via Merrill Lynch & Co.
Tweeter Home Entertainment Group Inc. (TWTR) – 2 million shares via BT Alex.Brown Inc.
Verisign Inc. (VRSN) – 2.4 million shares via Morgan Stanley Dean Witter.

MUNICIPALS
Tuesday
Los Angeles Wastewater System – $88.3 million of revenue bonds at noon.
Maricopa County Community College, Ariz. – $104.2 million of general obligation bonds at noon.

Wednesday
Chesterfield County, Va. – $75.0 million of general obligation bonds at 11 a.m.
Los Angeles County Metropolitan Transit Authority – $124.9 million of revenue bonds at noon.

One Day in the Week
Alameda Corridor Transportation Authority, Calif. – $650 million of taxable revenue bonds via PaineWebber.
Alaska International Airport System – $179 million of revenue bonds via Merrill Lynch.
Clackamas County Health Facility, Ore. – $100 million of revenue bonds via Merrill Lynch.
Denver Regional Transportation District – $50 million certificates of participation via PaineWebber.
Illinois Health Facilities Authority – $240 million of revenue bonds via Merrill Lynch.
New York State Dormitory Authority, Methodist Hospital – $60 million of revenue bonds via Bear Stearns.
New York City Industrial Development Authority – $85 million of revenue bonds via Merrill Lynch.
New York State Dormitory Authority, Hamilton College – $53 million of revenue bonds via Lehman Brothers.
New York State Dormitory Authority, Menora Home – $78.6 million of revenue bonds via Goldman, Sachs.
Phoenix, Ariz. – $163 million of general obligation bonds via Prudential Securities.
Rio Rancho, N.M. – $73 million of water & sewer revenue bonds via George K. Baum.
San Diego Redevelopment Agency, Calif. – $52 million of revenue bonds via Prudential.
Shelby County, Tenn. – $62.2 million of general obligation bonds via Morgan Keegan.
Tampa, Fla. – $100 million of revenue bonds via Merrill Lynch.

Municipal Bond Index
Merrill Lynch Muni Master
Week ended Tuesday, February 9, 1999

The following index is based on major municipal issuers having bonds with amounts outstanding of at least $50 million, an investment grade rating and issuance within the last five years. The chart shown displays the market weighted average yield to worst* of each index. The index is calculated by Merrill Lynch, based on pricing obtained from Standard & Poor's J.J. Kenny Co.

— MUNI MASTER BOND INDEX —
4.78   −0.01

— REVENUE BONDS —
Sub-Index   4.93   −0.01

	02-09		Change In Week
— 22-52 YEAR REVENUE BONDS —			
AAA-Guaranteed.....	4.88	−	0.02
Airport	5.02	−	0.04
Power.....................	4.87	−	0.02
Hospital..................	4.94	−	0.01
Housing- Single Family	5.26	+	0.01
Housing- Multi Family	5.06	+	0.01
Miscellaneous	n/a		n/a
Pollution Control/ Ind. Dev.	4.61	−	0.02
Transportation.......	4.88	−	0.01
Water	4.90	−	0.03
Advance Refunded ..	3.86	+	0.04
— 12-22 YEAR GENERAL OBLIGATIONS —			
Sub-Index 4.62 +0.00			
Cities......................	4.66	+	0.00
Counties	3.61	+	0.03
States	4.61	+	0.00
Other Districts	n/a		n/a

The transportation category excludes airports; other districts include school and special districts.

*-assuming the least advantageous maturity for each issue in each index.

Municipal bond buyers should always determine if the issuing agency can call (redeem) the bond before maturity. It may wish to do so when interest rates are low in order to issue new debt at lower rates. Meanwhile, the purchaser is forced to find another investment at a disadvantageous time. Therefore, an investor that plans to hold a bond until maturity should not purchase a bond that is callable before that date.

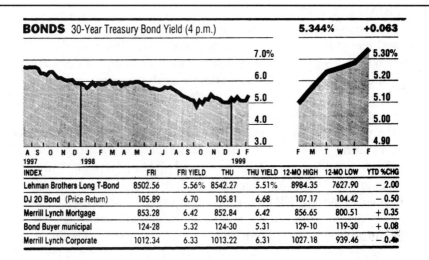

INDEX	FRI	FRI YIELD	THU	THU YIELD	12-MO HIGH	12-MO LOW	YTD %CHG
Lehman Brothers Long T-Bond	8502.56	5.56%	8542.27	5.51%	8984.35	7627.90	− 2.00
DJ 20 Bond (Price Return)	105.89	6.70	105.81	6.68	107.17	104.42	− 0.50
Merrill Lynch Mortgage	853.28	6.42	852.84	6.42	856.65	800.51	+ 0.35
Bond Buyer municipal	124-28	5.32	124-30	5.31	129-10	119-30	+ 0.08
Merrill Lynch Corporate	1012.34	6.33	1013.22	6.31	1027.18	939.46	− 0.4

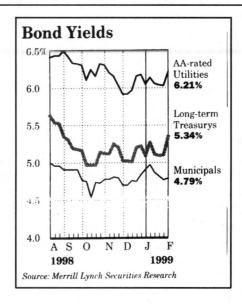

Source: Merrill Lynch Securities Research

TRACKING THE BOND MARKET

It's now time to wrap up this discussion by detailing how you can use the *Journal* every day to follow the bond market. You should begin your daily analysis of bond-market activity with a glance at the **Bonds** reports on the first page of the third section under **Markets Diary** (see the excerpt from the Monday, February 8, 1999 edition on page 251), which lists five important indexes that track bond-market performance and provide current yields. The graph portrays the yield on the bellwether **30-Year Treasury Bond**. **The Lehman Brothers Long T-Bond** tracks long-term Treasury securities. The **DJ 20 Bond** index provides the average price and yield of 10 public utility bonds and 10 industrial bonds. You became acquainted with it in the discussion of NYSE bonds. The **Merrill Lynch Mortgage** index covers mortgage-backed securities such as Ginnie Maes, Fannie Maes, and Freddie Macs. **The Bond Buyer municipal** index is compiled by *The Bond Buyer*, a publication that specializes in fixed-income securities, and covers AA-rated and A-rated municipal bonds. The **Merrill Lynch Corporate** bond index, like the Dow index, is a corporate bond composite.

The **Bond Yields** chart appears in Monday's *Wall Street Journal* with the **Credit Markets** article, as shown in the sample on page 251 from the Monday, February 8, 1999 issue. It depicts three series: the top line portrays the yield paid by financially healthy public utilities on debt instruments maturing in 10 years or more, the second series depicts the yield on 15-year and longer Treasury bonds, and the bottom line shows municipal bond yields.

The *Journal* publishes its **Bond Market Data Bank** (find it in the front-page index of the first and last sections) daily toward the center of Section C, as in the example from the Monday, February 8, 1999 issue on pages 253 and 254. The data bank thoroughly covers the bond market for the preceding trading day and contains more information than you may ever want to know.

Finally, you can compare the yield on a variety of long-term instruments by using the **Yield Comparisons** table that appears daily with the **Credit Markets** article; also check the yield on the entire range of Treasury securities in the **Treasury Yield Curve** (see the excerpts form the Monday, February 8, 1999 issue on page 255). Notice the normal shape of the yield curve: Yields increase with length of maturity.

MUTUAL FUNDS

If you recall the discussion of mutual funds in Chapter 9, you will remember that mutual funds often specialize in particular types of investments. Bond funds are mutual funds that invest primarily in debt instruments, permitting you to diversity your bond investments without venturing a large

BOND MARKET DATA BANK   2/5/99

BOND YIELDS

Source: Telerate, 4:00 p.m. Eastern time

	TREASURY ISSUES*			MUNICIPAL ISSUES† (Comparable Maturities)			
				Aaa	TAX	MUNI/TREAS	52-WEEK RATIO
MATURITY	COUPON	PRICE	YIELD	YIELD	EQUIV.	YIELD RATIO	HIGH	LOW
01/31/01	4.500	99.15	4.784	3.25	4.71	67.9	87.1	65.9
11/15/01	5.875	102.20	4.860	3.45	5.00	71.0	86.3	68.0
11/15/03	4.250	97.14	4.857	3.65	5.29	75.1	91.1	71.1
11/15/08	4.750	98.18	4.936	4.05	5.87	82.1	94.7	76.3
11/15/28	5.250	98.19	5.344	4.95	7.17	92.6	100.7	85.7

* Most recent auctions.   † From Delphis Hanover. Tax equiv. based on 31% bracket.

MAJOR INDEXES

HIGH	LOW (12 MOS)		CLOSE	NET CHG	% CHG	12-MO CHG	% CHG	FROM 12/31	% CHG
U.S. TREASURY SECURITIES		(Lehman Brothers indexes)							
5649.67	5213.19	Intermediate	5593.95	-- 7.04	-- 0.13	+ 365.51 +	6.99	-- 20.24	-- 0.36
8984.35	7627.90	Long-term	8502.56	-- 39.71	-- 0.46	+ 784.32 +	10.16	-- 173.71	-- 2.00
1809.29	1590.38	Long-term(price)	1677.43	-- 8.13	-- 0.48	+ 56.06 +	3.46	-- 44.60	-- 2.59
6372.83	5738.34	Composite	6222.90	-- 14.45	-- 0.23	+ 454.10 +	7.87	-- 55.33	-- 0.88
U.S. CORPORATE DEBT ISSUES		(Merrill Lynch)							
1027.18	939.46	Corporate Master	1012.34	-- 0.88	-- 0.09	+ 68.41 +	7.25	-- 4.82	-- 0.47
730.73	675.27	1-10 Yr Maturities	723.42	-- 0.37	-- 0.05	+ 45.99 +	6.79	-- 2.06	-- 0.28
827.57	743.59	10+ Yr Maturities	809.09	-- 1.23	-- 0.15	+ 60.02 +	8.01	-- 6.71	-- 0.82
507.98	469.49	High Yield	504.19	+ 0.01	-- 0.00	+ 14.27 +	2.91	+ 3.95	+ 0.79
737.70	678.22	Yankee Bonds	727.39	-- 0.27	-- 0.04	+ 45.21 +	6.63	-- 3.08	-- 0.42
TAX-EXEMPT SECURITIES		(Bond Buyer; Merrill Lynch: Dec. 31, 1986 = 100)							
129-10	119-30	Bond Buyer Municipal	124-28	-- -2	-- 0.05	+ -28 +	0.71	+ -3	+ 0.08
147.74	135.91	7-12 yr G.O.	147.15	-- 9.08	-- 0.05	+ 9.89 +	7.21	+ 1.76	+ 1.21
153.16	140.80	12-22 yr G.O.	152.57	+ 0.02	+ 0.01	+ 10.56 +	7.44	+ 1.12	+ 0.74
147.55	135.78	22+ yr Revenue	146.51	+ 0.07	+ 0.05	+ 8.93 +	6.49	+ 0.76	+ 0.52
MORTGAGE-BACKED SECURITIES		(current coupon; Merrill Lynch: Dec. 31, 1986 = 100)							
317.20	290.32	Ginnie Mae(GNMA)	314.53	-- 0.10	-- 0.03	+ 23.33 +	8.01	-- 0.69	-- 0.22
311.38	285.93	Fannie Mae(FNMA)	309.15	-- 0.04	-- 0.01	+ 22.53 +	7.86	-- 0.08	-- 0.03
189.61	174.65	Freddie Mac(FHLMC)	188.24	-- 0.03	-- 0.02	+ 13.11 +	7.49	-- 0.06	-- 0.03
BROAD MARKET		(Merrill Lynch)							
835.13	766.79	Domestic Master	826.05	-- 0.94	-- 0.11	+ 56.45 +	7.33	-- 3.24	-- 0.39
939.99	853.58	Corporate/Government	923.47	-- 1.67	-- 0.18	+ 65.39 +	7.62	-- 6.45	-- 0.69

TAX-EXEMPT BONDS

Representative prices for several active tax-exempt revenue and refunding bonds, based on institutional trades. Changes rounded to the nearest one-eighth. Yield is to maturity. n-New. Source: The Bond Buyer.

ISSUE	COUPON	MAT	PRICE	CHG	BID YLD	ISSUE	COUPON	MAT	PRICE	CHG	BID YLD
Alameda Corr TA Ca	4.750	10-01-25	95⅜	...	5.04	Jefferson Parish Hsp	5.000	07-01-28	96⅜	...	5.22
Alameda Corr TA Ca	5.000	10-01-29	98⅜	...	5.07	LA Stad & Expo Hotel	5.000	07-01-26	97⅞	...	5.14
Alaska Intl Arpts	5.000	10-01-24	96⅝	...	5.22	MA Bay Trans Auth Gen	5.000	03-01-28	97⅞	...	5.14
Ca Hlth Fac Fin Auth	5.350	08-15-28	102⅝	...	5.20	Mass Tpk Auth Ser A	5.000	01-01-37	97	-- ⅛	5.18
CA Hlth Fin Rev 98 Ser	5.000	10-01-20	97	-- ⅛	5.23	Mo. Hlth & Ed Fac	5.000	05-15-38	95⅜	-- ⅛	5.28
California GO Ser 98	4.750	12-01-28	95½	...	5.04	Monty BMC Spc Care	5.000	11-15-29	96⅞	-- ⅛	5.20
Chgo Ill Sls Tx Rev	5.375	01-01-30	101⅞	...	5.12	NJ Hlth Cr Rev Ser 9	5.000	07-01-24	98⅞	-- ⅛	5.08
Cll Pgf Sd Transit WA	4.750	02-01-28	94⅜	-- ⅛	5.12	NJ Hlth Fin Rev Ser 9	4.750	07-01-28	95¼	-- ⅛	5.06
Denver Colo Arpt	5.000	11-15-25	97¼	...	5.19	NJ Trans Trust Fund	4.500	06-15-19	93⅞	-- ⅛	4.98
Denver Sch Dist #1	5.000	12-01-23	98⅝	-- ⅛	5.10	No East Ind Sch Dist	4.500	10-01-28	91¼	...	5.07
Det Cty Sch Dist MI sch	4.750	05-01-28	94½	...	5.11	NYC Muni Wtr&Swr	4.750	06-15-31	94⅜	-- ⅛	5.08
Florida St Bd of Ed	4.500	06-01-23	92½	-- ⅛	5.03	Orge Co FL Trst Dev Tax	4.750	10-01-24	95⅜	...	5.07
Grpvn-Colv Sch TX	5.000	08-15-29	97⅞	...	5.13	Phil PA Go Ser 98	5.000	03-15-28	98	...	5.13
Highld Co Hlth FL	5.250	11-15-28	97¼	-- ⅛	5.44	Phila Sch Dist Pa	4.750	04-01-27	94½	-- ⅛	5.11
Hono HI Wastewtr	5.000	07-01-23	98¼	...	5.13	Pub Hwy Auth Colo	5.000	09-01-26	98¼	-- ⅛	5.12
Houstn Ind Sch Dis Tx	4.750	02-15-26	94⅞	-- ⅛	5.10	Puerto Rico Pub Improv	5.000	07-01-28	98¾	+ ⅛	5.11
Houstn Ind Sch Dist Tx	5.000	02-15-24	98⅜	...	5.12	Sacramento Cty Fin Auth	4.750	05-01-23	95¾	...	5.05
Huston Tx Airport Sys	5.000	07-01-25	97⅝	...	5.20	Wash Hlth Care Auth	5.000	11-15-28	96⅞	-- ⅛	5.20
Fl Hlth Fac Auth19	5.000	01-01-25	96¾	...	5.22	Wash Hlth Care Fac	5.000	10-01-28	97	...	5.20
Fl Hlth Fac Auth19	5.125	01-01-28	98	⅛	5.26	Wayne Chrtr Co MI Airp	5.000	12-01-28	97	...	5.20

Continued

MORTGAGE-BACKED SECURITIES

Indicative, not guaranteed; from Bear Stearns Cos./Street Pricing Service

		PRICE (Mar) (Pts-32ds)	PRICE CHANGE (32ds)	AVG LIFE (years)	SPRD TO AVG LIFE (Bps)	SPREAD CHANGE	PSA (Prepay Speed)	YIELD TO MAT.*
30-YEAR								
FMAC GOLD	6.0%	98-06	− 01	9.2	141	− 10	150	6.33%
FMAC GOLD	6.5%	100-09	unch	7.9	158	− 11	180	6.49
FMAC GOLD	7.0%	101-24	+ 01	5.4	172	13	290	6.59
FNMA	6.0%	98-03	− 01	9.1	140	− 10	150	6.32
FNMA	6.5%	100-07	+ 01	7.9	156	− 12	180	6.47
FNMA	7.0%	101-24	+ 01	5.3	167	− 13	290	6.54
GNMA	6.0%	98-11	− 02	10	136	− 9	125	6.29
GNMA	6.5%	100-15	unch	8.6	154	− 11	160	6.46
GNMA	7.0%	102-00	+ 01	6.9	174	− 12	210	6.63
15-YEAR								
FMAC GOLD	6.0%	99-30	unch	5.3	116	− 13	180	6.03%
FNMA	6.0%	99-26	unch	5.3	116	− 12	180	6.02
GNMA	6.0%	100-08	+ 01	5.6	109	13	150	5.96

*Extrapolated from benchmarks based on projections from Bear Stearns prepayment model, assuming interest rates remain unchanged. †-Price.

COLLATERALIZED MORTGAGE OBLIGATIONS

Spread of CMO yields above U.S. Treasury securities of comparable maturity, in basis points (100 basis points = 1 percentage point of interest)

MAT	SPREAD	CHG FROM PREV DAY
SEQUENTIALS		
2-year	120	− 25
5-year	150	− 17
10-year	170	− 12
20-year	137	− 10
PACS		
2-year	100	− 15
5-year	125	− 18
10-year	144	− 14
20-year	123	− 11
VNMA 953 1-E †		102-08
VNMA 961 1-E		101-02
VNMA 962 1-E		101-04

GUARANTEED INVESTMENT CONTRACTS

Source: T. Rowe Price GIC Index

	1 YEAR RATE CHG	2 YEARS RATE CHG	3 YEARS RATE CHG	4 YEARS RATE CHG	5 YEARS RATE CHG
High	5.35% +0.03	5.73% +0.02	5.86% +0.03	5.92% +0.04	6.01% +0.05
Low	5.26 +0.04	5.17 +0.01	5.36 +0.03	5.39 +0.03	5.42 +0.04
INDEX	5.30 +0.04	5.54 +0.03	5.68 +0.05	5.76 +0.04	5.84 +0.05
TOP QUARTILE RANGE	5.35% 5.35%	5.73% 5.67%	5.86% 5.80%	5.92% 5.85%	6.01% 5.94%
SPREAD vs. TREASURYS	+0.68	+0.73	+0.78	+0.84	+0.97

GIC rates quoted prior to 10:30 am (Eastern) net of all expenses, no broker commissions. Rates represent best quote for a $2-$5 million immediate lump sum deposit with annual interest payments. Yield spreads based on U.S. Treasury yields, as of 10:30 am (Eastern), versus the index rate unadjusted for semi vs. annual interest payments. CHG reflects change in rate from previous day. INDEX is average of all rates quoted. Universe is investment grade.

INTERNATIONAL GOVERNMENT BONDS

Prices in local currencies, from Telerate.

	COUPON	MATURITY (Mo./yr.)	PRICE	CHANGE	YIELD*
JAPAN (3 p.m. Tokyo)					
#129	6.50%	03/01	112.09	+ 0.02	0.66%
#156	3.40	03/04	108.49	− 0.48	1.60
#202	2.00	03/09	96.28	− 1.54	2.46
#39	2.60	03/19	91.49	− 2.55	3.31
UNITED KINGDOM (5 p.m. London)					
	8.00%	12/00	105.60	+ 0.05	4.76%
	6.50	12/03	109.59	+ 0.13	4.28
	9.00	10/08	136.97	+ 0.21	4.29
	6.00	12/28	128.81	− 0.33	4.28

	COUPON	MATURITY (Mo./yr.)	PRICE	CHANGE	YIELD*
GERMANY (5 p.m. London)					
	3.00%	12/00	100.08	+ 0.03	2.95%
	3.75	08/03	102.07	+ 0.11	3.25
	3.75	01/09	99.81	+ 0.26	3.77
	5.625	01/28	113.97	+ 0.68	4.73
CANADA (3 p.m. Eastern Time)					
	5.00%	12/00	100.20	− 0.03	4.886%
	8.50	04/02	110.03	− 0.02	5.032
	6.00	06/08	106.78	+ 0.00	5.087
	8.00	06/27	138.44	+ 0.20	5.351

*Equivalent to semi-annual compounded yields to maturity

Total Rates of Return on International Bonds

In percent, based on J.P. Morgan Government Bond Index, Dec. 31, 1987=100

	LOCAL CURRENCY TERMS INDEX VALUE	1 DAY	1 MO	3 MOS	SINCE 12/31	U.S. DOLLAR TERMS INDEX VALUE	1 DAY	1 MO	3 MOS	SINCE 12/31
Japan	189.26	− 0.73	− 1.51	− 6.86	− 1.03	202.83	− 1.37	− 2.68	− 3.47	− 1.16
Britain	344.45	+ 0.20	+ 0.46	− 5.48	+ 0.60	299.25	+ 0.23	− 0.58	+ 3.96	− 0.93
Germany	228.46	+ 0.17	+ 0.28	+ 3.17	+ 0.83	206.83	+ 0.14	− 3.95	− 1.28	− 3.09
France	305.31	+ 0.20	+ 0.19	+ 3.37	+ 0.68	279.33	+ 0.17	− 4.03	− 1.13	− 3.23
Canada	310.02	+ 0.01	− 0.24	+ 1.93	− 0.45	270.74	+ 0.49	+ 1.96	+ 4.03	+ 2.74
Netherlands	243.47	+ 0.17	+ 0.31	+ 3.40	+ 0.90	220.07	+ 0.14	− 3.92	− 1.00	− 3.01
ECU-a	260.41	+ 0.01	+ 0.89	+ 3.97	+ 1.02	247.21	− 0.02	− 3.36	− 0.91	− 2.90
Global-b	264.79	− 0.08	− 0.25	+ 0.94	− 0.07	246.77	− 0.17	− 2.07	− 0.32	− 1.54
EMBI+-c	134.55	− 1.60	− 5.58	− 2.67	− 2.91	134.55	− 1.60	− 5.58	− 2.67	− 2.91

a-Dec. 31, 1989=100   b-18 int'l gov. markets   c-external-currency emerging mkt. debt. Dec. 31, 1993=100.

YIELD COMPARISONS

Based on Merrill Lynch Bond Indexes, priced as of midafternoon Eastern time.

	2/5	2/4	—52 Week— High	Low
Corp.-Govt. Master	5.54%	5.51%	6.13%	4.84%
Treasury 1-10yr	4.93	4.89	5.77	4.19
10+ yr	5.54	5.50	6.12	4.86
Agencies 1-10yr	5.58	5.55	6.19	4.71
10+ yr	5.89	5.86	6.44	5.22
Corporate				
1-10 yr High Qlty	5.65	5.64	6.27	5.08
Med Qlty	6.20	6.19	6.53	5.59
10+yr High Qlty	6.36	6.33	6.81	5.91
Med Qlty	6.85	6.83	7.22	6.46
Yankee bonds(1)	6.38	6.37	6.69	5.87
Current-coupon mortgages (2)				
GNMA 6.00%	6.31	6.31	6.81	5.79
FNMA 6.00%	6.37	6.36	6.77	5.87
FHLMC6.00%	6.39	6.38	6.80	5.89
High-yield corporates	10.01	10.00	10.81	8.17
Tax-Exempt Bonds				
7-12-yr G.O. (AA)	4.12	4.11	4.86	4.05
12-22-yr G.O. (AA)	4.64	4.64	5.25	4.50
22+yr revenue (A)	4.96	4.96	5.37	4.67

Note: High quality rated AAA-AA; medium quality A-BBB/Baa; high yield, BB/Ba-C.

(1) Dollar-denominated, SEC-registered bonds of foreign issuers sold in the U.S. (2) Reflects the 52-week high and low of mortgage-backed securities indexes rather than the individual securities shown.

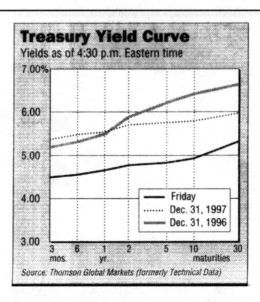

Treasury Yield Curve
Yields as of 4:30 p.m. Eastern time

— Friday
······ Dec. 31, 1997
▬▬ Dec. 31, 1996

Source: Thomson Global Markets (formerly Technical Data)

Source: *The Wall Street Journal*, February 8, 1999. Reprinted by permission of *The Wall Street Journal*, ©1999 Dow Jones & Company, Inc. All rights reserved.

sum of capital. For example, new Ginnie Mae issues require a $25,000 minimum investment, which would be out of the reach of the small investor. Mutual funds pool large sums of money in order to invest in instruments like Ginnie Maes, from which small individual investors can then benefit.

Recall as well Chapter 9's description of two types of mutual funds. Open-end funds issue shares as needed, while closed-end fund's shares are limited and fixed. Once all the shares are sold, no more shares will be issued. On Mondays the *Journal* reports on **Closed-End Funds** (find them in the last section's index), as in the example from the Monday, February 8, 1999 edition (pages 257, 258, and 259). Note the variety of bond funds reported here.

CONCLUSION

If all this detail has set your head swimming, regain your perspective by recalling that stocks' and bonds' values should move together in the long haul and that both are paper investments that thrive in low inflation.

CLOSED-END FUNDS

Friday, Febuary 5, 1999

Closed-end funds sell a limited number of shares and invest the proceeds in securities. Unlike open-end funds, closed-ends generally do not buy their shares back from investors who wish to cash in their holdings. Instead, fund shares trade on a stock exchange. The following list, provided by Lipper, shows the ticker symbol and exchange where each fund trades (A: American; C: Chicago; N: NYSE; O: Nasdaq; T: Toronto; z: does not trade on an exchange). The data also include the fund's most recent net asset value, share price and the percentage difference between the market price and the NAV (often called the premium or discount). For equity funds, the final column provides 52-week returns based on market prices plus dividends. For bond funds, the final column shows the past 12 months' income distributions as a percentage of the current market price. Footnotes appear after a fund's name. a: the NAV and market price are ex dividend. b: the NAV is fully diluted. c: NAV is as of Thursday's close. d: NAV is as of Wednesday's close. e: NAV assumes rights offering is fully subscribed. v: NAV is converted at the commercial Rand rate. w: Convertible Note-NAV (not market) conversion value. y: NAV and market price are in Canadian dollars. All other footnotes refer to unusual circumstances; explanations for those that appear can be found at the bottom of this list. N/A signifies that the information is not available or not applicable.

Fund Name (Symbol)	Stock Exch	NAV	Market Price	Prem /Disc	52 week Market Return
General Equity Funds					
Adams Express (ADX)	♠N	31.72	26³/₈	– 16.8	13.9
Alliance All-Mkt (AMO)	N	45.56	48⁹/₁₆	+ 6.6	65.8
Avalon Capital (MIST)	O	N/A	18¹/₂	N/A	23.3
Baker Fentress (BKF)	♠N	19.62	15⁷/₁₆	– 21.3	3.1
Bergstrom Cap (BEM)	A	206.84	186¹/₂	– 9.8	37.6
Blue Chip Value (BLU)	♠N	10.08	10	– 0.8	5.3
Central Secs (CET)	A	28.89	25	– 13.5	–11.7
Corp Renaissance (CREN)-c	O	9.43	7⁵/₁₆	– 22.5	19.4
Engex (EGX)	A	9.84	7⁷/₈	– 19.9	–19.7
Equus II (EQS)	♠N	21.30	15³/₄	– 26.1	–36.8
Gabelli Equity (GAB)	N	11.62	11³/₄	+ 1.1	9.9
General American (GAM)	♠N	33.53	31	– 7.5	37.7
Librty Allstr Eq (USA)	N	13.94	12¹/₄	– 8.5	7.6
Librty Allstr Gr (ASG)	♠N	12.73	11⁵/₁₆	– 11.2	–0.1
MFS Special Val (MFV)	N	15.08	15¹¹/₁₆	+ 4.0	–13.3
Morgan FunShares (MFUN)-c	O	7.60	8	+ 5.3	33.3
Morgan Gr Sm Cap (MGC)	♠N	11.36	9¹/₂	– 16.4	–8.6
NAIC Growth (GRF)-c	C	12.34	10¹/₄	– 13.9	–26.5
Royce Micro-Cap (OTCM)	♠O	9.60	8¹/₄	– 14.1	–15.7
Royce Value (RVT)	♠N	14.91	13⁵/₈	– 8.6	–2.9
Salomon SBF (SBF)	N	18.87	18¹/₄	– 4.3	20.7
Source Capital (SOR)	N	45.66	48⁷/₁₆	+ 7.1	0.6
Tri-Continental (TY)	♠N	33.95	28⁷/₁₆	– 16.2	19.8
Zweig (ZF)	N	11.77	10¹/₂	– 10.8	–9.9
Specialized Equity Funds					
C&S Realty (RIF)	♠A	7.32	8¹/₂	+ 16.1	–11.5
C&S Total Rtn (RFI)	N	11.88	13¹/₁₆	+ 9.9	–10.1
Chartwell D & I (CWF)	N/A	N/A	13¹¹/₁₆	N/A	N/A
Delaware Gr Div (DDF)	N	15.12	17¹/₈	+ 13.3	1.0
Delaware Grp Gl (DGF)	N	15.43	15¹/₄	– 2.4	–9.4
Duff&Ph Util Inc (DNP)	N	9.79	11	+ 12.4	11.5
Emer Mkts Infra (EMG)	♠N	9.43	7⁹/₁₆	– 19.8	–32.7
Emer Mkts Tel (ETF)	N	N/A	9⁵/₈	N/A	–16.1
First Financial (FF)	N	9.17	8¹¹/₁₆	– 5.2	–34.3
Gabelli Gl Media (GGT)	N	13.62	11¹⁵/₁₆	– 12.3	44.8
H&Q Health Inv (HQH)	♠N	19.60	14³/₈	– 24.1	–12.2
H&Q Life Sci Inv (HQL)	♠N	16.22	12¹/₂	– 22.9	–10.3
INVESCO Gl Hlth (GHS)-a	N	20.36	19³/₈	– 4.8	29.8
J Han Bank (BTO)	N	10.77	9¹/₂	– 14.7	–18.8
J Han Pat Globl (PGD)-a	N	14.53	13	– 10.5	2.7
J Han Pat Sel (DIV)-a	♠N	16.38	15¹/₂	– 5.4	7.5
Nations Bal Tgt (NBM)	N	10.29	9³/₁₆	– 9.5	2.8
Petroleum & Res (PEO)	♠N	32.79	30¹/₈	– 8.1	–12.4
SthEastrn Thrift (STBF)	N	22.53	19⁹/₁₆	– 13.2	–22.7
Thermo Opprfunty (TMF)	A	9.13	6³/₄	– 27.4	–33.7
Tuxis Corp (TUX)	N	16.45	15³/₄	– 4.3	6.0
Preferred Stock Funds					
J Han Pat Pref (PPF)-a	♠N	13.83	12³/₈	– 10.5	–7.6
J Han Pat Prm (PDF)	♠N	10.44	9³/₄	– 6.6	5.0
J Han Pat Prm II (PDT)	♠N	12.91	11³/₄	– 8.9	–1.3
Preferred Inc Op (PFO)	♠N	12.58	11¹³/₁₆	– 6.1	4.3
Preferred IncMgt (PFM)	♠N	15.07	12¹/₄	– 20.0	–11.9
Preferred Income (PFD)	♠N	15.52	14¹¹/₁₆	– 5.3	2.5
Putnam Divd Inc (PDI)	N	11.49	10¹/₂	– 8.6	5.2
Convertible Sec's. Funds					
Bancroft Conv (BCV)	♠A	26.49	22³/₈	– 15.5	4.8
Castle Conv (CVF)	A	25.86	22	– 14.9	–6.4
Ellsworth Conv (ECF)-a	N	11.17	9¹¹/₁₆	– 13.2	7.2
Gabelli Conv Sec (GCV)	N	11.56	11³/₁₆	– 3.2	13.3
Lincoln Conv (LNV)-c	♠N	16.68	14¹/₁₆	– 15.3	–14.1
Putnam Conv Opp (PCV)	N	23.41	22¹/₂	– 3.4	9.8
Putnam Hi Inc Cv (PCF)	N	8.52	9	+ 5.6	–10.2
TCW Conv Secs (CVT)	N	9.63	9⁵/₁₆	+ 1.9	9.8
VK Conv Sec (VXS)	N	24.37	20⁵/₈	– 15.3	2.6
World Equity Funds					
AIM Eastern Euro (GTF)	N	7.81	6¹/₈	– 21.5	–45.8
ASA Limited (ASA)-cv	N	16.63	16¹³/₁₆	+ 1.1	–25.7
Argentina (AF)	N	11.44	8¹¹/₁₆	– 24.0	–29.4
Asia Pacific (APB)	N	7.77	6⁵/₁₆	– 18.8	–32.2
Asia Tigers (GRR)	N	7.62	6³/₁₆	– 18.8	–30.1
Austria (OST)	♠N	11.86	10¹/₂	– 11.5	17.4
BGR Prec Metals (BPT.A)-cv	T	13.93	9¹³/₃₂	– 32.5	–20.7

| | Stock | Market | Prem | 52 week |
Fund Name (Symbol)	Exch NAV	Price	/Disc	Market
Brazil (BZF)	N	12.41	10³/₁₆	– 16.9	–36.2
Brazilian Equity (BZL)	♠N	N/A	3⁹/₁₆	N/A	–52.5
Cdn Genl Inv (CGI)-y	♠T	14.80	13¹/₄	– 10.5	–12.3
Cdn Wrld Fd Ltd (CWF)-cy	T	5.78	4³/₄	– 17.8	–1.0
Central Eur Eqty (CEE)	♠N	16.72	13¹/₂	– 19.3	–24.1
Central Eur Value (CRF)	N	13.07	10¹/₄	– 21.6	–5.8
Centrl Fd Canada (CEF)-c	♠A	4.10	3³/₄	– 8.5	–15.3
Chile (CH)	N	12.04	9¹/₄	– 23.2	–25.6
China (CHN)	N	8.52	7	– 17.8	–39.1
China, Greater (GCH)	♠N	6.77	5¹/₂	– 18.8	–41.6
Clemente Global (CLM)	N	14.35	13⁹/₁₆	– 5.5	29.9
Dessauer Glbl Eq (DGE)	N	14.63	14	– 4.3	19.4
Economic Inv Tr (EVT)-cy	T	44.13	104	+ 135.7	2.4
Emer Mkts Grow (N/A)	z	40.57	N/A	N/A	N/A
Emerging Mexico (MEF)-c	N	6.29	5¹³/₁₆	– 7.6	–39.6
Europe (EF)	N	19.49	18¹⁵/₁₆	– 2.8	29.6
European Warrant (EWF)-c	N	18.74	16¹/₁₆	– 14.3	18.2
F&C Middle East (EME)-c	N	16.87	13⁵/₁₆	– 21.1	–17.6
Fidelity Em Asia (FAE)	♠N	9.99	8¹⁵/₁₆	– 10.5	–16.8
Fidelty Ad Korea (FAK)	N	6.80	5³/₄	– 15.4	0.0
First Australia (IAF)	A	9.34	7¹/₄	– 22.4	2.1
First Israel (ISL)	N	13.84	11³/₄	– 17.8	–5.7
First Philippine (FPF)	N	7.40	6¹/₈	– 17.2	–22.2
France Growth (FRF)	N	16.61	14¹/₈	– 14.9	42.0
Germany Fund (GER)	♠N	15.82	14¹/₄	– 9.9	25.8
Germany, Emer (FRG)	N	13.84	13³/₁₆	– 4.7	41.1
Germany, New (GF)	N	15.35	12¹/₄	– 21.0	9.8
Global Small Cap (GSG)	A	15.95	13¹/₁₆	– 18.1	–10.7
Herzfeld Caribb (CUBA)	O	4.72	4¹¹/₁₆	– 0.6	–5.1
India Fund (IFN)	N	10.26	7⁵/₈	– 25.6	7.1
India Growth (IGF)-d	N	12.17	9	– 26.0	–8.3
Indonesia (IF)	♠N	2.52	3⁷/₈	+ 54.0	–46.0
Irish Inv (IRL)	N	22.21	20¹¹/₁₆	– 6.8	21.3
Italy (ITA)	N	17.96	14¹¹/₁₆	– 16.8	22.6
Jakarta Growth (JGF)	N	1.96	2¹/₈	+ 8.7	–54.0
Japan Equity (JEQ)	N	6.52	7¹/₂	+ 15.0	–4.0
Japan OTC Equity (JOF)	N	5.38	5³/₄	+ 6.9	–1.1
Jardine Fl China (JFC)	N	6.46	5¹/₁₆	– 20.6	–46.0
Jardine Fl India (JFI)-c	♠N	7.79	5¹¹/₁₆	– 27.0	–20.8
Korea (KF)	N	9.43	9¹/₈	– 3.2	2.2
Korea Equity (KEF)	N	3.89	3³/₄	– 3.6	–4.8
Korean Inv (KIF)	N	4.95	4¹/₄	– 14.1	–16.1
Latin Am Sm Cos (LLF)	N	5.92	N/A	N/A	N/A
Latin Amer Disc (LDF)	N	7.64	6¹/₄	– 18.2	–46.0
Latin Amer Eq (LAQ)	N	N/A	7¹/₄	N/A	–43.9
Latin Amer Inv (LAM)	♠N	N/A	8⁹/₁₆	N/A	–37.6
Malaysia (MF)	N	2.92	4³/₁₆	+ 43.5	–53.4
Mexico (MXF)-c	N	N/A	11⁷/₁₆	N/A	–38.2
Mexico Eqtv&Inc (MXF)-f	N	6.64	5¹/₈	– 22.7	–41.9
Morgan St Africa (AFF)	N	12.46	9¹/₄	– 25.8	–18.9
Morgan St Asia (APF)	N	8.76	7³/₈	– 15.8	–12.4
Morgan St Em (MSF)	N	10.48	8⁷/₁₆	– 19.5	–31.5
Morgan St India (IIF)	N	10.49	7¹/₂	– 28.5	–11.8
Morgan St Russia (RNE)	N	13.04	10¹/₂	– 19.5	–51.7
New South Africa (NSA)	♠N	10.48	9¹⁵/₁₆	– 5.2	–22.8
Pakistan Inv (PKF)	N	2.27	1¹¹/₁₆	– 25.6	–62.0
Portugal (PGF)	N	18.79	16⁵/₈	– 11.5	19.8
ROC Taiwan (ROC)	N	6.35	5⁷/₁₆	– 14.3	–35.9
Royce Global Trust (FUND)	♠O	5.06	4¹/₄	– 16.0	–19.1
Scud Spain & Por (IBF)	N	13.79	13⁷/₁₆	– 2.5	18.9
Scudder New Asia (SAF)	N	10.91	9⁹/₁₆	– 14.7	–16.8
Scudder New Eur (NEF)	N	21.79	20	– 8.2	36.7
Singapore (SGF)-c	♠N	7.52	7³/₁₆	– 4.4	–12.9
Southern Africa (SOA)	N	12.06	9⁷/₈	– 18.1	–26.4
Spain (SNF)	N	17.70	16¹/₈	– 8.9	43.0
Swiss Helvetia (SWZ)	♠N	18.41	15⁵/₈	– 15.1	13.3
Taiwan (TWN)-c	N	13.77	11³/₁₆	– 18.7	–36.6
Taiwan Equity (TYW)-c	N	9.74	7⁵/₈	– 21.7	–36.0
Templeton China (TCH)-c	N	7.12	5¹/₂	– 22.8	–31.9
Templeton Dragon (TDF)	N	8.91	7	– 21.4	–34.6
Templeton Em App (TEA)-c	N	10.72	8¹⁵/₁₆	– 16.6	–26.3
Templeton Em Mkt (EMF)	N	8.51	10⁵/₁₆	+ 19.7	–19.0
Templeton Russia (TRF)-c	N	7.60	9⁹/₁₆	+ 22.5	–64.9
Templeton Vietnm (TVF)	N	8.60	7	– 18.6	–22.2
Thai (TTF)	N	3.55	6³/₄	+ 90.1	–26.0
Thai Capital (TC)	N	3.03	4³/₈	+ 44.6	–26.2
Third Canadian (THD)-cy	T	20.72	16¹¹/₂₂	– 21.1	–10.9
Turkish Inv (TKF)	N	5.65	4¹¹/₁₆	– 17.0	–24.6
United Corps Ltd (UNC)-cy	T	66.95	46¹/₄	– 30.9	4.9
United Kingdom (UKM)	♠N	N/A	14	N/A	5.3
Z-Seven (ZSEV)	O	7.68	7³/₄	+ 0.9	–2.5

| | Stock | Market | Prem | 12 Mo Yield |
Fund Name (Symbol)	Exch NAV	Price	/Disc	1/29/99
U.S. Gov't. Bond Funds					
ACM Govt Inc (ACG)-a	N	N/A	8⁷/₈	N/A	9.9
ACM Govt Oppty (AOF)-a	N	8.21	7¹¹/₁₆	– 6.3	8.0
ACM Govt Secs (GSF)-a	N	N/A	8³/₈	N/A	10.4
ACM Govt Spec (SI)-a	N	N/A	6¹/₁₆	N/A	8.8
Excelsior Income (EIS)-c	N	18.80	16¹/₁₆	– 11.5	6.2
Kemper Int Govt (KGT)	N	7.76	7³/₁₆	– 1.7	8.0
MFS Govt Mkts (MGF)	N	7.43	6⁷/₁₆	– 13.3	7.2
MSDW Govt Inc (GVT)	♠N	9.48	8³/₄	– 7.7	6.7
RCM Strat Glbl (RCS)	N	11.39	9⁷/₈	– 13.3	9.5
U.S. Mortgage Bond Funds					
2002 Target Term (TTR)-c	N	15.09	14¹/₄	– 5.6	6.1
Amer Sel Porl (SLA)-ac	N	13.07	12¹/₁₆	– 7.7	8.6

Continued

Fund Name (Symbol)	Stock Exch	NAV	Market Price	Prem /Disc	52 week Market Return
Amer Str Inc II (BSP)-ac	N	13.07	11 7/8	– 9.1	8.5
Amer Str Inc III (CSP)-ac	N	12.45	11 3/4	– 5.6	8.5
Amer Str Income (ASP)-ac	N	12.92	11 3/4	– 9.1	8.2
BlckRk 1999 Term (BNN)-c	N	10.09	9 13/16	– 2.8	4.4
BlckRk 2001 Term (BLK)-c	N	9.59	9 1/16	– 5.5	4.8
BlckRk Adv Term (BAT)-c	N	10.99	9 13/16	– 10.7	6.9
BlckRk Income (BKT)-c	N	7.94	6 15/16	– 12.6	8.1
BlckRk Inv 09 (BCT)-c	A	14.54	13 3/16	– 9.3	7.5
BlckRk Inv Q Tm (BQT)-c	N	9.48	8 7/8	– 6.3	6.2
BlckRk Str Tm (BGT)-c	N	10.02	9 3/16	– 8.3	5.6
BlckRk Tgt Tm (BTT)-c	N	10.15	9 3/4	– 3.9	5.9
Heritage US Govt (HGA)-c	N	12.11	10 1/4	– 15.4	7.7
Hyperion 1999 Tm (HTT)-c	N	7.36	7 1/4	– 1.5	5.9
Hyperion 2002 Tm (HTB)-c	N	9.16	8 3/8	– 8.5	5.7
Hyperion 2005 (HTO)-c	N	9.69	8 13/16	– 9.1	6.3
Hyperion Tot Rtn (HTR)-c	N	9.99	8 9/16	– 14.3	8.7
Inc Opp 1999 (IOF)	N	N/A	9 3/4	N/A	5.9
Inc Opp 2000 (IFT)	N	N/A	9 13/16	N/A	6.3
Liberty 1999 (LTT)	N	9.14	8 7/8	– 2.8	4.1
Mentor Income (MRF)-c	N	9.88	8 9/16	– 13.4	8.6
Nations 2003 (NGI)	N	9.85	9 3/16	– 6.7	6.1
Nations 2004 (NGF)	N	9.99	9 5/16	– 6.8	6.3
PIMCO Comm Mtg (PCM)-c	♣N	13.74	13 5/8	– 0.8	9.0
TCW/DW Term 2000 (TDT)-a	♣N	9.90	9 5/8	– 2.7	5.8
TCW/DW Term 2002 (TRM)-a	♣N	10.29	9 11/16	– 5.8	6.7
TCW/DW Term 2003 (TMT)-a	♣N	10.33	9 7/16	– 8.6	6.6
Investment Grade Bond Funds					
1838 Bd-Deb (BDF)	N	22.28	21 1/4	– 4.6	7.6
All-American Tm (AAT)-c	N	13.87	13 1/8	– 5.3	7.5
Circle Income (CINS)-c	O	11.95	11 1/4	– 5.9	7.1
Current Inc Shs (CUR)	♣N	13.32	12	– 9.9	6.9
Fortis Secs (FOR)	N	9.15	8 3/4	– 4.4	8.3
Ft Dearborn Inc (FTD)	♣N	16.36	15 7/8	– 2.9	6.4
Hatteras Income (HAT)	N	15.94	14 7/16	– 9.4	7.5
INA Investments (IIS)	N	19.15	17 1/8	– 10.5	5.4
Independence Sq (ISIS)-c	O	18.24	16 7/8	– 7.5	7.7
MSDW Income Secs (ICB)-a	♣N	18.41	18 5/8	+ 1.2	7.1
Montgomery St (MTS)	N	19.95	19 7/8	– 0.4	7.0
Pac Amer Income (PAI)	N	15.44	16 1/8	+ 4.5	7.1
Pioneer Int Shs (MUO)	N	13.64	14 1/16	+ 3.1	7.5
Transam Income (TAI)	N	25.32	27 1/8	+ 7.1	6.9
VK Bond Fd (VBF)	N	21.03	20 1/4	– 3.7	7.2
Vestaur Secs (VES)-c	N	14.61	14 11/16	+ 0.5	7.1
Loan Participation Funds					
AIM Floating Rt (N/A)	z	9.85	N/A	N/A	N/A
Cyprstr Sen Flt (N/A)	z	N/A	N/A	N/A	N/A
E V Senior Inc (EVF)	N	10.12	9 9/16	– 5.5	N/A
EV Adv Sen Flt (N/A)	z	9.98	N/A	N/A	N/A
EV Classic Sr (N/A)	z	9.96	N/A	N/A	N/A
EV Prime Rate (N/A)	z	9.98	N/A	N/A	N/A
Franklin Flt Rt (N/A)	z	9.95	N/A	N/A	N/A
Merrill Sen Fl (N/A)	z	N/A	N/A	N/A	N/A
N Am Sen Flt B (N/A)-a	z	N/A	N/A	N/A	N/A
N Am Sen Flt C (N/A)-a	z	N/A	N/A	N/A	N/A
Pilgrim Prime Rt (PPR)	♣N	9.28	9 7/16	+ 1.7	8.6
Prime Income (N/A)	z	9.90	N/A	N/A	N/A
S Roe Flt Rt (N/A)-a	z	10.02	N/A	N/A	N/A
S Roe Inst Flt (N/A)-a	z	10.02	N/A	N/A	N/A
Trav Corp Loan (TLI)	N	15.12	N/A	N/A	N/A
VK Prime Rt (N/A)-ac	z	9.93	N/A	N/A	N/A
VK Sen Flt Rt (N/A)		10.08	N/A	N/A	N/A
VK Sen Inc Tr (VVR)	N	10.10	9 1/2	– 5.9	N/A
High Yield Bond Funds					
BlckRk Hi Yld Tr (BHY)	N	15.15	14 1/2	– 4.3	N/A
CIGNA High Inc (HIS)	N	6.38	7 1/2	+ 17.6	11.6
CIM High Yld (CIM)	A	7.01	6 3/4	– 3.7	10.1
Colonial Intmdt (CIF)	♣N	6.60	6 9/16	– 0.6	10.5
Conseco Str Inc (CFD)	N	13.97	13 15/16	– 0.2	N/A
Corp Hi Yld (COY)	♣N	N/A	12 1/16	N/A	11.5
Corp Hi Yld II (KYT)	N	N/A	11 1/4	N/A	12.2
Corp Hi Yld III (CYE)	N	N/A	12 1/16	N/A	10.3
DDJ Cndn Hi Yld (HYB.UN)-y	T	23.94	19 45/64	– 17.7	11.1
DLJ High Yield Bd (DHY)-c	N	8.89	9 5/16	+ 4.7	N/A
Debt Strategies Fd II (DSU)	N	N/A	8 1/16	N/A	N/A
Debt Strategies Fd III (DBU)	N	N/A	8 7/8	N/A	N/A
Debt Strategies Fund (DBS)	N	N/A	7 13/16	N/A	11.8
Dryfs Hi Yld Str (DHF)	N	12.07	12 9/16	+ 4.1	N/A
Franklin Univ (FT)	N	9.38	9 1/8	– 2.7	9.9
High Inc Opp (HIO)	♣N	11.37	10 7/16	– 8.2	10.3
High Yld Income (HYI)	N	7.04	7 3/16	+ 2.1	10.0
High Yld Plus (HYP)-f	N	7.50	7 1/8	– 4.9	11.7
Kemper High Inc (KHI)	♣N	8.93	10	+ 12.0	9.0
MSDW Hi Inc (YLD)-a	♣N	4.07	4 3/4	+ 16.7	12.3
MSDW Hi Inc II (YLT)-a	♣N	4.56	4 15/16	+ 8.3	12.7
MSDW Hi Inc III (YLH)-a	♣N	4.97	5 9/16	+ 11.9	12.1
Managed High Inc (MHY)	♣N	10.97	10 3/16	– 7.1	10.1
Managed High Pls (HYF)	N	12.76	12 9/16	– 1.6	N/A
Managed High Yld (PHT)	N	12.33	11 3/4	– 4.7	10.6
Morgan St Hi Yld (MSY)	N	13.75	15 5/16	+ 11.3	8.8
New Amer Hi Inc (HYB)	N	4.15	4 3/8	+ 5.5	11.9
Pacholder (PHF)-cg	♣A	15.45	16 1/16	+ 3.9	11.4
Prospect St High (PHY)-g	♣N	8.13	9	+ 10.7	13.6
Putnam Mgd HiYld (PTM)	N	12.46	14 3/8	+ 15.4	9.4
S B Hi Inc II (HIX)	N	13.20	12 5/8	– 4.3	N/A
Salomon HIF (HIF)	N	12.78	14 1/4	+ 11.5	10.2
Senior Hi Inc (ARK)	N	N/A	8 1/16	N/A	10.9
VK High Inc (VIT)	N	5.85	6 9/16	+ 12.1	10.9
VK High Inc II (VLT)	N	7.58	8 3/4	+ 15.4	10.9
Zenix Income (ZIF)	N	6.12	6	– 2.0	12.0
Other Domestic Taxable Bond Funds					
ACM Mgd $ (ADF)-a	N	N/A	9 7/8	N/A	14.9
ACM Mgd Income (AMF)-a	N	N/A	8 5/8	N/A	9.8
Allmerica Secs (ALM)	N	11.93	11 1/8	– 6.7	7.4
BEA Income (FBF)-a	♣N	7.76	7 11/16	– 0.9	9.2

Fund Name (Symbol)	Stock Exch	NAV	Market Price	Prem /Disc	52 week Market Return
BEA Strategic Gl (FBI)-a	♣N	9.18	8 9/16	– 6.8	10.7
Bexil Corp (BXL)-s	A	14.24	12 7/8	– 9.6	9.3
CNA Income (CNN)-c	N	9.73	10 5/16	+ 6.0	9.3
Colonial Intrmkt (CMK)	♣N	10.97	10 1/16	– 8.3	9.2
Duff&Ph Util Cor (DUC)	N	14.55	15 1/8	+ 4.0	7.8
Franklin Mul-Inc (FMI)	N	10.47	9 1/2	– 9.3	7.9
J Han Income (JHS)	♣N	16.61	15 15/16	– 4.0	7.1
J Han Investors (JHI)	♣N	21.76	21 9/16	– 0.9	7.1
Kemper Multi Mkt (KMM)	♣N	10.29	9 1/16	– 12.0	8.7
Kemper Strat Inc (KST)	♣N	13.02	15 1/4	+ 17.1	11.9
Lincoln Income (LND)-c	♣N	13.29	13 3/4	+ 3.5	7.5
MFS Charter (MCR)	N	10.33	10	– 3.2	8.3
MFS Intmdt (MIN)	N	7.66	6 13/16	– 11.1	7.4
MFS Multimkt (MMT)	N	7.28	6 9/16	– 9.9	9.1
MassMutual Corp (MCI)	N	N/A	24 15/16	N/A	6.5
MassMutual Part (MPV)	N	N/A	12 5/16	N/A	7.6
Op Fd Multi-Sec (OMS)	N	9.97	8 5/8	– 13.4	9.4
Putnam Mas Inc (PMT)	N	8.33	8 3/16	– 1.7	9.2
Putnam Mas Int (PIM)	N	8.02	8 1/16	+ 0.5	8.8
Putnam Prem Inc (PPT)	N	8.00	8 1/8	+ 1.6	9.0
USLife Income (UIF)	N	10.61	10 1/16	– 5.2	7.6
VK Income Tr (VIN)	N	7.85	7 5/16	– 6.9	8.8
Zweig Total Rtn (ZTR)	♣N	8.33	8 9/16	+ 2.8	8.8
World Income Funds					
Alliance Wld $ (AWG)-a	♣N	8.84	10 1/2	+ 18.8	13.3
Alliance Wld $ 2 (AWF)-a	N	8.24	9 1/16	+ 10.0	14.7
BlckRk North Am (BNA)-c	N	12.11	10 1/16	– 16.9	8.4
Dreyfus Str Govt (DSI)	N	10.12	9	– 11.1	8.2
Emer Mkts Float (EFL)	N	10.12	11 15/16	+ 18.0	14.3
Emer Mkts Inc (EMD)	N	9.68	10 1/4	+ 5.9	23.2
Emer Mkts Inc II (EDF)	N	8.50	9 3/16	+ 8.1	17.4
First Aust Prime (FAX)	A	6.96	5 7/8	– 15.5	10.4
First Commonwlth (FCO)	N	13.52	10 15/16	– 19.1	8.7
Global Hi Inc $ (GHI)	N	12.96	10 9/16	– 18.5	10.9
Global Income Fund (GIF)	A	6.13	5 7/16	– 11.3	13.7
Global Partners (GDF)	N	10.97	11 3/8	+ 3.7	15.6
Kleinwort Aust (KBA)	♣N	8.43	6 11/16	– 20.6	7.4
Morg St Em Debt (MSD)	N	6.87	7 3/16	+ 4.7	16.7
Morgan St Glbl (MGB)	N	9.64	8 13/16	– 8.6	13.3
Salomon SBG (SBG)	N	9.09	9 1/16	– 0.3	9.4
Salomon SBW (SBW)	N	9.71	10 3/16	+ 4.9	17.5
Scudder Glbl High Inc (LBF)	N	5.36	4 13/16	– 10.3	26.8
Strategic Gl Inc (SGL)	N	13.45	11 3/4	– 12.6	9.2
Templeton Em Inc (TEI)	N	10.90	9 5/16	– 14.6	13.4
Templtn Gl Govt (TGG)	N	7.50	6 5/8	– 11.6	9.1
Templtn Glbl Inc (GIM)	N	7.98	6 7/8	– 13.8	8.6
Worldwide $Vest (WDV)	♣N	N/A	5 1/16	N/A	21.8
National Muni Bond Funds					
ACM Muni Secs (AMU)-a	N	13.41	13 7/8	+ 3.5	6.2
Amer Muni Income (XAA)-ac	N	15.29	13 15/16	– 8.8	5.4
Amer Muni Tm II (BXT)-ac	N	11.61	11 9/16	– 0.4	5.4
Amer Muni Tm III (CXT)-ac	N	11.52	11 7/16	– 0.7	5.0
Amer Muni Tm Tr (AXT)-ac	N	11.42	11 3/8	– 0.4	5.7
Apex Muni (APX)	N	10.57	10 3/16	– 3.6	6.3
BlckRk Ins 2008 (BRM)	N	17.19	15 3/4	– 8.4	5.1
BlckRk Ins Muni (BMT)	N	11.29	11 5/16	+ 0.2	5.8
BlckRk Inv Q Mun (BKN)	N	15.62	15 3/4	+ 0.8	5.2
BlckRk Muni Tgt (BMN)	N	11.27	10 15/16	– 2.9	5.7
Colonial Hi Inc (CXE)	♣N	8.47	8 7/16	– 0.4	6.1
Colonial Inv Gr (CXH)	♣N	11.53	11 1/4	– 2.4	5.7
Colonial Mu Inc (CMU)	♣N	7.59	8 1/8	+ 7.1	6.1
Dreyfus Income (DMF)	A	9.55	8 15/16	– 6.4	6.9
Dreyfus St Munis (LEO)	N	10.05	9 1/8	– 9.2	7.0
Dreyfus Str Muni (DSM)	N	9.43	9 1/16	– 3.9	7.2
Duff&Ph Util TF (DTF)	N	16.50	16 1/2	0.0	5.9
EATON VANCE MUNI INC TR (EVN)	N	14.95	15 1/16	+ 0.8	N/A
Greenwich St Mun (GSI)	N	11.85	10 13/16	– 8.8	5.4
Ins Muni Income (PIF)	N	15.71	14 1/8	– 10.1	5.4
Inv Grd Muni Inc (PPM)	N	17.04	16 1/16	– 5.8	5.7
Kemper Muni Inc (KTF)	♣N	12.36	12 3/8	+ 0.2	7.0
Kemper Strat Mun (KSM)	♣N	12.18	12 5/16	+ 1.1	6.1
MFS Muni Inco (MFM)	N	8.49	8 9/16	+ 0.8	6.6
MSDW Ins Bd (IMB)-a	♣N	15.51	15 7/8	+ 2.4	6.1
MSDW Ins Mun Inc (IIM)-a	♣N	15.34	14 7/8	– 3.0	5.4
MSDW Ins Sec (IMS)-a	♣N	15.84	14 15/16	– 5.7	5.3
MSDW Ins Tr (IMT)-a	♣N	15.94	15 7/16	– 3.1	6.1
MSDW Muni Inc (TFA)-a	♣N	10.15	8 7/8	– 12.5	5.6
MSDW Muni Inc II (TFB)-a	♣N	10.30	9 3/16	– 10.8	5.4
MSDW Muni IncIII (TFC)-a	♣N	10.01	8 7/8	– 11.3	5.5
MSDW Muni Op (OIA)-a	♣N	8.79	9 7/16	+ 7.4	6.1
MSDW Muni Op II (OIB)-a	♣N	9.04	8 3/4	– 3.2	6.1
MSDW Muni Op III (OIC)-a	♣N	10.01	9 7/16	– 5.7	6.4
MSDW Muni Prem (PIA)-a	♣N	10.25	9 1/16	– 11.6	6.0
MSDW Qual Inc (IQI)-a	♣N	16.10	15 3/8	– 4.5	5.9
MSDW Qual Inv (IQT)-a	♣N	15.44	15 1/8	– 2.0	6.1
MSDW Qual Sec (IQM)-a	♣N	14.93	14	– 6.2	5.4
Managed Munis (MMU)	♣N	12.34	11	– 10.9	4.8
Managed Munis 2 (MTU)	N	12.28	11	– 10.4	4.8
Merrill Hi Inc (N/A)	z	10.79	N/A	N/A	N/A
Merrill Mun Str (N/A)	z	10.60	N/A	N/A	N/A
Muni Partners (MNP)	N	14.98	13 3/4	– 8.2	5.9
Muni Partners II (MPT)	N	14.52	13 1/16	– 10.1	5.8
MuniAssets (MUA)	N	14.50	14 3/16	– 2.1	5.9
MuniEnhanced (MEN)	N	11.96	12 1/16	+ 0.8	5.3
MuniHoldings (MHD)	N	16.11	16 5/16	+ 1.2	5.7
MuniHoldings II (MUH)	N	15.23	14 13/16	– 2.8	N/A
MuniInsured (MIF)	A	10.02	9 13/16	– 2.1	5.1
MuniVest (MVF)	A	10.11	10 1/8	+ 0.2	5.8
MuniYield (MYD)	♣N	15.52	16 1/8	+ 3.9	5.9
MuniYield Ins (MYI)	N	15.72	16	+ 1.8	5.5
MuniYield Qual (MQY)	N	15.55	15 3/16	– 2.3	5.8
MuniYld Qual II (MQT)	N	14.70	15 1/4	+ 3.7	5.8
Municipal Adv (MAF)	N	15.19	14 1/16	– 7.4	5.7
Municipal High (MHF)	♣N	9.73	9 5/8	– 1.0	6.4

Continued

Fund Name (Symbol)	Stock Exch	NAV	Market Price	Prem /Disc	12 Mo Yield 1/29/99
MuniHoldings Ins (MUS)	N	15.46	15 1/4	− 1.4	N/A
Munivest II (MVT)	N	14.80	14 1/2	− 2.0	5.8
Nuveen Ins Opp (NIO)	◆N	15.93	16 3/4	+ 5.1	5.8
Nuveen Ins Pr 2 (NPX)	◆N	14.12	13 1/4	− 6.2	5.4
Nuveen Ins Qual (NQI)	◆N	15.83	15 5/8	− 1.3	6.0
Nuveen Inv Qual (NQM)	◆N	15.94	15 11/16	− 1.6	6.2
Nuveen Muni Adv (NMA)	◆N	15.78	16	+ 1.4	6.2
Nuveen Muni Inc (NMI)	N	12.03	12 1/8	+ 0.8	5.8
Nuveen Muni Mkt (NMO)	◆N	15.88	16 3/16	+ 2.0	6.2
Nuveen Muni Val (NUV)	N	10.27	9 15/16	− 3.2	5.3
Nuveen Perf Plus (NPP)	◆N	15.37	14 3/4	− 4.0	6.4
Nuveen Pr (NPI)	◆N	15.55	15 3/8	− 1.1	5.7
Nuveen Pr 2 (NPM)	◆N	16.08	16 5/8	+ 3.4	5.7
Nuveen Pr 4 (NPT)	◆N	15.04	14 15/16	− 0.7	5.6
Nuveen Pr Ins (NIF)	◆N	16.10	16 7/16	+ 2.1	5.6
Nuveen Pr Mun (NPF)	◆N	15.72	16 3/8	+ 4.2	6.0
Nuveen Qual (NQU)	◆N	15.78	16 9/16	+ 4.9	6.2
Nuveen Sel Mat (NIM)	◆N	12.02	11 3/4	− 2.2	5.3
Nuveen Sel Qual (NQS)	◆N	15.64	16	+ 2.3	6.1
Nuveen Sel TF (NXP)	N	15.69	16 1/4	+ 3.6	5.7
Nuveen Sel TF 2 (NXQ)	◆N	15.54	15 7/8	+ 2.2	5.7
Nuveen Sel TF 3 (NXR)	◆N	15.09	15 3/8	+ 1.9	5.6
Putnam Hi Yld (PYM)	N	10.12	10 3/16	+ 17.2	6.4
Putnam Inv Gr (PGM)	N	11.97	14 1/8	+ 18.0	7.1
Putnam Inv Gr II (PMG)	N	14.16	15 1/4	+ 7.7	6.4
Putnam Inv GrIII (PML)	A	13.47	13 1/2	+ 0.2	5.9
Putnam Mgd Inc (PMM)	N	9.77	10 13/16	+ 10.6	7.1
Putnam Muni Opp (PMO)	N	14.23	15 3/16	+ 6.7	6.0
Putnam TxFr Hlth (PMH)	N	14.87	14 5/8	− 1.6	6.2
SB Intmdt Muni (SBI)	A	10.66	10	− 6.2	5.5
SB Muni (SBT)	A	15.89	14 5/8	− 7.9	5.5
Seligman Qual (SQF)	N	15.11	13 11/16	− 9.4	6.4
Seligman Sel (SEL)	◆N	12.31	11 13/16	− 4.1	6.3
VK Adv Muni (VKA)	N	16.93	16 1/4	− 4.0	5.9
VK Adv Muni II (VKI)	A	14.70	13 1/2	− 8.2	5.6
VK Inv Gr Muni (VIG)	N	10.58	10 13/16	+ 2.2	6.3
VK Muni Inc Tr (VMT)	N	10.34	10 13/16	+ 4.5	6.3
VK Muni Opp II (VOT)	N	15.08	14 1/8	− 6.3	5.6
VK Muni Opp Tr (VMO)	N	17.63	16 9/16	− 6.1	5.5
VK Muni Trust (VKQ)	N	16.80	16 5/16	− 2.9	5.8
VK Sel Sect (VKL)	A	N/A	13 1/16	N/A	5.6
VK Strat Sec (VKS)	N	14.83	13 13/16	− 6.9	5.7
VK Tr Ins Muni (VIM)	N	17.22	17 7/16	+ 2.0	5.6
VK Tr Inv Grd (VGM)	N	17.53	16 3/16	− 6.6	6.1
VK Value Muni (VKV)	N	15.66	14 5/8	− 6.6	5.6

Single State Muni Bond

Fund Name (Symbol)	Stock Exch	NAV	Market Price	Prem /Disc	12 Mo Yield 1/29/99
BlckRk CA Ins 08 (BFC)	N	17.26	15 3/4	− 8.7	4.9
BlckRk CA Inv (RAA)	A	15.47	16 1/16	+ 3.8	5.5
BlckRk FL Ins 08 (BRF)	N	16.60	16 7/16	− 1.0	5.3
BlckRk FL Inv (RFA)	N	15.77	15	− 4.9	4.9
BlckRk NJ Inv (RNJ)	A	14.90	14 1/2	− 2.7	4.9
BlckRk NY Ins 08 (BLN)	N	16.86	16	− 5.1	5.4
BlckRk NY Inv (RNY)	A	15.68	15 5/8	− 0.3	5.2
Dreyfus CA Inc (DCM)	A	9.63	10 1/4	+ 6.4	5.5
Dreyfus NY Inc (DNM)	A	9.90	9 13/16	− 0.9	8.3
EV CA Muni Inc (CEV)	N	14.94	15	+ 0.4	N/A
EV FL Muni Inc (FEV)	N	14.96	15 5/8	+ 4.4	N/A
EV MA Muni Inc (MMV)	N	14.93	15 2/16	+ 1.7	N/A
EV MI Muni Inc (EMI)	N	14.95	15 1/16	+ 0.8	N/A
EV NJ Muni Inc (EVJ)	N	14.96	15 1/4	− 1.1	N/A
EV NY Muni Inc (EVY)	N	14.94	15 1/8	+ 0.8	N/A
EV OH Muni Inc (EVO)	N	14.94	15 1/4	+ 0.8	N/A
EV PA Muni Inc (EVP)	N	14.95	15 1/4	+ 2.0	N/A
Greenwich St CA (GCM)	A	14.39	13 1/8	− 8.3	5.0
MA Hlth & Educ (MHE)	A	14.07	15	+ 6.6	5.1
MSDW CA Ins (IIC)-a	◆N	14.90	14 7/16	− 3.1	5.3
MSDW CA Qual (IQC)-a	N	14.58	14 1/2	− 0.5	5.2
MSDW IN Ins CA (ICS)-a	N	15.71	15 1/16	− 4.1	5.1
MSDW NY Qual (IQN)-a	◆N	14.70	13 3/4	− 6.5	5.3
Minn Muni Income (MXA)-ac	A	15.19	14 9/16	− 4.1	5.3
Minn Muni Tm (MNA)-ac	N	11.15	11 1/16	− 0.8	5.9
Minn Muni Tm II (MNB)-ac	N	10.94	11	+ 0.5	5.3
MnHdgs CA In III (MCF)	N	14.77	15	+ 1.6	N/A
MnHdgs CA Ins II (MUC)	N	15.39	15 1/16	− 2.1	N/A
MnHdgs CA Ins IV (CIL)	N	N/A	N/A	N/A	N/A
MnHdgs FL In III (MFD)	N	14.80	14 7/16	− 2.4	N/A
MnHdgs FL Ins II (MUF)	N	15.32	15	− 2.1	N/A
MnHdgs FL Ins IV (MFR)	N	N/A	N/A	N/A	N/A
MnHdgs MI Ins (MCG)	N	N/A	N/A	N/A	N/A
MnHdgs NJ In III (MNJ)	N	N/A	N/A	N/A	N/A
MnHdgs NJ Ins II (MWJ)	N	14.65	14 1/2	− 1.0	N/A
MnHdgs NY In III (MNK)	N	N/A	N/A	N/A	N/A
MnHdgs NY Ins II (MNU)	N	14.70	15 1/16	+ 2.4	N/A
MnHldgs Ca Ins (CLH)	N	15.76	15 1/2	− 1.6	5.6
MnHldgs FL Ins (MFL)	N	15.58	15 13/16	+ 1.5	5.4
MnHldgs NY (MHN)	N	15.89	15 5/8	− 1.6	5.5

Fund Name (Symbol)	Stock Exch	NAV	Market Price	Prem /Disc	12 Mo Yield 1/29/99
MnHldgs NY Ins (MUJ)	N	15.37	14 3/4	− 4.0	N/A
MuniVest FL (MVS)	N	14.15	13 7/8	− 1.9	5.5
MuniVest MI Ins (MVM)	N	14.47	13 3/4	− 5.0	5.4
MuniVest NJ (MVJ)	N	14.72	14 7/16	− 1.9	5.4
MuniVest PA Ins (MVP)	N	13.64	13 3/8	− 1.9	5.3
MuniYield AZ (MZA)	A	14.11	14 1/8	+ 0.1	5.2
MuniYield CA (MYC)	N	15.50	16 1/4	+ 4.8	5.5
MuniYield CA Ins (MIC)	N	15.06	15 7/8	+ 5.4	5.1
MuniYield FL (MYF)	N	15.20	15 7/8	+ 4.5	5.3
MuniYield FL Ins (MFT)	N	15.29	15 15/16	+ 4.3	5.3
MuniYield MI (MYM)	N	15.27	16	+ 4.8	5.5
MuniYield MI Ins (MIY)	N	15.70	15 1/2	− 1.3	5.4
MuniYield NJ (MYJ)	N	15.54	16 1/2	+ 6.2	5.5
MuniYield NJ Ins (MJI)	N	15.70	16 3/4	+ 3.9	5.3
MuniYield NY Ins (MYN)	N	15.56	16 1/4	+ 4.4	5.4
MuniYield PA (MPA)	N	15.44	16 5/16	+ 5.6	5.5
MuniYld CA Insll (MCA)	N	15.48	16 7/16	+ 6.2	5.2
MuniYld NY Insll (MYT)	N	15.36	14 13/16	− 2.5	5.4
Munholdings NY (MUN)	N	15.36	14 13/16	− 2.7	N/A
New York TE Inc (XTX)	A	9.73	9 1/8	− 6.2	5.1
Nuveen AZ Pr (NAZ)	N	15.69	16 3/4	+ 6.8	5.1
Nuveen CA Inv Q (NQC)	◆N	16.03	16 13/16	+ 4.9	5.9
Nuveen CA Mkt (NCO)	◆N	16.31	17 11/16	+ 8.5	5.8
Nuveen CA Perf (NCP)	◆N	15.93	17 9/16	+ 10.2	5.9
Nuveen CA Pr (NCU)	◆A	14.34	14 3/8	+ 0.3	5.3
Nuveen CA Qual (NUC)	◆N	16.43	17 1/4	+ 3.8	5.9
Nuveen CA Sel (NVC)	N	15.92	16 1/4	+ 3.6	5.9
Nuveen CA Val (NCA)	N	10.35	10	− 3.4	5.3
Nuveen CT Pr (NTC)	◆N	14.83	16 1/16	+ 8.3	5.1
Nuveen FL Inv Q (NQF)	◆N	15.75	17	+ 7.9	5.8
Nuveen FL Qual (NUF)	◆N	16.10	16 1/16	− 0.2	5.8
Nuveen GA Pr (NPG)	◆A	14.83	16 1/4	+ 8.3	5.0
Nuveen Ins CA (NPC)	◆N	16.41	16	− 2.5	5.2
Nuveen Ins CA 2 (NCL)	◆N	14.99	14 13/16	− 1.2	5.2
Nuveen Ins FI (NFL)	◆N	15.88	15	− 5.5	5.2
Nuveen Ins NY (NNF)	◆N	15.56	16 5/8	+ 6.3	5.2
Nuveen InsCA Sel (NXC)	◆N	15.39	15 5/16	− 0.1	5.2
Nuveen InsNY Sel (NXN)	◆N	15.07	15 1/8	+ 0.4	5.3
Nuveen MA Pr (NMT)	◆N	15.12	16 5/8	+ 10.0	5.3
Nuveen MD Pr (NMY)	◆N	14.84	15 3/4	+ 6.1	5.0
Nuveen MI Pr (NMP)	◆N	15.51	15 9/16	− 2.1	5.5
Nuveen MI Qual (NUM)	◆N	16.00	16 13/16	+ 5.1	5.7
Nuveen MO Pr (NOM)	◆A	14.70	15 1/16	+ 2.4	5.2
Nuveen NC Pr Inc (NNC)	◆N	14.66	16 1/8	+ 10.0	5.0
Nuveen NJ Pr (NQJ)	◆N	15.74	16 11/16	+ 6.0	5.8
Nuveen NJ Pr (NNJ)	◆N	15.56	15 13/16	− 1.6	5.6
Nuveen NY Inv (NQN)	◆N	15.66	17 7/16	+ 11.4	6.0
Nuveen NY Perf (NNP)	◆N	16.08	17 1/2	+ 8.8	6.2
Nuveen NY Qual (NUN)	◆N	15.69	16 3/8	+ 4.4	5.7
Nuveen NY Sel (NVN)	◆N	15.73	17	+ 8.1	5.9
Nuveen NY Val (NNY)	◆N	10.21	10 1/8	− 0.8	5.3
Nuveen OH Qual (NUO)	◆N	16.90	18 1/2	+ 9.5	5.4
Nuveen PA Inv (NQP)	◆N	15.98	17 5/16	+ 8.3	6.0
Nuveen PA Pr 2 (NPY)	◆N	15.10	16 1/16	− 6.0	5.5
Nuveen TX Qual (NTX)	N	15.97	15 7/8	− 0.6	5.8
Nuveen VA Pr (NPV)	N	15.22	16	+ 5.1	5.2
Nuveen VA Pr (NPW)	◆A	15.34	14 3/4	− 3.8	5.4
Putnam CA Inv Gr (PCA)	A	15.70	16 1/8	+ 2.7	5.5
Putnam NY Inv Gr (PMN)	A	14.21	14 1/2	+ 1.6	5.8
VK Adv PA Muni (VAP)	N	17.66	16 15/16	− 4.1	5.8
VK CA Muni (VMC)	A	10.50	11	+ 4.8	5.9
VK CA Qual (VQC)	N	17.69	17 13/16	+ 0.7	5.6
VK CA Value (VCV)	N	16.72	15 13/16	− 5.4	5.2
VK FL Muni Opp (VOF)	A	15.21	14 3/4	− 3.0	5.2
VK FL Qual (VFM)	N	17.18	17 5/16	+ 0.1	5.6
VK Inv Grd CA (VIC)	N	17.12	17 9/16	+ 2.6	5.6
VK Inv Grd FL (VTF)	N	17.78	18	+ 1.2	5.6
VK Inv Grd NJ (VTJ)	N	18.10	18	− 0.6	5.3
VK Inv Grd NY (VTN)	N	17.78	17 1/4	− 3.0	5.6
VK Inv Grd PA (VTP)	N	17.83	16 7/8	− 5.3	5.9
VK MA Value (VMV)	N	15.86	15 11/16	− 1.1	5.1
VK NJ Value (VNJ)	A	15.88	14 7/16	− 6.3	5.2
VK NY Qual (VNM)	N	17.37	16 7/16	− 6.1	5.7
VK NY Value (VNV)	N	16.20	15	− 7.4	5.3
VK OH Qual (VOQ)	N	17.46	18 1/2	+ 6.0	5.5
VK OH Value (VOV)	A	15.66	14 3/4	− 8.2	4.9
VK PA Qual (VPQ)	N	17.20	17 1/4	+ 0.3	6.0
VK PA Value (VPV)	N	15.98	14 5/8	− 8.4	5.3
Voyageur AZ (VAZ)	A	15.44	15 3/4	− 0.4	5.0
Voyageur CO Ins (VCF)	A	15.35	14 13/16	− 3.5	5.0
Voyageur FL Ins (VFL)	A	15.78	14 15/16	− 5.3	5.1
Voyageur MN I (VMN)	A	15.56	16 3/8	+ 6.9	5.6
Voyageur MN II (VMM)	A	15.08	15 1/16	− 0.1	5.5
Voyageur MN III (VYM)	A	14.09	14 1/2	+ 2.9	5.5

f-Rights offering in process. g-Rights offering announced. h-Data have been adjusted for rights offering. j-Rights offering has expired, but data not yet adjusted. o-Tender offer in process. Source: Lipper

MONEY-MARKET
INVESTMENTS

INTRODUCTION

MAYBE THE RISK AND BOTHER OF INVESTING IN STOCKS, BONDS, AND COMMODITIES INHIBIT YOU. If that's so, you may be satisfied with an investment whose yield just covers the rate of inflation, provided that you can readily convert it to cash. In other words, you want your money's purchasing power to be unchanged a year or two from now, and you want the assurance that you can get your hands on your money at will.

Many circumstances might justify this point of view. Everyone's future involves some degree of uncertainty. If you are retired, your nest egg may have to meet unexpected medical bills. You don't want to be penalized for cashing out in a hurry. And investors of every age may wish to park their money for brief periods in anticipation of other planned uses of their funds. Whatever the situation, you might have a number of good reasons not to tie up your funds in riskier investments, even if they offer higher returns.

If you wish to make a short-term investment that is relatively risk-free and can be quickly converted to cash, the money market offers a variety of selections that range from one day to one year and may be obtained for large or small amounts. Most of these are probably familiar to you: bank savings accounts, interest-bearing checking accounts (money-market checking accounts), certificates of deposit, money-market mutual funds, and Treasury bills (T-bills). Market forces determine their yields, and the markets for all are interrelated.

As a general rule, the greater the liquidity (ease with which it is converted into cash) and safety of an investment, the lower the yield. A smaller investment commitment and a shorter maturity also reduce the yield.

This chapter describes the money-market investments available to individual investors and shows you how to track those investments in *The Wall Street Journal.*

CONSUMER SAVINGS AND INTEREST-EARNING CHECKING ACCOUNTS

Your interest-earning checking account or savings account at the bank or savings and loan company (S&L) is a short-term liquid investment, because you can withdraw your funds quickly and easily with relatively few restrictions. Moreover, these accounts are insured up to $100,000 by the Federal Deposit Insurance Corporation (FDIC). In the hierarchy of short-term interest rate yields, consumer checking and savings rates tend to be on the bottom because of their liquidity and safety and because of the inertia that prevents many savers from shopping for the higher yields available on alternative investments.

BANK MONEY-MARKET ACCOUNTS

You can open a money-market account with a minimum daily balance ranging from $500 to $5,000, depending on the bank. This is a highly liquid investment, because you can withdraw from the account at any time simply by writing a check, although most banks have restrictions regarding the number and frequency of checks written. These accounts offer relatively low yields because of their check-writing privileges, although the yields do tend to be a little higher than on savings accounts due to higher required minimum balances. They are also insured up to $100,000 by the FDIC.

Every Thursday *The Wall Street Journal* publishes **Consumer Savings Rates** (check the third section's index), a listing prepared by the *Bank Rate Monitor* that reports on the average rate paid by 100 banks on the previous day for a variety of money-market and certificate of deposit (CD) accounts. See the page 263 excerpt from the Thursday, February 4, 1999 *Journal.* According to this report, *Money-Market Deposits* paid 2.19 percent on February 3, 1999, *Interest Checking* paid 0.98 percent, and a variety of certificates of deposit, as well as U.S. Savings Bonds, earned more.

On Wednesday of each week, in the *Journal's* last section, you can follow **Banxquote Money Markets** together with **High Yield Savings** and **High Yield Jumbos** (see the excerpt from the Wednesday, February 3, 1999

Consumer Savings Rates	
Money Market Deposits-a	2.19%
Interest Checking-a	0.98%
Six-month Certificates-a	4.06%
One-year Certificates-a	4.21%
Thirty-month Certificates-a	4.26%
Five-Year Certificates-a	4.40%
U.S. Savings EE Bonds-b	4.60%
U.S. Savings I-Bonds-b,c	5.05%

a-Average rate paid yesterday by 100 large banks and thrifts in the 10 largest metropolitan areas as compiled by Bank Rate Monitor.
b-Three-month interest penalty if redeemed before five years.
c-For I-Bonds bought from November 1998 through April 1999; applies for the first six months after issue.

Source: *The Wall Street Journal*, February 4, 1999. Reprinted by permission of *The Wall Street Journal*, ©1999 Dow Jones & Company, Inc. All rights reserved.

Journal on page 264). The Banxquote Money Markets report lets you compare your yield on a variety of money-market accounts and certificate of deposit accounts at different maturities with the average earned nationally (U.S. Bank Average) and in six key states: New York, California, Pennsylvania, Illinois, Texas, and Florida. You can also find the weekly change in the national average. In the week ended Tuesday, February 2, 1999, for instance, the average short-term three-month account earned 3.61 percent and had fallen 0.01 percent from the previous week. The **High Yield Savings** figures represent the rates available at individual institutions for accounts requiring a small minimum balance (some as low as $500), and the **High Yield Jumbos** are rates offered with minimum balances of $95,000 to $100,000.

Every Wednesday, accompanying the **Banxquote Money Markets** report, *The Wall Street Journal* publishes a brief article summarizing certificate of deposit yields for the week. See the example on page 265.

Banks and S&Ls created the money-market accounts to stem withdrawals of funds lost to competing money-market mutual funds offering higher rates than savings accounts. Although interest paid by the money-market accounts fluctuates with short-term market rates, these accounts do not enjoy yields as high as those paid by money-market mutual funds. Your account will, however, be insured by the FDIC, which is not the case with money-market mutual funds. Remember: The smaller the risk, the smaller the reward.

BANXQUOTE® MONEY MARKETS

Tuesday, February 2, 1999

AVERAGE YIELDS OF MAJOR BANKS

NEW YORK	MMI*	One Month	Two Months	Three Months	Six Months	One Year	Two Years	Five Years
Savings	2.05%			3.95%	3.97%	3.97%	4.02%	4.19%
Jumbos	3.33%	3.32%	3.34%	4.07%	4.12%	4.13%	4.19%	4.32%
CALIFORNIA								
Savings	2.58%			4.00%	4.09%	4.12%	4.15%	4.26%
Jumbos	3.17%	4.37%	4.37%	4.44%	4.49%	4.57%	4.62%	4.75%
PENNSYLVANIA								
Savings	2.90%			2.76%	3.09%	3.55%	4.10%	4.36%
Jumbos	3.89%	4.65%	4.43%	3.92%	4.15%	4.25%	4.50%	4.63%
ILLINOIS								
Savings	2.33%			3.99%	4.13%	4.21%	4.26%	4.45%
Jumbos	3.51%	4.35%	4.35%	4.37%	4.42%	4.48%	4.55%	4.72%
TEXAS								
Savings	3.43%			3.27%	3.88%	3.90%	4.02%	4.28%
Jumbos	3.95%	4.14%	4.17%	4.24%	4.23%	4.25%	4.38%	4.60%
FLORIDA								
Savings	2.55%			3.07%	3.38%	3.57%	3.77%	4.03%
Jumbos	4.24%	3.99%	4.07%	4.32%	4.40%	4.45%	4.64%	4.70%
U.S. BANK AVERAGE								
Savings	3.03			3.61	4.01	4.14	4.21	4.40
Jumbos	3.69	3.95	3.99	4.14	4.34	4.39	4.40	4.56
WEEKLY CHANGE (in percentage points)								
Savings	+0.01			−0.01	−0.01	−0.01	....	+0.01
Jumbos	+0.01	−0.03	−0.02	−0.02	−0.01	−0.02	....	....

SAVINGS CD YIELDS OFFERED THROUGH LEADING BROKERS

	Three Months	Six Months	One Year	Two Years	Five Years
BROKER AVERAGE	4.73%	4.65%	4.90%	5.00%	5.23%
WEEKLY CHANGE	−0.06	....	+0.10	....	+0.05

*Money Market Investments include MMDA, NOW, savings deposits, passbook and other liquid accounts.
Each depositor is insured by the Federal Deposit Insurance Corp. (FDIC) up to $100,000 per issuing institution.
COMPOUND METHODS: c-Continuously. d-Daily. w-Wkly. m-Mthly. q-Qrtly. s-Semi-annually. a-Annually.
SIMPLE INTEREST: si-Paid Monthly. e-Paid Semi-annually. y-Paid at Maturity.
OTHER SYMBOLS: APY-Annual percentage yield. F-Floating rate P-Prime CD. T-T-Bill CD.

BD-Broker-Dealer. pp-Priced below par.
Day BASIS: A-Actual/Actual. B-30/360. C-Actual/360.
The information included in this table has been obtained directly from broker-dealers, banks and savings institutions, but the accuracy and validity cannot be guaranteed. Rates are subject to change. Yields, terms and capital adequacy should be verified before investing. Only well capitalized or adequately capitalized depository institutions are quoted.
z-Unavailable.

HIGH YIELD SAVINGS

Small minimum balance/opening deposit, generally $500 to $25,000

Money Market Investments*	Rate		APY	Six Months CDs	Rate		APY
Advanta Natl, Wilmingtn DE	5.05%	dA	5.18	NeT.B@Nk, Alpharetta GA	5.07%	dA	5.20
Bankfirst, Sioux Falls SD	5.05%	mA	5.17	Providian Bk, Salt Lake Cty UT	5.06%	dA	5.19
NeT.B@Nk, Alpharetta GA	5.00%	dA	5.13	Providian National, Tilton NH	5.06%	dA	5.19
Chase Manhttn USA, Wilmgtn DE	4.93%	dA	5.05	Telebank, Arlington VA	4.98%	dA	5.11
Keybank USA, Albany NY	4.90%	dA	5.02	New South FSB, Birmingham AL	5.05%	siA	5.11
One Month CDs	**Rate**		**APY**	**One Year CDs**	**Rate**		**APY**
New South FSB, Birmingham AL	5.00%	siA	5.12	Bankfirst, Sioux Falls SD	5.16%	dA	5.30
Southn Pac Bk, Los Angeles CA	4.75%	dA	4.86	NeT.B@Nk, Alpharetta GA	5.12%	dA	5.25
Bluebonnet Savings, Dallas TX	4.70%	siA	4.80	Providian Bk, Salt Lake Cty UT	5.12%	dA	5.25
Pacific Crest, San Diego CA	4.64%	siA	4.75	Capital One FSB, Glen Allen VA	5.12%	dA	5.25
Safra National, New York NY	4.16%	dA	4.25	Providian National, Tilton NH	5.12%	dA	5.25
Two Months CDs	**Rate**		**APY**	**Two Years CDs**	**Rate**		**APY**
New South FSB, Birmingham AL	5.00%	siA	5.11	Capital One FSB, Glen Allen VA	5.41%	dA	5.56
Southn Pac Bk, Los Angeles CA	4.80%	dA	4.92	Bankfirst, Sioux Falls SD	5.30%	dA	5.44
Bluebonnet Savings, Dallas TX	4.70%	siA	4.79	Keybank USA, Albany NY	5.30%	dA	5.44
Pacific Crest, San Diego CA	4.64%	dA	4.75	Providian Bk, Salt Lake Cty UT	5.26%	dA	5.40
Safra National, New York NY	4.40%	dA	4.50	Providian National, Tilton NH	5.26%	dA	5.40
Three Months CDs	**Rate**		**APY**	**Five Years CDs**	**Rate**		**APY**
New South FSB, Birmingham AL	5.10%	siA	5.20	Providian Bk, Salt Lake Cty UT	5.64%	dA	5.80
Telebank, Arlington VA	4.95%	dA	5.07	Capital One FSB, Glen Allen VA	5.64%	dA	5.80
Keybank USA, Albany NY	4.90%	dA	5.02	Providian National, Tilton NH	5.64%	dA	5.80
Southn Pac Bk, Los Angeles CA	4.85%	dA	4.97	Advanta Natl, Wilmington DE	5.50%	dA	5.65
Chase Manhttn USA, Wilmgtn DE	4.74%	dA	4.85	Keybank USA, Albany NY	5.50%	dA	5.65

HIGH YIELD JUMBOS

Large minimum balance/opening deposit, generally $95,000 to $100,000

Money Market Investments*	Rate		APY	Six Months Jumbo CDs	Rate		APY
Advanta Natl, Wilmingtn DE	5.20%	dA	5.34	NeT.B@Nk, Alpharetta GA	5.07%	dA	5.20
Bankfirst, Sioux Falls SD	5.05%	mA	5.17	Providian Bk, Salt Lake Cty UT	5.07%	dA	5.20
First Signature, Portsmouth NH	5.01%	dA	5.14	Providian National, Tilton NH	5.07%	dA	5.20
NeT.B@Nk, Alpharetta GA	5.00%	dA	5.13	Advanta Natl, Wilmingtn DE	5.05%	siA	5.11
Keybank USA, Albany NY	4.95%	dA	5.07	Metropolitan Bank, Oakland CA	5.05%	siA	5.11
One Month Jumbo CDs	**Rate**		**APY**	**One Year Jumbo CDs**	**Rate**		**APY**
New South FSB, Birmingham AL	5.00%	siA	5.12	Advanta Natl, Wilmingtn DE	5.30%	siA	5.30
First Federal, Santa Monica CA	4.80%	siA	4.91	Bankfirst, Sioux Falls SD	5.16%	dA	5.30
Heritage Bank, Holstein IA	4.79%	yA	4.90	Republic Bank, Ann Arbor MI	5.15%	mA	5.27
EAB, Uniondale NY	4.76%	dA	4.87	Providian Bk, Salt Lake Cty UT	5.13%	dA	5.26
Advanta Natl, Wilmingtn DE	4.75%	siA	4.85	Capital One FSB, Glen Allen VA	5.13%	dA	5.26
Two Months Jumbo CDs	**Rate**		**APY**	**Two Years Jumbo CDs**	**Rate**		**APY**
New South FSB, Birmingham AL	5.00%	siA	5.11	Capital One FSB, Glen Allen VA	5.42%	dA	5.57
Advanta Natl, Wilmingtn DE	4.85%	siA	4.95	Bankfirst, Sioux Falls SD	5.30%	dA	5.44
Mission Savings, Riverside CA	4.85%	siA	4.95	Keybank USA, Albany NY	5.30%	dA	5.44
EAB, Uniondale NY	4.81%	dA	4.93	Providian Bk, Salt Lake Cty UT	5.27%	dA	5.41
First Federal, Santa Monica CA	4.80%	siA	4.90	Providian National, Tilton NH	5.27%	dA	5.41
Three Months Jumbo CDs	**Rate**		**APY**	**Five Years Jumbo CDs**	**Rate**		**APY**
New South FSB, Birmingham AL	5.10%	siA	5.20	Providian Bk, Salt Lake Cty UT	5.65%	dA	5.81
First Federal, Santa Monica CA	5.00%	siA	5.09	Capital One FSB, Glen Allen VA	5.65%	dA	5.81
Providian National, Tilton NH	4.94%	dA	5.06	Providian National, Tilton NH	5.65%	dA	5.81
Advanta Natl, Wilmingtn DE	4.95%	siA	5.04	Keybank USA, Albany NY	5.50%	dA	5.65
Keybank USA, Albany NY	4.90%	dA	5.02	Eastern Savs, Hunt Valley MD	5.51%	mA	5.65

Additional information on deposits and loans for all 50 states is available in the BanxQuote® Banking Center in The Wall Street Journal Interactive Edition at http://wsj.com

For BanxQuote® Dealer Market and Institutional CDs see Telerate pages 22300-99.

Source: BanxQuote Inc., N.Y. N.Y. Tel. 212-643-8000.

The average three-month account earned 3.61% in the week ending February 2, 1999 →

Three-Month Broker Average 4.73% →

New South FSB →

CD Yields Were Mixed in Week

By a WALL STREET JOURNAL *Staff Reporter*

NEW YORK—Yields on certificates of deposit were mixed for the latest week.

The average yield on six-month, "jumbo" CDs, which typically require deposits of $95,000 or more, slipped to 4.34% from 4.35%, according to a weekly index prepared by BanxQuote Inc. On five-year jumbos, the average held at 4.56%, the information service said.

Average yields on small-denomination "savings" CDs in some popular maturities were mixed. The yield on the average six-month CD fell to 4.01% from 4.02%, while the average five-year CD yield rose to 4.40% from 4.39%, BanxQuote said.

Yields on broker-sold CDs were mixed. According to BanxQuote, the average yield three-month CD dropped to 4.73% from 4.79%, while the six-month CD yield grew to 4.90% from 4.80%. The average five-year CD yield rose to 5.23% from 5.18%.

MONEY-MARKET MUTUAL FUNDS

Investment companies establish mutual funds to pool the capital of many investors and thus create a large shared portfolio of investments. (Recall the earlier discussions of mutual funds in Chapter 9.) Individuals invest in mutual funds by purchasing shares in the fund, and the return on the portfolio is passed through to the investor according to the number of shares held. An enormous variety of mutual funds is available, designed for different types of investors and bearing a wide variety of yields.

Money-market mutual funds invest principally in short-term investment instruments such as Treasury bills, commercial paper, bank certificates of deposit, bankers acceptances, and other liquid assets denominated in large amounts and therefore unavailable to the small investor. A money-market mutual fund permits you to participate in the return on a variety of short-term investments and enjoy the benefits of diversification without employing large sums of your own capital. You also take advantage of the professional management skills of the investment company.

Most money-market mutual funds are *no-load funds*. They do not charge a sales commission fee, because they are directly marketed by the investment company. However, "management" fees are subtracted from the yield you receive. Money-market mutual funds are issued and trade at a par value of one dollar. The dividends you receive are expressed as percentage yield.

Although money-market funds sell their shares for a dollar each, most have minimum investment requirements ranging from $1,000 to $25,000. As an incentive, many money-market funds also have check-writing privileges. Although these funds are not insured by the federal government, they are safe

and liquid investments whose yields tend to be higher than the yields on bank money-market accounts.

In the early 1980s, when the Federal Reserve applied a chokehold on the economy and interest rates climbed to the sky, money-market mutual funds became popular among investors and savers. Since banks and S&Ls were, at the time, prohibited from offering above-passbook rates to small depositors, huge sums poured into the money-market funds as their yields climbed above the legal passbook minimums. When the interest rate ceilings were removed from small denomination accounts at banks and S&Ls, and these accounts began to offer rates that moved with market conditions (and thus competed with the money-market mutual funds), some investors deserted the money-market funds. Once again, however, money-market fund (not insured) rates generally outdo those at the banks (insured) and consequently remain very popular.

Money-Market Funds

Each Friday in the third section, *The Wall Street Journal* publishes an article on *money-fund assets*. The report from the Friday, February 12, 1999 *Journal* (see page 267) informs you that money-fund assets rose in the latest week.

Every Thursday in the third section the *Journal* publishes a report and a chart called **Yields for Consumers** that compares money-market fund yields with yields on bank certificates of deposit and money-market accounts and provides a report on the size of money-market funds' assets. The Thursday, February 4, 1999 excerpt on page 268 reports little change in short-term interest rates. Notice that the average maturity of the investments in these funds (T-bills, CDs, commercial paper, etc.) remained the same. If they think interest rates will fall, many fund managers lock in longer yields on longer maturities in order to enjoy those higher yields for as long as possible; they choose shorter maturities when they believe rates will rise. Since the length of maturity did not change, money-fund managers apparently expected little fluctuation in interest rates.

Money-Market Mutual Funds, published every Thursday in the *Journal*, lists the most popular money-market mutual funds (see the index on page C1). Several statistics are given for each: the average maturity (in days) of the investments in the fund, the 7-day yield for the week (average yield), and the total assets in millions of dollars as of the previous day. (See the example from the Thursday, February 4, 1999 *Journal* on page 269.)

You can track the performance of your money-market mutual fund and most others with this report. For instance, on page 270 you can see that *Merrill Lynch's Cash Management Account* had an average maturity of 75 days, a yield of 4.52 percent, and assets of $59.558 billion. Finally, note that tax-exempt funds are listed separately and have lower yields.

Money-Fund Assets Grew $578 Million In the Latest Week

By a WALL STREET JOURNAL Staff Reporter

WASHINGTON—Money-market mutual-fund assets rose $578 million to $1.4513 trillion in the week ended Wednesday from a revised $1.4508 trillion, the Investment Company Institute said.

Assets of 918 retail-class shares increased $3.94 billion to $858.37 billion, the trade group said. Among retail-class

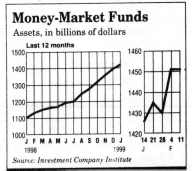

Money-Market Funds
Assets, in billions of dollars

Source: Investment Company Institute

shares, assets of the 566 taxable shares rose $4.02 billion to $705.81 billion, while assets of the 352 tax-exempt shares decreased $80.4 million to $152.56 billion.

Assets of the 752 institutional-class shares decreased $3.36 billion to $592.96 billion. Among institutional-class shares, assets of the 588 taxable shares fell $2.97 billion to $542.29 billion, while assets of the 164 tax-exempt shares fell $390 million to $50.67 billion.

CERTIFICATES OF DEPOSIT

Certificates of deposit (CDs) are like savings accounts for which you receive a "certificate of deposit" from the bank or savings and loan company. Banks and S&Ls issue certificates of deposit to compete with Treasury bills and commercial paper for the investor's dollar. CDs that have maturities of one year or less are part of the money market.

CDs offer higher rates than bank money-market accounts, but you pay a price in penalties for early withdrawal of funds. Jumbo ($90,000–$100,000)

Money-Fund Yields Were Mixed

By a WALL STREET JOURNAL Staff Reporter
NEW YORK—Yields on taxable and tax-free money-market funds were mixed in the latest week.

The average seven-day compound yield on taxable money funds edged up to 4.51% from 4.50% in the week ended Tuesday, according to IBC's Money Fund Report, an Ashland, Mass., newsletter. Compound yields assume reinvestment of dividends.

Assets of the 902 taxable funds rose $8.3 billion to a record $1.214 trillion. Of that figure, institutional investors added about $5.5 billion.

The average seven-day simple yield on taxable funds inched up to 4.41% from 4.40%; the average 30-day simple yield dipped to 4.44% from 4.48%. Average maturity of taxable funds' investments, which include commercial paper (short-term corporate IOUs) and Treasury bills, held at 54 days.

The average seven-day compound yield on tax-free money funds slipped to 2.38% from 2.45% in the latest week. The latest yield is equivalent to a taxable 3.72% for an investor in the 36% tax bracket and to 3.97% for someone in the 39.6% bracket.

Assets of 449 tax-exempt funds rose $13.2 million to a record $195.33 billion. The average portfolio maturity stayed at 42 days.

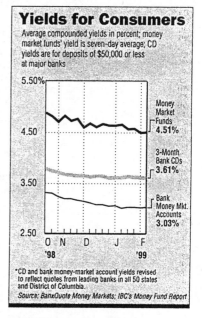

Yields for Consumers

Average compounded yields in percent; money market funds' yield is seven-day average; CD yields are for deposits of $50,000 or less at major banks

Money Market Funds 4.51%

3-Month Bank CDs 3.61%

Bank Money Mkt. Accounts 3.03%

*CD and bank money-market account yields revised to reflect quotes from leading banks in all 50 states and District of Columbia.
Source: BanxQuote Money Markets; IBC's Money Fund Report

IBC's Money Fund Report is published by IBC Financial Data Inc., a subsidiary of IBC USA Information Services Inc.

certificates purchased through a broker are the only exception, and then only if the broker can sell the CD to another investor. When you tie up your funds until maturity, the CD becomes a non-liquid asset. This disadvantage is offset to some extent by FDIC deposit insurance.

You can often get a higher CD rate from your broker than your local bank or S&L, because your broker can shop nationally for the highest CD rate. You won't pay a fee for this service, because the bank pays the broker.

Every Wednesday *The Wall Street Journal* publishes an article on current certificates-of-deposit yields which accompanies the **Banxquote Money Markets** table. Page 265 provides an example from the Wednesday, February 3, 1999 issue.

MONEY MARKET MUTUAL FUNDS

Fund	Avg. Mat.	7 Day Yield	Assets
AALMny	59	4.30	276
AARP HQ	29	4.27	571
AAdMileP	45	4.12	106
AAdvGovP	27	3.97	88
AAdvMMPlat	45	4.25	835
ABN AMROGovl	42	4.37	92
ABN AMRO Gvt	42	4.69	398
ABN AMROInv	44	4.41	223
ABN AMRO MM	44	4.77	1261
ABN AMRO Trs	29	4.37	307
AFD ExRsv A	18	3.99	166
AFD ExResB	18	3.48	166
AFD ExResC p	18	3.73	74
AIM MMCshRes	28	3.91	1221
ARKGvtA	34	4.39	76
ARK GvIn II	34	4.55	198
ARK MMIn II	43	4.71	176
ARKMM A	43	4.78	455
ARKMM A	43	4.55	213
ARKUSG A	34	4.62	1801
ARKUST A	80	4.19	284
ARKUST A	80	3.96	22
ARKUST C	80	4.12	147
AZMunCTIns	54	2.35	32
AccUSGov	47	4.43	173
ActAsGv	63	4.43	850
ActAsMny	73	4.62	15406
Advantus a	69	4.05	50
AetnaAdvs	58	4.74	176
Aetna Sel	58	4.74	280
AlexBwn	36	4.30	3560
AlxBTr	44	3.86	810
AlgerMM	20	3.93	333
AlliaGenMu	29	1.95	46
AlliaGov	41	4.08	46
AlliMMass	37	1.91	50
AlliaPrime	50	4.16	746
Alli TrResv	38	3.61	816
AlliaCpRs	55	4.19	10051
AlliaGvR	46	4.02	6199
AlliMny	59	4.16	1541
AmAAdGvl	27	4.78	35
AmAAdMMI	45	4.96	1318
AmPerCsh	53	4.41	501
AmPerTrs	1	4.01	408
AmAAdGvP	27	4.43	106
AmAAdMMP	45	4.67	301
AmAAdGvM	27	4.34	31
AmAAdMMM	45	4.56	122
AmSthInstPri	24	4.72	129
AmSouthPrC	50	4.31	137
AmSouthPrP	50	4.41	558
AmSouthUSP	49	[illegible]	306
AonMMktY	37	4.77	797
ArchMMInst	36	4.32	48
ArchMMInvA	36	4.32	231
ArchMM Tr	36	4.32	708
ArchTreaTr	44	3.65	210
ArchUSTrInvA	44	3.65	24
Armada Gvl	40	4.43	985
ArmadaGvR	40	4.28	577
Armada MMI	31	4.61	2753
Armada MMR	31	4.46	1075
ArmadaTrA p	49	3.91	66
Armada Trsyl	49	4.06	304
AMF MM Pt	3	4.69	77
Atlas USTrs	73	3.68	57
AutCsh	54	4.54	1759
AutGvt	37	4.23	2235
AuGvSvc	44	4.38	836
AutCshCII	54	4.37	748
AutTreasC	52	3.94	272
BB&T PrimTr	60	4.50	52
BB&T UST Tr	44	4.18	264
BNYHam TrHm	37	4.54	196
BNYHmltTrPr	37	4.29	521
BNY Hmltn	48	4.78	1500
BNY HmltnPr	48	4.53	580
BT InstCash	42	4.79	2628
BT InstCshRv	42	4.85	3357
BT Inst Trsy	39	4.53	1801
BT InvCash	42	4.28	237
BT InvTrsy	39	4.03	292
BT InvMMkt	42	4.68	420
BT LqdAsst	51	4.95	3397
Babson	50	4.21	39
BearST Prime	39	4.85	321
BedfdGv	62	4.01	139
BdfdMM	56	4.19	926
BenhmCap	81	4.14	3292
BenhmGvAg	53	4.43	529
BenhmPrCR	67	4.68	235
BenhmPrmGv	43	4.47	82
BenhmPrime	70	4.57	2864
BishopStA	66	4.70	259
BishopStTrea	60	4.45	272
BRInst	55	4.75	2079

Fund	Avg. Mat.	7 Day Yield	Assets
EvgrnMM A	67	4.36	5433
EvgrnMM B	67	3.66	67
EvgrnMM Y	67	4.66	1861
EvgrnNJMuA	2	1.91	98
EvgrnPaA	16	2.34	98
EvgSelMktl	65	4.99	2347
EvgSelMktIS	65	4.74	2257
EvgSelMu I	3	2.59	140
EvgSelMu IS	3	2.84	1022
EvgSelTrsyl	46	4.65	1979
EvgSelTrsyIS	46	4.40	1593
EvgSelUSTrl	50	4.39	552
EvgrTreasA	39	4.10	3446
EvgrTreasY	39	4.40	1066
ExcelsiorGvt	14	4.59	581
ExcelsiorMny	36	4.64	879
ExcelsrMM	81	4.89	193
ExcelsiorTry	29	4.24	509
ExpMM	53	4.40	180
ExpMMInst	53	4.65	77
FThirdComP A	37	4.18	53
FThirdComP I	37	4.47	411
FThirdGov A	51	4.15	479
FThirdGov I	51	4.29	265
FThirdTO	37	4.37	1016
FFTW	83	4.89	28
FIMMDom I	39	4.92	2368
FIMMDomII p	39	4.77	373
FIMMDomIII	39	4.67	517
FIMMGov I	38	4.90	4505
FIMMGovII	38	4.75	298
FIMMGovIII	38	4.65	785
FIMMMM I	45	4.97	14357
FIMMMMII	45	4.82	117
FIMMMMIII	45	4.72	839
FIMMTrOnlyII p	80	4.42	54
FIMMTrOnIII p	80	4.33	146
FIMMTrOnly I	80	4.57	1036
FIMMTry I	34	4.65	4533
FIMMTryII	34	4.50	342
FIMMTryIII	34	4.40	3731
FdShtUS	37	4.52	368
FedMstr	52	4.66	487
FidCashRes	45	4.84	32178
Fid FDIT	40	4.71	2950
FidGvRes	47	4.67	1446
FidPrimeDlyl	41	4.55	3696
FidRetGov	44	4.70	3850
FidRetMM	46	4.88	9337
FidSpGov	48	4.67	862
FidSpMM	45	4.83	9755
FidSpUSTr	74	4.31	2156
FidTryDlyl	27	4.20	1201
FidSelMM	43	4.56	828
FidTryCR	37	3.95	637
59WallStTreas	60	3.86	204
59WallStMM	51	4.51	1093
FInvTrUSGvt	40	4.77	220
FInvTrUSTrs	41	4.44	104
FinSqFed	50	4.76	4222
FinSq Gov	49	4.78	3366
FinSq POF	56	4.92	7825
FinSqTrsy	40	4.27	395
FinSq TOF	44	4.59	5231
FinSq MMF	57	4.92	8613
FinSq PMMF	43	4.85	767
FstAmGvObD	41	4.31	333
FstAmGvObY	41	4.46	952
FstAmTrObD	43	4.22	3842
FstAmGvObA p	41	4.15	456
FstAmPrObA	43	4.38	4152
FstAmPrObY	43	4.71	6343
FstAmPrObD	43	4.56	313
FstAmTrObA p	43	4.12	33
FstAmTrObY	43	4.37	1816
FirstChCshRvS	59	4.39	111
FirstChUSTrRvS	74	3.93	59
FirstCshRsvIII	61	4.41	64
FtInvCs	60	4.33	167
First Muni	26	2.44	52
FstOmahaGv	66	4.10	116
First USGv	54	4.54	96
First USTrs	54	4.37	19
FirstUSTrsyIII	54	4.15	51
FsrInstMn	47	4.71	1918
FirstrMM	52	4.38	290
FirstrUSGov	44	4.22	259
FirstarUST	53	3.76	99
FlexInst	71	4.93	938
FlexFd	71	4.73	198
Fortis A	52	4.18	177
ForumDACI	53	4.88	44
Forum DAG Obl	57	4.69	29
ForumDAGI	44	4.73	33
ForumDAGIS	44	4.48	7
ForumDAT Obl	41	4.39	139
Founders	19	4.09	94

Fund	Avg. Mat.	7 Day Yield	Assets
JPMrgInstSvFd	52	4.54	17
JPMrgInstTrsy	58	4.62	435
JPMorganFed	52	4.53	641
JPMrgInstIPr	58	4.72	709
JPMorganPr	58	4.71	3093
JanneyMntGv	62	3.98	412
JanneyMont	56	4.16	1038
JanneyMnt NY	26	2.16	29
JanusGovt	36	4.34	201
JanusGvtInst	36	4.79	630
Janus MM	40	4.50	1518
JanusMMInst	40	4.95	5402
JHanCashRs	38	4.26	29
JHan MMB	30	3.19	168
JHanMMA	30	4.04	388
KentGovInst	58	4.59	181
KentInst	58	4.57	781
KentMIInst	55	2.51	302
LegMUS	68	4.19	410
LegMCR f	72	4.30	1570
Lexingt a	17	3.98	88
LibtyUS	39	3.97	595
LindnerGvt	53	4.43	48
Liq Ins Gv	43	4.66	129
LiqInt	47	4.79	2190
LiqInstSec	68	4.23	189
LiqCshTr	2	4.67	510
LiveOakGen	65	4.16	805
LiveOakGov	44	3.95	77
LuthrnBr	55	4.14	529
MASCashRes	64	4.80	164
MFS CashA	42	3.97	95
MFSCashC p	42	2.80	88
MFSGovMonA	40	4.18	50
MFSMonMkA	35	4.20	1141
MMktProFdInv	42	4.19	92
MSD&T Gvt	48	4.56	440
MSD&T Prime	39	4.64	497
MSDWitrLqAst	76	4.53	17136
MSDWitrUS	55	4.14	1020
MainStay A	60	4.42	149
MainStay B	60	4.42	426
MainStay Inst	53	4.69	185
MainStayInstSrv	53	4.44	3
ManagersMM	58	4.62	1815
Map Gvt	8	4.32	4
Marshall A	37	4.81	1733
Marshall B	37	4.51	103
MasterWorks	70	4.62	206
MentorUSGCshI	22	4.85	108
ML CBAMon	77	4.40	2623
ML CMAGv	74	4.30	3798
ML CMAMn	75	4.52	59558
MerLyRdy	76	4.53	6659
MerLyRet	69	4.76	13766
ML CMATr	77	3.96	2548
MerLyUSA	77	4.11	661
ML US Tr	77	3.86	61
MerLyRetII p	69	4.56	560
MileTrObInst	27	4.65	1475
MileTrObInv	27	4.45	290
MHLIRSel	31	4.96	1198
MonarchCInst	53	4.52	244
MonarchCUniv	53	4.91	83
MonarchCInv	53	4.26	216
MonarchGInst	57	4.32	565
MonarchGUniv	57	4.71	314
MonarchTrs	41	3.89	107
MonarchTrInst	41	4.27	89
MonMMgt f	55	4.03	79
MonMkTrst	50	4.65	418
MontGovResR	48	4.52	798
MSDW Mony	63	4.57	2200
MosaicGvtTr	39	4.07	50
Munder A	38	4.08	12
MundCashA	40	4.33	143
MundCashK	40	4.43	930
MundCashY	40	4.58	342
MundLiqPlus	41	4.06	79
MunderMMY	38	4.33	77
MundTreasA	13	3.93	12
MundTreasK	13	4.03	61
MundTreasY	13	4.18	36
NatnsPrPrA	41	4.91	2688
NatnsCRsAdv	39	4.70	876
NatnsCRsCap	39	4.95	5045
NatnsGPrA	57	4.58	286
NatnsGRsAdv	37	4.43	101
NatnsGvPrB	57	4.33	2
NatnsMRsLiq	13	2.37	54
NatnsPrDaly	41	4.41	2643
NatnsPrIncC	41	4.66	11
NatnsPrInvB	41	4.66	760
NatnsTrDaly	39	4.03	210
NatnsTrInvB	39	4.28	262
NatnsTrPrA	39	4.53	775
NatnsTRsAdv	39	4.37	344
NatnsTRsCap	39	4.62	462

Fund	Avg. Mat.	7 Day Yield	Assets
PIFTmp	44	4.89	15577
PIFMnCADlr	20	2.00	147
PIFFedDlr	46	4.48	32
PIFFedTrDlr	48	4.47	44
PIFMCsDlr	47	2.49	111
PIFMuniDlr	31	2.30	58
PIFTrsTrDlr	55	4.01	454
PIFTpCshDlr	61	4.62	438
PIFTmpDlr	44	4.64	345
PruCdGvt	49	4.48	778
PruGvt	49	4.16	621
PruPILP A	56	4.97	346
PruPILP I	56	5.02	1944
PruMart	67	4.50	6409
PruSMM	51	4.60	310
PruTr	55	4.01	359
PruMMrtZ	67	4.63	211
Putnm MMA	57	5.06	3036
QltyCsh	36	4.00	265
RNC Liq	80	4.30	44
RegionsTreIn	56	3.71	101
RegionsTreTr	56	3.96	502
RepGov Cl A	63	4.16	1236
RepMMA	37	4.68	107
RepMMY	37	4.93	88
ReserPITT	15	4.32	244
ResrveUSTrs	63	3.73	329
ResrveFd Gvt	4	3.83	734
ReserveFd	22	4.14	3430
RiggsPrmY	57	4.42	304
RiggsTrsY	18	4.03	133
RdSqMM	51	4.57	1727
RdSqUS	55	4.48	581
RshFGI	45	3.72	546
RydexUSGvtA	25	3.52	338
RydexUSGv	25	4.02	894
SEI DIT MMA	56	4.96	1326
SEI DITGovA	56	4.85	204
SEI DIT MMC	56	4.46	136
SEI DITGovB	56	4.55	30
SEI DITGvIIA	58	4.83	926
SEI GovCNI	56	4.20	1108
SEI LqTr A	61	4.42	589
SEI LqGv A	59	4.50	96
SEI LqPr	53	4.76	1339
SEI DITPrmA	57	4.97	4398
SEI DITPrmB	57	4.67	276
SEI DITTrsA	50	4.63	300
SEI DITTrIIA	46	4.27	463
SEI DITTrIIB	46	3.98	130
SGCowenStdResv	56	4.52	1609
SITMMkt	33	4.49	43
SSgAMMA f	50	4.64	7803
SSgAPrm	47	4.85	3266
SSgAUSGvtA	52	4.57	1438
SSgAUSTry	35	4.63	1137
STIPrQuTr	48	4.55	2094
STIUSGvTr	13	4.20	441
STIUSGvIv	13	4.05	64
Safeco f	71	4.42	219
SalomonInst	41	4.91	139
SansomSt	56	4.61	645
SaratogaFd	67	4.08	45
SchbValAdv	65	4.82	23543
SchwabGCR	41	4.06	27
SchwabIntl	65	4.63	424
SchwbRetir	59	4.46	215
SchwbGv	60	4.38	2249
SchbMM	63	4.47	28888
Schb UST	80	4.15	2118
Scout MFed	15	4.49	329
Scout MPrm	21	4.34	670
ScudMMSerInst	27	4.90	1996
ScudGovMMInst	28	4.64	91
ScudGovMMMgd	28	4.48	33
ScudMMSerMgd	27	4.81	376
ScudPremium	27	4.84	857
ScudCshIn	27	4.20	1173
Scud UST	25	4.17	421
SecurityCsh	54	4.07	78
SelectGv	40	4.21	127
SeligmnCshA	34	3.84	337
SeligmanCshB	34	2.82	26
SeligmnCshD	34	2.82	70
SentinelUST A	68	3.77	100
ShtTrmIncoA	66	4.15	1139
ShTrInUS	37	3.89	819
SmBarCash	64	4.50	42890
SmBarGvt	50	4.41	5648
SmBarInstGA	39	4.67	149
SmBarRetir	51	4.51	1729
SmBarInstCA	64	4.88	1051
SoTrustTres	8	4.31	659
Stagecoach A	60	4.38	8568
StagecoachGvtA	39	4.31	60
StagecoachPrmI	63	4.87	1410
StageNatlIn	40	2.37	23
StagecoachPrmA	63	4.38	545

Merrill Lynch's Cash Management Account

Source: *The Wall Street Journal*, February 4, 1999. Reprinted by permission of *The Wall Street Journal*, ©1999 Dow Jones & Company, Inc. All rights reserved.

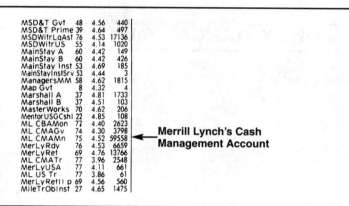

MSD&T Gvt	48	4.56	440
MSD&T Prime	39	4.64	497
MSDWitrLqAst	76	4.53	17136
MSDWitrUS	55	4.14	1020
MainStay A	60	4.42	149
MainStay B	60	4.42	426
MainStay Inst	53	4.69	185
MainStayInstSrv	53	4.44	3
ManagersMM	58	4.62	1815
Map Gvt	8	4.32	4
Marshall A	37	4.81	1733
Marshall B	37	4.51	103
MasterWorks	70	4.62	206
MentorUSGCshl	22	4.85	108
ML CBAMon	77	4.40	2623
ML CMAGv	74	4.30	3798
ML CMAMn	75	4.52	59558
MerLyRdy	76	4.53	6659
MerLyRet	69	4.76	13766
ML CMATr	77	3.96	2548
MerLyUSA	77	4.11	661
ML US Tr	77	3.86	61
MerLyRetll p	69	4.56	560
MileTrObInst	27	4.65	1475

← Merrill Lynch's Cash Management Account

On the same day, the *Journal* publishes the more comprehensive **Banxquote Money Markets**, **High Yield Savings**, and **High Yield Jumbos** discussed earlier. Return to the Wednesday, February 3, 1999 example on page 264 (and blown up on page 271). It reports CD interest rates by locale, maturity, and size. Note that CDs are quoted by rate and yield in the "high yield" portions of the table. The more frequently interest is compounded, the higher the yield for each rate.

It pays to shop, too. You can see on pages 264 and 271 that, while the *average three-month CD* paid 3.61 percent, the *broker average* was 4.73 percent, and that *New South Federal Savings Bank in Birmingham, Alabama* paid 5.10 percent.

TREASURY BILLS
Our national debt made the news when it stopped growing (at least temporarily) in 1999. Treasury bills (T-bills) constitute about a quarter of the total national debt, and this huge dollar volume makes Treasury bills one of the most important short-term investment instruments.

The U.S. Treasury borrows by selling bills at auction (primary market) every Monday in New York, and in the following day's *Journal* you will find a summary at the end of the **Credit Markets** article on the U.S. Treasury's Monday auction of 13- and 26-week bills (see the indexes at the front of the first and last sections). An example drawn from the Tuesday, February 9, 1999 edition of the *Journal* appears on page 272.

Treasury bills are sold on a discount basis. Buyers pay less than the $10,000 face value (par value), the amount they will receive when the bill

HIGH YIELD SAVINGS
Small minimum balance/opening deposit, generally $500 to $25,000

Money Market Investments*	Rate		APY	Six Months CDs	Rate		APY
Advanta Natl, Wilmingtn DE	5.05%	dA	5.18	NeT.B@Nk, Alpharetta GA	5.07%	dA	5.20
Bankfirst, Sioux Falls SD	5.05%	mA	5.17	Providian Bk, Salt Lake Cty UT	5.06%	dA	5.19
NeT.B@Nk, Alpharetta GA	5.00%	dA	5.13	Providian National, Tilton NH	5.06%	dA	5.19
Chase Manhttn USA, Wilmgtn DE	4.93%	dA	5.05	Telebank, Arlington VA	4.98%	dA	5.11
Keybank USA, Albany NY	4.90%	dA	5.02	New South FSB, Birminghm AL	5.05%	siA	5.11
One Month CDs	Rate		APY	One Year CDs	Rate		APY
New South FSB, Birminghm AL	5.00%	siA	5.12	Bankfirst, Sioux Falls SD	5.16%	dA	5.30
Southn Pac Bk, Los Angeles CA	4.75%	dA	4.86	NeT.B@Nk, Alpharetta GA	5.12%	dA	5.25
Bluebonnet Savings, Dallas TX	4.70%	siA	4.80	Providian Bk, Salt Lake Cty UT	5.12%	dA	5.25
Pacific Crest, San Diego CA	4.64%	dA	4.75	Capital One FSB, Glen Allen VA	5.12%	dA	5.25
Safra National, New York NY	4.16%	dA	4.25	Providian National, Tilton NH	5.12%	dA	5.25
Two Months CDs	Rate		APY	Two Years CDs	Rate		APY
New South FSB, Birminghm AL	5.00%	siA	5.11	Capital One FSB, Glen Allen VA	5.41%	dA	5.56
Southn Pac Bk, Los Angeles CA	4.80%	dA	4.92	Bankfirst, Sioux Falls SD	5.30%	dA	5.44
Bluebonnet Savings, Dallas TX	4.70%	siA	4.79	Keybank USA, Albany NY	5.30%	dA	5.44
Pacific Crest, San Diego CA	4.64%	dA	4.75	Providian Bk, Salt Lake Cty UT	5.26%	dA	5.40
Safra National, New York NY	4.40%	dA	4.50	Providian National, Tilton NH	5.26%	dA	5.40
Three Months CDs	Rate		APY	Five Years CDs	Rate		APY
New South FSB, Birminghm AL	5.10%	siA	5.20	Providian Bk, Salt Lake Cty UT	5.64%	dA	5.80
Telebank, Arlington VA	4.95%	dA	5.07	Capital One FSB, Glen Allen VA	5.64%	dA	5.80
Keybank USA, Albany NY	4.90%	dA	5.02	Providian National, Tilton NH	5.64%	dA	5.80
Southn Pac Bk, Los Angeles CA	4.85%	dA	4.97	Advanta Natl, Wilmingtn DE	5.50%	dA	5.65
Chase Manhttn USA, Wilmgtn DE	4.74%	dA	4.85	Keybank USA, Albany NY	5.50%	dA	5.65

New South FSB →

matures and is redeemed by the U.S. Treasury. If bidding is strong and the price is high, the effective rate of interest will be low, and vice versa.

To understand how this works, place yourself in the role of a buyer and study the example below. If you pay $9,750 for a bill maturing in 91 days (about a quarter of a year), your effective annual yield is approximately 10 percent. Remember, $250 in a quarter-year is the equivalent of $1,000 in a year, or 10 percent of a $10,000 base. (Use $10,000 as the base for calculating the discount rate, rather than $9,750, because Treasury bills' yields are usually quoted on a discount basis; that is, the discount—$250—is measured against face value—$10,000.) If strong bidding drives the price to $9,875, your yield falls to 5 percent. If weak bidding or selling pressure permits the price to fall to $9,500, the effective yield rises to 20 percent. The more you pay for the Treasury bill, the lower your yield, and vice versa.

Face (redemption) value	$10,000	$10,000	$10,000
Selling Price (note: prices falling)	$9,875	$9,750	$9,500
Discount (difference)	$125	$250	$500
Approximate Yield (discount rate) (note: yield rising)	5%	10%	20%

Take a moment to review the method used to compute the discount rate in the bottom row of the above table. The following calculations show how the 10 percent rate was obtained. Discount rate (yield) = Discount divided

In late when-issued trading yesterday, the five-year note was trading at 4.80%, the 10-year note was at 4.93%, and the 30-year bond was at 5.27%.

Uncertainty about the reopening of the 10-year note has resulted in a much tighter yield spread between the current note and the when-issued note. The so-called roll is less than one-hundredth of a percentage point compared with five-hundredths of a percentage point for the five-year roll and eight-hundredths of a percentage point for the 30-year roll.

The Treasury Department will reopen the current 4.75% November 2008 10-year note if the issue's price at 9 a.m. EST on auction day isn't below $98 per $100 face amount. If the price falls below that level, the department will then sell a new 10-year note.

With the current issue trading only 21/32 above the $98 cut-off price, it is still very much in doubt whether the issue will be reopened or not.

Separately, the Treasury sold 13-week and 26-week bills. Here are the results:

All bids are awarded at a single price at the market-clearing yield. Rates are determined by the difference between that price and the face value.

On Monday, February 8, 1999 the U.S. Treasury auctioned 13-week bills in the primary market at a price of $9,888.30 and a discount of $111.70 for a discount rate of 4.420% and a coupon equivalent of 4.53%

	13-Week	26-Week
Applications	$24,950,979,000	$24,091,447,000
Accepted bids	$7,506,479,000	$7,513,664,000
Accepted noncompet'ly	$1,386,186,000	$1,200,312,000
Auction price (rate)	98.883 (4.420%)	97.765 (4.420%)
Coupon equivalent	4.531%	4.585%
Bids at market yield	48%	46%
Cusip number	912795BL4	912795CK5

Both issues are dated Feb. 11. The 13-week bills mature May 13, 1999, and the 26-week bills mature Aug. 12, 1999.

by par value × Time factor multiplier (which is needed to generate the annual rate).

$$\text{Approximate discount rate (yield)} = \frac{\text{Discount}}{\text{Face or par value}} \times 4 \quad \text{(Because 91 days are about a quarter of a 365-day year)}$$

$$= \frac{\$250}{\$10,000} \times 4$$

$$= 2.5\% \times 4$$

$$= 10\%$$

The true discount-rate formula is very close to this approximation. The "time factor multiplier" is somewhat different, because the "year" is 360 days. Returning to the example, the discount rate would be calculated as follows:

$$\text{Discount rate} = \frac{\text{Discount}}{\text{Par value}} \times \text{Time multiplier}$$

$$\frac{\$250}{\$10,000} \times \frac{360}{91}$$

$$= 0.0989$$

$$= 9.89\%$$

You can see that the true discount rate of 9.89 is less than the 10 percent approximation calculated above, because the time multiplier ($\frac{360}{91}$) is less than 4.

The discount rate is only an approximation of the true yield to maturity or coupon equivalent. In the first place, the purchase price of the T-bill was $9,750, not $10,000. In the fraction below, $9,750 replaces $10,000. And secondly, a year is 365 days, not 360. Thus, the correct time multiplier is $\frac{365}{91}$.

Now calculate the actual yield, called the investment yield to maturity, for the same example.

$$\text{Yield to maturity} = \frac{\text{Discount}}{\text{Purchase price}} \times \text{Time factor}$$

$$= \frac{\$250}{\$9,750} \times \frac{365}{91}$$

$$= 0.1029$$

$$= 10.29\%$$

You can see that the discount rate of 9.89 percent is less than the true yield of 10.29 percent, because the discount is expressed as a percentage of the purchase price rather than par, and the year is calculated at 365 rather than 360 days.

Why are T-bills quoted on a discount rather than true-yield basis? Because the arithmetic is much easier to deal with, and that was important years ago before the advent of data-processing equipment.

Now that you understand the relationship between the discount rate and the yield to maturity (coupon equivalent), look at the illustration on page 272 from the Tuesday, February 9, 1999 *Journal*. Potential buyers submitted $24,950,979,000 in bids, of which the Treasury accepted $7,506,479,000. The auction provided $9,888.30 (98.883 percent of face value) for each $10,000 bill auctioned on Monday, February 8, 1999, for a discount of $111.70, a discount rate of 4.420 percent, and a coupon-equivalent yield of 4.531 percent. Note that the Treasury accepted 48 percent of the bids for the 13-week bill. Also, $1,386,186,000 worth of bids were accepted noncompetitively, meaning the buyers were willing to accept whatever price the auction generated.

Here is how you calculate the discount rate using the Treasury-auction figures on page 272.

$$\text{Discount rate} = \frac{\text{Discount}}{\text{Par value}} \times \text{Time multiplier}$$

$$= \frac{\$111.70 \text{ (i.e., } \$10,000 - \$9,880.30)}{\$10,000} \times \frac{360}{91}$$

$$= 0.04420$$

$$= 4.420\%$$

You can also compute the true (coupon-equivalent) yield as follows:

$$\text{Yield to maturity} = \frac{\text{Discount}}{\text{Purchase price}} \times \text{Time factor}$$

$$= \frac{\$111.70}{\$9,888.30} \times \frac{365}{91}$$

$$= 0.04531$$

$$= 4.531\%$$

Your motivation for buying Treasury bills is probably quite simple: You have idle cash on which you wish to earn an interest return. If you and all other bidders for Treasury bills have ample funds and are eager to buy, you will drive the price close to $10,000 and earn a low rate of return. If you and

all other bidders do not have ample funds, you can be enticed only by a very low price for the right to receive $10,000 in 91 days, and you will earn a high rate of return.

Now, this discussion has been presented as if you could participate in the bidding for Treasury bills. Well, you can't. The auction is conducted in New York by the Fed, acting as the Treasury's agent, and bidding is conducted by large firms that deal in, and make a market for, Treasury bills. They bid for the bills at the weekly Monday auction (primary market), so they can resell them at a markup on any business day (secondary market).

You *can* go to your local regional Federal Reserve Bank and buy Treasury bills, but you'll have to do so noncompetitively at the average rate (discount) established at the New York auction. (For instance, the 4.420 percent discount rate and 4.531 yield in the example on page 272.) Note that the Treasury accepted $1,386,186,000 of bids noncompetitively on Monday, February 8, 1999. These were bids made directly to the Fed by individuals and small institutions who could not participate in the auction.

There are two ways to buy T-bills from the Fed: Immediately or by opening an account that permits purchases at a later date.

If you want to purchase Treasuries right away, obtain what is called a "Tender" form from the Fed or your bank, fill out the "Direct Deposit" section, and include a money order or certified check for $10,000. The Fed will mail you your change (the discount) and return the $10,000 at maturity (91 days).

If you wish to open an account to purchase Treasuries in the near future, complete and return the "New Account Application." Once the application is received and you are given an account number, you can then contact the Fed by phone and purchase Treasuries with a tender offer and certified check for the exact amount.

If you purchase a Treasury bill from the Fed, you must hold it to maturity, which is not the case if you have purchased it from your bank or broker in the secondary market. Your bank or broker can sell it on the open or secondary market for you at any time, but be prepared to pay a flat fee of $25 to $50 per transaction. In order to gain clients with large assets, however, some brokerage houses do not charge a fee if an investor purchases more than $100,000 of Treasury bills.

The Wall Street Journal reports on activity in the secondary market each day, under the heading **Treasury Bonds, Notes & Bills**. Find this table by using the index on the front page or the index on the first page of Section C.

Look at the excerpts from the Thursday, February 4, 1999 *Journal* on pages 276 and 277. The data represents quotations for Wednesday, February 3, 1999. Keep in mind that these bills are auctioned on Mondays, issued

TREASURY BONDS, NOTES & BILLS

Wednesday, February 3, 1999

Representative and Indicative Over-the-Counter quotations based on $1 million or more.

Treasury bond, note and bill quotes are as of mid-afternoon. Colons in bond and note bid-and-asked quotes represent 32nds; 101:01 means 101 1/32. Net changes in 32nds. Treasury bill quotes in hundredths, quoted in terms of a rate discount. Days to maturity calculated from settlement date. All yields are to maturity and based on the asked quote. Most recently auctioned treasury bonds and notes, and current 13-week and 26-week bills are boldfaced. For bonds callable prior to maturity, yields are computed to the earliest call date for issues quoted above par and to the maturity date for issues quoted below par. n-Treasury note. i-Inflation-indexed. wi-When issued. iw-Inflation-indexed when issued; daily change is expressed in basis points.

Source: Dow Jones/Cantor Fitzgerald.

U.S. Treasury strips as of 3 p.m. Eastern time, also based on transactions of $1 million or more. Colons in bid-and-asked quotes represent 32nds; 99:01 means 99 1/32. Net changes in 32nds. Yields calculated on the asked quotation. ci-stripped coupon interest. bp-Treasury bond, stripped principal. np-Treasury note, stripped principal. For bonds callable prior to maturity, yields are computed to the earliest call date for issues quoted above par and to the maturity date for issues below par.

Source: Bear, Stearns & Co. via Street Software Technology Inc.

GOVT. BONDS & NOTES

Rate	Maturity Mo/Yr	Bid	Asked	Chg.	Ask Yld.
5	Feb 99n	99:31	100:01	....	3.86
8 7/8	Feb 99n	100:02	100:04	....	4.50
5 1/2	Feb 99n	100:00	100:02	....	4.45
5 7/8	Feb 99n	100:01	100:03	....	4.35
5 7/8	Mar 99n	100:05	100:07	+ 1	4.33
6 1/4	Mar 99n	100:06	100:08	....	4.49
7	Apr 99n	100:13	100:15	....	4.45
6 3/8	Apr 99n	100:12	100:14	+ 1	4.42
6 1/2	Apr 99n	100:13	100:15	+ 1	4.41
6 3/8	May 99n	100:13	100:15	+ 1	4.59
9 1/8	May 99n	101:05	101:07	+ 1	4.56
6 1/4	May 99n	100:14	100:16	....	4.61
6 3/4	May 99n	100:19	100:21	....	4.60
6	Jun 99n	100:17	100:19	+ 1	4.48
6 3/4	Jun 99n	100:26	100:28	+ 1	4.51
6 3/8	Jul 99n	100:24	100:26	+ 1	4.50
5 7/8	Jul 99n	100:17	100:19	+ 1	4.63
6 7/8	Jul 99n	101:01	101:03	+ 1	4.58
6	Aug 99n	100:21	100:23	+ 1	4.61
8	Aug 99n	101:22	101:24	+ 1	4.61
5 7/8	Aug 99n	100:20	100:22	+ 1	4.62
6 7/8	Aug 99n	101:05	101:07	+ 1	4.66
5 3/4	Sep 99n	100:20	100:22	+ 1	4.65
7 1/8	Sep 99n	101:16	101:18	+ 1	4.65
6	Oct 99n	100:27	100:29	....	4.64
5 5/8	Oct 99n	100:19	100:21	....	4.69
7 1/2	Oct 99n	101:30	102:00	....	4.68
5 7/8	Nov 99n	100:27	100:29	+ 1	4.66
7 7/8	Nov 99n	102:11	102:13	....	4.67
5 5/8	Nov 99n	100:22	100:24	....	4.67
7 3/4	Nov 99n	102:12	102:14	....	4.67
5 5/8	Dec 99n	100:24	100:26	-1	4.69
7 3/4	Dec 99n	102:20	102:22	....	4.67
6 3/8	Jan 00n	101:14	101:16	....	4.73
5 3/8	Jan 00n	100:18	100:20	-1	4.72
7 3/4	Jan 00n	102:27	102:29	....	4.71
5 7/8	Feb 00n	101:03	101:05	....	4.71
8 1/2	Feb 00n	103:22	103:24	-1	4.72
5 1/2	Feb 00n	100:24	100:26	....	4.71
7 1/8	Feb 00n	102:13	102:15	....	4.72
5 1/2	Mar 00n	100:25	100:27	-1	4.73
6 7/8	Mar 00n	102:10	102:12	....	4.72
5 1/2	Apr 00n	100:26	100:28	-2	4.73
5 5/8	Apr 00n	101:00	101:02	....	4.72
6 3/4	Apr 00n	102:10	102:12	-1	4.74
6 3/8	May 00n	101:30	102:00	-1	4.73
8 7/8	May 00n	104:31	105:01	-2	4.75
5 1/2	May 00n	100:29	100:31	-1	4.73
6 1/4	May 00n	101:27	101:29	-1	4.74
5 3/8	Jun 00n	100:25	100:27	-1	4.74
5 7/8	Jun 00n	101:14	101:16	-1	4.75
5 3/8	Jul 00n	100:27	100:29	....	4.74
6 1/8	Jul 00n	101:28	101:30	-1	4.76
6	Aug 00n	101:24	101:26	-1	4.76
8 3/4	Aug 00n	105:24	105:26	-2	4.77
5 1/8	Aug 00n	100:15	100:17	-2	4.77
6 1/4	Aug 00n	102:05	102:07	-1	4.76
4 1/2	Sep 00n	99:17	99:19	-1	4.76
6 1/8	Sep 00n	102:02	102:04	-1	4.77
4	Oct 00n	98:21	98:23	-2	4.77
5 3/4	Oct 00n	101:18	101:20	-1	4.76
5 3/4	Nov 00n	101:19	101:21	-1	4.76
8 1/2	Nov 00n	106:07	106:09	-2	4.76
4 5/8	Nov 00n	99:23	99:25	-2	4.75
5 7/8	Nov 05n	105:13	105:15	-12	4.91
5 5/8	Feb 06n	104:04	104:06	-12	4.91
9 3/8	Feb 06	125:29	126:03	-11	4.94
6 7/8	May 06n	111:21	111:25	-11	4.93
7	Jul 06n	112:14	112:18	-12	4.96
6 1/2	Oct 06n	109:17	109:21	-12	4.97
3 3/8	Jan 07i	97:10	97:11	+ 2	3.76
6 1/4	Feb 07n	108:11	108:13	-12	4.97

U.S. TREASURY STRIPS

Mat.	Type	Bid	Asked	Chg.	Ask Yld.
Feb 99	ci	99:28	99:28	....	4.81
Feb 99	np	99:28	99:28	+ 1	5.12
May 99	ci	98:24	98:24	+ 1	4.63
May 99	np	98:24	98:24	+ 1	4.63
Aug 99	ci	97:19	97:19	....	4.66
Aug 99	np	97:19	97:19	....	4.66
Nov 99	ci	96:15	96:15	....	4.68
Nov 99	np	96:14	96:15	....	4.71
Feb 00	ci	95:09	95:10	....	4.73
Feb 00	np	95.10	95:11	....	4.70
May 00	ci	94:07	94:08	....	4.70
May 00	np	94:05	94:06	....	4.76
Aug 00	ci	93:03	93:03	....	4.73
Aug 00	np	93:01	93:02	....	4.77
Nov 00	ci	92:01	92:02	....	4.72
Nov 00	np	91:31	92:00	....	4.76
Feb 01	ci	90:30	90:31	– 1	4.72
Feb 01	np	90:30	90:31	– 1	4.72
May 01	ci	89:28	89:29	– 1	4.73
May 01	np	89:28	89:29	– 1	4.73
Aug 01	ci	88:25	88:27	– 1	4.74
Aug 01	np	88:25	88:26	– 1	4.75
Nov 01	ci	87:24	87:25	– 1	4.75
Nov 01	np	87:23	87:25	– 1	4.76
Feb 02	ci	86:19	86:21	– 4	4.79
May 02	ci	85:18	85:20	– 4	4.80
May 02	np	85:16	85:18	– 4	4.82
Aug 02	ci	84:17	84:19	– 4	4.80
Aug 02	np	84:14	84:16	– 4	4.84
Nov 02	ci	84:00	84:03	– 5	4.64
Feb 03	ci	82:18	82:21	– 2	4.79
Feb 03	np	82:18	82:21	– 2	4.79
May 03	ci	81:18	81:21	– 2	4.80
Aug 03	ci	80:23	80:26	– 2	4.76
Aug 03	np	80:21	80:25	– 2	4.77
Nov 03	ci	79:26	79:30	– 2	4.75
Feb 04	ci	78:21	78:25	– 4	4.80
Feb 04	np	78:29	79:01	– 4	4.74
May 04	ci	77:23	77:27	– 5	4.81
May 04	np	77:25	77:29	– 4	4.79
Aug 04	ci	77:04	77:08	– 4	4.72
Aug 04	np	76:26	76:30	– 4	4.80
Nov 04	ci	75:21	75:25	– 6	4.86
Nov 04	bp	75:12	75:16	– 10	4.93
Nov 04	np	75:23	75:27	– 4	4.84
Feb 05	ci	74:17	74:22	– 5	4.90
Feb 05	np	74:24	74:28	– 5	4.86
May 05	ci	73:18	73:22	– 5	4.92
May 05	bp	73:14	73:18	– 5	4.95
May 05	np	73:28	74:00	– 6	4.86
Aug 05	ci	72:20	72:25	– 6	4.93
Aug 05	bp	72:16	72:20	– 6	4.96
Aug 05	np	72:26	72:31	– 6	4.89
Nov 05	ci	71:27	72:00	– 6	4.91
Feb 08	ci	63:11	63:16	– 6	5.09
May 08	ci	62:14	62:19	– 6	5.11
Aug 08	ci	61:20	61:26	– 6	5.11
Nov 08	ci	60:21	60:26	– 6	5.15
Feb 09	ci	59:19	59:25	– 6	5.20
May 09	ci	58:22	58:28	– 6	5.22
Aug 09	ci	57:24	57:30	– 6	5.25
Nov 09	ci	56:30	57:03	– 6	5.27
Nov 09	bp	56:11	56:17	– 6	5.36
Feb 10	ci	55:30	56:04	– 6	5.31
May 10	ci	55:01	55:07	– 7	5.34
Aug 10	ci	54:07	54:12	– 7	5.35
Nov 10	ci	53:12	53:18	– 7	5.37
Feb 11	ci	52:19	52:25	....	5.38
May 11	ci	51:25	51:31	....	5.40
Aug 11	ci	50:31	51:05	....	5.42
Nov 11	ci	50:05	50:11	....	5.44
Feb 12	ci	49:11	49:18	....	5.46
May 12	ci	48:20	48:26	....	5.48
Aug 12	ci	47:27	48:01	....	5.49
Nov 12	ci	47:04	47:10	....	5.51
Feb 13	ci	46:12	46:18	....	5.52
May 13	ci	45:21	45:28	....	5.54
Aug 13	ci	44:30	45:04	....	5.55
Nov 13	ci	44:08	44:14	....	5.57
Feb 14	ci	43:16	43:22	....	5.59
May 14	ci	42:26	43:00	....	5.60
Aug 14	ci	42:05	42:11	....	5.61
Nov 14	ci	41:15	41:22	....	5.63
Feb 15	ci	40:27	41:01	+ 1	5.63
Feb 15	bp	41:11	41:17	+ 1	5.56
May 15	ci	40:07	40:13	+ 1	5.65
Nov 24	bp	24:09	24:15	– 1	5.54
Feb 25	ci	23:28	24:01	– 1	5.55
Feb 25	bp	24:01	24:07	– 1	5.52
May 25	ci	23:18	23:24	– 1	5.55
Aug 25	ci	23:08	23:14	– 1	5.54
Aug 25	bp	23:13	23:19	– 1	5.52
Nov 25	ci	23:01	23:06	– 1	5.53
Feb 26	ci	22:20	22:25	– 1	5.55
Feb 26	bp	23:01	23:06	– 1	5.48
May 26	ci	22:11	22:17	– 1	5.54
Aug 26	ci	22:02	22:08	– 1	5.54
Aug 26	bp	22:09	22:15	– 1	5.50
Nov 26	ci	21:26	22:00	– 1	5.53
Nov 26	bp	22:00	22:06	– 1	5.50
Feb 27	ci	21:23	21:29	– 1	5.49
Feb 27	bp	21:27	22:01	– 1	5.47
May 27	ci	21:07	21:13	– 1	5.53
Aug 27	ci	21:07	21:13	– 1	5.48
Aug 27	bp	21:13	21:18	– 1	5.45
Nov 27	ci	21:15	21:21	– 1	5.39

TREASURY BILLS

← **Treasury Bills**

Maturity	Days to Mat.	Bid	Asked	Chg.	Ask Yld.
Feb 11 '99	7	4.23	4.15	–0.19	4.21
Feb 18 '99	14	4.19	4.11	–0.17	4.17
Feb 25 '99	21	4.19	4.11	–0.19	4.18
Mar 04 '99	28	4.34	4.26	–0.16	4.33
Mar 11 '99	35	4.32	4.28	–0.15	4.36
Mar 18 '99	42	4.34	4.30	–0.12	4.38
Mar 25 '99	49	4.32	4.28	–0.13	4.36
Apr 01 '99	56	4.37	4.33	–0.11	4.42
Apr 08 '99	63	4.36	4.34	–0.11	4.43
Apr 15 '99	70	4.39	4.37	–0.10	4.47
Apr 22 '99	77	4.39	4.37	–0.12	4.47
Apr 29 '99	84	4.39	4.37	–0.10	4.47
May 06 '99	**91**	**4.38**	**4.37**	**–0.03**	**4.48**
May 13 '99	98	4.34	4.32	–0.11	4.43
May 20 '99	105	4.36	4.34	–0.09	4.46
May 27 '99	112	4.38	4.36	–0.10	4.48
Jun 03 '99	119	4.35	4.33	–0.10	4.45
Jun 10 '99	126	4.37	4.35	–0.09	4.48
Jun 17 '99	133	4.37	4.35	–0.09	4.48
Jun 24 '99	140	4.35	4.33	–0.09	4.47
Jul 01 '99	147	4.34	4.32	–0.09	4.46
Jul 08 '99	154	4.35	4.33	–0.09	4.47
Jul 15 '99	161	4.35	4.33	–0.09	4.48
Jul 22 '99	168	4.38	4.36	–0.08	4.51
Jul 29 '99	**175**	**4.34**	**4.32**	**–0.03**	**4.47**
Aug 05 '99	182	4.39	4.38	–0.02	4.54
Aug 19 '99	196	4.40	4.38	–0.06	4.54
Sep 16 '99	224	4.39	4.37	–0.06	4.54
Oct 14 '99	252	4.40	4.38	–0.04	4.55
Nov 12 '99	281	4.40	4.38	–0.04	4.56
Dec 09 '99	308	4.39	4.37	–0.03	4.56
Jan 06 '00	336	4.38	4.36	–0.01	4.56
Feb 03 '00	364	4.37	4.36	....	4.57

← **91-Day T-Bill** (May 06 '99)

Source: *The Wall Street Journal*, February 4, 1999. Reprinted by permission of *The Wall Street Journal*,

On Wednesday, February 3, 1999, the 91-day T-bill rate on the open (secondary) market was 4.38% for bills auctioned on Monday, February 1, 1999, to be issued on Thursday, February 4, 1999, and maturing 13 weeks later on Thursday, May 6, 1999.

TREASURY BILLS

Maturity	Days to Mat.	Bid	Asked	Chg.	Ask Yld.
Feb 11 '99	7	4.23	4.15	– 0.19	4.21
Feb 18 '99	14	4.19	4.11	– 0.17	4.17
Feb 25 '99	21	4.19	4.11	– 0.19	4.18
Mar 04 '99	28	4.34	4.26	– 0.16	4.33
Mar 11 '99	35	4.32	4.28	– 0.15	4.36
Mar 18 '99	42	4.34	4.30	– 0.12	4.38
Mar 25 '99	49	4.32	4.28	– 0.13	. 4.36
Apr 01 '99	56	4.37	4.33	– 0.11	4.42
Apr 08 '99	63	4.36	4.34	– 0.11	4.43
Apr 15 '99	70	4.39	4.37	– 0.10	4.47
Apr 22 '99	77	4.39	4.37	– 0.12	4.47
Apr 29 '99	84	4.39	4.37	– 0.10	4.47
May 06 '99	**91**	**4.38**	**4.37**	**– 0.03**	**4.48**
May 13 '99	98	4.34	4.32	– 0.11	4.43
May 20 '99	105	4.36	4.34	– 0.09	4.46
May 27 '99	112	4.38	4.36	– 0.10	4.48
Jun 03 '99	119	4.35	4.33	– 0.10	4.45
Jun 10 '99	126	4.37	4.35	– 0.09	4.48
Jun 17 '99	133	4.37	4.35	– 0.09	4.48
Jun 24 '99	140	4.35	4.33	– 0.09	4.47
Jul 01 '99	147	4.34	4.32	– 0.09	4.46
Jul 08 '99	154	4.35	4.33	– 0.09	4.47
Jul 15 '99	161	4.35	4.33	– 0.09	4.48
Jul 22 '99	168	4.38	4.36	– 0.08	4.51
Jul 29 '99	**175**	**4.34**	**4.32**	**– 0.03**	**4.47**
Aug 05 '99	182	4.39	4.38	– 0.02	4.54
Aug 19 '99	196	4.40	4.38	– 0.06	4.54
Sep 16 '99	224	4.39	4.37	– 0.06	4.54
Oct 14 '99	252	4.40	4.38	– 0.04	4.55
Nov 12 '99	281	4.40	4.38	– 0.04	4.56
Dec 09 '99	308	4.39	4.37	– 0.03	4.56
Jan 06 '00	336	4.38	4.36	– 0.01	4.56
Feb 03 '00	364	4.37	4.36	.....	4.57

on Thursdays, and mature 13 weeks later (also on a Thursday). Thus, using the report in the February 4, 1999 *Journal*, you know that the latest 91-day bill included in the report was auctioned on Monday, February 1, 1999, to be issued on Thursday, February 4, 1999. It will mature 13 weeks later on Thursday, May 6, 1999. (Note the bold-face type for the 13- and 26-week maturity dates.)

On February 3, 1999 that bill carried a discount rate (bid) of 4.38 percent. This figure is located in the row opposite the date under the column headed "Bid." Buyers (bidders) paid a price (less than $10,000) that would yield 4.38 percent if the Treasury bill were held to maturity and cashed in for $10,000. Sellers on February 3, 1999 were asking a higher price (lower interest rate), equivalent to 4.37 percent. The last column gives a true yield of 4.48 percent. (The other maturity dates are for older bills and for bills with maturities of more than 91 days.)

It is now time to complete this discussion of short-term interest rates with a description of how you can track the yield on your own interest-earning investments and compare them with market rates.

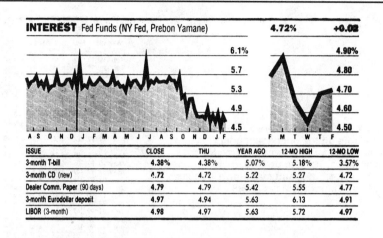

INTEREST Fed Funds (NY Fed, Prebon Yamane)			4.72%		+0.02
ISSUE	CLOSE	THU	YEAR AGO	12-MO HIGH	12-MO LOW
3-month T-bill	4.38%	4.38%	5.07%	5.18%	3.57%
3-month CD (new)	4.72	4.72	5.22	5.27	4.72
Dealer Comm. Paper (90 days)	4.79	4.79	5.42	5.55	4.77
3-month Eurodollar deposit	4.97	4.94	5.63	6.13	4.91
LIBOR (3-month)	4.98	4.97	5.63	5.72	4.97

TRACKING SHORT-TERM INTEREST RATES

Every day you can use the **Markets Diary** report on the left side of the first page of the *Journal*'s last section (C1) to follow some of the most important short-term interest rates. Consult the excerpt form the Monday, February 8, 1999 edition above, starting with the chart labeled **Interest**, which displays the *federal funds* rate for the preceding 18 months. This is the rate banks charge one another for overnight loans of reserves in amounts of $1 million or more. The federal funds rate was 4.72 percent on Friday, February 5, 1999. Four more interest rates follow. Except for Treasury bills, which were discussed above, these quotes are for instruments purchased by financial institutions in very large amounts. Nonetheless, they provide a good daily snapshot of current short-term rates. Note that the yields increase with increased risk and reduced liquidity. The Friday, February 5, 1999 rates were *3-month T-bills*, 4.38 percent; new *3-month Certificates of Deposit*, 4.72 percent; 90-day *Dealer Commercial Paper* (short-term corporate debt), 4.79 percent; *3-month Eurodollar deposit* ("dollar" denominated deposits held at European banks), 4.97 percent; and 3-month *LIBOR* (London Interbank Offer Rate), 4.98 percent.

You can follow an even larger array of interest rates each day in **Money Rates**, a report that lists the current yields on most of the major money-market interest-rate instruments. Look for it in the front-page index of the first and last sections. The example from the Thursday, February 9, 1999 *Journal*

on page 280 reports the rates for Monday, February 8, 1999. **Money Rates** tracks the following domestic rates: *Prime Rate* (the rate banks charge their corporate customers), *Discount Rate* (the rate the Federal Reserve charges its member banks), *Federal Funds*, *Call Money* (rates banks charge brokers), *Commercial Paper*, *Dealer Commercial Paper* (commercial paper sold through dealers), *Certificates of Deposit*, *Bankers Acceptances* (rates on bank-backed business credit used to finance international trade), *Treasury Bills*, *Overnight Repurchase Rate* (the dealer financing rate for overnight sale and repurchase of Treasury securities), *Federal Home Loan Mortgage Corp.* and *Federal National Mortgage Association* (yields on a variety of mortgages), and *Merrill Lynch Ready Assets Trust* (a money-market mutual fund). **Money Rates** also tracks foreign money-market rates, including: *Euro Commercial Paper* (European commercial paper), *London Late Eurodollars*, *London Interbank Offered Rates*, *Euro LIBOR* (similar to LIBOR), *Euro Interbank Offered Rates* (similar to LIBOR), and *Foreign Prime Rates*. These interest rates are discussed more thoroughly below.

Federal Funds Rate

Banks lend reserves to one another overnight at the federal funds rate. This practice is profitable for lender banks, because they earn interest on funds ($1 million or more) that would otherwise be idle, and it is profitable for the borrower banks, because they acquire reserves that enable them to make additional loans and still meet their reserve requirement.

Notice that under *Federal Funds* in the **Money Rates** column on page 280, four different percentages are listed: 4⅞ percent high, 4⅝ percent low, 4¾ percent near closing bid, and 4⅞ percent offered. These numbers show that during trading on Monday, February 8, 1999, 4⅞ percent was the highest interest rate proposed by a potential lender bank, and 4⅝ percent was the lowest interest rate proposed by a prospective borrower. The last two percentages describe the state of trading near the end of the day: lender banks were offering 4⅞ percent, and borrower banks were bidding 4¾ percent. Use the closing bid (4¾ percent) when following this interest rate.

This rate is closely watched as an indicator of Federal Reserve monetary policy. A rising federal-funds rate is a sign that the Fed is draining reserves from the banks via its open market operations, forcing some banks to borrow excess reserves from other banks and thereby driving up the federal funds rate. A falling rate would indicate an easy money policy. But beware: Sharp fluctuations occur from day to day. This is such a short-term market that the rate changes on an "as needed" basis.

MONEY RATES

Monday, February 8, 1999

The key U.S. and foreign annual interest rates below are a guide to general levels but don't always represent actual transactions.

PRIME RATE: 7.75% (effective 11/18/98). The base rate on corporate loans posted by at least 75% of the nation's 30 largest banks.

DISCOUNT RATE: 4.50% (effective 11/17/98). The charge on loans to depository institutions by the Federal Reserve Banks.

FEDERAL FUNDS: 4 7/8% high, 4 5/8% low, 4 3/4% near closing bid, 4 7/8% offered. Reserves traded among commercial banks for overnight use in amounts of $1 million or more. Source: Prebon Yamane (U.S.A.) Inc.

CALL MONEY: 6.50% (effective 11/18/98). The charge on loans to brokers on stock exchange collateral. Source: Telerate.

COMMERCIAL PAPER placed directly by General Electric Capital Corp.: 4.82% 30 to 38 days; 4.79% 39 to 53 days; 4.82% 54 to 126 days; 4.79% 127 to 144 days; 4.80% 145 to 199 days; 4.78% 200 to 270 days.

EURO COMMERCIAL PAPER placed directly by General Electric Capital Corp.: 3.10% 30 days; 3.07% two months; 3.05% three months; 3.00% four months; 2.99% five months; 2.99% six months.

DEALER COMMERCIAL PAPER: High-grade unsecured notes sold through dealers by major corporations: 4.82% 30 days; 4.83% 60 days; 4.83% 90 days.

CERTIFICATES OF DEPOSIT: 4.61% one month; 4.67% two months; 4.73% three months; 4.96% six months; 5.05% one year. Average of top rates paid by major New York banks on primary new issues of negotiable C.D.s, usually on amounts of $1 million and more. The minimum unit is $100,000. Typical rates in the secondary market: 4.87% one month; 4.90% three months; 4.95% six months.

BANKERS ACCEPTANCES: 4.78% 30 days; 4.77% 60 days; 4.77% 90 days; 4.75% 120 days; 4.75% 150 days; 4.75% 180 days. Offered rates of negotiable, bank-backed business credit instruments typically financing an import order.

LONDON LATE EURODOLLARS: 4 15/16% - 4 7/8% one month; 5 1/4% - 5 3/16% two months; 5 5/16% - 5 1/4% three months; 5 5/16% - 5 1/4% four months; 5 5/16% - 5 1/4% five months; 5 11/32% - 5 9/32% six months.

LONDON INTERBANK OFFERED RATES (LIBOR): 4.93813% one month; 5.0000% three months; 5.04406% six months; 5.18751% one year. British Bankers' Association average of interbank offered rates for dollar deposits in the London market based on quotations at 16 major banks. Effective rate for contracts entered into two days from date appearing at top of this column.

EURO LIBOR: 3.15828% one month; 3.11469% three months; 3.04938% six months; 3.03141% one year. British Bankers' Association average of interbank offered rates for euro deposits in the London market based on quotations at 16 major banks. Effective rate for contracts entered into two days from date appearing at top of this column.

EURO INTERBANK OFFERED RATES (EURIBOR): 3.156% one month; 3.107% three months; 3.044% six months; 3.026% one year. European Banking Federation-sponsored rate among 57 Euro zone banks.

FOREIGN PRIME RATES: Canada 6.75%; Germany 3.11%; Japan 1.500%; Switzerland 3.125%; Britain 5.50%. These rate indications aren't directly comparable; lending practices vary widely by location.

TREASURY BILLS: Results of the Monday, February 8, 1999, auction of short-term U.S. government bills, sold at a discount from face value in units of $10,000 to $1 million: 4.42% 13 weeks; 4.42% 26 weeks.

OVERNIGHT REPURCHASE RATE: 4.78%. Dealer financing rate for overnight sale and repurchase of Treasury securities. Source: Telerate.

FEDERAL HOME LOAN MORTGAGE CORP. (Freddie Mac): Posted yields on 30-year mortgage commitments. Delivery within 30 days 6.81%, 60 days 6.85%, standard conventional fixed-rate mortgages; 5.625%, 2% rate capped one-year adjustable rate mortgages. Source: Telerate.

FEDERAL NATIONAL MORTGAGE ASSOCIATION (Fannie Mae): Posted yields on 30 year mortgage commitments (priced at par) for delivery within 30 days 6.75%, 60 days 6.80%, standard conventional fixed rate-mortgages; 5.70%, 6/2 rate capped one-year adjustable rate mortgages. Source: Telerate.

MERRILL LYNCH READY ASSETS TRUST: 4.55%. Annualized average rate of return after expenses for the past 30 days; not a forecast of future returns.

CONSUMER PRICE INDEX: December, 163.9, up 1.6% from a year ago. Bureau of Labor Statistics.

Investor's Tip

- Follow the federal funds chart under Interest in the Markets Diary on page C1, because it presents a weekly average that smoothes out sharp daily movements.

Commercial Paper

Money Rates above lists 4.82 percent as the going rate for 54- to 126-day commercial paper on Monday, February 8, 1999. Commercial paper is short-term, unsecured debt issued by the very largest corporations. It is the equivalent of the Treasury bill, so in order to attract investors, its rate of interest has to be higher.

Corporations issue commercial paper to avoid the higher interest rate (prime rate) levied by banks on business borrowers, and it is issued for maturities up to 270 days. There are very large minimums set on commercial paper purchases (often in excess of $1 million), and this instrument is very popular with money-market funds.

Prime Rate
This is the rate that large commercial banks charge their best corporate customers. Although it does not change as frequently as other market rates, it is an important indicator of supply and demand in the capital markets. Banks raise the prime rate whenever they have difficulty meeting the current demand for funds or when the Federal Reserve drains away their reserves through its open market operations.

Bankers Acceptances
Bankers acceptances are used to finance international trade. Large institutions, investment companies, and money-market mutual funds purchase bankers acceptances because they offer high yields for relatively short periods of time. Individual investors benefit from the higher yields when they invest in funds that include these instruments.

Call Rates
The call rate is the rate that banks charge brokers, who generally add 1 percent on loans to their clients.

Key Interest Rates
Every Tuesday, under the heading **Key Interest Rates**, the *Journal* reports the weekly average of most important interest rates, including long-term rates. See the example on page 282 from the Tuesday, February 9, 1999 edition of the *Journal*. In the week ended Friday, February 5, 1999 *Treasury bills* averaged 4.40 percent; *Commercial paper* 4.76 percent; *Certificates of Deposit*, 4.88 percent; and *Federal funds*, 4.75 percent. Once again, notice the interest rate hierarchy.

Short-Term Interest Rates Chart
The *Journal* provides a **Short-Term Interest Rates** chart each Thursday in the daily **Credit Markets** report (consult the front-page index of the first and last sections for location of the *Credit Markets* article), as in the example from the Thursday, February 4, 1999 edition on page 282. The **Short-Term Interest Rates** chart portrays Federal Funds, 3-Month Commercial Paper, and 3-Month T-Bill rates over the past six months.

Key Interest Rates

Annualized interest rates on certain investments as reported by the Federal Reserve Board on a weekly-average basis:

	Week Ended:	
	Feb. 5, 1999	Jan. 29, 1999
Treasury bills (90 day)-a	4.40	4.35
Commrcl paper (Non-Finl., 90 day)-a	4.76	4.75
Commrcl paper (Finl., 90 day)-a	4.80	4.78
Certfs of Deposit (Resale, 3 month)	4.88	4.86
Certfs of Deposit (Resale, 6 month)	4.91	4.87
Federal funds (Overnight)-b	4.75	4.66
Eurodollars (90 day)-b	4.83	4.83
Treasury bills (one year)-c	4.61	4.51
Treasury notes (two year)-c	4.73	4.59
Treasury notes (three year)-c	4.75	4.58
Treasury notes (five year)-c	4.76	4.56
Treasury notes (ten year)-c	4.84	4.67
Treasury bonds (30 year)-c	5.26	5.12

a-Discounted rates. b-Week ended Wednesday, Feb. 3, 1999 and Wednesday, Jan. 27, 1999. c-Yields, adjusted for constant maturity.

Source: *The Wall Street Journal*, February 9, 1999. Reprinted by permission of *The Wall Street Journal*, ©1999 Dow Jones & Company, Inc. All rights reserved.

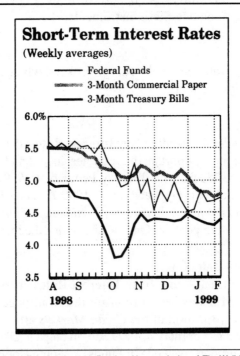

Short-Term Interest Rates

(Weekly averages)

——— Federal Funds

▓▓▓▓ 3-Month Commercial Paper

——— 3-Month Treasury Bills

Source: *The Wall Street Journal*, February 4, 1999. Reprinted by permission of *The Wall Street Journal*, ©1999 Dow Jones & Company, Inc. All rights reserved.

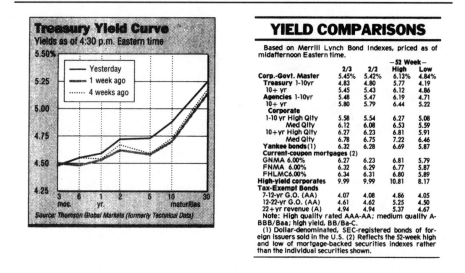

YIELD COMPARISONS

Based on Merrill Lynch Bond Indexes, priced as of midafternoon Eastern time.

	2/3	2/2	−52 Week− High	Low
Corp.-Govt. Master	5.45%	5.42%	6.13%	4.84%
Treasury 1-10yr	4.83	4.80	5.77	4.19
10+yr	5.45	5.43	6.12	4.86
Agencies 1-10yr	5.48	5.47	6.19	4.71
10+yr	5.80	5.79	6.44	5.22
Corporate				
1-10 yr High Qlty	5.58	5.54	6.27	5.08
Med Qlty	6.12	6.08	6.53	5.59
10+yr High Qlty	6.27	6.23	6.81	5.91
Med Qlty	6.78	6.75	7.22	6.46
Yankee bonds(1)	6.32	6.28	6.69	5.87
Current-coupon mortgages (2)				
GNMA 6.00%	6.27	6.23	6.81	5.79
FNMA 6.00%	6.32	6.29	6.77	5.87
FHLMC6.00%	6.34	6.31	6.80	5.89
High-yield corporates	9.99	9.99	10.81	8.17
Tax-Exempt Bonds				
7-12-yr G.O. (AA)	4.07	4.08	4.86	4.05
12-22-yr G.O. (AA)	4.61	4.62	5.25	4.50
22+yr revenue (A)	4.94	4.94	5.37	4.67

Note: High quality rated AAA-AA; medium quality A-BBB/Baa; high yield, BB/Ba-C.
(1) Dollar-denominated, SEC-registered bonds of foreign issuers sold in the U.S. (2) Reflects the 52-week high and low of mortgage-backed securities indexes rather than the individual securities shown.

Source: *The Wall Street Journal*, February 4, 1999. Reprinted by permission of *The Wall Street Journal*, ©1999 Dow Jones & Company, Inc. All rights reserved.

Treasury Yield Curve

The yield curve charts the relationship between interest rates and length of maturity for all debt instruments at a particular time. A normal yield curve slopes upward, so that longer-term investments have higher yields. Thus, short-term Treasury bill rates are usually lower than long-term Treasury bond rates. Abnormal yield curves can be flat, inverted, or peaked in the middle (higher short-term rates than long-term rates).

The Wall Street Journal publishes a **Treasury Yield Curve** chart daily with the **Credit Markets** article. See the excerpt from the Thursday, February 4, 1999 edition above. You can see the normal pattern of rising rates associated with longer maturities.

A **Yield Comparisons** table accompanies the chart.

CONCLUSION

If the risk and bother of investing in stocks, bonds, and commodities seems excessive to you, a wide variety of relatively risk-free and highly liquid money-market instruments is available to you. Use *The Wall Street Journal*'s data services to check the hierarchy of rates, and then choose the instruments that's right for you.

P A R T

FINE-TUNING: REFINING YOUR SENSE OF THE ECONOMY AND THE RIGHT INVESTMENT DECISION

13

LEADING ECONOMIC INDICATORS

N OW THAT YOU HAVE EXAMINED THE BUSINESS CYCLE in detail and learned to use *The Wall Street Journal*'s statistical series, you may be looking for a device to make analysis somewhat easier. Perhaps, while wading through the stream of data, you felt the need for a single indicator that could predict changes in the business cycle. You wanted something akin to the meteorologist's barometer, to inform you of rain or shine without a detailed examination of cloud formations.

Unfortunately, economists have never agreed on a single economic indicator to predict the future. Some indicators are better than others, but none is consistently accurate; all give a false signal on occasion. To deal with this, economists have devised a composite, or combination, of statistical series drawn from a broad spectrum of economic activity, each of which tends to move up or down ahead of the general trend of the business cycle. These series are referred to as leading indicators because of their predictive quality, and 10 have been combined into the *composite index of leading economic indicators*.

The components of the index are:

1. Average weekly hours of production of non-supervisory workers, manufacturing.

2. Average weekly initial claims for unemployment insurance.

3. Manufacturers' new orders in 1992 dollars, consumer goods and materials industries.

4. Vendor performance—slower deliveries diffusion index.

5. Manufacturers' new orders in 1992 dollars, non-defense capital goods industries.

6. New private housing units authorized by local building permits.

7. Stock prices, 500 common stocks.

8. Money supply—M2—in 1992 dollars.

9. Interest rate spread, 10-year Treasury bonds less federal funds.

10. University of Michigan index of consumer expectations.

There are three general criteria for inclusion in the index. First, each series must accurately lead the business cycle. Second, the various series should provide comprehensive coverage of the economy by representing a wide and diverse range of economic activity. And, third, each series must be available monthly, with only a brief lag until publication, and must be free from large subsequent revisions.

The leading indicators meet these criteria, and weaving these series into a composite provides a statistic that is more reliable and less erratic than any individual component by itself.

Finally, the component indicators measure activity in physical units, current dollars, constant dollars, percentages, interest rates, and index form. This variety of measurements is reduced to an index with 1992 assigned a base value of 100. All other months and years are expressed as a percentage of the base year.

The September index, published in the Wednesday, November 4, 1998 issue of *The Wall Street Journal*, is representative. The series usually appears around the first of the month. The first and second paragraphs (see page 289) inform you that the index remained unchanged at 105.5 (1992 = 100) in September. The illustration on page 290 from the August 5, 1998 edition is an example of the front-page chart that frequently accompanies the article.

You can see from Chart 13–1 on page 291 that the index did a good job of forecasting recession except in 1981–1982 and 1990–91. For all other instances, the index forecast the downturn by at least five months. In 1981–82, you should observe that the two-month lead is a difficult call, because the index double-clutched just prior to the recession's start. The first pump on the clutch is at least a half-year before the downturn begins. For 1990–91 there was no advance warning, although the index had been lethargic in the late 80s. This lends credence to the observation made earlier that there might have been no recession in 1990–91 had it not been for the Persian Gulf crisis.

Key Economic Gauge Again Shows No Change

By a WALL STREET JOURNAL Staff Reporter

WASHINGTON—The Conference Board's index of leading economic indicators remained unchanged for the second consecutive month, reinforcing expectations that the economy's remarkable growth spurt during the past few years is nearing an end.

The index, designed to predict economic activity six to nine months in advance, languished at 105.5 in September, where it has been since July. The Conference Board, a private research group, noted that the latest readings are still significantly higher than they were a year ago.

"From the indicators, we don't see a recession looming," said Michael Boldin, the Conference Board's research director. But, he said, the economy may find it difficult to match the pace of growth it has enjoyed in recent years.

As a rule of thumb, three or more months of sustained declines in the index indicate the beginning of an economic contraction. Many forecasters foresee a slowdown in the economy in the coming months, but say it's too early to predict a recession.

Five components of the index fell in September; declining the most were stock prices, the spread between long-term and short-term interest rates, and building permits. Four components rose during the month, with money supply the most significant positive indicator.

The board's index of coincident indicators for September, which looks at the economy's current condition, held steady from August. The lagging indicators index, which looks at the past, fell 0.1%.

LEADING INDICATORS

Here are the net contributions of the components of the Conference Board's index of leading indicators. The index didn't change in September, standing at 105.5.

	Aug. 1998	Sept. 1998
Workweek	.00	.00p
Unemployment claims	.07	.03
Orders for consumer goods	−.01	.00p
Slower deliveries	.01	.03
Plant and equipment orders	.06	−.03p
Building permits	.03	−.05
Interest rate spread	−.03	−.10
Stock prices	−.15	−.11
Money supply, M2	.11	.24p
Consumer expectations	−.02	−.05

The seasonally adjusted index numbers (1992=100) for September, and the change from August, are:

Index of leading indicators	105.5p	0.0p
Index of coincident indicators	121.0p	0.0p
Index of lagging indicators	106.5p	−0.1p

The ratio of coincident to lagging indicators was 1.14, in September, the same as August.

p-Preliminary. R-revised.

Index of Leading Economic Indicators—First and Second Paragraphs

WASHINGTON—The Conference Board's index of leading economic indicators remained unchanged for the second consecutive month, reinforcing expectations that the economy's remarkable growth spurt during the past few years is nearing an end.

The index, designed to predict economic activity six to nine months in advance, languished at 105.5 in September, where it has been since July. The Conference Board, a private research group, noted that the latest readings are still significantly higher than they were a year ago.

Leading Indicators

Index (1992 = 100)

COMPOSITE OF KEY INDICATORS of
future economic activity fell in June to
105 of the 1992 average from 105.2 in May,
the Conference Board reports.

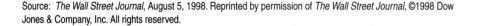

But you can also see the false alarms of 1962, 1966, 1984, and 1987. In
each case the index fell for at least three consecutive months, although no
recession followed.

The 1962 decline followed on the heels of President Kennedy's forced
rollback of Big Steel's price increase. The stock market went into shock and
business activity slowed, but you can see that the setback was brief. This
decline was clearly a random event and of no cyclical significance.

The indicators' 1966 setback was more like developments in the 1980s.
The Vietnam War had begun and inflation was climbing. The Fed tightened
in response, in order to raise interest rates and curb consumer and business
demand. Housing starts crashed, and it was "nip-and-tuck" for a while, but
the Fed quickly eased when alarm spread so that recession never took hold.

The Fed faced similar conditions and tightened in 1984 as the cycle
came roaring back from the 1981–1982 recession. The economy went into
the doldrums temporarily, and the leading indicators fell, but once again the
Fed eased as soon as inflation subsided and the economy emerged with only
a scratch.

CHART 13–1 Composite Index of 10 Leading Indicators

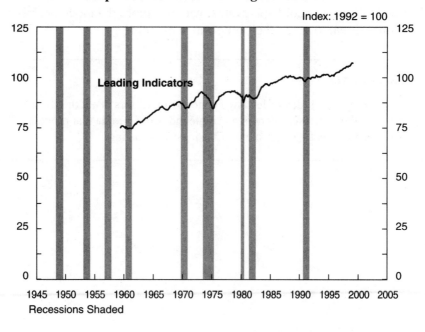

Index: 1992 = 100

1945 1950 1955 1960 1965 1970 1975 1980 1985 1990 1995 2000 2005
Recessions Shaded

Source: The Conference Board, *Business Cycle Indicators*, Series G0M910.

The October 1987 stock market crash was as severe as 1962's decline, but this time the market's own dynamic created the problem, rather than the actions of the president. Nonetheless, fears of recession swirled about for several months, and the composite index headed south. Soon, however, everyone realized the crash had nothing to do with the economy's fundamentals, and concern evaporated as the index snapped back.

To conclude, keep in mind that this statistic is not an analytical tool that permits you to probe beneath the cycle's surface in order to analyze its dynamic. The composite does not provide a step-by-step diagnosis that reveals the cycle's rhythm. It does not disclose the forces that lead from one set of conditions to another. It only averages a number of convenient series that are themselves leading indicators, but are otherwise unrelated.

This series is of interest solely because it provides an omen of future events. You need all the statistical reports appearing in the *Journal* in order to build an understanding of the timing, direction, and strength of the business cycle. After all, a meteorologist needs more than a barometer, and most

Americans who make decisions in the business community, or wish to be fully informed of current economic events, need far more than a crude, general directional signal to guide their long-range planning.

Investor's Tip

- The composite index of leading economic indicators is not the square root of the universe. There is no single index or formula that provides all the answers to the problem of business forecasting.

14

INVENTORIES

A DESTABILIZING FORCE

INVENTORIES ARE STOCKS OF GOODS ON HAND: raw materials, goods in process, or finished products. Individual businesses use them to bring stability to their operations, and yet you'll see that they actually have a destabilizing effect on the business cycle.

Businesses view inventories as a necessary evil. A manufacturer, wholesaler, or retailer, can't live from hand to mouth, continually filling sales orders from current production. Stocks of goods "on the shelf" are a cushion against unexpected orders and slowdowns in production. On the other hand, inventories are an investment in working capital and incur an interest cost. If the firm borrows capital to maintain inventories, the direct interest cost is obvious. Even if the firm has not borrowed, however, working capital tied up in inventories represents an interest cost. Any funds invested in inventories could have earned the going interest rate in the money market, and this loss can substantially crimp profits.

Therefore, business attempts to keep inventories at an absolute minimum consistent with smooth operations. For a very large business, literally millions of dollars are at stake. This is why you see modern automated cash registers (i.e., the ones that automatically "read" the black and white bar code on packages) in large chain supermarkets and retail establishments. These cash registers came into use not chiefly because they record your purchases more quickly (which of course they do), but because they also tie into a computer network that keeps track of inventories of thousands of items on a daily basis.

But why do inventories, so necessary to the smooth functioning of an individual business, exacerbate the business cycle?

Consider the upswing of the cycle first. As demand increases rapidly, businesses must boost production to meet the growing volume of orders. If they are not quick enough, and sales grow more rapidly than output, an unplanned drawdown of inventories will occur as orders are filled. This is known as involuntary inventory depletion. If inventories are severely depleted, shortages can result and sales may be jeopardized. To protect itself against such developments once it is confident of the unfolding expansion, business will boost output and defensively accumulate inventories more rapidly than its sales are growing. Since all firms are stockpiling to prevent shortages, industrial production increases more vigorously than it otherwise would, accentuating the cyclical expansion and the swift rise in capacity utilization. For the entire economy, production grows more rapidly than sales. This, of course, hastens the inevitable decrease in labor productivity and increase in unit labor costs associated with this phase of the cycle. Hence, inventory accumulation adds to inflationary pressures.

Now consider the downswing of the cycle. No firm willingly maintains production in a sales slump because unsold goods would pile up on the shelf. As sales weaken and fall, business curtails production in order to prevent involuntary inventory accumulation. Indeed, once business recognizes the severity of the slump, it will begin to liquidate the large volume of (now unnecessary) inventories built up during the previous expansion. These stockpiles of goods are no longer needed and can be disposed of. But as goods are sold from inventories, output and employment are reduced more than sales because orders can be filled from inventories rather than from current production. This aggravates the cycle's downturn.

Thus, inventories play an important destabilizing role in the cycle through their influence on industrial production, boosting output during expansion and depressing it during a slump. This destabilizing influence is compounded by inventory's impact on inflation. When rapid expansion is heightened by inventory accumulation, contributing to inflationary pressures, business firms increase their inventory buildup. They want to stockpile goods at current prices and sell them later at inflated prices. And when inventory liquidation in a recession contributes to deflationary pressures, falling prices can trigger a panic selloff, which drives prices down even more steeply.

Here's how it works. Business stockpiles goods during the expansionary phase of the cycle to prevent involuntary inventory depletion and shortages, and prices start to rise. Firms quickly discover that goods held in inventory increase in value along with the general rise in prices. They have an incentive to buy now while prices are low, hold the goods in inventory, and

sell them later at higher prices and profits. If prices are rising rapidly enough, widespread speculation can set in, which adds to the general increase in production and reinforces the inflation.

Recall, for example, the rapid increase in sugar prices in 1973–1974. Sugar manufacturers and industrial users of sugar (canners, soft drink bottlers, confectioners, and bakers) produced sugar and sweetened products and held them in inventory while their prices were low, hoping to make large profits from sales when their prices increased. This speculative stockpiling contributed to the price increase by bidding up production (and costs) out of proportion to sales.

Of course, when the inevitable contraction comes, liquidation of the inventory overhang helps halt the inflationary spiral. Businesses panic when faced with the prospect of selling at a price that will not recoup interest costs. If sufficiently severe, the selloff can force prices down. More important, output plummets and layoffs mount as orders are filled from the shelf. Liquidation continues until inventories are in proper relation to sales.

Thus, speculative inventory accumulation and liquidation become a self-fulfilling prophecy. Firms pile up inventories in anticipation of a price increase, and the large volume of orders bids prices upward. When the recession begins, firms sell inventories in haste, afraid of a drop in prices, and the selloff forces prices downward.

Now you understand why inventories and their relationship to sales are such important economic indicators. They not only confirm the stage of the cycle, they also provide advance warning of turning points and of the strength or severity of impending boom and bust.

And you also understand the irony that inventories exacerbate the business cycle, even though individual businesses use inventories to smooth operations. Production will rise more rapidly than sales during cyclical expansion, the difference accumulating as inventories, thereby forcing capacity utilization and costs up more rapidly, intensifying the expansion and hastening inflation and recession. After recession begins, firms will reduce output more rapidly than the drop in sales, drawing upon inventories to make up the difference. Therefore, the cycle's downswing will be more severe.

RECENT EXPERIENCE

Inventory accumulation and liquidation reinforce the business cycle. The consumer sets the cycle's pace; inventories exacerbate it. The cyclical experience of the early 1970s will serve as an illustration, followed by an examination of more recent developments.

To begin with, *The Wall Street Journal* publishes the Commerce Department's inventory, sales, and inventory/sales ratio data around the middle of each month (see page 296).

Business Inventories Fell 0.1% in May, The First Decline in Almost Two Years

By ROYCE T. HALL

Staff Reporter of THE WALL STREET JOURNAL

WASHINGTON—Business inventories decreased in May for the first time in almost two years, providing further evidence of a midyear economic slowdown.

The Commerce Department said business inventories fell 0.1% in May, compared with a modest 0.1% increase in April. The May drop in inventories largely reflected a sharp 1% decline in retail inventories as sales climbed 1.2%, the department said.

The tepid two-month performance follows a booming first quarter, in which businesses increased their inventories by a massive $106 billion. Indeed, that huge buildup was a major factor in the first quarter's 5.4% surge in gross domestic product and led most forecasters to project slower growth at an annual rate for the rest of the year as companies draw down stockpiles.

"The last few quarters have seen inventory build up very rapidly," said Ian Shepherdson, chief economist for New York-based HSBC Securities Inc. "There's been this thought that, sooner or later, there has to be some correction. It now looks as though it might be beginning to happen." Though the economy isn't plunging into recession, Mr. Shepherdson said the inventory numbers show that "some of the froth on the top of the economy is now not going to be there."

Still, analysts said they don't expect the pattern of falling inventories to continue through the end of the year. "It's just a second- and third-quarter phenomenon," said David Orr, chief capital-markets economist with First Union Corp., Charlotte, N.C.

Tim Martin, senior economist at Charlotte-based NationsBank, also said that while the inventory slowdown probably would continue through the third quarter, a lot depends on the General Motors Corp. strike. "It's hard to imagine the GM strike will last through the fourth quarter," he said. "They'll be building up their inventory as quickly as they can because they'll be pretty far depleted."

Another factor likely to prevent a deep cut in inventories is that consumer spending has continued to be strong. Indeed, despite the earlier buildup in inventories, the ratio of inventory to sales remained a relatively lean 1.38 to 1 in May—the same level as in April—and has hovered near that record-low level since the beginning of last year.

Separately, the Labor Department reported that prices of goods purchased by U.S. importers declined in June, falling 0.5% from May amid a drop in petroleum and nonpetroleum prices.

The drop, the largest in three months, was fueled primarily by slumping petroleum prices, which declined 3.9% from May. Prices of nonpetroleum imports declined 0.3%.

BUSINESS INVENTORIES

Here is a summary of the Commerce Department's report on business inventories and sales in May 1998. The figures are in billions of dollars, seasonally adjusted:

	(billions of dollars)		
	May 1998	April 1998	May 1997
Total business inventories	1,065.80	1,067.02	1,023.28
Manufacturers	461.56	461.13	443.46
Retailers	326.70	329.95	319.57
Wholesalers	277.54	275.93	260.26
Total business sales	774.20	773.41	742.07
Inventory/sales ratio	1.38	1.38	1.38

Statistical Summary

In the excerpt on page 297 from the *Journal*'s Thursday, July 16, 1998 edition, the statistical summary at the end of the article informs you that inventories were $1,065.80 billion, sales were $774.20 billion, and inventories were 1.38 times sales. The accompanying first-page chart mapped total inventories.

Inventories and sales are straightforward concepts. The inventory-sales ratio tells you how many months it would take to sell off inventories at the prevailing sales pace. You can calculate the ratio by dividing monthly inventory

Statistical Summary—End of Article

BUSINESS INVENTORIES

Here is a summary of the Commerce Department's report on business inventories and sales in May 1998. The figures are in billions of dollars, seasonally adjusted:

	(billions of dollars)		
	May 1998	April 1998	May 1997
Total business inventories	1,065.80	1,067.02	1,023.28
Manufacturers	461.56	461.13	443.46
Retailers	326.70	329.95	319.57
Wholesalers	277.54	275.93	260.26
Total business sales	774.20	773.41	742.07
Inventory/sales ratio	1.38	1.38	1.38

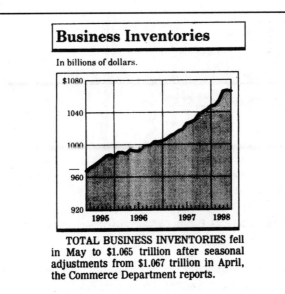

Business Inventories

In billions of dollars.

TOTAL BUSINESS INVENTORIES fell in May to $1.065 trillion after seasonal adjustments from $1.067 trillion in April, the Commerce Department reports.

by monthly sales. Typically, inventories have been roughly 1.5 times sales over the cycle. A rise in the ratio indicates that inventories are growing out of proportion to sales and that inventory liquidation and recession are imminent. A fall in the ratio informs you that sales are outpacing inventory growth and that economic expansion is under way. This is a key indicator; you should follow it closely.

CHART 14–1 Manufacturing and Trade Inventory/Sales Ratio, and Change in Book Value of Manufacturing and Trade Inventories

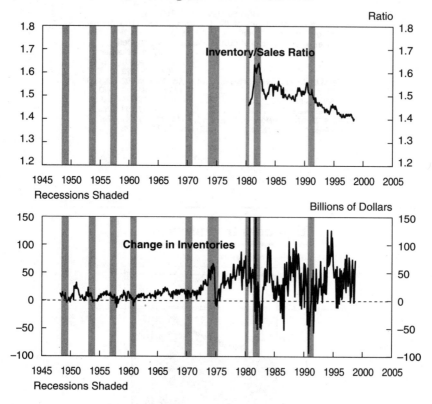

Source: The Conference Board, *Business Cycle Indicators*, Series A0M031. U.S. Department of Commerce, Bureau of the Census.

Return to the *Journal* article after examining the inventory cycle of the early 1970s (see Chart 14–1 above). This cycle concluded with a good example of inventory accumulation and speculation followed by inventory liquidation. To trace these events, follow the steep rise in inventories from 1972 through 1974 and the 1975 liquidation.

As increasing demand boosted sales, 1973 displayed all the symptoms of the expansion-to-peak phase of the cycle: strong and rapidly growing sales, strained capacity utilization and slower deliveries, and a rising rate of inflation. Under these circumstances, business sought to defend itself against possible shortages by adding to inventories more rapidly than sales grew. Speculation began. Business boosted inventories in the expectation of rising prices, hoping to make a profit as goods increased in value. This inten-

sified inflationary pressure (recall sugar), as a share of production went on the shelf instead of toward satisfying consumer demand. You can see that the inventory run-up dwarfed all other postwar increases up to that date.

As the cycle's peak approached, in 1974, sales stopped growing and unplanned inventory accumulation became a problem. Business firms had to deal with ever-larger stockpiles of goods. Sensing that a selloff was around the corner, they tried to bring inventories under control. Unfortunately, this was more easily said than done. Orders had to be canceled and production curtailed more than once because business underestimated the situation's severity.

But beginning in late 1974 and continuing into 1975, inventory liquidation finally began. Under panic conditions, business desperately dumped goods on the market. Other postwar recessions had been mild by comparison. Industrial production plunged, as business firms cut output sharply and filled the meager volume of orders from overstocked inventories. Two million workers were laid off between the fall of 1974 and the spring of 1975, and the unemployment rate brushed 10 percent. There is no doubt that inventory accumulation and liquidation played a key role in the recession's harshness.

Unlike the cycle of the early 70s, the 1981–82 recession can't be used as a typical example of inventory accumulation and liquidation because of the Fed's role in aborting the 1981 recovery. Sales were doing well and the inventory-sales ratio was low when the Fed's tight money policy clamped a vise on the economy in 1981. Sales shrank and involuntary inventory accumulation drove up both inventories and the inventory-sales ratio. As soon as possible, business began a massive inventory liquidation program that continued through early 1983. As you can tell from Chart 14–1 on page 298, a desperate bout of inventory liquidation accompanied the worst recession since World War II.

Recovery began as soon as the Fed provided easier credit conditions. And you can see that business did not wait long before it began restocking its depleted inventories. Massive inventory accumulation contributed impressively to the economy's explosive growth immediately after the 1981–82 recession, yet sales were so strong that the inventory-sales ratio declined throughout 1983 and remained low in 1984. There was no indication that inventory growth had outstripped sales or that the economy was near a cyclical peak.

Nevertheless, the Fed became concerned that the recovery and expansion were proceeding too rapidly. It fine-tuned the slowdown of mid-84, and inventory accumulation began to subside. By 1985 and early 1986, economic conditions were slack and inventory accumulation had fallen to a moderate level.

To a large extent, the inventory run-up of 1984 and the subsequent drop to a moderate pace in 1985–86 were a one-time reaction to the extreme inven-

tory depletion during the 1981–82 recession. These developments were not part of the ordinary cyclical scene; they were a reaction to the credit conditions imposed on the economy by the Fed. In a way, the decks were cleared for a resumption of normal cyclical patterns by the second half of the 80s.

As the economy's pace improved in the late 80s, inventory accumulation picked up once again. Although inflation, and perhaps speculation, was minimal, inventory accumulation turned robust by 1988 and then declined as the Fed tightened up once again. By the end of the decade, circumstances were similar to 1985–86: A jump in interest rates had led to slack conditions and the absence of inventory buildup.

Then Iraq invaded Kuwait, and the economy plunged into recession. Businesses were caught by surprise, and the inventory-sales ratio climbed as unsold goods piled up on shelves. But businesses brought the unintended inventory accumulation under control by sharply reducing inventories in 1991. By early 1992, the inventory-sale ratio was back to normal levels and inventories had begun to expand once again.

Another glance at Chart 14–1 on page 298 will demonstrate the 1990–91 recession's peculiar nature. No signs of serious speculation, such as a rising inventory-sales ratio, can be seen before the recession's start. Even after the slump begins, and despite massive inventory liquidation, the inventory-sales ratio's rise is moderate by the standard of previous recessions. Many observers ventured that the ratio's relatively smooth sailing provided evidence of business's better inventory-control methods and that relatively low inventory levels coming out of recession meant a snappy recovery and expansion.

They were wrong. Recovery was sluggish and expansion late.

THE OUTLOOK

By the end of the 1990s, the inventory-sales ratio fell to an unusually low level as sales gains continued to outstrip inventory growth. By the end of the decade it appeared that business's improved inventory-control methods had made a visible difference in the inventory-sales ratio's historical record

Return to the July 16, 1998 *Journal* article on pages 296 and 297. It informs you of a 1.38 inventory-sales ratio, and Chart 14–1 on page 298 confirms that this was a very low figure. This is partly a consequence of the improved technology that enables business to keep a closer watch over its inventories. But it's also a sign of a lean economy.

How long will the inventory-sales ratio remain low, and how long will it be before inventory accumulation exacerbates the expansion and contributes

to the next recession? By the end of the 1990s the inventory-sales ratio had fallen to a remarkably low level. Yet the possibility remained that business might begin stockpiling for self-protection and speculation, or that an unexpected weakness in sales could contribute to inventory accumulation. In which case, a rising inventory-sales ratio would be a dead giveaway that the cycle was peaking. Despite the inventory-sales ratio's decline for the better part of a decade, its subsequent rise could still signal the onset of recession.

Investor's Tip

- Watch these figures carefully. If boom conditions drive inventories out of moderate proportion to sales and the inventory-sales ratio rises rapidly and exceeds 1.6, you know recession can't be far behind.

C H A P T E R

BUSINESS CAPITAL EXPENDITURES

WHY BUSINESS INVESTS

JOHN MAYNARD KEYNES COULD NOT HAVE KNOWN AMERICA'S MODERN CONSUMER ECONOMY when he wrote his General Theory in 1936 (see Chapters 3 and 5). Keynes assumed the absence of any dynamic in British consumer expenditures and believed consumption behaved passively, expanding and contracting with consumer income. As far as Keynes was concerned, business investment determined the cycle's dynamic. So Keynes built his theory of aggregate economic activity around the forces that determine business investment in plant and equipment.

But business's expenditures on factories, warehouses, offices, machinery, and equipment, like its accumulation of inventories, reinforce the business cycle; they do not lead it. Business waits for its signal from the economy before committing its capital. Similarly, only after the expansion is over does business begin to cut back on capital expenditures in anticipation of reduced sales.

There are six principal factors influencing business decisions to spend on new plant and equipment.

First, old facilities may wear out and need to be replaced.

Second, the rate of capacity utilization may be high. Putting it simply, if sales are strong, business will invest in new machinery and equipment in order to have the capacity necessary to fill the orders. During a recession, however, the rate of capacity utilization is low and business has more than enough plant

and equipment on hand to satisfy the low volume of orders. Why add to plant and equipment when the existing level is already more than adequate?

Third, old facilities, whether fully utilized or not, will be scrapped and replaced by new facilities if operating costs can be sufficiently reduced through innovation in the process of production. Competition leaves business no choice: If equipment is no longer cost-effective, it must be replaced, even though it could still be used.

Fourth, new plant and equipment may be required to produce a new or redesigned product, even if existing facilities are operating at full capacity and have a continued useful life. Model and style changes have forced the automobile industry to spend billions replacing still-functional equipment, for instance.

Fifth, spending on plant and equipment is sensitive to current and anticipated profits. Business will invest in additional facilities if it expects long-range profit growth beyond any short-run cyclical fluctuation. In addition, profits plowed back into the business provide the cash flow necessary to finance capital expenditures. A recession will limit business's ability to finance capital expenditures; and expansion will generate the necessary cash flow.

The final factor is interest rates. Business must borrow to finance plant and equipment expenditures if internally generated funds are not adequate. When interest rates are very high, the cost of borrowing may be prohibitive, and so business firms postpone or cancel their capital expenditure plans. Or they may feel that, for the time being, they can get a better return by investing their own funds at high rates of interest than by making expenditures on new productive facilities.

Keep these factors in mind when evaluating business's capital expansion plans and their role in the current cycle. You can keep abreast of capital expenditures by following a series published monthly in *The Wall Street Journal*: the Commerce Department report on new orders for nondefense capital goods.

NONDEFENSE CAPITAL GOODS

The Wall Street Journal publishes the previous month's preliminary data for nondefense capital goods on the Thursday or Friday of the next-to-the-last week of the month, such as the Thursday, March 26, 1998 release (see page 305), and then publishes the final report about a week later. You will have to keep your eyes open for the preliminary figures, because they are part of an overall report on durable goods. The revised data, appearing a week later, is included with a general release on factory orders. The Friday, April 3, 1998 article on page 306 is a good example.

Durable-Goods Orders Fell 1.7% in February

By JOHN SIMONS
Staff Reporter of THE WALL STREET JOURNAL

WASHINGTON—New orders for manufactured durable goods fell 1.7% in February, after a 1.5% rise in January, dragged down by a sharp drop in aircraft orders by civilian and military customers.

Orders for durable goods — items built to last for more than three years — have fallen twice in three months, the Commerce Department said. Orders for aircraft and related equipment fell 34% last month. Excluding that volatile component, however, new orders actually rose 0.5% in February, for the third consecutive month.

Some economists found it difficult to draw any broad conclusions from the report. Others used it to support their previously held beliefs about the effect of the Asian financial crisis on the U.S. economy.

Jerry Jasinowski, president of the National Association of Manufacturers, for example, said the drop in aircraft orders is more proof that "manufacturers are starting to feel the heat from the Asian crisis." But while the Asian crisis is certainly having an effect on American business, some economists were less alarmed.

David Orr, an economist with First

Durable Goods
In billions of dollars

Union in Charlotte, N.C., said the report was inconclusive in terms of offering insight on the Asia crisis. "This is undoubtedly going to be a slower year," said Mr. Orr, adding that February's durable orders report is somewhat "enigmatic and ambiguous. My hunch here is that there isn't much of a slowdown [related to Asia]."

James F. O'Sullivan, an economist with Morgan,Guaranty Trust Co. in New York, found some good news in the new durables numbers, noting that the report's key gauge of business investment — orders for

nondefense capital goods (excluding aircraft) — "is showing signs of growing again. Those orders are up 17.9% at an annual rate for the quarter to date, more than making up for the 4.2% decline in [the final quarter of 1997]," he said.

Another notable February decrease occurred in orders for electronic and electrical equipment. Orders for those goods fell 2.7% in February, the first drop since November. February's largest increase came from the industrial-machinery and equipment segment, which has been rising for the last three months. Those orders rose 3.2% in February after posting a 2.2% gain in January. All figures are seasonally adjusted.

Here are the Commerce Department's latest figures on new orders for durable goods (seasonally adjusted, in billions):

	Feb.	Jan.	% Chg.
Total	$184.02	$187.19	− 1.7%
Primary Metals	$15.36	$15.04	+ 2.1%
Nonelect. machinery	$36.55	$35.41	+ 3.2%
Electrical machinery	$30.39	$31.24	− 2.7%
Transportation equip.	$41.64	$45.49	− 8.5%
Capital goods	$54.57	$59.44	− 8.2%
Non-defense	$49.17	$51.95	− 5.4%
Defense	$5.40	$7.48	−27.8%

Statistical Summary

Statistical Summary—End of Article

Here are the Commerce Department's latest figures on new orders for durable goods (seasonally adjusted, in billions):

	Feb.	Jan.	% Chg.
Total	$184.02	$187.19	− 1.7%
Primary Metals	$15.36	$15.04	+ 2.1%
Nonelect. machinery	$36.55	$35.41	+ 3.2%
Electrical machinery	$30.39	$31.24	− 2.7%
Transportation equip.	$41.64	$45.49	− 8.5%
Capital goods	$54.57	$59.44	− 8.2%
Non-defense	$49.17	$51.95	− 5.4%
Defense	$5.40	$7.48	−27.8%

You will notice that the statistical summary at the end of the March 26, 1998 article above states that orders for nondefense capital goods were $49.17 billion. The statistical summary at the end of the April 3, 1998 article on page 306 presents a revised figure of $49.57 billion.

This series presents new orders received by manufacturers of durable goods other than military equipment. (Durable goods are defined as those having a useful life of more than three years.) Nondefense capital goods represent approximately one fifth to one third of all durable goods production. The series includes engines; construction, mining, and materials han-

Factory Orders Fell 0.9% in February; Jobless Claims Drop

By Elizabeth Daerr
Staff Reporter of The Wall Street Journal

WASHINGTON — Factory orders slipped moderately in February, but demand for manufactured goods still remained strong indicating continued strength in the U.S. economy.

The 0.9% drop in orders followed a 0.6% increase in January, the Commerce Department reported. Excluding the volatile

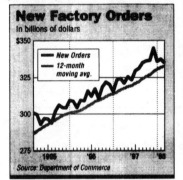

New Factory Orders
In billions of dollars

Source: Department of Commerce

transportation sector, however, orders increased 0.2% in February.

"It's better to look at the trend" excluding transportation, said economist Marilyn Schaja of Donaldson, Lufkin & Jenrette, New York. "That trend is up."

The figures were adjusted for seasonal factors, but not for inflation.

As part of its report, the Commerce Department also revised upward the preliminary estimate for February factory orders for durable goods that was announced last week. Orders for durable goods, big-ticket items made to last more than three years, fell 1.1% for the month, instead of the previously reported 1.7% decline.

Again excluding the volatile transportation sector, durable goods rose 1.9% in February. This included orders for primary metals and industrial machinery that each rose 2.8% for the month. Those sectors, which include construction, mining and computers, have increased for the third-consecutive month.

But because of falling orders from Asia, aircraft orders plunged 32.8% for the month. Although autos and parts were up a solid 4.2%, the transportation sector reported an overall 7.8% loss.

Factory orders for nondurable goods fell 0.5% in February.

Separately, the Labor Department reported jobless claims dropped by 5,000 to 309,000 for the week ended Saturday. That brings the four-week moving average to 308,250 and marks the eighth consecutive week that it remained under 310,000.

"With the economy operating at near full employment, a constricted labor supply should limit job gains," said Daniel Friel of NationsBank Corp., Charlotte, N.C.

Here are the Commerce Department's latest figures for manufacturers in billions of dollars, seasonally adjusted.

	February 1998	January 1998	%Chg.
All industries	334.84	337.76	− 0.9
Durable goods	185.36	187.48	− 1.1
Nondurable goods	149.48	150.28	− 0.5
Capital goods industries	55.23	59.65	− 7.4
Nondefense	49.57	52.11	− 4.9
Defense	5.65	7.54	− 25.1
Total shipments	337.50	333.65	+ 1.2
Inventories	457.58	455.12	+ 0.5
Backlog of orders	542.90	545.56	− 0.5

Statistical Summary

Statistical Summary—End of Article

Here are the Commerce Department's latest figures for manufacturers in billions of dollars, seasonally adjusted.

	February 1998	January 1998	%Chg.
All industries	334.84	337.76	− 0.9
Durable goods	185.36	187.48	− 1.1
Nondurable goods	149.48	150.28	− 0.5
Capital goods industries	55.23	59.65	− 7.4
Nondefense	49.57	52.11	− 4.9
Defense	5.65	7.54	− 25.1
Total shipments	337.50	333.65	+ 1.2
Inventories	457.58	455.12	+ 0.5
Backlog of orders	542.90	545.56	− 0.5

dling equipment; office and store machinery; electrical transmission and distribution equipment and other electrical machinery (excluding household appliances and electronic equipment); and railroad, ship and aircraft transportation equipment. Military equipment is excluded because new orders for such items do not respond directly to the business cycle.

Chart 15–1 (see below) provides a good illustration of the relationship between nondefense capital goods orders and the business cycle. We track orders rather than shipments in order to obtain maximum advance notice of business cycle developments and turning points.

By the late 80s, nondefense orders hovered around $35 billion and had advanced rapidly over the past half-decade. Yet you should notice, in a development remarked upon earlier in the discussion on inventories, that the 1980s expansion stumbled in the middle and end of the decade. Then nondefense orders dropped into the $30 billion range with the 1990–91 recession.

Orders for nondefense capital goods surged again in the 1990s, rising to over $50 billion. They began to lose steam at the end of the decade, in what some observers believed was a sign that the boom of the 90s was coming to an end.

CHART 15–1 Orders for Nondefense Capital Goods

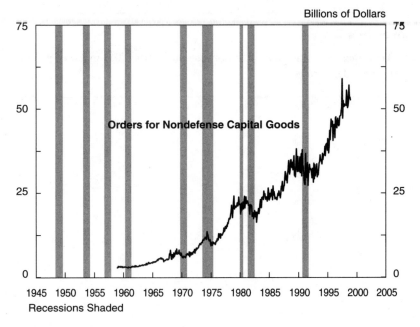

Source: The Conference Board, *Business Cycle Indicators*, Series A1M027.

SUMMARY

Business capital expenditures' role in the business cycle changed in the post-World War II era. Through the end of the 1970s, business capital expenditures, like inventory accumulation, reinforced the cycle rather than initiated it. Business responded to consumer orders by adding plant and equipment. As the expansion developed into the peak of the cycle and productive capacity became strained, business added facilities and equipment. Their completion swelled the level of demand and contributed to generally inflationary conditions.

After recession began, businesses typically canceled some of the investment projects, although most were completed, and these expenditures eased the downturn. Time elapsed before a new cycle's expansionary phase encouraged another round of capital expenditures. But until that occurred, depressed levels of plant and equipment expenditures restrained demand and prevented the economy from heating up too quickly. When capital expenditures did recover, the economy once again approached the cycle's peak.

But the cycle developed differently in the 1980s and 1990s than it had in the 1970s. Business capital expenditures now played a more important role in their own right. Such capital expenditures did not merely respond to consumer demand, they now drove the cycle forward.

Investor's Tip

- Treat these statistics like inventory accumulation: Too much of a good thing is dangerous.

C H A P T E R

U.S. INTERNATIONAL TRANSACTIONS

POSTWAR PERSPECTIVE

THE PHRASES OF INTERNATIONAL COMMERCE WERE CONTINUOUSLY IN THE NEWS DURING THE 1990s. Foreign exchange rates, devaluation, IMF, NAFTA, balance of trade, and the other terms used to discuss America's international economic relations can certainly be defined and described in the context of current events. But to understand them thoroughly, you must think back to World War II. Most of our modern international economic institutions were formed at the end of the war and immediately afterward, when the American dollar assumed the central role in the world's economy that it still plays today. Take the time to review postwar international economic developments before plunging into the current data and terminology.

In the summer of 1944, in the resort town of Bretton Woods, New Hampshire, well before World War II came to a close, the United States hosted a conference to plan international monetary affairs for the postwar years, since the Allies were already certain of victory. The United States knew that the war was taking a drastic toll on the rest of the world's economies, while the U.S. economy was growing stronger. Both victor and vanquished would need food, fuel, raw materials, and equipment, but only the United States could furnish these requirements. How were other nations to pay for these imports? They had very little that Americans wanted. If they sold their money for dollars in order to buy goods from us, the strong selling pressure on their

currencies and their strong demand for dollars would drive their currencies down in value and the dollar up. Soon the dollar would be so expensive, in terms of foreign currency, that the rest of the world could not afford to buy the American goods necessary to rebuild.

It would have been very easy to say that this was everyone else's problem, not ours, but America's statesmen knew that it was our problem as well. This lesson had been learned the hard way during the aftermath of World War I. Following that war, the United States had washed its hands of international responsibilities; consequently, the world economy had suffered a severe dollar shortage. Many nations were forced to devalue their currencies. Other nations used gold in desperation to settle their accounts with the United States, so America ended up with most of the world's gold supply. Moreover, each nation sought shelter in shortsighted protectionist devices, shattering the world economy. Economic nationalism spilled into the diplomatic arena, where its malevolent force accelerated the world into the second global war.

Determined to avoid these mistakes the second time around, the United States convened the Bretton Woods Conference to anticipate such problems and establish institutions to handle them. The conference's principal task was to prevent runaway depreciation of other currencies after the war. It therefore created the International Monetary Fund (IMF), a pool of currencies to which all nations (but mostly the United States) contributed and from which any nation could borrow in order to shore up the value of its own currency. If a nation's currency was under selling pressure, and weak and falling in value compared to other currencies, buying pressure designed to drive its price upward could be implemented with strong currencies borrowed from the IMF. For instance, Britain could borrow dollars from the IMF to buy pounds, thus supporting the price of the pound.

The dollar was pegged to gold at $35 an ounce, and all other currencies were pegged to the dollar (e.g., a dollar was worth a fixed number of francs or pounds). At the time, the United States had most of the world's gold and other nations had hardly any, so the entire system was tied to gold through the U.S. dollar. This system of fixed exchange rates was constructed to provide stability in international economic relationships. Traders and investors knew exactly what a contract for future delivery of goods or future return on investment was worth in terms of the foreign exchange in which a contract was written. There was no incentive to speculate on shifting exchange rates, which could wipe out profit margins or generate large losses.

To draw an analogy, consider a shipment of oranges from California to New York and investments made by Californians on the New York Stock Exchange. Californians must be concerned about the price of oranges in

New York and the price of a share of stock on the exchange, but they need not be concerned about fluctuations in the value of New York currency versus California currency, since both states use dollars.

Now think how much more difficult selling and investing in New York would be for Californians if the exchange rate between their currencies fluctuated. The diplomats wished to avoid precisely that problem after World War II, and that's why the Bretton Woods Conference established the IMF and a system of fixed exchange rates.

Unfortunately, after the war, the U.S. balance-of-trade surplus (the amount by which the revenue of all exports exceeds the cost of all imports) created a greater dollar shortage than the conference had anticipated. Other nations were continually selling their currencies in order to buy American dollars with which to purchase American goods. Selling pressure forced down the price of other currencies despite the IMF, which was not large enough to bail them out, and many of these currencies faced runaway depreciation against the dollar.

The United States responded to this crisis with the Marshall Plan. George C. Marshall, a career soldier, had been chairman of the Joint Chiefs of Staff during the war. At the war's end, President Truman appointed him Secretary of State. Marshall understood that a shortage of essential items such as food, fuel, raw materials, and machinery and equipment hobbled Europe's recovery. Only the United States could supply Europe's needs in sufficient quantities. He further understood that the dollar shortage prevented Europe from importing what it needed from the United States.

He proposed, and President Truman and Congress approved, a plan whereby the European nations drew up a list of their needs and the United States gave (not loaned) them the dollars they required to satisfy those needs. This reduced the strain on Europe's balance of payments and freed their currencies from the pressure of devaluation. American exports, of course, benefited, as our dollars bounced right back to us for purchases of American goods.

By the time of the Korean War, everyone was talking about the "economic miracle of Europe." The Marshall Plan had been extended to victor and vanquished alike, probably history's greatest example of benevolence as enlightened self-interest. The United States had learned from its mistakes following World War I. Isolationism was myopic; the United States had to play an active role in world affairs. And our generosity would be repaid many times over, as foreign markets for our goods recovered rapidly.

The Marshall Plan became a cornerstone of American foreign policy. The United States provided the rest of the world with desperately needed dollars in this and also a number of other ways, not all of them purposeful. For

example, the United States began to maintain a substantial military presence overseas, and our foreign bases salted their host countries with dollars when native civilians were employed at the bases and American personnel spent their paychecks. In addition, American business firms resumed overseas investing, especially in Europe, spending dollars to purchase subsidiaries and to build facilities. Finally, Americans started to travel abroad in great numbers, seeding Europe with funds. All of these activities meant that dollars were sold for foreign exchange (foreign currency), and so they helped offset the constant sale by other nations of their currency in order to buy American goods.

Furthermore, whenever foreign banks, businesses, or individuals received more dollars than were immediately required, they were delighted to deposit those dollars in either American or foreign banks in order to hold them for a rainy day. Since dollars were in vigorous demand because of the continuing need to buy American exports, those dollars could always be sold in the future, and, meanwhile, they were a handy private reserve.

To summarize, there were four principal outflows of dollars from the United States: foreign aid (such as the Marshall Plan), foreign investment, military presence overseas, and tourism. Two principal influxes of foreign exchange offset these outflows: foreign purchase of American exports, which greatly exceeded our purchases of imports, and foreigners' willingness to hold dollars as a liquid investment. The four outflows of dollars (roughly) equaled the two influxes of foreign exchange.

By the late 50s and early 60s, however, some foreign banks, businesses, and individuals found that they had more dollars than they could use. They did not wish to buy American goods, and they had found making other investments more attractive than holding dollars, so they decided to sell them.

The United States did not have to rely on the IMF to support the dollar and maintain a fixed exchange rate between the dollar and other currencies. Rather, the U.S. Treasury stood ready to redeem dollars with gold whenever selling pressure on the dollar became heavy: The United States propped up the price of the dollar relative to other currencies by buying the dollar for gold. Since a foreign holder of dollars could buy gold at $35 per ounce and sell that gold for foreign exchange anywhere in the world, there was no need to sell dollars below the fixed rate of exchange. Whenever the dollar fell a little, foreigners would buy gold with their dollars and cash that gold in for other currencies at full value, which kept the dollar up. And the U.S. price of $35 per ounce of gold set the world price for gold, simply because the United States had most of the world's supply. As more and more dollars were redeemed for it, a stream of gold started to leave the United States.

American holdings of gold were cut almost in half by the time increasing alarm was voiced in the early 60s.

An alternative solution had to be found, or else the U.S. supply of gold would disappear. The foreign central banks stepped in and agreed to support the price of the dollar as part of their obligation to maintain fixed exchange rates under the Bretton Woods agreement. They had potentially limitless supplies of their own currencies. If a bank, business, or individual in another nation wanted to sell dollars, and this selling pressure tended to force the price of the dollar down in terms of that nation's currency, the foreign central bank would buy the dollars for its currency and thus support the price of the dollar.

Neither the U.S. Treasury or the Federal Reserve System could support the dollar in this way, because neither had limitless supplies of foreign currency. As long as the foreign central banks were willing to buy and accumulate dollars, private citizens, banks, and businesses in other countries were satisfied. In this way, the system of fixed exchange rates survived.

However, by the late 60s and early 70s the situation had once again become ominous. The United States no longer had a favorable balance of trade. Other nations were selling more to, and buying less from, the United States. America's favorable balance of trade had been the single big plus in its balance of payments, offsetting the outflows of dollars mentioned earlier: foreign aid (the Marshall Plan), American tourism, foreign investment, and the American military presence overseas. Now the dollar holdings of foreign central banks began to swell ever more rapidly, as their citizens liquidated dollar holdings. These central banks realized that they were acquiring an asset that ultimately would be of little value to them. Having been put in a position of continually buying dollars they would never be able to sell, they insisted that the United States do something to remedy the situation.

The French suggested that the dollar be officially devalued as a first step, because it had had a very high value in terms of other currencies ever since World War II. They reasoned that if the dollar were worth less in terms of other currencies, American exports would be cheaper for the rest of the world, imports would be more expensive in the United States, and thus the U.S. balance of trade would shift from negative to positive as the United States exported more and imported less. In addition, if foreign currencies were more expensive, Americans would be less likely to travel and invest overseas. This would partially stem the dollar hemorrhage. Others suggested that the foreign central banks stop supporting (buying) the dollar and that the dollar be allowed to float downward to a more reasonable level as foreigners sold off their holdings.

For many years, the United States resisted both devaluation and flotation, until, in a series of developments between 1971 and 1973, the U.S. ceased redeeming the dollar for gold and permitted it to float. It promptly fell, relative to other currencies, because foreign central banks no longer felt obliged to purchase it in order to support its price.

At the same time, the price of gold increased, because the United States would no longer redeem dollars with gold. The willingness of the United States to sell gold virtually without limit at $35 per ounce had kept its value from rising, but now the price of gold could increase according to the forces of private supply and demand. Consequently, it fluctuated with all other commodity prices, rising rapidly during the general inflation at the end of the 1970s and then falling with commodity prices after 1980.

The dollar fell until the summer of 1973, and then it fluctuated in value until the end of the 1970s. Although foreign central banks no longer felt an obligation to buy dollars, they occasionally did so to keep it from plummeting too far or too fast. They took this action in their own interest at the suggestion of exporters, who knew that a low value for the dollar and a high value for their own currencies made it difficult to export to the United States. Nevertheless, by the end of the 70s the dollar's value was at a postwar low.

The history of the dollar in the 1980s was a roller-coaster ride. At first, the dollar's value headed steeply up and rose to a new postwar high by mid-decade. After that it fell once again, so that by the late 80s and early 90s it had retreated back down to its late 70s level. For the remainder of the 1990s the dollar fluctuated around this low point. What caused these ups and downs, and what does the future hold? You can find an answer in *The Wall Street Journal*'s coverage of the U.S. current account, the U.S. balance of trade, and foreign exchange rates.

These few statistical series portraying America's international transactions have generated more confusion in public perception than perhaps any others, but you will see that they are really not difficult to grasp and follow on a regular basis.

THE U.S. INTERNATONAL ACCOUNT AND BALANCE OF TRADE

In order to comprehend the *U.S. International Account*, think of yourself as representing the United States in all dealings with the rest of the world. If you wish to do business with the rest of the world, you must buy its currencies (called *foreign exchange*). Likewise, in order to do business in the United States, the rest of the world must buy dollars.

Now set up an accounting statement. The left side will include all the uses you had for all the foreign exchange you purchased. The right side of the account will include all the uses for the dollars that the rest of the world pur-

chased. The two sides must balance: *For every dollar's worth of foreign exchange that you buy with a dollar, the rest of the world must use a dollar's worth of foreign exchange to buy that dollar.* There are no leaks. It is impossible for you to buy any amount of foreign currency without the seller of that currency buying an equivalent value of dollars. It doesn't matter what you do with the foreign exchange you bought, nor what they do with the dollars they bought (even if both of you do *nothing* with your newly purchased money). The international account merely records what both parties do with their funds.

Congratulations. You have just constructed an international account.

U.S. International Account

Money going out (–)	Money coming in (+)
Uses by United States for all foreign exchange purchased with U.S. dollars	Uses by rest of world for all U.S. dollars purchased with foreign exchange

Once the accounting statement has been set up, you may add other details. Each side of the statement will have a *current account* and a *capital account*. Subdivide the current account into merchandise trade, services, and foreign aide; subdivide the capital account into private investment and central bank transactions.

U.S. International Account

U.S. purchase of foreign money (debit) (–)	Foreign purchase of U.S. money (credit) (+)
Current account payments by United States to rest of world	Current account payments to United States by rest of world
Goods and services imports by United States	Goods and services exports by United States
Merchandise trade imports	Merchandise trade exports
Services for which United States pays rest of world	Services United States sells rest of world
Foreign aid payments by United States to rest of world	Foreign aid payments by rest of world to United States
Capital account outflows of funds from United Sates	Capital account inflows of funds to United States
Private investment by United States in rest of world	Private investment by rest of world in United States
Central Bank transactions such as Fed buys foreign currencies	Central bank transactions such as foreign central banks buy dollars

To summarize: The left side of this account (*debit*) shows what you, representing the United States, are doing with the foreign exchange you purchased with American dollars. The right side of the account (*credit*) shows what the rest of the world is doing with the dollars it purchased with its money. Remember, *the two sides must be equal*; a transaction can take place only if things of equal worth are exchanged. Although the *total* for each side must be equal, however, the individual categories need not be. Thus, you can balance one category against another in order to arrive at a merchandise trade balance, goods and services balances, and so on. Each category in the international account will be examined in turn.

The Current Accounts

Balance on Goods and Services

Merchandise Trade
You can use the foreign exchange you have purchased to buy foreign goods, and the rest of the world can use dollars to buy American goods.

Thus, if you import goods into the United States, you have incurred a debit (–), because you have sold dollars to buy foreign currency in order to make the transaction; in other words, money has left the United States. On the other hand, if the rest of the world buys American goods, you have earned a credit (+). It is customary to talk about the *balance on merchandise trade* by netting imports against exports to determine whether we have an export (+) surplus or an import (–) deficit.

Services
If you use your dollars to buy foreign currency in order to travel in a foreign country, or to use a foreign air carrier, or to pay interest on a foreign debt, all this would be classified as an outflow of funds, or a debit (–). On the other hand, if the rest of the world uses the dollars it buys to travel in the United States, or to fly with an American air carrier, or to pay interest on a debt to the United States, that flow of money into the United States would be a credit (+).

If the net credit (+) or debit (–) balance on this account is added to the credit (+) or debit (–) balance of the merchandise trade account, this subtotal is referred to as the *balance on goods and services*.

Foreign Aid
If you use the foreign money you have purchased to make a gift to the rest of the world, that's a debit (–); if the rest of the world uses the dollars it has

purchased to make a gift to the United States, that's a credit (+). Until the Persian Gulf war, and our request to our allies that they compensate us for Operation Desert Storm, foreign aid had always been a debit (–) entry for the U.S. But in 1991 it temporarily switched to credit (+) and, as you will see, made a big difference in our international transactions that year.

When the foreign aid transaction is combined with the balance on goods and services, it completes the *balance on current account*, which will be a debit (–) balance or a credit (+) balance, depending on whether more funds flowed out of or into the United States.

The Capital Accounts

Private Investments

As a private investor, you may wish to sell U.S. dollars and buy foreign exchange in order to make an investment somewhere else in the world. This could be a direct investment in the form of plant and equipment expenditures or the purchase of a foreign company, or it could be a financial asset, either long-term or short-term. (Stocks and bonds, for instance are long-term investments, while a foreign bank account or a holding in foreign currency is a short-term investment.)

Any of these transactions will be a debit (–) in the American account, because dollars have left the United States. Conversely, when a private investor in another country sells foreign exchange in order to have U.S. dollars to make a direct or financial investment in the United States, whether long-term or short-term, this is classified as a credit (+).

Central Bank Transactions

If, as a representative of the Federal Reserve System, you sell dollars in order to buy foreign currency, this too is a debit (–), and when foreign central banks buy dollars, it is a credit (+).

These central bank transactions conclude the discussion of international transactions components.

A further point must be made before you plow into the data. References are constantly being made to deficits or surpluses in the balances on trade, goods and services, and current account. Now and then you may encounter a comment about a deficit or a surplus in the international account, despite this chapter's assertion that it always balances. How can you explain this apparent paradox?

Trade, goods and services, and current account are easy. You already know that there can be a surplus (+) or a deficit (–) in these separate accounts. But how could anyone speak of a deficit in the total international account

when it *must always balance*? Because that is the shorthand way of saying that the nation's currency is under selling pressure and that the value of the currency will fall unless some remedial action is taken.

For instance, at the time the foreign central banks supported the value of the dollar, their purchases of dollars constituted a "plus" (+) in the American balance of payments, because they sopped up the excess dollars that their own economies didn't need. (Had they not done so, the dollar would have fallen in value.) Obviously, if you remove a plus from an accounting system that is in balance, what remains has a negative bottom line. Since a remedial action made the account balance, and since without it the account would have been negative, reference was made to a deficit in the U.S. International Account.

When the United States still sold gold internationally in order to redeem the dollar, these sales were plus (+) entries in our international account. If you wonder why the loss of gold is a plus, remember that anything sold by the United States is a plus because the rest of the world must pay us for it. When you remove gold sales from the international account, the remaining items must net out to a negative balance. Therefore, people often referred to the size of the U.S. gold loss as the deficit in the U.S. International Account.

And now for one final tip before you look at the data: Keep your eyes on the money. That's the best way to determine whether something is a plus (+) or minus (−) in the international account. If *we* pay for it, it's a minus, because money is going out. If *they* pay for it, it's a plus.

The Wall Street Journal regularly publishes two Commerce Department reports dealing with the U.S. International Account and the balance of trade that will be useful to you.

1.   *Current account* figures for the previous *quarter* appear in the third week of the last month of each quarter.
2.   *Monthly balance-of-trade* figures for the previous month are also released in the third week of each month.

According to the first paragraph of the Thursday, December 10, 1998 *Balance on Current Account* article on pages 319 and 320, the U.S. current-account deficit was $61.3 billion in the third quarter of 1998.

Use Chart 16–1 on page 320 to focus on recent international account developments. (Note that this chart displays annual, not quarterly, data.)

First, the merchandise trade balance dropped like a stone in the early 80s, dragging the current-account deficit with it.

Second, the merchandise-trade deficit stopped falling in the late 80s, halting the deterioration in the current-account balance.

U.S. Current-Account
Deficit Widens to Record

By ROBERT S. GREENBERGER
Staff Reporter of THE WALL STREET JOURNAL

WASHINGTON—The U.S, current-account deficit swelled to a record $61.3 billion in the third quarter, reflecting an ailing global economy that is eroding U.S. sales and profits abroad.

Current-Account Deficit

The latest figure was the fourth consecutive record quarterly deficit and followed the second period's seasonally adjusted $56.69 billion current-account gap, the Commerce Department reported. Meanwhile, the annual current-account deficit appears headed toward a record, which would surpass 1987's $168.01 billion gap.

The current account is the broadest measure of the U.S. trade picture, including transactions involving goods, services and investment income.

Unsettling conditions abroad shrank the surplus on services, normally the strongest sector of U.S. trade. The services surplus narrowed to an adjusted $18.61 billion from $20.57 billion in the second quarter. "Our service exports got clobbered by the problems around the world, and I wouldn't be surprised to see that continue," said David Levy, vice chairman of the Jerome Levy Economic Institute, in Mount Kisco, N.Y. Among service categories, travel to the U.S. dropped nearly $2 billion.

At the same time, the deficit on U.S. investment income widened to an adjusted $5.46 billion from $3.38 billion in the second quarter, as the profits of U.S. companies' foreign units fell. Although the global malaise began in Asia nearly 18 months ago, the weakness in profits has spread to Latin America and even parts of Europe, analysts said. Mr. Levy said earnings also were affected by currency fluctuations and were particularly weak in the manufacturing sector abroad.

Analysts weren't surprised by the report, given global conditions. Indeed, the vibrant U.S. economy has become the buyer of first and last resort for many ailing nations that are trying to export their way back to economic health. The world's economic plight would be far worse if the U.S. weren't playing this role.

Still, a flood of imports to the U.S. has

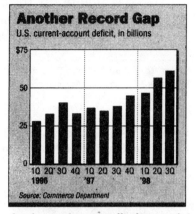

Another Record Gap
U.S. current-account deficit, in billions

Source: Commerce Department

already caused some layoffs—for example in the steel industry—and protectionist pressures are building. The steel industry and its major union have launched a high-profile campaign demanding that the White House and Congress curtail imports. They also have brought unfair-trade cases against steelmakers from Japan, Russia and Brazil, charging that steel is being "dumped" in the U.S. market at unfairly low prices and is hurting domestic producers. If the Commerce Department and International Trade Commission uphold the charges, duties would be imposed.

Meanwhile, Clyde Prestowitz, president of the Washington-based Economic Strategy Institute, warns that continually expanding trade deficits aren't economically sustainable. As the overall trade deficit widens, the U.S. must borrow more money to finance the gap. So far, other nations have been willing to invest and lend here, as the U.S. remains the soundest economy. But, Mr. Prestowitz says, "at some point we've got to get the rest of the world back on a growth track."

"If you borrow enough, sooner or later your credit rating goes down," he adds. And, noting that the common European currency will be launched in January, he says "there could be attractive alternative places to invest, and that would make it more costly for us to finance our deficit."

Current-Account Deficit—First Paragraph

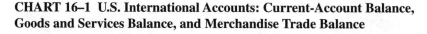

WASHINGTON—The U.S. current-account deficit swelled to a record $61.3 billion in the third quarter, reflecting an ailing global economy that is eroding U.S. sales and profits abroad.

Source: *The Wall Street Journal,* December 10, 1998. Reprinted by permission of *The Wall Street Journal,* ©1998 Dow Jones & Company, Inc. All rights reserved.

CHART 16–1 U.S. International Accounts: Current-Account Balance, Goods and Services Balance, and Merchandise Trade Balance

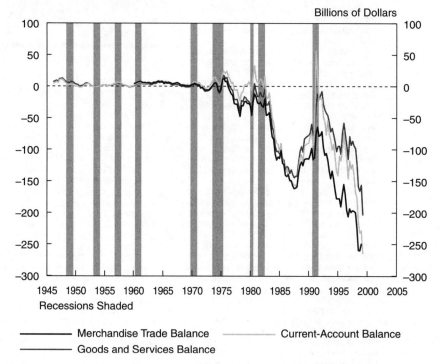

Source: The Conference Board, *Business Cycle Indicators,* Series A0Q622, U.S. Department of Commerce, Bureau of Economic Analysis

Third, the current-account balance moved back above zero in 1991, although the merchandise-trade balance lagged behind.

Service income—such as the net earnings that the United States receives from foreign investments, the sale of banking, transport, and insurance services, and foreign tourism in the United States—comprises most of the gap between the current account and merchandise trade balance. Notice that, until the late 70s and early 80s, U.S. service earnings grew so rapidly that the balance on current account remained positive (+) despite a negative (–) merchandise trade balance.

Then the U.S. merchandise trade balance and the balance on current account dropped off the end of the world, so that by the mid-80s both numbers exceeded $150 billion at annual rates. The following circumstances can explain this development.

1.   The Fed's contractionary, anti-inflationary stand in the early 80s drove U.S. interest rates above world-market levels. Consequently, Americans were reluctant to sell dollars, and the rest of the world was eager to buy them. Strong demand for the dollar drove its price up, making imports relatively attractive to Americans and our goods relatively less attractive to the rest of the world.

2.   Even after U.S. interest rates fell, the dollar remained an attractive haven because of President Reagan's perceived pro-business position and the fear of left-wing governments elsewhere. A strong dollar hurt our balance on merchandise trade.

3.   Recovery from the 1981–82 recession proceeded earlier and more swiftly in the U.S. than in the rest of the world. Therefore, our demand for imports grew more rapidly, because American incomes grew more rapidly.

4.   As the U.S. led the world out of recession, our economy attracted foreign investment, further boosting the dollar and hurting our trade and current-account balances.

At this point you should return to page 315 and review the International Accounts statement. If the current account is negative, as it was all through the 1980s, then the capital account must be positive. Otherwise, the international accounts cannot balance. But a positive balance on capital account means that the rest of the world is acquiring American assets. In other words, if we buy Toyotas, they buy Rockefeller Center.

Put it in simple terms. If we export $2 and import $3, the rest of the world has at its disposal an additional dollar. Why? Because the rest of the

world earned $3 selling goods to us, but used only $2 to buy our goods. Keeping the extra dollar in its pocket constitutes a foreign investment by the rest of the world in the U.S. But of course, the rest of the world won't just keep the dollar in its pocket. Instead, it will purchase U.S. Treasury securities or a baseball team, or some other investment.

The U.S. ran a balance-of-trade and current-account surplus for most years in the first three-quarters of the 20th century and thereby became the world's greatest creditor nation. Reversing the example in the previous paragraph, we had extra money to invest in the rest of the world. But after 1980 we became the world's greatest debtor nation, as the flow of capital into the U.S. offset our deficit in the current account.

By the mid-1980s, President Reagan and his advisers viewed the situation with alarm. Free traders, they didn't want Congress imposing tariffs in order to reduce imports. So, we proposed that our major trading partners dump some of the dollars they had accumulated in the 1970s, thereby forcing down the dollar's value. As our export prices fell and import prices rose, the problem would take care of itself.

This agreement, negotiated at New York's Plaza Hotel in 1985, became known as the Plaza Accord and began to work in 1987. You can see from Chart 16–1 on page 320 that our trade and current account balances began to improve in 1987 and that by the early 90s these deficits had shrunk considerably.

But they had help. Europe's economies began to break out of their malaise by the end of the 80s. As their incomes grew more rapidly, so did their imports of American goods. This helped stabilize our balance of trade.

In any event, you can see that even though the dollar had fallen all the way back down to its pre-1980 level, our balance-of-trade deficit persisted in the early 1990s and then continued to escalate toward the end of the decade. The dollar's fall had not cured America's trade imbalance. Obviously, more was involved than the dollar's value and the relative health of other economies.

But one last point remains regarding the current account before turning to the trade data in *The Wall Street Journal*. Our balance on current account popped back up above zero briefly in 1991 because of payments made to us by our Desert Storm allies. Those payments offset the continued trade deficit and momentarily pushed the current account into the black.

You can use the *Journal* to follow the Commerce Department's monthly merchandise-trade report. The Thursday, November 19, 1998 article provides data for September 1998 (see pages 323 and 324).

According to the second paragraph and the statistical summary at the end of the article, the United States ran a $14.03 billion trade deficit in September 1998 due to exports of $77.13 billion and imports of $91.16 billion.

U.S. Trade Deficit Narrowed in September

Large Jump in the Sales Of Aircraft, Automobiles Helped Reduce the Gap

By ROBERT S. GREENBERGER
And ALEJANDRO BODIPO-MEMBA
Staff Reporters of THE WALL STREET JOURNAL

WASHINGTON—Thanks to a big jump in sales of U.S.-made aircraft and automobiles, the U.S. trade deficit narrowed in September. But economists don't expect such sales to continue, suggesting the deficit will resume its record-setting pace for the rest of the year.

The Commerce Department reported that the gap between what the U.S. sells overseas and buys there fell to a seasonally adjusted $14.03 billion in September, down from a revised $15.9 billion in August. The smaller gap was attributed to stronger exports of civilian aircraft sales, which tend to be volatile, and increased overseas sales of autos and auto parts, reflecting a rebound from last summer's General Motors Corp. strike.

Analysts said the narrower-than-expected deficit is the second piece of economic news in the past few days that seems to indicate that economic growth in the third quarter was more brisk than had been previously projected. On Tuesday, the Commerce Department reported that business inventories shot up 0.6% in September, much higher than the rate the government used when it compiled its initial estimate of third-quarter economic growth last month.

Based on yesterday's report, along with Tuesday's inventories release, some economists believe the government will revise third-quarter growth upward. Nations-Bank, for example, said inflation-adjusted gross domestic product probably grew at an annual rate of 4% in the third quarter, rather than the government's earlier estimate of 3.3%.

Separately, the Labor Department said that in October the price of all imported goods rose 0.2%, up slightly from September. But excluding petroleum goods, import prices remained unchanged for the first time in 12 months. In a year-over-year comparison, however, prices were down 3.9% from 1997.

Regarding the trade deficit, Brian Horrigan, senior economist at Loomis Sayles & Co., a Boston investment counseling firm, called the September figure "a fluke." He noted that civilian-aircraft sales soared to $4.04 billion in September from $2.04 billion in August, more than accounting for the overall rise in exports. He added that most other ma-

Trade Deficit

Regional Trade Balances

U.S. merchandise trade balances by region; in billions of U.S. dollars, not seasonally adjusted.

	SEPT. 1998	AUG. 1998	SEPT. 1997
Japan	–$5.07	–$5.20	–$5.10
Canada	– 2.34	– 1.67	–'1.15
China	– 5.90	– 5.91	– 5.52
Western Europe	– 1.76	– 2.21	– 1.34
Mexico	– 1.45	– 1.76	– 1.38
NICs*	– 2.52	– 2.63	– 1.98
South/Central America	+ 0.68	+ 0.98	+ 0.72

*Newly industrialized countries: Singapore, Hong Kong, Taiwan, South Korea.   Source: Commerce Department

Continued

jor export categories—including food, industrial supplies and other capital goods—were either flat or below August levels.

In September, imports declined slightly to an adjusted $91.16 billion from $91.33 billion in August. That reflects the currency devaluations in Asia that have resulted in lower prices of imports. Many economists expect, however, that the volume of imports soon will increase, as foreign goods become increasingly more competitive here. That, in turn, would have an impact on U.S. employment.

Indeed, David Levy, director of forecasting at the Jerome Levy Economic Institute's forecasting center, says the U.S. goods-producing sector already is feeling the impact. Citing, Labor Department statistics, he says employment for this sector has fallen to 25,183,000 in October from 25,339,000 in April. Mr. Levy adds that other factors were at work during that period, but that the pattern is clear.

He warns that the combination of import competition and weak U.S. export markets will mean "increased pullbacks by domestic goods producers in employment and capital investment." President Clinton, who is expected to arrive in Japan today, will emphasize the need for Japan to reform and stimulate its economy "and

open its markets to fair trade," he said before leaving Washington yesterday.

Meanwhile, the Labor's Department's report for October, shows that the index of imported consumer-goods prices, which had fallen or remained flat for the previous seven months, rose 0.3% last month. The increase, which was the largest jump in the index since a 0.4% rise in December 1995, reflects the recent turnaround in the U.S. dollar.

The price of all imported goods rose 0.2% in October from a revised 0.1% increase in September, affected largely by price increases for imported petroleum. It was the second consecutive monthly increase in the index, following 10 months of declines.

Prices of petroleum and petroleum products jumped 5% in October, compared with a 3.6% increase in September. Petroleum prices, though, are down 31.9% for the year ended in October.

Here are the Commerce Department's monthly trade figures, in billions of dollars.

	September 1998	August (R) 1998
Total Exports	77.13	75.43
Goods	55.87	53.86
Services	21.25	21.56
Total Imports	91.16	91.33
Goods	76.47	76.60
Services	14.69	14.73
Overall trade balance	-14.03	-15.90
Goods	-20.60	-22.74
Services	6.57	6.84d1

Statistical Summary

Trade Deficit—Second Paragraph

The Commerce Department reported that the gap between what the U.S. sells overseas and buys there fell to a seasonally adjusted $14.03 billion in September, down from a revised $15.9 billion in August. The smaller gap was attributed to stronger exports of civilian aircraft sales, which tend to be volatile, and increased overseas sales of autos and auto parts, reflecting a rebound from last summer's General Motors Corp. strike.

Statistical Summary—End of Article

Here are the Commerce Department's monthly trade figures, in billions of dollars.

	September 1998	August (R) 1998
Total Exports	77.13	75.43
Goods	55.87	53.86
Services	21.25	21.56
Total Imports	91.16	91.33
Goods	76.47	76.60
Services	14.69	14.73
Overall trade balance	-14.03	-15.90
Goods	-20.60	-22.74
Services	6.57	6.84d1

U.S. Trade Deficit

In billions of dollars, seasonally adjusted.

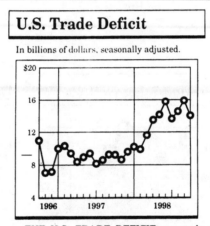

THE U.S. TRADE DEFICIT on goods and services rose in September to a seasonally adjusted $14.03 billion from a revised $15.90 billion in August, the Commerce Department reports.

Investor's Tip

• There is no long-run correlation between our balance of trade and the stock market's performance. If the trade figures improve, less and less attention will be paid to them.

FOREIGN EXCHANGE RATES

Each day *The Wall Street Journal* publishes several reports on foreign exchange trading activity. Start with the report on the last section's first page, under the **Markets Diary** heading, labeled **U.S. Dollar**. The excerpt below from the Monday, January 18, 1999 issue is an example. The chart provides a record of the dollar's value compared with a trade-weighted average of 19 currencies. Below that is a record of the dollar's value against five major currencies and the Euro.

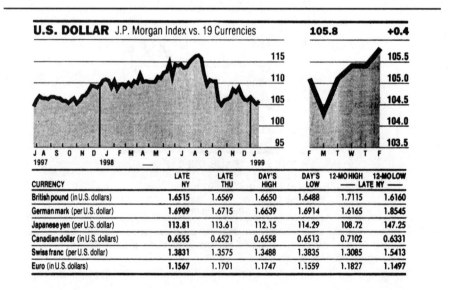

CURRENCY	LATE NY	LATE THU	DAY'S HIGH	DAY'S LOW	12-MO HIGH LATE NY	12-MO LOW
British pound (in U.S. dollars)	1.6515	1.6569	1.6650	1.6488	1.7115	1.6160
German mark (per U.S. dollar)	1.6909	1.6715	1.6639	1.6914	1.6165	1.8545
Japanese yen (per U.S. dollar)	113.81	113.61	112.15	114.29	108.72	147.25
Canadian dollar (in U.S. dollars)	0.6555	0.6521	0.6558	0.6513	0.7102	0.6331
Swiss franc (per U.S. dollar)	1.3831	1.3575	1.3488	1.3835	1.3085	1.5413
Euro (in U.S. dollars)	1.1567	1.1701	1.1747	1.1559	1.1827	1.1497

The *Journal* also publishes daily a table on **Currency Trading** (check the front-page index of the first and last sections under **Foreign Exchange**). The Monday, January 18, 1999 table appears on page 328. You can use it to keep abreast of the dollar's value against a wide range of currencies. For instance, on Friday, January 15, 1999, the British pound was worth approximately $1.65, the Canadian dollar about $0.65, the French franc approximately $0.17, the German mark approximately $0.59, the Japanese yen about ⁹⁄₁₀ of a cent, and the Swiss franc approximately $0.72.

You can see that these quotations portray the value of a single unit of foreign exchange in terms of the American dollar. However, foreign currencies are usually quoted in units per American dollar. Thus on Friday, January 15, 1999, the dollar was worth 113.81 Japanese yen and 1.69 German marks.

Most foreign exchange trading is conducted by banks on behalf of their customers. Banks will also provide future delivery of foreign exchange for customers who want a guaranteed price in order to plan their operations and limit risk due to exchange-rate fluctuation. The price for future delivery is known as the forward rate, and you can see forward quotes for the major currencies immediately beneath the current rate.

On Mondays, the *Journal* also provides exchange rates for major currencies in terms of each other's value and a weekly comparison of the dollar's value against almost every currency in the world. See **Key Currency Cross Rates** on page 328 and **World Value of the Dollar** from the Monday, January 18, 1999 issue on pages 329 and 330.

Recall the brief outline of the dollar's postwar history presented earlier.

Chart 16–2 on pages 331 and 332 provides graphic evidence of the dollar's fall in terms of most foreign currencies since the mid 1980s. The dollar's index value dropped from roughly 140 to 100; and in terms of other currencies the dollar fell from approximately 0.92 to 0.62 British pounds, 260 to 125 Japanese yen, 10 to 6 French francs, 3.3 to 1.7 German marks, and 2,000 to 1,650 Italian lira. But the U.S. dollar did rise from 1.3 to 1.5 Canadian dollars.

The dollar fell to its post-World War II low against most currencies in the late 70s (see Chart 16–2) because of severe inflation here at home and its impact on our trade balance. The merchandise-trade balance sank dramatically, as rising prices impeded our ability to sell and whetted our appetite for imports (see Chart 16–1 on page 320). Since people in the rest of the world needed fewer dollars (because they weren't buying as many of our goods) and we needed more foreign exchange (because we were buying more of their goods), the dollar's value plunged. The dollar's rally in the early 80s was a two-phase process. The first phase in 1981–82 had two major causes.

CURRENCY TRADING

Friday, January 15, 1999

EXCHANGE RATES

The New York foreign exchange mid-range rates below apply to trading among banks in amounts of $1 million and more, as quoted at 4 p.m. Eastern time by Telerate and other sources. Retail transactions provide fewer units of foreign currency per dollar. Rates for the 11 Euro currency countries are derived from the latest dollar-euro rate using the exchange ratios set 1/1/99.

Country	U.S. $ equiv. Fri	U.S. $ equiv. Thu	Currency per U.S. $ Fri	Currency per U.S. $ Thu
Argentina (Peso)	1.0011	1.0002	.9990	.9998
Australia (Dollar)	.6315	.6330	1.5835	1.5798
Austria (Schilling)	.08406	.08503	11.896	11.760
Bahrain (Dinar)	2.6525	2.6525	.3770	.3770
Belgium (Franc)	.02867	.02901	34.875	34.476
Brazil (Real)	.6993	.7576	1.4300	1.3200
Britain (Pound)	1.6515	1.6569	.6055	.6035
1-month forward	1.6500	1.6554	.6061	.6041
3-months forward......	1.6484	1.6537	.6066	.6047
6-months forward......	1.6472	1.6525	.6071	.6052
Canada (Dollar)	.6555	.6521	1.5255	1.5336
1-month forward.......	.6547	.6521	1.5275	1.5336
3-months forward......	.6549	.6520	1.5270	1.5337
6-months forward......	.6577	.6523	1.5205	1.5329
Chile (Peso).............	.002094	.002102	477.50	475.75
China (Renminbi)	.1208	.1208	8.2790	8.2789
Colombia (Peso).........	.0006311	.0006294	1584.42	1588.80
Czech. Rep. (Koruna) ...				
Commercial rate.......	.03252	.03269	30.753	30.586
Denmark (Krone)........	.1558	.1576	6.4170	6.3437
Ecuador (Sucre)				
Floating rate............	.0001406	.0001406	7113.00	7113.00
Finland (Markka)	.1945	.1968	5.1403	5.0814
France (Franc)...........	.1763	.1784	5.6709	5.6060
1-month forward.......	.1766	.1787	5.6623	5.5975
3-months forward......	.1771	.1792	5.6454	5.5811
6-months forward......	.1780	.1800	5.6182	5.5548
Germany (Mark)	.5914	.5983	1.6909	1.6715
1-month forward	.5923	.5992	1.6882	1.6690
3-months forward......	.5941	.6009	1.6832	1.6641
6-months forward......	.5971	.6038	1.6747	1.6563
Greece (Drachma)	.003597	.003602	278.00	277.60
Hong Kong (Dollar)	.1291	.1291	7.7482	7.7479
Hungary (Forint)	.004582	.004615	218.26	216.67
India (Rupee)	.02353	.02353	42.500	42.498
Indonesia (Rupiah)	.0001132	.0001153	8835.00	8675.00
Ireland (Punt)	1.4695	1.4857	.6805	.6731
Israel (Shekel)	.2442	.2446	4.0953	4.0877
Italy (Lira)	.0005974	.0006043	1673.96	1654.79

Country	U.S. $ equiv. Fri	U.S. $ equiv. Thu	Currency per U.S. $ Fri	Currency per U.S. $ Thu
Japan (Yen)...............	.008787	.008802	113.81	113.61
1-month forward	.008787	.008802	113.81	113.61
3-months forward......	.008788	.008803	113.80	113.60
6-months forward......	.008789	.008804	113.78	113.58
Jordan (Dinar)...........	1.4094	1.4114	.7095	.7085
Kuwait (Dinar)	3.3167	3.3167	.3015	.3015
Lebanon (Pound).........	.0006631	.0006629	1508.00	1508.50
Malaysia (Ringgit-b)	.2632	.2632	3.8000	3.7998
Malta (Lira)	2.6110	2.6110	.3830	.3830
Mexico (Peso)				
Floating rate.............	.09785	.09421	10.220	10.615
Netherland (Guilder)....	.5249	.5310	1.9052	1.8834
New Zealand (Dollar) ...	.5414	.5395	1.8471	1.8536
Norway (Krone)..........	.1336	.1343	7.4862	7.4463
Pakistan (Rupee)	.02002	.02038	49.950	49.070
Peru (new Sol)	.3051	.3175	3.2775	3.1500
Philippines (Peso).......	.02587	.02600	38.655	38.455
Poland (Zloty)...........	.2820	.2809	3.5460	3.5600
Portugal (Escudo)	.005773	.005839	173.23	171.25
Russia (Ruble) (a)	.04570	.04662	21.880	21.450
Saudi Arabia (Riyal)	.2664	.2666	3.7535	3.7506
Singapore (Dollar)	.5958	.5951	1.6785	1.6805
Slovak Rep. (Koruna) ...	.02720	.02740	36.762	36.492
South Africa (Rand)	.1642	.1623	6.0910	6.1600
South Korea (Won)	.0008449	.0008432	1183.60	1186.00
Spain (Peseta)	.006952	.007032	143.85	142.20
Sweden (Krona)	.1275	.1284	7.8452	7.7875
Switzerland (Franc)......	.7230	.7366	1.3831	1.3575
1-month forward	.7255	.7392	1.3785	1.3529
3-months forward......	.7297	.7435	1.3705	1.3450
6-months forward......	.7362	.7502	1.3584	1.3330
Taiwan (Dollar)	.03105	.03100	32.204	32.255
Thailand (Baht)	.02699	.02710	37.050	36.905
Turkey (Lira)	.00000311	.00000311	321253.00	321179.00
United Arab (Dirham) ..	.2723	.2723	3.6730	3.6730
Uruguay (New Peso)				
Financial...............	.09183	.09217	10.890	10.850
Venezuela (Bolivar)	.001755	.001758	569.75	568.75
—	—	—		
SDR	1.4073	1.4041	.7106	.7122
Euro	1.1567	1.1701	.8645	.8546

Special Drawing Rights (SDR) are based on exchange rates for the U.S., German, British, French , and Japanese currencies. Source: International Monetary Fund.

a-Russian Central Bank rate. Trading band lowered on 8/17/98. b-Government rate.

The Wall Street Journal daily foreign exchange data from 1996 forward may be purchased through the Readers' Reference Service (413) 592-3600.

Key Currency Cross Rates Late New York Trading Jan 15, 1999

	Dollar	Euro	Pound	SFranc	Guilder	Peso	Yen	Lira	D-Mark	FFranc	CdnDlr
Canada..............	1.5255	1.7645	2.5194	1.1030	.80072	.14927	.01340	.00091	.90220	.26900	....
France..............	5.6709	6.5596	9.3655	4.1002	2.9766	.55489	.04983	.00339	3.3539	....	3.7174
Germany............	1.6909	1.9558	2.7925	1.2225	.88752	.16545	.01486	.00101	....	.29816	1.1084
Italy	1674.0	1936.3	2764.5	1210.3	878.64	163.79	14.708	....	990.0	295.18	1097.3
Japan	113.81	131.64	187.96	82.286	59.737	11.136	....	.06799	67.309	20.069	74.605
Mexico	10.22	11.821	16.878	7.3892	5.3644	....	.08980	.00611	6.0442	1.8022	6.6994
Netherlands	1.9052	2.2037	3.1464	1.3775	....	.18642	.01674	.00114	1.1267	.33595	1.2489
Switzerland	1.3831	1.5998	2.2842	....	.72597	.13533	.01215	.00083	.81798	.24389	.90665
U.K.	.60551	.70039	....	.43779	.31782	.05925	.00532	.00036	.35811	.10677	.39693
Euro	.86453	.——	1.4278	.62507	.45378	.08459	.00760	.00052	.51129	.15245	.56672
U.S.	....	1.1567	1.6515	.72301	.52489	.09785	.00879	.00060	.59141	.17634	.65552

Source: Telerate

World Value of the Dollar

The table below, compiled by Bank of America, gives the rates of exchange for the U.S. dollar against various currencies as of Thursday January 14, 1999. Unless otherwise noted, all rates listed are middle rates of interbank bid and asked quotes, and are expressed in foreign currency units per one U.S. dollar. The rates are indicative and aren't based on, nor intended to be used as a basis for, particular transactions.
BankAmerica International doesn't trade in all the listed foreign currencies.

Country (Currency)	Value 1/14	Value 1/7	Country (Currency)	Value 1/14	Value 1/7
Afghanistan (Afghani -c)	4750.00	4750.00	Falkland Islands (Pound *)	1.6585	1.6429
Albania (Lek)	139.95	140.00	Fiji (Dollar -31)	1.9538	n.a.
Algeria (Dinar)	61.1608	60.8189	Finland (Markka -16)	5.0964	n.a.
Andorra (Peseta -7)	142.619	n.a.	France (Franc -8)	5.6226	n.a.
Andorra (Franc -8)	5.6226	n.a.	French Guiana (Franc -8)	5.6226	n.a.
Angola (Readjust Kwanza)	257128.00	257128.00	French Pacific Isl (C.F.P. Franc)	102.229	102.1726
Antigua (E Caribbean $)	2.70	2.70	Gabon (C.F.A. Franc)	562.26	561.95
Argentina (Peso)	0.9998	0.9998	Gambia (Dalasi)	11.10	11.105
Aruba (Florin)	1.79	1.79	Germany (Mark -12)	1.6764	n.a.
Australia (Australia Dollar)	1.5848	1.5789	Ghana (Cedi)	2350.00	2345.00
Austria (Schilling -14)	11.795	n.a.	Gibraltar (Pound *)	1.6585	1.6429
Azerbaijan (Manat)	3950.00	3950.00	Greece (Drachma)	278.855	277.79
Bahamas (Dollar)	1.00	1.00	Greenland (Danish Krone)	6.3835	6.3829
Bahrain (Dinar)	0.38	0.38	Grenada (E Caribbean $)	2.70	2.70
Bangladesh (Taka)	48.50	48.50	Guadeloupe (Franc -8)	5.6226	n.a.
Barbados (Dollar)	2.0113	2.0113	Guam (U.S. $)	1.00	1.00
Belgium (Franc -9)	34.578	n.a.	Guatemala (Quetzal)	6.9902	6.7316
Belize (Dollar)	2.00	2.00	Guinea Bissau (C.F.A. Franc -23)	562.26	561.95
Benin (C.F.A. Franc)	562.26	561.95	Guinea Rep (Franc)	1300.00	1300.00
Bermuda (Dollar)	1.00	1.00	Guyana (Dollar)	151.80	151.80
Bhutan (Ngultrum)	42.47	42.572	Haiti (Gourde)	16.5875	16.5875
Bolivia (Boliviano -o)	5.66	5.65	Honduras Rep (Lempira -d)	14.02	14.015
Bolivia (Boliviano -f)	5.67	5.66	Hong Kong (Dollar)	7.7484	7.7484
Botswana (Pula)	4.5916	4.4191	Hungary (Forint)	217.49	214.57
Bouvet Island (Norwegian Krone)	7.4774	7.358	Iceland (Krona)	69.26	69.40
Brazil (Real)	1.3016	1.2102	India (Rupee -m)	42.47	42.572
Brunei (Dollar)	1.6805	1.6763	Indonesia (Rupiah)	8835.00	8000.00
Bulgaria (Lev)	1676.47	1675.10	Iran (Rial -o)	3000.00	3000.00
Burkina Faso (C.F.A. Franc)	562.26	561.95	Iraq (Dinar -o-26)	0.3109	0.3109
Burma (Kyat)	6.1119	6.1078	Ireland (Punt * -5)	1.481	n.a.
Burundi (Franc)	491.22	490.72	Israel (New Shekel)	4.0835	4.0786
Cambodia (Riel)	3870.00	3870.00	Italy (Lira -13)	1659.68	n.a.
Cameroon (C.F.A. Franc)	562.26	561.95	Ivory Coast (C.F.A. Franc)	562.26	561.95
Canada (Dollar)	1.5355	1.5145	Jamaica (Dollar -o)	36.65	36.65
Cape Verde Isl (Escudo -20)	94.71	94.515	Japan (Yen)	112.745	111.97
Cayman Islands (Dollar)	0.8333	0.8333	Jordan (Dinar)	0.709	0.709
Centrl African Rp (C.F.A. Franc)	562.26	561.95	Kenya (Shilling)	61.50	62.10
Chad (C.F.A. Franc)	562.26	561.95	Kiribati (Australia Dollar)	1.5848	1.5789
Chile (Peso -m)	477.96	470.88	Korea, North (Won)	2.20	2.20
Chile (Peso -o)	471.65	470.57	Korea, South (Won -q-30)	1183.50	n.a.
China (Renminbi Yuan)	8.279	8.2796	Kuwait (Dinar)	0.3018	0.3017
Colombia (Peso -o-2)	1588.00	1540.50	Laos, People DR (Kip)	4203.50	4203.50
Commnwlth Ind Sts (Rouble -m-17)	22.905	23.35	Latvia (Lat)	0.5687	0.5709
Comoros (Franc)	421.695	421.4625	Lebanon (Pound)	1508.00	1508.00
Congo, People Rp (C.F.A. Franc)	562.26	561.95	Lesotho (Maloti)	6.2225	5.82
Costa Rica (Colon)	272.31	271.71	Liberia (Dollar)	1.00	1.00
Croatia (Kuna)	6.2914	6.2769	Libya (Dinar -21)	0.45	n.a.
Cuba (Peso -1)	23.00	23.00	Liechtenstein (Franc)	1.3617	1.3843
Cyprus (Pound *)	2.0056	2.0056	Lithuania (Litas)	4.0016	4.0015
Czech (Koruna)	30.773	29.914	Luxembourg (Lux.Franc -11)	34.578	n.a.
Denmark (Danish Krone)	6.3835	6.3829	Macao (Pataca)	8.0041	8.0041
Djibouti (Djibouti Franc)	177.72	177.72	Madagascar DR (Franc)	5220.00	5220.00
Dominica (E Caribbean $)	2.70	2.70	Malawi (Kwacha)	43.95	44.0164
Dominican Rep (Peso -d)	15.925	15.85	Malaysia (Ringgit -q)	3.7999	n.a.
Ecuador (Sucre -o-4)	7130.00	7001.50	Maldive (Rufiyaa)	11.77	11.77
Ecuador (Sucre-d-4)	7135.00	7001.50	Mali Rep (C.F.A. Franc)	562.26	561.95
Egypt (Pound)	3.41	3.4087	Malta (Lira *)	2.6554	2.6396
El Salvador (Colon -d)	8.755	8.755	Martinique (Franc -8)	5.6226	n.a.
Equatorial Guinea (C.F.A. Franc)	562.26	561.95	Mauritania (Ouguiya)	204.905	204.285
Estonia (Kroon)	13.4179	13.4064	Mauritius (Rupee)	24.725	24.71
Ethiopia (Birr -o)	6.9875	6.9875	Mexico (New Peso)	10.70	9.815
Faeroe Islands (Danish Krone)	6.3835	6.3829	Monaco (Franc -8)	5.6226	n.a.

Continued

Country (Currency)	Value 1/14	Value 1/7	Country (Currency)	Value 1/14	Value 1/7
Mongolia (Tugrik -o-29)	817.61	817.61	Seychelles (Rupee)	5.478	5.478
Montserrat (E Caribbean $)	2.70	2.70	Sierra Leone (Leone)	1571.00	1571.00
Morocco (Dirham)	9.3018	9.307	Singapore (Dollar)	1.6805	1.6763
Mozambique (Metical)	11495.00	11495.00	Slovak (Koruna -15)	36.681	n.a.
Namibia (Rand -c)	6.2225	5.82	Slovenia (Tolar)	160.9957	161.8442
Nauru Islands (Australia Dollar)	1.5848	1.5789	Solomon Islands (Solomon Dollar)	4.9285	4.9603
Nepal (Rupee)	67.925	67.925	Somali Rep (Shilling -d)	2620.00	2620.00
Netherlands (Guilder -10)	1.889	n.a.	South Africa (Rand -c)	6.2225	5.82
Netherlands Ant'les (Guilder)	1.79	1.79	Spain (Peseta -7)	142.619	n.a.
New Zealand (N.Z.Dollar)	1.8575	1.8489	Sri Lanka (Rupee)	68.535	68.46
Nicaragua (Gold Cordoba)	11.2426	11.1245	Sudan Rep (Pound -c)	1960.00	1960.00
Niger Rep (C.F.A. Franc)	562.26	561.95	Sudan Rep (Dinar)	196.00	196.00
Nigeria (Naira -o)	21.886	21.886	Surinam (Guilder)	401.00	401.00
Nigeria (Naira -m)	91.40	95.75	Swaziland (Lilangeni)	6.2225	5.82
Norway (Norwegian Krone)	7.4774	7.358	Sweden (Krona)	7.854	7.8381
Oman, Sultanate of (Rial)	0.385	0.385	Switzerland (Franc)	1.3617	1.3843
Pakistan (Rupee -27)	50.70	n.a.	Syria (Pound)	46.25	46.25
Panama (Balboa)	1.00	1.00	Taiwan (Dollar -o)	32.225	32.17
Papua N.G. (Kina)	2.1097	2.1075	Tanzania (Shilling)	685.00	685.00
Paraguay (Guarani -d)	2855.00	2850.00	Thailand (Baht)	37.195	36.425
Peru (New Sol -d)	3.3025	3.19	Togo, Rep (C.F.A. Franc)	562.26	561.95
Philippines (Peso)	38.70	38.15	Tonga Islands (Pa'anga)	1.5767	1.5888
Pitcairn Island (N.Z.Dollar)	1.8575	1.8489	Trinidad & Tobago (Dollar)	6.2525	6.2525
Poland (Zloty -o)	3.544	3.494	Tunisia (Dinar)	1.0922	1.0934
Portugal (Escudo -6)	171.844	n.a.	Turkey (Lira)	323941.00	320485.00
Puerto Rico (U.S. $)	1.00	1.00	Turks & Caicos (U.S. $)	1.00	1.00
Qatar (Riyal)	3.6405	3.6408	Tuvalu (Australia Dollar)	1.5848	1.5789
Repub of Macedonia (Denar)	52.0044	51.6051	Uganda (Shilling -l)	1233.50	1233.50
Republic of Yemen (Rial -a-25)	136.66	136.66	Ukraine (Hryvnia -18)	4.18	n.a.
Reunion, Ile de la (Franc -8)	5.6226	n.a.	United Arab Emir (Dirham)	3.673	3.6729
Romania (Leu)	11242.00	11266.00	United Kingdom (Pound Sterling *)	1.6585	1.6429
Rwanda (Franc)	320.63	320.63	Uruguay (Peso Uruguayo -m)	11.01	10.835
Saint Christopher (E Caribbean $)	2.70	2.70	Vanuatu (Vatu)	127.91	128.50
Saint Helena (Pound Sterling *)	1.6585	1.6429	Vatican City (Lira -13)	1659.68	n.a.
Saint Lucia (E Caribbean $)	2.70	2.70	Venezuela (Bolivar -d-3)	568.50	566.25
Saint Pierre (Franc -8)	5.6226	n.a.	Vietnam (Dong -o-28)	13885.00	13841.00
Saint Vincent (E Caribbean $)	2.70	2.70	Virgin Is, Br (U.S. $)	1.00	1.00
Samoa, American (U.S. $)	1.00	1.00	Virgin Is, US (U.S. $)	1.00	1.00
Samoa, Western (Tala)	2.9647	2.9481	Yugoslavia (New Dinar -19)	10.0615	n.a.
San Marino (Lira -13)	1659.68	n.a.	Zaire Rep (New Zaire)	217500.00	217500.00
Sao Tome & Principe (Dobra)	2390.00	2390.00	Zambia (Kwacha)	2620.00	2565.00
Saudi Arabia (Riyal)	3.751	3.7507	Zimbabwe (Dollar)	43.20	39.40
Senegal (C.F.A. Franc)	562.26	561.95			

*U.S. dollars per National Currency unit. (a) Free market central bank rate. (b) Floating rate. (c) Commercial rate. (d) Free market rate. (e) Controlled. (f) Financial rate. (g) Preferential rate. (h) Nonessential imports. (i) Floating tourist rate. (j) Public transaction rate. (k) Agricultural products. (l) Priority rate. (m) Market rate. (n) Essential imports. (o) Official rate. (p) Exports. (n.a.) Not available.

(1) Cuba, 13 January 1999: 08/11/96: specific rate for FX houses only. (2) Colombia, 13 January 1999: Columbian Peso FX rate band raised by 9% on 09/15/98. (3) Venezuela, 13 January 1999: 12/11/95, Bolivar devalued by approximately 41%. (4) Ecuador, 13 January 1999: Ecuador Sucre devalued by 15% on 09/15/98. (5) Irish Rep., 13 January 1999: As of 1/1/99, currency running fixed in parallel with Euro. (6) Portugal, 13 January 1999: As of 1/1/99, currency running fixed in parallel with Euro. (7) Spain, 13 January 1999: As of 1/1/99, currency running fixed in parallel with Euro. (8) France, 13 January 1999: As of 1/1/99, currency running fixed in parallel with Euro. (9) Belgium, 13 January 1999: As of 1/1/99, currency running fixed in parallel with Euro. (10) Netherlands, 13 January 1999: As of 1/1/99, currency running fixed in parallel with Euro. (11) Luxembourg, 13 January 1999: As of 1/1/99, currency running fixed in parallel with Euro. (12) Germany, 13 January 1999: As of 1/1/99, currency running fixed in parallel with Euro. (13) Italy, 16 September 1992: Lira leaves ERM (14) Austria, 13 January 1999: As of 1/1/99, currency running fixed in parallel with Euro. (15) Slovak, 13 January 1999: Koruna floating as of 10/01/98 effective devaluation 6%. (16) Finland, 13 January 1999: As of 1/1/99, currency running fixed in parallel with Euro. (17) Russia, 13 January 1999: redenominated: 1 Ruble = 1,000 old Rubles, 01/01/98. (18) Ukraine, 13 January 1999: Ukraine Hyvernia devalued on 09/21/98. (19) Yugoslavia, 13 January 1999: Dinar devalued by 81.81% to 6.0 to the DEM from 3.3 on 3/98. (20) Cape Verde, 13 January 1999: 07/01/97, new rate from Banco Cape Verde. (21) Libya, 13 January 1999: Lybia Dinar devalues 18% on 12/09/98. (22) Djibouti, 13 January 1999: Djibouti Franc 05/20/97 now quoting the official rate. (23) Guinea-Bissau, 13 January 1999: Guinea Bissau Peso 05/02/97 now using the CFA Franc. (24) Angola, 3 July 1995: New currency called the Readjusted Kwanza introduced. (25) Republic of Yemen, 7 January 1996: Official Riyal exchange rate abolished. (26) Iraq, 17 November 1995: Market and Official rates now quoted for Iraq (27) Pakistan, 13 January 1999: Pakistan devalues rupee by 8.5% on 10/16/97. (28) Vietnam, 13 January 1999: Vietnam Dong devalued 5% on 02/16/98, new central rate 11.8. (29) Mongolia, 13 January 1999: Mongolian Tugrik now quoting the market rate (30) Korea, South, 13 January 1999: South Korean Won free floating as of 12/16/97. (31) Fiji, 13 January 1999: Fiji Dollar devalued 20% as of 01/22/98. For further information please contact your local branch of Bank of America..

Further information available at BankAmerica International. Source: Bank of America Global Trading, London

CHART 16–2 Foreign Exchange Rates

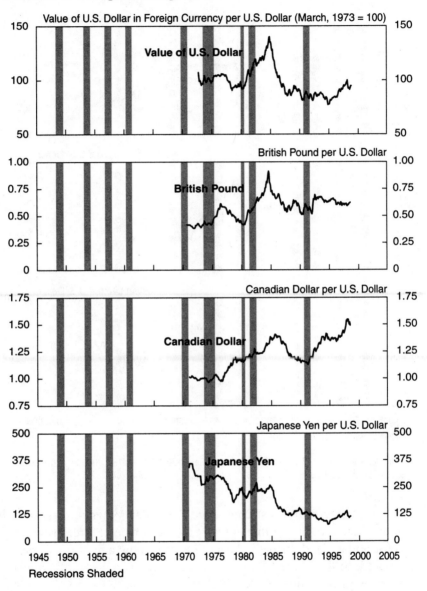

Value of U.S. Dollar in Foreign Currency per U.S. Dollar (March, 1973 = 100)

Value of U.S. Dollar

British Pound per U.S. Dollar

British Pound

Canadian Dollar per U.S. Dollar

Canadian Dollar

Japanese Yen per U.S. Dollar

Japanese Yen

Recessions Shaded

Continued

CHART 16–2 Foreign Exchange Rates (continued)

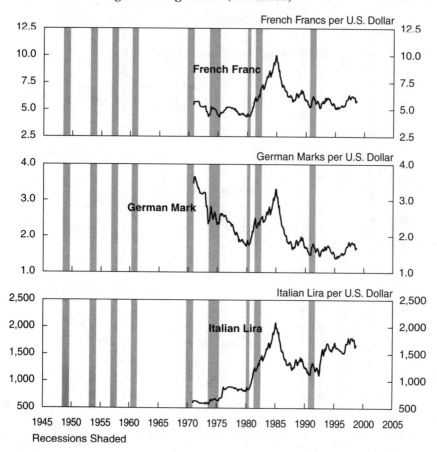

Source: The Conference Board, *Business Cycle Indicators*, Series U0M750, U0M752, U0M753, U0M755, U0M756, U0M757, and U0M758.

First, high interest rates strengthened the dollar. When interest rates in the United States are higher than interest rates elsewhere, foreign exchange is sold for dollars, and the capital accounts will show a net flow of private investment into the United States. The Fed's tight money policy pushed interest rates in the United States higher than those in Europe and Japan, prompting heavy dollar purchases by foreign investors who wished to enjoy the high interest rates available here. (See the list of reasons on page 321 for the U.S. current-account deficit in the early 1980s.)

Second, the U.S. balance on current account improved dramatically until late 1982 because of rapidly growing service income and despite a

sharply negative balance of trade. This positive element in the U.S. international accounts not only generated a flow of dollars into the United States, but also encouraged private businesses and individuals in the rest of the world to invest in dollars, because they believed that the dollar would remain strong in the future.

The second phase in 1983–84 is somewhat more complex. The interest rate differential between the United States and the rest of the world had narrowed since mid-1982, while the balance on current account deteriorated rapidly due to the plunge in our merchandise trade balance (see Chart 16–1 on page 320). Under these circumstances, the dollar's value should have fallen.

Nevertheless, it improved because of the continuing flow of investment dollars into the United States and the continuing reduced flow of our investment dollars to the rest of the world. The rest of the world believed America to be the safest, most profitable home for its funds. To foreigners (indeed, to many Americans), President Reagan symbolized America's protection of, and concern for, business interests. Certainly, the United States was a secure haven: Investments would not be expropriated, nor would their return be subject to confiscatory taxation. And the return was good; even if the interest rate differential between here and abroad had narrowed, U.S. rates were still higher than those in most other countries. Moreover, profits had been strong, and the stock market reflected this. Foreign investors who had a stake in American business were rewarded handsomely.

Thus, the dollar remained strong because the huge net capital flow into the United States bid the dollar's price up and forced other currencies down. The rise in the dollar's value, together with the quicker economic expansion here than abroad, depressed our exports and stimulated our imports. Consequently, the deterioration in our merchandise trade balance in 1983 and 1984 was a result of the dollar's appreciation, not a cause of it.

But by 1985 the merchandise trade balance had deteriorated to such an extent, while American interest rates continued to slide, that the dollar began to weaken. Foreign demand for our currency was not strong enough to offset our demand for the rest of the world's currencies. In addition, we began to pressure our major trading partners, requesting their assistance in reducing our trade deficit by driving the dollar's value down. They (i.e., their central banks) complied by agreeing to the Plaza Accord and sold dollars, contributing to the dollar's slide. As a result, by the late 80s, the dollar had lost most of the increase of the early 80s.

The dollar stabilized at the end of the decade because our balance-of-trade deficit stopped growing due to rapid export growth. American interest rates rose, and foreign central banks actively supported the dollar once

again. These developments stimulated dollar purchase and helped halt the dollar's decline. The foreign central banks had begun to respond to their own industrial interests and were no longer willing to let the dollar fall in order to protect our markets.

The dollar remained low throughout the 1990s, depressed by the continuing deterioration in America's balance of trade. As the American economy operated at higher levels and grew faster than its trading partners', it drew vast quantities of imports. Americans sold dollars in order to purchase foreign goods, and the dollar's value remained depressed.

Then the tiger economies of East Asia and the Asian Pacific Rim slipped into financial chaos in the summer of 1997. That began a year long upward trend for the U.S. dollar as it gained 10 percent against the 19 currencies tracked on page C1 of the *Journal* (see pages 326 and 331). Then in mid-1998 the dollar began to slide again until it had lost all of its recent gains. By the beginning of 1999, the dollar's value was back where it had been in mid-1997. But what influences drove the dollar back down? First, the worst of the Asian crisis was over and the panic had stopped. Second, U.S. imports surged while exports stalled. Weak demand for the dollar pushed it back down. As U.S. trade deficits swell, it appears that the dollar will continue to weaken at the end of the decade.

Investor's Tip

• This brief history should warn you how difficult it is to predict the dollar's value and the course of international economic events. That's why foreign exchange speculation is not for amateurs. Even some pros go broke doing it.

SUMMARY AND PROSPECT

S O WILL THE DOW HIT 30,000 BY THE YEAR 2010? That depends on the course of inflation, the business cycle, and corporate earnings.

We seem to have tamed both inflation and the business cycle in the 1980s and 1990s. Those decades ended with records of solid expansion, low unemployment, and low inflation, interrupted only by the recession of 1990-91. Escalating debt and inflation and the business cycle's roller-coaster ride appeared to be mere relics of the past, confined to the years 1965 through 1980. Could it be that those years, with all their problems, were an exception, a kind of rough patch that is now behind us? Once again, we must turn to the historical record for some perspective.

The early 1960s followed the Eisenhower years, which President Kennedy and his advisers criticized severely for sluggish economic performance and too many recessions. They excoriated the fiscal policy of President Eisenhower's administration and the monetary policy of the Federal Reserve for excessive concern with inflation and complacency about slow

economic growth and unemployment. These critics charged that, because of the attempt to restrain demand in order to combat "creeping inflation," the economy's growth rate had fallen and recovery from frequent recessions in the 1950s had been weak.

Yet the Eisenhower years had been the best of times for stock-market investors. The Dow climbed from 200 in 1950 to almost 1,000 in 1965, a five-fold increase in 15 years. Some said that stocks had been a good hedge against the negligible inflation of those years. In truth, they had done well because of inflation's absence.

But as the middle 60s approached, the economy rapidly gained steam. The low level of inflation (inherited from the Eisenhower years) and the Fed's easy money policy (in response to Kennedy administration requests) were the most important ingredients in the rapid economic expansion that began in the 1960s.

Modest increases in the CPI permitted strong growth in real consumer income. As a result, consumer sentiment steadily improved. This, together with the ready availability of loans at low interest rates, prompted consumers to resort to record levels of mortgage borrowing and consumer credit. Home construction and automobile production set new highs. Business responded by investing heavily in new plant and equipment, so that general boom conditions prevailed by the middle of the decade.

The tax cut proposed by President Kennedy has received most of the credit for this prosperity. Inconveniently, however, it was not enacted until 1964, after his death, and it is difficult to understand how an expansion that began in 1962 can be attributed to a tax cut two years later.

The expansion's relaxed and easy progress was its most important early feature. There was no overheating. Housing starts, auto sales, consumer credit, and retail sales gradually broke through to new highs. By 1965, there had been three solid years of expansion, reflected in a strong improvement in labor productivity and a solid advance in real compensation.

The problems began in the late 60s, when the Fed did not exercise enough restraint on the boom. Its half hearted measures were too little and too late. Most observers blamed the Vietnam War for the inflation, but the federal deficit never exceeded $15 billion in the late 60s. Meanwhile, private borrowing hit $100 billion annually, thereby dwarfing federal fiscal stimuli. Private borrowing and spending on residential construction, autos, and other consumer durables and business capital expenditures—not federal borrowing and spending on the Vietnam War—generated the inflation of the late 60s.

As the inflation progressed, it created a nightmare for stock and bond holders in the 1970s. During the entire decade, their investments did not

gain in value; some even fell. Meanwhile, real estate boomed and gold and other precious metals went through the roof.

And as you know from the earlier discussion, the Fed's attempts to deal with inflation remained inadequate throughout the 70s, so that its stop-go-policies only exacerbated inflation over the course of the cycle.

It was not until Paul Volcker persuaded the Fed to take a stand in the early 80s with a policy of continued restraint that inflation was brought under control and stability ensured for the rest of the decade. By the end of the 80s, Americans enjoyed better economic conditions than at any time since the early 60s.

The 1990s began with recession, as had the 1980s. Then, just like the 80s, the 90s embarked upon a sustained expansion through the end of the decade. The Fed's firm reins kept inflation low, so that production, employment, and profits gained strongly in a climate of low inflation. The stock market tripled, as it had in the 80s.

But there was a key difference. The stock market suffered a severe correction in 1987. Share prices raced ahead of earnings per share in 1987, boosting the price/earnings ratio and instigating a crash that halved that ratio. However, there was no such correction in the 1990s. Share prices similarly climbed faster than earnings per share and the price/earnings ratio increased once again, but the crash never came.

Some thought the fundamentals had changed dramatically and that a new-age economy had altered investors' ground rules. Others expressed reservations. Could corporate earnings continue their robust climb after a decade of expansion? Could share prices continue spiraling upward more rapidly than earning per share?

True, the Fed's change in direction in the early 1980s means that the years from 1965 to 1980 were an anomaly, a bad patch that is now behind us. The Fed managed to wrestle inflation to the mat, so that the rate of price increases fell steadily throughout the 80s and 90s removing investors' worst fears. Yet that does not mean that the business cycle has become a relic of the past, that earnings can climb forever, or that the price/earnings ratio can do the same. A day of reckoning could lay ahead.

A P P E N D I X

STATISTICAL SERIES PUBLISHED IN *THE WALL STREET JOURNAL* IN ALPHABETICAL ORDER

Chapter Introduced	Series Description	Publication Schedule
9	American Stock Exchange composite transactions	Daily
11	Amex bonds	Daily
16	Balance on current account	Quarterly
16	Balance of trade	Monthly
12	Banxquote money markets	Weekly
11	Bond-market data bank	Daily
11	Bond yields (chart)	Weekly
9	Canadian markets (stocks)	Daily
7	Capacity utilization	Monthly
10	Cash prices (commodities)	Daily
11	Closed-end bond funds	Weekly
9	Closed-end funds (stocks & bonds)	Weekly
10	Commodities (article)	Daily
10	Commodity indexes	Daily
6	Consumer confidence	Monthly

339

Chapter Introduced	Series Description	Publication Schedule
6	Consumer credit	Monthly
12	Consumer-savings rates	Weekly
6	Consumer-price index	Monthly
9	Corporate-dividend news	Daily
8	Corporate profits (Commerce Department)	Quarterly
8	Corporate profits (*The Wall Street Journal* survey)	Quarterly
11, 12	Credit markets (article)	Daily
11	Credit ratings	Daily
16	Currency trading	Daily
9	Digest of earnings report	Daily
9	Dow Jones averages (six-month charts)	Daily
10	Dow Jones commodity indexes (chart)	Weekly
9	Dow Jones U.S. industry groups	Daily
9	Dow Jones world industry groups	Daily
15	Durable-goods orders	Monthly
7	Employment	Monthly
6	Existing-home sales	Monthly
15	Factory orders	Monthly
5	Federal budget	Monthly
16	Foreign exchange (article)	Daily
9	Foreign markets (stocks)	Daily
10, 11, 12	Futures-options prices	Daily
10, 11, 12	Futures prices	Daily
7	GDP	Quarterly
11	Government-agency issues	Daily
11	High-yield bonds	Daily
6	Housing starts	Monthly
9	Index-options trading	Daily
7	Industrial production	Monthly
9	Insider-trading spotlight	Weekly
14	Inventories	Monthly

| 16 | Key-currency cross rates | Daily |
Chapter Introduced	**Series Description**	**Publication Schedule**
11, 12	Key interest rates	Weekly
13	Leading indicators	Monthly
9	Leaps—long term options	Daily
9	Listed-options trading	Daily
9–12	Markets diary	Daily
12	Money-fund yields	Weekly
12	Money-market funds (chart)	Weekly
12	Money-market mutual funds	Weekly
12	Money rates	Daily
11	Municipal-bond index	Weekly
9	Mutual-fund quotations	Daily
9	Mutual-fund scorecard	Daily
9	NASDAQ national-market issues	Daily
9	NASDAQ small-cap issues	Daily
6	New-home sales	Monthly
11	New-securities issues	Daily
6	New-vehicle sales	Monthly
11	New York exchange bonds	Daily
9	NYSE composite transactions	Daily
9	NYSE highs/lows	Daily
9	Odd-lot trading	Daily
6	Personal income	Monthly
8	P/E Ratios	Weekly
7	Producer price index	Monthly
7	Productivity	Quarterly
7	Purchasing-management index	Monthly
6	Retail sales	Monthly
11	Securities-offering calendar	Weekly
9	Short interest (stocks)	Monthly
12	Short-term interest rates (chart)	Weekly
9	Stock-market data bank	Daily

Chapter Introduced	Series Description	Publication Schedule
11, 12	Treasury-bill auction	Weekly
11, 12	Treasury bonds, notes, and bills	Daily
11, 12	Treasury yield curve	Daily
11	Weekly tax-exempts (bonds)	Weekly
10	World markets (stocks article)	Daily
16	World value of the dollar	Daily
12	Yields on CDs	Weekly
11, 12	Yield comparisons	Daily
12	Yields for consumers (chart)	Weekly

STATISTICAL SERIES PUBLISHED IN *THE WALL STREET JOURNAL* IN CHAPTER ORDER

Chapter Introduced	Series Description	Publication Schedule
5	Federal budget	Monthly
6	Consumer confidence	Monthly
6	Consumer credit	Monthly
6	Consumer price index	Monthly
6	Existing-home sales	Monthly
6	Housing starts	Monthly
6	New-home sales	Monthly
6	New-vehicle sales	Monthly
6	Personal income	Monthly
6	Retail sales	Monthly
7	Capacity utilization	Monthly
7	Employment	Monthly
7	GDP	Quarterly
7	Industrial production	Monthly
7	Producer price index	Monthly
7	Productivity	Quarterly

Chapter Introduced	Series Description	Publication Schedule
7	Purchasing-management index	Monthly
8	Corporate profits (Commerce Department)	Quarterly
8	Corporate profits (*The Wall Street Journal* survey)	Quarterly
8	P/E Ratios	Weekly
9	American Stock Exchange composite transactions	Daily
9	Canadian markets (stocks)	Daily
9	Closed-end funds (stocks & bonds)	Weekly
9	Corporate dividend news	Daily
9	Digest of earnings report	Daily
9	Dow Jones averages (six-month charts)	Daily
9	Dow Jones U.S. industry groups	Daily
9	Dow Jones world industry groups	Daily
9	Foreign markets (stocks)	Daily
9	Index-options trading	Daily
9	Insider-trading spotlight	Weekly
9	Leaps—long term options	Daily
9	Listed-options trading	Daily
9	Mutual-fund quotations	Daily
9	Mutual-fund scorecard	Daily
9	NASDAQ national market issues	Daily
9	NASDAQ small-cap issues	Daily
9	NYSE composite transactions	Daily
9	NYSE highs/lows	Daily
9	Odd-lot trading	Daily
9	Short interest (stocks)	Monthly
9	Stock-market data bank	Daily
9–12	Markets diary	Daily
10	Cash prices (commodities)	Daily
10	Commodities (article)	Daily
10	Commodity indexes	Daily

Chapter Introduced	Series Description	Publication Schedule
10	Dow Jones commodity indexes (chart)	Weekly
10, 11, 12	Futures-options prices	Daily
10, 11, 12	Futures prices	Daily
10	World markets (stocks article)	Daily
11	Amex bonds	Daily
11	Bond-market data bank	Daily
11	Bond yields (chart)	Weekly
11	Closed-end bond funds	Weekly
11, 12	Credit markets (article)	Daily
11	Credit ratings	Daily
11	Government-agency issues	Daily
11	High-yield bonds	Daily
11, 12	Key interest rates	Weekly
11	Municipal-bond index	Weekly
11	New-securities issues	Daily
11	New York exchange bonds	Daily
11	Securities-offering calendar	Weekly
11, 12	Treasury-bill auction	Weekly
11, 12	Treasury bonds, notes, and bills	Daily
11, 12	Treasury-yield curve	Daily
11	Weekly tax-exempts (bonds)	Weekly
11, 12	Yield comparisons	Daily
12	Banxquote money markets	Weekly
12	Consumer savings rates	Weekly
12	Money-fund yields	Weekly
12	Money-market funds (chart)	Weekly
12	Money-market mutual funds	Weekly
12	Money rates	Daily
12	Short-term interest rates (chart)	Weekly
12	Yields for consumers (chart)	Weekly
12	Yields on CDs	Weekly
13	Leading indicators	Monthly

Chapter Introduced	Series Description	Publication Schedule
14	Inventories	Monthly
15	Durable-goods orders	Monthly
15	Factory orders	Monthly
16	Balance on current account	Quarterly
16	Balance of trade	Monthly
16	Currency trading	Daily
16	Foreign exchange (article)	Daily
16	Key-currency cross rates	Daily
16	World value of the dollar	Daily

LISTING OF STATISTICAL SERIES ACCORDING TO *THE WALL STREET JOURNAL* PUBLICATION SCHEDULE

Day of Month Usually Published in *The Wall Street Journal*	Series Description	Chapter Introduced
	Quarterly	
Middle of last month of quarter	Balance on current account	16
25th	GDP	7
25th of last month of quarter	Corporate profits (Commerce Department)	8
A month after end of quarter	Productivity	7
Two months after close of quarter	Corporate profits (*The Wall Street Journal* survey)	8
	Monthly	
1st	Leading indicators	13
1st week	Consumer confidence	6
1st week	Factory orders	15
1st week	New-home sales	6
1st week	Purchasing-management index	7

Day of Month Usually Published in *The Wall Street Journal*	Series Description	Chapter Introduced
5th	New-vehicle sales	6
Monday of 2nd week	Employment	7
2nd week	Consumer credit	6
Middle of 2nd week	Retail sales	6
Midmonth	Capacity utilization	7
Midmonth	Consumer price index	6
Midmonth	Industrial production	7
Midmonth	Inventories	14
Midmonth	Producer price index	7
3rd week	Balance of trade	16
17th to 20th	Housing starts	6
20th	Short interest (stocks)	9
Thursday or Friday of next-to-last week	Durable-goods orders	15
Last week	Existing-home sales	6
Last week	Federal budget	5
Last week	Personal income	6
	Weekly	
Monday	Bond yields (chart)	11
Monday	Closed-end bond funds	11
Monday	Closed-end funds (stocks & bonds)	9
Monday	Dow Jones commodity indexes (chart)	10
Monday	P/E Ratios	8
Monday	Securities offering calendar	11
Tuesday	Key interest rates	11, 12
Tuesday	Treasury-bill auction	11, 12
Tuesday	Weekly tax-exempts (bonds)	11
Wednesday	Banxquote money markets	12
Wednesday	Insider trading spotlight	9
Wednesday	Yields on CDs	12

Day of Month Usually Published in *The Wall Street Journal*	Series Description	Chapter Introduced
Thursday	Consumer-savings rates	12
Thursday	Money-fund yields	12
Thursday	Money-market funds (chart)	12
Thursday	Money-market mutual funds	12
Thursday	Short-term interest rates (chart)	12
Thursday	Yields for consumers (chart)	12
Friday	Municipal-bond index	11

Series Description—Daily	Chapter Introduced
American Stock Exchange composite transactions	9
Amex bonds	11
Bond-market data bank	11
Canadian markets (stocks)	9
Cash prices (commodities)	10
Commodities (article)	10
Commodity indexes	10
Corporate dividend news	9
Credit markets (article)	11, 12
Credit ratings	11
Currency trading	16
Digest of earnings report	9
Dow Jones averages (six-month charts)	9
Dow Jones U.S. industry groups	9
Dow Jones world industry groups	9
Foreign exchange (article)	16
Foreign markets (stocks)	9
Futures-options prices	10, 11, 12
Futures prices	10, 11, 12
Government-agency issues	11
High-yield bonds	11
Index-options trading	9

FURTHER REFERENCES*

These references were selected to assist you with further research into the many topics covered in this book. Given the flood of new Internet-based information in recent years, a special effort was made to highlight timeless classics—and perspective-building information—of particular value in organizing and managing a long-term investment master plan. Many of these books and services enjoy a wide following among private and institutional investors, alike.

In certain cases, a book may be out-of-print, but copies will be available in bookstores, libraries or through the catalogs listed herein. All McGraw-Hill titles are available in bookstores, in many catalogs, or directly from McGraw-Hill Publishing at 1-800-2-MCGRAW.

ASSOCIATIONS AND CLUBS

American Association of Individual Investors
(312) 280-0170 / www.AAII.com

Member benefits include the monthly *AAII Journal* with detailed articles on wide ranging investment and financial planning topics. Numerous extra books and support services are also available.

*The author gratefully acknowledges the assistance of Robert H. Meier of DeKalb, Illinois, in compiling these references.

American Institute for Economic Research
(413) 528-1216 / Fax: (413) 528-0103
www.aier.org

The institute publishes close to 40 special reports and books on investment basics, estate planning, insurance, the behavioral sciences, and economics. The twice-monthly *Research Reports* newsletter is known for its comprehensive business-cycle condition forecasts.

Oxford Club
(800) 992-0205 / Fax: (410) 223-2652
www.oxfordclub.com

The twice-monthly member newsletter includes global portfolio recommendations. In addition, frequent bulletins and chapter meetings keep members current on everything from wealth-protection strategies to foreign real estate. Affiliate clubs are located in London, Paris, and Bonn.

BONDS AND MONEY MARKET

All About Bonds and Bond Mutual Funds
by Esmé Faerber. McGraw-Hill.

Without getting bogged down in needless technicalities, all the basics of bonds and bond funds are covered. This revised edition contains new material on bond mutual funds, tax-free municipal bonds, and international bonds and bond funds.

Bond Market Rules—50 Axioms to Master Bonds for Trading or Income
by Michael B. Sheimo. McGraw-Hill.

The first of its kind, this book is packed with solid, actionable advice and insights to increase bond-portfolio profits — whether for conservative income or aggressive growth.

BOOK CATALOGS

Books of Wall Street
(800) 253-0900 / Fax: (802) 658-0260
www.fraserbooks.com

One of the largest and most comprehensive selections of business and finance catalogs, including new editions of long out-of-print classics. Investment newsletters are also listed, especially those using contrary-opinion decision models.

Laissez Faire Books
(800) 326-0996
http://laissezfaire.org

World's largest selection of books on free-market economics, plus benchmark titles in personal finance, offshore tax and estate planning, socioeconomic trends, and children and money.

CHARTING & TECHNICAL SERVICES

Chartcraft, Inc.
(914) 632-0422 / Fax: (914) 632-0335

The Chartcraft *Point & Figure Monthly Chart Book* includes more than 3,500 common stocks on the New York, American and OTC exchanges, 42 industry bullish-consensus charts, data for 185 more industry groups, major option and world indexes, and much more. Although not as well-known as bar charting, point & figure charting is considered more reliable by many practitioners.

Technical Analysis of Stocks & Commodities
(800) 832-4642 / Fax: (206) 938-1307
www.traders.com

This monthly magazine is the single best source for "how-to" articles, the latest indicator-reliability studies, and new software and data bases.

Topline Investment Graphics
(800) 347-0157 / Fax: (303) 440-0147
www.jcarder@topline-charts.com

The company offers an extensive selection of custom chart formats and data combinations for tracking markets and optimizing indicators. The company does not sell data.

CHILDREN AND MONEY

Gifting To People You Love
by Adriane G. Berg. New Market Press. $24.95

The complete family guide to making gifts, bequests, and investments for children.

National Center for Financial Education
(619) 232-8811 / www.ncfe.org

The one-stop source for virtually everything in print to help children learn how to become better savers and investors.

CYCLES

New Classics Library
(800) 336-1618 / Fax: (770) 536-2514
www.elliottwave.com

Newsletters and books on the Elliott Wave Theory and cycles in general. For cycle basics, start with *The Wave Principle of Human Social Behavior and the New Science of Socionomics* by Robert Prechter.

FINANCIAL PLANNING

How to Pay Zero Estate Taxes
How to Pay Zero Taxes
by Jeff A. Schnepper. McGraw-Hill.

The two foundation references to discover every practical tax break the IRS allows.

International Association for Financial Planning
(888) 806-PLAN / (404) 845-3660
www.planningpaysoff.com

The Association provides a set of eight brochures on important planning topics free of charge, including guidelines for choosing a financial adviser. The topics also are covered on their web site.

Smart Questions to Ask Your Financial Advisers
by Lynn Brenner. Penguin Putnam, Inc.
www.penguinputnam.com

FOREIGN CURRENCIES

Information Line
(800) 831-0007 / Fax: (301) 881-1936
www.assetstrategies.com

This newsletter is published free of charge by Asset Strategies International, a major foreign-currency and precious-metals dealer. Prominent economists and money managers are interviewed, and U.S. dollar and inflation forecasts are regularly issued along with investor protection alerts.

FINANCIAL HISTORY

It Was a Very Good Year - Extraordinary Moments in Stock Market History
by Martin S. Fridson. John Wiley & Sons.

Against the Gods—The Remarkable Story of Risk
by Peter L. Bernstein. John Wiley & Sons.

The fascinating story of how risk has been measured, forecast, and controlled since the Renaissance.

INTERNATIONAL INVESTING

The Global Investment Strategist
(514) 499-9706 / Fax: (514) 499-9709

A full spectrum service for the serious international investor. Features include a quarterly strategy outlook, weekly bulletins, monthly asset allocation recommendations, and Internet access to up-to-date charts and indicators, plus regular teleconferences.

World Brief Monthly Journal
(800) 959-2397 / Fax: (818) 386-9012
www.lintz.net

Nicknamed "The Pink" because of the color paper used, the newsletter features comprehensive recommendations for all major foreign stock and bond markets, currencies, precious metals, and much more.

MUTUAL FUNDS

Mutual Fund Rules—50 Essential Axioms to Explain and Examine Mutual Fund Investing
by Michael B. Sheimo. McGraw-Hill.

Covering everything from types of mutual funds and how they differ, to tips and techniques for avoiding fraud and hidden charges, it's must reading for anyone owning mutual funds.

ONLINE INVESTING

Mining for Gold on the Internet
by Mary Ellen Bates. McGraw-Hill.

Must-reading. Take maximum advantage of hundreds of free financial and software web sites. Sample web sites are illustrated, and valuable pointers given on using the Net to manage personal finances.

Online Investor
(800) 778-8568 / subscribe@onlineinvestor.com
www.onlineinvestor.com

A bimonthly magazine that rates and reviews hundreds of new financial web sites every year.

OPTIONS

IPS Short Course in Futures and Options
by Investor Publishing Services
(800) 345-7026 / Fax: (312) 341-7945

Offered free as a public service, this report distills all the option basics and vital trading rules down to a few pages of easy-to-read explanations.

PRECIOUS METALS

The Moneychanger
(931) 722-3135 / Fax: (931) 722-3166

A monthly newsletter featuring in-depth interviews with precious-metal economists and portfolio managers, insightful analysis of political forces impacting precious-metals prices, and in-depth technical analysis of gold, silver, platinum, and palladium.

PRIVACY

Privacy 2000
by Mark Nestmann. Pathway Books.
(888) 295-2770 / Fax: (603) 357-2073

e-mail: pbs@top.monad.net

An exhaustive survey and analysis of domestic and international laws, regulations, government emergency powers, and court decisions impacting financial privacy. Ideal for anyone seeking legal ways to enhance personal or business privacy.

PSYCHOLOGY

International Institute of Trading Mastery
(919) 362-5591 / Fax: (919) 362-6020
www.iitm.com

One-of-a-kind personal psychological profiling, home-study courses, seminars, and the monthly *Market Mastery* newsletter to successfully overcome the many hidden psychological barriers to profitable trading and investing.

REAL ESTATE

Getting Started in Real Estate
by Michael and Jean Thomsett. John Wiley & Sons.

STOCK MARKET

Alexander Paris Report
(800) 416-7479 / Fax: (312) 634-6350

This newsletter uses a proprietary, free-market credit-cycle model to pinpoint business cycle and stock sector leadership transitions, with specific stock recommendations.

How to Read a Financial Report
by John A. Tracy. John Wiley & Sons.

Now in the fifth edition, this popular guide gives investors the basics needed to intelligently decipher company annual reports and financial statements.

Stock Trader's Almanac
(201) 767-4100 / Fax: (201) 767-7337
www.hirschorganization.com

The annual *Wall Street* classic. Combines a desk calendar, daily diary and valuable market tips such as the best trading days and calendar periods to buy and sell stocks; also the results of probability studies, and dozens more insights every month of the year.

The Hulbert Financial Digest
(703) 750-9060 / Fax: (703) 750-9220
www.hulbertdigest.com

The world's most widely followed advisory-services performance tracking service. In addition to ranking over 60 stock, commodity and mutual fund newsletters, the service features in-depth sector, cyclical, and new-issue performance updates.

Stock Index Futures & Options
by Susan Abbott Gidel. John Wiley & Sons.

The benchmark reference on the most popular stock-index futures and option contracts on 20 U.S. and 18 foreign exchanges. Includes valuable trading guidelines.

What Works on Wall Street
by James P. O'Shaughnessy. McGraw-Hill.

One of the most valuable investment books of all time. Never before have so many factual, unbiased, and surprising findings on what portfolio strategies actually work—and how well—been presented in one place. Importantly, the book also warns of popular market folklore with no basis in fact.

Winning the Loser's Game
by Charles D. Ellis. McGraw-Hill.

A revised and updated edition of *Investment Policy*, a financial magnum opus considered essential reading for professionals, this edition is tailored for individual investors. The books details how to manage stock market holdings to maximize lifetime financial success through five stages, from earning and saving through investing and estate planning and gifting.

TECHNOLOGY AND TRENDS

Tech Stock Alert
(800) 877-8847 / Fax: (504) 837-4885

Specializing in small- and mid-cap stocks with exceptional growth potential, it is widely followed by private investors and portfolio managers alike. The monthly newsletter covers biotechnology, computers, software, telecommunications, the Internet, semiconductors, and technology mutual funds.

TRADING SYSTEMS

Trade Your Way To Financial Freedom
by Van K. Tharp. McGraw-Hill.

In simple English, the book quickly and simply reveals how to pick the optimum trading system, and details the vital but little known key to trading profits: trading for expectancy rather than accuracy. This book is of exceptional value, no matter what the investment time horizon – from day trading to decades-long master portfolio planning.

I N D E X